Heroes Never Die!

The Italian Peplum Phenomenon 1950-1967

Heroes Never Die!

The Italian Peplum Phenomenon 1950-1967

By Barry Atkinson

Midnight Marquee Press, Inc.
Baltimore, Maryland, USA; London, UK

Copyright © 2017 by Barry Atkinson
Interior Layout by Gary J. Svehla
Cover Design by Aurelia Susan Svehla
Copy Editor Linda J. Walter

Without limiting the rights under copyright reserved above, no part of this publication may be reproduced, stored in or introduced into a retrieval system, or transmitted, in any form, or by any means (electronic, mechanical, photocopying, recording or otherwise), without the prior written permission of the copyright owner or the publishers of the book.

ISBN 9781936168699 (color version)
ISBN 9781936168750 (black and white version)
Library of Congress Catalog Card Number 2016916579
Manufactured in the United States of America
First Printing January, 2018

DEDICATION AND QUOTES

"This war will never be forgotten. Nor will the heroes who fought in it." *Troy*, 2004

To Anna, Frieda, Phoebe, Betty, Charlie and Fudge. Animals really are a man's best friend.

To the countless technicians and artists whose endeavors in bringing this vast body of work to cinema audiences have gone unnoticed over the past 50 years. Like the heroes that formed the pivotal centerpieces in their productions, their labor, artistry and vision in the field of peplum must never be allowed to die.

"He has the strength of hell!" *Samson and Delilah*, 1949

"There are things unknown in the black tents of Allah that I shall teach you." *Flame of Araby*, 1951

"The only reward of a slave is scars." *Spartacus*, 1953

"Send her back to Sparta. Her name is death!" *Helen of Troy*, 1956

"What a gloomy song. When they're covered in flames, they'll sound more cheerful." *Aphrodite, Goddess of Love*, 1958

"Marry me and I'll free your people." *Pia of Ptolomey*, 1958

"I'm less than a man and more than half a monster." *The Black Archer*, 1959

"Only a madman could cross the Alps." *Hannibal*, 1959

"There is no room for weakness in this world. One must strike first, or be destroyed." *Herod the Great*, 1959

"It's force which is the only law." *Judith and Holofernes*, 1959

"To breathe the same air as Cleopatra—even that's too good for a Roman." *The Legions of Cleopatra*, 1959

"Careful. You'll tear my peplum." *Messalina Venus Empress*, 1960

"We are men without a country—but not without honor!" *Pirates of the Coast*, 1960

"If we're in the hands of women, who wants to escape, huh?" *Queen of the Amazons*, 1960

"It has been a month since my sword tasted blood!" *Revak, the Slave of Carthage*, 1960

"Murder. What an ugly expression for lips that are so lovely." *Robin Hood and the Pirates*, 1960

"My sword is my love." *Terror of the Red Mask*, 1960

"It's more difficult to understand women than to beat an army." *Goliath Against the Giants*, 1961

"A supreme race born of the blood of Uranus!" *Hercules and the Conquest of Atlantis*, 1961

"Marriage or the scaffold." *The Invincible Gladiator*, 1961

"Yes, he's mad! Mad with love!" *The Last of the Vikings*, 1961

"Let's go find the Mole Men." *Maciste, the Strongest Man in the World*, 1961

"He's no man, he's a demon!" *The Revenge of Ursus*, 1961

"100 pieces of silver or we raze your village to the ground." *Swords Without a Flag*, 1961

"I intend to put a foot of steel through your stomach." *The Terror of the Seas*, 1961

"No woman is worth the blood that has been shed in these nine years—least of all Helen." *The Trojan War*, 1961

"Achilles. A fighting machine created to kill." *The Fury of Achilles*, 1962

"My wedding gift to you will be the head of your father's murderer." *Gladiators 7*, 1962

"Women never admit their real weight or their age." *The Golden Arrow*, 1962

"Hurry. It's the end of the world. You must do something." *Maciste Against the Headhunters*, 1962

"Leave me to my pleasure or die!" *Sodom and Gomorrah*, 1962

"How can a Roman centurion be the son of a slave?" *The Son of Spartacus*, 1962

"I've heard so much of this little jewel of the desert, I've decided I want her." *The Son of the Sheik*, 1962

"Attack me." "With pleasure." *Swordsman of Siena*, 1962

"A woman's tongue is far deadlier than the sword." *The 300 Spartans*, 1962

"Go, you strumpet of death." *The Black Duke*, 1963

"The man commands. The woman gives birth. The slave works. This is the order of things." *Brennus Enemy of Rome*, 1963

"Why can't those miserable idiots just die quietly without disturbing our pleasure?" *The Hero of Babylon*, 1963

"You're the cruelest woman I've ever met. Also the most beautiful." *I, Semiramis*, 1963

"I could eat a raw praetorian!" *The Ten Gladiators*, 1963

"Caesar doesn't need dead heroes." *The Giants of Rome*, 1964

"And if they're thirsty, give them a drink of blood. Their own, of course." *Maciste at the Court of the Czar*, 1964

"I'm going to burn your face. Then you can sleep forever." *Maciste in Genghis Khan's Hell*, 1964

"The sword becomes you much more than a mirror." *Maciste in King Solomon's Mines*, 1964

"Ask for any reward. Even the death of a human being." *Maciste, Gladiator of Sparta*, 1964

"Go rot in a ditch. I'm the boss here." *The Revenge of Spartacus*, 1964

"Whenever you get tired of her, you can throw her away—the way I got rid of your mother." *Revenge of the Gladiators*, 1964

"Would you give me a little kiss, Hercules?" *Samson Against the Black Pirate*, 1964

"I want to see the terror of death in his eyes." *Sinbad Against the Seven Saracens*, 1964

"You want her? You take her!" *The Two Gladiators*, 1964

"Ursus is a zombie at my command!" *Ursus, the Terror of the Kirghiz*, 1964

"Not every man can be as handsome or courageous as Zorro." *Zorro the Rebel*, 1966

"You trust this man?" "Like my own brother." "You killed our brother." "That is why I trust him." *The Brigand of Kandahar*, 1967

"Her soul is an empty vessel. Only Roman blood can fill it!" *Centurion*, 2010

"I'm really not that interesting; I just played that kind of guy on film … That was easy … Living is tough." Roger Browne to author, February 2015

And to Jan, my wife, for using countless hours of her precious spare time in tracking down many, many peplum rarities and obscurities that otherwise would not have appeared in the pages of this book. Her patience in having to sit through most of them has been truly monumental!

TABLE OF CONTENTS

10   Foreword

18   Chapter 1: The Forefathers: *Captain from Castile* 1947, *Fabiola* and *Samson and Delilah* 1949

22   Chapter 2: The Hollywood Epic: Demetrius, Helen and Lower-Budget Influences 1946-1959

47   Chapter 3: Before Hercules: Italian Pepla 1950-1956

72   Chapter 4: Hail Hercules! The Rise of Peplum 1957-1959

100   Chapter 5: Hercules 1960-1965

113   Chapter 6: Maciste 1960-1965

133   Chapter 7: Samson 1961-1964

137   Chapter 8: Goliath and Ursus 1961-1964

148   Chapter 9: Ancient Greece

163   Chapter 10: The Gladiators

174	**Chapter 11: Ancient Egypt and Biblical**
186	**Chapter 12: Ancient Rome**
211	**Chapter 13: Babylon and the Middle East**
228	**Chapter 14: The Barbarians and the Pagans**
239	**Chapter 15: The Pirates**
253	**Chapter 16: Swashbucklers, Historical and Costume Dramas**
296	**Chapter 17: The Conquerors and the Vikings**
303	**Chapter 18: Zorro and The Musketeers**
310	**Chapter 19: It Wasn't Only the Italians**
333	**Chapter 20: The Spirit Lives On**
334	**Chapter 21: Index of Film Titles**
341	**Chapter 22: Source References /Author Biography**

Foreword

Peplum n. (in Ancient Greece) A woman's loose outer tunic or shawl. (Greek: Peplos) Mantle; A robe of state worn over the shoulder. pl. pepla/peplums

How did the peplum explosion that occurred in Italian cinema between 1958 and 1965 (its productive years) come into being? What were its origins? Why, like a multicolored firework burning brightly in the night sky, did it flare up and die out so quickly? All those 20-something cinemagoers who reveled in Ridley Scott's $103,000,000 *Gladiator* (Universal, 2000), Oliver Stone's $155,000,000 *Alexander* (Warner Bros., 2004), Antoine Fuqua's $120,000,000 *King Arthur* (Touchstone, 2004), Wolfgang Petersen's $175,000,000 *Troy* (Warner Bros., 2004), Ridley Scott's $130,000,000 *Kingdom of Heaven* (20th Century Fox, 2005), Zak Snyder's $65,000,000 *300* (Warner Bros., 2006), Ridley Scott's $140,000,000 *Exodus: Gods and Kings* (20th Century Fox, 2014), Paul W.S. Anderson's $80,000,000 *Pompeii* (TriStar, 2014) and Noam Murro's $110,000,000 *300: Rise of an Empire* (Warner Bros., 2014) were probably totally oblivious to the fact that over four decades back, the Cinecitta film studios in Rome were busy churning out scores of such movies under the banner of the sword and sandal epic, but on much lower budgets and without the aid of computerized effects. These boisterous, dusty Mediterranean-looking Italian sub-epics may have been program fillers on American and British cinema circuits, but they struck a chord with the public, if not the scornful critics who, unable to get to grips with this new-fangled foreign product and through a great deal of misconception on their part, slated sword and sandal to a man. Critical derision notwithstanding, these films were extremely popular during their heyday despite their obvious Latin roots, compounded by poor dubbing bestowed upon them by British and American distributors, filling smoky theaters on rainy Saturday afternoons, quite often double-billed with an English co-feature to balance the mix, and given restrictive (to English kids) A-ratings. And what you saw is what you got—those thousands of warriors on the march were made up of thousands of extras, not a few hundred multiplied by digital trickery. Likewise, the massive walls they were marching against were specially built for the occasion, not conjured up on a computer. Those mighty coliseums were actual ancient monuments, centuries-old stadia chosen by location hunters for authenticity (the same went for medieval castles and fortresses). Floggings, whippings and lashings were explicit, screened in gory detail (Britain's film censor would *not* condone views of backs being whiplashed—scenes had to be done face toward the camera), while battles, fights and duels were hard, bloody and violent, upsetting the censor in their graphic portrayal (often shot in close-up, and featuring both women and children) of death by sword, saber, scimitar, cutlass, dagger, axe, knife, spear, mace, javelin, lash, pike, rocks, arrow, lance, net and trident, club, fire, pitchfork, suffocation, white hot iron, lions, burning at the stake, strangulation by armlock and assorted torture devices Edgar Allan Poe would have approved of, everything filmed in vivid colors and backed by thunderous scores—and practically all came in some form of widescreen process to heighten the visceral viewing experience. Nearly every movie had the obligatory "sword embedded in abdomen," "arrow through the neck," "slash across the face," "back shredded by the cat-o'-nine-tails," "torso/face scarred by glowing brand," "several arrows in the torso," "body carved by the whip," "blood seeping through armor" and "spear in the chest" moment, a level of brutalism and outright nihilism unheard of at the time and generally avoided in today's cinema. This hard graft style of filmmaking gave the Italian sword and sandal movie, or to give it its Greek nomenclature, the peplum, a sweaty, gritty realism that super-spectacles like *Gladiator*, *Alexander*, *Troy* and *Kingdom of Heaven* didn't possess and couldn't hope to match despite their enormous budgets, assembled as they were with the aid of 21st-century CGI effects and in a climate of strict censorial codes of behavior.

Genre foundations date back to the early years of the Italian film industry and blockbusters *Quo Vadis* (1913 and 1924), *The Last Days of Pompeii* (1913), *Fabiola* (1913 and 1918) and 1914's 148-minute *Cabiria*, made on a colossal budget of (for the time) $200,000. From 1914-1927, 28 movies featuring strongman Bartolomeo Pagano in the role of Maciste, Italy's original mythical muscleman, were produced (this includes *Cabiria*, when the character was first introduced) but the vogue then entered into a decline of sorts, pushed into the shadows

Brad Pitt as Achilles in *Troy*

by the brief emergence of the postwar Italian neorealism movement, a creative period in which the Italian school of filmmaking got down to basics, reflecting on the poverty, exploitation, misery, bigotry and depression felt among the poorer working classes and often featuring non-professional actors in crucial roles. Key works in this field include Roberto Rossellini's *Rome, Open City* (1945), Vittorio De Sica's *Bicycle Thieves* (1948), Roberto Rossellini's *Germany, Year Zero* (1948), Giuseppe De Santis' *Bitter Rice* (1949) and Vittorio De Sica's *Umberto D.* (1952). To counteract this stark, pessimistic portrayal of Italian street life, filmmakers once again turned to the country's mythological heritage and the ancient spectacle to alleviate the gloom. Here could be found those Adonis-like heroes of old that audiences would be in tune and identify with, to once again raise their mood to one of optimism after the calamity that befell the country during World War II. Whereas a neorealist movie would, say, on an Ancient Roman or Greek canvas, focus on exposing the dark side of man's nature and present the scenario in downbeat, gritty black-and-white, the spectacle would portray it in color and, later on, widescreen, glorifying the narrative through sheer escapism—it would, in fact, create a simplified, purer world of heroes versus villains without delving too deeply into social injustice, a celebration of heroic values (and overt masculinity) where good always triumphed over evil and at tremendous odds; fairy tales for adults, as many have termed them, led by a figurehead in the shape of an iconic bodybuilder, a larger-than-life persona endowed with superhuman strength that cinemagoers could look up to. Plotlines were rigidly structured and rarely deviated from what some might perceive as a form of stubborn inflexibility—in fact, you would be perfectly justified in leveling the accusation that virtually the same recurring story and plot hooks were utilized throughout pepla to the point that you knew exactly what was about to happen before it *did* happen, umpteen variations on a single theme. And that was the challenge faced by the movie technicians ... how to present those well-worn themes in a fresh guise from one production to the next in order to keep peplum-happy punters rolling in through the theater doors. All credit must go to them; in most cases, they succeeded, in spades.

Some critics have claimed that a homoerotic element existed within pepla, particularly in the mythical strongman/gladiator movies where little was worn, underwear was basic and on full view, pumped-up oiled muscles were on display and studded leather predominated—never was the male of the species more heavily promoted in the "body beautiful" stakes than in peplum! True, I have seen a lot of films where the scantily clad male backside and an actor's nipples have been the focus of undue attention from the camera rather than what else is occurring at the time, but even if such connotations did/do exist, it surely is in the mind of the viewer, not the director concerned! In olden times, males and females didn't wear a great deal of clothing due to the hot climates they inhabited, a fact mirrored by the multitude of film companies striving for genuineness in their wardrobe/costume departments. Let's just leave it at that!

Also existing within pepla was an undeniable cruel streak toward women and animals. I have mentioned this where it appears in a certain production and won't dwell on it here. Censorship on the Continent in those days appeared to be quite lax when it came down to it; many of the harrowing scenes in, say, Siro Marcellini's *The Hero of Babylon* would either be trimmed in Britain, even today, or the film handed an adult "18" certifi-

Bartolomeo Pagano played mythical strongman Maciste in *Cabiria*.

cate, an attestation in some ways, albeit a disturbing one, of how savage peplum could be over 50 years ago. However, busty, leggy and extremely attractive females at the mercy of all kinds of ghastly physical abuse made for good box-office receipts, something that most fans wouldn't argue with. These films were made by the hot-blooded, temperamental Italians, not the more conservative Americans and English, and it shows in many a peplum outing.

There was a definite crossover period between the darker neorealism and the lighter pepla, termed by director Vittorio Cottafavi "neo-mythologism." Alessandro Blasetti's *Fabiola* (1949), Marcel L'Herbier and Paolo Moffa's *The Last Days of Pompeii* (1950), Ferruccio Cerio's *The Sack of Rome* (1953) and Riccardo Freda's *Spartacus* (1953), for example, were all produced in black-and-white, more neorealist in outlook than straightforward spectacle. But spurred on by the success of Cecil B. DeMille's *Samson and Delilah* (1949) and Mervyn LeRoy's *Quo Vadis* (1951), Italian sword and sandal swiftly dropped the neorealist ambience and the gravitas, focusing on lavish kitsch-filled mayhem, also branching out into *cappa e spada* (swashbuckling) and historical costumers, the new product advertised in lurid poster artwork plastered in hyperbolic publicity blurbs and overblown slogans. The term "peplum" was coined following the international spotlight cast on Pietro Francisci's *The Labors of Hercules* in 1957/1958; the movie took the overseas market by storm despite a universal critical drubbing. A new, and rather unique, genre was born, *Hercules* having a snowball

Italian neorealism: German persecution of Italians in Roberto Rossellini's *Rome, Open City*.

effect; over 300 films poured forth from a profusion of Italian studios before the bubble burst in 1966/1967, due mainly to decreasing budgets, increasingly regurgitated storylines and the burgeoning Spaghetti Western. Traditional pepla of the mythological hero variety (Hercules; Maciste; Samson; Goliath; Ursus) spread outwards, encompassing within its varied framework Fantasy, Gladiators, Ancient Rome, Greek Mythology, Ancient Egypt, Barbarians, Vikings, Cavaliers, Babylon, the Middle East, Pirates, Knights, Swashbucklers, Conquerors, Costume Dramas, Historical Dramas and Biblical mini-epics, many featuring a well-known character such as Zorro, Robin Hood, Cleopatra, the Three Musketeers and Julius Caesar, a welter of Italian adventure and fantasy features which knew no bounds, an eruption of cheesy, blood-soaked hokum spread over seven to eight years that vanished as quickly as it had begun. The great (*The Trojan War*) rubbed shoulders with the not-so-great (*Zorikan the Barbarian*) to the downright awful (*The Normans*), but even the worst of the bunch are interesting to view these days as, apart from a brief resurgence in the 1980s, kicking off with Arnold Schwarzenegger's *Conan the Barbarian* (1982), Italian pepla produced during the peak period of 1958-1965 are veritable "one-offs," never repeated but often imitated. The aim of this study is to uncover and bring to light, over the course of 400-plus feature films, the cult of the sword and sandal, torch and toga, sword and spear, sword and sorcery, cloak-and-dagger, swashbuckler (*cappa e spada*), *fusto*, or *fusti* (musclemen) and blood and sand movie, from its early beginnings, *Fabiola* in 1949, to *Massacre in the Black Forest* in 1967. In putting a name to a face, hopefully a new generation of cinemagoers will be encouraged to become interested in learning about the long-forgotten exploits of musclemen Steve Reeves, Gordon Mitchell, Dan Vadis, Alan Steel, Brad Harris, Gordon Scott, Kirk Morris, Ed Fury, Mark Forest, Richard Harrison, Peter Lupus, Howard Ross, Reg Park, Samson Burke, Iloosh Khoshabe et al., and exotic babes Chelo Alonso, Gianna Maria Canale, Gloria Milland, José Greci, Isabelle Corey, Wandisa Guida, Helga Liné, Bella Cortez, Daniela Rocca, cousins Moira and Liana Orfei, Leonora Ruffo, Rosalba Neri, Hélène Chanel and Lisa Gastoni, actors and actresses that starred in colorful, exciting, enjoyable, sometimes very dark and violent, occasionally just plain daft, fodder with large helpings of "camp" to spice things up.

Composers were prolific in pepla, producing scores as memorable as anything to come out of Hollywood. Between them, the "big six," Carlo Franci, Carlo Savina, Carlo Rustichelli, Francesco De Masi, Angelo Francesco Lavagnino and Carlo Innocenzi, knocked out over 150 scores between 1958 and 1966, a prodigious output showing no signs of decline in excellence from one production to the next. Music that stirred the blood, aroused the senses and brought tears to the eyes in sweeter-than-sweet leitmotifs during the quieter/romantic interludes. 99 percent of Italian pepla covered in this book are embellished with a great, at times memorable, soundtrack. Likewise, cinematographers dressed their productions in luxurious colors; Mario Bava wasn't the only highly distinguished artist in this field—Alvaro Mancori, Luciano Trasatti, Augusto Tiezzi, Tino (Clemente) Santoni, Pier Ludovico Pavoni, Julio Ortas, Raffaele Masciocchi and many, many others conveyed rich shades and textures to the silver screen that outside of their native country would have earned them a clutch of Oscars; paintings by Old Masters come to life in front of your very eyes. As with the soundtrack, lavish color photography is par for the course in Italian sword and sandal and *cappa e spada*. The same goes for pithy scripts, often laced with dark humor, usually at the expense of the persecuted Christians, as in this priceless retort from Vladimir Medar (playing Nero) in *The Fire of Rome*: "An unforgettable sight. Rome illuminated by the Christians!" I've listed 55 great one-liners in my Dedication—many more will be included throughout the coming chapters!

In writing this volume, I have experienced in no short measure a whole raft of insurmountable problems relating to research on the lost cinematic world of pepla. Over a 63-year span spent in watching every kind of genre movie imaginable at the cinema, on television, on tape, on boxed film reels and on digital disc—war, Western, comedy, social drama, sci-fi, horror, *film noir*, fantasy, musical, cartoon, crime, adventure, romance, biographs, epic—I have *never* come across a category of feature film that has been so badly, and sadly, neglected and treated with a worrying lack of respect by the media as Italian peplum. It's as though the entire misunderstood (and unrecognized) genre has been swept under the carpet, to lie hidden in obscurity for decades, gathering dust. DVD issues, right across the board, are extremely limited in availability (an anomaly in our "let's get everything onto disc" age; some have literally disappeared off the face of the Earth) and, for the most part, in a lamentable state of digital transfer: Pan and scan replacing widescreen/letterbox 2.35:1 aspect ratio; color washed out, faded or reduced to one tint, usually red; poor sound/dialogue synchronization; black-and-white replacing color altogether (I have watched around a dozen films where this has occurred); and many prints "wobbly" and blurred, as if viewed through jelly—flotsam and jetsam making for ragged, scuzzy viewing on an unprecedented scale. Best available digital copies in excellent quality can be obtained from Italy, Greece, Germany (this country's DVDs are of spick and span quality) and France, but these are in Italian, Greek, Spanish, German and French dialogue with no subtitles. For British viewers, French VHS tapes containing some of the scarcer pepla can only be watched in black-and-white due to the incompatible French SECAM system; this can be remedied back

Italian neo-mythologism: Roman persecution of Christians in Alessandro Blasetti's *Fabiola*.

to color at a cost. A lot of obscure pepla can be acquired in Italian/Spanish/French-spoken dialogue containing Greek subtitles, taken from old Greek tapes; I have also come across subtitles in Russian, Polish, Czechoslovakian, German, Dutch, Portuguese and Arabic. Collectors would do well to trawl German, Greek and Italian sites for hard-to-finds, particularly Germany who sporadically issue thin-on-the-ground pepla in their original color that are only available in black-and-white elsewhere. It is *very* rare to lay hands on a pristine, dubbed/subtitled (in English) widescreen/letterbox DVD copy of an Italian peplum feature—when you do, it's like a breath of fresh air!

Mario Tota's 1961 production *Suleiman the Conqueror* and Nick Nostro's *La cieca di Sorrento* (1963) both sum up this (to the fan) deplorable state of affairs which in all probability will never be rectified. In Tota's movie, we have a marvelously constructed epic of the old school, featuring terrific battle scenes, a magnificent Francesco De Masi score, moving human drama and a real breadth of vision that has been allowed to languish in the vaults. Not available officially, gray market DVDs are pan and scan, the color dulled, with jumps in continuity. This marvelous picture will probably never be seen in its original magnificence, a criminal shame. And that's the trick in watching peplum, to actually *enjoy* what you're viewing and give the film a fair hearing—you *have* to exercise a great deal of imagination and place yourself in an auditorium of over 50 years ago, envisaging a film like *Suleiman the Conqueror* as it was meant to be presented to the public on the big silver screen, in Totalscope and Eastmancolor, totally free of blemishes. It's difficult, but only then can you begin to appreciate the amount of artistry and hard work that went into pictures like these and give it the critique it deserves.

The same can be said about *La cieca di Sorrento*, commonly known as *Revenge of the Black Knight*. Originally shown in Techniscope/Technicolor, current ultra-obscure prints, though mercifully still in widescreen, exhibit the following: Vertical and horizontal scratches; black-and-white changing to brown-and-white and even dark mauve; erratic breaks and sudden jumps in continuity and film movement; blurred, out-of-focus ghosting of images; a "muddiness" in the center of screen; wonky soundtrack; shadows on the edges; and countless random marks from start to finish. Some may fight shy of watching *any* feature film in that condition; for the writer engaged in researching pepla, it represents the norm rather than the exception to the rule. Therefore, out of the countless rare pepla detailed in the following chapters, I nominate Nick Nostro's once vibrant costume swashbuckler as the worst case of a peplum film transfer to digital disc that I have had the misfortune to sit through. Like *Suleiman the Conqueror*, it will never be seen as how it was meant to be seen, all those decades ago.

Films are reviewed under their Italian release dates, not the dates they appeared in other countries, which could differ by two to three years. In some instances, a title is entered under the year it was copyrighted and completed and had its release date postponed for a few months, the classic example being Guido Malatesta's *Maciste Against the Headhunters* (*Colossus and the Headhunters*). Various online sites quote release dates as 1960, 1962, 1963 and even 1965. In fact, the movie was finalized toward the end of 1962 but, due to production hassles and another project the director was working on, not released in Italy until January 1963. Therefore, in this instance, Malatesta's hokey *Maciste* opus appears under 1962, the year it was finally wrapped up.

Then there is the genuine difficulty in establishing role identity and production details; making sense while sifting through a mass of conflicting, contradictory information can, to the film writer, be a real headache. Source material/statistics/data is nonexistent, inadequate, scant and/or simply wrong. Internet sites can be notoriously inaccurate and inconsistent when it comes to peplum film credits, a marked lack of attention regarding the proper facts, either giving incorrect actors' names against incorrect character names, omitting a character name altogether or simply listing the actors' names in alphabetical order, *not* in the order of importance they appeared in the actual film (a leading actor whose surname starts with a "T" can find himself near the bottom of a list, while a minor actor whose surname starts with a "B" near the top). Key technicians are missing in "cast and crew" sections while synopses are so muddled that you are left wondering whether the movie has ever been seen at all. Let's give some examples of this: In Francesco De Feo's *The Revenge of the Iron Mask*, Michel Lemoine's role of Andrea is switched (in some reviews) with that of Pietro Albani as Marco, thereby creating plot confusion by having Lemoine romancing his own sister (Wandisa Guida); Lemoine is also incorrectly spelled as Lamoine, and Albani as Albano. And Andrea Bosic *doesn't* go off to fight the French with a bucket-mask over his head in the end as suggested. Sergio Grieco's plots to *The Mysterious Swordsman* and *The Black Devil* are often interchanged while Andrea Aureli is listed on two sites as Rhia in *Maciste Against the Monsters* when in fact he was the King of the Droods and Rhia, a woman, was played by Birgit Bergen! In *The Prince in the Red Mask*, Armando Trovajoli wrote the music, not, as some sites state, Carlo Innocenzi. *The Defeat of the Barbarians* had director Piero Regnoli's young daughter, Daniela, in the part of Prince Albert; she was *not* Moira Orfei's black maidservant, played by Beryl Cunningham, as accredited on some sites. Online photos can also throw you off track: Kirk Morris and Hélène Chanel pictured in *Valley of the Thundering Echo* turn up somewhere else as being from *The Ruler of the Desert*; an image of Mark Forest from one of his seven *Maciste* outings is listed as a still from a *Hercules* picture, and so on, and so forth. These are the challenges facing the writer engaged on peplum research who wishes to present the true picture, not one based on incorrect analysis passed on over the years.

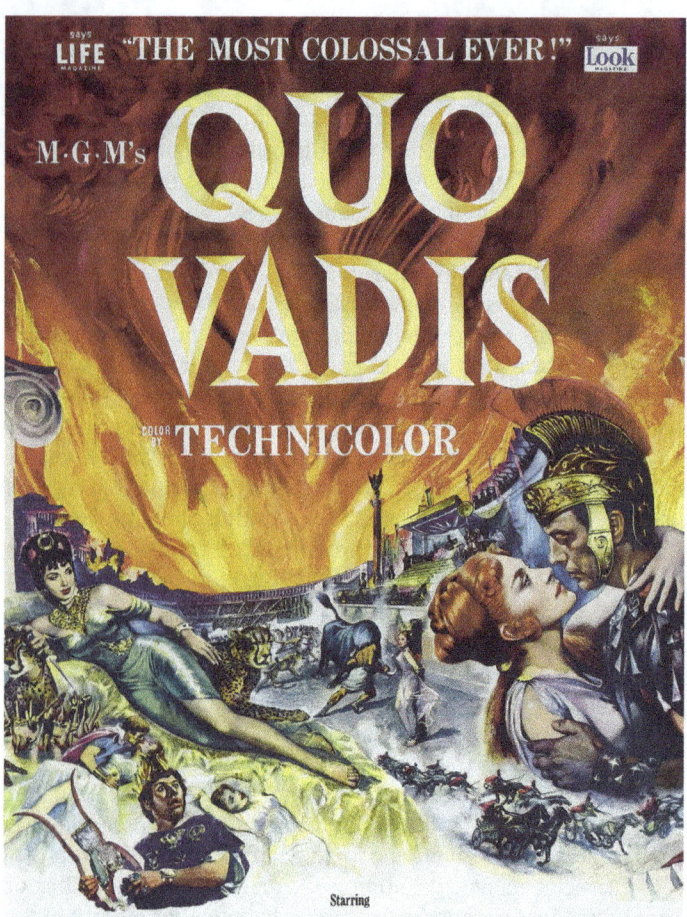

The Americanized versions issued by Embassy Pictures (AVCO Embassy) and Medallion are the worst culprits, especially *The Sons of Hercules* TV syndicated series, only showing the *Son of Hercules* U.S. title, the leading actors and director's name in the truncated credits and nothing else, the producer being the one that is most commonly ignored. Spellings can be a minefield, both in actors' and characters' names: Georges Marchal becomes George Marshall, Hedy Vessel, Edy Vessell and Conrado San Martin, Conrado Sanmartin. In *Maciste and the Queen of Samar*, the chief moon man, depending on what source you look at, be it film, book or Internet article, is variously named Rudolphis, Redolphis, Rodolphes, Redolphus or Rodopes. Christopher Lee in *Hercules at the Center of the Earth* can be found as Lico, or Lyco, or Licos, or Licho—take your pick of any. Italian names ending in "ius" become "io," or vice versa, or differ drastically from what is heard on dubbed discs. In non-Italian prints, the Anglicization of names, particularly directors, is quite often found; Antonio Margheriti morphs into Anthony Dawson, Umberto Scarpelli into Richard McNamara. And many Italian players adopted American names, as will be seen throughout the book; for instance, José Greci was sometimes listed as Susan Paget/Liz Havilland, Mimmo Palmara as Dick Palmer. The changing of titles is legendary within the sphere of pepla, some films containing as many as four replacement names *after* the original Italian title—*The Devils of Sparti-*

vento and *Revak, the Slave of Carthage* are prime examples of this. Italian film titles tended to reflect more aesthetically the production's contents, emphasizing the main character(s), U.S. versions pandering to the masses by going for the jugular and not giving any indication as to what the picture was all about: *Judith and Holfernes* was altered to *Head of a Tyrant*, *Genoveffa of Brabant* became *The Revenge of the Crusader*, *Rosamund and Alboino* changed to *Sword of the Conqueror*, *Romulus and Remus* was known as *Duel of the Titans*, *Maciste at the Court of the Great Khan* became *Samson and the Seven Miracles of the World* and *The Last Gladiator* morphed into *Messalina Against the Son of Hercules*. In all probability, the average cinemagoer will never have heard of any of these titles (*The Tyrant of Lydia Against the Son of Hercules*? What's all that about?), while newcomers to pepla may be utterly perplexed by the plethora of alternative names many sword and sandal movies come under—for instance, Cineluxor's 1964 offering, *Valley of the Thundering Echo*, can be found listed on various online sites as *Hercules of the Desert*, *Maciste and the Women of the Valley* and *Desert Raiders*, depending on which country the picture was released in—but it shouldn't be confused with *The Ruler of the Desert* (1964), also known as *Desert Raiders*; both films star Kirk Morris and have near-enough the same production team, but *are* different! And how many films with the title of *Revenge of the Gladiators* can a peplum fan take!

Main character names are included where appropriate and if available. On occasions where (a) no character names are listed anywhere, (b) the film is in a foreign language lacking subtitles or (c) in such a condition as to render speech inaudible, there will be no character names, or the odd one. And character names can differ, from one country's print to another—Marco in one can become Marcellus in another!

Peplum movies were produced by independent film companies on small to medium budgets; unless acting as a distributor, the giant Hollywood corporations of Columbia, MGM, Warner Bros., Paramount, 20th Century Fox and their ilk are notable by their absence in chapters 3-18 of this book, which deal exclusively with Italian pepla. Even Romana Film, founded in 1946 and one of the larger of the pack, was small fry compared to, say, an outfit the size and substance of Universal-International. Companies such as Panda Film, Illiria Film, Jonia Film, Titanus, Flora Film, Explorer Film '58, Artix Cinema, Leone Film, Liber Film, Jork Film, Filmes Rome, Rosa Film, Rodes Cinematografica, San Paolo Films, Itala Film, Avala Film, SpA Cinematografica, CIRAC, Alta Vista, Atlantica, Adelphia, Capi Film, Prometeo Film, Lux Film, Oro Film, Athena Cinematografica, Excelsa Film, Galatea Film, Walmar Cinematografica, Ambrosiana and Atenea have long since disappeared off the cinematic map and remain today in obscurity, as does most of their product.

Throughout the chapters, I have headed each film using the English language title with the original Italian release title in brackets, followed by alternative titles as applicable. Not all Italian film titles translate literally into English, but the majority do. As an illustration of this, *Giovanni dalle bande nere* translates as *John from the Black Bands*, which is *not* a release title, has never existed as such and has never been screened in a cinema under that name *in English*. Therefore, to clarify matters, I have listed the film under its English title of *The Violent Patriot*. Similarly, the Italian title for *Swordsman of Siena* is *La congiura dei dieci*, which translates as *The Conspiracy of the Ten*—but the film has *never* been screened under this *English* translation.

Most of the pictures examined don't present this problem and match Italian titles with English/European names, both formally and informally, as with *Hercules at the Center of the Earth* (*Ercole al centro della terra*) which is formal, or *Captain Phantom* (*Capitan Fantasma*) which is informal; here, Fantasma can mean "ghost" or "phantom," the latter being the common usage. Another anomaly that can occur is that of the Italian title used extensively worldwide in a country's own dialect in preference to the English language release title, a case in point being *The Tomb of the Kings* (*Il sepolcro dei re*). The English title was *Cleopatra's Daughter*, but many countries stuck with *The Tomb of the Kings* or the similar *The Tomb of the Pharaoh* (s). To simplify this apparent confusion, I have, within the body of a movie analysis, referred to the film title that I feel the reader will be more comfortable with. Hopefully, cross-referencing the index at the back will alleviate any headscratching. The main Italian production company comes first and other production companies follow, if more than one country was involved in the shooting and finance. Various permutations of widescreen/color and original running times are included, the times in brackets denoting the length screened elsewhere; quite often, these films were trimmed for worldwide distribution, either by the censor or the distributor. As these pictures were Italian in origin, the Italian title, however strange and unknown it may appear to the peplum novice, gets first nod. Ratings given to each production are as follows:

✞✞✞✞✞ Classic peplum

✞✞✞✞   Excellent

✞✞✞   Good

✞✞   Average

✞   Poor

I have been fortunate in catching a handful of pepla at the time they were released in the United Kingdom in their natural habitat, a cinema. In September 1955, my father took me to see 20th Century Fox's follow-up to *The Robe*, *Demetrius and the Gladiators*, which carried an "A" certificate in England. For the benefit of non-British readers, the United Kingdom had three film classifications during the 1950s/1960s: The infamous "X," suitable for over-16s only; the "A," suitable for over-14s only, but if under 14, you could watch the movie accompanied by an adult; and the "U," suitable for all. These are the ratings that will be used throughout this book in relation to how the British Board of Film Censors viewed the Italian pepla genre motion pictures for what they deemed "adult content" on first release. *Demetrius* was pretty bloodthirsty fare for its day, hence its "A" rating, a lot more down-to-earth and realistically violent than *The Robe*'s pedestrian-paced dramatics had managed to be (*The Robe* was heavily promoted by the Fox publicity machine as the first to be shot in CinemaScope), a tasty dish for an enthusiastic audience to get their teeth into in its gritty portrayal of life in the gladiatorial arena, lorded over by Jay Robinson's camp, utterly mad Caligula; beefy Victor Mature played a Greek slave. Budgeted at $4,000,000, *Demetrius* was one of the many lavish, highly successful Hollywood Biblical blockbusters that the Italian film industry would base their lower-budgeted sword and sandal epics on from 1957 onward, so, in a way, Delmer Daves' captivating take on Ancient Roman brutality was the first

Beefcake represented by Alan Steel

peplum movie I ever saw in a cinema. The first peplum *proper*, that is an Italian feature with unrecognizable foreign actors as opposed to recognizable American actors, came in the form of two in quick succession, *Goliath and the Barbarians* (billed with *The Day They Robbed the Bank of England*) and *The Last Days of Pompeii* (with *The Steel Bayonet*), caught within the space of a fortnight in December 1960. Both starred the mighty Steve Reeves and were A-rated, both were in widescreen and dazzling color and both suffered from appalling dubbing. And these weren't the only torch and toga movies I caught in a movie theater. Between June 1961 and December 1965, I sat through 34 others (Italian, American and English) as follows with their co-features at the time; the titles (in bold) are those bestowed upon them by their British distributors:

Hercules c/w (coupled with) **Hercules Unchained**

The Thief of Baghdad c/w ***The Giant of Marathon***

The 3 Worlds of Gulliver c/w ***Sword of Sherwood Forest***

Morgan, the Pirate c/w On the Fiddle

The Colossus of Rhodes

Sign of the Gladiator c/w ***Zarak***

Son of Samson c/w Serious Charge

Sodom and Gomorrah

Guns of the Black Witch c/w ***The Bandit of Zhobe***

Last of the Vikings c/w House of Mystery

The Phantom of the Opera c/w ***Captain Clegg***

Mysterious Island c/w ***The Pirates of Blood River***

Belmonte Castle was one of many real-life fortresses used by peplum filmmakers.

Glamour represented by Helga Liné

The Wonders of Aladdin c/w *Watch Your Stern*
Hercules at the Center of the Earth c/w *Destry*
Fury at Smugglers' Bay c/w *The Minotaur*
Jason and the Argonauts c/w *Siege of the Saxons*
Samson and the 7 Miracles c/w *Double Bunk*
Constantine the Great c/w *Mrs. Gibbon's Boys*
Marco Polo c/w *The Young and the Cool*
Nights of Rasputin c/w *Corridors of Blood*
The Scarlet Blade c/w *The Son of Captain Blood*
The Devil-Ship Pirates c/w *The Secret Seven*
The Son of Spartacus c/w *Gladiators 7*
Jason and the Golden Fleece c/w *Mystery Submarine*
The War Lord

At the time, I viewed the Italian efforts with a mixture of enjoyment and "what on earth is this all about?" puzzlement, oddball foreign actioners that, in a packed auditorium, were noisy and colorful, difficult to take in and fully understand because of the dubbing and sheer *unfamiliarity* of what was on offer. I applauded the fact that they were different without realizing how they were conceived and by whom—the Italian spectacle didn't conform to the way the Americans or the British would have presented it, deviating from the norm in so many ways. It is only now, after sitting through scores of them, that I can acknowledge and raise my hat to the enormous, almost staggering, amount of effort and toil that went on during those years in order to bring this immense body of work to the silver screen. From a film history point of view, the labors of these Italian filmmakers, like the labors of Hercules, must not be allowed to, as so many victims do in peplum, fester in the vaults, or fade from the pages of movie compendiums.

So enter a bygone world where handsome mythological heroes sporting bulging, gleaming muscles pick up colossal polystyrene boulders, topple polystyrene walls, handle tree trunks like matchsticks, take on lions barehanded, break chains, bend bars, demolish walls, rescue damsels in distress, have two beautiful women vying for their attention and lead rebel groups in overthrowing power-hungry usurpers; where said damsels in distress, when rescued, whisper "I'll be your slave" into their savior's ear; where ancient cultures clash, one civilized and the other uncivilized; where outlandish cardboard monsters dwell in garish underground grottos; where kings are ousted by devious second-in-commands; where wicked, femme fatale queens scheme and rule their kingdoms in fear; where you have the test, or trial, of strength; where every castle has at least one secret passage and a trapdoor; where the narrative is often punctuated by an exotic, flesh-revealing dance; where leading men are impossibly handsome and leading women impossibly gorgeous; where the Monte Gelato falls and the Lapilli quarries are used extensively for location shooting; where comic relief comes in the form of a dwarf; where most bouts of action commence with a cry of "Follow me!" followed by "Die, you dog!"; where Zorro, Robin Hood and the Three Musketeers crop up in unfamiliar surroundings; where the ultimatum of "Marry me and I'll spare him/her/them" is a common threat; where heroes are cornered/encircled by a ring of swords/spears/lances/pikes, *the* classic "We've gotcha!" shot; where villages are razed to the ground by heathen hordes; where heroines in peril hide in convents; where heroes go incognito dressed as friars; where caves, caverns and grottos predominate, either as rebel hideouts or the entrance to subterranean realms of ancient races; where real-life castles, palaces, galleons and amphitheaters are used instead of painted backdrops, models and computer mock-ups; where castles and palaces contain a pit full of snakes, rats or crocodiles; where gigantic sets have been constructed by the hand of man; where slaves are sent to work on the gristmill; where extended tavern brawls are plentiful; where the governor's daughter is packed off to a nunnery if she misbehaves; where battle scenes last up

The Devil-Ship Pirates went the rounds in England with *The Invincible Seven* (aka *The Secret Seven*).

to 10 minutes or more; where crusading avengers wear black/red masks; where bad guys wear red cloaks/capes; where arranged marriages are rudely interrupted, much to the relief of the bride who didn't want to wed her villainous bridegroom in the first place; where eavesdroppers spy from inside statues; where flamboyant costume design dazzles the senses; where maidens flaunt ample bosoms and flash shapely thighs; where the hero is falsely accused of the murder of his fiancée's father; where arena clashes and mortal combat fights are uncompromisingly rough, tough, bloody and brutal; where people fall in love a minute after meeting one another; where fiendish torture devices are straight from the pages of Edgar Allan Poe; where cruelty toward animals and the fairer sex is not entirely suitable for sensitive souls; where scenes of mass destruction equal, if not better, the CGI cataclysms prevalent in today's cinema; and where practically every picture on offer contains a fabulous score, superb color photography and is incisively directed to ensure maximum excitement on an adrenalin-pumping level. Welcome, then, to the wonderful world of Italian peplum cinema—whether what on offer is brilliant or otherwise, and on occasion defies all sense of logic, you will not fail to be intrigued and entertained by motion pictures that come served on a platter containing huge portions of flamboyancy, kitsch, schlock and, let's not forget, *expertise*, guilty pleasures by the score. It's an unrepeatable, distinctive and in many ways divorced from mainstream viewing experience, a "once in a cinematic lifetime" genre that has been kept under wraps for far too long; let us hope that in some small way, this book will give these movies, and the people who participated in them, the airing they so richly deserve, and enlighten those cinemagoers to whom the word "peplum" remains, in 2017, a complete and utter mystery.

1
The Forefathers: *Captain from Castile* 1947, *Fabiola* and *Samson and Delilah* 1949

Captain from Castile, *Fabiola* and *Samson and Delilah*—three major motion picture events produced toward the end of the 1940s that were the templates, in their own individual fashions, for the pepla boom: the first for its swashbuckling values, the second for its gladiatorial/Ancient Rome themes and the third for introducing a muscleman as the main hero. Lengthy and expensive, these can lay claim to be the forefathers of the pepla movement and still make for hugely enjoyable viewing today; time hasn't diminished their power and capacity to entertain an audience one iota.

Darkly handsome Tyrone Power is the *Captain from Castile*.

Captain from Castile

20th Century Fox (US); Technicolor; 141 mins; Producer: Lamar Trotti; Director: Henry King ✝✝✝✝✝

There isn't a single battle scene in *Captain from Castile*, but don't let that put you off. Executive producer Darryl F. Zanuck's $4,000,000 1947 adaptation of Samuel Shellabarger's popular (of its day) 1945 novel, set in Spain and Mexico in 1518, is the supreme Hollywood swashbuckling romantic adventure, containing a whole stack of pointers that were to be employed repeatedly throughout the Italian *cappa e spada* movement; Fox's extravagant picture, above all others of the period, is a veritable blueprint of all that was to follow in the genre. Darkly handsome Tyrone Power, no stranger to the swashbuckler, having starred in, among others, *The Mark of Zorro* (Fox, 1940), *The Black Swan* (Fox, 1942) and *Son of Fury* (Fox, 1942), played wronged nobleman Pedro De Vargas, escaping from the clutches of ruthless Inquisition agent John Sutton (Diego De Silva) after his 12-year-old sister had been brutally tortured and murdered on a trumped-up charge of heresy. Joining Power is his mother, father, sidekick Lee J. Cobb (Juan) and, in her film debut, peasant girl Jean Peters (Catana). Power, Cobb and Peters decide to sail to the New World and enlist in Hernando Cortez's conquistadors who are embarking on an expedition to relieve Aztec Emperor Montezuma of his legendary treasure trove and conquer the Aztec empire. Alighting on Mexican shores, the trio join up with strict disciplinarian Cesar Romero (Cortez), busy driving his men ever westward despite continual warnings from Montezuma's ambassadors to "leave our land" and protests from the Governor in Cuba, alarmed at the Spaniard's relentless quest for gold. Power eventually marries Peters and is badly injured in a plot to undermine Romero's command and steal his stockpile of valuables. Sutton, run through by Power's rapier thrust in Spain, turns up as the king's emissary, having survived, and old wounds are reopened. Indian slave Jay Silverheels (Coatl), nursing a grudge against Sutton, strangles him to death in his tent and the film ends with Romero's army, plus Peters holding her newborn infant, continuing their journey to confront Montezuma and his riches.

A nobleman falsely accused of heresy, his family and possessions destroyed by an evil-minded competitor; Power's "she who mustn't be touched" fiancée (Barbara Lawrence), a passionless woman more in love with the idea of being in love than true love itself; the lady eventually wed to ne'er-do-well Sutton for money and prestige in an arranged marriage she doesn't, on this occasion, object to; a peasant girl besotted with a man far above her station; Gothic-style dungeon scenes; Power trapped against a wall by a dozen lances; horseback chases through woods; a sojourn beside a picturesque waterfall (shot at Uruapan, Michoacan, Mexico); Cobb disguised as a friar to elude capture; the questioning of Christian beliefs; native pageantry; authentic costumes; a secret temple door; a fight to restore family honor; and Power reprieved at the last minute for the murder of Sutton. It's all there, in one form or another, vignettes and themes that would form the basis for the tidal wave of Italian swashbucklers that gathered pace from 1950 onward. Add to this Alfred Newman's magnificent Oscar-nominated score (his romantic leitmotifs are achingly poignant, his rousing marching theme uplifting the senses), wonderful, atmospheric cinematography by Arthur E. Arling and Charles G. Clarke, Henry King's camera lingering on the eminently photogenic pairing of Power and Peters as they perform an emotion-charged flamenco dance (the couple had a brief fling off-set) and one of cinema's most mesmerizing fade-outs, Romero's massed forces swarming across the Mexican landscape as a volcano belches dark, slowly spreading vapors in the distance (filming took place in the vicinity of the active Paricutin volcano near Uruapan, which erupted during shooting; its dense plume of smoke can first be detected in the 101st minute) and you have the cinematic equivalent of a storybook come vividly to life, presented in oodles of grand, colorful Hollywood flamboyancy; a vivid costume swashbuckler that, like a good book, that can be savored and indulged in over and over again.

Fabiola [*Fabiola*] aka *The Fighting Gladiator*
Universalia Film (Italy/France); B&W; 164 (96) mins; Producer: Salvo D'Angelo; Director: Alessandro Blasetti ✝✝✝✝✝

Samson and Delilah
Paramount (US); Technicolor; 131 mins; Produced and Directed by Cecil B. DeMille ✝✝✝✝✝

Two films that were released in 1949 and produced several thousand miles apart can be cited as the prototypes of the peplum sword and sandal/muscleman movement that gained momentum from the mid-'50s onward, bursting into life in 1957/1958 with Steve Reeves' first *Hercules* feature: Alessandro Blasetti's *Fabiola* and Cecil B. DeMille's *Samson and Delilah*. Both contain the fundamental components that were to figure strongly in countless peplum features to come: beefcake actors, beautiful women, gladiators, the persecution of Christians, pagan dances, opulent sets, authentic costumes, dwarfs, violent deaths, clashes in the arena, wicked villains, subjugation of the people and brutal sadism on a spectacular scale. While DeMille's three million dollar Old Testament tale unashamedly wallowed in old-fashioned Hollywood kitsch, Blasetti's one million dollar Ancient Rome opus was a lot darker in mood, presented in fashionable Italian postwar neorealism style, keeping to the black-and-white format that gave this genre its renowned stark, gritty feel. Yes, *Fabiola* and *Samson and Delilah* should be regarded as the two major pre-1950 influences that spawned a host of sword and sandal imitators, yet poles apart in looks, ideas and execution, *Fabiola* opting for character depth over out-and-out spectacle, *Samson and Delilah* quite the reverse, concentrating on comic book escapism. But perhaps that was a good thing. They offered filmmakers, eyeing up the potential for their own projects, totally different slants and angles on what were to become much-favored familiar themes, yet at the same time portraying their leading heroes, Rhual and Samson, as strong, upright, muscle-packed citizens fighting unjust causes, becoming champions for the oppressed. Both movies did big business at the box-office—*Fabiola*, in its severely edited form, made over a million dollars profit in America when shown in 1951, while DeMille's opus, as expected from the undisputed master of the expensive, flamboyant epic, raked in a fortune.

On its 1951 U.S. release, *Fabiola* was screened in a dubbed, 96-minute edit. The original Italian length came in at 183 minutes, but this appears to be no longer available; the European cut of 164 minutes is generally acknowledged as the true representation of Blasetti's masterpiece, obtainable in Italian only, lacking subtitles. For those not conversant in Italian, view the heavily butchered, incomprehensible, dubbed U.S. version to grasp who among the dozens of players is who, and doing what, then relax and take in the 164-minute picture, picking up the shorn 68 minutes as you go along. Filmed twice during the silent era (1913 and 1918), *Fabiola* tells the story of the tempestuous love affair between Henri Vidal (Rhual) and Michele Morgan (Fabiola), set during the period of Roman persecution and hostility toward Christians. The scenario is austere and dialogue-driven, Blasetti cramming his shots with multitudes of characters and their motivations, each slotting effortlessly into the richly woven tapestry of events. Vidal, on a secret mission to spread the word of the nascent Christianity movement throughout Rome, is falsely accused of murdering friend Michel Simon (as Fabius Severus) during a prolonged feast in which the garrulous senator unwisely expounds his sympathies for Christians and freedom from slavery in front of his guests, among whom lurk several enemies. Morgan is his daughter, she and Vidal falling passionately in lust after a heated midnight meeting on a beach (the couple had an off-set romance, so what you saw is what you got!). The moment when Vidal first sets eyes on her standing beside a garden pool like a white marble statue is straight out of a Jean Cocteau fantasy ("You looked like a goddess."), enhanced by Enzo Masetti's wonderfully evocative music and Mario Craveri and Ubaldo Marelli's imaginative lighting. Densely plotted, *Fabiola*

Third choice Victor Mature and screen goddess Hedy Lamarr as *Samson and Delilah*

encompasses within its very broad canvas the lovers' seemingly doomed relationship, the quest to discover Simon's real killer, the introduction of a pair of corrupt politicians in Louis Salou (Fulvius) and Paolo Stoppa (Pronsul Manlius Valerian), devout Christian leader Sergio Tofano (Luciano), Morgan's close companion Elisa Cegani (Sira), Franco Interlenghi as young bully-cum-assassin Corvino and Massimo Girotti's honest Sebastian, a centurion on the side of the god-fearers, all played out against a backdrop of seething unrest.

It's a heady, deeply involving (and moving), complex brew for connoisseurs of well-crafted cinema, where 100 percent concentration is required—nothing less will suffice to digest all that it has to offer. French beauty Morgan's glacial blonde features and inner strength light up the screen, while Vidal's finely sculptured body is shown to its best advantage in the movie's first half, the actor wearing nothing but a white wraparound. There are spells of bloody violence: Girotti's execution, tied to a tree and peppered with arrows, is harrowing, but not half as harrowing as the plight of Christian slaves in the supercharged finale. Herded by the hundreds into a packed arena (the sequences here resemble Jews resignedly trooping to the gas chamber, Blasetti's undisguised dig at Nazi German atrocities), they're thrown into fiery pits, nailed to crosses, stabbed, flogged, burned alive, have limbs amputated by axe, hung on stakes, dragged by horses and fed to hungry lions, 15 minutes of nerve-shredding savagery unequalled since its day; imagine *Dante's Inferno* come to gruesome life in the Roman arena. Salou promises Vidal that the nonstop carnage will cease if he fights as a gladiator; Vidal agrees, but refuses to finish off his opponents with his trident.

God's intervention, together with the arrival of Emperor Constantine's legions, spells doom for Salou's vicious regime, Vidal and Morgan reunited in love as the jubilant crowds, sick of the mass slaughter of innocents, embrace their newfound religion.

Steer clear of that dreadful 96-minute print as you will need assistance in figuring out who is who—the sheer scale of cuts renders it an uncoordinated shambles. For example, when Morgan visits Vidal in a cell, it happens after 70 minutes in the edited cut, and 108 minutes in the full version, 38 minutes having been excised for U.S./U.K. release. Matters get worse. The arena sequences occur, in the original, after 138 minutes; in the edited print, 82 minutes. Various characters and scenes have been omitted, or inserted out of place, mainly Franco Interlenghi's role as a psychotic boyish killer. His is a major part in the narrative, slaying by slingshot those who cross Salou's path; in the shortened version, he appears for a second on a balcony, about to hurl a missile at Simon, and briefly at the end, and that's it. Also missing: the initial five minutes of Vidal journeying to Rome from his home village, the bustle of merchants on the harbor front, a suggestive dance routine, an interlude in a school where children are taught the ways of God, much of the trial to determine Simon's killer, many catacomb interludes, the body of a boy callously murdered by Interlenghi shown to Vidal imprisoned in his cell, Cegani's death scene, exposed breasts on display in the arena, plus a woman having her hand chopped off and other glimpses of barbarism. Whether in Italian or not, *Fabiola* has to be relished in its entire, 164-minute length, its visual scope, sweep, concepts, artistic grandeur and busy content the benchmark for everything that followed in Italian sword and sandal spectacle, an essential cinematic experience dating from the industry's golden age. Note: A year after filming, Vidal married Morgan, the handsome French actor dying tragically from a heart attack in 1959, at only 40 years of age.

Never let it be said that Cecil B. DeMille didn't know how to tell a story and put on a show. Modern-day historians tend to deride his films, forgetting that the man came from a vastly different cinematic climate from that of today. His big-budget epics, with big stars to match, were conceived during Hollywood's Golden Age; DeMille's Broadway theatrical background ensured that every dollar he spent could be seen up there, on the big screen, his philosophy being: Never mind what the critics say, the public love 'em. DeMille was a one-off; no one has ever replaced him or his movies, which *did* have their faults: an over-reliance on obvious stage sets, occasionally clumsy back-projection work, slow pace and cliché-ridden dialogue. And once in a while, he produced a rare flop: *Unconquered* (1947), his five million dollar colonial yarn that preceded *Samson and Delilah*, failed to ring cash tills, despite the presence of leading man Gary Cooper. So the Hollywood showman turned to the Old Testament for his next blockbuster; Biblical/religious epics could always guarantee success, especially when given the DeMille treatment. For the role of Samson, 22-year-old unknown Steve Reeves was screen-tested in 1948 and told to lose 15 pounds, but he turned down the offer to concentrate on a bodybuilding/weightlifting career—his star was still on the horizon; Burt Lancaster was also considered for the part (Reeves admitted, in later interviews, that he never rated Mature's portrayal of Samson). Hefty six-foot-two Victor Mature, 36 at the time, was third choice, playing opposite screen goddess Hedy Lamarr as Delilah. *Samson and Delilah* was the biggest box-office hit of 1949, won two Oscars, was nominated in three other categories and remains one of the director's most memorable pictures. Unlike *Fabiola*, don't expect anything remotely cerebral to tax the thought processes, simply relax and revel in George Barnes' lush color photography, Victor Young's glorious score, Jesse Lasky, Jr. and Fredric M. Frank's pithy dialogue, George Sanders (the Saran of Gaza) acting everyone else off screen, Lamarr's sultry sexiness and the final destruction of the Temple of Dagon, one of cinema's greatest-ever set pieces. Conversely, like *Fabiola*, the ingredients were all there in DeMille's barnstormer for the oncoming peplum revolution to seize on: the character of Samson, his supernatural strength, his battle against evil, his entrapment by a beautiful, scheming woman, his redemption through an "invisible god," his opposition to tyranny—these were the key factors, the catalysts, that were to propel the heroic figures of Hercules and his brethren into the public arena from the mid-to-late 1950s onwards. MGM's *Quo Vadis*, released two years later and another major influence on pepla, may have provided the arena spectacle—but *Samson and Delilah* provided the all-important muscleman.

Danite hunk Mature from Zorah, dreaming of liberty for his people, is due to marry Philistine Angela Lansbury (Semadar), loved by soldier Henry Wilcoxon (Ahtur), even though Lamarr, first seen provocatively sitting on a wall eating plums, has her eyes on him, as does virtuous Olive Deering (Miriam), a native villager. Out on a lion hunt, Mature strangles one of the beasts (a distressing scene that wouldn't make it past the censor today); sneering Wilcoxon arrives with his charioteers, labels Mature a "brawling troublemaker" and challenges him to fight his champion, William "Wee Willie" Davis. Mature does just that, making mincemeat out of him. Later, at a pre-wedding celebration, Lansbury reveals to guests the answer to one of Mature's riddles; annoyed, he storms off. Wilcoxon marries Lansbury, Mature wrecks *their* wedding reception by demolishing the room and its revelers ("He has the strength of hell!"), Lansbury killed in the affray. Making the mistake of spurning Lamarr's clutches, Mature goes on the run, giving himself up after a year as tax collectors are putting his people under the yoke because of his disappearance; roped to a chariot, he prays to God, breaks his bonds, overturns the chariot and smashes the skulls of a thousand soldiers with the lower jawbone of an ass, a tremendous sequence from DeMille. Now Sanders' courtesan, even though the cad doesn't trust her an inch, Lamarr announces that she will seduce Mature on the promise of 1,100 pieces of silver each from several tribe leaders and discover the secret of his great strength. What, she wonders, is his weakness? Mature and youngster Russ Tamblyn, robbing the rich to pay the poor, still being hammered by tax inspectors, espy her caravan; Mature enters her tent ("A silk trap baited with a woman."), falling under the vixen's spell ("Your kiss is the sting of death. You're a daughter of hell.") ... and who wouldn't; Lamarr's "come and get a taste of this" stance would be more than enough to have a whole army of Philistines groveling at her sandaled feet. Fate is not on the strongman's side; Samson foolishly letting slip that his dark mane lends him his incredible powers, Lamarr drugs his wine and cuts his flowing locks, although swiftly regretting her misdeed ("I'll never be free of you, Delilah," moans Mature). Mature is cornered (note that pose, Mature surrounded by spears; this would become *the* classic peplum shot) and chained, berating that "Philistine gutter rat," blinded with a red-hot sword and forced to work the gristmill, much to Lamarr's horror; she still yearns for his love, wanting to become his eyes in an idyllic home in Egypt. "The name of Delilah will be an everlasting curse on the lips of men," groans Mature, Sanders adding later, "No man leaves Delilah." Haunted by his grim predicament, she visits the broken Danite just as his strength returns. However, Mature elects not to go away with her—God has other plans. At the festivities next day within the Temple of Dagon, the jeering crowd and a swarm of malicious dwarfs taunt Mature; Deering pleads with Lamarr to show mercy. Her acid response? "I would rather see him dead than in your arms." Lamarr, ignoring Sanders' wishes, rushes to his aid, helping him to position himself between two giant stone columns supporting the mighty temple, leading to one of DeMille's, and cinema's, most riveting climaxes: Mature heaves against one column, the crowd falls silent, the stone gradually shifts off its pedestal, a woman screams, Sanders holds up his wine glass in salute to a brave warrior and the 50-foot idol, plus the massive temple walls, slowly crash down onto the panicking onlookers, a tremendous blend of model work and split-screen technique that, as I will mention throughout this book in other scenes of devastating mass destruction, could never be bettered by 21st-century CGI effects.

Captain from Castile, *Fabiola* and *Samson and Delilah* become three very contrasting motion pictures made by three very different kinds of filmmakers that had one thing in common. All were major evolutionary influences on the development of the pepla phenomenon, the precursors of what was to come, their material sourced in over 350 Italian films that were to appear from 1950 up to 1967, thus creating a genre that, as I have touched upon, remains forgotten and neglected to this day. Much more on that subject will be dwelt upon in further chapters.

2
The Hollywood Epic: Demetrius, Helen and Lower-Budget Influences 1946-1959

From 1951 through to 1959, Hollywood bombarded the movie-mad public with a host of expensive Biblical/historical epics produced on eye-watering budgets: *David and Bathsheba* (Fox, 1951: $3,000,000); *Quo Vadis* (MGM, 1951: $7,000,000); *The Robe* (Fox, 1953: $5,000,000); *Demetrius and the Gladiators* (Fox, 1954: $4,000,000); *The Egyptian* (Fox, 1954: $5,000,000); *The Silver Chalice* (Warner Bros., 1954: $4,500,000); *Land of the Pharaohs* (Warner Bros., 1955: $3,000,000); *The Prodigal* (MGM, 1955: $5,000,000); *The Ten Commandments* (Paramount, 1956: $13,000,000); *Alexander the Great* (United Artists, 1956: $5,500,000); *The Conqueror* (RKO-Radio, 1956: $6,000,000); *Helen of Troy* (Warner Bros., 1956: $6,000,000); *War and Peace* (Paramount, 1956: $6,000,000); *The Vikings* (United Artists, 1958: $5,000,000); *Ben-Hur* (MGM, 1959: $16,000,000); and *Solomon and Sheba* (United Artists, 1959: $5,000,000). These were the top-tier productions produced by the main studios that pulled in the fans, and the Italians took note, each and every one massively instrumental in the formation of the peplum spree just around the corner.

Out of these wallet-busting blockbusters, *Demetrius and the Gladiators* and *Helen of Troy* are the two that stand above the pack, embodying within their framework every key aspect of plot motif that would hold prominence in the grand Italian gladiator/Greek conflict films of the late '50s/mid-1960s: A muscular, heroic figure on the side of good; wars between opposing nations; persecuted Christians and Roman misunderstanding of their religion; the sacking of a city; gladiatorial training; combat in the arena; a mad emperor; a beautiful, ambitious empress-in-waiting; chariots thundering into battle; duels to the death; and attractive lovers caught up in a mighty conflict of their own making. These are what the Italians seized upon with a vengeance, two momentous motion pictures in their chosen field that, like *Captain from Castile*, *Fabiola* and *Samson and Delilah*, precipitated and accelerated the burgeoning pepla movement from 1957 onwards.

One of the earliest CinemaScope productions, Delmer Daves' vibrant Ancient Rome saga, *Demetrius and the Gladiators*, knocked spots off its predecessor, *The Robe*, carrying on from where Fox's worthy but occasionally pious feature ended: Greek freed slave Victor Mature (Demetrius) is tasked with caring for Jesus' robe by Michael Rennie (Peter the Fisherman) and finds himself enrolled in Ernest Borgnine's gladiator school after scuffling with praetorian guards. Mauled by three tigers in the arena, Mature is cared for by Susan Hayward (Messalina, wife of Claudius) and falls head-over-heels in lust with the voyeuristic man-eater, rapidly shedding his Christian beliefs, especially when girlfriend Debra Paget (Lucia), almost raped by Richard Egan during a gladiatorial feast, dies from shock. Mature eventually realizes the error of his ways after the robe restores Paget to life; in the arena, depraved emperor Jay Robinson (Caligula) receives a thoroughly deserved spear in the chest, Hayward takes up her position beside new ruler Barry Jones (Claudius) and Mature, with a promise that the Christians will be left alone, leaves the palace with Nubian buddy William Marshall to resume his Christian way of life with Paget.

As with many Italian Roman/gladiator features, great emphasis is laid on the Romans' aversion to Christianity ("How can they not be afraid to die?" rages Robinson) and their incom-

prehension of a people in adoration of an "invisible god." But whereas Hollywood treated the subject with a certain degree of reverence, the Italians didn't; catch any Italian peplum dealing with Christian discrimination (*The Last Days of Pompeii* [1959], *Revolt of the Slaves* [1961] and *Constantine the Great* [1961] are three examples) and you'll see a level of sadistic relish not found in American cinema. The same goes for the forum sequences. At one point, Mature slays five opponents in a fit of fury, Daves choosing to compose his combat sequences in longshot, thereby promoting to a paying audience the virtues of the high, wide and, at the time, novel CinemaScope format; the Italians went for in-your-face battering close-ups, as witnessed in the galvanizing opening quarter of an hour *The Invincible Gladiator* (1961), a genre classic. Likewise, Hayward's Messalina, while undeniably attractive, is no match for Belinda Lee's almost pornographic X-rated temptress in *Messalina Venus Empress* (1960) or Lisa Gastoni in *The Last Gladiator* (1964). An Italian version of *Demetrius and the Gladiators* would have been rougher around the edges, less polished, a lot bloodier, women sexier, bad guys badder and had more frantic camera movement. Having said that, Robinson's unhinged emperor Caligula is a one-off, never bettered, a self-deluded lunatic hated by all, slithering his bony frame from one palace room to the next and shouting commands in a high-pitched feminine squeak, a career-best performance. Add to this Franz Waxman's rousing score, Milton R. Krasner's gleaming cinematography, Philip Dunne and Lloyd C. Douglas' concise script, lavish sets and Mature in one of his more decisive roles and you have the ultimate Hollywood gladiator movie, 101 minutes of pure five-star popcorn entertainment that can be enjoyed frequently, of significant impact, like another of Mature's pictures, *Samson and Delilah*, to Italian peplum filmmakers. And like *The Robe*, it made an absolute fortune at the box-office.

Warner Bros.' *Helen of Troy* has come in for its fair share of flack over the years, mainly down to the uneven pairing of 31-year-old Jacques Sernas (as Paris) and 22-year-old Rossana Podesta (Helen) in the roles of the two lovers whose lustful act sparked off the 10-year Greek-Trojan conflict. But this was an American/Italian coproduction shot around Tuscany, Italy and in Rome's Cinecitta studios, so why not feature two homegrown players in the lead parts? Let's get one thing straight—there is absolutely nothing amiss with Podesta. First seen wading through the surf in a pink off-the-shoulder robe and sporting a blonde rinse, the woman once dubbed Italy's most beautiful actress would force any man to chance his luck with her, whether it led to all-out war or not; she remains the silver screen's loveliest Helen of Troy. On the other hand, lightweight Sernas was up against a formidable cast of British beefcake: Welsh hellraiser Stanley Baker an arrogant Achilles; Niall MacGinnis as glowering bully boy Menelaus; Torin Thatcher a scheming Ulysses; Robert Douglas' power-mad King Agamemnon; Harry Andrews' champion warrior Hector; Maxwell Reed's war-loving Ajax; Ronald Lewis' ebullient Aeneas; Robert Brown's argumentative Polydorus; Terence Longdon's spirited Patroclus; and Sir Cedric Hardwicke's wise King Priam. Placed beside this wealth of classical-trained talent, Sernas (11 peplum movies to his credit) sometimes looked totally bewildered and out of his comfort zone, never the most forceful of actors.

Director Robert Wise's interpretation stuck fairly closely to Homer's *Iliad*. Sernas, Prince of Troy, whisks Podesta, Queen of Sparta, off to his impregnable walled city after a failed peace mission to Sparta; instigated by enraged husband MacGinnis,

Rossana Podesta, one of Italy's most beautiful actresses, is the screen's loveliest *Helen of Troy*.

the Greeks follow hot on their heels in a thousand ships. The war drags on for 10 long years; Baker kills Andrews outside the walls of Troy and is then slain by a well-placed arrow fired by Sernas; the wooden horse allows the Greeks access to the walled city that they sack. MacGinnis duels with Sernas who's stabbed in the back by a soldier, and Podesta departs to Sparta in a galley with her detested spouse. Over 118 minutes, the pace never falters in this great-to-look-at epic filmed in CinemaScope and Warnercolor, and it has to be said that the first encounter between Greeks and Trojans, lasting nearly 10 minutes, places Wolfgang Petersen's similarly shot sequence in *Troy* firmly in the shadows. Twenty thousand armed extras carrying shields, swords, bows and lances troop up a beach cluttered with chariots, horses, cattle and towering war machines, a stupendous sight heightened by Max Steiner's magnificent score; as a prelude to a large-scale battle in ancient times, it has rarely been outdone for sheer visceral grandeur. Baker's savage tussle with Andrews is tightly edited, the climactic sacking of Troy tensely handled, John Twist and Hugh Gray's screenplay bristling with acerbic lines: Sernas to Andrews, as battle commences:

Cornel Wilde, holding a bow, and his old band of Merrie Men in *The Bandit of Sherwood Forest*

"Where's my place?" Andrews, bitingly: "Beside your Spartan woman!" "Send her back to Sparta. Her name is death!" warns prophetess Janette Scott (Cassandra) to the Trojan assembly, while Thatcher solemnly intones, after Baker perishes, "So dies Greek courage. But not Greek cunning." Acted to the maximum extent by all concerned (even Sernas does his best) and featuring an early appearance by French sex-kitten Brigitte Bardot as Podesta's handmaiden Andraste, *Helen of Troy* is an invigorating five-star spectacle that tells its well-trodden story with lashings of Ancient Greek style and panache. Wise's picture eventually led to the triumvirate of Italian sword and sandal epics dealing with those legendary events circa 1100 BC: Giorgio Ferroni's *The Trojan War* (1961), Marino Girolami's *The Fury of Achilles* (1962) and Giorgio Venturini's *The Legend of Aeneas* (1962), three essential peplum features of immensely enduring quality.

But look lower down the financial ladder and you'll discover many other movies made on medium budgets that were in their own way just as much a controlling factor, and just as inspirational, if not more so, than Tinseltown's mighty blockbusters. The selections I have chosen contain those selfsame traits that would be pounced on by the Italian studios and molded to suit their own storylines—the female pirate, mysterious masked avengers in black, Atlantis, Robin Hood, Zorro, Old Baghdad, Ali Baba, cloak-and-dagger, Ancient Egypt, Cleopatra, King Arthur's knights and barbarian hordes. Biblical potboilers, costume dramas, swashbuckling adventures, piratical hijinks on the high seas and Alan Ladd, Tony Curtis and Robert Wagner charging around Hollywood's version of Ye Olde English countryside in career-worst performances (depending on your point of view); perhaps this is where the peplum producers filched their ideas from, in addition to scrutinizing *Demetrius and the Gladiators*, *Helen of Troy*, *The Ten Commandments* and *The Vikings*. Check these titles out and you'll detect noticeable growth patterns in how plots were established, signature scenes, dialogue, imagery and narrative devices utilized time and time again by the Italian filmmakers; in all probability, the lower budget U.S. and U.K. "pepla" are the kind of programmers that formed the foundation for the Italian boom that was just over the horizon, waiting to be unleashed.

1946

The Bandit of Sherwood Forest

Columbia (US); Technicolor; 86 mins; Producers: Leonard S. Picker, Clifford Stanforth; Directors: Henry Levin, George Sherman ✧✧✧

Elderly Russell Hicks (Robin Hood), alarmed when Henry Daniell (Regent William of Pembroke) abolishes the 20-year-old Magna Carta, England's Charter of Liberties, and with it the common peoples' rights, summons his old band of longbow-waving Merry Men, together with son Cornel Wilde (Robert of Nottingham), to put paid to the tyrant's cruel regime. The boy king (Maurice Tauzin) is abducted and imprisoned in the tower, while Jill Esmond (the queen) and Anita Louise (Lady Catherine) are forced to flee the castle. Daniell, with toadying George Macready (Fitz-Herbert) hovering at his side, plans to have the lad pushed from the battlements and proclaim himself monarch of England. Wilde and Louise fall in love, both captured and incarcerated in cells and sentenced to death. Wilde invokes the law of trial by combat, hurling a sword into Daniell's midriff in a duel, while Hicks and the Merry Men, disguised as soldiers, take over the castle. At a ceremony, Tauzin, restored to the throne, knights Wilde and commands him to marry Louise, which he planned to do anyway.

More or less shot on the lines of a medieval Western in California's Simi Valley, *The Bandit of Sherwood Forest* makes for pleasurable viewing, far better than many of the numerous films to feature the man in green tights. Wilde is a dashing hero, Louise simply ravishing and Daniell and Macready make a devilish pair of hiss-boo villains. Less effective is Edgar Buchanan's Friar Tuck and Ray Teal's Little John. Filmed in bright Technicolor and driven by Hugo Friedhofer's bouncy music, this is one *Robin Hood* adventure that won't have you fidgeting in your seat.

Peplum influences: The Robin Hood character (popular in Italian cinema); several cries of "Follow me!"; a wicked usurper and his slimy second-in-command; Louise and Wilde falling in love a day after meeting; an imposing castle; a weapon thrown in deadly accuracy at an opponent; trial by combat; and a lengthy duel within a castle courtyard.

1947

Queen of the Amazons

Robert L. Lippert/Screen Art (US); B&W; 61 mins; Produced and Directed by Edward F. Finney ✧

Patricia Morison (Jean Preston) organizes a safari to search for her missing boyfriend, Bruce Edwards (Greg), thought held captive by a tribe of warmongering Amazons in Africa's remote "Forbidden Land." After adventures with lions, tigers, locusts and natives, they meet headstrong Amira Moustafa (Zita), the Queen of the Amazons, who wants Edwards as her mate to play house with. Cook J. Edward Bromberg, complete with pet raven and chattering monkey, is exposed as the brains behind a gang

Long-forgotten Amira Moustafa as the *Queen of the Amazons*

Louis Hayward and Janet Blair in *The Black Arrow*

of ivory poachers, Morison eventually giving up on drippy Edwards and hitching her skirts to big game hunter Robert Lowery (Gary). In a double wedding, Morison, Lowery, Moustafa and Edwards get spliced under an avenue of native lances.

A 1947 movie masquerading as a 1937 movie, the incredibly dated *Queen of the Amazons* consists of 33 percent stock wildlife footage, 66 percent bottom-of-the-barrel non-thrills, the kind of grade-Z clunker Edward D. Wood, Jr. would drum up in the 1950s. Never has 61 minutes appeared like 161 minutes; where was Jungle Jim when you so urgently needed him?

Peplum influences: Amazon queens of all shapes and sizes would showcase in many Italian productions in the years to come, eager to get their claws into a white man, but none so butch, or talkative, as the long-forgotten Amira Moustafa; a staged fight between bull elephants; and some excruciatingly awful dumb lines, such as … Edwards to Moustafa: "You're quite a queen." Moustafa: "Someone has to be boss, dear!"

1948

The Black Arrow aka *The Black Arrow Strikes*
Columbia (US); B&W; 76 mins; Producers: Edward Small, Grant Whytock; Director: Gordon Douglas ††††

After fighting for three years in the War of the Roses (1455-1485), Yorkist Louis Hayward (Sir Richard Shelton) returns to find his father dead, his estates in the hands of his vile uncle, George Macready (Sir Daniel Brackley). Paul Cavanagh, the father of Lady Janet Blair (Joanna Sedley), is a threat to Macready's ambitions and has been blamed for the murder but escaped execution, seeking refuge in the forest with Edgar Buchanan's band of Robin Hood-type Merry Men, who send messages via a black arrow, threatening to eliminate the four blaggards responsible for the killing one at a time. Hayward joins them in his determination to unmask his conniving uncle as the murderer and regain his estates, plus marrying Blair in the bargain.

The Black Arrow is a briskly directed, energetic, sub-Errol Flynn swashbuckler (although Hayward is no Errol Flynn) with bags of intrigue, swordplay and treachery, bolstered by a scorching Paul Sawtell score and deep black-and-white photography from Charles Lawton, Jr.

Peplum influences: a secret passage in the castle; the ultimatum made to Blair by Macready: "Marry me and he'll (Cavanagh) live"; Hayward cornered by a dozen crossbows, pepla's much-used "Gotcha!" moment; swordfights on staircases; a cave hideout; Blair secreted away in a convent; Hayward and Buchanan disguised as friars; a public bareback flogging; the trial by mortal combat, a bruising five-minute joust, Hayward (on white horse) defeating Macready (on black horse) by hurling a broken lance into his chest; and a final shot of Hayward and Blair kissing.

1949

Siren of Atlantis aka *Atlantis the Lost Continent*
United Artists (US); B&W; 75 mins; Producer: Seymour Nebenzal; Director: Gregg C. Tallas †††††

In flashback, Lieutenant Jean-Pierre Aumont (André) relates to a board of enquiry how the Tuareg captured both him and Captain Dennis O'Keefe (Jean Morhange) while searching for a patrol missing in the Sahara. At the foot of the Huggar Mountains, they encountered Maria Montez (Antinea), the legendary Queen of Atlantis, a bewitching, predatory man-eater ("You feed on death. A woman without heart.") who discards her lovers as soon as she becomes bored with them, their bodies turned into gold statues. Aumont lusts after Montez and is granted a brief fling but is cruelly brushed aside when she focuses her attentions on the aloof O'Keefe, turning to drink to ease his misery. In a row over Montez's favors, Aumont stabs O'Keefe to death and flees the lost city, making it back to the French Foreign Legion outpost. Exonerated for the killing (as nobody believes his story), Aumont, obsessed with Montez's beauty, rides into the desert to reunite with his love, perishing in a sandstorm, clasping her gold medallion in his dead fingers.

Maria Montez's finest hour, she shimmers and radiates "come and get me" desire in a third film adaptation of Pierre Benoit's novel *L'Atlantide*, adroitly directed by Tallas. Married

to Aumont in real life, her camp-filled performance, backed by imaginative art deco sets and backdrops, Oscar-winner (*Sunrise*, 1929) Karl Struss' diamond-hard photography and a wonderful score from Michel Michelet, ensures that The Caribbean Cyclone's monument to good old Hollywood kitsch remains untarnished after all these years, a genuine cult classic. The Italians remade it in 1961 as *Journey Beneath the Desert* (the U.S. title) and Montez went on to star in two obscure peplum movies, 1950's *The Thief of Venice* and 1951's *The Pirate's Revenge*, before her premature death in 1951, aged only 39.

Peplum influences: The Atlantis myth appeared in several pepla over the coming decade; lavish, ornate set design; a haughty, sex-mad queen; a lost city; an alchemist turning corpses into metal statues; the hero yearning for a love that will never be, expiring in the sands in a *Lost Horizon*-type tragic ending.

1950

Buccaneer's Girl aka The Pirate Captain

Universal (US); Technicolor; 77 mins; Producer: Robert Arthur; Director: Frederick de Cordova ✞✞✞

Stowaway guttersnipe Yvonne De Carlo is picked up from a ship after pirate Philip Friend has raided it; put ashore, she enrolls in Elsa Lanchester's New Orleans School for Genteel Young Ladies. Friend, a seafaring Robin Hood, is raiding and sinking the treasure-laden vessels of mountebank Robert Douglas, using the stolen loot to finance New Orleans' poorer seamen by buying up other vessels for their needs. Under the guise of Captain Kingston, he inveigles Douglas' soirées, snobbish fiancée Andrea King on his arm, and falls for De Carlo, a song and dance artist. After consigning three more of Douglas' galleons to the bottom of the ocean, Friend's true identity is discovered by King, and also his attraction for the vivacious singer. Out of spite, she marries Douglas and arranges for the capture and execution of her ex-boyfriend. In a fight with Douglas' guards, Friend is freed by his corsairs, led by De Carlo, and sails off for more adventures, cradling the vixen in his arms.

Light frothy fun sums up Universal's B-pirate flick featuring an on-form De Carlo (Deborah McCoy), a dashing leading man in Friend as Baptiste the pirate, a handful of poorly choreographed song and dance numbers, model galleons firing broadsides and the shortest tavern brawl/prison scrimmage in celluloid history. Worth a look just to see how vibrant color *used* to be presented to the public during Hollywood's heyday.

Peplum influences: a female tomboy pirate; a tavern brawl; galleons firing broadsides; a jilted fiancée turning the tables on her ex-lover; a catfight between De Carlo and King; escape from prison on execution day; flamboyant costume design; a final shot of Friend and De Carlo kissing on the ship's quarterdeck; and glorious Technicolor photography from Russell Metty.

Fortunes of Captain Blood

Columbia (US); B&W; 91 mins; Producer: Harry Joe Brown; Director: Gordon Douglas ✞✞

In the West Indies in the 17th century, Louis Hayward (Captain Peter Blood) moors his ship the *Avenger* in a secluded cove and infiltrates Tortuga, the island base of Governor George Macready, to rescue his crew, but he is taken prisoner and earmarked for slave labor. Disguised as a fruit seller, he forms a relationship with both perky Dona Drake (Pepita) and Macready's niece, disdainful Patricia Medina (Isabelita), who's engaged to mountebank Lowell Gilmore, after her for her money. Gilmore attempts to hand Hayward over to the authorities to claim a reward of 50,000 pieces of eight, but is run through by the corsair in an on-board duel; Macready's 40-gun galleon is taken over by Hayward's crew after they've escaped jail (the film's best sequence, shot in vaulted dungeons); Macready and his guards board the *Avenger* where the cannons have been tampered with; and in a cannonade, the *Avenger* is blown out of the water, Macready, injured, going down with the vessel. Medina is sent back to Tortuga, Hayward promising to join her in due course.

Philip Friend and Yvonne De Carlo in *Buccaneer's Girl*

Fortunes of Captain Blood is no great shakes in the swashbuckling department, strictly second-feature fodder, most of the action taking place on land, not at sea, although Gordon Douglas manages to inject a fair bit of vigor into the swordplay, when it occurs. Hayward and veteran heavy Macready sleepwalk through their roles, Drake shines as a flighty tavern wench and character actor Alfonso Bedoya puts in a crazy performance as Carmilio, the drunk-sodden prison overseer. Also, full marks to Paul Sawtell for a top-notch score, one that perhaps the picture didn't deserve. Okay viewing for a wet Saturday afternoon.

Peplum influences: Despite the so-so material, the influences are all there to see: Medina threatened to a life in a convent if she doesn't toe the line; a man engaged to a woman only because of her wealth; a cry of "The rest of you—follow me!"; swordfights in the dungeon; torture by tightening a leather band around the head; a flirty lass versus a haughty lady; and two galleons blasting away at each other in the final reel.

Rogues of Sherwood Forest

Columbia (US); Technicolor; 79 mins; Producer: Fred M. Packard; Director: Gordon Douglas ††

In 1215, the son of outlaw Robin Hood, the Earl of Huntingdon, teams up with the now older survivors of his father's original band of Merry Men to do battle with King John's soldiers; in order to purchase 5,000 troops from the Earl of Flanders, the king needs £100,000 in gold and raises extortionate taxes on the poor to obtain the funds. When the outlaws' repeated sorties prove too much, King John decides to marry off Lady Marianne to the Flemish warlord in lieu of payment. The king's thugs murder a number of rich barons, with the blame placed on the rebels who waylay the Earl of Flanders' wedding procession in Sherwood Forest. The Flemish leader is stabbed to death in a duel with Robin, and King John is subsequently forced to sign one of England's most famous political charters, the Magna Carta, at Runnymede. Sherwood Forest's jovial troublemakers are pardoned and Robin welcomes Marianne into his manly arms.

John Derek and his Merry Men salute the king in *Rogues of Sherwood Forest*.

Shot amid sunny scenery more used to the sight and sound of cowboys shooting at one another in umpteen Columbia Westerns of the period, with the entire cast speaking in Olde American accents, Gordon Douglas' entry into the never-ending list of low-budget *Robin Hood* potboilers is a pleasant-enough time waster, with John Derek so-so as the hero in green tights. George Macready's King John is too limp by far, Paul Cavanagh's Sir Giles and Lowell Gilmore's dastardly Earl of Flanders a much more forceful pair of varlets, while Diana Lynn's Marianne is decorative but vacant. The film is notable for being Alan Hale's final picture; the star of 250 features played Little John not only here but in *Robin Hood* (1922) and *The Adventures of Robin Hood* (1938), dying in January 1950 at the age of 57 soon after completion of this production. The set design, above all else, catches the eye, embellished in Charles Lawton, Jr.'s rich Technicolor hues.

Peplum influences: a joust where lance tips have been tampered with to enable the villain to win; Derek throwing a sword into a soldier's chest; a savage flogging; villagers under the yoke of persecution; messages sent by doves and arrows; acrobats and jugglers at a castle feast; the outlaws swooping down from trees onto startled soldiers; Derek trapped by a circle of crossbows; a marriage of inconvenience; beautifully rendered color cinematography; and a final few seconds showing Derek and Lynn kissing.

1951

Anne of the Indies

20th Century Fox (US); Technicolor; 81 mins; Producer: George Jessel; Director: Jacques Tourneur †††††

In the early 1700s, embittered Jean Peters, pirate boss of the *Sheba Queen*, wages a personal vendetta on the British fleet, a mission of revenge for the hanging of her brother in chains, showing no mercy for any prisoners taken; they're forced to walk the plank, including officers. During an explosive sea encounter, one captive is spared, mysterious Frenchman Louis Jourdan, who claims to own half of a map pointing the way to Captain Morgan's fabled treasure. Peters hires him as sailing master and allows her pent-up emotions to cave in, falling for his handsome charms, but he's not all that he appears to be. James Robertson Justice's suspicions are confirmed: Jourdan is a former French officer; on a promise made by the British stationed at Maracaibo of the return of his ship the *Molly O'Brien*, he has been tasked with bringing Peters to justice and, furthermore, he's married to Debra Paget. Enraged and feeling utterly rejected by this devastating news, Peters, after crossing swords with barrel-chested pirate captain Thomas Gomez, abducts Paget, blasts the *Molly O'Brien* out of the ocean in an engagement and dumps Jourdan and his wife on a tiny desert island, to perish in the heat. Full of remorse, she has second thoughts, sending the ship's doctor in a boat to give them provisions. Gomez's vessel, the *Revenge*, is then sighted. In a thunderous exchange of fire, the *Sheba Queen* is blown to bits and everyone on board killed, Peters going to meet her Maker in a blaze of glory.

They don't come that much more exciting than Jacques Tourneur's full-blooded swashbuckler; everything about *Anne*

Bedouin chief Jeff Chandler and Princess Maureen O'Hara smooch in *Flame of Araby*.

Peplum influences: Peters' hardheaded and hard-hearted pirate captain keeping her emotions, and her uncouth but loyal crew, in check, a once-in-a-lifetime star turn; thrilling clashes on the high seas; rowdy taverns; wrestling with an animal (in this case, a bear); and gorgeous color cinematography.

Flame of Araby
Universal (US); Technicolor; 77 mins; Producer: Leonard Goldstein; Director: Charles Lamont ✞✞✞

Bedouin chief Jeff Chandler is determined to rope wild black stallion Shazada, but also intent on owning the magnificent steed is Princess Maureen O'Hara from Tunis. When O'Hara's father is poisoned, her iniquitous cousin, Maxwell Reed, takes command of the city, promising to offer her hand in marriage to one of two oafish Barbarossa brothers, Lon Chaney, Jr. and Buddy Baer, the warlords and their pagan corsairs having invaded Tunis; whoever wins the Grand Taifa horse race can have her. When Shazada is caught and tamed, Chandler enters the race, emerges the victor and carries O'Hara off to play house Bedouin-style. As for traitor Reed, he's trampled to oblivion by the Barbarossa brothers' horses in revenge for their loss.

Chandler (Tamerlane), exchanging cowboy hats and Indian feathers for an Arab kufiya, charges around Lone Pine's towering rock formations with pals Dewey Martin and Royal Dano, somehow managing to keep a straight face; O'Hara's Titian tresses clash violently with her aquamarine gown; British heartthrob actor Reed's Prince Medina minces across set, lisping effeminately; and horror star Chaney's bushy ginger beard is a sight for sore eyes. Chandler calls O'Hara (Tanya) a "pampered wench," while she enticingly informs him as the curtain closes: "There are things unknown in the black tents of Allah that I shall teach you." All dressed up in Russell Metty's glowing colors, *Flame of Araby* is 100 percent Hollywood bunkum, nothing more, nothing less. But it *will* bring a smile to the face, making you wonder how on earth Universal got away with stuff like this all those years ago! Note: That beautiful ebony horse Black Diamond won the Animal Award of Excellence in 1952.

Peplum influences: the whole hokum-filled package. And if the Americans could shoot Arabian adventures in obvious non-Arabian locations such as Lone Pine and Bronson Canyon, why

Louis Jordan and Jean Peters in a publicity still for *Anne of the Indies*

of the Indies screams "pirate classic!": tremendous performances from Peters as Anne Providence ("I bear many scars from the English!"), Jourdan (Captain Pierre LaRochelle), Justice, Paget, Herbert Marshall (the caring doctor) and Gomez (he plays legendary Blackbeard); a riot of color courtesy of Harry Jackson; Franz Waxman's thumping score; a thoughtful script (Philip Dunne; Arthur Caesar) giving Peters' character, and her motivation, meaning and depth; and enough incident, plotting and set pieces to stock a film twice the length. "She's home at last. Let the sea keep her," intones Jourdan, mourning Peters' demise and gazing at her wrecked pride and joy, fitting, and moving, final words to *the* essential female pirate movie, one that has never been bettered.

The cast up to its frilly necks in a tavern scene from *The Highwayman*

Military tyrant Anthony Quinn and sidekick Arnold Moss from *Mask of the Avenger*

not the Italians in Lazio's Lapilli quarries and the Monte Gelato falls.

The Highwayman aka *The Masked Cavalier*

Allied Artists (US); Cinecolor; 82 mins; Producer: Hal E. Chester; Director: Lesley Selander ✝✝✝✝

Aristocrat-turned-masked highwayman Philip Friend ("Stand and Deliver!") is robbing the rich to pay the poor, using a tavern as his hideout and romancing innkeeper's daughter Wanda Hendrix. The dashing cavalier becomes embroiled in the machinations of ambitious Victor Jory and Charles Coburn, who profit from those consigned to the debtor's court and are both up to their frilly necks in the slave trade. Jory is married to Friend's ex-love, Virginia Huston, causing Hendrix to become jealous of their past relationship and worry over whether it will be rekindled. After several coach holdups and confrontations with the king's dragoons, Friend's mute assistant, who lusts after Hendrix, reveals Friend's hiding place to the authorities. In a duel to the death, Friend runs Jory through and rides off to the rescue of Hendrix, molested and tied to a bedpost by soldiers who have set an ambush for the highwayman. Hendrix manages to pull the trigger on a musket, killing herself; warned of the trap by the shot, Friend turns tail and is told by a comrade of Hendrix's sacrifice. Distraught at losing the girl he loved deep down, he purposely rides into crossfire, dying instantly. We last see his ghostly figure galloping through the gloom to the inn where he's reunited with the spirit of Hendrix.

Adapted from Alfred Noyes' 1906 poem *The Highwayman*, Lesley Selander's little-seen gem of a swashbuckler is a tad convoluted in parts, although containing several exciting moments, including an enthralling four-minute spell of rapier parrying between Friend (as Jeremy) and Jory as its climax. Composer Herschel Burke Gilbert utilizes snatches of music from Mendelssohn's Italian Symphony No. 4 to give the movie a classical feel, while Harry Neumann's Cinecolor photography bathes the action in period greens and oranges. And the mystical, almost moving, finale is unusual in a film of this type.

Peplum influences: a masked avenger, out to right wrongs; a gala ball; a nasty dungeon scene featuring torture by glowing-hot poker; a noblewoman yearning for her former lover; a girl of lower class dying for a love she thinks will never happen; duplicitous villains; and a powerhouse duel, performed minus any musical accompaniment to heighten the tension.

Mask of the Avenger

Columbia (US); Technicolor; 83 mins; Producer: Hunt Stromberg; Director: Phil Karlson ✝✝

Casamare, Italy 1848: Military tyrant Anthony Quinn, aided by sidekick Arnold Moss, is throwing his lot in with the approaching Austrian invaders, transferring finances received from the enemy into his own bank account. Quinn shoots a nobleman who has threatened him with exposure, faking the crime as the suicide of a traitor. The murdered man's son, John Derek, returning on leave from the Italian army, takes on the guise of the black-caped, black-hatted masked avenger, also called The Ghost of Monte Cristo, holding up coaches, infiltrating Quinn's castle by feigning injury and romancing Lady Jody Lawrance, resolved to clear his father's name, nail the tyrant and prevent the Austrian fleet from landing. By the end, he's managed to achieve all three, disposing of Quinn in a duel, with a little help from rapier-wielding Lawrance, and urging the townsfolk in successfully repelling the Austrian navy.

Charles Lawton, Jr.'s vibrant cinematography, sparkling costume design, a few swordfights and painted Italian castle backdrops try their best to enliven a flat-footed costumer from the usually reliable Phil Karlson; Derek (Captain Renato) appears listless, simply going through the motions and even Quinn (Viovanni) is less menacing than usual. Statuesque Lawrance perhaps comes off best in a swashbuckler you feel could always have been just that little bit more polished than it turned out.

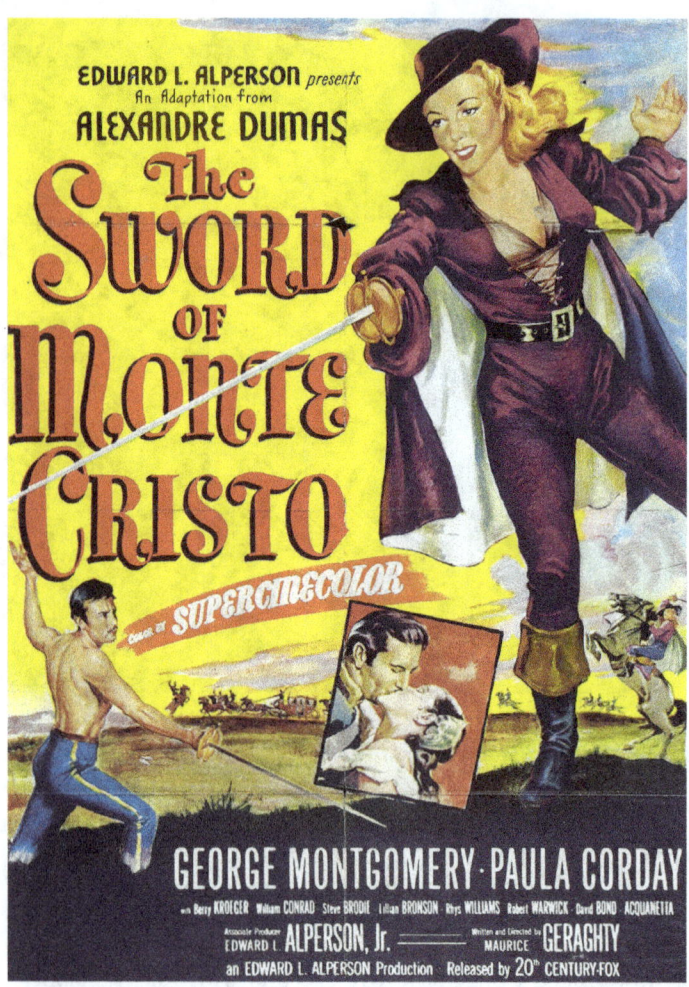

Renault of the dragoons (George Montgomery) eventually sides with the insurgents; the riches are located in a ruined monastery, the Masked Cavalier turning out to be none other than Corday. In a confrontation over the treasure chests, Kroeger falls backwards through a window to his doom; the jewels and gold are handed over to Bond, and Montgomery kisses Corday in front of a packed congregation.

Low-budget, maybe, but *The Sword of Monte Cristo* (it was screenwriter Maurice Geraghty's one and only feature film as director) rattles through its paces, ablaze with Jack Greenhalgh's deep, rich colors and bolstered by Raoul Kraushaar's rowdy score. Corday's Masked Cavalier, dressed all in black with wide-brimmed hat, resembles Vincent Price's mad sculptor alter-ego in *House of Wax* (Warner Bros., 1953), adding to the movie's unusual, but very welcome, Gothic qualities, as do the atmospheric dungeon scenes. Montgomery, a stalwart figure in many a fine '50s Western, brandishes a blade with aplomb, looking perfectly at ease in military garb as opposed to gun and holster in one of the better of the countless pictures based on the Alexandre Dumas novel.

Peplum influences: torture on the rack; a masked cavalier in black; several shouts of "Follow me!"; secret castle passages and hidden rooms; the search for lost treasure; Montgomery surrounded by lances, the peplum "You're cornered" shot; two brothers, one good, the other evil; and Montgomery hungrily kissing Corday as the curtain comes down, something which most, if not all, of the tall, good-looking actor's leading ladies didn't object to at the time!

Peplum influences: Derek's masked Zorro-type avenger would become a very familiar figure in many a peplum in the years to come; exceptional color and authentic wardrobe; a corrupt military official; eavesdropping from a secret passage; a son trying to restore his father's besmirched name; and Derek and Lawrance engaged in lip action as the end credits roll.

The Sword of Monte Cristo

Edward L. Alperson Prods./20th Century Fox (US); SuperCinecolor; 80 mins; Producer: Edward L. Alperson; Director: Maurice Geraghty ††††

In 1858, Louis Napoleon III (David Bond) rules France; his scheming, jealous brother, Charles La Roche (Berry Kroeger), covets the French throne, using bullying tactics to oppress the populace. A rebellion breaks out, the mysterious Masked Cavalier causing Kroeger and his thugs no end of problems. The Sword of Monte Cristo is hidden behind a painting in Lady Christianne's (Paula Corday) castle; on its hilt is an inscription that, once deciphered, pinpoints the whereabouts of Monte Cristo's fabled treasure. The Marquis de Montableau (Robert Warwick) is the only person able to untangle the code but won't give in to Kroeger's strong-arm methods in revealing it, including torture on the rack. Captain

1952

At Sword's Point aka **Sons of the Musketeers**

RKO-Radio (US); Technicolor; 81 mins; Producer: Jerrold T. Brandt; Director: Lewis Allen †††††

France, 1648: Following the death of Cardinal Richelieu, the country is in the hands of the ne'er-do-wells, out for all they

Cornel Wilde (wearing green) and Maureen O'Hara (far right) in a lobby card for *At Sword's Point*

can get. At her wits' end and aware that Robert Douglas (the Duke de Lavalle) plans to dispose of her young son and marry her protesting daughter, Gladys Cooper (Queen Anne) calls upon the services of Cornel Wilde, the son of legendary musketeer D'Artagnan, to rid France of this power-hungry mogul. Wilde approaches Alan Hale, Jr., the son of Porthos, Dan O'Herlihy, the son of Aramis and Maureen O'Hara, the *daughter* of Athos, to join him in protecting France's throne from Douglas and his cronies' conniving ploys. When the Musketeers are captured and tortured, the queen halts their execution, yielding to Douglas' demands that he marries Princess Nancy Gates. O'Hara is substituted as the bride on the wedding day and at the Golden Cockerel inn, the foursome's meeting place, news comes through that the queen has died. The Musketeers attempt to spirit young King Louis XIV from a monastery but are thwarted by two-timing countess June Clayworth. Signing up volunteers to form a musketeer army, Wilde and his companions storm Douglas' castle in the finale; the duke is run through in a duel, the boy king and Gates taking their places on the throne.

Directed with tornado-type pace by Lewis Allen, *At Sword's Point* is one of the early '50s finest offshoots from the Alexandre Dumas *Three Musketeers* novel: a memorable cast giving it 100 percent (Moroni Olsen, who appeared as the older Porthos, was the young Porthos in 1935's *The Three Musketeers*); rampaging duels, fights and set pieces; humor (especially when O'Hara, clad as a tomboy, has to share a bed with her three masculine compatriots); Ray Rennahan's rich color photography (he won Oscars for his work on 1939's *Gone With the Wind* and 1941's *Blood and Sand*); Roy Webb's thundering score; O'Hara dueling in a wedding dress; a succinct script ("My father's sword. Now I have a legend to live up to."); a harrowing torture sequence; Hale wrenching his chains from the cell wall; and lively incident a-plenty. Eighty-one minutes of pure Technicolored joy.

Peplum influences: the complete movie, including an early appearance of peplum's much-favored bed of spikes—Wilde pushes a guard onto the device in a prison skirmish scene.

The Golden Hawk

Columbia (US); Technicolor; 83 mins; Producer: Sam Katzman; Director: Sidney Salkow ††††

During the 17th century, in the Caribbean, French privateer Sterling Hayden benefits from the English and Spanish versus the French conflict by filling his ship, the *Golden Hawk*, with plunder. He's also on a personal mission to rid the seas of John Sutton, the Spaniard he holds responsible for the death of his mother. Commandeering English frigate the *Sea Flower*, Hayden pursues Sutton's 60-gun *Garza* across the high seas, taking captive feisty pirate wench Rhonda Fleming who rejects his romantic overtures, shooting him in the arm. Hayden then abducts Helena Carter, due to marry Sutton, holding her prisoner on the island of Cul de Sac for a ransom of 10,000 gold coins. The exchange made, Fleming, back on the scene, turns out to be captain of the British vessel *Witch*, although this is an alias as she's actually a wealthy plantation owner. After blowing up one of three Spanish warships sent to trap them, Hayden's buccaneers raid Fleming's Jamaican property; the French rearm the *Sea Flower* and a blazing assault is carried out on the Spanish fortress at Cartagena in which the enemy is defeated. Sutton turns out to be Hayden's father, his wife dying in an accident; Hayden forgives him and in turn is forgiven by Fleming, who plans to put a stop to his womanizing ways.

Publicity shot of feisty pirate wench Rhonda Fleming for *The Golden Hawk*

Never let it be said that cheapo producer Sam Katzman couldn't put together a decent pirate adventure on limited funds. *The Golden Hawk* bristles with broadside-blazing action, cutlass fights, romance and winning turns from the cast. Six-foot-five-inch Western/detective stalwart Hayden (Kit Gerardo) towers over his two leading ladies; Fleming gives good value for money in her dual roles of Captain Rouge and Lady Jane, while Carter radiates dark-haired allure as Bianca. A low-budget pirate flick of some merit, directed at a nippy pace by Salkow.

Peplum influences: numerous clashes on the high seas; the shelling of a fortress; a noblewoman masquerading as a pirate; a native dance; Hayden encircled by firearms; a rescue from dungeons; an exploding powder magazine; and Hayden and Fleming smooching as the picture ends.

Lady in the Iron Mask

20th Century Fox (US); SuperCinecolor; 78 mins; Producers: Walter Wanger, Eugene Frank; Director: Ralph Murphy †††††

On board ship, bound for America and the New World and married to a woman he doesn't love, Louis Hayward, starring as D'Artagnan, reflects on how he arrived at this unhappy situation. In flashback, Hayward and the Three Musketeers are asked by the French prime minister to intervene in the forthcoming marriage of Princess Anne to King Philip of Spain. Apparently, Anne is an imposter; the bride-to-be is in fact her twin sister Louise, the pair separated at birth. In later years, Anne, who bears a distinctive birthmark, was incarcerated in a dank dungeon, an iron mask clamped over her features. Hayward's task is to rescue the real heir to the throne and prevent the sham

Patricia Medina is saved by the Three Musketeers in *Lady in the Iron Mask*.

wedding from taking place. John Sutton (the Duke de Valdac) is determined to stop Hayward and his Musketeers from achieving their aim, the ambitious swine out to feather his own nest as a result of the French/Spanish alliance. After several stormy confrontations with Sutton's men, Hayward and the Musketeers, disguised in the king's livery, rescue Anne from her prison, remove the mask and gallop off, a price on their collective heads. Riding to Paris, Anne declares her love for Hayward, wishing to play house in England, but he knows it could never be. In Sutton's mansion, the twins finally meet and the duke finished off in a duel with Hayward. Anne weds a French count as she must marry into royal blood; D'Artagnan is knighted Chevalier of France and allowed to marry Louise as second choice. But on board ship, where we were at the start, Louise's dress accidentally rips, revealing a birthmark above her left knee—Hayward has hitched himself to Anne after all!

Unfortunately, as at the time of writing, color prints of this exceedingly rare slant on Alexandre Dumas' *The Man in the Iron Mask* do not exist, Oscar-winner (*Ship of Fools*, 1965) Ernest Laszlo's photography now shown in black-and-white; ironically, this in some ways enhances rather than detracts from the action. The dungeon torture chamber sequence, whereby Alan Hale, Jr. (Porthos) and Hayward grapple hulking Ed Wood regular Tor Johnson before flinging the brute into a lime pit, is straight out of a 1950s Gothic horror flick, even an Edward D. Wood, Jr. one, while the shadowy swordfights take on a *noir*-ish life of their own. Ralph Murphy includes a plethora of thundering, helter-skelter horse chases, adrenalin-pumping stuff (not a back-projection screen in sight), a smash-up-the-furniture inn ruckus inserted just for the hell of it, thrilling bouts of swordplay, and a telling performance from Patricia Medina in the role of both sisters. However, the film's undoubted major asset is Dimitri Tiomkin's score. One of Hollywood's most revered composers,

Tony Curtis and Piper Laurie pose for the camera in *Son of Ali Baba*

Tiomkin occasionally lent his genius to pictures of this caliber, thereby elevating them from the good to the great. However minor his soundtrack may have been in Murphy's energetic swashbuckler, it was always worth a listen, an aural backdrop to treasure, making *Lady in the Iron Mask* an obscure must-have on any fan's "want" list.

Peplum influences: the potent iron mask image figures in quite a few peplum costume dramas; rough and tumble tavern fights and brawls; a secret passage; lack of back-projection, a form of cinematic chicanery which the Italians, to their credit, tended to avoid; a lurid torture chamber; one of pepla's oft-quoted cries is heard twice: "Follow me!"; Hale breaking his chains from the walls; and a stupendous score from maestro Tiomkin.

Son of Ali Baba

Universal (US); Technicolor; 75 mins; Producer: Leonard Goldstein; Director: Kurt Neumann ††

In Ancient Persia, Tony Curtis as Kashma, the wayward son of Ali Baba (Morris Ankrum), is the one undisciplined member at a highly disciplined military academy, his attentions focused more on women than soldiering. Cunning caliph Victor Jory lusts after Ali Baba's treasure, sending Princess Piper Laurie to Bagdad under the guise of an escaped handmaiden, her instructions to snare Curtis and obtain the whereabouts of the riches; if she refuses, her imprisoned mother will be put to death. Curtis falls for her, arousing the jealousy of childhood sweetheart and female Robin Hood-type Susan Cabot. When Jory's son destroys Ankrum's palace, Hugh O'Brian, Curtis, Cabot, buddy William Reynolds, the sons of the 40 thieves and Curtis' fellow cadets band together to oust Jory and his mob and free Ankrum and Laurie's mother, both chained in a dungeon cell. Jory is killed, Curtis cuts down O'Brian in a duel, Ankrum is made the new caliph by the shah and Curtis decides to drop his womanizing ways by marrying Laurie.

Produced at a time when Curtis' looks counted more than his acting ability (which turned out to be considerable), *Son of Ali Baba* is empty pantomime fodder, lumbered with anachronistic dialogue from Gerald Drayson Adams (he scripted the similar *Flame of Araby*); "Here we are, boys!" shouts Curtis during one fracas. For Universal watchers, it's somewhat amusing to see O'Brian, Ankrum and Reynolds in Arabian garb instead of their usual milieu, Westerns and horror. Apart from Herman Stein's rousing title score, *Son of Ali Baba* is harmless and forgettable, cashing in on the leading man's boyish charms that made him, at the time, one of America's most swooned-over movie pinups.

Peplum influences: four cries of "Follow me!"; a lithesome dancer wearing a gold mask; two strongmen wrestling as court entertainment; scenic Old Baghdad backdrops; an evil caliph; and Curtis kissing Laurie in the final seconds.

The Story of Robin Hood and His Merrie Men

Disney/RKO-Radio (US/UK); Technicolor; 83 mins; Producer: Perce Pearce; Director: Ken Annakin ✟✟✟✟✟

Nottingham, 1190: Patrick Barr (King Richard the Lionheart) goes off to fight in the Crusades, leaving the kingdom in the hands of his devious brother, Hubert Gregg (Prince John) who, aided by Peter Finch (the Sheriff of Nottingham), immediately raises the foresters' taxes. In an archery contest, Richard Todd (Robin) is the winner, giving the golden arrow prize to Joan Rice (Maid Marian). Sick of Finch's tyranny, which reaches new heights when 100,000 marks has to be raised for the release of Barr, held captive by Saracens, Todd forms an outlaw band, all dressed in Lincoln green, determined to bring Finch to heel, their hiding place a forest cave. After several altercations between the two factions, Rice is imprisoned in Gregg's castle, Queen Martita Hunt's escort attacked by soldiers disguised as Todd's outlaws so that Finch and Gregg can reclaim that 100,000 mark fortune. Gaining access to the castle, Todd frees Rice and, following a duel, Finch is crushed to death in the drawbridge mechanism. Barr, dressed as a black knight, returns from the wars, granting gallant Todd and his "Merrie" Men a pardon and instructing the new Earl of Loxley to marry his pretty maiden.

Second only to Errol Flynn's classic *The Adventures of Robin Hood*, Disney's visually arresting interpretation of the legendary medieval tale cut out the fat, presenting a lean, mean narrative minus the usual doses of Disney syrupy sentiment, even including a few snatches of violence and graphic demise by arrow. A truly outstanding Britsh cast—Todd, Gregg, Finch, Rice, Hunt, Barr, James Robertson Justice (Little John), James Hayter (Friar Tuck), Elton Hayes (Alan-A-Dale), Anthony Forwood (Will Scarlett)—and authentic English locations at Burnham Beeches in Buckinghamshire came dressed up in

Guy Green's brightly lit photography, many scenes resembling a Middle Ages scrapbook. Ken Annakin directed with pace and dash, the dappled greenwood forest glades glowed in the sunlight, and Clifton Parker's score struck all the right notes, as did the movie itself. With minstrel Alan-A-Dale's tuneful ditties echoing in their heads, thousands of schoolkids went straight home after watching one of Disney's biggest box-office smashes of the '50s to concoct bows and arrows in their backyards, that is until the studios' just-as-successful *Davy Crockett: King of the Wild Frontier* appeared three years later, again featuring an unforgettable theme song for children to latch on to; bows and arrows were rapidly replaced by coonskin caps!

Peplum influences: the entire picture; the character of Robin Hood was to crop up in numerous Italian productions, even at one point having the hero in green tights pitting his wits against pirates!

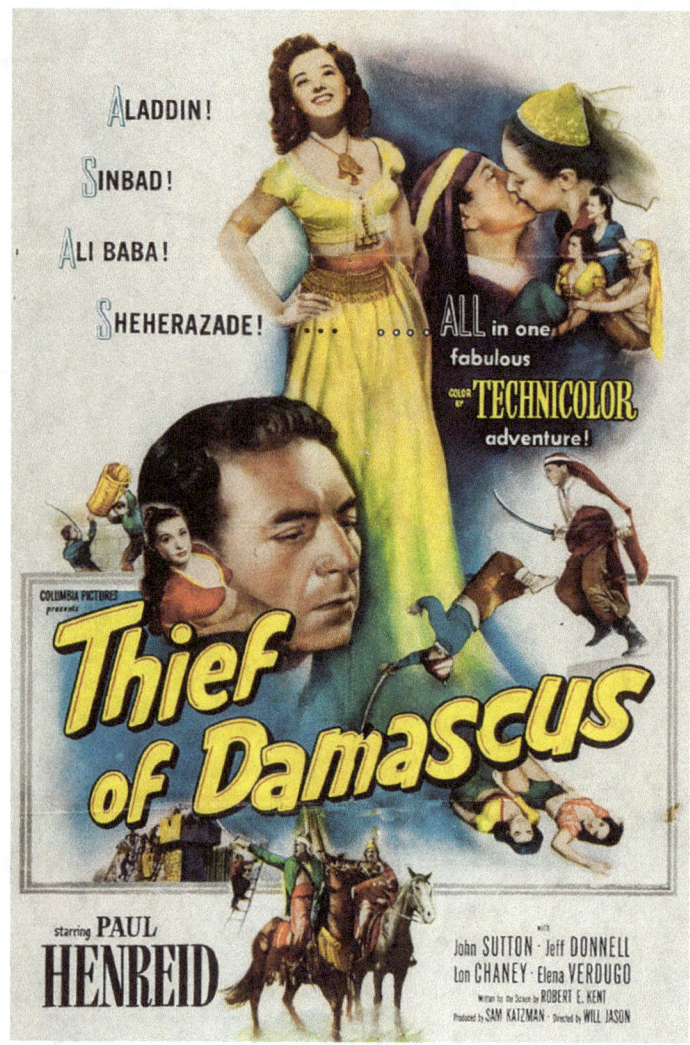

Rock Hudson attempts to pull *The Golden Blade* from a stone pillar.

California's striking Vasquez Rocks area, Will Jason's addition to the cycle of cut-price Arabian adventures is 78 minutes of enjoyable nonsense.

Peplum influences: Sinbad, Aladdin and Ali Baba—all three would appear in future peplum offerings; exotic dance routines; a cave retreat; the interruption of a public execution; opulent palaces; and a closing shot of Henreid planting a smacker on Gilbert.

1953

The Golden Blade aka ***The Sword of Damascus***
Universal (US); Technicolor; 79 mins; Producer: Richard Wilson; Director: Nathan Juran ✝✝✝

Rock Hudson (Harun of Basra) vows vengeance when his father is killed in a raid on their camp instigated by George Macready (Jafar). The evil grand vizier wants to create a war between Basra and Bagdad and usurp Caliph Edgar Barrier from the throne, installing son Gene Evans (Hadi) in his place, the caliph's unwilling daughter, Piper Laurie (Khairuzan), his chosen bride. In wily peddler Steven Geray's (Barcus) store, Hudson comes into possession of the fabled Golden Sword of Damascus, a magical weapon that can cut through solid metal and render him impervious to wounds. Romancing Laurie in secret, Hudson loses a jousting tournament when the swords are switched, Laurie having to wed Evans, the victor, thus arousing the jealousy of his mistress, handmaiden Kathleen Hughes. Barrier is murdered, Evans earmarked as the next caliph while Hudson and Laurie escape the palace guards. The magical sword then becomes embedded in a pillar and no one can pull it free—it must be removed to fulfill a prophecy regarding the rightful ruler of Baghdad. Hudson and Laurie return to the palace and, during a general melee, Hudson pulls the sword from the stone; the pillar cracks and the ceiling tumbles down, crushing Macready and Evans to death. Hudson is now down for the caliph's position, with Laurie at his side.

All dressed up in Maury Gertsman's dazzling Technicolor tones and blessed with John Rich's amusing screenplay, *The*

Thief of Damascus
Columbia (US); Technicolor; 78 mins; Producer: Sam Katzman; Director: Will Jason ✝✝✝

Under the cruel leadership of John Sutton, the Persians enter the city of Damascus, ruled by Philip Van Zandt (Ali Baba). Protected by a flag of truce, Princess Helen Gilbert, Baba's daughter, liaises with General Paul Henreid over fair treatment for the populace, but Sutton has other ideas; he insists on marrying Gilbert himself, placing her father in irons for good measure. Henreid, disturbed at Sutton's level of brutality, teams up with Lon Chaney, Jr. (Sinbad) and Robert Clary (Aladdin), hiding out with rebels in the legendary cave of the 40 thieves. Imprisoning Sutton's crack regiment inside the cavern, Henreid and his followers, concealed in empty olive barrels, stop the public execution of Gilbert, Zandt and Jeff Donnell (Scheherazade) and overthrow the Persians using deadly swords made from a special type of steel. Sutton is dispatched in a duel and Henreid ends up kissing Gilbert, now the new potentate of Damascus.

Many of the Hollywood studios in the early '50s were knocking out sub-Arabian Nights' fodder such as this, which was no better or worse than the rest of the pack. Above all else, *Thief of Damascus* demonstrated Lon Chaney's attempts to break away from horror roles; his Sinbad, complete with hip-wiggling Salome tattoo, was an amusing delight, not too deep maybe, but engaging all the same. Opening with a pulsating battle outside Damascus' impregnable walls and efficiently directed among

John Payne is one of the *Raiders of the Seven Seas*

Golden Blade is frivolous escapist fun that all and sundry must have enjoyed making, even Hudson who publicly denounced his early Universal output in interviews (Tony Curtis turned the part down; Hudson was third choice behind Farley Granger). It moves like a rocket thanks to Nathan Juran's sure-fire hand, and Universal starlet Laurie puts in a perky performance to match her leading man's tongue-in-cheek approach. They certainly don't knock 'em out like this anymore!

Peplum influences: invincible heroes immune to the cut of the blade occasionally cropped up in peplum, noticeably in 1965's *Kindar, the Invulnerable*; a magic sword; Hudson encircled by a ring of scimitars; a two-timing handmaiden; conjuring tricks at a lavish feast; a sexy dancer bewitching the hero; a jousting match; and instant death by falling masonry.

Raiders of the Seven Seas

United Artists (US); Technicolor; 88 mins; Produced and Directed by Sidney Salkow ††††

During the mid-1600s, pirate captain John Payne (Barbarossa), fleeing from his sultan warlord employer in Morocco, captures a Spanish galleon, enlisting the slaves as corsairs. Anthony Caruso is also taken on as first mate, even though crusty seadog Lon Chaney, Jr. (Peg Leg) doesn't trust him an inch. In Tortuga, Payne meets governor's daughter Donna Reed, engaged, contrary to her wishes, to Spaniard Gerald Mohr, a starchy officer continually at loggerheads with his archrival, Captain Henry Brandon. Payne's cutthroats sack the town and Reed is held prisoner, a ransom of 100,000 gold coins placed on her head. Payne then takes over Santa Maria, reducing Reed's ransom to 50,000 gold pieces. While engaged in a skirmish at sea, the pirates' base at Windward Bay is attacked, women and children slaughtered. Enraged at the massacre, Payne goes on the warpath, sinking one Spanish vessel after another, determined to wipe Havana off the map in reprisal, and releasing petulant Reed to Mohr for nothing. Mohr is given an extra 1,500 men to cope with Payne's corsairs who attack a fort, young Skip Torgerson plunging a blade into Brandon's chest. To gain a possible pardon, traitor Caruso murders Chaney and informs Mohr of the details of Payne's planned raid on Havana, paying with his life. In the taut battle for Havana, Mohr and his troops find themselves trapped on the shore, shelled by Payne's fleet, which once more consists of stolen Spanish warships. Mohr is arrested for treason and Reed finally succumbs to Payne's brusque charms, the two sailing off to the Americas for fresh adventures.

Like the Arabian Nights' cycle, Hollywood also ran a spate of low-budget pirate actioners in the early 1950s, of which *Raiders of the Seven Seas* was one of the better examples. Tons of incident and intrigue is boosted by the sight of Payne's muscle-packed hairy chest, Reed looking gorgeous, Lon Chaney again showing he could act with honors, Mohr and Brandon a couple of scowling villains and enough powder smoke to have you coughing into your handkerchief. Gleaming photography from W. Howard Greene and Paul Sawtell's robust seafaring score make this a high seas winner.

Peplum influences: a lashing on board ship; a cold-blooded arranged marriage; an over-the-top banquet; a montage of action shots; a traitor in the camp; several shouts of "Follow me!"; the introduction of a tough young lad as the captain's mate; humorous lines (Payne gazing at Reed for the first time: "You're what I've dreamt of for 60 salty celibate days!"); thundering sea clashes; a fine score; and Payne and Reed smooching on deck.

Serpent of the Nile aka *The Loves of Cleopatra*

Columbia (US); Technicolor; 81 mins; Producer: Sam Katzman; Director: William Castle ††††

In 44 BC, following the assassination of Julius Caesar, Commander Cassius, leader of the opposing Roman factions, commits suicide, his general, William Lundigan (Lucilius), al-

Raymond Burr (left), Rhonda Fleming and William Lundigan from *Serpent of the Nile*

lying himself to Raymond Burr (Marc Antony). Lundigan and Burr travel to Alexandria and meet Rhonda Fleming (Queen Cleopatra), Burr quickly falling for her bewitching charms. Fleming secretly desires to place her son on the hot seat in Rome as emperor; Lundigan is aware of this but Burr, intoxicated on too much wine and lust, refuses to act. Fleming's sister Arsinoe, causing trouble in a remote desert temple fortress, is murdered on orders from the Egyptian queen, Lundigan held under house arrest by Fleming, who views him as a threat to her ambitions. Burr, ignoring his lover's command, allows his loyal friend to return to Rome where Lundigan enlists in Octavius' legions. The Roman regiments successfully storm Alexandria's defenses; Burr does the honorable thing, falling on his sword, Fleming expiring from the bite of an asp.

Potted history made on the cheap, maybe, but why shell out over $40,000,000 on a four-hour epic, as Fox did in 1963, when you can relate the whole Cleopatra saga in 81 minutes on a budget a fraction of the cost, and with considerable expertise. *Serpent of the Nile* has got the lot: Henry Freulich's rich photography; a rousing stock score made up from the works of 13 composers; obvious but attractive painted matte backdrops; massive columned sets (left over from 1953's *Salome*); rattling pace; bruising battle sequences, chariots and horses thundering over the camera; flamboyant dances; a fight with a bear at a banquet; and Fleming ("The golden wench!") looking juicy in black eyeliner and ebony Egyptian wig. A slim-looking Burr is actually quite believable as Marc Antony, Lundigan on hand to prick the man's conscience over the task at hand instead of the commander ogling Fleming's figure-hugging outfits and bullet-bra. Dancer Julie Newmar, gilded in gold 11 years before Shirley Eaton in *Goldfinger*, writhes all over the floor in wild abandon, while Robert E. Kent's script is amusingly concise. "We are rulers of the world," states Michael Fox (Octavius) to Lundigan, to which he replies, "Rome *is* the world." "Are women ever conquered?" queries Burr to Lundigan, who informs Fleming, "You can best serve Rome with your death." "I've only two friends in the world," says Burr resignedly to Lundigan. "You and my sword," realizing that deep down, Fleming doesn't love him, she only yearns for power. Yes, on this occasion, Katzman plus Castle didn't spell disaster; *Serpent of the Nile* is an eminently enjoyable, cut-price *Cleopatra* opus, short, precise and very, very sweet.

Peplum influences: practically the complete Cleopatra deal; Egypt's promiscuous monarch and her sexually motivated shenanigans often formed the basis for numerous Italian movies set in Ancient Egyptian times.

Siren of Bagdad

Columbia (US); Technicolor; 73 mins; Producer: Sam Katzman; Director: Richard Quine ††

Magician Paul Henreid and sidekick Hans Conreid, in the middle of a conjuring trick, are attacked by bandits who swoop on their Arabian desert oasis, carrying off their two prime female attractions, Laurette Luez and Anne Dore. In Old Bagdad, Henreid and Conreid rescue their stooges from a slave market and are treated to an extravagant dance in Sultan Charles Lung's palace after performing for him. Wicked Grand Vizier George Keymas plans to marry off Princess Alexia to Lung for his own devious agenda, but Henreid helps the true heir to the throne, Gypsy Patricia Medina, to impersonate the princess and overthrow Keymas' tyrannical regime. Henreid finally uses his powers to defeat the bandit hordes converging on Bagdad and for good measure makes Keymas and Lung vanish in his magic box.

Where were Bob Hope and Bing Crosby when you so desperately needed them? *Siren of Bagdad*, retitled *Road to Bagdad*, would have been the perfect vehicle for Hope and Crosby's comedy aptitude; Henreid and Conreid (as Kazah the Great and Ben Ali) simply weren't up to the task in Richard Quine's silly satire on Middle Eastern hokum. Henry Freulich's color photography is superb, as are the costumes, while Luez's busty gold bikini-clad beauty is a delight, but the sight of Conreid changing into a woman, joining the dancing girls and mugging furiously, plus limp scimitar clashes, wears thin after 30 minutes, becoming a glossy pantomime pastiche that misfires on all counts.

Peplum influences: exotic, sexy dances featuring jugglers and acrobats; a secret cave hideout; bright-as-a-button Technicolor; an evil Grand Vizier; a true heir to the kingdom determined to regain her rightful place. The Italians occasionally came up with ridiculous skits on Bagdad and its heroes (Aladdin, Ali Baba, Sinbad, et al.), but nothing quite as dumb as what was on offer here.

Sword of Venus aka Island of Monte Cristo

RKO-Radio/American Pictures (US); B&W; 73 mins; Producers: Jack Pollexfen, Aubrey Wisberg; Director: Harold Daniels ††

Paris, 1832: Womanizing Robert Clarke (Robert Dantes), the son of the infamous Count of Monte Cristo, is toying with

his latest conquest, a married woman, under the eyes of three scoundrels led by Dan O'Herlihy (Danglars) who are planning to rob him of his capital and estates. Another of the trio, Catherine McLeod (Claire), arranges to be stranded on the road to Monte Cristo, knowing that Clarke will rescue her and start a romance. Clarke's valet, in with O'Herlihy on the scam, is shot dead by O'Herlihy, his body found with forged papers naming him as McLeod's fictitious husband. Tried for murder and sentenced to execution, Clarke, who has now fallen in love with McLeod, marries her in prison in the hope that the judge will be lenient. Instead, he's sent to the stone quarries for a life of hard labor. In a fight with a fellow prisoner, Clarke fakes his own death and escapes; his features hidden behind bandages after killing O'Herlihy's confederate Merrit Stone, the playboy confronts the ringleader and alcoholic lawyer William Shallert on the Isle of Monte Cristo. Spilling ink over documents entitling them to the Monte Cristo fortune, Clarke shoots O'Herlihy following a swordfight and is reunited with McLeod.

Hack director Harold Daniels rattled off this obscure B-swashbuckler in a couple of weeks on minuscule funds, casting B-actor Robert Clarke in the title role. A labyrinth plot, whereby characters continually impersonated other characters for their own ends, performed on shaky sets, resulted in a moderately interesting costumer enlivened by Charles Koff's deafening score. This is a U.S. peplum for purists only.

Peplum influences: Cheapskate pepla can be found among the plethora of bigger budgeted stuff; a wicked lady falling in lust with her chosen victim; changes in identity, including masked, horror-type, disguises; and a terrific score to cover up cracks in the narrative.

The Veils of Bagdad

Universal (US); Technicolor; 82 mins; Producer: Albert J. Cohen; Director: George Sherman ✞✞

Bagdad, 1560: Victor Mature (Antar), an agent acting for Suleiman the Magnificent, head of the Ottoman Empire, infiltrates the court of Pasha Leon Askin who, with Grand Vizier Guy Rolfe (Kasseim), is stirring up trouble with the hill tribes in order to put a spoke in the Turkish conqueror's works. Taken on by Rolfe after saving his escort from a bandit ambush (a put-up job; the bandits are all Mature's pals), Mature falls for Princess Mari Blanchard (Selima), whose father was murdered by Rolfe; Rolfe's sex-starved wife, Virginia Field, also longs for the beefy warrior to whisk her away. After assorted skirmishes within the palace walls, Mature's men, dressed as wrestlers, defeat the palace guards; Rolfe is sent to Allah with a sword in his guts, Mature, made pasha when Askin abdicates, gets a marriage proposal from Blanchard and Field departs with a chest overflowing with gold, promising Mature that if he ever tires of the princess, she's his for the taking.

Probably one of the many films in his repertoire that Mature never had fond memories of, *The Veils of Bagdad* retains its action set pieces on sound sets and is muddily photographed, unusual for a cinematographer of Russell Metty's repute; director Sherman was more at home with his Universal Westerns (*Border River*; *War Arrow*; *Chief Crazy Horse*) than when working on gimcrack material like this. Notwithstanding James *The Thing* Arness shining as Mature's hefty compatriot and a joint score

The colorful court of Leon Askin in *The Veils of Bagdad*

Rosemarie Bowe, Miss Montana 1951, added the sizzle to *The Adventures of Hajji Baba*

from Herman Stein and Henry Mancini brimming with spicy flavors, Universal's Middle Eastern romp is one of the least interesting of the innumerable low-budget *Bagdad* offerings to have emerged from the Hollywood studios during this heady period, despite Mature's heavyweight screen presence.

Peplum influences: dances and acrobats during a banquet; a public whiplashing; the whole Bagdad shtick; and Mature himself, seized upon by filmmakers to star in a number of peplum features, some good, some indifferent.

1954

The Adventures of Hajji Baba

Allied Artists/20th Century Fox (US); CinemaScope/DeLuxecolor; 94 mins; Producer: Walter Wanger; Director: Don Weis ☦ or ☦☦☦☦☦

Handsome young masseur/barber John Derek (Hajji Baba) becomes embroiled in a series of chaotic adventures when he encounters petulant, pampered, preening, self-centered Elaine Stewart (Princess Fakzia) hoisted away from the Persian city of Ispahan to be married against her will to Paul Picerni (Prince Nurel-Din). After being captured in the desert and escaping from a tribe of Amazons known as the Turcomanos, and caught up in the stratagems of crafty slave merchant Thomas Gomez (Osman), Derek slays Picerni in a fight to the finish, marrying Stewart with her father's blessing.

Most definitely a prime contender for Hollywood's number one "so bad it's essential" 1950s helping of hokum-filled balderdash, Don Weis' Arabian frolic has everything on offer for lovers of trash-laden guilty pleasures: Nat "King" Cole warbling "Hajji Baba" in a ghostly echo throughout the action, the song written by Dimitri Tiomkin and Ned Washington; Tiomkin's strident soundtrack (why was a composer of his magnitude roped into scoring *this* picture?); flame-haired Amazon queen Amanda Blake digging her claws into perpetually grinning Derek; stunning Lone Pine mountain scenery; "Miss Montana 1951" Rosemarie Bowe performing an erotic dance, then dragging only-too-willing Derek off to her tent; the Turcomanos warriors astride on horseback, lassoing their opponents around the neck with cloth streamers; Derek pole-vaulting onto his steed; sexy, half-naked slave girls in cages; Stewart at the mercy of her vengeful ex-handmaiden, strung up to fry in the sun; and a steamy finale, loved-up Stewart, looking drop-dead gorgeous on her wedding night and playing seductively to the audience, demanding that her new husband stop waving at the crowds and come back to bed immediately—for her, once is certainly *not* enough!

Peplum influences: the entire madly entertaining kit and caboodle. The Italians were just as capable at knocking out sky-high camp as the Americans—just check Vittorio Sala's utterly bonkers offering *Queen of the Amazons* (1960) and you'll see what I mean.

The Black Knight

Warwick Films/Columbia (US/UK); Technicolor; 85 mins; Producers: Irving Allen, Albert R. Broccoli; Director: Tay Garnett ☦

Alan Ladd (John), a humble blacksmith/swordmaker employed by Harry Andrews (the Earl of Yeonvil), and friend to André Morell (Sir Ontzlake), takes up arms when Peter Cushing and his Saracen hordes, disguised as Vikings, sack the Earl's castle and set their sights on Camelot. Patrick Troughton (King Mark of Cornwall) is in league with Cushing, while Patricia Medina (Lady Linet), Andrews' daughter, doesn't realize that the mysterious Black Knight, who appears from nowhere and upsets Cushing's plans *and* saves her from ritual sacrifice at Stonehenge, is none other than meek and mild Ladd. In a mighty battle for supremacy, the Saracens are defeated, Ladd hurling Cushing off Camelot's walls; he's then knighted by Anthony Bushell (King Arthur) for his valiant efforts and gets betrothed to Medina.

Often cited as the worst Arthurian adventure movie ever made, *The Black Knight* is chaotically bad. Let's list the reasons: an anachronistic plot; clumsy attempts to make five-foot-six Ladd appear taller than six-foot-two Andrews in their joint scenes; a terribly conceived polystyrene Stonehenge set; erratic chop-and-changes in continuity location work, from Black Park, Buckinghamshire to Castell Coch, South Glamorgan, Wales, to Manzanares Castle, Madrid, to Avila's town walls, to Castilla y Leon, Avila; Peter Cushing wearing a Viking helmet; Medina, in blonde wig, subjecting herself to one of cinema's most inept sacrificial sequences; Ladd's obvious stunt double swinging across Camelot's great hall on a rope; and a cheesy curtain closer—Bushell to Ladd: "Name your heart's desire," the Hollywood actor turning to Medina with a big sloppy grin on his face. Looking completely out of his comfort zone among a contingent of authoritative British actors and woefully miscast, it's true what they all say: Alan Ladd doth not a good English knight maketh.

Peplum influences: the whole skew-whiff travesty on English historical legend. And if the British and Americans could

get it all so completely and utterly wrong, so could the Italians: Check out Tanio Boccia's *The Revenge of Ivanhoe* (1965) as a prime example of English history going to the dogs.

The Black Shield of Falworth
Universal (US); CinemaScope/Technicolor; 99 mins; Producers: Robert Arthur, Melville Tucker; Director: Rudolph Maté ††††

In the reign of Henry IV, Tony Curtis (Myles), the heir to the estates of Falworth, travels to Mackworth Castle with sister Barbara Rush (Meg) and is enrolled as a squire of arms by Herbert Marshall (the Earl of Mackworth), Dan O'Herlihy (Prince Hal) and teacher Torin Thatcher. Marshall and O'Herlihy are aware of Curtis' origins; his father was wrongly charged with cowardice by David Farrar (the Earl of Alban) and murdered by him for his property. Curtis romances Janet Leigh (Lady Anne), betrothed to Farrar's evil son, Patrick O'Neal; Farrar is stirring up trouble between Marshall and Ian Keith (King Henry), wishing to lay his hands on the Mackworth fortune. Told of his true identity and determined to clear the tarnished name of Falworth, Curtis, now a knight, challenges Farrar to trial by combat, plunging his sword into his hated enemy's armpit in a fiercely fought contest. Farrar's gorillas are overthrown in a struggle, Curtis' friend Craig Hill dispatching O'Neal. Curtis has the satisfaction of seeing the Falworth coat of arms restored and Leigh on his arm.

Newlyweds Curtis and Leigh, Hollywood's golden couple of the time, made an engaging duo in Universal's $1,000,000 medieval frolic (their first CinemaScope production) that manages to delight the senses, even if for the most part the action takes place within the confines of Marshall's castle. Curtis, in beige tights and Bronx accent, displays his acrobatic skills as well as a nice line in self-deprecating humor, and the bruising clash between him and Farrar to the sound of sword and mace clashing on armor and shields is a classic. Vibrant color (Irving Glassberg) and a knights-of-old score (Frank Skinner, Hans J. Salter, Herman Stein) add to a picture that belies its dodgy reputation among critics; this stands as one of Curtis' finest, most appealing, moments from the mid-1950s.

Peplum influences: a dastardly earl hoodwinking a king; lessons in court etiquette; love trysts between a commoner and a girl from the upper class; and trial by combat. A great deal of the movie is talkative, focusing on the Curtis/Leigh romance, something which the Italians dwelt on at some length in their period costumers, long before the days when audiences demanded a thrill every minute to keep them both amused and awake.

Captain Kidd and the Slave Girl
United Artists (US); CCA Color; 84 mins; Producers; Jack Pollexfen, Aubrey Wisberg; Director: Lew Landers †††

Released from London's Newgate Prison by crafty James Seay (the Earl of Bellomont), Anthony Dexter (Captain William Kidd) and hook-handed buddy Alan Hale, Jr. set sail on the *In-*

Newlyweds Janet Leigh and Tony Curtis in an off-set moment during the filming of *The Black Shield of Falworth*

Eva Gabor and Anthony Dexter on board James Seay's vessel in *Captain Kidd and the Slave Girl*

dian Queen with a bunch of untrustworthy lubbers in search of Captain Morgan's treasure. Seay's vessel, the *Empress*, follows at a discreet distance; the earl and his partners in deception are anxious to grab the treasure, planting Eva Gabor on board the *Indian Queen* with instructions to romance Dexter and wheedle out of him the exact location where the fortune is buried. Dexter cottons on to what Gabor is up to, drawing incorrect maps of the site to throw her, and any other snoopers, off the scent. Abandoning his mutinous crew on an island, Dexter alights on Turtle Island, bumping into Michael Ross (Blackbeard) and his gang of roughneck captains, including Sonia Sorel (Anne Bonney), a fiery pirate lass; she sets her sights on Dexter, instantly falling for him. When the three chests of treasure are unearthed, a struggle for ownership between Seay's crew, Ross' corsairs and the duo of Dexter and Hale results in Sorel being shot dead, the *Empress* exchanging broadsides with the *Indian Queen*, Hale fatally wounded and both ships going up in flames when a cargo of dynamite explodes, Morgan's treasure consigned to the bottom of the ocean. Rescued in a boat by the English, Dexter and Gabor make plans to start a new life together in a foreign port.

Okay, a lot of this Lew Landers' pirate flick, containing a breezy Paul Sawtell score, is performed on studio sets, but the narrative moves like wildfire, a picture that both kids and adults would still enjoy today. Dexter makes a bold Captain Kidd, Hale (always good value for money) barges his burly weight around, Gabor, Zsa Zsa's younger sister, squeaks and preens, not Tinseltown's greatest actress by any stretch of the imagination, while Sorel's vibrant star turn makes you wonder why she didn't get more similar roles in Hollywood—she certainly acts Gabor off the screen. Unfortunately, current DVD issues come in black-and-white, not color.

Peplum influences: Sorel falling in love with Dexter a couple of hours after meeting him; a full-blooded score to punctuate the action; buried treasure, usually Captain Morgan's; a female pirate, as tough to handle as the male of the species; vessels blowing sky-high; and Dexter and Gabor (still in her crumpled, stained white dress) smooching as the film closes.

The Men of Sherwood Forest

Hammer/Exclusive (UK); Eastmancolor; 77 mins; Producer: Michael Carreras; Director: Val Guest ††

In 1194, Patrick Holt (King Richard) is on his way back to England from Germany, details of his arrival secreted inside a silver toy. Two bandits steal the object; Don Taylor (Robin Hood) is assigned the task of retrieving it and hopefully staving off a treacherous coup by Douglas Wilmer, David King-Wood and Harold Lang to usurp the throne from the king. Aided by Reginald Beckwith (Friar Tuck) and Eileen Moore (Lady Alys), Taylor infiltrates King-Wood's castle disguised as a troubadour to try to prevent the attempt on the king's life. Holt disembarks on a beach-traveling inland; a scuffle in Marley Woods proves the downfall of Wilmer and company, the Merry Men coming to the rescue of the monarch. Taylor is given permission to hunt for deer in Sherwood Forest, Moore already betrothed to one of Holt's fellow crusaders—so the greenwood savior doesn't get the leading lady!

Hammer's first picture in color featured Errol Flynn lookalike Taylor as the outlaw donning, on this occasion, red tights, doing his utmost to enliven an uninspiring effort (he's constantly laughing his head off) filmed in the setting of East Sussex's imposing Bodiam Castle. A couple of movies away from one of

his, and Hammer's, most influential successes, *The Quatermass Experiment* (1955), Val Guest seemed to be going through the motions: no Sheriff of Nottingham, no Maid Marion and no Peter Cushing or Christopher Lee. Beckwith's comical gambling routines get tiresome after a while, gamine Moore more of a tomboy than lady, the swordplay is lackluster compared to later Hammer *Robin Hood* outings, and six-foot-seven inch-tall Bernard Bresslaw, in his film debut, ambles around on set, playing a buffoonish guard, matching the production's none-too-serious tone. On the positive side, classical composer Doreen Carwithen's Olde English score is delightful.

Peplum influences: As with *The Story of Robin Hood and His Merrie Men*, the fabled folk hero in Hammer's watered-down family version was a favored character with the Italians, either as Robin Hood himself or a Robin Hood-type champion of the people.

Prince Valiant

20th Century Fox (US); CinemaScope/Technicolor; 100 mins; Producer: Robert L. Jacks; Director: Henry Hathaway
✝✝✝✝

Robert Wagner (Prince Valiant), son of Donald Crisp, the exiled King of Scandia and of Viking blood, travels to the court of Brian Aherne (King Arthur) at Camelot to become a knight and then come to grips with the Viking hordes, led by Sligon, busy raiding the coast where his father resides. Befriending Sterling Hayden (Sir Gawain), he becomes involved with the Black Knight, a mysterious figure in cahoots with the Vikings. James Mason (Sir Brack) turns out to be the knight; aggrieved at being overlooked as the leader of the round table, he wants to wrest control from Aherne. Falling for Janet Leigh (Lady Aleta), Wagner eventually penetrates the Viking stronghold where Leigh, Crisp and his mother (Mary Philips) are being held captive. Wagner and Christian Vikings commanded by Victor McLaglen (Boltar) overthrow Sligon and his warriors in a fierce confrontation, the prisoners freed. At Camelot, Wagner accuses Mason of treachery in front of Aherne and kills him in a duel. Knighted for his efforts, he's now in a position to wed Leigh.

Great score from Franz Waxman; lovely cinematography by Lucien Ballard; four authentic British castle locations; a thrilling three-minute clash between Wagner and Mason; and a strong cast—*Prince Valiant* is vintage Hollywood filmmaking masquerading as English history with one big question in mind: Would it have worked even better without Wagner in the lead? Resembling an undernourished pageboy with attitude, he leapfrogs around set, demolishing foes three times his size and shouting, in a broad American accent (broader than Tony Curtis' in *The Black Shield of Falworth*), dialogue such as "Sire, I have found your traitor. The Black Knight." Set beside the likes (and box-office clout) of Mason, McLaglen, Crisp and six-foot-five Hayden (who dwarfs him), he appears at times a little too eager to please. Notwithstanding Wagner and whether he fitted the role or not, *Prince Valiant* is a vibrant costumer of the old school, maintaining pace and interest from start to finish.

Peplum influences: Real-life castles were used to great effect, something which the Italians were partial to over painted backdrops; Vikings; Leigh in love with Wagner after one day; a tremendous jousting display, the victor promised the lady's

Debra Paget and Jeffrey Hunter pose as the lovers in *Princess of the Nile*.

hand; a wicked knight; Christians to be burned on the cross; an exciting, climactic duel, the ring of metal echoing throughout the castle halls.

Princess of the Nile

20th Century Fox (US); Technicolor; 71 mins; Producer: Robert L. Jacks; Director: Harmon Jones ††††

Halwan, in the Upper Valley of the Nile, 1249 AD: Bedouin overlord Michael Rennie (Rama Khan), aided by Edgar Barrier (the Shaman), plans to wed Debra Paget (Egyptian princess Shalimar) and worm his way into the court at Bagdad. Jeffrey Hunter (Prince Haidi), son of Bagdad's caliph, visits Halwan on his way home and becomes embroiled in a plot to oust Rennie and his occupiers from power, while the rebels, a gang of thieves, are led by none other than Paget posing as Taura, a dancing wench at the Tambourine tavern. Gaining access to the palace rooms via a secret water-filled gallery, Paget fends off Rennie's advances while the insurgents perpetually harass Rennie's troops. Hunter wants to track down the man responsible for knifing his best friend; Rennie is the culprit, giving Paget an ultimatum: "I'll spare your people and restore your father to the throne if you marry me." During a mass skirmish, Rennie falls on the point of a lance, the Bedouins are routed and Hunter and Paget kiss in front of an adoring crowd of vagabonds.

Shot in dazzling color by Lloyd Ahern and scripted by Gerald Drayson Adams, who specialized in this kind of sub-Arabian Nights' fluff, *Princess of the Nile* represents 71 minutes of no-holds-barred kitsch containing many points of reference aped by the peplum makers. Paget, 21, looks absolutely gorgeous, as does Hunter (!), while Rennie's hiss-boo Bedouin is pantomime villainy at its best. The film's corny and highly entertaining.

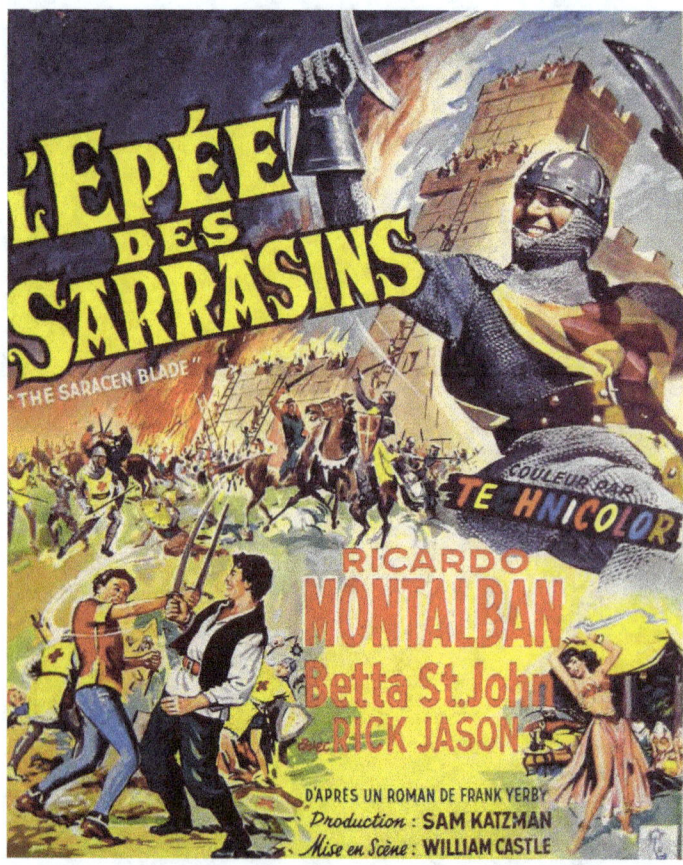

A Belgian movie poster for *The Saracen Blade*

Peplum influences: several shouts of "Follow me!"; the introduction of a dwarf (Billy Curtis) into the proceedings—diminutive actors like Curtis appeared in countless pepla over the coming years; a secret passage into a palace; sexy, thigh-revealing dances; the oft-used peplum ultimatum of "Marry me, and they'll be spared"; vivid color photography; beautiful handmaidens (Paget has five); thieves turned good (note regular heavy Jack Elam among them); a fine Middle Eastern score (Lionel Newman); knockabout fight sequences; villains called "dogs"; a pet lion in a cave; and exotic Arabian sets.

The Saracen Blade

Columbia (US); Technicolor; 76 mins; Producer: Sam Katzman; Director: William Castle ††††

In 15th-century Italy, blacksmith Guy Prescott's wife dies in childbirth. Twenty years later, her son, Ricardo Montalban (Pietro Donati), meets Prescott during a siege in which rebels unsuccessfully try to overcome the forces of Michael Ansara (Count Alesandro Siniscola). Wishing to enrol in the Saracens, Montalban joins the Siniscola court as a vassal, falling for Betta St. John (Lady Iolanthe) who's engaged to be married to Rick Jason (Enzio Siniscola). On the eve of her arranged wedding, St. John gallops off with Montalban; they're apprehended, Montalban flung into a dungeon, St. John married to Jason. St. John frees her one true love; Whitfield Connor (Emperor Fredrick II), who was born at the same hour as Montalban, befriends him during a manhunt in the forest. The two bond; Montalban once more finds himself in the Siniscola court, marrying Ansara's cousin Carolyn Jones before leaving for the Crusades. Montalban returns as a knight with slave girl Pamela Duncan; in a jealous rage, Ansara, who desired Jones, stabs her to death. Incensed, Montalban, against Connor's express wishes, declares war on the Siniscolas and in a revolt, Jason is killed, Montalban running Ansara through with his curved blade. Stripped of his land and titles by Connor for staging an uprising, Montalban rides off with St. John to begin a new life for himself.

Katzman and Castle come up with the goods again in a rousing Arabian swashbuckler that belies its low budget. Hairy chest bared to the four winds, Montalban romps through the colorful action with zest and a grin on his face, matched by a beautifully judged performance from Carolyn Jones as man-eater Elaine, turned on by Montalban's rough, masculine charms. Bags of action (stock footage is used in some sequences), intrigue and romance are put together with energetic relish by William Castle in a picture that doesn't contain a single boring second.

Peplum influences: The entire movie and its style—this is about the nearest Hollywood could get to an Italian peplum feature in the 1950s without it being Italian in origin.

Sign of the Pagan

Universal (US); CinemaScope/Technicolor; 92 mins; Producer: Albert J. Cohen; Director: Douglas Sirk ††††

Centurion Jeff Chandler (Marcian), on his way to Constantinople, is captured by Jack Palance (Attila the Hun) but spared death; Palance wants the soldier to teach his warriors the art of Roman combat. Chandler escapes on Palance's prize steed. In Constantinople, he meets Jeff Morrow (General Paulinus), who is in disagreement with George Dolenz's (Emperor Theodosius) toadying up to the barbarians; Dolenz is in a secret alliance with Palance, paying 5,000 gold coins a year for patrolling his borders, and wants nothing to do with Rome. Palance, on the other hand,

desires Rome for himself, inciting tribal chieftains into a state of war as long as they leave the Christians alone; the warlord is deeply superstitious over this new god they worship. In a palace coup, Dolenz is forced to abdicate, his sister Ludmilla Tchérina taking command as empress. Palance's forces march away from Rome after bad omens from Persian astrologer Edward Franz and are halted in a ruined town; during a battle, Palance is put to the sword by Allison Hayes, one of his embittered wives who was appalled at Palance's brutal slaying of his own daughter, Rita Gam, during an argument. The pagans defeated, Tchérina and Chandler become the new rulers of Constantinople.

The role model for the cycle of peplum barbarian/pagan features, *Sign of the Pagan*, budgeted at $1,300,000, is an invigorating actioner boasting lavish sets, a strong cast, an unsubtle, sledgehammer score from Hans J. Salter and Frank Skinner, bright color courtesy of Russell Metty, screen heavy Leo Gordon (minus hair) as a rampaging Hun and Palance (who was to star in three Italian pepla) on full throttle.

Peplum influences: Like *The Saracen Blade*, Sirk's Huns versus Romans feature is Italian peplum by any other name, such is its all-round prestige and, of course, the mighty presence of six-foot-four Jack Palance, with those looks born to play a pagan warlord.

1955

The Purple Mask

Universal (US); CinemaScope/Technicolor; 82 mins; Producer: Howard Christie; Director: H. Bruce Humberstone ✟✟✟

France 1803: A new Scarlet Pimpernel in the form of The Purple Mask is kidnapping Republicans and demanding ransoms of 10,000 gold louis to aid the Royalist cause. At a ladies' shop, Colleen Miller (Laurette) and Angela Lansbury are working undercover for the Royalists; Miller's important father is due to be guillotined, so they hatch a plan to produce a fictitious Purple Mask and have him captured, a diversionary tactic to enable the man to be saved. Tony Curtis (Rene) is chosen, the gadabout cadet in a dancing/fencing school—and he's the real Purple Mask! Miller's starchy admirer, Gene Barry (Captain Laverne), smells a rat while top-ranking swordsman Dan O'Herlihy (Brisquet) is brought out of retirement to deal with Curtis, disguising himself as a governor to trap the man who has become a thorn in Robert Cornthwaite's (Napoleon) side. After numerous games of bluff and counter-bluff, Curtis, Miller, Lansbury and several Royalists are saved from the guillotine by Royalists dressed as Republican dragoons; granted safe passage to England by Cornthwaite, Curtis waltzes off with Miller on his arm, vowing to return.

Before Tony Curtis got down to more serious roles, he starred in harmless programmers such as *The Purple Mask*, his disarming masked avenger breezing through a costumer low on violence, high on derring-do, saturated in Irving Glassberg's dazzling Technicolor cinematography. The picture also ably demonstrated Curtis' deft light comedic touch and his enviable attraction to the female cast, who appear all faint every time he appears on set. An appetizing swashbuckler for all ages, the charismatic leading man makes it look all so easy.

Peplum influences: A masked avenger with a foppish alter-ego was an important central figure in many a peplum, in particular the Italian *Zorro* features; a secret room behind a sliding panel; last-minute intervention at a public execution; rebels disguising themselves as soldiers; and stellar color photography.

The Scarlet Coat

MGM (US); CinemaScope/Eastmancolor; 101 mins; Producer: Nicholas Nayfack; Director: John Sturges ✟✟

Cornel Wilde (left) and Michael Wilding get turned on by the charms of Anne Francis in *The Scarlet Coat*.

During the American Revolution, 1780, American intelligence officer Cornel Wilde (Major John Boulton) poses as a deserter and infiltrates the British lines, his assignment to unmask a spy known as Gustavus. Befriending Michael Wilding (Major John Andre) and suspicious doctor George Sanders (Jonathan Odell), he romances Wilding's girlfriend, Anne Francis, becoming involved in one bout of subterfuge after another until Robert Douglas (General Benedict Arnold) is unmasked as the turncoat rebel. Wilding, a counterspy, is hanged at the end, Wilding's mission complete.

John Sturges' toothless colonial costume drama is a film most would only want to catch once. Two solitary spells of rapier parrying and a limp confrontation on board ship brighten up a dialogue-driven narrative that confuses if you're not familiar with this particular period of American history. Wilde, Wilding, Sanders and John McIntire (General Robert Howe) turn in solid performances (Francis appears uneasy with her material) and the leafy, rustic Sleepy Hollow locations are nicely photographed by Paul C. Vogel, but in all honesty, the movie goes nowhere at a snail's pace; it's earnest, worthy but patently unexciting.

Peplum influences: Period spies and traitors cropped up in many latter-day pepla, but in far livelier confections than MGM's turgid, overlong offering.

1956

Zarak

Warwick Films/Columbia (UK); CinemaScope/Technicolor; 99 mins; Producer: Phil C. Samuel; Director: Terence Young
✝✝✝

On India's North West frontier, Victor Mature (Zarak), following a row with his father over Anita Ekberg's charms, is banished from his tribe and becomes a fearsome bandit chieftain, waging war against the British garrisons commanded by Michael Wilding (Major Michael Ingram). Allying himself to cousin Peter Illing (Ahmad), he raids the town of Ziarat and Fort Abbott with a 50,000 rupee price tag on his head, but eventually falls out with his slippery partner. After several bloody confrontations, Wilding is captured by Illing's warriors and marked down for decapitation; Mature, a haunted man, full of remorse for killing holy prophet Finlay Currie, takes his place and is whipped to death by Illing's soldiers. Wilding's reinforcements arrive on the scene and defeat Illing's warriors; peace is returned to the region.

Any movie that contains around 20 minutes of stirringly staged battle sequences (and a terrific rope bridge interlude) can't be all that bad, but viewed as a whole, *Zarak* is something of a mess, the narrative drifting all over the place from one incident and locale to the other (filming was carried out in Burma, India, Morocco and England). Love interest Ekberg performs two X-rated dance routines (what a body!) to the out-of-context sounds of a '40s cabaret number, her moments of passion with stone-faced Mature totally unconvincing. The cinematography (Ted Moore, Cyril J. Knowles and John Wilcox) is superb, as is William Alwyn's thunderous score; it's these plus points, together with tremendous battles and Mature's box-office clout, that lift *Zarak* out of its gaudy rut into the realms of a guilty pleasure.

Peplum influences: a rebel bandit; sexy dances; all-weapons-blazing confrontations; a leading lady with a body to die for; Victor Mature's hulking screen presence; and William Alwyn's fabulous score, echoes of which can be detected in the riveting arrangements of Italian composers Angelo Francesco Lavagnino (for *Ursus and the Tartar Girl*, 1961), and Francesco De Masi (in *Suleiman the Conqueror*, 1961).

Anita Ekberg flaunts her assets in *Zarak*.

Louis Jordan and Belinda Lee in *Dangerous Exile*

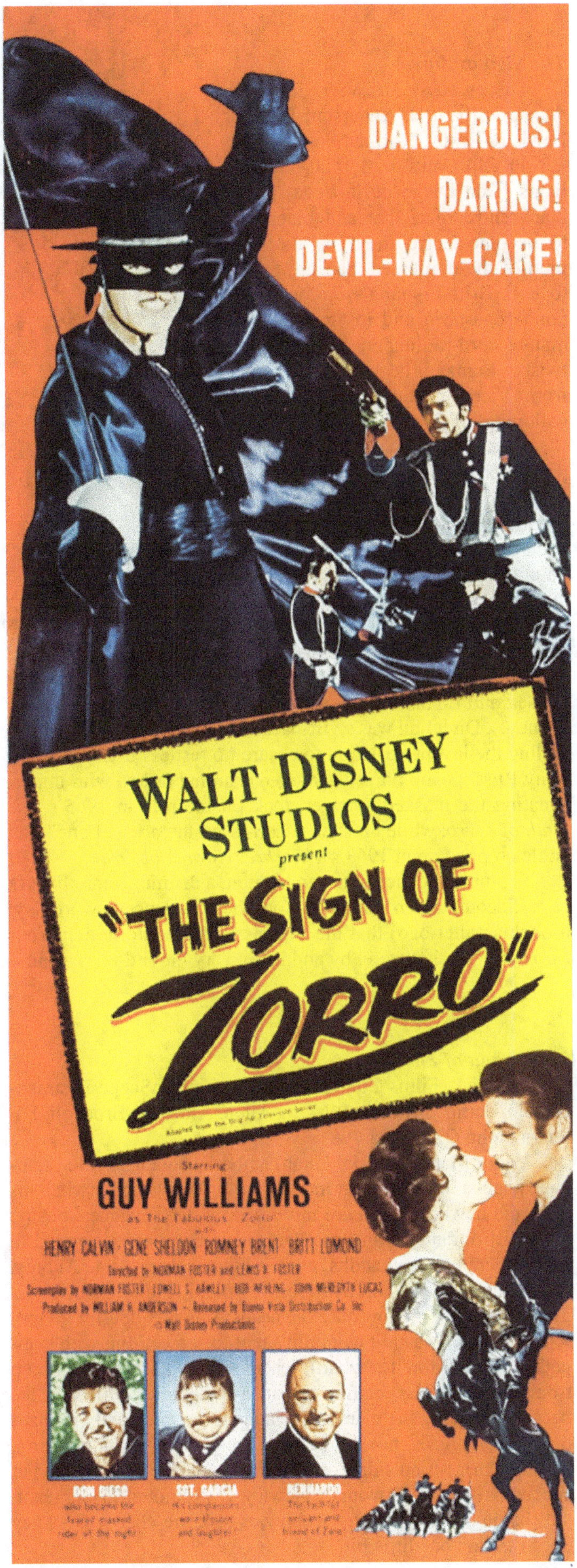

1957

Dangerous Exile

Rank (UK); VistaVision/Eastmancolor; 89 mins; Producer: George H. Brown; Director: Brian Desmond Hurst ††††

In 1795, during the war between England and Republican France, young Richard O'Sullivan (Louis XVII) is smuggled to Wales in a hot-air balloon, cared for by visiting American Belinda Lee (Virginia Traill) on bedridden Martita Hunt's island retreat. Frenchman Louis Jourdan (the Duke de Beavais), a Royalist, visits the boy; he placed his own son, who resembled O'Sullivan, in prison in order to save the future king from the guillotine. On his return to France, Jourdan discovers that his son has been murdered and given a sham king's funeral to fool the public into believing the heir to the crown is dead. Republican Keith Michell (Colonel St. Gerard), on learning that the young monarch still lives, sails to Wales in a warship to kill the monarch. In a cliff-edge struggle, British traitor Finlay Currie falls to his death, his female accomplice Anne Heywood shot in the back. Hunting for O'Sullivan in the castle, Michell is shot dead by Jourdan; the duke elects to stay on in Wales with Lee, who has fallen for him, and raise the boy king as his own.

Using Cornwall's striking Caerhays Castle as its focal point, *Dangerous Exile* is a smoothly shot costume drama featuring lurid moments of Hammer-type Gothicism in its Paris dungeon sequences, atmospherically photographed and lit by Geoffrey Unsworth (Oscars for *Cabaret* [1972] and *Tess* [1979]). Rank starlet Lee procured the lead role in *The Venus of Cheronea* (*Aphrodite, Goddess of Love*) the same year, her smoldering sex appeal all too evident; she went on to star in in a further four Italian peplum features (and one French) before her tragic death in 1961, aged only 25.

Peplum influences: a boy king hidden away for his own safety; dungeon sequences filmed in nightmarish horror style; swordfights composed in close-up for maximum impact; traitors and spies; Belinda Lee's upfront, pouting sexuality; a grand castle background; and Georges Auric's rousing soundtrack.

1958

The Sign of Zorro

Disney (US); B&W; 91 mins; Producer: William H. Anderson; Directors: Lewis R. Foster, Norman Foster ✝✝✝✝

In Old California, 1820, Guy Williams (Don Diego de la Vega) puts on black shirt, black hat and black mask to become Zorro the Fox, the champion of the oppressed, battling to bring to heel Britt Lomand's dastardly Captain Monastario and his gorillas. After many sword-rattling encounters and plot twists, Lomand is arrested on orders from Viceroy John Dehner, Williams galloping off for more adventures.

Eight episodes culled from Disney's popular *Zorro* TV series, which ran from 1957-1961, were cobbled together to produce one of cinema's liveliest, more coherent *Zorro* flicks, dashing Guy Williams in engaging form. Lack of a female lead wasn't missed in this instance. Apart from Williams, Gene Sheldon was amusing as Zorro's mute assistant, Bernardo; Henry Calvin's rotund Sergeant Garcia bumbled all over the set; and Lomand displayed mild brutality (after all, this was Disney!). Direction was swift-paced, William Lava's music propelling the inventive action to ensure no restless bums on seats. Tony Russel, who played a wanted criminal tasked with impersonating the masked avenger, took on the role in 1965's *The Oath of Zorro*, while the "three Zorros for the price of one" plot angle cropped up in 1963's *The Three Swords of Zorro*.

Peplum influences: As can be seen, a defining genre flick (a cave hideout; tavern skirmishes; provocative dances; swordplay; a bookish alter-ego) that the Italians latched onto in numerous *Zorro* movies that were, by and large, very hit-and-miss affairs.

1959

The Bandit of Zhobe

Warwick Films/Columbia (UK); CinemaScope/Eastmancolor; 81 mins; Producers: Irving Allen, Albert R. Broccoli; Director: John Gilling ✝✝

Victor Mature (Kasim Khan) embarks on a hate-filled rampage against the British on India's North West Frontier when his wife and newborn child are murdered by the Thuggees, posing as British infantry. Norman Wooland is the major assigned to halt Mature and his bandits, even if his daughter, Anne Aubrey, believes in Mature's motivations. Corporal Anthony Newley is given the job of making sure the headstrong lass doesn't go galloping off to the bandit chieftain's tent to shower him with sympathy. Walter Gotell (Azhad), leader of the Thuggees, stirs up trouble on all sides, knifing a British undercover officer in the back and placing the blame on Mature, who eventually realizes that the Thuggees, not the British, slaughtered his family. In a bloody skirmish outside Fort Murdoch, Mature kills Gotell but succumbs to a fatal wound; Newley is promoted to Sergeant, still having to watch over Aubrey, a task the cheery Cockney doesn't mind one little bit!

Victor Mature cuts up rough as *The Bandid of Zhobe*.

If you've seen *Zarak*, it's not really worth bothering with *The Bandit of Zhobe*, or, to be more precise, *Zarak II*. This film features the same sets, same locations, same plot and turbaned, hangdog Mature appearing fed up with the whole proceedings. Over 10 minutes' worth of stock footage from *Zarak* is used, mostly in the battle sequences, the production given a shambolic air by hurriedly jumping from one series of events to another, unevenly coordinated by director John Gilling. Among the cast, Newley stands out as the wisecracking corporal nursing lustful feelings toward Aubrey, which unfortunately for his libido aren't reciprocated.

Peplum influences: Mature, captured, suspended in a wooden cage, a favorite peplum imprisonment device; Aubrey rescued from being burned at the stake; a village massacre; Mature nabbed, encircled by rifles; Mature's ultimatum to Wooland when Aubrey is captured: "Her life for yours"; and a turbaned bandit chief carrying out raids on caravans.

3
Before Hercules: Italian Pepla 1950-1956

Peplum produced from 1950 to 1956 was in its embryonic stages and presents a slightly more serious, and more refined, take on what was to come, the accent focusing on characterization rather than full-blooded thrills and spills, although these are still there to be had. This is understandable—plots that would become over-familiarized to the point of tedium were excitingly different, some productions still keeping to the black-and-white format and standard screen size, resulting in a darker, thoughtful approach—almost peplum *noir*: From 1957 onwards, color and every permutation possible of the widescreen process would become the norm to rake in the punters and the money; spectacle would take pride of place over human drama, productions dominated by a muscular, handsome heroic figurehead. Costumers, swashbucklers, pirates, mass destruction, temptresses, barbarian warlords, Ancient Roman antics, Ulysses' adventures and a potted history of Jesus Christ can be found among early pepla, a sprinkling of familiar American actors/actresses involved, but in the main, there is a shortfall in the flamboyant, over-the-top brouhaha and brash, colorful activities that were the main staple of pepla circa 1957-1967, especially those falling into the *fusto* category; a plain sandwich as opposed to one filled to excess with large quantities of ham. However, they still make very interesting and compulsory viewing in what was very much a period of transition within the genre.

Georges Marchal and Marcel Herrand as they appeared in *Sins of Pompeii* (aka *The Last Days of Pompeii*)

1950

The Last Days of Pompeii [*Gli ultimi giorni di Pompei*] aka *Sins of Pompeii*

Universalia Film/Franco London Films (Italy/France); B&W; 110 (95) mins; Producer: Salvo D'Angelo; Directors: Marcel L'Herbier, Paolo Moffa ††††

The fourth full-length adaptation of Edward George Bulwer-Lytton's 1834 novel, set in 79 AD, marked one of the final films from veteran French director Marcel L'Herbier, whose output dated back to the silent era (*Rose-France*, 1919). Rarely thought about these days and overshadowed by Steve Reeves' colorful blockbuster of 1959, L'Herbier's early historical peplum disaster movie pivots around a convoluted romantic drama as its narrative, building on various intrigues until the 83rd minute when Vesuvius erupts and Pompeii is destroyed. For its curtain opener, Roman Vlad's noisy, operatic title music gives way to a montage of views showing Pompeii's stark ruins (you can almost hear and see the ghosts of those thousands of souls who perished in the inferno so long ago); we then have Georges Marchal (Lysias) slumped dazedly in a chair in chains at a tribunal. In flashback, events unfold leading up to his predicament. Handsome Marchal, a Greek, arrives in Pompeii on a chariot, with slave girl Adriana Benetti (Nidia) latching on to him when she faints in the street and he revives her. In the Egyptian Temple of Isis, High Priest Marcel Herrand (Arbax) is initiating his latest pupil, Roman noblewoman Micheline Presle (Hélene), into the older, more corrupt rites of his religion. Marchal speaks out to the crowds, many of who are Christians, warning of the dangers in idolizing a false god, an Earth tremor forecasting the doom to come. Marchal falls in love with Presle, also catching the eye of older, richer Laura Alex (Giulia), so now he has three tantalizing women vying for his attention. L'Herbier's camera glides from one ornate set to the other during the opening 30 minutes or so, Roger Hubert's superb cinematography highlighting every pillar, stone and statue into sharp contours, while Vlad's violin leitmotifs during the romantic interludes add to the air of Ancient Pompeian decadence in which the Roman nobles indulged themselves within Emperor Jacques Catelain's court. Pedestrian it may be to begin with, but this is atmospheric filmmaking of the first order.

Alex demands a love potion from Herrand to snare Marchal; jealous Benetti overhears their conversation, switches liquids and slips the substitute into the Greek's wine, with calamitous consequences. The potion, meant to drive a person insane, throws Marchal into a mad rage after one sip; charging off in his chariot, he's wrongly accused of murdering Benetti when the sinister priest stabs her to death after threatening to expose his foul deeds. Presle's brother witnesses the killing but at Marchal's trial fails to convince the judges of Herrand's guilt. In the arena (Verona's impressive Roman amphitheater, Italy's third largest, built in 30 AD to hold 20,000, was used,

Vittorio Gassman leads his troops in *The Lion of Amalfi*

as it is today for operatic concerts) Marchal confronts a hungry lion armed only with a dagger, slowly regaining his senses; the ground shakes, the sky darkens, the crowds stare in horror as Vesuvius erupts, the nervous beast backs off and the special effects team earn their pay by concocting a 10-minute cataclysm of astounding intensity—the Italians certainly knew how to pull off a sequence of mass destruction, and this is one of their greatest. Temples, walls and columns topple, roofs collapse, Herrand is crushed under the falling statue of Isis, cinders and sparks rain down on the terrified citizens, bolts of lightning hit the ground, buildings and people burst into flames and black, acrid smoke fills the thoroughfares (a telling shot of a hand scrabbling for jewelry in the rubble is inserted, flesh melting from bone as molten lava approaches). Marchal and Presle manage to escape to safety by boat and thus begin a new life together.

The main players in L'Herbier's carefully wrought Roman yarn tend to be dwarfed by their majestic surroundings (the huge sets from 1949's *Fabiola* were utilized) but still hold the attention right up to that pulverizing sequence of total devastation, thanks to solid, believable acting and pure film craftsmanship. Pristine prints can be obtained from France (no subtitles), a must-have addition for any fan inquisitive enough to want to learn about the genre's black-and-white fledgling period, several years before color and widescreen took precedence over personalities and plot.

The Lion of Amalfi [*Il leone di Amalfi*]

Laura Film/Oro Film (Italy); B&W; 89 mins; Producer: Mario Francisci; Director: Pietro Francisci

In 11th-century Italy, Norman adventurer Roberto Guiscard ousts the Lombards from Amalfi, murders the province's chief and imprisons his son, Mauro. Mauro is eventually freed by patriots and taken to Salerno where he becomes leader of a revolution to oppose Guiscard's equally brutal son, Ruggero, who has taken over the reins of power. He falls in love with Eleonora, the daughter of a chieftain and returns to Amalfi bent on revenge

A Spanish poster for *Son of D'Artagnan*

for his father's death. On the trip, Diana, daughter of a Greek nobleman, becomes infatuated with him, arousing the jealousy of Eleonora who sides with Ruggero and sets a trap for Mauro and his compatriots. Following a fierce skirmish, Ruggero and his men are overwhelmed and the despot is imprisoned; Amalfi is restored to peace and Mauro weds Diana.

Starring Vittorio Gassman and Elvi Lissiak as lovers Mauro and Diana, Carlo Ninchi as Roberto Guiscard, Sergio Fantoni his son Ruggero and Milly Vitale as scheming Eleonora, *The Lion of Amalfi*, Pietro Francisci's debut into the world of peplum, is commercially unavailable at the time of writing, on disc or tape.

Son of D'Artagnan [*Il figlio di d'Artagnan*]

Augustus Film (Italy); B&W; 86 mins; Producers: Raffaele Colamonici, Umberto Montesi; Director: Riccardo Freda

D'Artagnan's work-shy, pacifist son, Raoul, doesn't care much for following in his father's illustrious footsteps, content to be a humble novice in a monastery. But when an ambassador of the king seeks refuge in the monastery and is murdered by a mysterious knight, along with the head prior, he takes up the cape and sword (after a few fencing lessons), joining forces with his father to hunt down the gang of murderers who are causing the monarchy so much grief.

Played out on semi-comical lines, Riccardo Freda's rare swashbuckler, starring Carlo Ninchi as D'Artagnan senior, Piero Palermini as D'Artagnan junior, Peter Trent as the dastardly Duke of Malvoisin and Franca Marzi and Gianna Maria Canale

as the love interests, appears (as of 2015) to be lost in the mists of time.

The Thief of Venice [*Il ladro di Venezia*]
  Sparta Film (Italy); B&W/Sepia; 109 (90) mins; Producers: Robert Haggiag, Dario Sabatello; Director: John Brahm ✝✝✝

In 17th-century Italy, the invading Turkish army is closing in on Venice where Scarpa the Inquisitor, played with controlled menace by Massimo Serato, is busy climbing the ladder to political power, eliminating everyone who stands in his way, including the infirmed, elderly Doge (Duke). Noblewoman Francesca (Faye Marlowe) is being coerced into a marriage of convenience with the cruel brute, while in the streets and on the canals, the citizens are up in arms over Serato's repressive regime. Paul Hubschmid (billed as Paul Christian), Admiral Disani's second-in-command, arrives on a war-damaged galley with a contingent of slaves, realizing that Serato is not only going to withhold supplies to the navy but is intent on discrediting the admiral who happens to be Marlowe's father. Hubschmid (Alfiere) teams up, and falls in lust, with frisky tavern owner Tina (Maria Montez); she and her followers, including a number of freed galley slaves, are opposing Serato's aim to become the next Doge, knowing what it would spell for the city's poorer classes. Hubschmid then dons a mask and, in a number of escapades, robs the rich to obtain the necessary funds to arm the people against a possible Turkish attack. When Serato captures Montez, she is whipped,

An Italian poster for *The Black Captain*

strung up and suspended in a pit, but Hubschmid abducts Marlowe for a hostage exchange and promptly falls in love with her. The swap is made. On the day of Marlowe's extravagant marriage to Serato, Hubschmid's rebels storm the palace square and, in a raging battle, overthrow the guards; Serato is killed in a duel with Hubschmid, falling dead from the prow of a ship, the seafarer uniting with Marlowe, distraught Montez watching with the crowds as her boyfriend goes off with another woman.

The Thief of Venice is generally considered by fans to be the one film that showcases Maria "The Caribbean Cyclone" Montez at her fiery best: She flaunts, pouts, teases, giggles, kisses and tosses her mane of raven hair through those evocative Venetian backstreets, canals and alleyways (beautifully shot in shadowy sepia tones by Anchise Brizzi) with earthy feminine vitality. How Hubschmid's character can prefer winsome Marlowe to that spitfire is beyond belief! Tragically, Montez died a year after completing the picture, suffering a heart attack and drowning in her bath at age 39. In fact, she was four years Massimo

Anna Marie Ferrero (left) confronts Nelly Corradi in *The Count of Saint Elmo.*

Serato's senior who, at 34, was made to appear 10 years older, looking like a villain out of a 1920s horror film. Serato was a peplum regular, appearing in over 30 productions from 1947 (*The Rebel Prince*) through 1965 and taking on a wide range of roles, from lover to transgressor, a very much underrated actor within the realm of Italian cinema. Fast-moving but muddled, German director Brahm's moody costume romance is far more about Venice and Montez's charms than plot, an interesting, forgotten rarity from the dawn of pepla's early 1950s beginnings.

1951

The Black Captain [*Il capitano nero*]

Cooperative Tecnici Cinematografici (Italy); B&W; 92 mins; Producers: Federico D'Avack, Michelangelo Frieri; Directors: Giorgio Ansoldi, Alberto Pozzetti

In 16th-century Renaissance Italy, two noble families are up to their swords in a religious war, the Adinolfis and the Garlandis. In a violent coup, Count Marco Adinolfi's sister, Lucrezia, is raped by Giuliano Garlandi and seeks refuge in a convent. Two of Marco's brothers are also killed in the confrontation. Marco takes up arms in revenge for this evil act, eventually defeating Giuliano and treacherous Duke Fabrizzio Di Corvara, and marries damsel in distress Barbara Vivaldi, who was promised against her wishes to Di Corvara.

Starring American Stephen (Steve) Barclay as Marco, Paul Muller as Giuliano, Marina Berti as Barbara and Mario Ferrari as Di Corvara, this early swashbuckler, whose content at the time upset the Catholic Film Center, is unobtainable (as of 2015) on tape or disc.

The Count of Saint Elmo [*Il conte di Sant'Elmo*] aka *The Rebel of Naples*

Itala Film (Italy); B&W; 86 mins; Producer: Leopoldo Imperiali; Director: Guido Brignone ✝✝✝

In 1860 bandits hold up a coach carrying concert singer Bianca, on its way to Naples. Their masked leader forms an attachment to the woman and together they spend a night of passion

A cast member scooters to work wearing a Roman uniform on the Cinecitta backlot during the making of *Messalina.*

after she has been abducted and performed a song for the robbers. The masked rider is in fact the Count of Saint Elmo, forced into a life of banditry after his jealous rivals wrongly accused him of treason. The aristocrat, a revolutionary, breaks into the castle of Baron Cassano (also the police minister) to retrieve damaging evidence that could lead to the identity of his fellow patriots and falls in love with Laura, the baron's daughter; she's engaged, unwillingly, to Alberico Villalba, a treacherous duke who desires the baron's seat of power as well as his daughter. Laura helps the count evade the police, and later, she herself is the subject of a falsified kidnapping in order that a young bandit is freed in exchange. Bianca grows jealous when she learns of the relationship between the two and informs the baron and the police of her suspicions, that the masked bandit and the count are one and the same person. The count is arrested and flung into a cell; Bianca, realizing the error of her ways, organizes his escape. Alberico is killed in the skirmish, leaving the count and Laura to embark on a ship for Genoa, with her father's blessing.

A plotline that was reused *ad infinitum* in peplum costume dramas over the coming years, that of a scorned woman betraying her lover who's taken with another (check the story in 1955's *The Prince in the Red Mask*, almost identical to this one), was given an old-fashioned treatment in Guido Brignone's very obscure opus, available in lamentable prints of dubious origin. In one of his earliest peplum outings, Massimo Serato is stiffly convincing as the aristocrat-turned-thief, Anna Maria Ferrero gorgeously seductive as Laura; Tino Buazelli is the bumbling, wise old baron, while Italian opera singer Nelly Corradi is both vivacious and tuneful, treating the audience to a few random ditties. Much dashing here and there in castle rooms and cellars, striking backdrops shot around Itri in the province of Latina and a nice turn in villainy from Carlo Croccolo as Alberico—all factors contributing to a pleasing, hard to obtain, costumer that is solid without being overly passionate.

Messalina [*Messalina*] aka ***The Affairs of Messalina***
Filmsonor/Suevia Film/Produzione Gallone (Italy/France/Spain); B&W; 116 (95) mins; Producers: Carmine Gallone, Cesareo Gonzalez (uncredited); Director: Carmine Gallone †††††

At the time of its release the most expensive Italian film ever made, *Messalina* starred legendary Mexican actress-cum-diva Maria Félix, whose off-screen romantic liaisons were just as tempestuous as the woman she portrayed in Carmine Gallone's languid, compelling excursion into Rome circa 48 AD, Valeria Messalina, the artful wife of Emperor Claudio (Memo Benassi), the man she married at age 16. The first 57 minutes dealt with her haughty, imperious manner, all and sundry pampering to her every whim, and her legendary manipulation of men: main lover Georges Marchal (Caio Silvio); rebel leader Jean Chevrier (Valerio); a young boy smitten with her (he's discarded and murdered); and court advisor Jean Tissier (Mnester). Rarely moving out of the emperor's opulent palace and its luxurious gardens, Gallone's camera drifts elegantly from one columnated set to another, people wandering, milling, talking and indulging in decadent feasts, backed by Renzo Rossellini's haunting, melodic score (his title theme is a thriller), an hour dripping in Ancient Rome ambience. Disguised as a prostitute, Félix prowls the streets with her treasonous agenda, looking for signs of insurrection, listening to gossip, casting her eyes on dancer Delia Scala (Cinzia) and ruthlessly stabbing a rival streetwalker to death. Benassi, a dotard, puts up with his wife's loose morals, content to dream about dredging the port of Brindisi to enable the free flow of shipping. Scala is abducted and forced to dance in front of Félix and her retinue (a near-pornographic number featuring two young blond male fauns), flushing out boyfriend Erno Crisa (Timo), who's in league with Chevrier and his conspirators; Benassi, in the meantime, terrified of predictions that spell doom for Rome if he stays with the temptress, scuttles off to his secret quarters with a group of servile cronies, planning to rid himself of his sexually insatiable wife.

On the hour, we're treated to a 20-minute stadium event and you can see where all that money went—the amphitheater is colossal, packed with thousands of extras, Gallone shooting among the crowds on the packed terraces to impart an almost documentary air. First off is a race, riders standing astride two horses; then Crisa and slaves enter in chains; he's tied to a post and lions let loose. Scala rushes to his aid and, using her articles of faith, repels the beasts, setting Crisa free. One hundred gladiators troop in, pair off and clash violently, one of the goriest arena set pieces on celluloid: blades pierce flesh, tridents are rammed into faces, swords hack at limbs, the dead dragged off, leaving bloody furrows in the sand, all to the roars of the approving masses. Crisa is left to deal with champion Carlo Ninchi (Tauro) and is spared death by Marchal, who is beginning to realize what kind of a female monster he is sleeping with. But "you reap what you sow," and in the end, everyone turns against the evil empress. Devoted Tissier deserts her, as does Benassi and the once-loyal palace guards; Marchal is killed in an uprising and, to end her misery, Félix falls on Ninchi's sword, her body carried off in a wagon. Félix glows in the part of a darkly passionate historical figure few would find easy to like, a go-getter indulging in sexual freedom centuries before it became common practice. If in color, *Messalina* would have been hailed as a classic; as it stands, it still remains a classic of its type, Anchise Brizzi's masterful black-and-white photography a joy in itself, showing just what can be achieved in the non-color medium of cinema.

Husband and wife team Maria Montez and Jean-Pierre Aumont in *The Pirate's Revenge*

The Pirate's Revenge [*La vendetta del corsaro*] aka ***Duel Before the Mast***; ***Revenge of the Pirates***
Athena Cinematografica (Italy); B&W/Sepia; 95 mins; Producers: Luigi Carpentieri, Ermanno Donati; Director: Primo Zeglio †††

More romantic costumer than out-and-out swashbuckler, Primo Zeglio's long-forgotten pirate adventure, set in 1675, had Jean-Pierre Aumont (Captain Enrico Roccabruna) pitting his wits against the Governor of Maracaibo, Enrico Glori, who owns property stolen from the pirate chief; Aumont wants it back, together with Maracaibo's gold and the hand of Maria Montez (Consuelo), starring in her final film. Aumont and Montez (they were married at the time) meet during the rousing opener, when the pirate vessel attacks and ransacks a Spanish galleon, the pair forming an instant attraction. From then on, the scenario consists of a variety of romantic, rather than swashbuckling, vignettes as Aumont meets Montez in secret, learning that her maid, Milly Vitale (Luana), is his foster daughter, the girl up to her pretty neck in love trysts with Aumont's right-hand man, Roberto Risso (Miguel), even though she's promised to Glori. To darken the mood, Risso is captured midway through and strung up on a rack in a harrowing torture scene, released when Vitale pleads with token genre bad guy Paul Muller, Glori's devious deputy, to untie him; the snake is trying to pin Aumont and Risso down so that he can rise to power like his boss. In the closing stages pistol-packing Montez interrupts the forced wedding between Vitale and Glori; prisoners blow up the castle keep, and Muller with it, as Aumont's corsairs storm the governor's buildings. A mass fight ensues within Maracaibo's fortress walls, Glori dueling with the pirate leader and falling to his death from the battlements. Risso and Vitale, still wearing her bridal dress, tie the knot, leaving Aumont and Montez to smooch in each other's arms.

Carlo Rustichelli's second peplum score (*The Lion of Amalfi* was his first) is a belter as befits one of Italy's greatest of all film composers, while Gabor Pogany's photography shines, even in scratchy sepia prints. Montez starred in exactly the kind of part (that of a high-class lady) she protested about during the

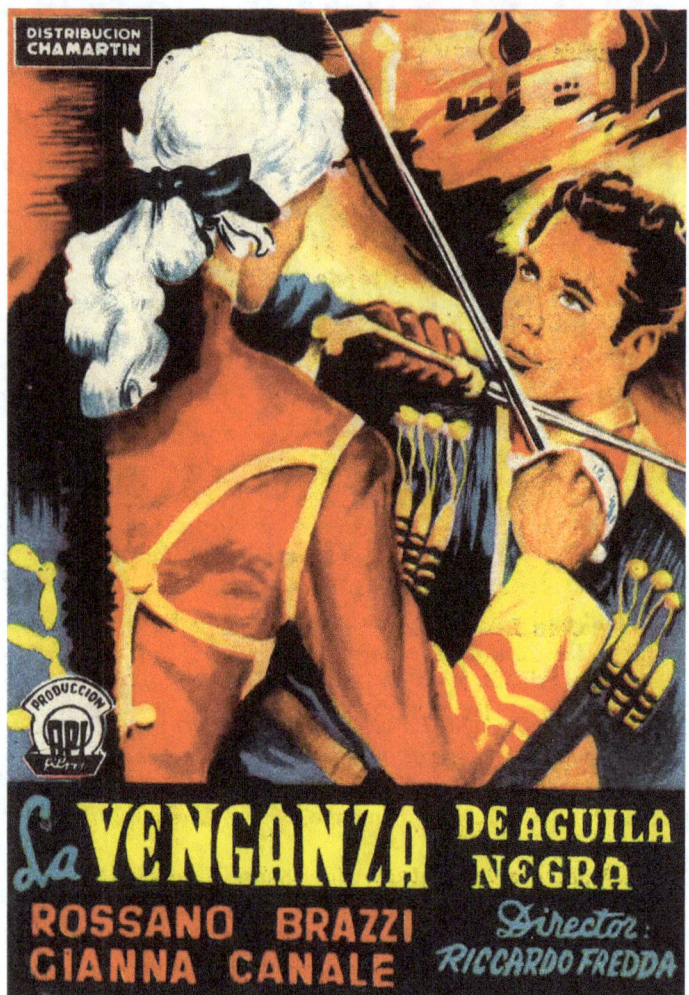

A Spanish poster for *Revenge of the Black Eagle*

years she spent with Universal-International; the firebrand was at her best playing exotic queens, wild Gypsies, sexy dancers and dusky natives rather than noblewomen shackled in flamboyant dresses. It reined in her fieriness, as it did here. Nevertheless, this was the last time the "Queen of Hokum" appeared on the silver screen, dying in her bath only a short time after shooting reached completion. (Note the extra in the 15th minute tripping over his feet and tumbling to the ground during a pirate raid, retained in the print. More unintentional cinematic *faux pas* are mentioned in other chapters.)

Revenge of the Black Eagle [*La vendetta di Aquila Nera*]

Associati Produttori Indipendenti Film (Italy); B&W; 97 mins; Producers: Carlo Caiano, Umberto Momi; Director: Riccardo Freda ††††

The character of Vladimir Dubrovskij first appeared in Freda's *The Black Eagle* (1946); Rossano Brazzi played him then and reprised the role in *Revenge of the Black Eagle*, a wonderfully exciting blend of thrills, spills, dark deeds and romance featuring, not only the finest of Freda's mastery of style, but his 24-year-old wife, the incomparable Gianna Maria Canale. Backed by a pulverizing Renzo Rossellini soundtrack and photographed in Toni Frenguelli's typically Italian stark monochrome shades, Freda's costume revenge drama is the precursor of what would become a very familiar genre plotline throughout the coming years, that of the nobleman whose family and estates have been destroyed by a power-mad arch villain. In 1951, the scenario was relatively fresh—this, combined with Freda's renowned directorial skills and solid acting from all involved, ensured that *Revenge of the Black Eagle*, rare to lay hands on these days, gripped from beginning to end, a highly satisfactory slice of swashbuckling derring-do that, in moments of high drama, drifted into dark, almost Gothic territory, as most of Freda's movies were wont to do.

At the end of the 18th century, Catherine the Great of Russia is dead, the Russian-Turkish conflict over. On the battlefield, Colonel Peter Trent (Igor) is accused of cowardice by Brazzi (the Black Eagle of the title) and imprisoned; Brazzi, who hasn't seen his wife for five years and never laid eyes on his son, heads for home, unaware that Vittorio Sanipoli (Prince Boris) has raided his castle, arranged for the murder of his wife and given his son Andre (Guido Sissia) to an innkeeper; he's also released Trent on condition he can court the colonel's sister Gianna Maria Canale (Tatiana), with a view to marriage, even though she cannot stomach the servile creep. Yes, it's a power struggle Freda hurls us into, Brazzi leading a band of guerrillas hiding out in the hills, determined to avenge the death of his wife, locate the boy, now mute due to shock after seeing his mother killed, and regain his property. After burning alive Dante Carapelli and his mob in a house (the perpetrators of the murder), he takes Canale hostage (much to the chagrin of admirer Franca Marzi) and rescues a mute five-year-old from a tavern (the cruel proprietor ties the lad to a beam and horsewhips him, a disturbing scene), not realizing the waif and stray is his son. Canale (looking radiant) falls in love with downcast Brazzi, while Sanipoli (a brilliant portrayal of downright evilness) stabs Trent in the back and blames the killing on Brazzi, to break up his relationship with Canale—she's now vowing revenge against the wronged Black Eagle! In the palace, the mute youngster is revealed to be Brazzi's offspring; Sanipoli, stooping to new depths, lures Sissia into a bear pit (a semi-horror sequence), the beast shot by Brazzi who holds the usurper at pistol-point ("A crow never wins against an eagle."). Jumped on and seized, Brazzi plus Sissia are sent to a Siberian labor camp, where, meeting with a sympathetic doctor, the Black Eagle feigns death after a severe flogging, escapes, grabs the boy and rides off to Moscow with his men, Sanipoli having just wedded Canale, the snake reneging on his agreement with her to set Brazzi and Sissia free. Unfortunately for the venomous prince, a shepherd witnessed the murder of Trent and tells all, Canale horrified at the monster she has married. Brazzi and company ride in, Canale is snatched and they charge away to the mountains, Sanipoli and a posse of Cossacks in hot pursuit. Brazzi draws a dagger on Canale, convinced she's brought him bad luck; Sissia yells in terror, his voice returning, and Brazzi puts the dagger down. In a frantic climax, Brazzi detonates a ruined building packed with dynamite, an avalanche wiping out the Cossacks; dueling to the death with Sanipoli on a precipitous ridge, the prince is run through, falling down the sheer cliff face-first into a pool. In the surroundings of a fountain-filled garden, Brazzi and Canale confess their love for each other, and peace at last returns to the Black Eagle's troubled world.

1952

At Sword's Edge [*A fil di spada*]

Panaria Film (Italy); B&W; 96 (79) mins; Producer: Francesco Alliata; Director: Carlo Ludovico Bragaglia

An Italian photobusta for *At Sword's Edge*

Tyrannical governor Don Sebastiano arranges the murder of a nobleman in order to take control of a South American province and begins a regime of oppression to subdue the downtrodden population. The nobleman had been commissioned by the King of Spain to investigate Don Sebastiano's corrupt affairs; womanizing swordsman Don Ruy takes on the task of bringing the dictator to heel, even when he's blamed for the killing. Don Ruy, of noble descent himself and friend of the murdered man, becomes a champion of the poor; arrested, the adventurer is released and joins up with a rebel group, forming a relationship with childhood friend Linda, sister of the deceased nobleman. As Don Ruy and his friends prepare to liberate the city, Linda, convinced that he killed her brother, informs the governor of their plans. A trap is set to capture Don Ruy and the insurgents; during a fierce struggle, Don Ruy kills Don Sebastiano in a swordfight. Linda, realizing that the swordsman was innocent all along, marries him in the end.

Starring Frank Latimore (Don Ruy), Milly Vitale (Linda), Pierre Cressoy (Don Sebastiano), Doris Duranti, Peter Trent, Enrico Glori, John Kitzmiller and Arturo Bragaglia (the director's brother), Carlo Ludovico Bragaglia's long-forgotten swashbuckler remains unavailable on disc and tape; a series of stills exist, which can be located on obscure online sites.

The Devil's Daughter [*La figlia del diavolo*]

Excelsa Film (Italy); B&W; 83 mins; Producer: Mario Borghi; Director: Primo Zeglio

In 1860, revolutionary leader Giuseppe Garibaldi's troops land in Marsala, Sicily and move on to Naples, the controlling Bourbons in disarray. Baron Tucci arrives to take part in the fight, a discredited Bourbon nobleman promised exoneration if he works as a spy against the liberation of Southern Italy. In Count Terzi's castle, Tucci persuades the count's second wife Donna Giulia, whom he once had an affair with, to murder her elderly husband to gain his inheritance for the pair to live on, which she does by means of an enforced heart attack, refusing to give the count, a leading liberal supporter, his medicine. The count's younger daughter Graziella hears an argument taking place between the two lovers; the baron attempts to kill her but she flees into the arms of a patriot, joining the conspirators in the Devil's castle. Baron Tucci informs the authorities of their whereabouts, culminating in the arrest of young doctor Adolfo Santagata, Graziella's fiancé and a key figure in the conspiracy. Sentenced to the gallows, he's saved from the noose when Garibaldi's cavalry storms the castle courtyard. Tucci the spy is dispatched, and Santagata is reunited with Graziella.

Starring Massimo Serato as the doctor, Marina Vlady as Graziella, Carlo Tamberlani, Paola Barbara, Roberto Risso and Franco Pastorino, *The Devil's Daughter*, based on true-life events known as The Expedition of the Thousand, remains commercially unavailable in 2015—only posters and photobustas exist on auction sites.

The Executioner of Lille [*Il boia di Lilla*] aka *Milady and the Musketeers*; *Vengeance of the Musketeers*

Atlantis Film/Venturini Film (Italy/France); B&W; 88 mins; Producers: Nino Martegani, Giorgio Venturini; Director: Vittorio Cottafavi ✝✝✝

A young Marina Vlady (*The Devil's Daughter*) relaxes with her record collection.

Spanish lobby card for *The Executioner of Lille*

Another take on Alexandre Dumas' *Three Musketeers* yarn (a blond, empty-headed D'Artagnan is virtually absent from the proceedings), Vittorio Cottafavi's version places the accent on French actress Yvette Lebon's highly dangerous Milady Anne de Winter and her rapid rise to power, from scrubbing floors in a convent to the confidante/spy of starchy Massimo Serato (Rochefort). She is pursued throughout the film by the dour-faced executioner of the title, Jean-Roger Caussimon, who has cause to hate her for a variety of reasons, in that manipulative Lebon wraps every man she meets around her little finger, including Caussimon's younger brother, officer Armando Francioli (he's smothering her in kisses two minutes after they meet, before hopping into her bed), and Rossano Brazzi, the Conte de la Frere, also known as Athos, one of the Musketeers.

At 42, Lebon still had the type of refined bone structure and voluptuous figure to make men lose their senses, and twice during the action, she's seen almost naked under bedsheets. The movie opens with Lebon about to plunge a dagger into Caussimon's daughter, Maria Grazia Francia—in flashback, events unfold leading up to this moment. Half-strangled and branded by the vengeful executioner, Lebon leaves a trail of destruction in her wake, Francioli hanging himself in a prison cell after she abandons him for Serato and a life of political entanglements, while the swashbuckling Musketeers only feature spasmodically in the occasional swordfight (why are English men-at-arms shown wearing Scottish kilts?). On orders from King Louis XIII, the foxy spy is put to the sword by Caussimon beside a river, a lonely death for such a beautiful woman, as Brazzi, who loved her, realizes with a tear in his eye watching the execution from the riverbank. Renzo Rossellini's score is unusually low-key for this composer, matching the melancholy mood and Cottafavi's careful pacing. It doesn't rank among the best of the Musketeer tales to hit the screen, but Lebon carries the day, turning in a fine performance, running the gamut of emotions: love, anger, tease and deviousness. Prints in Italian (no subtitles) are very difficult to lay hands on, as is Cottafavi's second of nine peplum outings, *Il cavaliere di Maison Rouge* (US: *The Glorious Avenger*), based on Dumas' 1845 novel. Released by Venturini Film in 1953 and also starring Lebon and Francioli in the lead roles (Cottafavi's two movies were shot back-to-back), this long-forgotten swashbuckler appears to exist in poster/photobusta form only, prints having seemingly disappeared off the cinematic map.

The Queen of Sheba [*La Regina di Saba*]

Oro Film (Italy); B&W; 110 (92) mins; Producer: Mario Francisci; Director: Pietro Francisci ✞✞✞✞✞

Pietro Francisci's second peplum (his first was 1950's *The Lion of Amalfi*) was designed to promote the talents, and more importantly the exotic looks, of 17-year-old Italian starlet Leonora Ruffo, playing Balkis, Queen of Sheba. Shooting in fetishistic close-up, the camera dwelling on her flawless complexion highlighted by huge, hypnotic almond eyes, we were left in no doubt that whatever the girl was like as an actress (she was pretty good, in fact), Ruffo could set all men's pulses racing with a flash of those eyes and a pout of those lips. Next to her smoldering charms, slender 18-year-old Gino Leurini (Prince Rehoboam, King Solomon's son) appeared in awe and out of his depth as her lover, a teenage hero overshadowed by a beautiful tigress in full bloom, even though he was a year older. *The Queen of Sheba* may have lacked action, apart from a blistering deciding battle fought outside the walls of Jerusalem, but the pacey narrative involved (thanks to incredible, jaw-dropping sets built on a colossal scale) expert playing, incisive direction,

A German pressbook depicts 17-year-old starlet Leonora Ruffo in all her exotic glory as Balkis, *The Queen of Sheba*.

An Italian poster for *The Three Pirates*

Nino Rota's evocative music (he won an Oscar for scoring *The Godfather Part II* in 1974), and Ruffo's sheer lust appeal.

In 1000 BC, benign King Solomon of Jerusalem (Gino Cervi), worried over rumblings from Arabia concerning Sheba's hostile intentions, sends Leurini, under an alias, to Sheba protected by a stolen safe conduct note, mercenary Umberto Silvestri (Isachar) at his side, his job to ascertain if a war between the two countries is imminent. Leurini is engaged to Marina Berti (Princess Zamira), but once he meets Ruffo at Monte Gelato's waterfalls, Berti, also highly attractive, is quickly forgotten. In Sheba, Ruffo's father dies and she's proclaimed queen, bride to the sun god Shamash, meaning no man can ever touch her. Army leader Franco Silva (Kabaal), in love with Ruffo, fumes in impotent frustration, as does Leurini, while Silvestri is busy romancing pert Dorian Gray (Ati). Holding her emotions for Leurini in check against the need for conquest, power and glory, Ruffo is furious when she learns of his true identity; Leurini, Silvestri and Gray flee Sheba via a secret grotto as Ruffo, feeling deceived, masses her troops for an assault on Jerusalem. The battle is a humdinger, arrows, rocks, boiling pitch and spears raining down on the heads of the Shebans, fire destroying their war machines. Ruffo is captured following a clash with Leurini on horseback, taken to Cervi's palace but allowed to leave the city; riding to the Valley of Silence in penance, Ruffo is trailed by Leurini and Silva, who fight to the death. An avalanche (a real one by the look of it) buries Silva; as the mountain has "spoken," the queen is free of her obligation to her "stone lover" Shamash and marries Leurini, cementing relationships between Jerusalem and Sheba.

Sheba's palace, a 100-foot high edifice, was the work of art directors Giulio Bongini and William Cameron Menzies—Menzies was the man behind the staggering futuristic effects in 1936's *Things to Come*, and Sheba's massively ornate buildings (the interiors were just as impressive) mirrored his legendary efforts in Alexander Korda's sci-fi masterpiece. Vittorio Nino Novarese's costume design was authentically fabulous, Mario Montuori's needle-sharp monochrome photography throwing everything into crisp relief. A peplum long-lost classic, *The Queen of Sheba*'s only downside is Leurini, too juvenile-looking to be taken seriously as a macho warrior prince, or the male lead for that matter—Ruffo could have easily eaten him for breakfast! If you wonder why fans rave about Italian beauty within the sphere of pepla, check out Ruffo in this movie. She may not have fulfilled her potential, starring in five other peplum movies before bowing out of the film industry in 1969, but she exuded sultry screen magnetism as Queen Balkis, her one and only crowning achievement in Italian cinema.

The Three Pirates [*I tre corsari*]

Lux Film (Italy); B&W; 88 mins; Producers: Dino De Laurentiis, Carlo Ponti; Director: Mario Soldati

In the 17th century, Flemish Captain Van Gould, in the services of the Spanish, aids the Spaniards in taking control of Count Ventimiglia's estates and his imposing castle; the count is murdered by the tyrant, his three sons imprisoned and then deported to the West Indies, along with Isabella, daughter of the Spanish viceroy. On the sea voyage, their galleon is attacked by buccaneers; the brothers enlist with the corsairs to take out their revenge on the Spanish and Van Gould, becoming Enrico the Black Pirate, Rolando the Red Pirate and Carlo the Green Pirate. After many adventures in and around Tortuga and Maracaibo, the Black Pirate kills his hated enemy, and Isabella is rescued from the corsairs and gets wed to Enrico, who decides to give up piracy for a normal life.

Starring Ettore Manni as Enrico (the actor's first peplum), Renato Salvatori as Rolando, Cesare Danova as Carlo, Barbara Florian as Isabella and Marc Lawrence playing Van Gould, this early peplum piratical jaunt cannot be traced, as I write, either on disc or tape.

1953

Captain Phantom [*Capitan Fantasma*]

Athena Cinematografica (Italy); Ferraniacolor; 86 mins; Producers: Luigi Carpentieri, Ermanno Donati; Director: Primo Zeglio

In the early 19th century, Spain rejoices in victories over Napoleon Bonaparte's French forces. Aristocrat Miguel, the Duke of Canabil, is told at a celebratory banquet that his father, an admiral commanding the Spanish fleet, has turned traitor by handing his ships over to the enemy. Held in contempt by his own regiment, the duke swears to uncover the mystery; the man behind the misdeed is Don Inigo da Costa, a turncoat and captain of the *Asuncion*, out to take over as governor of Cadiz and bag Consuelo, the governor's daughter, into the bargain. Da Costa is eventually revealed to be the real traitor and eliminated in a duel with Miguel, who wins the hand of Consuelo.

An Italian poster for *Captain Phantom*

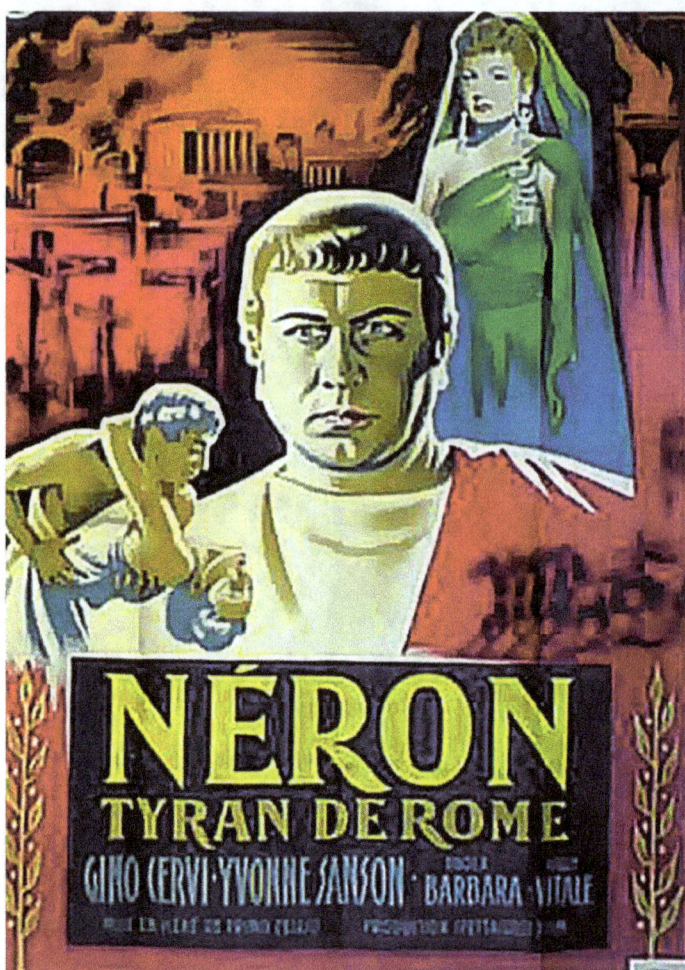

A French poster for *Nero and Messalina*

Starring Frank Latimore as Miguel (his second peplum), British heartthrob Maxwell Reed in the role of the villainous da Costa and Anna-Maria Sandri as the female lead, *Captain Phantom* is impossible to obtain today; an online eight-minute color clip existed in 2015 but has since been withdrawn.

Nero and Messalina [*Nerone e Messalina*] aka *Nero and the Burning of Rome*; *Nero, Tyrant of Rome*

Spettacolo Film (Italy); B&W; 106 mins; Producer: Gualtero Bagnoli; Director: Primo Zeglio

Due to the devious ruses of his mother Agrippina, licentious, unstable Nero sits on the imperial throne, disposing of all those who cross his path, including his first two wives and, eventually his own mother. A Christian slave girl, Atte, who tries unsuccessfully to persuade Nero to accept the Christian doctrine, tends to the emperor's third wife, Stabilia Messalina. Accidentally knocking over a lamp during an argument, the emperor inadvertently sets fire to Rome, blaming the destruction of the city on the Christians. Atte is executed for treason, leading to an uprising in which the mad ruler, hiding from the mob, is slain by a slave.

Starring Gino Cervi as Nero, Yvonne Sanson playing Messalina, Milly Vitale as Atte and Paola Barbara as Agrippina, *Nero and Messalina*, based on the 1949 novel by Harry Bluhmen, remains commercially unavailable on disc and tape at the time of this writing.

Phryne, Courtesan of the East [*Frine, cortigiana d'Oriente*]

P.A.M. (Italy); B&W; 101 mins; Producer: Alberto Manca; Director: Mario Bonnard ††††

Mario Bonnard's vibrant telling of the life of famous legendary Athenian courtesan Phryne starred statuesque Elena Kleus in the title role, the events occurring around 315 BC. Falsely accused of stealing a sacred necklace from the Temple of Demeter for opposing Mino Doro's (as Osco) tyrannical rule, Kleus' parents are put to death on orders from the slimy regent, Kleus sent packing to Athens and sold into slavery. Lamaco (Giulio Donnini), a soldier, buys her in an attempt to save her from a life of prostitution; ironically, he was the person who planted the stolen jewels in her parents' house, leading to their death. However, Kleus' alluring physical assets get noticed and she becomes a courtesan of considerable note, taking much wealth from her rich Athenian clients and learning many valuable political secrets, to be used when Alexander the Great's forces are converging on the city of Thebes. Kleus meets Iperide, a young ex-alcoholic orator (Pierre Cressoy), and they fall in love. Alexander plunders and destroys Thebes, Kleus planning to rebuild the city with her acquired affluence and assist the destitute population, but the council rejects her offer, accusing her of promoting her own scandalous talents, and she's arrested during a pagan dance in honor of the goddess Demeter. Cressoy acts as her defense, up against not only the council but pimp Donnini who is finally exposed by mute slave John Kitzmiller (Nabus) as the man who secreted the incriminating necklace in her home. Kleus

Spanish lobby card for *Phryne, Courtesan of the East*

is eventually exonerated of any crime, with Donnini condemned to death and the rebuilding of Thebes gets underway.

Giulio Bonnard (the director's brother) wrote a full orchestral score to match Mario Albertelli's deep photography in a racy (for 1953) and rare peplum featuring crowded, opulent sets, lengthy orgasmic masked dance routines and flashes of nudity, the accent on dialogue-driven political intrigue and connivance over spectacle. Thebes was depicted as an art deco city (unusually, a model was used) and there were plenty of sacrifices on offer to appease the bloodthirsty. In her first of only four film appearances, Kleus shone as Phryne, emoting wanton desire beautifully while flaunting her plunging neckline to perfection. Scratchy tapes taken from an old Italian television broadcast are difficult to locate, a shame as Bonnard's mini-epic presents peplum in its transitional, black-and-white stage before color and widescreen took priority.

Prisoner in the Tower of Fire [*La prigioniera della torre di fuoco*]

L.I.A. Film (Italy); B&W; 87 mins; Producers: Nello Di Paolo, Fernando Moscato; Director: Giorgio Walter Chili

We open on the Italian province of Emilia in the 15th century. A war breaks out between two feudal families, the Maltivoglios and the Peplis, while the Turks are invading the country. During a battle, Cesco Maltivoglio saves the life of Marco Pepli, the two rivals swearing eternal friendship despite family hostilities. Back home, Cesco discovers that his sister, Bianca, has been kidnapped and imprisoned in a castle tower following a row between the families, resulting in the death of one of his siblings. Also locked in the tower is Germana della Valle. Both Cesco and Marco fall in love with the girl, leading to a further parting of the ways,

Marco enlisting the aid of Cesare Borgia to get rid of the Maltivoglio clan. Germana returns Marco's affections—when Cesco finds out, he feels betrayed and incarcerates his friend in a dungeon. Cesare Borgia's troops besiege the castle, Cesco and Marco again joining forces to repel the invaders who enter the fortress via a hidden tunnel. Cesco is mortally wounded in the assault and dies, but not before attending the wedding of Marco and Germana, the two families having joined together in peace.

Starring Ugo Sasso as Cesco, Carlo Giustini as Marco, Milly Vitale as Germana, Rossano Brazzi as Cesare Borgia and Elisa Cegani as Bianca, the ultra-rare *Prisoner in the Tower of Fire* is unobtainable on disc or tape; posters and photobusta stills are displayed on online auction sites, going for exorbitant amounts of money.

The Sack of Rome [*Il sacco di Roma*] aka The Barbarians; The Pagans; Blood Over Rome

Laura Film/Oro Film (Italy); B&W; 87 (83) mins; Producer: Mario Francisci; Director: Ferruccio Cerio ✝✝✝

In 1527, under the orders of King Charles V, 20,000 Spanish and French troops converge on Rome to conquer a city which itself is in turmoil: A pair of prosperous families, the Orsinis and the Colonnas, are at loggerheads over territorial rights, heedless to the threat of invasion on their doorstep. Massimo Colonna and Angela Orsini plan to wed but Tancredi Serra, a conniving official who wishes to marry the girl, interrupts their nuptials. During a duel of honor, Serra's confederate murders Angela's father and Massimo receives the blame. He flees Rome as the enemy's demand of 400,000 gold ducats to cease hostilities is rejected; feeling insulted, they launch an advanced guard strike. In a mighty skirmish, Rome's walls are breached and atrocities

Italian photobusta for *Prisoner in the Tower of Fire*

An Italian poster for *The Sack of Rome*

committed, with many titled patricians cooperating with the Spanish. Angela is told that Massimo wasn't her father's killer; Massimo returns to Rome with a force of devoted plebeians, runs Serra through with his rapier and helps defeat the Spanish in a pitched battle on Castle Sant'Angelo's ramparts. Rome emerges triumphant, the Spanish withdraw in disarray and Massimo weds Angela, bringing peace and harmony to the two feuding families.

Two prominent fortresses feature in Ferruccio Cerio's sluggish costumer, both having connections with the true-life events depicted: Castello Orsini-Odescalchi near Lazio, constructed in the 10th century and seen at the beginning; and Castel Sant'Angelo near Rome, built for Emperor Hadrian circa 135 AD, and the actual site of the final engagement between Roman defenders and the Spanish army. A lengthy opening overhead crane shot of armed infantry slogging through mud promises much, but you have to persevere for 40 minutes before any action occurs; we're plunged into *Romeo and Juliet* domain, Cerio throwing the spotlight on the troubled Massimo (Pierre Cressoy)/Angela (Hélene Rémy) liaison and in-fighting between the two high-ranking households. Also in the mix is a secondary (and somewhat superfluous) plotline focusing on artist Luigi Tosi's stormy relationship with dark-haired model Annamaria Bugliari. Rascally Franco Fabrizi is an old pal of Cressoy's, a mercenary who sides with the Spanish for plunder but changes his allegiances in the final reel, while peplum regular bad guy Vittorio Sanipoli plays Serra, a mountebank out for his own ends, regardless of who gets hurt. Vividly photographed by Tonino Delli Colli (the initial sequences resemble a Hollywood 1940s romantic drama), *The Sack of Rome* was released in Britain in 1956 carrying an "A" certificate after cuts demanded by the censor, notably in the scenes showing victorious enemy soldiers on a rampage in the streets of Rome, raping, killing, torturing, looting and torching buildings with over-the-top relish. The two main battles are grittily staged (bodies falling onto the camera lens), almost akin to World War II footage, there are a couple of hectic swordfights and Cressoy makes a dashing, heroic leading man; overall, though, the picture meanders and appears a lot longer than its 80-odd minutes, basically a love story tagged onto a backdrop of conflict that doesn't fully maintain interest due to the director's slack handling of the narrative.

The Ship of Condemned Women [*La nave delle donne maledette*] aka ***Ship of Lost Women***
Minerva/Excelsa Film (Italy); Gevacolor/B&W; 101 (93) mins; Producer: Alfredo De Laurentiis; Director: Raffaello Matarazzo ††††

For the first 38 minutes, *The Ship of Condemned Women* is a bore. In the late 1700s, haughty married noblewoman Tania Weber (Isabella) has her baby (the result of an affair) murdered; a poor relation, May Britt (Consuelo), is asked to shoulder the blame to prevent a family scandal. Defended in court by young lawyer Ettore Manni (Da Silva), she's found guilty and sentenced to 10 years penal servitude in a labor camp. Talkative and flat,

Gianna Maria Canale reclines in splendor as Vittorio Sanipoli and Ludmilla Tchérina look on in Spartacus.

the pace flagging, one might be tempted to call it a day, but that would mean missing the movie's outlandish pièce de résistance in the last 20 minutes. On board a penal ship bound for the colonies, Britt is flung below deck with a pack of female convicts living in unsanitary conditions, all under the thumb of heartless captain Luigi Tosi (Fernandez). Weber sets sail with them, her elderly husband the ship's owner, and Manni stows away to help Britt who he knows is innocent of the crime, besides which he's already in love with the unfortunate girl. Britt, sick with worry, is confined to the infirmary, then dragged on deck to be flogged, Manni already having been discovered and brutally whiplashed, thus setting the scene for that over-the-top finale.

At this point, director Matarazzo suddenly pulls out all the stops, the scenario erupting into a hurricane of unintentionally hilarious melodramatics: Outraged at Britt's callous treatment, the women, led by Kerima (unaccountably, the sexy Algerian belly dancer received star billing) decide to mutiny; grabbing the cell keeper's keys, they unlock the gates and storm above deck. Their solution to win the sailors over is to stage an orgy, throwing themselves at the sex-starved crew who, amazed at their good fortune, drop their weapons posthaste, making a beeline for those heaving breasts and flashing thighs. Women and men (those few still on Tosi's side) fire at each other; in a confrontation below decks, amid much lewd behavior, Tosi is stabbed to death by Weber who, in turn, is flogged so viciously that she expires. A fierce storm brews—Manni and Britt escape in a boat while the ship and its cargo of lovelies goes up in flames, everyone praying to God for forgiveness. Back on dry land and in court, Britt is exonerated, free to play house with Manni.

This was the second of good-looking Manni's 20 excursions into pepla (the first, Mario Soldati's *The Three Pirates* [1952], is impossible to come by) and is only available (in 2015) as a black-and-white print with Greek subtitles (the picture was originally issued in some parts of Europe in monochrome). Nino Rota's seafaring score is pleasant in a film of two halves, one mundane, one wildly excitable, similar in content to 1961's *The Mutiny*. At least it's different from the norm, an early exploitation offering that deserves a color release to show off all that brazen female flesh to its full advantage. Note: On July 27, 1979, Manni, aged only 52, died from a gunshot wound; it is now believed he committed suicide over the loss of his girlfriend, Austrian actress Krista Nell, who died from leukemia in 1975 at the age of 28.

Spartacus** [Spartaco]* aka ***Sins of Rome, Story of Spartacus
API/Es Establissments Sinag (Italy/France); B&W; 103 (75) mins; Producer: Carlo Caiano; Director: Riccardo Freda ✞✞✞✞✞

Seven years before Stanley Kubrick/Universal's $12,000,000 *Spartacus*, Riccardo Freda's more intense version concerning a massive slave revolt circa 74 BC hit Italian screens, a full 28 minutes longer than drastically edited versions currently available on rare DVDs (producer Carlo Caiano was the father of Mario Caiano, director of seven peplum features from 1962-1965). Distributed by RKO-Radio in America, Freda's film was presented, like *Fabiola* before it, in neorealist style, not Hollywood gloss, a succession of grainy black-and-white imagery shot in a ferocious manner quite unknown in movies of this type outside of Italy, the director's pace only abating during the scorching love scenes between Massimo Girotti (Spartacus) and Gianna Maria Canale (Sabina). Canale's refined bone structure, perfect profile and sheer beauty was photographed in full frame soft-focus by Gabor Pogany to represent the kind of glamour portraits found inside the pages of movie magazines—the lady was an absolute stunner, and both Freda and Pogany took advantage of the fact. (The actress, married to Freda, came second in the Miss Italia beauty contest of 1947 and was often cited as Italy's answer to Ava Gardner.)

Canale also had the movie's best lines (screenplay: Maria Bory, Jean Ferry, Gino Visentini): "My feet are more important than all your foolish thoughts and even your existence," she haughtily sneers at slave Ludmilla Tchérina (as Amitys). "You are mine. They've put a price on your head," she tells Girotti. "They want you. But not as much as I do." She goes on: "How wonderful to feel you tremble with hate and desire." No wonder with words like these whispered in his ear, and Canale's supple body draped all over his, the Thracian slave forgets all about the revolt and falls hook, line and sinker into the web of desire spun by the temptress. "The slaves are such a nuisance," she yawns as one is whipped in her garden, interrupting another lust session; Girotti, who at last remembers what he was put on this Earth for, rides back to his rebel legions to take up duties and resume his crusade against Rome.

On trial for striking Vittorio Sanipoli (Marcus Virilius Rufus), who has just slain Tchérina's protesting elderly Thracian father ("Nobody can stop the Romans!" the thug growls), Girotti is ordered by Carlo Ninchi (Crassus) to attend gladiator training school under the severe tutorship of Umberto Silvestri (Lentulus). Cinecitta's gigantic sets (built for an international fair in 1943) dwarf a cast of thousands in the opening scenes, a breathtaking sight. In the arena stands a galley, dancers enacting a story that's broken up by a score of rampaging lions let loose, Freda's camera right in among the prowling beasts, perhaps one of the most vividly realistic "lions in the arena" sequences ever

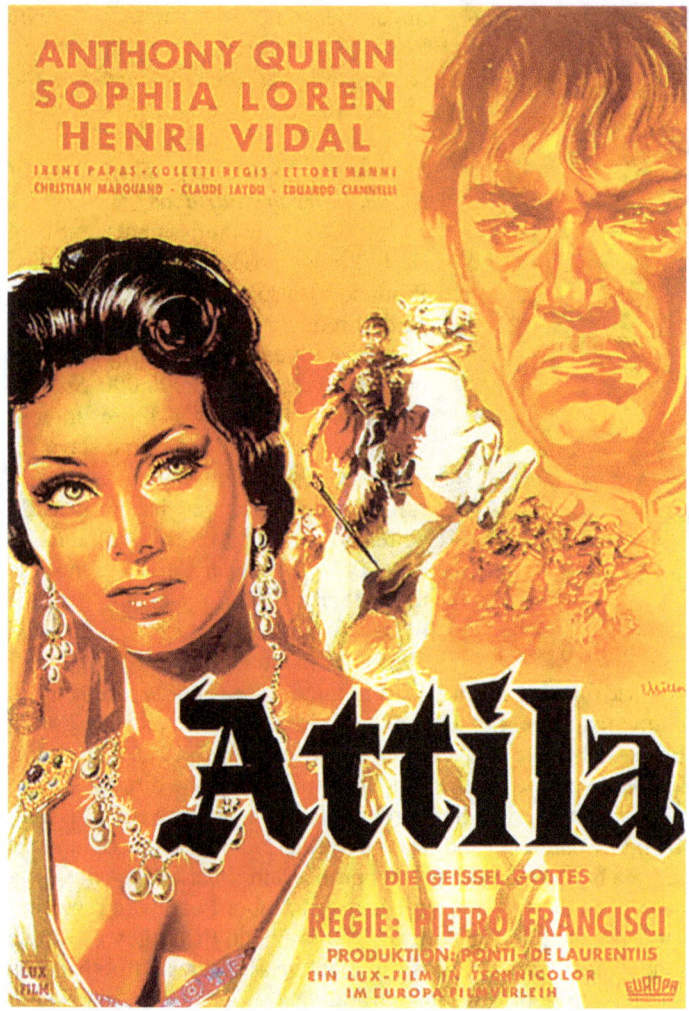

filmed. Girotti leaps into the bedlam, sends the big cats packing, is declared a hero but turns down an offer of freedom from Ninchi unless slaves are given theirs. During a fierce struggle with the men-at-arms using flaming torches as weapons, brutal slave master Silvestri is murdered and the gladiators, plus slaves, escape via a canal, Girotti heading the revolt with Tchérina and artful Yves Vincent (Octavius) at his side. After the interlude with Canale in her villa, Girotti spurs his ragtag troops on ("The only reward of a slave is scars," he reminds them) and, at the Battle of Vesuvius, defeats the Roman army in a resounding victory, leaving over 2,000 dead. Canale tries one more throw of the dice in winning back Girotti from his cause and the arms of Tchérina ("I love you. I'll die without you.") but is rejected; in a bloody skirmish outside Rome (Freda has horses racing over his camera, mud spattering the lens for maximum impact), the rebellion is quashed. Tchérina finds her beloved dying on the corpse-strewn battlefield, a deeply moving closing few minutes: "I led you to disaster, not to victory," he groans, handing her his sword. "One day, this will be victorious," she says as the film ends.

Freda's assured, fluid camerawork brought Ancient Rome to starker life than many of the film's Technicolored cousins. Renzo Rossellini's strident score is a foretaste of the marvelous soundtracks that were to come in the following years by the likes of Carlo Innocenzi, Carlo Rustichelli, Angelo Francesco Lavagnino and Francesco De Masi. Okay, it may not have the multi-million dollar pomp of Kubrick's legendary sword and sandal opus, and no big stars appear to match Kirk Douglas,

Laurence Olivier, Jean Simmons and Tony Curtis, but Freda's *Spartacus*, a key production among the vanguard of movies that paved the way for the peplum invasion four years away, scores highly in different areas and on different levels, a heated, darker-than-dark portrayal of slaves versus the might of Rome, and a love that could never be, which deserves a full-length release to place it among the greats of the genre.

1954

Attila [*Attila, il flagello di Dio*] aka ***Attila the Hun***

Lux Film/Compagnie Cinématographique (Italy/France); Technicolor; 80 (77) mins; Producers: Dino De Laurentiis, Carlo Ponti; Director: Pietro Francisci ††

Budgeted at $100,000, *Attila*'s distribution rights were snapped up by American producer Joseph E. Levine, who spent an additional $500,000 on promotion, the film eventually grossing $2,000,000; he would later perform the same feat with *The Labors of Hercules*. An all-star cast included Anthony Quinn in the title role, Henri Vidal as Roman general Aethius, Ettore Manni (unrecognizable as Bleda, Quinn's brother), Irene Papas, Quinn's mistress (Grune) and 20-year-old Sophia Loren (Honoria), living up to her reputation as "The World's Most Beautiful Woman," a title bestowed on several Italian actresses during the 1950s. That talent, combined with Enzo Masetti and Raoul Kraushaar's thumping score and Aldo Tonti's vibrant color photography, should have guaranteed a barbarian winner, but it failed to do so.

Apart from brief opening footage of the heathens on a rampage and the aftermath (bodies strung up; corpses littering the streets; buildings ablaze), the first 20 minutes dwelt on lengthy negotiations in the Hun's encampment between Vidal, Quinn (who wants war) and Manni (he desires peace). The pace drags, picking up slightly in the Roman town of Ravenna where sickly, weak mother's boy Claude Laydu (Emperor Valentiniano) and his pet leopard are being treated to a dance. Colette Régis is the elderly empress mollycoddling her crybaby son who behaves like a five-year-old, while ambitious Loren wants to rule in Laydu's place. On the 40th minute, Quinn murders Manni during a wild boar hunt; the Huns go on the march, Vidal's peace deal is in tatters and Loren decides to offer herself to Quinn on a platter to stop hostilities and plant her shapely derriere on the Roman throne. No happy ending in this movie—during the final assault on Ravenna, defended by Vidal's legions (lively, but only four minutes long, woefully short by peplum standards), Loren is stabbed to death in a cart, and Vidal slain on the battlefield. And the closing sequence is as blatant a piece of Christian propaganda you are ever likely to encounter on celluloid. Quinn and his victorious hordes converge on a procession of cross-bearing Christians led by Pope Leo I. Quinn (on a black horse) confronts the pontiff (on a white horse), there's a clap of thunder and, worried, the superstitious pagan chief backs off, riding away as a giant cross appears in the sky; good triumphs over evil, plain and simple.

Loren's sophisticated looks and acting talent appear wasted in this 80-minute Hun potboiler; Quinn chews the scenery, something he was very good at (how can Loren kiss the uncouth warlord when his mouth is full of half-eaten meat?), but it's all done and dusted in quick-fire time and leaves no lasting impression. The barbarian cycle of features from 1960 onwards were far superior to this lackluster effort (just look at Sergio Grieco's

Errol Flynn and Gina Lollobrigida cozy up on the set of *Crossed Swords*.

The Queen of the Tartars and you'll see what I mean), and made on a fraction of *Attila*'s cost.

Crossed Swords [*Il maestro di Don Giovanni*]

Viva Film (Italy/US); Pathécolor; 83 mins; Producers: Vittorio Vassarotti, Barry Mahon, Errol Flynn; Directors: Milton Krims, Vittorio Vassarotti ✝✝

Leaping out of a bedroom window, leaving two distraught ladies behind, one of Hollywood's most notorious Lotharios made his appearance in a garishly photographed (Jack Cardiff) Renaissance pseudo-comedy that, if leading man Errol Flynn had not starred in it, would have passed into the annals of obscurity years ago, if it hasn't done so already. *Crossed Swords*, as it was known when distributed by United Artists in America and Britain, is Flynn's hardest-to-come-by picture, produced at a time when Warner Bros. had terminated his contract because the 44-year-old actor suffered from financial problems and long-term alcohol abuse. Mirroring his own *The Adventures of Don Juan* (Warner Bros., 1948), a preposterous plot had the town of Sedona decreeing that any man aged 20 and over not married must be punished as, following a recent war, the birth rate is too low (not that this would stop a man of Flynn's reputation!). Flynn (Renzo, the "romantic grasshopper") has teamed up with Cesare Danova (Ranieri) to stop Roldano Lupi (Pavoncello), aided by mercenary Riccardo Rioli and bumbling official Alberto Rabagliati (Nadia Gray plays his persevering wife), from usurping the Duchy from Danova's father, Pietro Tordi. Gina Lollobrigida, Danova's busty sister (Francesca), is one of many females vying for Flynn's attention (and getting it), determined to pin the gadabout down with a firm commitment of wedded bliss before that blessed proclamation is read to the public.

Alessando Cicognini and Gino Marinuzzi, Jr.'s busy classical overture score, clearly taking its inspiration from Erich Wolfgang Korngold's Oscar-winning music from one of Flynn's greatest successes, *The Adventures of Robin Hood* (Warner Bros., 1938), is thoroughly wasted in Milton Krims' not-so-jolly caper (it was the screenwriter's one and only stab at directing), where flamboyant costumes spoke louder than the lame dialogue. Much scampering about and giggling occurs among the decorative women (Flynn, looking slightly shopworn, still had what it takes in *that* department!), and tomfoolery elsewhere jars with brief snatches of violent fistfights, dueling, and a bruising clash with bamboo poles. However, the final confrontation between still-rakish Flynn and slobbering Lupi is brilliantly staged, the old swashbuckler suddenly shedding the years in a grand piece of swordplay. What a pity the preceding 75-odd minutes couldn't have been presented in the same thrilling vein. Beautiful color photography and a quality score would have been far better served in something a lot more worthwhile than Flynn's solitary contribution to the world of the Italian costumer.

The Loves of Three Queens [*L'amante di Paride*] aka *The Face That Launched a Thousand Ships*

Cine del Duco (Italy); Technicolor; 97 mins; Producers: Victor Pahlen, Hedy Lamarr; Directors: Marc Allégret, Edgar G. Ulmer ✝✝✝

A traveling band of players in Italy, the Theater Romani, puts on sketches relating to famous historical heroines, each featuring actress Lyala in the lead role. On tour an unseen admirer finally gives her up so that she can continue to delight audiences with her performances.

Hollywood sex goddess Hedy Lamarr took on all three principal roles in *The Loves of Three Queens*.

Rhonda Fleming faces public execution in the city square, wrongly accused of murder in *The Queen of Babylon*.

In 1938, MGM supremo Louis B. Mayer described Austrian actress Hedy Lamarr as the world's most beautiful woman. In 1954, aged 40, she still retained her radiant looks and, to prove it, she partly financed this portmanteau movie based on three notorious women of history, casting herself in the lead roles: Genevieve of Brabant, Empress Josephine and Helen of Troy. Originally slated at over three hours, the film was edited to a more palatable 97 minutes; French filmmaker Roger Vadim contributed toward the script, Marc Allégret replaced Edgar G. Ulmer after Ulmer's falling out with Lamarr on set and an international cast selected—see if you can spot British actors Terence Morgan and John Fraser among the sea of Latin faces. Each story began life on stage, then segued effortlessly into real-life action, much like the revolutionary technique employed by Laurence Olivier so successfully in *Henry V*.

The first story, "Genevieve of Brabant," concerns Genevieve, married to Count Siegfried who's away in the wars. Pregnant and wrongly accused of adultery by spurned nobleman Golo, who lusts after her, she is taken into the forest to be murdered but is spared death. Let loose in the woods, Genevieve brings up her son for five years among animals, living in a cave, until her husband discovers her, realizes she has been wronged and takes her back. Note: This story was the foundation for 1964's excellent *Genoveffa of Brabant*, aka *The Revenge of the Crusader*, and had been filmed in 1947 by Primo Zeglio for Vi-va Film. Rossano Brazzi also starred in the French/Italian production of *The Mistress of Treves* (*La leggenda di Genoveffa*; Venturini Film, 1952), yet another version of the much-loved fable, with Anne Vernon playing Genoveffa/Genevieve. *The Mistress of Treves* is not available on tape or disc as of 2015.

Story two, "Napoleon and Josephine," was the shortest and most talkative, dealing with the constant bickering going on between Napoleon Bonaparte (Gérard Oury) and Empress Josephine. Basically, the French conqueror doesn't trust his coquettish wife an inch in the company of other men and needs to further his own career by marrying into royalty; they were publicly divorced in 1810.

The final segment, and the longest at nearly 40 minutes, "The Face That Launched a Thousand Ships," presented the viewer with a potted history of the Trojan wars, Massimo Serato playing Paris opposite Lamarr's Helen of Troy ("Are you a goddess or a mortal woman?"), hence the Italians focusing on this particular colorful segment for the main title, stills and posters. The Trojan conflict was all somehow packed in: a montage of battles; the Greek fleet of 1000 ships; the wooden horse; a sumptuous palace; and a truly commendable reimagining of the walls of Troy, an archaic structure of towering, irregular-placed building blocks, both highly unusual and striking when compared to other depictions of the city in costlier productions. The wooden horse sequence and the sacking of Troy were expertly organized by the effects department.

Overall, Lamarr's homage to her own matchless beauty comes off well, nowhere near the disaster written about elsewhere. True, the camera spends an inordinate amount of screen time zooming up on her face, but with looks like hers, who can really have cause to complain. Her acting verges on the emotive on occasions, but this was a Hollywood legend in her prime, so allowances should be made. Nino Rota's score is tremendous, as is the bright-as-a-button photography courtesy of John Allen, Desmond Dickinson, Fernando Risi and Guglielmo Lombardi. A one-off for those who appreciate a dose of idiosyncratic cinema once in a while; they don't come any quirkier than *The Loves of Three Queens*.

The Queen of Babylon [*La cortigiana di Babilonia*] aka *Semiramis, Slave Queen*; *The Slave Woman*

Rialto/Panthéon Prods. (Italy/France); Ferraniacolor; 109 mins; Producer: Nat Wachsberger; Director: Carlo Ludovico Bragaglia ††††

31-year-old Hollywood star Rhonda Fleming starred opposite Ricardo Montalban in Carlo Ludovico Bragaglia's colorful chunk of Middle Eastern hooey, photographed in glorious hues by Gabor Pogany and driven by Renzo Rossellini's almost classical-sounding music (20th Century Fox distributed the movie worldwide). Around 800 BC (not 600 BC as quoted in the blurbs), the cruel King Assur of Assyria (Roldano Lupi) governs Babylon. At a court meeting, Chaldean leader Montalban (Amal) refuses to kneel and pay subservience to the tyrant. "Submit and I'll pardon you," snaps Lupi, but Montalban and his men turn tail and walk off. Ambushed, Montalban kills an entire posse of soldiers but is wounded, treated by goat-herder Fleming (Semiramis) beside the picturesque wooded scenery of the Monte Gelato falls. Hiding in a cave, the Chaldean falls in love with the shepherdess, who is almost raped and then captured in a savage raid on her village. In Babylon, she's chosen to be a dancer by Lupi's scheming second-in-command, Carlo Ninchi (Sibari), her beauty catching the king's eye. Contrary to her wishes, the couple wed, much to king's favorite Tamara Lees' disgust, Fleming now elevated to the position of powerful joint ruler, although she still loves Montalban, festering in the palace dungeons and whiplashed before being sent to work in a quarry. Lupi is murdered by ambitious Ninchi and henchman Furio Meniconi, Fleming cast as the culprit and sentenced to burning at

An Italian poster for *The Son of Man*

the stake. On the day of execution in the square, Montalban, who has broken out of the quarry and rejoined his Chaldeans, storms the city with his warriors, rescuing Fleming; during a skirmish, Ninchi topples backwards into a pool full of crocodiles, eaten alive, and the Assyrians are overthrown. Fleming resumes her seat on the throne, the crowds roaring their approval, Montalban kneeling at her feet—whether or not they resume their rocky relationship is open to conjecture.

This is the kind of picture that once packed 'em in on a Saturday night in the '50s, audiences wallowing in a good old-fashioned love story overlaid with various intrigues set in distant times. It's low on action, but so were many similar films of the period. (How much action is there, for example, in 1963's four-hour *Cleopatra*? Very little.) What mattered most for the price of a ticket was believable acting, dialogue that wasn't too risible, a score that touched the emotions, fabulous ancient sets to feast the eyes on and color that dazzled. *The Queen of Babylon* (its more common title) scored on all counts. Montalban and Fleming, given their material, project strength as the doomed lovers while Lupi, Ninchi and Meniconi, all dressed to the nines, ham it up to the hilts of their swords as the scowling villains of the piece. Rossellini manufactures some wonderful leitmotifs, especially in the romantic interludes, Pogany's artful use of color imbuing the archaic exterior/interior designs in deep, rich textures. And those crocodiles the slaves have to grapple look frighteningly real. Peplum's much-used shout of "Follow me!" is heard throughout and it's rather novel to see redhead Fleming strip down to a Babylonian bikini and strut her stuff in front of a drooling Lupi. Semiramis was revisited in 1963, Yvonne Furneaux taking on the role in *I, Semiramis* (*Slave Queen of Babylon*), a slightly racier version than what was on offer here. A gratifying, expertly paced reminder of how sword and sandal storytelling virtues used to be portrayed on the silver screen without the constant need for ear-shattering, rapidly edited set pieces, a regrettable trend in the "thrill-a-minute" climate of 21st-century cinema.

The Son of Man [*Il figlio dell'uomo*] aka *Jesus, the Son of Man*

Parva/San Paolo Films (Italy); B&W; 68 mins; Producers: Emilio Cordero, Virgilio Sabel; Director: Virgilio Sabel ✝✝✝

Documentary filmmaker Virgilio Sabel, winner of two awards for Best Short Film (Venice Film Festival 1950: *Millesimo di millimetre* [1950]; National Syndicate of Film Journalists 1952: *Metano* [1951]), directed a pared-to-the-bone revisionist essay on the life of Christ, shooting in unusual locations (the towns of Peschici and Rhodes Garganico; Capoiale beach, Apulia; the lakes at Lesina and Varano, Apulia) and utilizing the willing participation of local farmers/fishermen (their faces are portrayed behind the opening credits). Commencing with a 20-minute spell showing a naked Adam (handsome Antonio Casali) and Eve (lovely Franca Parisi) up to no good in the Garden of Eden (complete with serpent), the voice-over narrative, leafing through the pages of the Bible, flashes forward to Jesus' birth in the stable, the visit of the three wise men, his preaching, raising Lazarus from the dead, his brutal flogging at the hands of the Romans, the crucifixion and the resurrection— Jesus (Eugenio Valenti) rising up to heaven in white robes, watched in awe by his disciples.

South American actress Fiorella Mari played the Madonna, while Jenny Maggeti starred as Mary Magdalene in an experimental interpretation so downbeat as to be virtually unwatchable. However, composer Renzo Rossellini and cinematographer Oberdan Troiani expertly guide us through Sabel's avant-garde framing of major scenes and Expressionistic sets; and Mel Gibson's $30,000,000 *The Passion of the Christ* (Fox, 2004) wasn't the first to depict Jesus' terrible treatment prior to his execution—the whipping and crucifixion scenes in Sabel's radical effort are, for the time it was made, unflinchingly graphic. So rare as to be almost extinct, *The Son of Man*, although produced with a dignity worthy of its reverential subject matter, is of interest to purists only.

Theodora, Empress of Byzantium [*Teodora, imperatrice di Bisanzio*] aka *Theodora, Slave Empress*

Lux Film/Lux Compagnie Cinématographique de France (Italy/France); Eastmancolor; 91 (88) mins; Produced and Directed by Riccardo Freda ✝✝✝✝

Told in flashback, Georges Marchal (Emperor Justinian) relates how, as a young man, he became infatuated with tempestuous plebeian street thief Gianna Maria Canale (Theodora) after seeing her dance in a tavern and marrying her, only to find that Roman patricians resented the waif's unexpected rise to power so much that they plotted to have the pair murdered.

Taking place in 547 AD during the time of the flourishing Byzantine Empire, when the peasant classes (plebeians) wore

Street thief turned empress Gina Maria Canale shows off her stunning beauty in this lobby card for *Theodora, Empress of Byzantium*.

the empire. The film closes where it began, Marchal reflecting on his life with Canale, who suddenly appears at his side, older and wiser.

Two Nights With Cleopatra [*Due notti con Cleopatra*]

Excelsa Film/Rosa Film (Italy); Ferraniacolor; 78 mins; Producer: Giuseppe Colizzi; Director: Mario Mattoli † or ††††† for Sophia Loren lovers

The year 31 BC: Cleopatra, Queen of Egypt, wishes to visit her lover, Marc Antony, for a night of passion, but High Priest Tortul forbids it; it is sacrilege to leave the palace on the night of the Feast of Isis. The queen's problem is resolved when Tortul, strolling in the marketplace, alights on slave girl Nisca, Cleopatra's blonde double. The queen hurries off for a bout of lovemaking while Nisca is planted in her place. Cesarino, a bumbling would-be conspirator, sneaks into the palace, mistakes Nisca for the real article and proceeds to woo her, showing the girl a signet ring copied from

green and the upper classes (patricians) wore blue, Freda used the same technicians and vast sets from *Spartacus* and cast his wife in the central role, a role she made the most of. In modern vernacular, Canale's flighty character was a "tease," leading men on to the point of frustration, a case of "look but don't touch." Marchal is only allowed physical intimacy when he rescues her from the cells and they wed ("Take your hands off me. You can have me if you marry me!"), triggering a chain of turbulent events. Rebel plebeian Renato Baldini (Arcas) loves her, failing to understand that she married Marchal to free slaves from bondage and grant them an amnesty ("I represent the voice of the people."); Canale's sister, Irene Papas, is jealous of her good fortune, becoming slippery councilor Henri Guisol's courtesan so that she can blacken her name within the confines of the emperor's court; Loris Gizzi and Roger Pigaut join in the coup to oust Marchal and Canale; and Nerio Bernardi plays General Valerius, solidly behind Canale and her tenet. It's a very busy-looking scenario presented by cinematographer Rodolfo Lombardi and Freda in glorious vibrant colors, Canale first flaunting her curvaceous figure in a dance routine beautifully scored by Renzo Rossellini, but it's also too talkative in parts, the gifted filmmaker displaying his wife's vivacity to the detriment of dramatic thrust. Things liven up with a fantastic, blood-pumping chariot race, a forerunner to *Ben-Hur*'s Oscar-winning set piece (snippets were used in 1963's *Maciste, the World's Greatest Hero*); Canale begins to throw her weight around once on the throne ("These sandals are gold. I prefer to wear red."); Baldini organizes a rebellion to quell the patricians (lions and leopards are let loose, mauling the guards); and Canale is falsely accused of having an affair with Baldini, whom she loves, but only "like a brother." In the cellars, encircled by 14 lances (a classic peplum shot that would occur many times over the coming years), Canale is saved from strangulation by a hulking blind guard when Bernardi and his legions enter the city of Ravenna and expose Guisol, Pigaut and Gizzi as collaborators against

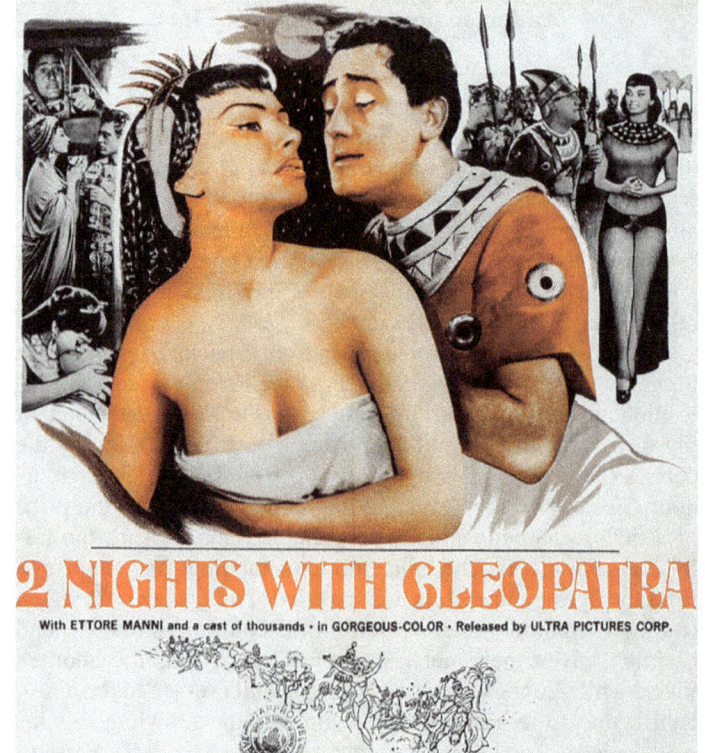

19-year-old starlet Sophia Loren smolders as Queen Cleopatra in *Two Nights With Cleopatra*.

the one that Cleopatra gave to Marc Antony many years ago. Marc Antony warns the queen of a plot to overthrow her, led by the corps of Octavian, ready to march on Egypt, and gives her his ring so that on her return to the palace, she can match it with Cesarino's and he can be arrested. The following night, Nisca is flung into the dungeons for impersonating Cleopatra but freed when evil Tortul is unmasked as the court traitor. Cesarino gets the bona fide Cleopatra drunk, she collapses against a pillar (dead?) and the pint-sized Romeo waltzes off with Nisca.

Mario Mattoli specialized in cock and bull leg-pull movies; he directed seven *Toto* features in his career as well as *Maciste Against Hercules in the Vale of Woe* (1961), itself a sendup of peplum values. *Two Nights With Cleopatra* was specifically tailored to showcase the glamorous features of 19-year-old starlet Sophia Loren (a finalist in 1950's Miss Italia beauty contest); I defy any seasoned cinemagoer to name an actress of her age, at that period, that matched her phenomenally stunning looks and curvaceous physique. Loren possessed an unparalleled female splendor *and* she could act. "Can you think of a better way of going?" she haughtily tells her delectable handmaidens when yet another soldier is poisoned after spending the night in her bed (to help with her insomnia!). Not many would disagree with that sentiment; it's a wonder Mattoli's lens didn't steam over when focusing on those fabulous contours! Granted, the sets are magnificent, the photography (Karl Struss and Riccardo Pallottini) glowing and the score by Armando Trovajoli (often misspelled in film credits as Trovaioli) rewarding, but sets, color and music alone cannot carry a movie. Depending on your tastes in comedy, Italian funnyman Alberto Sordi, the male lead, is excruciatingly *unfunny*, his incessant mugging and clowning at odds with the spectacular backdrops, contrasting to Ettore Manni's somber Marc Antony and Paul Muller's artful high priest. And did they honestly say things like: "Don't worry, pussycat" in Ancient Egypt? Loren, playing both Cleopatra and Nisca, drifts from one situation to another with the regal bearing of a queen herself (probably celluloid's most vivacious Queen of Egypt) in a film that makes Fernando Cerchio's *Toto and Cleopatra* (1963) seem like a lost masterpiece. There is really only one reason, and one reason alone, to watch this mercifully short historical sex-spoof—Sophia Loren.

Ulysses [*Ulisse*]

Lux Film (Italy/US); Technicolor; 117 (102) mins; Producers: Dino De Laurentiis, Carlo Ponti; Director: Mario Camerini ††††

Produced on a budget of $500,000 (expensive for an Italian film studio) and distributed worldwide by Paramount, *Ulysses* was a sizeable box-office hit, perhaps, in hindsight, as important to the peplum genre as *The Labors of Hercules* would become three to four years later. Kirk Douglas plus Anthony Quinn meant rich pickings; both were highly bankable Hollywood stars, contributing greatly to the movie's success. A more or less faithful adaptation of Homer's *Odyssey* (Ben Hecht was one of seven screenwriters), the narrative unfolded in flashback: At the start, a minstrel sings of Ulysses' triumph over Troy, depicting the wooden horse deception and his violation of the Temple of Neptune, invoking the curse of prophetess Cassandra on his head. Ulysses, the King of Ithaca, has been absent for 10 years and wife Penelope (Silvana Mangano) has been forced into the unenviable position of choosing a successor from among 12 suitors ("You are much too young to sleep with your memo-

Umberto Silvestri (Polyphemus, the man-eating Cyclops) enters his cave to confront Kirk Douglas and friends in *Ulysses*.

ries."), strutting Antinuous of Cephalonia (Anthony Quinn) the prime candidate ("I've come to end your loneliness."). Her son Telemachus (Franco Interlenghi) boils with indignation as the nobles fight, squabble and barter over his mother's charms, not yet man enough to remedy the situation.

Mario Camerini then concentrates on Ulysses (Douglas fits the role like a glove). Washed ashore in the land of King Alicinous (Jacques Dumesnil) after his ship is wrecked, and suffering from loss of memory, Douglas is cared for by the king's daughter, Nausicaa (Rossana Podesta, a picture of radiant womanhood; it was her looks in this film that got her the leading role in Robert Wise's *Helen of Troy*), who falls in love with the handsome stranger. "He might be a god," states an aide. "I hope not," she replies. "I want him to be a man." During a games tournament, Douglas wrestles and defeats the king's champion, promising to wed besotted Podesta, but on the eve of their marriage, he wanders down to the shore, goes into a trance and another flashback, forming the narrative's backbone, follows as his past adventures seep back into his mind: a storm at sea, the statue of Neptune tossed overboard; the blinding of Polyphemus, the man-eating Cyclops in his cave (a lengthy, imaginative interlude given the budget); avoiding the Sirens who can drive sailors mad; his entrapment by enchantress Circe, the witch taking on the form of Penelope (Mangano played both parts); and

A Belgian poster for *The Golden Falcon*

meeting the spirits of those who fought with him in the Trojan wars. "I am Ulysses!" he cries, his memory returning. Granted a ship by Dumesnil, he sets sails for Ithaca and a confrontation with those 12 rowdy suitors. Disguised as a beggar, Douglas enters his palace, manages to draw his powerful bow which no one else can manage, fires an arrow through 12 axe heads and slays all 12 nobles, by arrow, sword, spear and axe, leaving the room littered with blood-soaked corpses. The King of Ithaca is finally reunited with wife and son, his odyssey at an end, forgiven by the gods.

It must be said that *Ulysses* is a slow-mover in parts, the Polyphemus episode of most interest to fantasy fans. However, Douglas was one of those movie legends who *never* turned in a bad performance, and he certainly doesn't disappoint here; this was the actor in his prime (38 at the time), rugged and muscular, his trademark flashing-grin almost hidden under a thick beard. So, take Douglas, Latin beauties Mangano and Podesata, Quinn in full villainous flow, inviting Mediterranean locations and stunning cinematography by Harold Rosson (he was nominated for five academy awards, including work on 1939's *The Wizard of Oz*) and you have one of pepla's archetypal heroic/myth offerings before the "Big Bang" of 1957/1958.

1955

The Golden Falcon [*Il falco d'oro*]

Po Film (Italy); Supercinescope/Ferraniacolor; 98 mins; Producer: Ottavio Poggi; Director: Carlo Ludovico Bragaglia ✝✝✝

In Tuscany in the 17th century the mysterious Golden Falcon is stirring up trouble between two feuding Siena noble families, the Montefalcos and the Della Torres. Widow Rose Alba (Gertrude Montefalco) knows full well that the Falcon is her wayward son, Massimo Serato, who's betrothed to Nadia Gray (Ines Della Torre) in the hope that hostilities will finally cease. However, tomboy Anna Maria Ferrero (Fiametta), the daughter of fencing master Enzo Musumeci Greco, is in love with Serato and does everything she can to break up the forthcoming nuptials, including taking on the guise of The Golden Falcon to bring Gray into disrepute, wielding a sword and lying about her fictitious childhood in which she claims she was abused by the Della Torre family. Serato is arrested and incarcerated for wrongful misdeeds toward the community, while stuffy Frank Latimore (Simone) wants to marry Gray, jealous of Serato's intentions. Eventually, after many comings and goings in the grand castle where most of the action takes place, Serato marries Gray and peace is restored between the two nobilities.

Filmed in and around Tuscany's medieval Montalcino Castle, *The Golden Falcon* is played, if strictly not for belly laughs, in sportive fashion, not to be taken too seriously. An abundance of clowning around in dungeons and one too many cases of "we've caught the wrong man" detract from what could have been a classic Renaissance swashbuckler, boosted by a terrific joint operatic score from Angelo Francesco Lavagnino and Ezio Carabella, plus Alvaro Mancori's sharp photography. Serato looks uncomfortable acting the fool; Latimore, dressed to the nines, is wooden as the chief villain; and it's left to Ferrero to carry the proceedings on her dainty shoulders, a one-woman show if ever there was one. Pristine DVD copies in Italian are now difficult to come across due to the closure of the company that produced them in 2008.

The Prince in the Red Mask [*Il principe dalla maschera rossa*] aka *The Red Eagle*

Scalera/Titanus (Italy); B&W; 84 (78) mins; Producers: Giovanni Addessi, Giuseppe Fatigati; Director: Leopoldo Savona ✝✝✝✝

The Italian province of Scala, late 16th century: Land and property belonging to Conte Filippo are seized in a bloody coup, the count murdered by Captain Alberico, acting for a gang of conspirators, all in the service of Duke Altichieri. For 10 years, the people under Alberico's iron rule are subjected to oppres-

Prison officer Livio Lorenzon (with hair, the actor's first peplum) threatens trussed-up Frank Latimore, the Red Mask, in *The Prince in the Red Mask*.

sion, torture, persecution and loss of goods until a mysterious red-masked avenger appears with his band of vigilantes, righting the wrongs enforced upon them in a series of raids on Alberico's thugs. In the castle gardens, Masuccio, the masked avenger and the son of the murdered count, meets Lady Isabella, who Alberico wishes to wed. At Masuccio's Gypsy camp bolt-hole, peasant girl Laura is in love with the rebel leader but, having met Isabella, his thoughts turn elsewhere. Alberico, aware of the attraction between the two, masquerades as the masked rider, holds up a coach and murders Isabella's wealthy banker father, Gaspare, in front of her. Disguised as a Gypsy, Isabella infiltrates the rebel sanctum, determined to kill Masuccio, but when she learns the true facts about him and his background from a medallion he wears, she professes her love for the masked prince. Embittered Laura denounces the pair to Alberico and Masuccio is imprisoned in the dungeons, the threat of death hanging over his head if Isabella doesn't marry the tyrant. Torn with remorse at her wicked actions, Laura flirts with the guards, enabling the rebels to gain access into the castle. Masuccio is released; during a lengthy skirmish with soldiers, Laura is stabbed to death and Alberico pierced by a blade after a duel with the deposed heir, toppling from the battlements. Duke Altichieri is driven from the castle and the cheering crowds salute Scala's rightful rulers, Masuccio and Isabella, joined together in love.

American Frank Latimore, 30 at the time, was up to his neck in costume swashbucklers during this period, Leopoldo Savona's classy entry into what would become a long line of "masked avenger" outings, a fine example of how to present formulaic material in a fresh guise. Assisted by deep black-and-white photography from Vincenzo Seratrice (especially in the wonderfully lit castle sequences at the end), Armando Trovajoli's Spanish-based score (the composer's flamenco guitar leitmotif during Yvonne Furneaux's dance routine is sublime), location work at the massive Italian hilltop fortress of Castello di Torrechiara near Parma and a likeable turn from Latimore, *The Prince in the Red Mask* (another peplum rarity, available in Italian with Greek subtitles) gallops through the paces with verve, no one scene ever outstaying its welcome. There are several boisterous swordfights, Maria Fiore (Isabella) competes with Furneaux in the "who's the better looking" stakes and the climactic four-minute duel to the finish between Latimore and villain Elio Steiner, each armed with swords, pikestaffs and daggers, is a great piece of swashbuckling cinema, benefiting from a combination of Savona's tight edits and Seratrice's artistic backlighting. And keep a look out for one of the genre's most famous (and most employed) of all bad guys, Livio Lorenzon (billed as Livio Arden, playing the chief prison officer) sporting hair! This was the master of skulduggery's first of 37 peplum outings, a reliably familiar face (minus that hair!) that would enliven many a sword and sandaler/swashbuckler in the years to come.

The Red Cloak [Il mantello rosso]

Trio Film/Franca Film (Italy/France); Cinepanoramic/Ferraniacolor; 102 mins; Producer: Elios Vercelloni; Director: Giuseppe Maria Scotese ✟✟✟

In 16th-century Pisa, a tyrant, Flemish Captain of the Guards Raniero d'Anversa, rules over the oppressed people and obtains taxes under the continuing threat of violence. Laura Lanfranchi, engaged against her wishes to be married to the despot, makes the acquaintance of Luca de Bardi, a banker's son posing as an artist, and he decides to paint her portrait, the pair falling in

A Spanish poster for *The Red Cloak*

love. Luca then takes on the guise of the avenging masked Red Cloak—his father, Cosimo de Bardi, has been assassinated by d'Anversa's hyenas and he seeks retribution. The audacious Red Cloak leads a succession of daring sorties on the city's enemies, fighting in the streets at night and waylaying coaches during the day, a ransom placed on his head, but is undone by Laura when he welcomes a beautiful Gypsy girl, Stella, to his home to sit for him. Laura spots the two together, jumps to the wrong conclusion and, seething with jealousy, informs her father that the wedding to d'Anversa will proceed as planned. The Red Cloak and his rebels abruptly disturb the wedding reception, d'Anversa backing away from a confrontation as Luca makes his escape. Laura begins to see through the painter's disguise; he's eventually captured, tortured and condemned to death. Saro, Luca's friend, organizes a revolt and The Red Cloak is saved on the way to his execution; in the ensuing struggle, Luca kills d'Anversa in a duel and is at last free to carry on his relationship with Laura.

Faded, ragged DVD copies in pan and scan do little justice to Scotese's moderately thrilling, and uncommonly lengthy, costumer (and Adalberto "Bitto" Albertini's color tones) featuring Bruce *King Kong* Cabot in the heavyweight part of snarling thug d'Anversa; Fausto Tozzi plays the dashing hero Luca while English-born Patricia Medina (Laura) loses out to Lyla Rocco (Stella) in the "ravishing beauty" stakes. And there are a lot of what would become familiar faces in the supporting cast—Giacomo Rossi-Stuart, Giulio Battiferri and the Fantasia brothers,

Italian photobusta for *Knight of the Black Sword*

Franco and Andrea (both are listed as fencing coaches, an art they were adept at). Gino Marinuzzi, Jr.'s music thunders away in the background to a standard, yet lively enough, swashbuckler that is very difficult to obtain these days.

1956

Knight of the Black Sword [*Il cavaliere dalla spada nera*]
Romana Film (Italy); Ferraniacolor; 86 mins; Producer: Fortunato Misiano; Directors: Ladislao Kish, Luigi Capuano (uncredited) ††††

Count Ludwig weds Countess Laura in a lavish ceremony; stepping out onto the castle steps, he's slain by a crossbow arrow through the neck, the killer leaving behind his weapon and a jewel from his sword's guard. The countess vows revenge, and following the count's death, the local populace is set upon by The Marquis of Altamura's flunkies, their livestock and homes ransacked—the blaggard was responsible for the murder and desires marriage to Laura, thereby coming into her fortune and her lands. But he hasn't reckoned on a mysterious figure named The Masked Cavalier, who comes to the aid of the oppressed, carving a ragged furrow on the foreheads of his enemies as his calling card. The young widow arranges a falcon hunt to flush out the culprit and has suitors lining up at her feet, including Marco, the handsome young Count of Montefalcone. Due to the marquis' continual harassment, Laura and her friend Livia are forced to leave her castle after he has thrust himself upon her; the marquis then receives the point of the masked swordsman's mark on his forehead after they duel. In a final confrontation with his foe, the caped swordsman proves, in front of Laura, that the jewel found at the scene of the crime belongs to the rogue's sword; the two clash and the marquis is run through. The swordsman removes his mask to reveal himself as Marco, whom Laura loved all along. The couple are last seen galloping across a sunlit meadow to start a future together as man and wife.

Hungarian Ladislao Kish was given an opportunity to direct this ultra-rare swashbuckler after a career hiatus of 12 years, his previous movie being Titanus/Sabaudia Film's *Finalmente si* in 1944. Luigi Capuano (his first of 16 peplum movies; 17 if you include 1971's *Zorro, Rider of Vengeance*, which is outside the scope of this book) helped him out, the pair concocting a sedate, handsomely dressed romantic-themed *cappa e spada* that has two things going for it: dazzling photography in the Italian Ferraniacolor process by Augusto Tiezzi; and Carlo Innocenzi's beautifully melodic title theme music, one of the finest to be scored in the medium of peplum, redolent of times gone by. Stephen Barclay, born in Baltimore, Maryland, played Marco, a makeshift gray mask draped over his head, his redlined black cape swirling in the breeze, leaping to the defense of the lovely Marina Berti (as Laura; the two had starred together in 1951's *The Black Captain*), while Otello Toso put in a suitably foul performance playing the iniquitous marquis. The numerous swordfights and tavern brawls were mostly performed without Innocenzi's musical accompaniment, lending them a curiously unfinished quality. Kish seemed content simply to let his camera drift around the Lazio landscape, taking in wooded glades, dappled orchards, farmsteads, the Monte Gelato waterfalls and all those decorative costumes; the grand Castello Piccolomini di Balsorano fortification was used as the castle setting, seen mostly in longshot. It's true, *Knight of the Black Sword* is languid, leisurely and not overly exciting, like a dress rehearsal for the real thing, but somehow, the picture exerts a strange and sleepy timeless charm that many others of its ilk do not possess, akin to a snapshot of the past captured on celluloid. Good quality DVDs can be obtained from certain German suppliers, dubbed in German but lacking subtitles.

Michael Strogoff [*Michele Strogoff*]
Illiria Film/Les Films Modernes/Produzione Gallone (Italy/France); CinemaScope/Technicolor; 111 mins; Producer: Emile Natan; Director: Carmine Gallone †††

Adapted from Jules Verne's 1876 novel, *Michael Strogoff* is a sprawling outdoor yarn containing a very thin plot. In the mid-1800s, Russia is being harassed by the Tartar hordes. Captain Curt (Curd) Jurgens (Strogoff) is given a vital message from the Czar to deliver to a troop detachment at Irkutsk, Genevieve Page (Nadia) posing as his wife to divert attention from their mission. Tartar chieftain Valéry Inkijinoff, meanwhile, has abducted Jurgen's elderly mother and had her whipped to death. Confronted by her brutal execution in the Tartar encampment, Jurgens is caught and, following a provocative dance, blinded with a red-hot saber, the papers stolen. Jurgens and Page escape back to the palace of Grand Duke Jacques Dacqmine, where Jurgens, his sight restored, kills imposter/traitor Henri Nassiet and helps the Russians overcome the barbarians in a fierce struggle. The picture closes with Jurgens dispatching Inkijinoff in a duel and getting wed to Page.

The accent here is on scenic splendor as opposed to meaningful drama; filming took place in the wilds of Yugoslavia, most of the action and battle sequences (featuring boats and rafts) occurring on the wide, turbulent River Drina, cinematographer Robert Lefebvre conjuring up some splendid panoramic shots of the sparsely wooded countryside. Marshal Tito's Yugoslavian cavalry units were hired to take part in the climactic skirmish on land which appears curiously limp, hundreds of horsemen and

infantry milling around doing very little—the director should have given all concerned a rocket (the same can be said of Jurgens' tame duel with Inkijinoff). Out of the cast, only Sylva Koscina, playing a Gypsy in love with Jurgens, injected her part with a modicum of fire, the rest content to meander through a historical tapestry suitable for the whole family, nice to look at with commendable period feel but devoid of any real emotional depth.

The Mysterious Swordsman [*Lo spadaccino misterioso*]

Po Film (Italy); Cinepanoramic/Ferraniacolor; 90 (78) mins; Producer: Ottavio Poggi; Director: Sergio Grieco ††††

An entertaining, vintage swashbuckler that can only be found today in its edited form, with Greek subtitles and English dubbing, starring Frank Latimore as Count Riccardo Argentari, who turns into a masked highwayman in order to put to rest Gérard Landry's (Ubaldo, the Duke of Roka Montana) plans of siding with the invading Spanish, busy routing the local population, to feather his own nest. Basically, Sergio Grieco's picturesque swashbuckler (his second in 1956) plays like an adventure romance interrupted by bouts of perky swordplay. Latimore, refusing to enter into Landry's schemes, loves Fiorella Mari (Laura), daughter of a count who's murdered on Landry's orders because he too won't go along with the duke's treacherous collaboration with the Spanish. Landry subsequently fabricates the facts to Mari, lying by stating that before he died, the count gave his blessing to their betrothal—he also desires her to be his wife, and wicked Tamara Lees (as Vialante) lusts after Latimore, determined that Mari won't get her claws into him. When Landry starts throwing his weight around, Latimore dons a full-faced black mask and assumes the persona of The Elusive Swordsman ("The swordsman will protect you!"), robbing the rich to pay the poor, leading to a profusion of skirmishes in woods and Landry's hilltop fortress (Castello Piccolomini, or Castello Di Balsorano, in the Italian province of L'Aquila was used for location shooting). There's a drunken, semi-orgy scene, Spaniard Andrea Aureli and his retinue groping a number of half-undressed nubile strumpets, while another dances provocatively on a table. A particularly vicious torture sequence also appears when Lees abducts Mari; the girl is stretched on the rack, then whipped unconscious. In the concluding melee, Lees, in a struggle with Mari, falls through a stair rail onto a bed of upturned spears, while Latimore polishes off Landry following a thrilling, four-minute swordfight in a quarry. Latimore and Mari end up in each other's arms, as expected.

Renato Del Frate's striking color tones have more or less made it intact on surviving, ultra-rare DVDs, as has Ezio Carabella's insidious score, enlivening an easy-on-the-eye actioner directed with purpose by Grieco, featuring a highly watchable turn by Latimore and Landry as hero and villain, two of their keener performances in pepla.

Orlando and the Knights of France [*Orlando e i paladini di Francia*] aka **Roland the Mighty**

Italgamma (Italy); Gammascope/Eastmancolor; 110 (99) mins; Produced and Directed by Pietro Francisci †††

In 778 AD, Emperor Charlemagne's knights are in conflict with the Saracen hordes led by Ugo Sasso and Mimmo Palmara. During a bloody skirmish (the film's lively curtain raiser) the Paladin knights retrieve a sacred picture of the Madonna, and a shaky peace is forged between the two blocs. But Sasso isn't happy, sending his secret weapon into the Frankish camp to set the knights against each other—daughter Rosanna Schiaffino, a raven-haired seductress guaranteed to bring any male's blood

An Italian photobusta for *The Mysterious Swordsman*

The Italian Peplum Phenomenon 1950-1967

A French poster for *Orlando and the Knights of France*

to boiling point. Sure enough, the plan works: Rik Battaglia (Orlando), the moody, introspective head knight, gets hot under his suit of armor at the very sight of the girl swanning around camp, while compatriot Fabrizio Mioni feels almost the same. In a head-scratching love triangle, Sasso offers Schiaffino's hand in marriage to Mioni, who has just saved the king's daughter, Lorella De Luca, from a wild boar goring (at the Monte Gelato falls) and, in the space of two minutes, has fallen in love with her—and she's betrothed to Battaglia, who loves Schiaffino! This quandary is further exacerbated by Battaglia donning Mioni's armor and defeating Palmara in a jousting contest, Mioni taking the credit; not only has this ended war, but the winner gets to marry Schiaffino, and once again, it's the reluctant Mioni whose feelings lie elsewhere. When the deception is discovered by traitor Vittorio Sanipoli (the knight has one eye on the royal throne), the Saracens see red; Palmara fights Mioni and wounds him, Battaglia rides out to locate his missing friend on the eve of his marriage and by doing so upsets the king, who promptly replaces him with Sanipoli, now chief knight. The whole mess ends with Palmara and his forces decimated in a canyon. Sanipoli, deluding himself that he's the new French king, is taken care of by Sasso, who has no time for treacherous rats. At a confrontation between his warriors and the Paladin knights, he delivers Sanipoli's sword as evidence of the man's betrayal and death and rides off, as do the two pairs of lovers, Battaglia and Schiaffino, and Mioni and De Luca, each couple sharing a mount.

Flamboyant costumes and heraldic tournaments, photographed by Mario Bava and scored by Angelo Francesco Lavagnino, highlight a vaguely disappointing pageant molded around the Battle of Roncevaux Pass in the Pyrenees in which Orlando's divisions were overrun by the Basques. Leads Battaglia and Mioni are okay but not brilliant, certainly no match for Sasso and Palmara's sneering brigands, and the romantic entanglements tire after a while. Director Francisci was on the cusp of greater things to come—his *The Labors of Hercules* was just around the corner, ready to light the fuse and blow the whole peplum scene wide open. *Orlando and the Knights of France* gives some indication of *Hercules*' strong suits but is a mite overlong in places, action substituted by too much mooning around by the four would-be lovers, who don't exactly set the screen on fire charisma-wise.

The Slaves of Carthage [*Le schiave di Cartagine*] aka **The Sword and the Cross**; **The Slave Girls of Carthage**
Societa Italiana Cines/Yago Films (Italy/Mexico/Spain); Cinetotalscope/Ferraniacolor; 87 (82) mins; Producer: Gregorio Walerstein; Director: Guido Brignone ††

Tarsus, in the Roman province of Cilicia, 120 AD: Unsmiling Gianna Maria Canale (as Julia) gets nasty in Guido Brignone's entry into the Romans versus Christians area of pepla, playing a vindictive go-getter seething with spite and jealousy when her ambitious fiancé, consul Rubén Rojo (Flavius), takes a shine to Carthaginian slave Marisa Allasio (Lea), one of two Christian sisters (one blonde, one brunette) bought in the slave market by tribune Jorge Mistral (Marcus) and presented to her as a gift. Whipped and bullied by their stern-faced crone of a maid, the girls (looking swell in matching jade costumes) submit to harsh treatment, Allasio tortured and blinded in a dungeon on orders from Canale (appropriately dressed in black to highlight her evilness). Canale then takes up a much-coveted seat of power beside Rojo, when elderly proconsul Fernando (more commonly billed as Nando) Tamberlani, her father, is murdered. She blames the Christian rabble for his sudden demise and orders their persecution—they're herded into an arena, whipped, kicked to the ground, burned on the cross and peppered with arrows. Mistral, in love with Allasio, sympathizes with the Christians and their doctrine, but is betrayed by a shepherd, imprisoned and sentenced to die on the cross. Freed, he races to the rescue with friend German Cobos and their men, just as a mass burning at the stake is due to take place in a makeshift arena. Allasio, her sister Ana Luisa

A French poster for *The Slaves of Carthage*

Peluffo and other Christians are saved; Canale, in pursuit of the liberators, falls from her chariot, trampled to death. In a duel on a beach, Rojo does the honorable thing and falls on Mistral's sword, his body collapsing in the waves. Mistral, declared the new proconsul, weds blind Allasio because of her purity, and Cobos gets hitched to her sister.

Like many other movies that strayed into this particular area of pepla, *The Slaves of Carthage*, despite its grand sets, dazzling color (Adalberto "Bitto" Albertini) and rousing score (Enzo Masetti) comes across as rather dull. Scenes of the poor, downtrodden Christian slaves working treadmills, holding pious gatherings, added to talkative political intrigue in the senate do little to alleviate the mood of gloom, and that goes for Canale, swanking around on set in her finery with a look of thunder clouding those finely chiseled features. And if Allasio gets blinded by a glowing rod of iron, why isn't there a single sign of any scarring on her? Mistral and Cobos grin a lot, while Rojo appears unconvincingly theatrical as a bad guy. It's Canale who steals the show, even if not the faintest hint of a smile creases her lovely face. The film's credentials belie the fact that what we have here is a good-to-look-at but ultimately very average, pedestrian-paced sword and sandal potboiler. Brignone would nail his material much more forcibly, and successfully, in 1959's *Sign of Rome*.

Vittorio Gassman as Giovanni De Medici, *The Violent Patriot*

The Violent Patriot [*Giovanni dalle bande nere*]

Po Film (Italy); Cinepanoramic/Ferraniacolor; 95 (84) mins; Producer: Ottavio Poggi; Director: Sergio Grieco ✟✟✟

The first of Sergio Grieco's 12 pepla dealt loosely with the real-life exploits of unruly mercenary leader Giovanni De Medici (1498-1526), who led his Black Bands (so-called because of the black stripes on their insignia) against the French troops of Frances I, defeating them and then finding himself up to his eyes in treachery when Italian nobles decide to ally themselves to German invaders for profit. Argentinian Gérard Landry, who featured in all three of Grieco's 1956/1957 Renaissance swashbucklers and went on to star in a career total of 15 pepla, was bad guy Gasparo, jealous of Giovanni's success to the point of hatred, doing his utmost to engineer events to his advantage so that the mercenary boss is eliminated. Vittorio Gassman starred as Giovanni, a cruel hothead who "ruled by terror, like the law of wild beasts" and didn't believe in God, even though friendly friar Philippe Hersent acted as his conscience. Two women figured in his anarchic day-to-day existence—Anna Maria Ferrero (Anna) and Constance Smith (Emma). Smith is the noblewoman who falls in love with him within an hour of their meeting, not realizing he's the captain stuck with that violent reputation; while peasant girl Ferrero, rejected by Gassman, hooks up with Landry in order to teach her ex-lover a lesson.

Grieco's costume adventure is high-spirited fare without ever reaching the heights, a couple of battles chucked into the romantic twists and turns to keep the audience on their toes, the narrative helped on its way by Roberto Nicolosi's drum-laden score. Loris Gizzi and Andrea Aureli (his first of over 30 pepla; he had an uncredited part in *Ulysses*) play a couple of dastardly barons switching allegiances at the drop of a plumed hat; Smith blames Gassman for the death of her brother and mother when his men, contrary to explicit orders, embark on a drunken rampage in Caravaggio, Landry behind the whole affair (her brother's death, his head smashed with a rock, is particularly nasty; and some of the graphic rape scenes were trimmed outside of Italy). Landry stabs Ferrero after she spurns his groping, living long enough to inform Gassman that the two-timing rat plans to ambush his mercenaries in the defile at Borgoforte. The Italians overcome the French in the final clash but sustain heavy losses (including Gassman's horse-faced sidekick Silvio Bagolini). Gassman, injured in the right leg, staggers to a monastery wrecked by vandals and, in an unsparing struggle with Landry who has tailed him, beats the turncoat to death with a candlestick (another vicious scene); he's then reunited with Smith, who forgives him. (Note: As a result of this wound, Giovanni's leg was amputated in the field and he died five days later from septicemia.)

Watch out for the extreme form of Italian military punishment for those disobeying a leader's command—the Decimation. Following their misdeeds in Caravaggio, Gassman's troops are lined up, every 10th man beheaded. Rarely seen (DVDs are black-and-white, pan and scan), *The Violent Patriot* is a moderately entertaining costumer with Gassman and Landry in watchable form. As for the ladies, fiery dark-haired Ferrero, displaying oodles of cleavage, is a far better bet than staid blonde Smith, buttoned up to the neck, making you wonder why volatile Gassman chose stiff nobility over earthy sensuality; perhaps it was a case of meeting the challenge!

4
Hail Hercules! The Rise of Peplum 1957-1959

Wrapped up and completed in December 1957 and released in Italy in February 1958 (worldwide distribution occurred in 1959), Pietro Francisci's *The Labors of Hercules* was the bomb that blew wide open the immensely popular Italian trend toward peplum moviemaking en masse; it all began in earnest from that point onward. Black-and-white standard screen format was replaced by all manner of color and all manner of widescreen to ensure maximum pleasure for sword and sandal and *cappa e spada*-mad audiences everywhere. Budgets were raised and beefcake actors employed to take on the pivotal roles of the musclebound superheroes required to carry the action and become a film's central focusing point, one that punters could identify with. Costumers, swashbucklers, pirates, seductive temptresses, Ancient Egyptian shenanigans, gladiators, Biblical and historical events, Ancient Rome, barbarians, cavaliers, legendary conquerors, cataclysmic destruction, medieval derring-do, romantic drama, desert warriors and Robin Hood-type characters spewed forth unabated from both major and minor Italian studios. Names which up until now had been relatively unfamiliar to filmgoers became better-known: Livio Lorenzon, Chelo Alonso, Gérard Landry, Gianna Maria Canale, Jacques Sernas, Arturo Dominici, Georges Marchal, Paul Muller, Giacomo Rossi-Stuart, Philippe Hersent, Gabriele Antonini, Wandisa Guida, Alberto Lupo, Carlo Tamberlani, Franco Fantasia, Mimmo Palmara, Ettore Manni, Massimo Serato, Andrea Aureli and Arnoldo Foà, to name but a few. And those captivating waterfalls set within enchanting wooded scenery, the Monte Gelato cascades, cropped up time and time again. Directors, producers, actors, actresses, scriptwriters, composers, cinematographers and technicians pooled their collective skills, rolled up their sleeves, took on the challenge and got down to fabricating, on an unparalleled scale and over (in cinematic terms) a comparatively short period of activity, what would become a great many classics-in-the-making. Peplum proper, as we now term it, started right here!

1957

The Black Devil [*Il diavolo nero*]

Po Film (Italy); Supercinescope/Ferraniacolor; 83 (78) mins; Producers: Ottavio Poggi, Nino Battiferri; Director: Sergio Grieco ††

Sergio Grieco's 16th-century costumer was not one of his best; currently scarce DVDs come in muddy black-and-white and pan and scan, which doesn't help. Putting that aside, *The Black Devil* is an early, yet curiously tired, addition to the series of "wicked usurper plans to rule the Duchy in medieval Italy" movies that proliferated during the early to mid-'60s, made by the same team behind the much better *The Mysterious Swordsman* and *The Violent Patriot*. Andrea Aureli played Lorenzo, trying to manipulate a marriage between the old duke's daughter, Milly Vitale (Isabella), and a nephew of King Charles V; this will enable Aureli to rule Roccabruna in tandem with the Spanish aggressors who run the country. A gang of Spanish-hating rebels led by Maurizio Arena (Ruggero) are attempting to overthrow Aureli's brutal regime, assisted by a mysterious swordsman in black, his face masked by a balaclava, The Black Devil ("A vulgar bandit," Aureli calls him). Leonora Ruffo is Stella, foster-daughter of a rebel, who, as it turns out, is the real Isabella, The Black Devil relating to Arena (shown in flashback) how 15 years ago, the heir to the principality was taken from court after her father was poisoned by Aureli; the *other* Isabella is a fraud, stolen from a Gypsy camp. Arena loves Ruffo, the genuine Isabella ("We can live happily in the sunlight," she coos in one too many sloppy love scenes), while The Black Devil loves the pretender. Duchess Nadia Gray (Lucrezia), Aureli's mistress, does her best to rid herself of both girls for her own greedy ends, while pint-sized buffoon Ughetto Bertucci ruins the limp action scenes with bouts of silly horseplay.

Gérard Landry, 45 at the time, starred as The Black Devil and his foppish alter-ego, Osvaldo; he huffs and puffs his thickset frame through the set pieces as though his inner batteries were functioning on low power, not pepla's most graceful of swashbucklers or most convincing of actors. Aureli and Ruffo appear off-form, the narrative, even at 80 minutes, drags and the only two items of interest on Grieco's agenda are seeing Ruffo tied up in a dungeon over a pit of starving rats (she's savagely smacked across her lovely face by the jailor, emphasizing the Italian "cruelty toward women" theme found in many of these films) and Landry and Aureli fighting to the death on a beach littered with boats, rather than in a castle. The movie finishes in a welter of "I love you's" and "My darling, my darling's" as Landry, Vitale, Arena and Ruffo kiss, hug and slobber, the Spanish menace all but forgotten. And you will quickly forget this uninspiring picture, too, even if you can lay your hands on a copy.

Italian photobusta for *The Black Devil*

assassin José Guardiola (Kamal), who has just stuck a dagger in *her* father's back. By this time, Montalban has amassed an army composed of tribes loyal to the uprising; the combined force assaults the palace walls, Guardiola's jackals are wiped out, the black-clad killer dies at the hands of Montalban and Sevilla is rescued from a burning tower. The final curtain falls on the couple just wed, Montalban holding high the Scimitar of the State to declare himself as the new Sultan to a joyous assembly

Moonlight trysts at the Temple of Ra, multiple floggings, the graphic torture by fire and rack of Franca Bettoia (as Suleika; this scene is cut from some prints), caravan raids, much sneaking about in palace rooms and a rousing nine-minute battle— *The Desert Lovers* is an entertaining package featuring Montalban in top form, one of the least-remembered roles in his lengthy career. Guardiola's loathsome quisling makes the flesh crawl, while Sevilla is one in a long line of dark-haired, exotic-looking peplum beauties that adorn these productions to perfection. The other bonus is Michel Michelet's energetic score, harking back to the full orchestral Hollywood soundtracks of the '30s and '40s, a tremendous piece of work all film music aficionados will treasure. More or less remade in 1962 as *The Son of the Sheik* with Gordon Scott in the title role, *The Desert Lovers* is worth tracking down, even though a pan and scan transfer sabotages the original CinemaScope format.

The Labors of Hercules [*Le fatiche di Ercole*] aka **Hercules**

Galatea/O.S.C.A.R. (Italy); Dyaliscope/Eastmancolor; 104 mins; Producer: Federico Teti; Director: Pietro Francisci ††††

This is the starting block for the peplum phenomenon that flourished and eventually died out at the beginning of 1967. To cash in on the critical and commercial success of *Ulysses*, Pietro Francisci decided to shoot his own mythological muscleman saga based on the exploits of Hercules, the Son of Zeus (or Jupiter in Roman-based flicks), a demigod endowed with superhuman strength, Cecil B. DeMille's *Samson and Delilah* an obvious source reference. Mimmo Palmara, beefy enough, was considered for the title role until Francisci's daughter spot-

A Spanish poster for *The Desert Lovers*

The Desert Lovers [*Gli amanti del deserto*] aka **Desert Warrior**

Films Benito Perojo/Parc Film/Rialto Film (Italy/Spain/France);CinemaScope/Eastmancolor; 91 (87) mins; Producers: Carlo Infascelli, Benito Perojo; Directors: Goffredo Alessandrini, Fernando Cerchio, Leon Klimovsky, Gianni Vernuccio ††††

A flashy larger-than-life desert adventure that employed four directors to bring the romantic action to the big screen, Mexican actor Ricardo Montalban stars as Prince Said, the son of a murdered sultan fighting to regain his right to the dynasty. Atmospherically filmed in Egypt, the ancient pyramids and Sphinx forming a dramatic background to the action, Montalban makes a masculine hero, baring his hairy chest to the blinding sun and the almond eyes of Carmen Sevilla; she's Princess Amina, the daughter of Sheik Ibrahim (Gino Cervi), illegal claimant to the throne, the man responsible for the death of Montalban's father. Following a succession of amorous encounters, the girl becomes so besotted by the rebel's intrepid charms that she doesn't let on her true identity until the final 10 minutes after escaping from Cervi's palace, refusing to marry

Steve Reeves as Hercules gets frisky in this American lobby card for *The Labors of Hercules*.

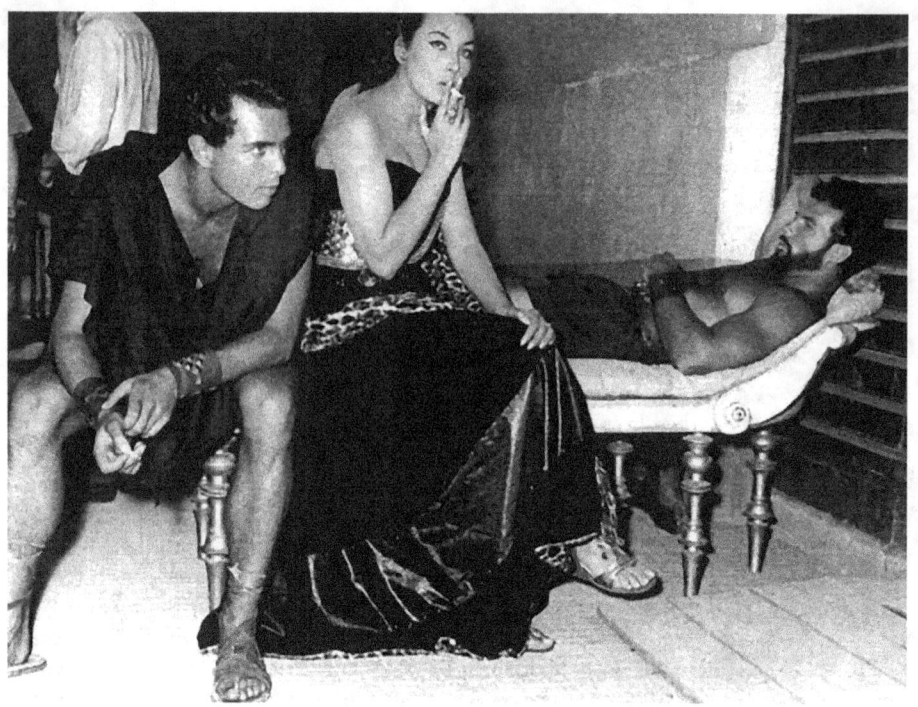

Fabrizio Mioni (left), Gianna Maria Canale and Steve Reeves take a break on the set of *The Labors of Hercules*.

ted Steve Reeves in Richard Thorpe's musical comedy *Athena* (MGM, 1954), playing Ed Perkins, a weightlifter (Mr. Universe of 1950) entering a bodybuilding contest ("Daddy, I think I have your Hercules," she is reported as saying). Reeves, Mr. Universe himself of 1950, had the requisite good looks and awesome physique—Palmara was given a secondary role and Reeves promptly hired, the resulting film (completed in December 1957 after a three-month shoot and released in February 1958) setting the Italian box-office on fire. American producer Joseph E. Levine noted the sensation it was creating on the Continent, bought the U.S. distribution rights for $120,000 and took a gamble, lavishing $300,000 of Warner Bros.' cash on promotion and advertising, more, in fact, than *The Labor of Hercules*' original production costs. The gamble paid off, profits of over $5,000,000 rolling in when it was issued in the States in July 1959 (taking in reissues, the film's eventual profit was close to $40,000,000). A new genre was born, Reeves elevated to iconic status and later to become (with Sophia Loren) the highest paid actor in Europe—he received $10,000 for *Hercules*, his salary skyrocketing to $250,000 per picture in the 1960s. Yet he only starred in one other picture featuring the invincible demigod, 1959's *Hercules and the Queen of Lydia* (*Hercules Unchained*), claiming years later that he didn't want to be typecast, production values in the first two *Hercules* outings, in his opinion, being far superior to those that followed. Reeves' *Hercules* peplum features still remain today the two highest-grossing Italian movies ever made.

A pivotal moment in pepla then, acting as a box-office barometer for others to match, but how great, and how important to sword and sandal, is *The Labors of Hercules*? The narrative is divided up into two parts: Hercules' journey to the city of Iolcus to champion King Pelias, whose throne is in danger from usurpers; and his adventures with Jason and the Argonauts in their quest for the Golden Fleece in Colchis. The first 50 minutes moves like wildfire, Reeves first seen ripping a tree out of the ground and hurling it at Sylva Koscina's (Iola, the king's daughter) careering chariot, establishing him as one muscle-packed hero not to be messed with. As quick as one of Zeus' bolts of lightning, the pair fall in love. In Iolcus, weak-willed Pelias (Ivo Garrani), influenced by devious Eurysteus (Arturo Dominici), turns against Reeves when Iphitus, his son (Palmara), who is deeply jealous of Reeves' athletic skills, is killed by a lion (the scene where Reeves strangles the big cat was copied directly from *Samson and Delilah* and highlighted a trait of vicious cruelty toward animals found in many Italian peplum productions). Reeves is then ordered by Garrani to "meet the Cretian Bull in battle," defeating the rampaging beast but failing to win back his respect and that of Koscina, both blaming him for Palmara's death.

After 50 minutes, Reeves casts off in the *Argo* with the Argonauts in search of the Golden Fleece, Dominici aboard to stir up trouble along the way. It's on the hour that the film drags its sandals for almost 20 minutes—dropping anchor, Jason (Fabrizio Mioni) and selected crew members disembark on the Isle of Amazons, inhabited by leggy, lustful women, their leader sex-starved Queen Antea (graceful Gianna Maria Canale in her prime). Despite the natural wonders of the Monte Gelato falls making their appearance, nothing much happens, the men lounging, drinking and carousing, unaware that they're like lambs to the slaughter: Reeves and Gabriele Antonini (a youthful Ulysses) drag them back (they're all drugged) to the *Argo* and the voyage continues. On the shores of Colchis, the crew is pounced upon by a tribe of apemen (Reeves sends them scattering) and Mioni grabs the Golden Fleece, slaying the dinosaur-type monster that keeps watch over it (Godzilla's roar was used as a sound effect). On their return to Iolcus, the Argonauts discover that Dominici has stolen the Fleece; Garrani refuses to acknowledge Mioni as the rightful heir to the throne and Reeves is chained to a dungeon wall. When Garrani's cavalry attacks the Argonauts, Reeves yanks his fetters free, throttles Dominici, beats off the guards with his massive chains (Francisci accused Reeves of not trying hard enough in this scene. "If they don't get hurt, they don't get paid," he yelled) and, in another nod of gratitude to *Samson and Delilah*, brings the palace walls crashing down on the heads of the army. Garrani, guilt-ridden, drinks poison, Mioni is crowned king and Reeves and Koscina, back in each other's arms, sail off for further adventures.

Highlighted by Mario Bava's deep color schemes (especially in the cave sequences and richly detailed set design) and containing snatches of Bebe and Louis Barron's music from *Forbidden Planet* (1956) amid Enzo Masetti's rowdy score, *The Labors of Hercules* contains all the plot and narrative motifs that were to crop up on countless occasions, not only in the *Hercules* movies but in the *Maciste* features and other strongmen excursions. Here, they were fresh—later on, they would become formulaic in the extreme. *The Labors of Hercules* is quintessential Reeves (a pristine, widescreen digital makeover would be appreciated), but bettered in the follow-up, *Hercules and the Queen of Lydia*.

Spanish poster for *Pirate of the Half Moon*

Pirate of the Half Moon [*Il corsaro della mezzaluna*]

Glomer Film (Italy); Totalscope/Eastmancolor; 95 mins; Producer: Enzo Merolle; Director: Giuseppe Maria Scotese ✞✞✞

Fresh from playing Joshua in *The Ten Commandments*, American John Derek crossed the ocean to star as Nadir in Scotese's loose-at-the-seams pirate yarn, a nautical adventure ranging from lukewarm thrills to romance to semi-comedy and back again, not to be taken seriously. He's a nobleman turned corsair, on a personal calling to find the man responsible for the death of his family; information tells him that the murderer is skulking away somewhere in a coastal stronghold, so Derek and his seadogs are investigating one castle after another to flush the man out. Camillo Pilotto is Baron Alfonso di Camerlata, in charge of the fortress Derek is seeking, Captain of the Guards Alberto Farnese (Alonzo) the person he is hunting. As soon as the pirate boss ingratiates himself into the castle, posing as a stargazer, the scenario shifts from Derek making a beeline for Lady Ingeborg Schöner (Angela), whom Farnese wants to marry, to the arrival of Spanish infanta Gianna Maria Canale (Caterina) and her cortege, meeting Pilotto and his cronies who are bemoaning their lack of funds, unable to stave off a pirate attack due to lack of gunpowder. Derek shows his true colors, instructing his schooner to fire a broadside every hour, hoping this will force the baron to capitulate to his demands: Smuggle Canale aboard his ship and hold her for ransom in exchange for the man who "destroyed my family." In the fortress, Farnese threatens Schöner with life in a convent if she refuses to wed him and Canale is captured but released when Derek learns from his tortured, dying brother that Farnese is the wanted killer. In a ruse to enter the castle walls, Derek and his rovers disguise themselves as Canale's entourage, gallop into the courtyard, partake in a fight and then flee through a secret passage. King Carlo V turns up, Derek chases Farnese in a carriage, the two roll in the waves and Derek drowns his enemy: "To the sea I commit you."

It's a mildly entertaining pirate flick for a wet Sunday afternoon's viewing, directed with a lack of tension or surprise in the plot department. Derek is so-so as the dashing hero, Canale haughtily aloof playing the complaining duchess, while Farnese's villain isn't anywhere near nasty enough to hiss and boo at. Prints are hard to find—pan and scan, plus atrocious color, is what you'll get if you can obtain a copy. As we will observe throughout this book, this is the norm, rather than the exception, with movies coming under the peplum banner, a sad state of affairs that will probably never be rectified.

The Venus of Cheronea [*La venere di Cheronea*] aka ***Aphrodite, Goddess of Love***; ***Goddess of Love***

Faro Film/Prora/Rialto (Italy/France); Totalscope/Ferraniacolor; 90 (68) mins; Producer: Giampaolo Bigazzi; Directors: Fernando Cerchio, Viktor Tourjansky ✞✞✞

Basically a vehicle to promote the talents (or, more precisely, the voluptuous curves) of Rank Organization starlet Belinda Lee, *The Venus of Cheronea*'s minuscule plot revolves around three main characters: Lee (as Aphrodite), Jacques Sernas (Macedonian captain Laertes) and sculptor Massimo Girotti, playing Prassitele. Girotti is sculpting a statue of Aphrodite, using Lee as his model; Sernas, on the run from the Greeks, is wounded and found lying on a beach by Lee; taken back to hide and recover in Girotti's opulent palace, the couple falls in love, much to the anger of Girotti, who also loves her. And that's it. Enraged Girotti forces Lee to leave his home and cozies up to the Greeks, Lee dishes out her charms in a grim Greek military brothel, fending off a sea of eager, grabbing hands, while Sernas organizes a mass Macedonian offensive on the Greek regiments, reclaiming Lee as she is about to throw her

Belinda Lee poses by the shore in preparation for playing Aphrodite in *The Venus of Cheronea*.

Bring on the dancing girls! One of pepla's favorite sequences gets another airing in *Aphrodite, Goddess of Love*.

lovely body off a cliff; the pair kiss and cuddle overlooking a sunlit sea to the sound of a full orchestral fanfare.

To their credit, over this slight framework, directors Cerchio and Tourjansky weave some kind of magic. The set design is out of this world, Girotti's palace a forest of marble columns, ornamental ponds and flamboyant statues adorning each and every room, beautifully lit by cinematographer Arturo Gallea. We get to inspect Lee's naked back twice, there's one lively battle sequence to stir things up, backed by Michel Michelet's pounding drums score, and Girotti is stabbed a dozen times by Macedonian soldiers for collaborating with the enemy. On the downside, too many shots of waves crashing on rocks are inserted to hike up the dramatic romantic theme and predatory Lee looks as though she could eat vacuous Sernas for breakfast. It is possible to obtain mint-condition widescreen prints of the movie in its 87-minute edit, unfortunately in Italian with no subtitles, giving some idea of what the grandeur prevalent throughout the production appeared like on the big silver screen. Ironically, it was followed by the more extravagant (and better) *Aphrodite, Goddess of Love* in 1958, Irene Tunc starring as the woman all men desired. Devon-born Lee (this was the first of her five peplum outings) took on the roles of two other legendary temptresses, Lucretia Borgia (in 1959) and Messalina (in 1960), these parts perhaps mirroring her turbulent private life (she had a penchant for older married men). On March 12, 1961, at the age of 25, she was tragically killed in a car crash in San Bernardino, California, cutting short a film career that could have led to much greater acclaim.

1958

Aphrodite, Goddess of Love [*Afrodite, dea dell'amore*] aka ***Slave Women of Corinth***; ***Slave of the Orient***
Schermi Produzione (Italy); Schermiscope/Ferraniacolor; 91 mins; Producers: Alberto Manca, Adriano Merkel; Director: Mario Bonnard ††††

67 AD: Emperor Nero has ordered work to start on construction of the Corinth Canal, cutting the Isthmus that connects the Greek mainland to the Peloponnese Peninsula; Roman governor Ivo Garrani (Antigono) and deputy Giulio Donnini (Erasto) are in charge of the workforce, sculptor Anthony Steffen (Demetrio) assigned with the job of modeling a statue of Aphrodite in homage to the gods. Simonide's taxation laws are repealed; the Corinthian's land and homes are to be destroyed, making way for the canal, while merchants are going to have to cough up 50 percent of their revenue to help finance the project, leading to civil unrest. Anyone caught arguing will be arrested or exterminated. Cue for an epic on a grand scale, depicting the evolution of one of Rome's major engineering feats? Well, not exactly. Among a group of female slaves, bought by Arab trader Andrea Aureli, are statuesque Irene Tunc (as Diala) and Isabelle Corey (Lerna). Tunc, an arch seductress and ex-courtesan, comes to the attention of Garrani, who takes her as his mistress; Corey, a devout Christian, is hired as Tunc's handmaiden. When both women fall in love with young Steffen, jealous passions rise to the surface and we are in Roman soap opera territory, a welter of plot twists and turns, intrigues and back-stabbings making the senses whirl. The picture is nicely dressed up in Tino (Clemente) Santoni's flashy Ferraniacolor tones, Giovanni Fusco's brash score providing a lively aural surround.

Sergio Leone, as well as participating in the script, assisted Mario Bonnard on the action scenes, but although these are few and far between, the movie still holds the attention, thanks to Tunc's star turn as Steffen's muse; he plans to use her body for Aphrodite's figure, but also use Corey's for the goddess's face. Tunc dances, pouts, arches her eyebrows, flashes her legs (there's a steamy, near-nude bath scene), smothers herself in scent and twists everyone around her bejeweled fingers in her rapid rise from slave girl to Queen of Corinth, Garrani's wife (Clara Calamai) having been conveniently dispatched by arrow. Donnini lusts after her, and Bonnard introduces a "persecuted Christians" angle popular at the time with audiences (*Ben-Hur*'s entire plot was founded on this one subject). As expected, Steffen joins the Christians after Corey has elbowed boyfriend Matteo Spinola out of the way, the pair joining in prayer meetings held in a large sea-cave. Tunc enlists Donnini's aid in eradicating Corey and the Christians, throwing the lot into prison, where they will be burned to death ("What a gloomy song. When they're covered in flames, they'll sound more cheerful," sniggers Garrani when he hears the prisoners singing a sorrowful hymn). Then the plague strikes: People drop dead like flies, Tunc desperately tries to prevent the Christians from being roasted alive when she learns that Steffen is among their number and stern-faced Massimo Serato arrives from Rome to take up office; Nero has been murdered, his reign of iniquity over, and there is to be no more ill-treatment of the Christian brethren. Donnini is arrested, Garrani hits the marble floor, dead from the plague, and Tunc poisons herself; the rains come, purifying the atmosphere, and Steffen, Corey by his side, both saved from the fire, gazes upon Aphrodite's unfinished statue: "Diala. The symbol of a goddess who no longer exists," states the artist as he leads his intended bride away from the palace and Corinth.

A great cast includes Livio Lorenzon (billed as Silvio Lorenzon), peplum stalwart Carlo Tamberlani (the genre's chief character actor, along with brother Nando, when it came to portraying the elderly) and likeable John Kitzmiller, playing

An Italian poster for *Captain of Fire*

Tomoro, Tunc's black servant who sympathizes with the Christians. Talkative, maybe, but more character-driven than most peplum actioners, and, in consequence containing more depth, *Aphrodite, Goddess of Love* is lavish to look at and highly enjoyable, the equivalent of a centuries-old gossip magazine come to life on the big screen. Current VHS copies are in pristine condition, complete with subtitles.

Captain of Fire [*Capitan Fuoco*] aka *Captain Falcon*; *Robin Hood, the Rebel*

Transfilm Prod./Austria Film (Italy/France); Cinepanoramic/Ferraniacolor; 86 mins; Producer: Emimmo Salvi; Director: Carlo Campogalliani ††

Finding work difficult to come by in Hollywood, Lex Barker relocated to Europe in 1957 and resumed a successful film career on the Continent up to his untimely death from a heart attack in 1973, at only 54 years of age. *Captain of Fire*, more commonly known as *Captain Falcon*, was the first of his nine peplum feature films; it was also director Carlo Campogalliani's first in the genre. Both would do a lot better in the years ahead. Dressed in lace-up white shirt, green feather-fronted shorts, red hat and brown leather boots, Barker played Pietro, a Robin Hood-type figure (hence the German title), in the manner of a dilettante, looking as though he had just stepped out of a Manhattan gay club. Initially spotted sitting in a tree with pal Furio Meniconi, Barker gets embroiled in a plot by Massimo Serato (Baron Oddo di Serra) to grab Contessa Rossana Rory's (Elena) principality from under her dainty feet, aided by a pair of dagger-wielding thugs, Livio Lorenzon (Manfredo) and Paul Muller (Rusca), two of pepla's greatest villains. Becoming a fly in Serato's ointment, Barker is lusted after by peasant girl Anna Maria Ferrero, takes up residence in a cave, is blamed for the death of Rory's father (Herbert A.E. Bohme), tackles Serato's marauders, tries to woo the icy contessa and unites the villagers in a mission to terminate Serato's reign. The fights are slackly handled by the director, almost half-hearted attempts at swordplay, not helped by composer Carlo Innocenzi's least memorable peplum soundtrack (the opening and closing marching choral hubbub is painful to the ears). Following a lengthy skirmish on a towering cliff face beneath Barker's polystyrene grotto (Serato, not given a great deal to do in the first half, finishes off Lorenzon with an arrow, the surly captain standing in the way of his ambitions), Campogalliani, on the hour, goes for a quick wrap within the surrounds of Rory's castle, now in the hands of Serato. The baron is about to announce his marriage to the contessa, but not before Barker, tied to a stake in the center of the great hall, is almost blinded by torch flame. The rebels surge into the hall, Barker breaks loose, pasty-faced Muller (resembling a black-clad vampire) stabs Ferrero, and the Mullern receives a dagger in *his* back, and Serato stumbles onto Barker's blade in a swordfight. The curtain closes on Barker and Rory kissing as the crowds roar their approval.

Interestingly, Barker, Lorenzon and Bohme would all go on to star in *The Knight of 100 Faces* (1960), another Barker Robin Hood caper. *Captain Falcon* seems to have had all concerned trying to find their feet—Campogalliani, rather sloppy on this occasion, would direct two undisputed classics of the genre in the new decade, *Maciste in the Valley of the Kings* (*Son of Samson*, 1960) and *Ursus* (1961), while Barker displayed his energetic versatility and cheerful charisma to greater effect in productions such as *Son of the Red Corsair* (1959), *Pirates of the Coast* (1960) and *The Executioner of Venice* (1963). Adalberto "Bitto" Albertini's vivid color hues are a valid reason to watch, the noted cinematographer being one of pepla's greatest exponents of the art across a wide range of material. And the female leads should have been swapped—blonde Rory is too much of a haughty goody-goody for the likes of devil-may-care Barker; he should have ended up with the much more down-to-earth Ferrero. The movie is a light, fluffy and inconsequential stepping-off board for the leading man and director's joint career paths in peplum.

The Count of Matera—The Tyrant [*Il conte di Matera-Il tiranno*]

Romana Film (Italy); Totalscope/B&W; 85 mins; Producer: Fortunato Misiano; Director: Luigi Capuano †††

During the French-Spanish troubles of the early 1500s, Count Giovanni Carlo Tramontano, a native of St. Anastasia near Naples and up to his eyes in debt, moved his court to the province of Matera, where the over-zealous tyrant governed with a rod of iron, exacting unreasonable taxes and duties from the disgruntled populace until murdered on December 29, 1514. Luigi Capuano's movie related the true series of events in brisk fashion, peplum favorite-to-be Giacomo Rossi-Stuart (Duke Paolo), the dashing young rebel leader, coming to the aid of his sister, Wandisa Guida (Gisella), ousted from the family home with their elderly father by Otello Toso (here named Rambaldo

Wandisa Guida and Aldo Bufi Landi in *The Count of Matera—The Tyrant*

Tramontano) and his mob of bullies. Most of the action takes place inside the count's opulent castle—intrigues, plots, two graphic tortures on the wheel, daring escapes from dungeon cells and a very suggestive dance routine coming on the 25th minute, where a lass drapes her legs over Toso's quivering body. All very formulaic, but Capuano was capable enough in knowing how to put this kind of material together with verve and pace, so the action never lags, the narrative boosted by Michele Cozzoli's vibrant score. Although Tramontano was actually assassinated in an alley near the cathedral, here he's dispatched by slimy henchman Paul Muller, stabbed in the back; Muller then undergoes a five-minute duel with Rossi-Stuart, expiring on the point of his sword. Toso's daughter, Virna Lisi, is spared after the villagers have ransacked the castle, peace is restored to Matera and Rossi-Stuart marries Emilia Diaz in a mass wedding ceremony in front of a bishop and his dignitaries.

Interestingly, Capuano chose to shoot in black-and-white, using the village of Matera for location filming. Leading man Toso had worked with the director on another early peplum, *Knight of the Black Sword*, and tragically died in a car accident in 1966, at only 52 years of age.

Jerusalem Set Free [*La Gerusalemme liberata*] aka *The Mighty Crusaders*

Max Film (Italy); Supercinescope/Ferraniacolor; 97 (88) mins; Producer: Ottavio Poggi; Director: Carlo Ludovico Bragaglia †††

In the 10th year of the War of the Crusades, knights led by Francisco Rabal (Tancredi), Rik Battaglia (Rinaldo) and Philippe Hersent (Geoffrey of Bouillon) converge on Jerusalem to purge the city of occupying heathen Persians and liberate Christian hostages, without reckoning on the fact that they'll become entangled in the machinations of three beautiful conniving princesses, each capable of upsetting their battle strategies: Sylva Koscina (Clorinda, a Persian), Gianna Maria Canale (Armida, a Damascan) and Livia Contardi (Erminia, an Antiochian).

Shorn of almost 10 minutes, leading to jumps in continuity, *Jerusalem Set Free* is made further confusing by Bragaglia's uncoordinated direction, an abundance of furtive meetings jamming up the works, his camera flitting from Rabal/Koscina's numerous liaisons outside the city walls to the Battaglia/Canale relationship in Damascus. Moreover, rejected Contardi bemoans to all that she loves Rabal yet Koscina has had the audacity to steal the White Knight from her, visiting the crusaders' camp and sowing the seeds of dissension. To add to the confusion, the crusaders fall out over a vital leadership issue, Rabal riding off with his men in a huff while loose-cannon Battaglia is imprisoned in Damascus after falling foul of Canale's sudden whims and seduction techniques; if he doesn't marry her, she'll kill a Christian a day. With everything going on, it's a wonder Jerusalem was ever liberated … but it is after a storming siege involving battle towers, the Persians downing arms, suffering heavy casualties. And lovesick Contardi finally gets the man of her dreams, seen arm-in-arm with Rabal after the fighting has ceased.

Bragaglia's crusaders opus has many fine touches: Roberto Nicolosi's noisy, insistent score; combat beside Monte Gelato's waterfalls and mill buildings where Koscina meets her maker (Rabal baptizes her before she succumbs); a beautifully composed segment showing a sinewy dancer sensuously flashing her thighs against a backdrop of ornamental fountains, dripping in Eastern atmosphere; a glowering star turn from Andrea Aureli as the brutish Persian commander Koscina refuses to wed; the King of Persia's opulent palace; a slogging, sweaty duel fought with deadly mace/axe weapons between Aureli and Rabal, last-

Italian photobusta for *Jerusalem Set Free*

A French poster for *Pia of Ptolomey*

ing so long that it ends in stalemate; an uplifting ending, Christians and crusaders gathered together in prayer, a giant golden cross illuminating the sky; and Koscina, in female warrior guise, sporting mauve tights. But overall, the production carries a disconcerting air of sloppiness, leaving audiences to figure out, in many instances, exactly what is taking place (especially the pitch-black night assault by Persians on the war towers). Acting-wise, Canale's ice-cold egotistical princess triumphs over Koscina and Contardi, those sharp-as-a-knife cheekbones are set hard to perfection, while Aureli's bull-headed infidel puts Rabal and company firmly in the shade. It's good—but we are left with the feeling that more tightly edited, the movie could have been a whole lot better.

Pia of Ptolomey [*Pia de' Tolomei*]

Do.Re.Me. Roma Film/Procinex (Italy/France); Supercinescope/Ferraniacolor; 102 (95) mins; Producer: Carlo Infascelli; Director: Sergio Grieco ✞✞✞✞✞

Romeo and Juliet set in Siena, Italy, during the Middle Ages. Supposedly based on factual events, Grieco's darkly shot obscurity tells of two opposing factions, the Guelphs and the Ghibbelines, fighting for control of one of the country's wealthiest cities. Tyrannical Nello Della Pietra (a rich performance from character actor Arnoldo Foà) is ruler of the occupying forces of the Ghibbelines, lusting for power *and* winsome Guelph, Pia (Ilaria Occhini); she, in turn, loves young painter Ghino (Jacques Sernas), also a Guelph. Dressed in black and sporting red tights, a pack of vicious dogs at his heels, Foà chews the scenery, scuttling from room to room like a demented Richard III and putting to instant torture or death anybody who even dares argue with him. In the shadows lurks another of the principal players in this heated melodrama, Bella Darvi, widow of Foà's brother, who wants the blackguard all to herself. A war breaks out, Sernas leading the revolt, but the Guelphs are quashed; Occhini's father is killed, Sernas is wounded and smirking Foà orders mass executions. The despot then steals the Ptolomey family's gold to finance a new army, enslaves 500 civilians and issues the standard peplum ultimatum to Occhini: "Marry me and I'll free your people." She reluctantly agrees ("He's capable of killing them all."), thinking Sernas dead, but the painter turns up after the wedding vows, unable to believe what his eyes are seeing. At a clandestine meeting, she informs her crestfallen lover of the bald truth: "I'm tied to him forever." Scheming Darvi overhears the conversation and tells Foà who, seething with rage, immediately incarcerates his new bride in a gloomy citadel situated in murky marshland beset by storms.

It's at this 60-minute point in the film that *Pia of Ptolomey*, for the remainder of its length, takes on all the aspects of a Roger Corman Edgar Allan Poe '60s production. Saturated in Tino (Clemente) Santoni's deep mauves (shot in Ferraniacolor, a process developed in Italy that closely resembled Cinecolor and Anscocolor) and backed by Carlo Rustichelli's somber, droning tonalities which lodge themselves in the brain and won't let go, we are now firmly in Gothic mystery/romance territory, the action (if you can call it that) centered on this eerie, misty locale, and no other. The narrative becomes imbued with an air of impending calamity as Sernas manages to scale the battlements, gaining access to his beloved's cell. There's much skulking around stone corridors as a mad nun watches over the prisoner. Foà wrings his hands in anguish, missing Occhini terribly, not knowing whether he has done the right thing, while in the wings, Darvi plots to rid herself of the two lovers. It all ends in tragedy: "Duce! Duce!" wails Occhini mournfully, surreally threading her unsteady way through the bogs like a lost soul in search of Sernas. Foà confronts her in the darkness and stabs out, instantly regretting his misdeed; Sernas finds her, groaning in pain, and carries her off toward the camera, Foà and treacherous Darvi sinking to their deserved deaths in a quagmire. "Her life became a legend," intoned a voice-over at the very beginning, but what actually happened to Pia of Ptolomey is never fully explained here.

Slow-moving but dripping in haunting atmosphere (the Gothic/Renaissance set design is faultless), Sergio Grieco's emotive, long-lost mood piece may lack all-out sword and sandal thunder, but that doesn't make it any less interesting to peplum aficionados. As at the time of writing (2015), decent prints in widescreen, with subtitles, are impossible to come by. Perhaps one day …

The Pirate of the Black Hawk [*Il pirata dello sparviero nero*]

Emmepi/Comptoir Francais CFPC (Italy/France); Supercinescope/Ferraniacolor; 72 mins; Producers: Carlo and Giorgio Pescino; Director: Sergio Grieco ✞✞✞✞

Originally presented in America as a black-and-white feature in 1961 (distributed by Roger Corman's Filmgroup), Sergio Grieco's salty sea saga, set in the 15th century, can now (2015) be found online in color and widescreen. Gérard Landry starred as Riccardo, pirate captain of the *Black Hawk*, pitting his wits against Manfred, the Duke of Monteforte, who has mustered

an army of Saracen corsairs in his personal ambition to lord it over the Duchy unmolested. Andrea Aureli played Manfred with over-the-top manic glee, a performance of uncurbed ham from one of pepla's most renowned character actors, first spotted disposing of the old duke's family in a gun-blazing opening episode, except for Lady Mijanou Bardot (Brigitte Bardot's younger sister) and 12-year-old Piero Giagnoni (as Hector, her kid brother), the true heir to the monarchy. Both escape death by the skin of their teeth, thanks to Landry's intervention. During festivities (two strongmen wrestle in front of the revelers, an old peplum standby), the Saracen mogul's body is carried into the castle and dumped in front of Aureli's horrified guests; Landry has boarded the Saracens' boat and wiped them out. To get his own back, Aureli and creepy sidekick Giulio Battiferri arrange for Landry's village to be razed to the ground; the women are rounded up and cast into jail, awaiting execution if the *Black Hawk*'s boss doesn't turn himself in.

Grieco's lively confection is plot-heavy for a seafaring jaunt of this nature, no bad thing as most pirate films from this period tended to be on the lighter side. Aureli plots, schemes and cackles like a lunatic. He covets Bardot, his cousin, over mistress Pina Bottin, reckoning that wedlock to her will bring him much-needed esteem in the eyes of the populace. Bottin, aware of this, latches onto corsair betrayer Germano Longo, planning to dispose of Aureli, marry him and, in her own words, "We'll become absolute rulers." It all falls apart when the deceitful lovers are caught; Longo is run through, Bottin stabbed by Battiferri. Bardot gets hitched to Aureli, petrified of his warning ringing in her ears, "If you don't marry me, the boy (Hector) will disappear," narrowly avoiding being groped in the bridal suite and submitting to his lust by giving her repugnant new husband drugged wine before bedtime. Landry and company, disguised as French diplomats, worm their way into the castle, Battiferri smells a rat and sailor Ettore Manni, Giagnoni, Bardot and Eloisa Cianni find themselves locked in a cell slowly filling with water. Landry's buccaneers storm the battlements, Manni and company are saved from drowning, Battiferri perishes and Aureli is dragged along a beach by Landry on horseback, fetching up on a lethal barrier of spikes. Giagnoni is proclaimed the Duke of Monteforte and, job completed, Landry, Bardot, Manni and Cianni sail off toward the blue horizon to play house. All credit to composer Roberto Nicolosi for producing a memorable score to match the action in an enjoyable pirate caper whose only downside is Landry, a little too mature at 46 to be playing a chivalrous, romantic hero. Manni or Longo would have fared much better in the role.

The Revolt of the Gladiators [*La rivolta dei gladiatori*] aka *The Warrior and the Slave Girl*

Alexandra/Atenea/Comptoir Francais CFPC (Italy/Spain/France); Supercinescope/Eastmancolor; 88 mins; Producer: Virgilio De Blasi; Director: Vittorio Cottafavi ✝✝✝✝✝

An early masterwork from Cottafavi whose themes and ideas were to crop up in scores of sword and sandal feature films to come over the next seven years. A Roman (named, of course, Marcus) comes to the salvation of a repressed nation ruled by a cruel female dictator, the downtrodden people venting their hatred and frustration at the regime they are forced to live under. Ettore Manni played the upright Roman, posted to an Armenian outpost in 200 AD to quell a gladiator revolt. En route, Georges Marchal's (Asclepio) rebels ambush the squad, but they are released, Manni taking two female captives of his own, one being the slave girl of the title, tigerish Mara Cruz (Zahar). Once at his destination (the fort and pal-

A Spanish poster for *The Revolt of the Gladiators*

An Italian photobusta for *The Sword and the Cross*

The Sword and the Cross [*La spada e la croce*] aka ***Mary Magdalene***

Liber Film (Italy); Supercinescope/Ferraniacolor; 102 (88) mins; Producer: Ottavio Poggi; Director: Carlo Ludovico Bragaglia
✝✝✝

Former Hollywood screen vamp Yvonne De Carlo starred as Mary Magdalene, going from harlot to devout follower of Christ, shedding lovers like leaves in the wind when Jesus of Nazareth takes precedence over her sordid love life. An interesting but occasionally turgid take on the political, historical and religious scene at the time of emerging Christianity, De Carlo emoted like crazy as the courtesan with a conscience, flitting half-naked between the arms of earnest Roman Jorge Mistral (Caio Marcello) and hissable Massimo Serato (Anan), the nobleman who provides a roof over her lovely head in return for sexual favors. Andrea Aureli cropped up as Barabbas the thief, raiding caravans loaded with Roman tribute, while delicious Rossana Podesta played De Carlo's deeply religious (and righteous) sister Martha. Philippe Hersent was Pontius Pilate, the man trying his hardest to govern the ungovernable Jews in Jerusalem, with Rossana Rory wasted as his glamorous wife, more glamorous, it has to be whispered, than the slightly shopworn leading lady (De Carlo was 36 at the time of filming).

Among the countless movies to have been made on the life of Christ, Bragaglia's potted account of events was no better or worse than many others, reasonably exciting one minute, too pious (and therefore too boring) by far the next. It's the old cinematic trade-off—sin, without doubt, is a great deal more watchable, and bankable, than virtuousness. Hersent wants to restore military order to a population that regards the Romans as "the enemies of the Lord" and pulls down the Roman eagle in defiance; Mistral is puzzled as to exactly why the Jews get so impassioned with this strange Galilean. When De Carlo performs a highly salacious dance in front of Jesus's father, tied to a pillar in Serato's palace, the look the holy man gives her virtually paralyzes her on the spot; from then on, she rejects all men, visited by the headless spirit of Jesus on her balcony. "I love you," says De Carlo to Mistral, followed by "I want you" to Serato, ending up with "Don't touch me" to both, Jesus now the number one man in her life, especially after the proclaimed Messiah raises her brother Lazarus (Mario Girotti aka Terence Hill) from the dead ("Lazarus is saved. Your faith has saved him."). The picture closes with Jesus' crucifixion, De Carlo, a woman now free of vice, kneeling at the cross as storm clouds gather, denoting God's wrath.

Current DVD issues are pan and scan, Raffaele Masciocchi's rich color photography suffering as a result, the version 14 minutes shorter than the original. Watch out for that expansive white-stoned quarry (the old Lapilli quarry, near Lazio) and the spacious mined, square-fronted portals of the Salone caverns, also near Lazio, that Aureli and his bandits hide away in—these man-made features would appear in dozens of peplum movies over the following years, a favored haunt of Italian moviemakers, as familiar to fans of the genre as the picturesque Monte

ace are impressively constructed), the compassionate centurion frees dozens of slaves shackled in a large stone pit and becomes embroiled in intrigue and narrow escapes, Gianna Maria Canale (Princess Amira) and shifty minister Rafael Duran stirring up trouble between the Shi'ites and Armenians while administering poison to the young king, Fidel Martin (Osro); he's the main obstacle to Canale placing her shapely rear on the hot seat and has to be done away with.

Shot in bright colors by Mario Pacheco, with a standard blustering score from Roberto Nicolosi, Cottafavi's energetic caper delivers the goods at full pelt, piling on one incident after another over a commendably brief running time, cutting right back on dwarf Salvatore Furnari's loony antics (this is one of the few peplum flicks where a dwarf gets killed) to prevent hiccups in the flow. There's a much-too-realistic scuffle with a lion in the arena, head-battering gladiatorial hand-to-hand combats, an unfrequented hideout in the ornate Tomb of the Kings, where Martin is taken to recover, a scene where Cruz, tied to cell bars, is brutally lashed by Canale, and the sight of Manni's affable partner, Rafael Luis Calvo, bringing the ceiling of the prison crashing down onto the heads of the guards. It's fast and furious, Marchal joining forces with Manni's legionnaires to eliminate the Shi'ites in a pumped-up finale, Canale torn to shreds by her three pet tigers; likeable ruffian Calvo unfortunately expires from two arrow wounds, while Duran receives a dagger in the back. Martin survives his poisoning and Manni hooks up with tomcat Cruz; the picture ends with the grand funeral of Marchal, hundreds watching from the rocks as he's laid to rest in the Tomb of the Kings.

Scarcely known outside of their native Italy, directors of the caliber of Cottafavi were every bit as capable as their American counterparts, as shown by this tightly woven actioner. A veritable template for what was to follow in the Roman/Gladiator genre of pepla, *The Revolt of the Gladiators* can be obtained in a full-length pristine widescreen edition (with English dubbing) from various obscure outlets if you're prepared to hunt around for a copy.

Van Heflin, the self-proclaimed Czar Peter III, languishes behind bars in *Tempest*.

Gelato waterfalls would become.

Tempest [***La tempesta***]

Gray Film/Société Nouvelle Pathé (Italy/France); Technirama/Technicolor; 121 mins; Producer: Dino De Laurentiis; Directors: Alberto Lattuada, Michelangelo Antonioni (uncredited) ††

Distributed worldwide by Paramount, this expensive adaptation of two Alexander Pushkin tales, *A History of Pugachev* (1834) and *The Captain's Daughter* (1836), was given a critical pasting on its U.S. release in 1959. The ingredients are all set in place for a classic historical adventure to unfold on the grand scale: In Russia, 1870, Catherine II (a venomous Viveca Lindfors) rules with an iron glove. Geoffrey Horne (Piotr Griniev) is sent packing to remote Fort Bjelogorsk for being drunk on parade duty, picking up frozen Van Heflin (Pugachev) en route and reviving him with vodka and a new fur coat. Heflin is a rebel leader opposed to Lindfors' harsh measures, the self-proclaimed Czar Peter III, his people living a life of hardship under the monarch's reign, which he intends to put right. At the fort, Horne meets Captain Robert Keith's daughter, Silvana Mangano (Masha), and they fall in love, even though she's betrothed to would-be traitor Helmut Dantine. Heflin's Cossacks attack the fort and annihilate the garrison; Mangano's parents are brutally executed and Horne finds himself a pawn in the titanic struggle between Russia's two opposing political ideologies, plus having to contend with Dantine's burning hatred, the officer siding with the Cossacks, determined to claim Mangano as his own.

Aldo Tonti photographed the narrative in rich rustic colors, numerous snowy scenes resembling the covers of Christmas cards, and the enthralling six-minute battle for Fort Bjelogorsk (over 5,000 Yugoslavian soldiers were hired to take part in filming) is a humdinger, one of the genre's finest. Heflin chews the scenery, growling through a dense orange beard, and Lindfors' cold-hearted empress is as frigid as the Russian steppes. Taking these into consideration, why, then, has *Tempest* languished in the vaults (it's not officially available on disc) while other Russian-based epics such as *Doctor Zhivago* (MGM, 1965) have reaped the plaudits? The answer lies principally in the miscasting of Horne in the central role; the 25-year-old actor was deficient in both the magnetism, gravitas and presence called for, appearing to be all at sea in much of his screen time, especially when pitted against a player of Heflin's standing. He was too fresh and innocent looking to carry the picture, a babe among real dirty, begrimed fighting men, and it dragged the film down (he was just as ineffectual in 1960's *Joseph Sold By His Brothers*, although marginally better in 1961's *The Corsican Brothers*). *Tempest* also suffered from an anticlimactic ending: Following another lengthy battle in which Heflin's hordes are crushed, Horne is carted off to St. Petersburg and jailed for being a deserter and traitor, to await execution. Ice-queen Lindfors ignores Mangano's pleas for his life but finally releases him when Heflin tells her the young officer was always faithful to her cause. The curtain goes down on Heflin, in irons, shambling to the gallows. These closing scenes are drawn-out and tedious—finishing soon after that tremendous battle would have been the note to go out on, a bang instead of a whimper. It's great to look at, but one is left with the feeling that *Tempest*, despite its high production values, is one of those niggling movies that somehow misses the mark, lacking that vital spark to bring it to vibrant, memorable life and lodge it in the mind of fans. It remains unremembered to this day.

1959

The Battle of Marathon [***La battaglia di Maratona***] aka ***The Giant of Marathon***

Titanus/Lux/Galatea (Italy/France); Dyaliscope/Eastmancolor; 92 (90) mins; Producer: Bruno Vailati; Directors: Jacques Tourneur, Mario Bava †††††

Within the space of two years, Steve Reeves had become the iconic figurehead of a whole new, slightly bizarre and certainly *different* form of cinematic entertainment with which to whet a mass audience's appetite. Customers were now in a position to say, "I'm off to see the new Steve Reeves picture tonight." That's how far the ex-bodybuilder had progressed on his meteoric rise to stardom, becoming almost a household name. *The Battle of Marathon*, released worldwide by MGM as *The Giant of Marathon*, is quintessential Reeves. From that opening credits pose of him poised to throw a javelin, tanned torso and muscles rippling in the sunlight, you know that this movie, above all others, is the one that showcases that magnificent frame to its full advantage. In the United Kingdom, Tourneur and Bava's saga of Greeks in defiance of Persians narrowly escaped the prohibitive

A French poster for *The Battle of Marathon*

"X" certificate when issued in 1961 (as did Reeves' *The Terror of the Barbarians*, aka *Goliath and the Barbarians*, in 1960). With a few minor edits, it was granted an "A" classification. Tourneur fell ill during filming and couldn't cope with the action sequences; Bava, in charge of cinematography and visual effects, took over directorial duties, filming the grand battle between Greeks and Persians at five frames per second; speeded up, the result brought a frenetic energy and realism to the conflict, a blur of bodies, armor and blood, Bava in some instances deploying his camera at ground level, horses and chariots flying overhead and crashing onto sharpened stakes, taking punters by the scruff of the neck, right into the heart of the fighting instead of viewing it from the sidelines. The terrific finale, whereby Reeves and the sacred guard disable the Persian fleet by planting 30-foot sharpened stakes on the seabed to rip open the flotilla's keels, was similarly orchestrated; it's during this section that the British censor's scissors came into use, images of divers skewered on lances, the water turning crimson with blood, deemed too strong for U.K. consumption (some less-gory shots were retained in the print.)

These were the high points; in between, *The Battle of Marathon* took its time in getting off the ground in a tale (traced back to factual events circa 490 BC) of Greek Olympic champion Phillipides (Reeves) falling in love with Andromeda (a delectable Mylene Demongeot, wearing one of peplum's shortest skirts) and entreating the Spartans, Greece's sworn agressors, to come to their aid in defeating Daniele Vargas' Persian hordes. Intrigue comes in the shape of untrustworthy official Teocrito (Sergio Fantoni), cohabiting with long-suffering mistress Daniela Rocca but betrothed to Demongeot, consul Ivo Garrani's daughter; the heel wants to side with Vargas for political gain. Reeves and Demongeot meet, kiss and fall in love almost within seconds (*too* immediately, even by peplum standards!). Rocca, sick of being slapped around the face by despicable Fantoni, also loves Reeves, a romance doomed from the start; and military commander Alberto Lupo forms a regiment to combat the Persians (Lupo, Fantoni and Garrani all appeared in Anton Giulio Majano's classic horror thriller from 1960, *Seddok, Son of Satan*). The spectacular battle set piece gets underway on the 46th minute, an explosive, bloody eight-minute affair culminating in Reeves pushing huge boulders down upon Vargas' troops. Rocca is killed for spying but manages to gasp Vargas' invasion plans to Reeves, who uses his marathon skills to run the whole distance to Athens, organize the sacred guards (all 100 of them, attired in white loincloths) and forestall the Persian fleet until the Spartans (initially antagonistic to the alliance) arrive, which they do in the closing minutes. Driven back into the sea, Fantoni having fallen into the jaws of a fighting craft, the invaders leave for home, Reeves galloping off into the sunset with the blonde of his dreams (Sergio Ciani, aka Alan Steel, had a minor part as well as standing in for Reeves' body double, the second of his 14 pepla).

A fair-sized success in Britain, *The Battle of Marathon* was produced on a heftier budget than most and it shows. Set design, Bava's renowned

An Italian poster for *The Black Archer*

The Italian Peplum Phenomenon 1950-1967

photography and skill behind the camera, Roberto Nicolosi's exciting score and charismatic Reeves at the top of his game all guarantee a good time in one of the genre's key motion pictures, and one of the most memorable Reeves ever appeared in.

The Black Archer [L'arciere nero]

Diamante (Italy); Schermiscope/Ferraniacolor; 91 mins; Producer: Dino Sant'Ambrogio; Director: Piero Pierotti ✝✝ (✝✝✝✝✝ for Livio Lorenzon's performance)

There's only one reason, and one reason alone, for catching Piero Pierotti's baffling *cappa e spada*—Livio Lorenzon. Dressed entirely in black, hobbling painfully on a deformed left leg, his left arm twisted up to his chest, a small hump causing him to stoop, the veteran of 37 peplum features (he died in a traffic accident, at only 48, in 1971) chews the scenery, relegating everyone else to the role of bit player. It's a typical Lorenzon character part, that of a tyrannical despot (Lodrosio) lusting after both power and the arms of a woman who doesn't want to know, all the time scheming to have his enemies eliminated with the help of an assassin. Extremely hard to obtain nowadays, *The Black Archer*, without Lorenzon's scowling façade to prop it up, wouldn't be worth a dime: He's that good, maybe his best-ever (but least-remembered) peplum movie.

Gérard Landry plays Corrado, a man hunting for the killers of his father. Escaping from a bunch of black-gloved heavies, he encounters Gypsy Fulvia Franco at the Monte Gelato waterfalls who reads his fortune; as he rides off on her horse, ungratefully stating, "Your words are as meaningless as a flight of crows," she whispers, "Oh spirits that be, protect him. He is so young, so handsome and his heart is pure." Not altogether true. Landry was running to fat and *not* your average screen idol, too old to be playing the role of a dashing hero. Franco is arrested, interrogated and tortured by Lorenzon's hyenas, the "Devil's Hoofprint," as he is known, bemoaning his fate: "I'm less than a man and more than half a monster," a line of dialogue taken straight out of a 1940s Universal-International horror outing. And staggering around on set with the aid of a stick, he *looks* in real agony, almost sweating with exertion. His cousin, Erno Crisa, romances the Gypsy, released on condition that she work undercover to determine what those crafty insurgents are hatching at the not-so-secret discussion groups held in their rebels' den, a rowdy tavern. From there on in, we have one of those pictures where you are not quite certain who is doing what, all and sundry charging here, there and everywhere on horseback, stopping for swordfights and involving themselves in a totally incomprehensible plot. Federica Ranchi (Ginerva) is the damsel that Lorenzon, Crisa and Landry all make a beeline for (no prizes for guessing who ends up the winner), masked androgynous femme fatale Carla Strober plays a black-clad assassin and blank-faced Landry (terrible in his love scenes) reinvents himself as The Avenging Arrow, although spending most of his time mixing it with the bad guys. "Marry me and I'll spare him," spits Lorenzon to Ranchi, issuing pepla's stock ultimatum after she implores her deformed suitor not to execute her wooden-as-a-plank lover. In rides the new prince regent and Lorenzon's evil deeds (whatever they were) are exposed. Strober has a lance, complete with banner, buried in her chest, Crisa bites the dust in a duel, Franco succumbs to an arrow after telling Landry, "I shall die happy … I have always loved you Corrado. Farewell," while crippled Lorenzon, caught like a rat in a trap, scuttles down the castle steps, goes to mount his horse, gets his mal-

A French poster for *Cavalier in the Devil's Castle*

formed foot caught in the stirrup and is dragged to his death. As expected, Landry, his ripped, bloodstained shirt revealing a paunch, cradles Ranchi in his arms, the crowds cheer and to the sound of Tarcisio Fusco's music (a great score, by the way) and the action ends on the "King of the Peplum Villains" Livio Lorenzon's show, and nobody else's.

Cavalier in the Devil's Castle [Il cavaliere del castello maledetto] aka Cavalier of the Devil's Castle; Cavalier in Devil's Castle

Romana Film (Italy); Totalscope/Ferraniacolor; 86 (80) mins; Producer: Fortunato Misiano; Director: Mario Costa ✝✝✝

In medieval Italy, heinous Massimo Serato (Captain Ugone) and unprincipled Livio Lorenzon (Guidobaldo) are running the population ragged: Taxes are hiked up to ridiculous levels, crops are demanded for the aristocracy and revenue from sales goes straight into Lorenzon's coffers. But the downtrodden peasants have their own knight in shining armor in the form of The Masked Cavalier, a mysterious protector wearing a full-faced steel helmet who leaps to their rescue at any given moment, wielding his deadly blade and staging a revolt, picking off Serato's men like flies. As well as trying to cope with this enigmatic nuisance, Serato is desperate to marry his cousin, Luisella Boni (Contessa Isabella), to form a union between their respective provinces, cold-shouldering mistress Irene Tunc, the woman bristling with indignation as she watches her smarmy lover make plans to wed less-than-enthusiastic Boni behind her back.

That's the plot in a nutshell, a standard peplum costume *cappa e spada* before the genre got into full swing a year later.

Boni's father is incarcerated in a dungeon under threat of death, Serato lying to her as to his whereabouts by blaming his disappearance on The Masked Cavalier. Lorenzon prowls around his decorative palace rooms doing very little besides glare and growl, and The Masked Cavalier leads a posse of Serato's men into a gorge where they're wiped out by spears, arrows, boulders and fire. Court prankster-cum-minstrel Luciano Marin (Gianetto) unveils himself as the more masculine Masked Cavalier in the closing minutes ("You masked blaggard!" roars Serato), as Lorenzon receives a fatal sword thrust and Tunc wedges a dagger into Serato's back, his just reward for two-timing her. And Marin winds up with Boni as his new bride, even if the reticent damsel has only set eyes on him a couple of times in his more immature moments (without that cumbersome helmet concealing those boyish features).

Mario Costa directed this frothy confection with fervor, inserting sporadic bouts of swordplay to cover over the cracks in the paper-thin plot, one-dimensional characters and clichéd dialogue. Michele Cozzoli's music also lifted the movie out of the rut. Unfortunately, prints in Ferraniacolor and Totalscope are no longer available; rough-looking DVD copies come in monochrome, veteran cinematographer Augusto Tiezzi's work (he participated in over 20 peplum features) lost to the fans, a situation that has befallen many films included in this book and, again, one that will probably never be remedied.

The Devil's Cavaliers [*I cavalieri del diavolo*]

Galassia Cinematografica (Italy); Eastmancolor; 92 (83) mins; Producers: Argy and Edoardo Robelli; Director: Siro Marcellini ✝✝✝

Frank Latimore took on the lead role in Siro Marcellini's heavy-footed swashbuckler, the plotline (not yet stale) of which would feature in scores of similar movies churned out during the oncoming decade. Adventurer Latimore (Captain Richard Stiller) and his small band of rowdy mercenaries return from a 10-year war to France, coming to the aid of Contessa Emma Danieli (Louisa) after she falls from her bolting horse ("Richard! You are my Saint George," she simpers at him in an awful [to U.K. ears] twee English-dubbed accent). The blossoming Latimore/Danieli relationship (they're first seen smooching by the Monte Gelato falls, then dancing at a palace ball) arouses the envy of Andrea Aureli (the Duke De Vas); he's busy climbing the ladder of power in his black tights to gain absolute rule of the province alongside ambitious cousin Baroness Gianna Maria Canale (Elaine), desiring the blonde contessa's hand in marriage as the icing on his cake; Aureli views Latimore as "the obstacle in my plans" in overthrowing the King of France. Fencing champion Andrea Fantasia is unable to finish Latimore off, but when the captain is wounded in a swordfight, he's cared for in a castle storeroom, first by Danieli, then by Canale, who hankers after him. In the 38th minute, Canale is shot dead, a real shame that this highly watchable actress has to leave the scenario so abruptly (wide-eyed but vacuous Daniele is certainly no match for her lofty virtuosity); Daniele and her brother, Anthony Steffen, are tried and found guilty of murder. Latimore and his men (Mirko Ellis and José Jaspe are two of the rogues) are holed up in a convent under surveillance, but Latimore sneaks out and heads for the castle where he's arrested, ending up chained to the wall in a torture chamber, Danieli subjected to peplum's prime threat from Aureli: "Marry me, and his life will be spared." Ellis, Jaspe and company escape from the convent via a rope, free their leader and, in a fracas, Aureli's lieutenant, Franco Fantasia, is run through (brother Andrea has already been taken care of). The movie picks up in the finale, a rousing jousting tournament to judge who is top dog: Latimore (gold armor) and Aureli (black armor) slug it out (that armor must have been heavy, judging by the exhaustion on the participant's faces) until the dastardly duke bites the dust. The final shot is of Latimore, Danieli and comrades riding off down an avenue of trees into the sunset.

An Italian photobusta for *The Devil's Cavaliers*

Strikingly filmed at the Castello di Ostia near Rome, *The Devil's Cavaliers* is difficult to obtain these days, Luciano Trasatti's photography reduced to a pink/mauve-tinged parody of what it once was. Carmine Rizzo's score pummels along in the background, doing its best to energize an indifferent performance from Latimore. The easygoing American starred in 10 peplum movies, beginning in 1952 with Carlo Ludovico Bragaglia's *At Sword's Edge*, finding his career niche in the overseas film market rather than the United States. Here, he's merely adequate; a host of future peplum stars would outshine him in this kind of actioner. A side note: Andrea and Franco Fantasia are listed in the credits as "fencing masters." The acting brothers were both highly proficient in the art of swordplay and taught many of their fellow players how to wield a rapier. (Franco instructed most of his *El Cid* co-stars on how to handle a sword.)

A Spanish lobby card for *Hadji Murad The White Devil*

Hadji Murad The White Devil [*Agi Murad il diavolo bianco*] aka *The White Warrior*

Majestic Film/Lovcen Film (Italy/Yugoslavia); Dyaliscope/Technicolor; 91 (85) mins; Producer: Mario Zama; Director: Riccardo Freda ††

Adapted from Leo Tolstoy's final novel, written between 1896-1904, which in turn was founded on the exploits of a legendary Chechen figurehead, Riccardo Freda's beautiful-to-look-at historical essay (photography: Mario Bava), distributed worldwide by Warner Bros., was dialogue-driven, short on action and slow-moving. Freda had four assistant directors working with him: Bava, uncredited, was one, Leopoldo Savona another; it was Savona who cooperated with Freda on 1961's *The Mongols*. Bava's imaginative color schemes, as expected, enriched each frame of film (the hunt for Steve Reeves in the forest, sunlight streaming through the trees, is visually breathtaking). But perhaps Freda and Bava were not ideally suited to the standard peplum all-action format; true, they brought a certain depth of character and artistic integrity to the genre and, in doing so, transcended the usual sword and sandal clichés, but at the expense of blood and thunder, and blood and thunder is what audiences of the day required for their money, not endless bouts of speech, however artistically creative those talkative sequences might have been. In this respect, *Hadji Murad The White Devil* would have had a paying audience shifting around in their seats, waiting for things to spring into life; ultimately, they were to be left discontented (Reeves relates how he sat around a campfire with seven of his co-stars who spoke in Italian, Yugoslav, Serb and other assorted languages; yet this disparity in dialects never prevented them from acting off each other for the good of the production).

Set in the Caucasus region, 1850, Steve Reeves played the titular hero, a widower leading his Chechen fighters against the might of Russia, ruled by Tsar Nicholas I (Milivoje Zivanovic). King Shamil (Nikola Popvic) treats Reeves like a son, agreeing that in order to gain control of the Black Mountains, war must continue to be waged. Tribal chieftain Renato Baldini (Ahmed Khan) hovers in the background, desiring both the throne and Reeves' promised woman, Giorgia Moll (Sultanet), detesting his rival's popularity. The only slice of action occurs after 25 minutes: Reeves' rebels successfully attack the fortress of Tabarasan, dynamiting its foundations and wiping out the garrison, over and done with in five hectic minutes. Back in the Chechen stronghold, Freda lays on one of pepla's weirdest dance routines during a celebratory feast, three minutes of madcap prancing by men and women armed with swords, backed by an equally odd Russian-type tune from Roberto Nicolosi. It's here that Reeves strips off to reveal the physique that propelled him to stardom, wrestling with a fellow strongman. He then falls out with Popvic over the ill-treatment of prisoners, rides off with a splinter group, is caught by Gérard Herter's (Prince Sergi Vorontzov) hyenas in a forest, shot twice, pinioned on the ground by a dozen bayonets (that archetypal peplum image) and taken to Russian headquarters where he's tortured (whip and poker) in an attempt to force his signature on a peace agreement. Meanwhile, Baldini murders Popvic, plumps his backside on the throne and threatens to behead Reeves' 12-year-old son if Moll doesn't marry him. After extricating himself from the sensuous charms of Scilla Gabel, married to stuffed-shirt martinet Herter and longing for the Chechen leader's muscular arms to enfold her, Reeves jumps through a window with a pal, rides through a packed ballroom, throws Gabel a yellow flower in fond remembrance of a love that could never be and heads for the hills, rallying together a powerful force. His men burst in on Baldini's wedding ceremony. In a struggle over a rocky cliff, Baldini and Reeves slug it out, the bogus king slain by Reeves whose son is released. The picture closes with Reeves carrying Moll in his arms, marching toward the camera to tumultuous cheering from his devoted supporters.

Hannibal [*Annibale*]

Liber Film (Italy); Supercinescope/Eastmancolor; 100 (95) mins; Producer: Ottavio Poggi; Directors: Carlo Ludovico Bragaglia, Edgar G. Ulmer ††

Almost as heavy going as the initial 14-minute trek over the Alps, *Hannibal* is a stodgy mini-epic that fails to catch fire and set the screen ablaze as it should. Victor Mature wasn't a lover of his own work and as Hannibal, the Carthaginian warrior who took on the might of Imperial Rome with 20,000 men plus a herd of elephants in 218 BC during the Second Punic War, he's solid but stiff, especially in his passionless love scenes with Roman lady Rita Gam (as Sylvia). Hannibal inflicted upon the Roman army their heaviest defeat of all time, at the Battle of Cannae in 216 BC, and it's this mighty 12-minute conflict, directed by Carlo Ludovico Bragaglia, that, not before time, breathes life into a static narrative flatly handled by Edgar G. Ulmer, doyen of countless American B-movies and an odd choice to participate

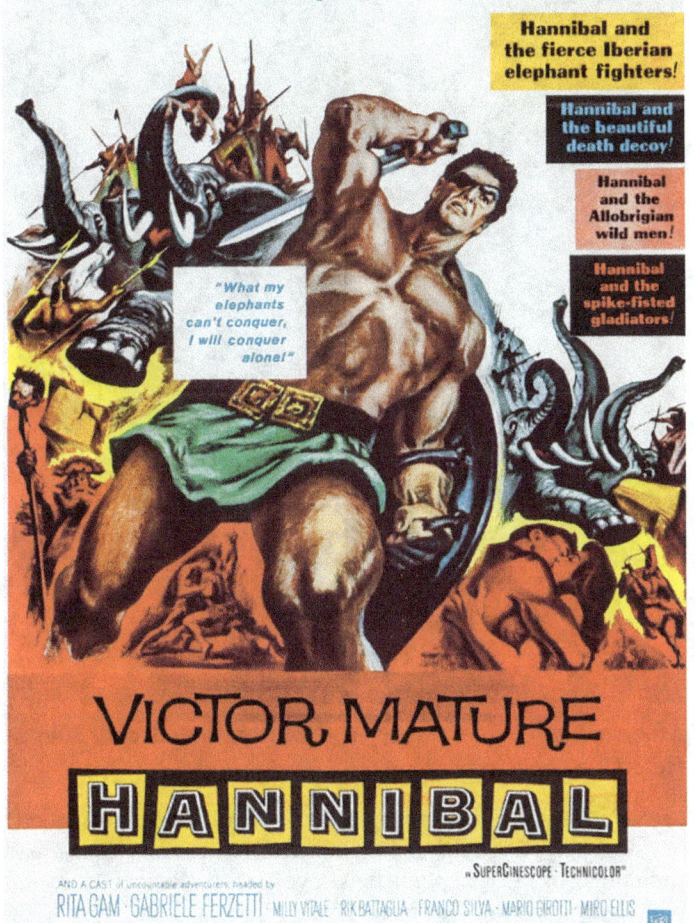

The mighty Steve Reeves flexes his muscles in Pietro Francisci's classic *Hercules and the Queen of Lydia*, one of the finest peplum features ever made.

in a picture of this nature, budgeted at $750,000.

That first segment plays almost like a silent movie, men and elephants struggling up precipitous, snow-covered slopes in driving sleet, some falling to their deaths (wolves feast on the corpses), others perishing through hunger and exhaustion, all to the sound of the keening wind and captains shouting "Keep moving." In Rome, consul Gabriele Ferzetti (Fabius Maximus) refuses to believe that Mature can pull off such a feat ("Only a madman could cross the Alps."); when news comes through that the Carthaginians are encamped on the hillside above the city, mobilization takes place, every man available to be drafted into the units. At this juncture in the proceedings, Ulmer introduces an unlikely romance between Mature and captive Gam, a liaison strongly opposed by his brothers, Rik Battaglia and Mirko Ellis, and Lieutenant Franco Silva. Gam is also lusted after by Roman soldier Terence Hill (billed as Mario Girotti) but he's much too immature for her tastes, likening him to a brother, not a potential lover. Silva even tries to manipulate stampeding elephants to trample the temptress to death, to no avail, while Ferzetti threatens her with banishment to the Temple of Vesta if she doesn't put a stop to all this nonsense. There follows that colossal battle, the Roman legions caught in a pincer movement and massacred, the riverbanks littered with their dead. Hill is slain, Silva decapitated and Gam, walking out on Mature because his estranged wife (Milly Vitale) has turned up with their young son, sentenced to be buried alive for fraternizing with the enemy; Ferzetti gives her poison to drink to lessen the ordeal. The movie ends with a narrator stating that Hannibal fought on for years, his son, who didn't follow in his father's footsteps, never knowing the bitterness (and loneliness) of command.

Unusually for a composer of his stature, Carlo Rustichelli provides a listless score that meanders along rather than nailing the action; in compensation, Raffaele Masciocchi's color photography is diamond sharp throughout. Sporting a black eye patch in the film's second half, Mature's heavy features remain frozen in time; he hardly smiles at all, not even when in a clinch with the delectable Gam. True, his size alone (and box-office clout) virtually guaranteed that he could carry a production on his broad shoulders, but if only he had put just a little bit more elbow grease into the role of one of history's greatest military commanders instead of making Hannibal appear like a six-foot-two-inch bore …

Hercules and the Queen of Lydia [*Ercole e la regina di Lidia*] aka **Hercules Unchained**

Galatea/Lux Film (Italy/France); Dyaliscope/Eastmancolor; 105 (96) mins; Producer: Bruno Vailati; Director: Pietro Francisci ✝✝✝✝✝

More tightly constructed than *The Labors of Hercules*, Steve Reeves' second appearance as the mythical he-man was a huge commercial success outside of Italy—and the critics took kindly to it as well. Pietro Francisci, spurred on by the trium-

The Italian Peplum Phenomenon 1950-1967

phant reception lavished on his first *Hercules* feature, seemed to have hit his stride, fashioning an invigorating concoction in which Reeves is caught up in a war of wits between two mentally unstable brothers, Mimmo Palmara (Polynices) and Sergio Fantoni (Eteocles). Fantoni is ruling Thebes, but for a year only: Under a pact made with Cesare Fantoni (Sergio's real-life father, playing Oedipus), it's now Palmara's turn to be king. The trouble is, Fantoni, behaving like a spoiled brat, doesn't want to relinquish the reins of power, too busy enjoying the sight of tigers mauling his enemies. As a result, Palmara's Argive forces are amassing to attack the city in six days, if Fantoni refuses to change his mind. En route to Thebes with Gabriele Antonini (Ulysses) and new bride Sylva Koscina (Iola), Reeves tussles with strongman Primo Carnera (Anteo the Giant), throwing him into a lake to defeat him (he's an Earth god). In Thebes, Fantoni accedes to Palmara's wishes, Reeves and Antonini heading back to Palmara's camp clutching a signed pledge. Stopping at a cave entrance, Reeves drinks the water of forgetfulness issuing from a carved face's eye; drugged, he's taken by boat to the Kingdom of Lydia and we enter a different phase of the narrative. Queen Omphale, played by utterly gorgeous Sylvia Lopez (she tragically died nine months after the film's release), uses her seductive charms to take on lovers, kill them and embalm their bodies. Reeves, not knowing who he is or what mission he's on, falls under her spell, Antonini pretending to be a deaf-mute to avoid being put to the sword. Languid smooching sessions beside Monte Gelato's striking cascades, X-rated pagan dances, Antonini trying to convince Reeves he's the mighty Hercules; yes, the pace slows, but the overall look is wonderful, Lopez's crystalline grotto domain beautifully lit by Mario Bava in a riot of dazzling colors, like the inside of a jewel box. It may be talkative, but Reeves seizes the chance to get under his character's skin, and those atmospheric, dazzling sets hold the attention and imagination throughout.

Once Reeves regains his memory (Lopez, in love with him, throws herself into a pool of blue embalming fluid in anguish at her loss), it's all systems go. Teaming up with the Argonauts, Reeves is enraged when mad Fantoni throws Koscina's family off the top of the city walls; entering the city, he wrestles with three ferocious tigers, smashing down a huge door to free prisoners, while outside, the two unhinged brothers decide to settle matters once and for all in a duel to the death, both expiring in a bloody clash fought with spears and axes, watched by cheering thousands. In the ensuing battle, Reeves, manning a chariot, pulls down three war towers (a terrific action sequence), Theban archers decimating Palmara's Argive warriors who turn tail and run; Reeves is reunited with Koscina as Carlo D'Angelo (Creonte, the High Priest) becomes ruler of Thebes, peace having been restored.

Big in scale, particularly the momentous end skirmish, and well-acted by the entire ensemble (Enzo Masetti's pumping score keeps things moving), *Hercules and the Queen of Lydia* is classic torch and toga entertainment, Reeves on spellbinding form; he chose to bow out of the *Hercules* franchise after this one, vowing he wouldn't go on playing the same character to the point where audiences became indifferent (future peplum star Sergio Ciani stood in for his body double in some scenes). Although a plethora of other beefcake actors took on the role over the next 16 entries, Reeves, above all others, is forever associated with the part, a testament to his screen charisma, handsome looks and legendary physique, attributes that brought Italian peplum to the attention of appreciative worldwide cinemagoers; he, alone, displayed the genre banner on his broader-than-broad shoulders. In most peplum fans' eyes, Steve Reeves was, and will always remain, *the* Hercules!

Alberto Lupo and Sandra Milo play husband and wife in *Herod the Great*.

Herod the Great [Erode il grande]
Vic/Faro/Explorer Film '58 (Italy/France); Totalscope/Eastmancolor; 93 (80) mins; Producers: Viktor Tourjansky, Giampaolo Bigazzi, Umberto Falciani, Piero Ghione; Director: Viktor Tourjansky (as Arnaldo Genoino) ♱♱♱

If you're an out-and-out action fan, look no further—*Herod the Great* contains no action scenes, not even a single sword/fistfight. Instead, it's a peplum biopic, detailing the final years of Herod, the paranoiac King of Judaea who had more to contend with in his own court than out on the battlefield, facing the Romans. The film is overloaded with intrigue, plotting and counterplotting, presented in an atmosphere of intimacy, as Herod manipulates his way through an entourage that would give a nest of vipers a bad name. Edmund Purdom starred as Herod and hammed the part up for all it was worth, a glorious, barnstorming performance depicting a troubled overlord teetering on the edge of self-doubt, depression and angst, never quite sure who is on his side, and who isn't. Within the realms of pepla, it remains one of the actor's most vital roles.

Marc Antony has committed suicide following his scandalous affair with Cleopatra; Commander Octavian (Massimo Girotti) is marching on Jerusalem to oust Purdom. The Jews are in revolt over Purdom's roughhouse measures and the king's armies have just suffered catastrophic losses at the Battle of Actium. "My kingdom is in ruins," moans Purdom in his magnificent stonewalled palace. "The city is waiting for my death." Miriam, his flame-haired wife, played by Sylvia Lopez (the ravishing actress whose wanton looks positively glowed and tragically died in 1959 from leukemia at only 26, having made only eight pictures, three of which were pepla) persuades Purdom, his mind "poisoned with suspicion," to meet Girotti and attempt to form a peace pact, thus setting in motion a convoluted chain of events that, while bereft on action, is wordy and involving to those who appreciate good old-fashioned melodrama. Lopez's black-clad witch of a mother, Elena Zareschi, spreads a vicious rumor that Purdom has been murdered by the Romans in an attempt to place her son, Andrea Giordana, on the throne; Purdom's craven, conniving son from a previous marriage (Corrado Pani) spreads a further lie that Purdom's trusted friend, Alberto Lupo, Captain Aronne of the Royal Guards, had a fling with Lopez and therefore, by default, she's an adulteress; Purdom, on his way to liaise with the Romans, instructs Lupo to kill Lopez *if* he is executed on Girotti's orders so they can be together in the afterlife, a fact twisted by Pani and related to Lopez in the form of a death threat, not as an act of love; Pani himself covets that throne; and Lupo, bad-mouthed and disgraced, is replaced as captain of the guards. When Purdom returns to the city (Girotti releases him to retain peace in Judaea) just as Giordana is about to be crowned, all hell breaks loose. Giordana is drowned in an ornamental pool (on Purdom's orders), Lopez rejects Purdom's advances ("I married a monster!") and Purdom, the seeds of doubt planted in his mind by his son, accuses his wife of adultery; she's subsequently stoned to death. Lupo is tortured with a red-hot poker but escapes from prison with the aid of his wife (Sandra Milo) and Pani (he bribes a guard, but then stabs him to maintain secrecy), and Purdom strangles the detestable Pani during a thunderstorm ("She was innocent! And you knew it!"). After dispatching a few treacherous lieutenants, Purdom gives the infamous instruction to "Kill all the newborn" on the eve of the birth of the new Messiah. Alone in his vast palace, his baby son gone, along with his empire, his beloved wife no more, Purdom succumbs to madness, collapsing on the court steps in agonizing death (Herod actually died from kidney failure in 4 BC, aged 70).

Carlo Savina's resounding score, Massimo Dallamano's brash cinematography and Russian director Viktor Tourjansky's deft handling of his material combine to lift this slab of Biblical history out of the rut of ordinariness into something just that little bit special. The entire cast act their socks off, especially Purdom and Lopez, the doomed couple setting the screen on fire with a mixture of inflamed passion, unbridled lust and mutual distrust. And in the incisive script (four writers contributed, including Tourjansky) Purdom speaks the standout line: "There is no room for weakness in this world. One must strike first, or be destroyed," a sentiment echoed through the centuries to this day.

Judith and Holofernes [*Giuditta e Oloferne*] aka *Head of a Tyrant*

Explorer Film '58/Faro (Italy/France); Totalscope/Ferraniacolor; 95 mins; Producer: Piero Ghione; Director: Fernando

Isabelle Corey with Massimo Girotti in an American lobby card for *Judith and Holofernes* (aka *Head of a Tyrant*)

Cerchio †††††

The Book of Judith in the Catholic Old Testament relates how Judith, a sexually charismatic Jewess, saved the city of Bethulia and its people from destruction by becoming Assyrian commander Holofernes' concubine, then cutting off the demigod's head, causing the enemy to flee the city in terror. Fernando Cerchio's telling of the events mixed Biblical fact with fiction by necessity (as most productions derived from the Bible do) in order to add spice to the fable, thereby making the picture more palatable to an audience. *Judith and Holofernes* is one of the more talkative of the pre-1960 pepla, based on Christian Friedrich Hebbel's 1840 tragedy *Judith*; four scriptwriters, including Cerchio and future hack director Guido Malatesta, came up with an educated screenplay that avoided the clichés, concentrating on the intense, short-lived relationship between Judith (Isabelle Corey) and Holofernes (Massimo Girotti). Unfortunately, due to the passage of time, Pier Ludovico Pavoni's color photography has suffered greatly on obscure DVD copies, the Ferraniacolor hues reduced to a muddy green in many sequences, although glimpsed on occasion. However, Carlo Savina's strident score (he composed 22 peplum soundtracks between 1959-1966), a tremendous backbone on which to enact the tragedy and believable performances from the entire cast, goes to make *Judith and Holofernes* a worthwhile experience to savor. Admittedly, Cerchio's involving movie is short on blood and guts action, but once in a while, it's a pleasure to escape the hue and cry of battle and indulge in ancient, intimate human drama, which is what Cerchio's feature is all about.

Girotti and his battle-hardened Assyrian plunderers, weary after three years of fighting, troop into Bethulia and take instant control on orders from King Nebuchadnezzar of Nineveh, demanding hospitality from the Council of Elders, the militia to be disbanded and the Assyrian god Ashur to be bowed down to, otherwise the city and its inhabitants will suffer dire consequences. Bethulia is now part of the great Assyrian Empire, he announces ("I now command you."): its people, its livestock, its property, its wealth. All his to do with whatever he so desires. Anyone foolish enough to disobey these regulations will be put to death and, to prove his word on the matter, three members of a household are dragged before his feet and dispatched with arrows. Gianni Rizzo, a servile toad-like merchant (Ozia) and wife Yvette Masson (Rispa) suck up to the enemy to save their own skins while the Jews, worried, start to organize a revolt led by Ricardo Valle (Isaac), given urgency when three palace sentries are found murdered. Girotti, resentful of all the simmering hatred aimed in his direction, has a proclamation read out in the streets: If, within four days, the assassins guilty of this crime refuse to give themselves up, Bethulia will be razed to the ground and every single citizen—man, woman, child—put to the sword. Corey, betrothed to kindly boyhood sweetheart Leonardo Botta (Gabriel), hatches a plan, deciding to worm her way into the palace, befriend the dictator, overcome his willpower, climb into his bed and murder him when his defenses are down. By doing so, she will become a divine saint, the most revered woman in all of Israel. But in her careful deliberations, Corey hasn't banked on that modern-day term "Fatal Attraction." Tarting herself up to the nines, she enters the palace, gyrates her torso through a teasing dance routine before Girotti, gets the iron-faced chief on his own, tells him that she wants to be his slave girl and promptly, against the grain, falls in lust with the muscular, battle-scarred warlord. The Jewess is now faced with a dilemma never before encountered in her chaste life: Does she proceed in her mission and kill a man she is beginning to understand, like and even love, or does she go away with him after he's conquered Egypt, to live, as he yearns for deep down, a peaceful existence near the sea?

An Italian photobusta for *The Kings of France* showing Chelo Alonso in her full glory

Granted, Corey and Girotti (his voice was dubbed by Frank Latimore) are no Elizabeth Taylor and Richard Burton, but their scenes together are charged with a certain degree of electricity, especially the moment when she approaches his sleeping form, dagger poised to strike, but can't carry it through, her emotions at the boiling point. The closer they get, the barriers coming down, the more he opens up. He's sick of war and wants it to end, dreaming of an all-encompassing Assyrian nation and admiring her courage ("You came here to kill me," he growls, handing her a short sword to call her bluff); they kiss, she responds, then backs off, crying, "I hate you! I hate you!" when, in fact, she feels the opposite. "You attract me," he admits, stating, "Its force which is the only law" when Corey pleads for him to show pity and cancel his order for the massacre deadline. Girotti even tells Corey to run away with Botta (who's horrified at his beloved's wanton behavior: "She's moved in with him!") to save themselves. "He's capable of forgiveness. I can make him change," the Jewess says to Botta, electing to stay with the Assyrian leader; they kiss feverishly, the girl turned on by his rough macho charm ("I love someone I don't even know," she muses, afterwards). Corey, bedecked in finery as a queen, moans, "I can't follow you and leave behind a cemetery," when Girotti asks her to be at his side when his army leaves for Egypt. Meanwhile, slimy Rizzo is murdered after being unearthed as a spy and Girotti's deputy, Renato Baldini, is both puzzled and angry at his master's softening attitude. "The soldiers are whispering," he informs Girotti who thunders back, "Who accuses me of weakness?" During a night of passion, the warlord, dozing and restful, whispers, "One day, we will sail together. I want to be with you," but in the morning, Corey, fighting her innermost sexual cravings for her fearsome lover *and* revulsion, delivers the final blow, knowing that his order for the slaughter of the innocents will proceed. ("That's the law of war. I must do it for the soldiers. Do you hate me?") On the palace steps, she holds high the decapitated head of the tyrant as twin thunderbolts crash to the ground; the watching troops scatter in abject horror at the sacrilegious loss of their chieftain, hounded out of the city by the Jews. In the palace, Corey, sobbing, declares to her friends that she's cursed in God's eyes for having slept with Girotti. "He was a monster," states Botta. "That monster. I loved him then. And I belong to him now," Corey wails, unable to come to terms with what she has done. But when her little brother wanders in, and the cheering crowds announce her as their savior, she finally realizes that her brutal act has saved the lives of thousands of people. With her family in tow, she leaves the city and returns home.

The Kings of France [*I reali di Francia*] aka **Attack of the Moors**

Schermi Produzione (Italy); Dyaliscope/Ferraniacolor; 88 (80) mins; Producer: Alberto Manca; Director: Mario Costa ✠✠✠✠

Chelo Alonso received top billing in Mario Costa's hokey medieval costumer but didn't get to perform one of her torrid dance routines; this was left to Gypsy girl Liana Orfei. In the 1400s, the Moors, led by Cesare Fantoni, are encroaching on Spanish and French soil, the movie opening with Rik Battaglia and Andrea Scotti (playing a French Lancelot) galloping to the Chateau Roux with the royal children, rescuing two Gypsies (Franco Fantasia and Gino Marturano) en route; the pair are about to be burned at the stake for thieving. Battaglia, Scotti and their Gypsy chums then become embroiled in one hair-raising stunt after another as they attempt to prevent the Warriors of

Islam from overrunning their lands.

Costa refuses to ease his foot off the accelerator pedal, the action unrelenting. Alonso, playing Moorish Princess Suleima, is captured by Battaglia (Roland), held as a hostage to guarantee the safety of the Royal family; Captain Gérard Landry is a betrayer, taking up with the Moors and murdering the French duke (Carlo Tamberlani) to enable him to rule the realm. Orfei (Jitana) falls in love with Battaglia ("My wonderful knight.") but he only has eyes for exotic Alonso; peplum's most instantly recognizable permanent fixture, Livio Lorenzon (as Basirocco), his characteristic bald head hidden under a flamboyant headpiece, strangles Fantoni (Alonso's assumed father) and assumes control of the Moorish forces. Scotti courts winsome aristocrat Luisella Boni. Unfortunately, composer Carlo Innocenzi (21 peplum scores from 1958 to 1962) creates an absolute racket with his soundtrack, the music raising the decibel count to uncomfortable levels, and hard-to-find DVDs have English dubbing clumsily overlaying the original Italian dialogue to the extent that you can hear both languages. "Marry me and you'll live," growls Lorenzon to Alonso who, in fact, is the daughter of a Spanish nobleman, not an Islamic heathen, and therefore a Christian (Lorenzon and Alonso disliked each other on and off set). Swordfights, clashes, romance, hidden fortress galleries, forest glades, Battaglia charging around in armor and heraldic knights in swanky regalia are set against the majestic backdrop of Northern Italy's fabulous Fenis Castle, the entire package dressed up in Augusto Tiezzi's lustrous cinematography. *The Kings of France* will appeal to everyone from eight to 80 or to those yearning for an entertaining knights and castle opus the way they used to make 'em. In the end, the infidels defeated, the King of France bestows honors on the entire cast, the Gypsy rogues are handed purses of gold, Scotti prepares to marry Boni and Battaglia (wooden but competent enough) announces that Alonso, trading in her black Moorish costume for a white virginal dress, will be his new countess.

An Italian photobusta for *Knight Without a Country*

Knight Without a Country [*Il cavaliere senza terra*]

Diamante (Italy); Cinepanoramic/Ferraniacolor; 86 (81) mins; Produced and Directed by Giacomo Gentilomo ††

Returning home from the wars, knight-cum-soldier of fortune Rolando (Gérard Landry) and his small band of fellow servicemen find monasteries and convents locked and barred to the public—a friar tells him that Rizziero, the Duke of Villalta (Franco Fantasia), now rules the land with a fist of iron and has ordered their closure ("A danger to us all!"). He's also planning to murder the King of France and place himself on the royal throne. Landry quickly gets to work—disguised as a turbaned merchant selling clothes and wares to two fine-looking contessas trapped inside Fantasia's castle, he infiltrates the fortress to try to figure out what's going on. Valeria Fabrizi (Contessa di Holten) loves Giacomo Rossi-Stuart (Ruggero), the other (Constance Smith as Laura, marriage material for Fantasia's ambitions) will very soon get to love Landry, her savior (and maid Wandisa Guida makes up a third beauty). Dressed to resemble a boy, Smith attempts an escape but fails—Landry then gains entrance to the castle, meets Smith and smuggles her out a second time. Enlisting rogue José Jaspe after defeating him in a duel out on the road, Landry, Rossi-Stuart and company hatch a plot to overthrow the tyrant, the arrival of suspicious captain Alberto Farnese precipitating Fantasia's eventual downfall. During a banquet in honor of the French monarch's visit, Landry, Rossi-Stuart and Jaspe are imprisoned below in a rapidly flooding cell. Breaking out, Landry thwarts the assassin who is about to plunge a dagger into the king's back. A furious bout of swordplay within the courtyard ends with Fantasia's demise; Landry is awarded the title of Knight of France by the king and gallops off with Smith and his compatriots.

Brightly photographed by Anchise Brizzi in the surrounds of the Castello di Ostia near Rome, *Knight Without a Country* is a static swashbuckler that contains very few action moments, simply a lot of talk and discussion. This review has been culled from a 20-minute film clip that was online in 2014, together with photobustas, stills, posters and a French Cinefoto book dating from 1959; as of April 2015, the movie is unavailable on tape or disc. Some online sites quote Alberto Farnese as playing Rizziero, which is incorrect; Fantasia was the villainous count (the two actors bore a slight resemblance to one another). And Fabrizi had a much bigger role than Guida, contrary to Internet cast/character listings. A stated running time of 111 minutes appears overly optimistic in view of the content; other sources put the length at 81-86 minutes. Will *Knight Without a Country* ever see the light of day? One can only hope and pray that it will.

The Last Days of Pompeii [*Gli ultimi giorni di Pompei*]

CI.AS./Domiciana/Procusa (Italy/Spain/West Germany); Supertotalscope/Eastmancolor; 103 (96) mins; Producer: Paolo Moffa; Directors: Mario Bonnard, Sergio Leone ††††

Adapted from Edward George Bulwer-Lytton's famous

An Italian poster for *The Last Days of Pompeii*

Leone's *Dollar* trilogy, forcing the British censor to slap "X" classifications on all three; *The Last Days of Pompeii* was slightly edited for U.K. release, given an "A" rating and put out on the circuits in September 1960, gathering healthy box-office receipts. Leone brought a dynamic energy to the oft-told tale, eliciting a superbly mean star turn from his leading man and excellent performances from the support cast. This glorious print acts as a double-edged sword. When revelling in the sheer opulence of it all, it acts as a stark reminder of the facts that well over 90 per cent of pepla have never made it this far and in all probability never will. As mentioned, the genre has been criminally neglected over the decades; what a pity that so many have never been given the digital restoration job they urgently deserve, as is the case here.

In 79 AD, Pompeii and neighboring Herculaneum were completely obliterated when Mount Vesuvius erupted, burying both towns under a layer of ash, stone, mud, cinders and lava several feet thick. Thousands of lives were literally erased in the cataclysm, one of the worst natural disasters of its kind on record. The eruption occurs on the 79th minute (honoring the year it happened), lasts for almost 14 minutes and doesn't disappoint. Burning cinders rain down from a glowering sky, the ground shakes, buildings and arches collapse onto a panicking populace, temples and forums topple, black smoke and methane gas fill the streets, houses are set ablaze, liquid mud bubbles through cracks, a crevasse opens under people's feet, water cascades from burst pipes and there's a mammoth rockslide. When it's more or less over, Leone frames a shot of thoroughfares choked with torn, bloodied corpses and broken masonry, an infant crying over its mother's inert body, a spellbinding, and moving, sight. Created in pre-CGI days, *The Last Days of Pompeii*'s earthquake sequence is one of the most spectacular moments of destruction ever committed to celluloid, everything achieved to remarkable effect *without* the aid of computers.

1834 novel, *The Last Days of Pompeii* remains one of pepla's crowning achievements and is one of Steve Reeves' best-known pictures. Fortunately, immaculately presented widescreen prints, English-dubbed with French subtitles, are available on the market, admirably showcasing this half-million-dollar production to its full advantage, in all its finery. "Dazzling" is a term used throughout this book to describe a particular cinematographer's work; here, the color is truly dazzling, of a type rarely seen in cinemas these days, Antonio L. Ballesteros dressing up the ornate sets in vivid hues that delight the eye. Mario Bonnard was taken ill on the first day of filming, Sergio Leone (one of five scriptwriters) more or less assuming directorial control, and it showed in the director's predilection for violence. In the opening few minutes, Reeves' father is murdered, his villa ransacked for gold, with men, women and even children brutally put to the sword; in another sequence, a horse is brought down, riddled with arrows. Scenes such as these would frequently crop up in 55 years later, CGI wizardry *was* used in Paul W.S. Anderson's 2014 "$80,000,000 B-movie" (*sic*) *Pompeii* and, give TriStar's technicians some credit, the results were breathtakingly good (this particular film contains many familiar peplum tropes within its framework and is well worth any fan's time).

Before that, the plot has Reeves (as Glaucus), returning to Pompeii with three buddies after six years in the wars, determined to enjoy wine, women and some peace, but instead finding himself caught up in a conspiracy against Rome; very quickly, Reeves, after visiting his ruined villa, is hell-bent on unearthing those responsible for the murder of his father. En route, he rescues waif-like Christine Kaufmann (Ioni) from an out-of-control speeding chariot (carrying out this stunt himself, Reeves badly injured his shoulder), saves likeable street thief Angel Aranda from a thrashing and sets about unmasking the hooded assassins who are persecuting the poor Christians, carving a crude cross on their properties (and corpses). Ice-blonde noblewoman

Anne-Marie Baumann, in tandem with high priest Fernando Rey, is behind the killings; she hates Rome *and* Christians (her entire family were slaughtered by Romans when she was a child). By placing the blame for the outbreak of slayings on the god-worshippers, she can feed them to the lions, steal their valuables and finance an army to march on Rome, her ultimate aim to become ruler.

Leone kept things on the boil quite expertly, and he was well aware that audiences of the time were in a high state of anticipation, anxiously waiting the fireworks to begin. Reeves, drunk, demonstrates his animal energy (and volatile temper) by smashing a table in two; the Temple of Isis, complete with concealed trapdoor, is the assassins' meeting place. Christians and their leader, Carlo Tamberlani, are stretched on the rack, flogged, tied to wheels and tormented with glowing pokers in a graphic torture scene; Guillermo Marin's consul is scared at the sight of blood, Baumann plunging a dagger in his heart when he talks about freeing the Christians. Burly Mimmo Palmara, a praetorian heavy, stars as Reeves' sworn enemy, a brazier thrust into his face during a scuffle; Barbara Carroll touchingly plays blind Nydia, girlfriend of Aranda. Reeves is severely wounded and cared for by Baumann, who takes a shine to him; and there's a splendid semi-finale before the big climax, taking place in the arena. The Christians are herded in, a lion set loose; Reeves dispatches the beast and two gladiators; then, to his dismay, 10 more gladiators armed with bows arrive. Marching forward, they draw their weapons and let loose their arrows, not at the Christians but at the watching nobility who die to a man—those gladiators are Reeves' followers in disguise! Suddenly, a massive tremor is felt, Vesuvius erupts, the crowds flee in terror and we have reached that much-expected centerpiece (Baumann and Rey are flattened by a falling pillar in the temple).

Some nice touches include Reeves yanking his chains from the prison wall, then forcing the cell door off its hinges; and when the handsome muscleman falls through the trapdoor, finding himself on the edge of a sewer harboring crocodiles, Angelo Francesco Lavagnino's leitmotif is the one the composer used when he scored the underwater sequences in 1961's *Gorgo*. Set and costume design is beyond reproach, right up there with the best of Hollywood, especially Isis' lofty temple and the arena sequences where thousands of spectators present us with a sea of differing colors. This is a marvelous sword and sandal extravaganza that still has the power to enthral fans over 50 years from its inception.

The Legions of Cleopatra [*Le legioni di Cleopatra*] aka *Legions of the Nile*

Alexandra/Atenea/Comptoir Francais CFPC (Italy/Spain/France); Supercinescope/Eastmancolor; 100 (91) mins; Producer: Virgilio De Blasi; Director: Vittorio Cottafavi ✝✝✝

20th Century Fox paid Alexandra Productions a million dollars to haul this film off the circuits and shelve it, concerned

Linda Cristal as Cleopatra in *The Legions of Cleopatra*

that Cottafavi's telling of the Cleopatra fable would detract from the massive publicity campaign surrounding their forthcoming magnum opus, *Cleopatra*. They needn't have worried—*The Legions of Cleopatra* couldn't hope to compete with the $30,000,000 Fox splashed out on their notorious epic, while Linda Cristal (Cleopatra) and Georges Marchal (Marc Antony) were no match for the virtuosity and star glamour of Elizabeth Taylor and Richard Burton. Having said that, Cristal's Queen of the Nile is a quite beguiling creature; darkly alluring, she plays her as a wanton slut inhabiting, incognito, the waterside inns and falling for centurion Ettore Manni (Curridio), sent to Alexandria by Emperor Caesar Octavian (Alfredo Mayo) to uncover exactly what Marchal is up to. Commencing in jokey fashion, Manni (posing as a gladiator) falling in with Conrado San Martin and clowning around in roughhouse tavern brawls, enlisting half-heartedly in gladiatorial training and rescuing a young lad and his sister (Maria Mahor) from slavery, the film gets down to hard basics when Manni, disguised as a legion commander, worms his way into Cristal's palace (a towering, ornately designed columned edifice) and confronts Marchal. We all know where the storyline leads from here—down the political path. Marchal is bewitched by the queen's charms and wants a cordial alliance put in place with Rome, his conscience pulling him in two directions; Mayo's units are marching on Alexandria to take control; and Manni can't decide which side of the fence to sit on, Rome or Egypt. Besides, he's fallen head over heels in love with belly dancer Bernice, aka Cleopatra; when the mysterious woman discloses her true identity, he accuses her of manipulation and she agrees with his verdict, cruelly discarding her admirer's feelings. "To breathe the same air as Cleopatra—even that's too good for a Roman," is her contemptuous put-down. Shattered by this unforeseen rejection, Manni rides out to meet Mayo at his campaign headquarters in the desert and discuss the Antony/Cleopatra liaison before the inevitable engagement on the plains outside Alexandria.

The French poster for *Revenge of the Borgias* (aka *The Night of the Great Attack*)

A couple of battle scenes featuring a cast of thousands fails to live up to their potential, over and done with too quickly, although the sight of Cristal charging across the corpse-littered battlefield on her 10-horse chariot to confront Mayo makes up for it. "She has no heart," remarks Manni, the Egyptian queen's priests ordering the torture and killing of every Roman sympathizer in Alexandria. We never witness either Marchal's death or Cristal's; he's found lying on the floor by Mayo when the Romans enter the city, Cristal slumped lifeless on her throne. Mission ended, Manni gallops off into the desert for new adventures, besotted Mahor by his side.

Incorporating no less than five scriptwriters, *The Legions of Cleopatra* was a sizeable hit in Italy and Spain when first issued, a colorful but ultimately superficial version of the Cleopatra saga. Mention must be made of Renzo Rossellini's atmospheric title theme, a lovely piece of music redolent of Ancient Egypt, which greatly enhances the picture, as does his soundtrack.

The Night of the Great Attack [*La notte del grande assalto*] aka *Revenge of the Borgias*

Italcaribe/Paris Interproductions PIP (Italy/France); Totalscope/Eastmancolor; 85 mins; Producers: Giuseppe Maria Scotese, Angelo Faccenna; Director: Giuseppe Maria Scotese ✝✝✝

Unavailable for years, *The Night of the Great Attack* has recently surfaced on a German triple DVD box set in a digitally restored widescreen version, German-dubbed. Although alternatively entitled *Revenge of the Borgias*, Cesare Borgia himself (played by Alberto Farnese) only flits in and out of the scenario, as does Duchess Caterina Sforza (Olga Solbelli), the woman whose land he's after—she only appears at the beginning and end. The story, set in 1488, mainly revolves around Solbelli's renegade nephew Marco (Sergio Fantoni) and his band of vagabonds (curiously dressed to resemble a cross between Robin Hood's Merry Men and pirates), Fabio (Giacomo Rossi-Stuart) and bad guy Zanco di Montforte (Fausto Tozzi). Fantoni and Tozzi both desire Rossi-Stuart's sister Isabella (Agnès Laurent, first seen stripping off her red tights for a spot of semi-nude bathing), while backstabbing Tozzi, assisted by toadying advisor Gianni Rizzo (repulsively oily in a red turban), is in cahoots with the Borgia clan. When Tozzi murders Rossi-Stuart (a sword hurled into his chest), Fantoni and his mountain bandits, their ranks boosted by hundreds of peasants in Stone Age garb, decide to oust the tyrant from his seat of power and prevent the Borgias from lording it over the land.

Scotese's medieval swashbuckler is a schizophrenic affair, not helped by Carlo Rustichelli's offbeat score, which sounds distinctly un-Italian, more like a Hollywood soundtrack from the 1940s. The mood veers from half-jocular (Farnese's resident court fool is a thorough nuisance) to Gothic grimness in the dungeon/torture sequences (Fantoni, chained and whipped, has his life spared if Laurent agrees to marry Tozzi); the director throws in a fiery two-timing Gypsy wench (Algerian actress Kerima as Maya), a rebel girl (Luisa Mattioli) in love with Fantoni, a tavern interlude and a harrowing gallows sequence before the big payoff, treating the audience to a spectacular 11-minute night assault on Tozzi's fortress (Turin's Fenis Castle was used in shooting the attack), a splendid piece of action cinema to rival the best in peplum. Rizzo the rat receives a spear through his heart and Fantoni duels with Tozzi after the fighting ends, while Farnese, who has arrived on the scene, instructs one of his bowmen to finish off the schemer. Solbelli and her warriors also turn up; Farnese admits defeat and rides away to his hilltop retreat, leaving Fantoni and Laurent to wander through a grassy meadow and play house. Pier Ludovico Pavoni's color photography brings the whole cockeyed exercise to vivid life (the location work around Turin's Piedmont region is spot-on), and likeable tough guys José Jaspe and Raf Baldassarre are on hand to back Fantoni up in his quest to get rid of Tozzi. This becomes passable peplum entertainment enlivened by a truly riveting battle sequence.

The Nights of Lucretia Borgia [*Le notti di Lucrezia Borgia*] aka *Nights of Temptation*

Musa Cinematografica/Fides (Italy/France); Totalscope/Eastmancolor; 109 mins; Producer: Mario Damiani; Director: Sergio Grieco ✝✝✝✝

Belinda Lee's second peplum outing went even further in promoting the actress' mouth-watering curves and wanton behavior, titillating window dressing for a salivating male audience. Half the movie is spent in Lee (as Lucretia) preening herself dressed only in a skimpy bedsheet, lolling on her bed in lust, flaunting her cleavage and fawning over the two males prominent in her life, Jacques Sernas (Federico) and Arnoldo Foà (Astorre)—there's even a nude silhouette shot as she steps out of a bath. The other half concentrates on Sernas' repeated rescue attempts in extricating damsel in distress Michele Mercier (Diana) from prison; she heads a gang of insurgents opposing the Inquisition methods employed by Lee's brother, Count Cesare Borgia (Franco Fabrizi), and his sadistic reign in the Italian province of Urbino. Sernas, a famed swordsman on his way to join Fabrizi's forces, snatches Mercier from soldiers in the opening minutes, dueling with the count's right-hand man Foà in court during revelry and debauchery; Lee casts her eyes on the young officer (the couple starred together in *The Venus of Cheronea*) and thereafter keeps would-be suitor Foà dangling on a string by giving him the odd peck on the cheek (she *does* allow him to tighten her gar-

Jacques Sernas tries his seduction techniques on pouting Belinda Lee in *The Nights of Lucretia Borgia*.

ter at one point, reducing him to jelly). In a scene dripping with X-rated sexual electricity, she seduces Sernas in her boudoir but seethes with jealousy on realizing that the swordsman's heart lies with Mercier, doing her utmost to sabotage the romance. In their hideout among archaic ruins, Nando Tamberlani and Mercier incite the rebels to action, spied on by Foà; Sernas is captured, accused of treachery, thrown into a cell and lashed savagely around his neck until Lee, hopelessly in love, frees him, showing him the way out via a secret passage. Then Mercier gets nabbed once more, strapped to a bench and undergoing a "Pit and the Pendulm"-type ordeal, a curved serrated blade inching closer toward her throat. Again, Sernas and the rebels sneak into the fortress, save Mercier and slip back out wearing masks; Lee spots them, shouts the alarm and Sernas fights Fabrizi in the corridor, slashing him across *his* neck in reprisal for his earlier treatment, but not killing him. Knowing that Sernas will never be hers, the hussy hitches her nightgown to another handsome young swordsman, Germano Longo, closing the door on a night of passion. Rejected Foà rides after Sernas, dispatched in a swordfight with the hero, who ends up in Mercier's arms.

Photographed in gorgeous colors by Massimo Dallamano, *The Nights of Lucretia Borgia* is Lee's *pièce de résistance*; perhaps at the time she wasn't the world's greatest actress, but with a body like hers, who cared about roleplaying and nuance. Sernas looks occasionally out of his comfort zone when she's busy eating him for breakfast, but so would many men in his sandals. This is a vintage dose of kitsch from the genre's up-and-coming period.

The Scimitar of the Saracen [*La scimitarra del saraceno*] aka ***The Pirate and the Slave Girl***; ***The Pirate's Captive***

Romana Film/SNC (Italy/France); Totalscope/Ferraniacolor; 99 (92) mins; Producer: Fortunato Misiano; Director: Piero Pierotti ✝✝✝

Ex-Tarzan star Lex Barker kitted himself out in rakish pirate costume to take on the role of Drakut the Dragon, a Venetian mischief-maker of the high seas, who has stolen not only vital war documents but the Governor of Rhodes' daughter, Graziella Granata (Bianca), in a raid on the *San Luca*, the vessel sunk without mercy. Massimo Serato (Captain Roberto Diego), an adventurer up to his eyes in money problems, wangles himself a pardon from the debtor's court if he can find a place on board Barker's ship *Sea Devil*, rescue the girl and retrieve those secret orders. Barker has other ideas. He plans to present the military papers to an African sultan in a trade for the title of Caliph, ruling the very oasis where Princess Miriam, played by delectable Chelo Alonso, resides with her entourage; the pirate chief also wants to marry the alluring vixen despite her haughty indifference to his advances.

There's a wealth of incident in Pierotti's jolly pirate caper (Barker's muscular presence makes for a memorable pirate scoundrel), proof that decades before the mega-budgeted *Pirates of the Caribbean* franchise, lavish seafaring adventures of this nature did exist, were just as entertaining and financed on far less money. What distinguishes *The Scimitar of the Saracen* from so many others is Augusto Tiezzi's use of the short-lived Ferraniacolor process, a garish combination of greens, oranges, reds and blues that adds a certain bizarre look to the sea sequences and intensifies the varicolored interior sets (Italy's first movie to be shot in this process was *Toto in Color*, 1952). Michele Cozzoli's rousing score underlines the pacey narrative as Serato is given 30 lashes for breaking into Barker's shipboard harem (a graphic flogging, not for the squeamish); Barker and his complement slog over desert wastes toward Alonso's oasis (the Monte Gelato falls; in the uncut print, Alonso stands full-frontal naked on a ridge, probably wearing a body stocking), which doubles as the pirates' stronghold, while foxy Alonso performs a blasphemous

An Italian photobusta for *The Scimitar of the Saracen*

A British poster for *Sign of the Gladiator* (aka *Sign of Rome*)

flamenco dance, offending her devout followers. The war plans are spirited away by Serato's painter pal and returned to the governor, and Serato takes flight with Granata (who's totally smitten with him) and the women, only to be picked up by Barker and imprisoned in the ship's hold. Following a well-staged sea battle, drenched in Tiezzi's over-bright color tones, a flotilla of small boats grapples with the *Sea Devil* and cutlass fights galore. Barker accidentally shoots Alonso dead; his ship slowly sinking from cannon shelling, the pirate sails off to his doom with Alonso's lifeless body clutched to his chest. Serato, Granata and the surviving women look on with a certain amount of sadness at his demise.

Sign of Rome [*Il segno di Roma*] aka *Sheba and the Gladiator*; *Sign of the Gladiator*

Glomer Film/Lux/Lyre (Italy/France/Yugoslavia/West Germany); Dyaliscope/Eastmancolor; 98 (85) mins; Producer: Enzo Merolle; Director: Guido Brignone ††††

The Cuban H-bomb meets the Swedish sex goddess. 38 minutes into *Sign of Rome*, Chelo Alonso (Erika), fourth on the cast list, performs a three-minute erotic dance (four minutes in the movie's unedited version) that almost steals Anita Ekberg's (playing Zenobia, Queen of Palmira) thunder. This was the hot tamale's first foray into the world of peplum and she certainly lit up the screen with those high cheekbones, pouting lips, mane of jet-black hair, plunging neckline and gyrating hips. Sensuous Ekberg, naturally, had her own plunging neckline to contend with, having great difficulty during some scenes in preventing her 44-inch chest from spilling out of her off-the-shoulder outfits (as was the case in 1960's *La Dolce Vita*, the actress' most memorable picture). Better known as *Sheba and the Gladiator* (Sergio Leone was one of five scriptwriters involved), Brignone's sword and sandal opus, set in 217 AD and blessed with ravishing color photography by Luciano Trasatti, especially in the opulent interior shots, centered on intrigue and subterfuge. Roman consul Georges Marchal (Marcus Valerius) poses as a gladiator, gets himself captured by Ekberg's warriors on purpose, winds up doing duty in a salt mine, is untied from the cross and inveigles himself into her court on the pretext that he will assist Ekberg in wiping out Rome, while secretly planning to suppress her tribe; and Ekberg's oily minister, Folco Lulli (Zemanzius), is planning to join forces with the Persians so that he can rule Palmira.

It's a full hour before the movie ups a gear and battle royal commences between the warriors of Palmira and Rome's legions, led by centurion Jacques Sernas (Julianus) and Alberto Farnese. By that time, Marchal has fallen in love with the queen and wants the Romans to accept a pact of non-aggression without bloodshed; Sernas has rescued vestal virgin (and next in line to the throne) Lorella De Luca (Bathsheba) from a throat-slitting and plans to marry her; and Lulli's attempt at ousting Ekberg have been thwarted by Marchal, who shoves a dagger into his well-upholstered tunic. Taking place in the Gorge of Jaffa, the brush between opposing sides is gritty and staged with brio, multiple spear carriers and catapults hurling flaming boulders raining death and destruction on Ekberg's army, who down arms and pull back in disarray; Ekberg, having lost the fight, petulantly lets fly with a war lance at her guileful lover but forgives him in the end after she's pardoned by the Roman senate—off they wander in each other's arms before the fadeout. Shorn by 13 minutes on international release, this multi-European venture was snapped up by American-International Pictures in late 1959, given a new title and promoted heavily on the back of *The Labors of Hercules*' box-office triumph in America; it raked in over a million dollars profit for AIP, reviving the company's flagging fortunes. The picture also did quite well in the United Kingdom, screened as *Sign of the Gladiator* and U-rated. A year down the line, Alonso, Sernas and Lulli were reunited in *The Queen of the Tartars* and this time around, the Cuban lovely received top billing!

Son of the Red Corsair [*Il figlio de corsaro rosso*] aka *Son of the Red Pirate*

Athena (Italy); Totalscope/Eastmancolor; 96 (90) mins; Producers: Luigi Carpentieri, Ermanno Donati; Director: Primo Zeglio †††††

This is Lex Barker's finest peplum hour. What a crying shame that Primo Zeglio's pulsating pirate actioner is only (2015) available from independent dealers in a monochrome pan and scan copy. To quote a modern-day idiom, *Son of the Red Corsair* would look "awesome" in widescreen and color, and hopefully one day it may be issued in its original form (Sergio Leone was assistant director). Thankfully to all soundtrack buffs, what *does* remain is Roman Vlad's brassy, in-your-face score. In Warner Bros.' classic *The Adventures of Robin Hood* (1938), Erich Wolfgang Korngold's Oscar-winning music punctuated the narrative, boosting the action scenes and calming down tunefully in the quieter moments. Here, Vlad achieves precisely the same deft mix in a soundtrack probably not recalled by aficionados but ranking as one of the genre's finest. If you're into lyrical film music, Vlad's *pièce de résistance* is as much a pleasure to listen to as the movie is to watch.

In the early 1800s, Count Henry of Ventimiglia (Barker) takes on the mantle of a notorious pirate, the scourge of the high seas, with one thing on his mind other than booty—justice. He seeks to avenge the death of his father, the infamous Red Corsair, and locate sister Vira Silenti (Neala), missing for 15 years. First seen against a background of cannon smoke as his vessel overpowers a Spanish galleon, Barker cuts a commanding figure, investing his devil-may-care character with real depth and passion; a fearsome handler of the sword one minute, a seducer the next, an expert at donning guises to gain entry incognito into places where he can obtain information about the crimes committed on his family. Over the course of 96 minutes, the movie packs everything in barring the kitchen sink: swordfights, romance, music, dance, mystery and limited doses of light comedic relief. On board ship, Barker's lieutenant (Saro Urzi) discovers Giorgio Constantini among the captured Spaniards, turned in by colluder Diego Michelotti; Constantini was the man who betrayed the Red Corsair to the authorities, leading to his death, and he knows where Silenti is. Also among the prisoners is Marquise Carmen di Montélimar, played by Sylvia Lopez, the Austrian-born ex-model turned actress, raised in Paris, and who was an out-and-out stunner *and* could put in a decent performance. She was not able to fulfill her potential due to her early death at the age of 26. Lopez appreciates Barker's stance of not relieving the passengers of their finery, as well as his good looks and strong physique, and quickly falls under his manly spell. Livio Lorenzon (with hair!) appears for a couple of minutes; molesting a female, he tussles with his captain and falls backwards into the sea. Meanwhile, in Maracaibo, Marquis Luigi Visconti (Lopez's uncle), the Governor of Panama, and sidekick Antonio Crast, the two lawbreakers responsible for the Red Corsair's death, are also hunting for Barker's sister; apparently, she's a half-Indian princess and filthy rich. Visconti wants to marry the girl to gain overall power of the region and lay his fat paws on her assets. The trouble is, young Luciano Marin (Miguel), Lopez's brother, loves Silenti, recognizable by a serpent tattoo on her right shoulder. Visconti's plan is to find Silenti, have her murdered, steal her fortune and substitute a stooge (dancer Vicky Lagos) in her place. But things go wrong when Silenti is located and the marquis decides he physically desires her, reckoning that she, not the imposter, would make an ideal wife. Lopez's life (she's strung up over a pit full of spikes in a dungeon, repeatedly whipped) hangs in the balance, the price to pay if Silenti doesn't consent to wed the portly, bullying miscreant.

In a densely plotted adventure, Barker's exploits in uncovering Visconti's misdeeds involves him wearing various disguises to fool the filibusters—at one stage, the sea rover is made Defender of Cartagena, the governor unaware of his true identity. Franco Fantasia, Lopez's cousin, is dispatched in a furious duel with Barker for insulting him, and Constantini is done away with by Michelotti after telling the marquis the whereabouts of the missing sister; in turn, he's shot dead by Barker. Even a captain of the guard is enlisted to champion the cause. Barker, with a cry of "I'm your brother," bursts in on the wedding ceremony of the marquis and Silenti just as she's about to say "I do"; she shoots Crast and Barker rescues Lopez from the torture chamber, Visconti toppling head-first into the pit of spikes. As the curtain closes on this rollicking costume spree, Marin marries

An Italian photobusta for *Son of the Red Corsair* featuring Lex Barker and Sylvia Lopez

Silenti. Judging by the looks on their faces, it will be Barker and Lopez's turn next! A stirring, well-crafted tribute to old-fashioned swashbuckling filmmaking virtues, the likes of which will never be experienced again.

Terror of the Barbarians [*Il terrore dei barbari*] aka ***Goliath and the Barbarians***

Standard Produzione/Alta Vista (Italy); Totalscope/Ferraniacolor; 100 (85) mins; Producer: Emimmo Salvi; Director: Carlo Campogalliani †††††

"568 AD. A time when, if you didn't fight or love, life was a very short and dull affair." So read the publicity slogans on billboards for *Terror of the Barbarians*. Well, there was plenty of fighting and loving in Steve Reeves' third peplum, the film that established him as the heroic musclemen supremo, one whose symbolic footsteps every bodybuilder harboring thoughts of taking up a movie career wanted to follow in, and aspire to. Like *The Battle of Marathon*, *Goliath and the Barbarians*, as it was more commonly known outside of Italy, ran into censorship problems when released in the United Kingdom in 1960, the British censor taking a dim view of images featuring overt bloody violence, particularly toward women who, in one sequence, are roughly assaulted, their clothing ripped. Shorn of several minutes, the picture was classified "A" instead of an "X," even though moments of savagery were retained in the print. More so than his first two *Hercules* flicks, *Terror of the Barbarians* placed Reeves on the world stage, a catalyst for the pelpum craze that followed in its wake.

The death of his father at the hands of rampaging barbarian hordes causes Reeves (as Emiliano) to forget all about his job as a woodcutter; the he-man turns nasty. "I will have my revenge. I swear it. His murderers will have no peace. I will fight as long as I live!" he thunders to sister Giulia Rubini (Lidia). Donning a wolf's mask and talons, he becomes, at first, a one-man army, striking terror into the invaders by meting out rough justice, de-

Goliath becomes Hercules in the Belgian poster for *Terror of the Barbarians*.

molishing them left, right and center in an outbreak of surprise sorties. After barbarian huntress Chelo Alonso (as Landa) has gyrated her fabulous figure through the first of two three-minute sensuous dance routines in front of a salivating Livio Lorenzon (aptly named Igor), we move to Verona. Bruce Cabot, of *King Kong* fame, is Alboino, a chieftain trying to keep his quarrelsome captains happy. Lorenzon, as odious as ever, is sent to Andrea Checchi's stockade with henchman Arturo Dominici to deal with the "Goliath" menace; Lorenzon readily agrees, planning to wed Alonso and get rid of Checchi (her father), so that he can rule the roost. On a hunting expedition in the woods, Alonso meets Reeves, reasoning that he's the mysterious Goliath; she can't keep her big brown eyes off his bulging biceps and soon, she's melting in those powerful arms, the pair smooching like mad (sizzling on-screen chemistry from the two main stars who were firm friends away from the cameras). Luciano Marin (as Marco), leading the rebels, reckons Reeves has gone soft in the head over a female. ("You've traded us for a woman!") Reeves agrees, sends Alonso packing ("I love you, but it isn't right.") and gets back to the business of wiping out the enemy.

In the stockade, Reeves gives everyone a chance to gape at that mighty superstructure of his in a "Test of Truth," a yoke slung around his neck, heaving on a rope against several men to prevent being speared to death, then tethered between two horses, bringing the steeds to heel. An attack on a barbarian detachment in a gorge, where Cabot's sacred golden crown is taken, is followed by the enraged warlord's reprisal. He plunders a village, director Campogalliani treating the audience to a man branded in the face, another staked to the ground and used for target practice, a third dispatched horribly by a row of blades pulled by horses and several more crucified, gory and gruesome. In the final, furious 10 minutes, Marin and his outlaws ride into the encampment, just as Checchi's devoted minions fight Lorenzon's hyenas; Dominici and Checchi die in the affray, Reeves and Lorenzon going head-to-head, the muscleman knocking the barbarian senseless, hoisting him above his head and hurling his body against the stockade wall, a brutal demise. The closing shot is of Reeves and Alonso, Marin and Rubini and their people riding away from the fortress to begin a more peaceful life.

Terror of the Barbarians was unusual in being filmed mostly on studio sets, giving it a stagy look that fans of the outdoor actioner might not appreciate. But this is an indispensable genre movie in every sense of the word and a highly successful one to boot (it played to packed houses in England), containing vivid color photography by Adalberto "Bitto" Albertini, a combined Carlo Innocenzi/Les Baxter throbbing, insistent score and vital performances from Reeves (powerful and sexy), Alonso (oozing lust appeal), Lorenzon and Dominici (both epitomizing devilish thuggery). This is tremendous entertainment for aficionados from the beginning of pepla's golden period.

The Volga Boatmen [*I battellieri del Volga*] aka **Prisoner of the Volga**; **The Boatmen**

Transmonde Film/ Fides/Omnia-Regina (Italy/West Germany/France); Totalscope/Eastmancolor; 102 (85) mins; Produced and Directed by Viktor (Victor) Tourjansky ††††

A peplum weepie set in Czarist Russia, *The Volga Boatmen* must count as American actor John Derek's most least-known film; it has never been afforded an official DVD release, only available on ultra-scarce gray market copies. Thankfully, these are in letterbox format, Mario Montuori's glorious inky color wash remaining more or less preserved, although lapsing into a pink and mauve tint on two short occasions. There's not a great deal of action to be had—the accent is firmly on characterization and period atmosphere and in this respect, Ukrainian Viktor Tourjansky delivers the goods, being no stranger to the subject. In 1928 he directed *Volga, Volga*, followed by *Volga in Flames* in 1934 and wrote the story together with most of the screenplay on this production.

On his wedding day, Captain Alexi Orloff (Derek) is horrified to learn that his bride of a few hours (Dawn Addams as Princess Tatyana) is pregnant—but not by him! The varlet responsible is her guardian, General Gerow (Wolfgang Preiss); he got her drunk one night, took advantage and has foisted his ward on Derek to avoid a public scandal. "Can you forgive me anything?" she cries before spilling the beans. The answer is no. "It isn't possible. I can't believe it," moans Derek, hitting Preiss at the reception and finding himself behind bars. Swiftly court martialed and stripped of his rank, Derek is shunted off to a Siberian labor camp, his former officers, headed by Charles Vanel, arrested for protesting their captain's harsh treatment; besides, they know the real reason behind Derek's banishment, as Preiss is fully aware. Ridden with guilt, Addams meets her victimized husband in a tavern after bribing the camp commandant with copious glasses of vodka and cash to let him out for a couple of hours; fleeing the inn, they gallop into dense woodland but she's shot, dying in Derek's arms (Norbert Glanzberg's sweet music highlights this moving scene). "Give her a Christian burial," Derek asks an aged priest, riding off and cared for by the Volga boatmen, Elsa Martinelli (Mascha) taking an instant shine to him in his hour of need despite rumors circulating that he murdered his wife for her wealth. Preiss learns of Derek's escape and Addams' demise, ordering Rik Battaglia and his troops to hunt the man down; Martinelli remains torn between her feelings for the despondent fugitive and those of her bullying father, caught up in a dispute with rival boatmen over pay and working conditions. Back in St. Petersburg, Preiss is relieved of his command as his own wife has testified against him, a cavalry regiment sent to the Volga to rescue Derek, now at the mercy of Battaglia's thugs. Preiss organizes his own band of renegades to put paid to the beleaguered captain; in a rooftop fight with Derek, the general falls backwards to his death. Vanel exonerates Derek of all past accusations, restores his rank and allows him to ride off with Martinelli: "I've got my reward," Derek grins, happy at last.

Steeped in Old Russia ambience, *The Volga Boatmen* is beautifully composed by Tourjansky, especially the opening lavish ballroom sequence. With an eye for gritty detail, the director expertly projects the audience into the grim realities of the harsh

A French poster for *The Volga Boatmen*

existence led by the impoverished boatmen as they towed their barges along the muddy banks of the Volga over a century ago. Martinelli turns in a touching performance as the dark-haired lass in love with an unfairly punished casualty of someone else's misdeeds, her intimate tete-a-tetes with Derek an absolute delight. In all probability, this beguiling movie will forever remain a long-lost gem, consigned to that cinematic graveyard that is the final resting place of many a peplum dating from the genre's pre-1960 period. What a shame. (Note: Although some online sites give the running time as 102 minutes, the DVD copy runs for 85 minutes with no obvious signs of editing or breaks in continuity. If there *is* a longer version, it may never be seen.)

5
Hercules 1960-1965

Following the international success of Steve Reeves' two seminal *Hercules* movies, a further 16 strongman adventures were produced between 1960 and 1965, 17 if you include *Maciste Against Hercules in the Vale of Woe* (1961), in which the Son of Zeus (or Jupiter) was featured (Frank Gordon played him); this is included in the chapter on Maciste. Mark Forest, Mickey Hargitay, Reg Park, Mike Lane, Brad Harris, Kirk Morris, Gordon Scott, Dan Vadis, Alan Steel and Peter Lupus stepped into Reeves' formidable sandals, the actor refusing to become typecast in the role. The name Hercules appeared on a number of English-dubbed versions of films originally released in Italy as Maciste, Samson, Ursus and Goliath adventures; these were never intended to be part of the *Hercules* series, the title altered for marketing strategies. As with most string of movies built around a single character and all containing near-similar storylines, the *Hercules* pictures declined in artistic merit as the decade wore on, Reg Park perhaps coming across as the most all-rounded "complete" Hercules, in screen presence, physique and just plain getting under the skin of the character. Dan Vadis was the most energetic, Mike Lane and Frank Gordon the least effective. In hindsight, these 16 *Hercules* pictures came off second-best to the *Maciste* movies, shot in tandem, which tended to be more hokey, complex, livelier and blessed with better scripts, as we will see later on. The titles are listed in order of their original Italian theatrical release dates, not dates issued elsewhere, which could differ by a couple of years in some cases.

1960

The Revenge of Hercules [*La vendetta di Ercole*] aka Goliath and the Dragon

Achille Piazzi and Gianni Fuchs Produzioni/CFPC (Italy/France); Totalscope/Technicolor; 87 mins; Producers: Achille Piazzi, Gianni Fuchs; Director: Vittorio Cottafavi †††††

The first of the '60s run of 16 *Hercules* features starred Brooklyn-born bodybuilder Mark Forest (Lorenzo Luis Degni) in *his* first major production (he had a bit part in Fox's *The Egyptian*, 1954), and a pivotal production at that. Successfully released in the United Kingdom in 1961 as *Goliath and the Dragon*, A-rated, director Vittorio Cottafavi's brightly colored confection is the embodiment of all that is schlock *fusto* peplum: Heroic strongman battles monsters and villains to restore justice to the people in a series of over-the-top action sequences guaranteed to keep audience enjoyment levels on a high. Mario Montuori's bold cinematography is breathtakingly gorgeous (his father was veteran cameraman Carlo Montuori), while Alexandre Derevitsky provides a grand score (Les Baxter tinkered with it for U.S. distribution). Cottafavi's movies were a lot pacier than most; he brought thundering movement, vigor and pictorial splendor to the masses and ranks as one of the genre's greatest exponents of the slam-bang set piece, of which *The Revenge of Hercules* has more than its fair share.

Forest (as Emilius, or Hercules) is first seen descending by rope into a misty labyrinthine cave system, killing a firebreathing three-headed dog, spotting a dragon (Jim Danforth supplied the stop-motion animation in the American cut) and grabbing the hallowed Blood Diamond from a winged bat creature. Meanwhile, scar-faced King Eurystheus (Broderick Crawford) and henchman Renato Terra are planning the downfall of Thebes, but ambassadors from five nations will only agree to join them if Forest is reported dead; they promptly turn heel and walk out when it's announced he's alive and heading their way to seek revenge for the death of his family. Forest's brother, Sandro Moretti (who bears a passing resemblance to Western movie star Audie Murphy), the rightful heir to Thebes' seat of power, is arrested, freed by girlfriend Federica Ranchi (Thea) and taken to Forest's villa simmering with resentment; Crawford has planted it in his mind that the muscleman is a traitor and not to be trusted.

From then on, nine scriptwriters do their best to both confuse and entertain the viewer in equal measures. Overlook the headache-inducing plot, just concentrate on the visuals. Ranchi is imprisoned in a Gothic-type dungeon, as is slave Wandisa Guida (Alcinoe), after refusing to poison Forest—he saves her from a marauding bear and she falls for him, even though he's married to Leonora Ruffo (the presence of Gaby André and

Mark Forest defeats the dragon and saves Leonora Ruffo in *The Revenge of Hercules*.

Carla Calò makes five attractive females in this picture). Forest restores the diamond to the God of Vengeance's forehead, later smashing it in anger when the gods decree that his wife has to be sacrificed in order for Thebes to be saved, pulling down the temple walls ("Collapse like my shattered dreams."). Ruffo is abducted by Polymorphous the Centaur; when Forest slays him, the gods are further provoked. She's then chained to a wall, food for the dragon; Forest dispatches the beast (good in longshot, the giant rubber head puppet prop not so good), using his brute strength to wreck the palace foundations, and with it Crawford's fortress, a spectacular scene given the film's medium budget. Terra receives a sword in the back from Crawford who's pushed into a pit of snakes by Guida, the slave girl dying in Forest's arms. Forest's Thebans and rebellious citizens take the city and, contrary to what the gods roared from above, Ruffo is reunited with Forest, Moretti going off to play house with Ranchi.

Forest, star of 12 peplum films, made a fine muscular Hercules (as he would with Maciste); he was blessed with the kind of looks women went for, a massively developed frame (watch him bring an elephant to its knees), charisma and at least he tried to act like a mythical demigod. Crawford, one of cinema's renowned bully boys, played the part of the king like a Hollywood gangster, throwing his bulk around, spitting feathers and snarling, not smiling once, while Cottafavi demonstrated his agility (and a certain amount of vision) with an extraordinary upside-down shot of Forest striding over the camera to confront the God of Vengeance, the scene staying in that peculiar position. Luckily for fans, a pristine print of *The Revenge of Hercules* is available on the market (never have the Monte Gelato falls and cascades looked lovelier), a rarity indeed in the world of peplum, which has never received the care and attention the genre deserves. Make the most of this gleaming copy, which shows the movie as it was presented theatrically—they don't come around all that often.

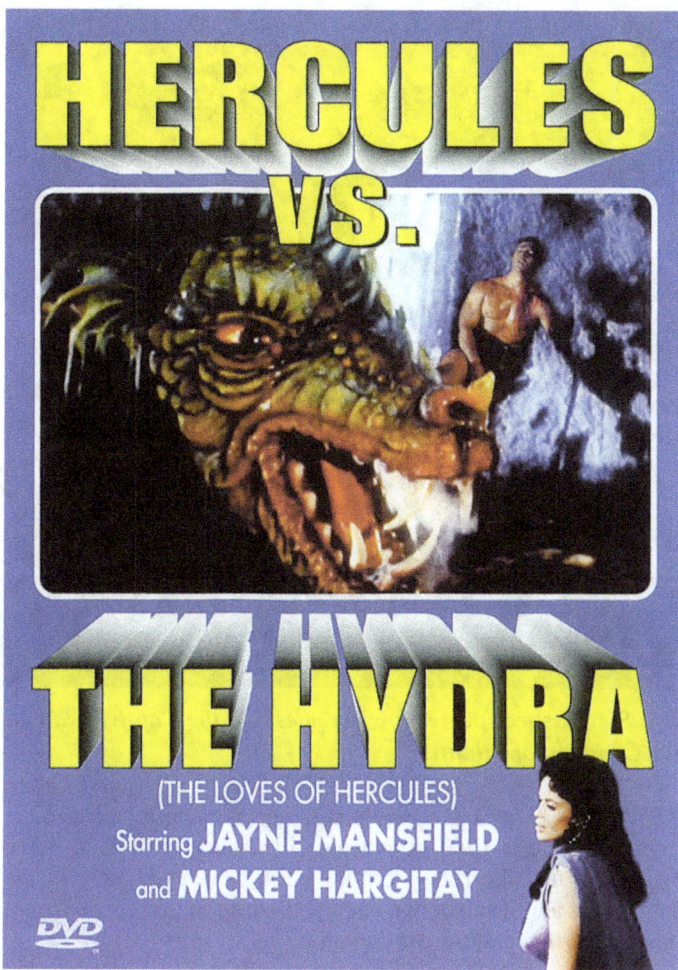

DVD cover for *Hercules vs. The Hydra* (aka *The Loves of Hercules*)

The Loves of Hercules [*Gli amori di Ercole*] aka Hercules vs. The Hydra

Grandi Schermi Italiani/Contact Org./P.I.P. (Italy/France); CinemaScope/Eastmancolor; 100 (97) mins; Producer: Alberto Manca; Director: Carlo Ludovico Bragaglia ✝✝✝

King Eurites of Oechalia orders the murder of Hercules' wife, Megara; Licos, who carries out the assassination, covets the throne and kills the king, telling his daughter Deianira that he died in battle. Hercules vows vengeance on Oechalia but spares Deianira, who has to undergo a trial for the gods to decide her implicit guilt. Deianira falls in love with Hercules after he prevents her being savaged by a ferocious bull, even though she's betrothed to Accolos. Licos stabs Accolos in the back, blaming the crime on Hercules, who he sees as a threat to his ambitions. To prove his innocence, Hercules pursues Philitetes, the murder's sole witness, to the cave of the Hydra. Hercules slays the monster but is seriously injured, a tribe of Amazons led by Queen Hippolyta tending his wounds. Hippolyta, who turns her ex-lovers into living trees, desires Hercules but he doesn't respond, so Maga, a sorceress, changes her appearance to that of Deianira, so that he may want her. Numaya, an Amazon in love with Hercules, tells him of the queen's deception. Hercules escapes the Amazons' domain, Numaya killed by Hippolyta who is strangled by one of the tortured, angry tree-men. In Oechalia, Licos' proposition to marry Deianira and share the throne is turned down, so she's imprisoned. Hercules stages an uprising against Licos' dictatorship; during a fierce battle, Licos drags Deianira into a cave inhabited by a monstrous apeman. The beast kills Licos before Hercules dispatches it with a boulder. On horseback, Hercules and Deianira set off to begin a new life together.

Husband and wife team Mickey Hargitay and Jayne Mansfield starred in a sword and sorcery *Hercules* adventure as scatty as the giant mechanical, three-headed, fire-breathing Hydra that the Son of Jupiter had to combat in reel four (created by Carlo Rambaldi). Hargitay possessed the physique and the looks but not the acting ability, and that went for Hollywood's self-styled "poor man's Marilyn Monroe," Mansfield (as Deianira *and* the altered Hippolyta), surrounded by a retinue of male beefcake slaves; the girl seemed to have great difficulty in preventing her 44-inch bust from spilling out of its skimpy support gown ("Tears are not a queen's privilege" is Mansfield's one memorable line). And get that Hollywood hairdo—black, then red, then purple! Elsewhere, Massimo Serato stole the performance honors as slimy Licos, resident peplum beauty Moira Orfei played Numaya, the Amazon yearning for Hargitay's wooden charms, and that big hairy apeman was straight out of a 1950s Sam Katzman *Jungle Jim* feature. Oechalia's columnar sets were impressive, as were the cave sequences and the Hydra itself, the combination of Bragaglia's pacey direction, Carlo Innocenzi's lively score and Enzo Serafin's vivid colors ensuring that the *Hercules* bandwagon kept on rolling. Overall, though,

A U.S. half-sheet poster for *Hercules and the Captive Women* (aka *Hercules and the Conquest of Atlantis*)

The Loves of Hercules vaguely dampens the spirits, mainly due to the fact that in 1960, audiences still retained visions of Steve Reeves in the title role. Hargitay wasn't even remotely in the same class and it showed; a stronger central performance would have lifted this picture considerably.

1961

Hercules and the Conquest of Atlantis [*Ercole alla conquista di Atlantide*] aka **Hercules Conquers Atlantis**; **Hercules and the Captive Women**

SpA Cinematografica/Comptoir Francais CFFP (Italy/France); Super Technirama 70/Technicolor; 101 (98) mins; Producer: Achille Piazzi; Director: Vittorio Cottafavi †††††

Leeds-born Roy "Reg" Park (Mr. Universe 1951, 1958, 1965 and runner-up to Steve Reeves in 1950) starred in five pepla before calling time on his brief movie career in 1965 (Park would become mentor to a young Arnold Schwarzenegger in 1972). The bearded Englishman bore a passing resemblance to both Reeves and Nigel Green, who played Hercules in Columbia's *Jason and the Argonauts* and on this, his first showing, put in a more positive performance than Mickey Hargitay, even though he spent the first 10 minutes dozing in idle bliss, ignoring the action taking place around him. In a deliciously delirious romp in which we are led to believe that Hercules wiped out Atlantis singlehanded, Park, Ettore Manni (Androloces of Thebes), Luciano Marin (Hylos, Son of Hercules) and dwarf Salvatore Furnari (Timoteo) venture on a perilous voyage to save Greece from destruction. The country is threatened by mists and mysterious forces ("A reign of blood and fire.") emanating from the west, and Greece's warring kings are willing to put aside their differences to defeat this unknown enemy; Park doesn't want to leave his wife, but Marin drugs him and somehow hauls his massive frame on board Manni's boat. Disembarking to take on water (the location at Palinuro, south of Naples, was seen in *Jason and the Argonauts* when Jason and his men fought Talos, the bronze giant), the crew mutiny, leaving the four to carry on. During a storm, Manni is washed overboard, the craft wrecked, the next port of call being the domain of Proteus, an evil wizard. Combating snakes, lions and vultures, Park slays a man in a baggy dinosaur suit; Proteus is destroyed (the cliffs run red with blood) and the fogs lift, Laura Efrikian (Princess Ismene) freed from captivity—her mother is Queen Antinea of Atlantis (Fay Spain), where the final half of the movie is played out.

Mario Bava had an uncredited hand in the striking visual effects (lit by Carlo Carlini's garish colors), coming to the fore when Park enters Atlantis to find Manni an amnesic zombie, an army of Mimmo Palmara robotic clones at Spain's beck and call. Mario Petri fumes as a high priest, bowing to the Great God Uranus, while Spain wishes to kill her own daughter. Prophecy states that Atlantis' ruler is doomed if she/he is survived by their offspring. The black-haired viper is out to conquer the world, hopefully with Park by her side ("I love you. Join me in the conquest of the world. Together we shall reign over men and gods."), a fleet of super-slaves ("A supreme race born of the blood of Uranus!") ready to sail on Greece. The source of Atlantis' power lies in a subterranean crater filled with the blood of Uranus. Park learns that sunlight will disrupt that power; by battering, with chains, a large cavity in a cavern roof, he causes an avalanche, the sun's rays striking the crater. A four-minute cataclysm ensues: A volcano erupts, tidal waves swamp the fleet, buildings and temples crumble in multiple explosions and Spain is crushed under falling masonry. Thebes, and Greece, are saved: Park, Manni (who has regained his memory), Marin and Efrikian (now a couple) cast off for home waters, Atlantis' deadly powers at an end.

A soldier dropped into an acid bath, turning into a skeleton; Park setting his chariot on fire, the 12 charging horses smashing down Spain's black-helmeted automatons; imaginative set design; a great climactic scene of destruction; and Spain vamping it up as the Atlantean bitch. The fifth *Hercules* outing, directed with panache by Vittorio Cottafavi, had it all, inserting (in U.S. prints) snatches of Hans J. Salter's musical cues from *Creature from the Black Lagoon* to liven up Gino Marinuzzi, Jr. and Armando Trovajoli's soundtrack. The *Hercules* movies were now becoming more fantasy-based, as was to prove the case with the second of Park's 1961 outings in the role, *Hercules at the Center of the Earth*, probably the archetypal *Hercules* fantasy/horror feature.

Hercules at the Center of the Earth [*Ercole al centro della terra*] aka **Hercules in the Haunted World**; **Hercules Against the Vampires**

SpA Cinematografica (Italy); Supertotalscope/Technicolor; 91 (76) mins; Producer: Achille Piazzi; Director: Mario Bava ††††

Style over substance? Style over sword and sorcery action? There's very little of either in Mario Bava's strikingly visual but strangely empty *Hercules* solo entry; it's as though the di-

An Italian poster for *Hercules at the Center of the Earth*

rector set out to make a fantasy/horror movie and included the mythological demigod as an afterthought. On Saturday, March 9, 1963, I caught the picture, A-rated in Britain, on a double bill with the Audie Murphy Western *Destry* (Universal, 1954) and couldn't make head or tail of it. All very dark, hollow sounding and *foreign*, with a convoluted myth-ridden narrative, poor dubbing and a clumsy monster—like many other 16-year-olds, I paid money to see Christopher Lee, although he only appeared at the beginning and end. But that was over 50 years ago. Now, through more seasoned eyes, you can appreciate the enterprise for what it set out to be, Bava's bold, creative attempt to bring something different to the *Hercules* genre, instead of presenting countless fights and feats of strength. Yet it's not the out-and-out classic whispered in some quarters. Franco Giacobini's lame attempts at comedy torpedo the fantasy mood (he plays Telemachus); Bava's gloomy lighting, though graced with his favorite pools of greens, blues and reds, renders the screen almost impenetrable at times; Procrustes the rock-monster resembles Tabanga, the rubbery tree-monster in *From Hell It Came* (Allied Artists, 1957); and wires can visibly be seen when Reg Park is under bombardment from the flying undead. Lee (King Lico) is as excellent as ever (he apparently enjoyed working on the film immensely) and Park's performance made one wish he had stuck with the title role more often than he did. A major bonus for music buffs, and one that is mainly overlooked by critics, is Armando Trovajoli's highly atmospheric music, which wouldn't have sounded out of place in a Hammer horror production—the composer's eerie tones match Bava's showy visuals to perfection, a macabre cascade of tonalities to delight the aural senses.

In order to save his ailing beloved, Leonora Ruffo (Deianira), held in a trance-like state under Lee's vampiric spell, and rid the land of threatening evil forces, Park and buddies George (Giorgio) Ardisson (as womanizing Thesius) and Giacobini journey to the Garden of Hesperides to retrieve a golden apple from a vast tree. Watched by tormented maidens, Park grabs the apple as his two comrades are threatened by lumbering Procrustes ("You must be longer so I will stretch you out till you fit the bed," it growls); Pluto's curse is lifted from Hesperides. Hurling the monster into a pile of boulders, Park and Ardisson (their daft friend is left safeguarding the apple) enter the gateway into a red-tinged Hades, the Kingdom of Pluto, a misty underworld of Gothic grottos where they're first met with the vision of a naked woman in chains, an enticing temptation to both men and a potent image used throughout Italian cinema. Park manages to cross a lake of molten lava to lay his hands on the sacred stone that will cure Ruffo; Ardisson slips into the lava, wakes and falls for Ida Galli (Persephone, Pluto's daughter), their romance offending the gods, a "profanity against the Kingdom of the Dead." After a stormy sea voyage, Park reaches Oechalia to find the land suffering from famine and pestilence. Black-clad Lee plans to drink virgin Ruffo's blood at a forthcoming lunar eclipse, thus immortalizing himself. To appease Pluto, Galli returns to Hades; summoned by Lee's satanic rites, the leprous undead rise from their coffins, attacking Park in Lee's ghostly haunt; the musclemen defeats the ghouls, throwing a boulder at the sorcerer and rescuing Ruffo. As the eclipse ends, Lee bursts into flames, his reign at an end, and prosperity returns to Oechalia.

Hercules at the Center of the Earth is wonderful to behold, yet it's a little too dense, its characters so divorced from reality that they fail to connect with the audience, like figures in another time and dimension. As mentioned, Bava's photography is very dark for most of the time, the dialogue echoing from afar; like a hallucinatory dream, it meanders through Hades' garish caverns, a cut-rate horror movie-cum-fantasmagorical one-off that would probably have had most peplum fans of the day yearning for the flash of blade and trident in sunlight, and Hercules putting his well-oiled muscles (as opposed to wits) to much better use.

1962

Ulysses Against Hercules [*Ulisse contro Ercole*] aka ***Ulysses vs. the Son of Hercules***

CCM/Fides (Italy/France); Totalscope/Eastmancolor; 105 (91) mins; Producer: Luigi Nannerini; Director: Mario Caiano
††††

Six-foot-five American ex-boxer Mike Lane stepped into Hercules' boots in his one and only peplum feature, ordered by the gods to bring Ulysses (Georges Marchal) to justice. The King of Ithaca has offended Jupiter by blinding the Son of Neptune, Polyphemus the Cyclops, and must atone for his crime. Lane says goodbye to betrothed Helen (Alessandra Panaro), leaving her at the mercy of a second would-be suitor, Prince Adraste (Raf Baldassarre), and sets off to apprehend Marchal, hiring Phoenician pirates to attack Marchal's craft and take him prisoner. During an onboard fire, Marchal escapes, Lane swimming after him. On shore, he waylays his exhausted quarry, the

Dominique Boschero plays the mysterious feather-clad queen in *Ulysses Against Hercules*.

two tramping over arid desert wastes and becoming involved in a stereotypical peplum adventure, exciting one minute, utterly preposterous the next.

First, they meet a mysterious queen (Dominique Boschero), ruling a race of gray-skinned, twittering bird-faced creatures. Reclining in her resplendent crystalline grotto, attired in white feathers (and very little else), Boschero takes a fancy to both men, deciding not to sacrifice them to her god, a giant vulture, at the rising of the full moon; instead, they will fight to the death, and she'll wed the victor. Tied to a tree during a wild ceremonial tribal dance, the pair burst their bonds and run like Hades, encountering an old hermit in a forest glade before Marchal manages to sneak away from slumbering Lane at night.

Marchal now enters the realm of King Lagos, played with over-the-top demented relish by Gianni Santuccio; the crazed monarch has an army of pug-ugly cavemen at his disposal (they resemble the mutants in Allied Artists' *World Without End*, 1956), ready to wage war on King Icarno (Raffaele Pisu), whose daughter Panaro just happens to be Lane's intended. Santuccio throws Marchal into a cell, while Lane organizes Pisu's forces to meet the Neanderthals on the open plain: swords versus clubs. Santuccio, on chariot, leads his cavemen against Lane's white-robed warriors, the five-minute affray a terrific piece of bloody action conjured up by Mario Caiano (his first of seven pepla), especially when Lane hoists Santuccio's chariot and hurls it at the enemy (note a stuntman falling off his horse in the 77th minute before battle commences). Lane strangles Santuccio, rushing back to the mad king's palace, tangling with a trio of barrel-chested cavemen and hauling on counterweights to prevent Marchal from being crushed under a slowly descending cell ceiling, a nerve-wracking moment of sweaty suspense, one of the best in pepla. Marchal feigns delirium (he probably didn't have to after undergoing this ordeal!); at nightfall, Baldassarre and his followers infiltrate Lane's camp, the rejected suitor making off with Panaro. Lane chucks boulders and logs at the soldiers, employing a two-footed drop kick; Marchal, restored to normality, chases after Baldassarre and slays the usurper in a brutal head-on duel. Lane, grateful to Marchal for saving his girl, prays

Brad Harris finds himself behind bars in *The Fury of Hercules*.

to Jupiter, asking him to relieve the king of any further suffering. A golden light fills the screen, a sign from the gods that Marchal has paid the price for blinding Polyphemus. Marchal sails off to Ithaca and his family, leaving Lane and Panaro on a sea wall, clasping hands.

Clean-shaven Lane (he played the bandaged monster in Allied Artists' 1958 horror movie *Frankenstein 1970*) was okay as Hercules, though not quite as muscle-packed as his predecessors and lacking impact. Marchal, on the other hand, was splendid as a thoughtful Ulysses, investing his troubled character with a depth and meaning not usually found in these kind of films. The star of this particular show was undoubtedly Mario Caiano—his creativity behind the camera helped forge all the oddball pieces of the jigsaw into a bizarrely entertaining whole (cuts in U.S. prints spoil the continuity on occasions), assisted by Angelo Francesco Lavagnino's fine score and Alvaro Mancori's vivid colors. Shot in the Canary Islands to give the picture a different look, *Ulysses Against Hercules* is fun-packed nonsense put over with oodles of style and dash.

The Fury of Hercules [*La furia di Ercole*] aka *The Fury of Samson*

CI.AS./Comptoir Francais CFFP (Italy/France); Totalscope/Eastmancolor; 97 mins; Producer: Mario Maggi; Director: Gianfranco Parolini ††††

Hercules (Brad Harris) arrives on his four-horse chariot in Arpad to find the king dead, Queen Comidia (Mara Berni) struggling to rule her people; military advisor Menistus (Serge Gainsbourg) and his cronies desire the throne and don't take kindly to the Son of Zeus poking his nose into their scheming. During a dance (performed by the Zagreb Opera Ballet), an unsuccessful assassination attempt is made on Hercules, who is then shown the remains of supposed traitors rotting in the dungeons by Daria (Luisella Boni, billed as Brigitte Corey), daughter of rebel leader Eridone (Carlo Tamberlani). Eridone's second daughter is

1963

Hercules Challenges Samson [*Ercole sfida Sansone*] aka **Hercules, Samson and Ulysses**

I.C.D. (Italy); Totalscope/Eastmancolor; 93 (88) mins; Producer: Joseph Fryd; Director: Pietro Francisci ††††

Iloosh Khoshabe/Richard Lloyd (left, as Samson) takes on Kirk Morris (Hercules) among the polystyrene temple columns in *Hercules Challenges Samson*.

The King of Ithaca, Laertes (Andrea Fantasia), asks Hercules (Kirk Morris) to slay a sea monster that is causing havoc among fishermen. Setting sail with Ulysses (Enzo Cerusico) and a handpicked crew, the monster is located (a giant growling sea lion, becoming pepla's, and celluloid's, poorest-ever sea beast) and harpooned; during a storm, the crew are washed ashore in Judaea, under the Philistine rule of Seren (Aldo Giuffre), whose mistress Delilah (Liana Orfei) desires all men. In Gaza (the city palace, a mighty ornate white stone edifice, is splendidly realized by the effects team) Hercules is mistaken for Samson (Iloosh Khoshabe, billed as Richard Lloyd), the scourge of the Philistines, and has to fight him to prove who he really is. But after a memorable clash amid a ruined temple, the two heroes form an alliance to overthrow the despot, while fending off the advances of Delilah.

Never have so many polystyrene columns, boulders and building blocks tumbled to the ground as frequently as they do in Pietro Francisci's two-for-the-price-of-one beefcake opus. The lengthy temple battle of the two mythical titans sequence is a hoot, Morris and Khoshabe cavorting among the ruins, lobbing pillars and massive carved lintels at each other, *and* bending metal poles, without breaking a sweat (note the electricity pylons in the background!); likewise, in the finale, they bring an entire temple crashing down on the heads of the Philistine army (adorned in WWII German helmets), a mind-boggling scene guaranteed to raise a smile. Orfei, arresting but not the silver screen's greatest Delilah, gets to bathe naked beside the Monte Gelato cascades, Khoshabe demonstrates his prowess with the javelin and axe, throwing two at a time and decimating Aldo Pini's troops (weird sound effects are used as the weapons fly through the air) and, as usual in a *Hercules* feature, Morris strangles a lion. The *Argo*, commanded by Fantasia, comes to the aid of Morris, Khoshabe and company in the climax, discharging rows of spears from a multiple spearcarrier, destroying the Philistines, Giuffre receiving a well-aimed javelin in his midriff. Morris is reunited with his wife, elfin Diletta D'Andrea, while Khoshabe swims back to the fatal charms of Orfei, unaware of what's in store for him!

On the whole, *Hercules Challenges Samson* is amusing fare, Morris and Khoshabe's gleaming muscles put to good use, but beware! On the half hour, Philistine thugs carry out a reprisal raid on a village; women are nailed to the walls (shot in close-up), people are hanged, children are put to the arrow and fleeing villagers are brought down with spears. One toddler trots out into the mayhem, callously shot with an arrow. It's a scene of

spared death in the Square of Sacrifices after Hercules (Samson in some prints), in a Trial of Truth, defeats a lion, an apeman and mute warrior Janak (Alan Steel). Alarmed at Menistus' growing power, Hercules joins the rebels in their mission to overthrow the undersized tyrant Daria, a spy working for the insurgents. Hercules is saved by Comidia, who loves him, from perishing in a pit of noxious fumes; she's killed as a result of her action. A climactic battle sees the rebels storming the city; Hercules calls upon Zeus to give him more strength and Menistus' troops, seeing their cause lost, desert the usurper in droves; he receives a volley of arrows in his breastplate, just reward for his treachery. Although Daria pleads with Hercules to stay, he rides off at the end as the gods have decreed further adventures for him.

"There's a chariot coming up to the gates." "How many men in it?" "There's only one. But his muscles are so big he might as well be two." Yes, Brad Harris made a decent Hercules, rugged-looking and beefy, lifting the film (as he did with that massive block of stone sliding down a ramp) out of its "seen it all before" rut into something special, putting in a solid star turn. Whether wrestling lions and that X-rated hairy apeman, tangling with Steel on a bed of spikes (he eventually wraps a metal bar round his neck), romancing Berni *and* Boni (some men had all the luck!), demolishing guards, chasing off three rampaging elephants or hurtling across country on his chariot pulled by four magnificent steeds, Harris was in fine fettle. Two secret passages, a rebel cave, Berni and Boni exuding allure and Gainsbourg (his final peplum) as weasely as ever (who would ever obey a command from *this* little tyke?); *The Fury of Hercules*, filmed in Yugoslavia, blessed with a pounding Carlo Innocenzi soundtrack and glowing cinematography courtesy of Francesco Izzarelli, is a fast-paced *Hercules* delight, one of the better of the entries in the series; Harris should have played the part more often, but chose not to.

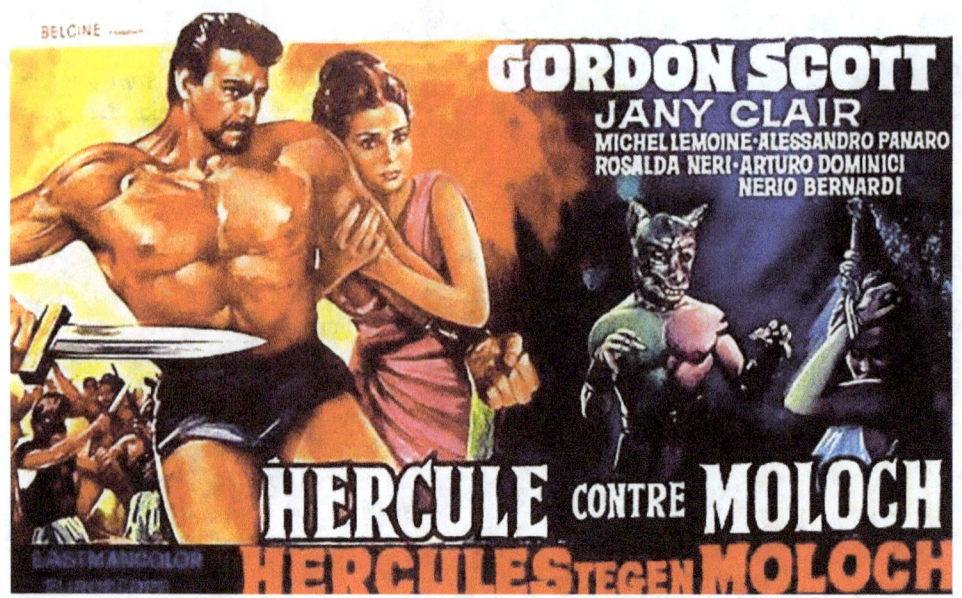
A Belgian poster for *Hercules Against Moloch*

sickening violence that doesn't sit well with the rest of the rather lighter antics, filmed in bright sunlight (Silvano Ippoliti), although Italian peplum cinema was full of barbaric moments like this; however, the carnage serves as a reminder of Khoshabe's equally violent counterattacks and motives. Angelo Francesco Lavagnino's noisy, overblown full orchestral score does its best to shatter the peace in a sword and sandal romp that is slow to get into gear; when Francisci engages the throttle, this is pure popcorn fodder for the less-discerning viewer.

Hercules Against Moloch [*Ercole contro Moloch*] aka *The Conquest of Mycenae*; *Hercules Attacks*

Explorer Film '58/Comptoir Francais CFFP (Italy/France); Euroscope/Eastmancolor; 102 (93) mins; Producer: Diego Alchimede; Director: Giorgio Ferroni †††

Hercules doesn't really figure in Giorgio Ferroni's semi-horror peplum—Gordon Scott plays Prince Glauco of Tiron who, in the 31st minute, informs Rosalba Neri (Demetra, Queen of Mycenae) that he's called "Hercules." Scott has infiltrated the new city of Mycenae (the old one is destroyed in an earthquake after the opening credits) posing as a captive, to put an end to Neri's reign of terror; not only does the lady with that refined Egyptian profile have sneering henchman Arturo Dominici (Pentheus) at her side, raiding neighboring cities for tribute and slave hostages, but a 20-year-old son so disfigured he inhabits a subterranean labyrinth wearing a hideous Minotaur mask, the god Moloch of the title; this screwed-up monster likes nothing better than to rip the faces of young virgins before shooting them with arrows, just for kicks ("You have lost your beauty," he grunts, raking their pretty faces with his fingernails). After all, his twisted mind reasons, if he's ugly, so should they be. Pumped up by Carlo Rustichelli's operatic soundtrack, *Hercules Against Moloch* comes complete with impressive set design (the Temple of the Earth Goddess is magnificent) and a few spirited action pieces, such as Scott and slave master Nello Pazzafini going head-to-head in the arena. But the big battle sequences have been filched from 1961's *The Trojan War* (also directed by Ferroni) and look out of place. Corrupt high priest Nerio Bernardi, poised to plunge a sacred dagger into sacrificial lamb Alessandra Panaro (Medea), is struck dead by a bolt of lightning, occurring frame-by-frame in Ferroni's *The Bacchantes* (1961), with Bernardi and Panaro again in the same roles, as priest and victim!

Dominici lusts after Panaro; Panaro loves Scott; Neri also fancies Scott; and Jany Clair (Deianira, a popular girl's name in *Hercules*' features) desires kindly Mycenaean Michel Lemoine. The film is a bit soap opera-ish at times, too much chat and plotting going on at the expense of muscular heroics; Scott doesn't get to show off his mighty frame once, and rarely smiles. The best moments are reserved for the closing moments: The Mycenaean army is defeated by Scott's rebels; below the palace, Moloch has Panaro chained to a wall, firing lighted arrows at her, his cult of screeching maidens beating out a frenzied rhythm on the drums; and he removes his mask, revealing grotesque horror features. In bursts Scott, wearing a massive plumed helmet, the caverns explode and crumble and Moloch takes on the he-man, burned to death when Scott kicks a brazier of hot coals over him. Panaro is declared the rightful queen, whispering "Glauco, my king!" to Scott, who at last gets to play house with at least one of the trio of lovelies populating this agreeable, though average, *Hercules* entry.

1964

Hercules the Invincible [*Ercole l'invincibile*] aka *Son of Hercules in the Land of Darkness*

Metheus Film (Italy); Techniscope/Technicolor; 85 (81) mins; Produced and Directed by Alvaro Mancori ††

Cinematographer Alvaro Mancori only directed two feature films, *Hercules the Invincible* being his one and only peplum. Claude Haroy is listed as photographer but that name was probably a pseudonym used by Mancori, a noted cinematographer who contributed immensely to a dozen pepla. Examples of his finest work can be seen in *Maciste Against the Vampire* (1961), *Toto and Cleopatra* (1963), *The Lion of St. Mark* (1963) and *I, Semiramis* (1963). As a photographer, he was among the best; as a director, not among the best. Dan Vadis, a real behemoth of an actor, played Argolese/Hercules in a skimpy tunic and skimpier beard, saving Spela Rozin (Princess Telca) from a lion mauling. Under tribal laws, Vadis can apply for her hand in marriage, but her father, Ugo Sasso (King Tedaeo), demands that the strongman first has to slay "The Dragon of the Mountain" and retrieve one of its teeth as a potent charm. Using footage from *The Labors of Hercules*, where Jason kills the dino-monster protecting the Golden Fleece (which can clearly be seen draped over a tree branch), Vadis grabs the tooth and returns to find Sasso's village destroyed. Queen Ella (Carla Calò), ruler of the underground city of Demios, is responsible; her minions, led by Ken Clark (minister Kabol), drink the blood of beautiful women to take on their attributes, and Calò has set her sights on Rozin for just that purpose. Pursued by a weird-looking bear-creature, Vadis and deeply annoying buddy John (Jon) Simons (Babar) set off to locate Rozin and her people, crossing a perilous stone bridge over a river of lava, avoiding traps and entering the kingdom to save the king and his daughter from being sacrificed.

Vadis looks the business here, always one of pepla's more energetic musclemen. Oiled six-pack to the fore, he wades into the guards, throwing them into the "Pit of Slime," breaks chains, skewers three soldiers with one almighty thrust of a spear, tangles with two elephants, pulls open a massive stone door that allows molten lava to flood the passages, bends prison bars and brings down the rock drawbridge in the closing stages; he also becomes the object of Calò's infatuated desires. Mancori's direction goes nowhere in the first 20 minutes and, up to the hour, the narrative is a shambolic mess, not helped by current ragged DVD prints. Vadis wanders from set to set looking dazed while the rest of the cast sit around Calò's ornate palace doing nothing much. Thankfully, the final 25 minutes picks up: Clark's malicious daughter, Maria Fiore (Melissa), stabs Calò in the back and assumes the role of queen, drinking a quantity of Rozin's blood from a goblet; the slaves are let loose, giving rise to umpteen clashes, Vadis at last in his combative element; and lava flows through the galleries which begin to cave in. Flore's final tragic moments, alone in her stately room, surveying her crumbling realm with mad serenity, the golden crown adorning her brunette beehive, horrified as the molten rock creeps slowly toward her ("Liquid of the earth—stay back," she shrieks), is pure melodrama, complemented by Francesco De Masi's tremendous music, becoming the best scene in the entire picture. Vadis hefts the stone bridge on his mighty shoulders and sends it crashing into the ravine; the enemy soldiers follow suit, and so does Clark after fighting with Vadis. The beefcake hero and Rozin walk arm in arm, grinning in love (and lust), the crowds celebrating their freedom.

During those final 25 minutes, the color photography is superb, Vadis squirming his bulk through narrow caverns lit in garish red; the underground city is also visually arresting, as is its destruction. But, up to this stage in the series, *Hercules the Invincible* is the weakest, least interesting of the *Hercules* flicks, lazy, uncoordinated and not particularly well acted. And an award must go to John Simons (an alias for an unknown Italian actor) as pepla's most irritating comical sidekick, his Toto-like antics totally scotching what could have been a passable sword and sandal fantasy; whether stuffing his cheeks with food, pulling faces, camping it up or dressing in soldier's garb and shouting orders to the guards, the little man's a veritable menace. He should have been consigned to the molten lava in reel one!

A Belgian poster for *Hercules the Invincible*

Hercules Against Rome [*Ercole contro Roma*]

Romana Film/Regina Films (Italy/France); Totalscope/Eastmancolor; 92 (85) mins; Producer: Fortunato Misiano; Director: Piero Pierotti †††

244 AD: Mansurio (Livio Lorenzon) on orders from Philip the Arab (Daniele Vargas) assassinates Emperor Gordian (Carlo Tamberlani). Ulpia (Wandisa Guida), the king's daughter, calls on Hercules (Alan Steel) for protection; the blacksmith is busy defending villages from Rosio (Andrea Aureli), whose mercenaries ally themselves to the praetorians, both parties aiming to gain control of the province of Ravenna. Philip is crowned ruler but comes up against an obstacle in the form of Lucio Trajan (Mimmo Palmara), Governor of Pannonia, Greece, who's in love with Ulpia. Hercules convinces Lucio to march his legions and counter Philip's army, thus ending the tyranny casting a shadow over Ravenna. In a mighty battle, the enemy forces are

An Italian photobusta for *Hercules Against Rome*

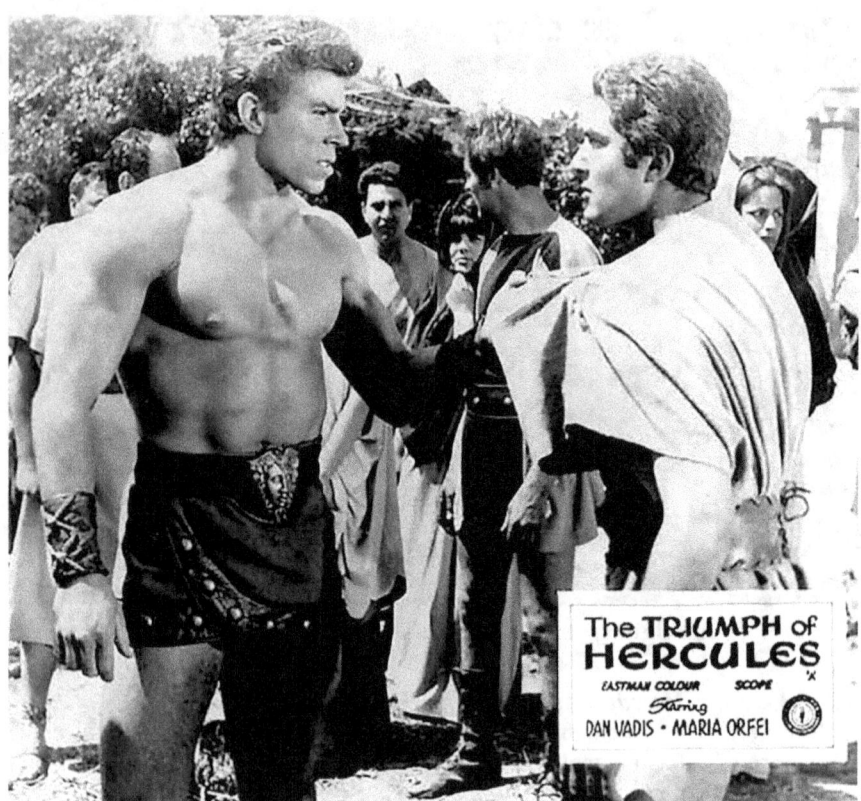
Dan Vadis displays his awesome physique in *The Triumph of Hercules*.

defeated, Lucio killing Philip. Ulpia is announced empress and Hercules rides away for further adventures.

A story that could have been written on a postage stamp is padded out by Steel's numerous energetic free-for-alls, fighting his macho way through one tavern/catacomb brawl after another, hurling all manner of objects at his opponents—doors, tables, boulders, sacks of grain and that old *Hercules* standby, a brazier of glowing embers. He also yanks his chains from a prison wall, smashes down the cell doors with a stone bench, upends a battering ram-cum-catapult war machine just for good measure, the ram's head making a useful weapon, and then he crushes Aureli under an anvil. A trio of snarling villains in Vargas, Lorenzon and henchman Nello Pazzafini is matched by a trio of beauties in Guida, Dina De Santis (Armenia, Steel's love interest) and Simonetta Simeone (Erica), as Pierotti hurls through the action to cover up familiarities in plot design, stock footage inserted for the battle sequences, a practice now becoming commonplace to cut down on production costs. There's nothing new on offer here, but *Hercules Against Rome* is tightly constructed and decently acted, with Steel putting in a muscular performance, a likeable Hercules in physique, looks and attitude that helps pass the 90-minute time pleasantly enough.

The Triumph of Hercules [Il trionfo di Ercole] aka Hercules vs. The Giant Warriors; Hercules and the Ten Avengers

Produzione Cinematografica/Unicité (Italy/France); Cromoscope/Eastmancolor; 95 (76) mins; Producers: Alberto Chemin, Vico Pavoni; Director: Alberto De Martino ††††

Dan Vadis shaved off that ridiculous wispy facial hair and demonstrated his trademark crouching "come and take me on" stance to great effect in his second *Hercules* outing, a vast improvement on *Hercules the Invincible*. Vadis almost verged on the vicious at times, hammering and battering his foes into submission, including seven (not 10) bronze bald musclemen conjured up from Hades by Pierre Cressoy's magic gold "Dagger of Jaia," a look of sheer glee lighting up his features, appearing to relish every single minute. Cressoy (Prince Melo) assassinates his uncle, the King of Mycenae, in the opening reel to gain control of the throne. "Send for Hercules," gasps the stricken monarch with his dying breath; learning of this, Cressoy heads off to a labyrinthine cave system where his mother, the sorceress Pasiphae (played by Moira Orfei, actually seven years younger than Cressoy!), hands a sacred dagger to her evil son, viewing Vadis in a mystical pool, busy erecting a new temple. In Mycenae, the grief-stricken populace stages a revolt at the death of their beloved king; Cressoy, by unsheathing the dagger, summons the seven indestructible warriors, all wearing studded dog collars, who go on a rampage, tossing the villagers in the air like rag dolls, Piero Lulli (Aristea, leader of the rebels, the actor on the side of good for a change) running in abject terror.

Vadis steps into the fray at a tournament given to decide who's to wed Marilù Tolo, the king's daughter, Ate. Cressoy has his slimy lieutenant, Howard Ross (Gordio, billed as Renato Rossini), earmarked for the suitor, his idea to have Ross marry Tolo, then finish them off to enable him to become total ruler. Ross, on his scythed chariot, defeats his foes, Vadis (The Son of Job in this picture) throwing down a challenge; in a ferocious clash, he pummels Ross senseless and throws his body onto a chariot blade, thus torpedoing Cressoy's plans. Vadis then fights the seven warriors of Jaia (a naughty monkey has taken the dagger from its sheath), wiping the floor with them. Not to be outwitted by his musclebound nemesis, Cressoy blames the king's murder on Lulli and the villagers, faking the abduction of Tolo. Enraged and taken in by Cressoy's deception, Vadis, in a moment of madness, destroys the settlement, uprooting trees, overturning huts, hurling millstones and pulling down a bridge; finally, he savagely beats Lulli into oblivion (a violent scene), realizing too late that he was wrong. Furious Zeus, as punishment, deprives him of his great strength and, during another barnstorming Vadis set-to in the palace, he's captured and flung in a cell. Now it's Tolo's turn to suffer torture in the arena: She's strapped to a plank, Vadis having to balance a huge counterweight beam filling with rocks on his shoulders to prevent her from being raised into a bed of spikes. His power sapping, a repentant Vadis calls on the gods for mercy; a thunderbolt rends the sky and his strength returns. Smashing the torture machine to pieces, Vadis flings the sacred dagger into a brazier, as Cressoy gallops off with Tolo to Orfei's domain. There, he's given another dagger with which to rally the bronze devils; Vadis tussles with them and pushes two pillars apart, the seven automatons from Hades crushed under tons of falling rock. Cressoy loses his footing on the rim of a fiery pit, plummeting to his doom. Orfei disguises herself as Tolo to hoodwink Vadis, both women crying for help on a crumbling cliff edge; Vadis, unsure of who's who, stares into their eyes, Orfei's orbs a bright orange giveaway. She tumbles onto the beach, expiring in the waves; Tolo is saved and, united with Vadis, the pair rule Mycenae.

Giuliano Gemma (left) and Mark Forest march into action in *Hercules Against the Sons of the Sun*.

An invigorating entry in the series, *The Triumph of Hercules* features Vadis in prime form, Alberto De Martino briskly rattling through the pared-to-the-bone action with stylistic dash; there's not an ounce of fat in this movie. Francesco De Masi provides a thumping score, while Pier Ludovico Pavoni's photography comes into its own during the fantasy-type cavern sequences. Number 13 in the *Hercules* franchise showed no signs of slowing down, even if every plot device was being put through the wringer to achieve a result that would still entertain an audience. Full credit to all concerned that by the middle of 1964 these sword and sandal *Hercules* outings maintained their freshness despite familiarities in content and design.

Hercules Against the Sons of the Sun [*Ercole contro i figli del sole*]

Wonder Films/Hispamer (Italy/Spain); Techniscope/Technicolor; 88 mins; Produced and Directed by Osvaldo Civirani ✝

The *Hercules* bandwagon spectacularly came off the rails in possibly the worse entry in the ongoing franchise, veteran filmmaker Osvaldo Civirani (he also cooperated on the cinematography with Julio Ortas, and the script) all at sea in a dafter-than-daft tale of shipwrecked Hercules, played by Mark Forest, landing on the shores of South America in the 1500s (several centuries out of his time zone) and becoming embroiled in a war between two rival Inca groups. A pumped-up Giuliano Gemma (Prince Maytha) saves Forest from an enemy attack; in return, the mythical hero enlists in Gemma's tribe, teaches them how to construct war machines with wheels ("You've never heard of wheels?" says Forest to Gemma) and wrests the throne at the city of Tiahuanaco from usurper Franco Fantasia (King Atahualpa) and his wife Angela Rhu. Along the way, Gemma's virgin sister, Anna-Maria Pace (Princess Hamara), is saved from a sacrificial stabbing; burly Carlo Latimer (Chaco) at first challenges Forest's strength, loses in a tangle and then befriends him; and José Riesgo, the true king, languishes in prison, talking to songbirds.

Granted, the colorful Inca costumes look fabulous, but fabulous costumes alone do not make a good movie, and this movie has shortcomings galore. That very familiar peplum shoreline setting leading to a series of white-stoned cliffs and small quarries is nothing like Bolivia or Peru; Fantasia, virtually unrecognizable under a layer of outlandish headgear and plumed outfits, appears deeply uncomfortable, probably wishing he was back in one of his more usual swashbuckling roles. The film features two six-minute dance routines (yes, two!), among the worst in pepla, uncoordinated, clumsy and unintentionally hilarious, Coriolano Gori's modernistic score compounding the awfulness of it all (his title music, on the other hand, is sublime); Civirani drags out some scenes to distraction (the flight from Tiahuanaco by Gemma and his warriors through a shallow river is a prime example) to bolster the running time. Forest brushes past a pillar that visibly moves, then topples the polystyrene block to the ground; three llamas are shown to try and convince the audience that we are *not* in Italy; and the final 12-minute battle is a ramshackle affair. Everyone except Forest wears long jet-black wigs, Riesgo (incorrectly listed as Fresco on many Internet film sites) falls on his own sword after consulting his feathered friend, Latimer gets a spear in the stomach, Gemma kills Fantasia in a climactic duel and Forest, beaming to the rejoicing populace, has the consolation of being stuck in Italy's answer to the Ancient Inca Empire by hitching up with Pace, a real doe-eyed beauty who only ever appeared in one other peplum, a bit part in *Brennus Enemy of Rome* (she quit the business after this picture). To rub salt into the wound, grainy monochrome stock footage of a herd of llamas, a golden eagle and the snow-capped Andes is tagged on at the end to further bamboozle us into believing that what we have just witnessed took place in South America, not the Lazio backlot.

Forest (who worked with Civirani on 1965's *Kindar, the Invulnerable*, a much better production) and Gemma must have had great difficulty in keeping the smiles off their faces and acting with a modicum of decorum when making this Herculean turkey, which can't even be classed as a guilty pleasure. More than once are guilty pleasures meant to be savored; once is more than enough for this particular *Hercules* outing.

Hercules, Samson, Maciste and Ursus: The Invincibles [*Ercole, Sansone, Maciste e Ursus; gli invincibili*] aka *Samson and His Mighty Challenge*; *Hercules Returns*

Senior Cinematografica/Films Régent/P.E. Films (Italy/Spain/France); Totalscope/Eastmancolor; 100 (94) mins; Produced and Directed by Giorgio Capitani ✝ for purists; ✝✝✝ for spoof lovers

Cartoon credits; Piero Umiliani's comedy '60s score; snatches of Beethoven's Fifth Symphony heard in moments of high (or low) drama; and Elisa Montés (Omphale) shouting to Hélène Chanel (Queen Numaya): "I would rather die than live with that brainless gorilla. You can have him," referring to Hercules' questionable beefy charms, which obviously don't turn her on. What we had here was a peplum spoof, a parody of sword and sandal where every plot device was played for belly laughs: the tavern dance; the oafish rebel leader; the bitchy queen; the

A French lobby card for *Hercules, Samson, Maciste and Ursus: The Invincibles*

trial of strength; the interfering dwarf; and four mythic heroes acting as if they hadn't got a single brain cell among them. In England, this would have been released as an 85-minute *Carry On Hercules*, part of the highly successful, long-running British *Carry On* series, with an appropriate cast to match (who would have played the four musclemen is anyone's guess); here, at 100 minutes, the result, if you're not into this kind of mickey-take, is an overlong bore that outstays its welcome after an hour. Did Pietro Francisci and Steve Reeves ever think that their 1957 trailblazer would come to *this* seven years later?

"Hercules, I gave you fair warning!" thunders Zeus as Alan Steel gallops toward the fleshpots of Lydia to sample the delights of its notoriously beautiful women, opting for a life of pleasure to one of virtue. Rescuing Montés from drowning in a fisherman's net, he takes the lass to Lydia and asks her mother, Chanel (overacting like mad), if they can marry. ("Love strikes like lightning to the son of a god.") The fiery princess, however, loves wimpy Luciano Marin (Enor), son of drunken warlord Livio Lorenzon (as Lico, he doesn't appear on set until 65 minutes has dragged by), using diminutive Arnaldo Fabrizio (Micron) to spin misleading prophecies about Hercules via the smoking mouth of the oracle. Steel has to prove who he is by dragging a wrecked boat full of gold out of the sea on the end of a rope; three emissaries are then sent to Palestine to bring back Samson (Nadir Moretti) so that he can defeat Steel and scotch his plans to wed Montés. "The strongest man in the world is Hercules. How do you expect me to fight myself?" says Steel on learning of this possible clash of the giants. The narrative then trips over its own sandals in a number of unfunny set pieces: Bad-tempered Roman slave Ursus (Yann Larvor) likes nothing better to do than demolish inns and force the proprietress to perform silly dances; Moretti is rendered useless when conniving Moira Orfei (Delilah) shears his locks; Maciste (Howard "Red" Ross) arrives on the scene to sort Larvor, and his foul mood, out; Lorenzon stumbles all over his settlement, cackling like a maniac; and Montés is almost burned at the stake by Lorenzon, who wants his boy to marry someone else. Weak-as-a-kitten Moretti is taken to Lydia against his will ("I'm weak. I don't wanna go to Lydia. I wanna go home!" he bawls to Ross and Larvor), defeated by Steel in a square ring of pink ribbon held by four maidens. The entire fatuous shebang ends in a mass scrum, Moretti having regained his powers. Sick of all the infighting, Zeus calls a halt (and not before time), decreeing that Montés gets hitched to her ineffectual lover, Steel, Larvor and Ross escorting Moretti back to face the wrath of his tempestuous wife. Spoof movies were nothing new, even in 1964, but why send up a genre that occasionally sent itself up without realizing it. Like *Hercules Against the Sons of the Sun*, Giorgio Capitani's goofy opus can only be viewed once by those with more serious inclinations who, at the time, were no doubt wondering whether the *Hercules* run of adventures had quite literally nowhere else to go, or had nothing new to say.

Hercules Against the Tyrants of Babylon [*Ercole contro i tiranni di Babilonia*]

Romana Film (Italy); Totalscope/Eastmancolor; 97 (86) mins; Producer: Fortunato Misiano; Director: Domenico Paolella ✝✝✝

In Ancient Babylon 3,000 years ago, a trio of tyrants—Salman Osar (Livio Lorenzon), his brother Azur (Tullio Altamura) and sister Taneal (Helga Liné)—govern the city. Among the hundreds of slaves incarcerated in subterranean dungeons is Esperia, Queen of the Hellenes (Anna Maria Polani). The winsome fugitive is much in demand—Salman Osar wants to kill her after he's had his wicked way; Azur desires marriage to cement an alliance and gain total rule; Taneal wishes her out of the way, regarding the lass as a threat to her own ambitions; King Phaleg of Assyria (Mario Petri) also fancies wedlock, the queen's army boosting his own forces, making him invincible; and Hercules (Peter "Rock Stevens" Lupus) is after rescuing his queen and returning her to Hellenes. Phaleg showers gifts on the three despots to ingratiate himself but is seduced by Taneal, giving away his real reasons for visiting Babylon when she drugs his wine. After a skirmish with Babylonian cavalry, Hercules meets Phaleg, advising him that Esperia needs to be rescued from the catacombs. Hercules and six of Phaleg's crack troops infiltrate Babylon and reach the gloomy dungeons via a secret gallery; behind a huge stone block, he finds Esperia among scores of female prisoners. At a feast, Hercules is ordered by Salman Osar to take on six beefy champions; the muscleman defeats three, realizing that the tyrants meant to put him out of the way as one of his opponents held a spiked club. After the slaves have been freed, Hercules works the winch in a vast chamber that tightens colossal chains attached to the city's foundations, bringing the walls of Babylon crumbling down on the populace. Salman Osar murders Azur but dies under falling masonry; in the desert, the released slaves overwhelm the Assyrians, Hercules beats Phaleg to death, Taneal poisons herself and the Son of Zeus is reunited with Esperia. Jointly, they lead their people away, marching toward Hellenes and a new life.

Hercules Against the Tyrants of Babylon was the last of the *Hercules* syndicate proper. The next, *Hercules the Avenger*, was a rehash of two previous outings starring Reg Park (*Hercu-*

An Italian poster for *Hercules Against the Tyrants of Babylon*

Liné). To spice things up, there's an "I am Spartacus!" moment when Lorenzon's mob whip dozens of female slaves tethered to stakes in an effort to unmask Esperia, the girls all shouting, "I'm the Queen of the Hellenes!" Containing an Angelo Francesco Lavagnino stock soundtrack (always worth a listen) plus glowing Augusto Tiezzi photography, *Hercules Against the Tyrants of Babylon* more or less completed the series, not perhaps with a bang, but certainly not with a whimper, Paolella ensuring that the pace never slackened and all involved performed to the best of their abilities.

1965

Challenge of the Giants [*La sfida dei giganti*] aka ***Hercules the Avenger***

Plaza Film/Schermi Riuniti (Italy); Techniscope/Technicolor; 86 mins; Producer: Armando Govoni; Director: Maurizio Lucidi ††

Structured around 20 minutes of footage culled from *Hercules and the Conquest of Atlantis* and *Hercules at the Center of the Earth*, the last of Reg Park's five peplum movies was a fantasy adventure designed to take in sequences from the earlier films (a cut-and-paste job if ever there was one), concoct a basic plotline and still make the end product appear cohesive, which it just about managed to do. When Park's son Xantos (Luigi Barbini) is mauled by a lion, not only is he badly injured, he's become a delirious lunatic, having to be strapped to his bed because his soul has been imprisoned in Hades. Park journeys to the nether regions to restore Barbini's tortured spirit while the Earth Goddess Gia sends her son Anteo (Giovanni Cianfriglia) to take Park's place among the mortals, the substitute Hercules sitting beside Leda, Queen of Syracuse (Gia Sandri), who has just rejected six totally unsuitable suitors for her hand in marriage; her realm is under threat from the Phoenicians and Carthaginians and she's looking for a protector, preferably in Hercules. Trouble is, Cianfriglia is a raving, murdering, uncontrollable maniac, spearing young maidens, wolfing down food and drink, bullying Sandri's treasurer, forcing himself on her, employing criminals as his personal bodyguard who terrorize the citizens and putting to death those who refuse to up their tribute by 100 percent—one young girl is even hung by a rope tied in her hair, her horrified

les and the Conquest of Atlantis* and *Hercules at the Center of the Earth*), while *Hercules and the Princess of Troy* was a TV-produced movie that was later given a limited cinema release. This was Lupus' first sword and sandal outing (he made four, three directed by Paolella), while Petri only had one more to go after this before calling it a day, 1964's *Goliath at the Conquest of Bagdad*, filmed back-to-back by the same team and also featuring Lupus, Liné and Polani in the cast. Paolella's gaudy offering was a considerable improvement on *Hercules, Samson, Maciste and Ursus: The Invincibles*, but how could it not be. Man-giant Lupus, rippling tanned torso gleaming under camera lights, hurls boulders, snaps weapons, shifts blocks, lassos ranks of archers and wields an enormous club with panache, a smile on his handsome face; Lorenzon is even more demented than normally, appearing intoxicated in most of his scenes ("Employ an army to destroy one man?" he roars when hearing of Hercules' escapades). Liné was one of the genre's true beauties and looks ravishing, Paolella closing in on her refined bone structure several times; the obliteration of Babylon is well-executed; Petri is solid as usual; and perhaps Polani comes off second-best, but not really queen material (unlike the more forceful

An Italian photobusta for *Challenge of the Giants*

Gordon Scott squares up to the fascinating bug-eyed sea creature in *Hercules and the Princess of Troy*.

At the beginning of 1965, American producer Joseph E. Levine announced plans to make 32 one-hour episodes featuring Hercules for the ABC network, based on the Son of Zeus' successful Italian exploits. A budget of $4,000,000 was penciled in, pulp producer/writer/director Albert Band taken on to steer the helm and Gordon Scott hired in the title role (it was to be the last of his 14 genre films), a mix of American and Italian actors in secondary parts. Ace effects technician Carlo Rambaldi was brought in to manufacture the sea monster and the first episode, *Hercules and the Princess of Troy*, was aired on September 12, 1965. It wasn't a hit with the public or critics and no further episodes were forthcoming, the film later playing as a second feature in some parts of Europe.

Was it worth all the effort? What we have here is a truncated *Hercules* adventure, half the length of a normal *Hercules* offering, accounting for a definite rushed feel to the narrative. Scott (looking very pumped-up), educated Paul Stevens (Diogenes) and up-for-a-fight Mart Hulswit (Ulysses) sail to the rescue of Diana Hyland (Princess Diana of Troy) when her dastardly uncle, Steve Garrett (Petra), kills the king and arranges for her to be the next sacrifice to the sea monster, thus enabling him to rule the city. Peplum bad guy Gordon Mitchell disappointingly figures only in the first couple of minutes as a pirate captain, a pity because Mitchell at his most ferocious was always worth the price of a ticket alone (he should have been allowed more screen time), while another genre favorite, Roger Browne (Ortag), injured by the creature, wears a Phantom of the Opera half-mask throughout (this was his final sword and sandal opus as well). You can't help wondering whether the likes of Andrea Aureli as Petra and Rosalba Neri as Diana would have added more flavor; Hyland and Garrett are adequate but lack the necessary Italian fire and spirit to bring life to their characters. Another peplum regular, blond George (Giorgio) Ardisson, was Leander, Hyland's intended husband. Cinematographer Enzo Barboni's bright colors add to the foreign location work (Italy and Yugoslavia), but Fred Steiner's music is strictly TV-oriented and rather mundane. Star of the show is undoubtedly Rambaldi's striking sea monster. A full-sized mechanical model worked by six motors and (for the time) complex circuitry, this cross between a giant caterpillar and a crustacean is a corny delight, lurching onto the beach to do battle with Scott who stabs the thing around 30 times before it expires. A bug-eyed beauty with claws, Rambaldi's creation wouldn't have looked out of place in a '50s B-creature feature, one of the most arresting in peplum, even though it resembles a fairground attraction! Fast-moving and enjoyable but all over in a flash, this would be the last occasion fans would see likeable, charismatic Gordon Scott in a loincloth pushing down stone pillars, one of the genre's genuine "greats," still in his prime, even though the picture betrayed its television origins in several underdeveloped areas.

father sobbing in agony. Needless to say, Great God Jove isn't happy with this state of affairs. When Park returns from his mission and Barbini regains his senses, his soul at rest, he confronts Cianfriglia after the city has been devastated in a cataclysm, the pair slugging it out for three minutes in a low-vaulted cavern. The sham Hercules is battered to death, leaving Park, wife Adriana Ambesi and their son to play happy families.

Director Lucidi uses extensive sequences from *Hercules at the Center of the Earth* to depict Park in the underworld searching for his son's phantom (some fresh footage was included), that movie's attack of the harpies scene brought forward to enable the musleman to combat something evil in his quest; likewise, the destruction of Atlantis from *Hercules and the Conquest of Atlantis* is a convenient method of wiping out the entire cast of *this* picture which, due to the awkward insertion of a plethora of filched shots, falls apart at the seams at this juncture in the narrative. If you haven't seen the first two movies, *Challenge of the Giants* works; if you have, it doesn't—you're only too aware that what you are watching is a composite of three separate, altogether different, features stitched together to form an overall unsatisfactory whole. Alvaro Mancori is listed as cinematographer, Mario Bava's work on the other two films ignored in the opening credits. Thanks to an unusually near-pristine letterbox DVD print, *Challenge of the Giants*, marking the end of the classic run of Italian *Hercules* features, is fine to watch from an aesthetic angle (after all, how many peplum outings look *this* good?), but as an example of sword and sandal filmmaking, it comes across as a cheese-paring exercise and a bit of a cheat in the bargain.

Hercules and the Princess of Troy aka **Hercules vs. the Sea Monster**

Embassy Television (Italy/US); Technicolor; 47 mins; Produced and directed by Albert Band ✝✝✝

6
Maciste 1960-1965

Spurred on by the worldwide box-office triumphs of Steve Reeves' first two *Hercules* films, Italian producers decided to revive the character of strongman Maciste, originally the star of 28 silent movies made between 1914 and 1927, a figure carved from classical Greco-Roman myth. *Maciste in the Valley of the Kings* was the first of 24 outings produced from 1960 to 1965. Mark Forest starred in seven, Kirk Morris six, Gordon Scott two, Alan Steel two and one apiece for Gordon Mitchell, Samson Burke, Ed Fury, Reg Park and Iloosh Khoshabe. Reg Lewis was in one but also appeared in the rarity *Maciste, Avenger of the Maya* along with Kirk Morris; the movie was a stitched-up job of footage taken from *Maciste Against the Monsters* and *Maciste Against the Headhunters*, which starred Lewis and Morris respectively. Renato Rossini (Howard Ross) played Maciste in the *Hercules* movie *Hercules, Samson, Maciste and Ursus: The Invincibles*. How mighty Maciste, the savior of the poor, starving, downtrodden and repressed, the righter of wrongs, arrived at various locales on the planet among the people he stood up for remains a perplexing mystery only hinted at; he was never given a history, an enigmatic, somewhat one-dimensional hero flitting from one situation to another, and in different time zones. This results in a lack of character depth, although in movies of this type, depth of character isn't really needed. How he brings about the downfall of the bad guys is all that counts. As with the *Hercules* movies, I have listed the *Maciste* films in order of their original Italian release dates.

1960

Maciste in the Valley of the Kings [*Maciste nella valle dei re*] aka *Son of Samson*; *Maciste the Mighty*

Panda Societa/Gallus Films/CICC (Italy/France/Yugoslavia); Totalscope/Technicolor; 94 (89) mins; Producers: Luigi Carpentieri, Ermanno Donati; Director: Carlo Campogalliani ✪✪✪✪✪

Egypt 500 BC: The Persians cruelly govern the subjugated people of the Nile. Kindly Pharaoh Armiteo I wishes to liberate those enslaved within the walls of the city of Tanis, but his scheming wife Queen Smedes has other ideas; the vixen plans to have her husband assassinated and throw in her lot with the invaders, leaving her to rule with an iron glove. Armiteo is murdered, the sovereign head of state appointing the Persian Grand Vizier as her second-in-command. Armiteo's humane son Kenamun, who lives among the poor and has fallen in love with peasant girl Nofret, returns to Tanis, only to be drugged by a magic pendant, the "necklace of forgetfulness," falling into the clutches of the consort; she's going to marry him and further her hold on Egypt. But the she-devil hasn't reckoned on Maciste, Son of Samson, the mysterious strongman "born from the rock," appearing out of nowhere; the musclebound hero in a yellow loincloth promises to lead a revolt against Smedes and her Persian buddies and restore Kenamun to the throne.

Mark Forest, hired for the first of the 24 *Maciste* features, had the honed physique, the good looks and the athleticism required for this responsible role, but possessed very little acting instinct, although, to his credit, he progressed in later outings. Forest was the second American actor after Steve Reeves to be recruited for Italian sword and sandal pictures, a move which prompted the short-lived "Society to Protect Italian Musclemen" to complain about foreign imported *fusti* stars taking up roles that could have been filled by homegrown bodybuilders. The only scene in which he appears remotely animated is when Chelo Alonso (Smedes) puts her Folies Bergere dancing experience to good use and performs one of her most raunchy numbers, a red veil swirling around her lithe figure as she belly dances provocatively over to Forest and seduces him; what red-blooded male wouldn't appear aroused at such a glorious sight! Carlo Campogalliani's Egyptian peplum confection is extremely gory in parts, especially the opening strike on a village; people burned at the stake, cut to pieces, set on fire and buried head and feet first in the sand (riders gallop over their protruding, battered heads). Forest gets to fight a lion, heave a couple of oversized boulders and a big millstone at the enemy, flip a ladder full of men into the river and worm his way into Alonso's court, the temptress eying his pecs lustfully, momentarily banishing from her mind her forthcoming sham nuptials to puny Angelo Zanolli (as Kenamun), Carlo Tamberlani (Armiteo) conveniently done away with by Zvonimir Rogoz, the wily vizier. The young pharaoh walks around in a complete daze, unaware of his intended's

U.S. half-sheet poster for *Son of Samson* (aka *Maciste in the Valley of the Kings*)

Gordon "born from the rock" Mitchell admires a reclining Chelo Alonso in *Maciste in the Land of the Cyclops*.

devious plotting. The director conjures up some riveting set pieces: the raising of a giant stone obelisk by hundreds of toilers (pinched unashamedly from Cecil B. DeMille's *The Ten Commandments*); women, bound and blindfolded, scythed down by a bladed chariot; and a tremendous battle sequence waged on the plains (an axe in the head; poles rammed into torsos; a pronged fork plunged into a mouth), Forest pulling down a bridge to save the villagers from being overrun and massacred. The all-blazing climax has Zanolli relieved of the mystical necklace and regaining his senses, enough to remember that Federica Ranchi (Nofret) was his sweetheart; the freedom fighters storm the city, Rogoz expires and bewitching Alonso meets her end by falling into a pool full of crocodiles. As for Forest, he has the charms of dark-haired beauty Vira Silenti to find solace in; she's been drooling over those biceps ever since laying eyes on him in the 20th minute and thinks he's a god.

It's fast, it's furious, it's bloody and it's fun, composer Carlo Innocenzi providing a thundering score and cinematographer Riccardo Pallottini suffusing the luxurious sets and Ancient Egyptian panoramas in pin-sharp color. *Maciste in the Valley of the Kings* is pure 100 percent classic peplum, a thumping series opener; even Forest's awkward performance fails to spoil the party. After all, this is Chelo Alonso's show, and boy, does she make the most of it!

1961

Maciste in the Land of the Cyclops [*Maciste nella terra dei ciclopi*] aka **Atlas in the Land of the Cyclops**; **Atlas Against the Cyclops**; **Monster from the Unknown World**

Panda Film (Italy); Dyaliscope/Eastmancolor; 100 (95) mins; Producers: Luigi Carpentieri, Ermanno Donati; Director: Antonio Leonviola ††††

Gordon Mitchell (born Charles Allen Pendleton; a clairvoyant forecast he would be given his pseudonym and have a great career in Italy) took on the *Maciste* persona in the first of his run of 15 pepla. The rugged-looking actor would perfect his trademark snarling, bulldozing style later on in such genre classics as *The Fury of Achilles* (1962) and *Brennus Enemy of Rome* (1963); in Antonio Leonviola's cheesy schlock fantasy, he did little more than grin and pose, his massive frame causing busty Chelo Alonso (Queen Capys of Sadok) to go weak at the knees and drool like a schoolgirl nursing an almighty crush. Vicious, cold-hearted Alonso is a cursed woman, the victim of Circe's vengeance; centuries ago, Ulysses outwitted the enchantress and Polyphemus, the one-eyed giant, and her thirst for revenge lives on. Only by the Cyclops devouring the last descendant of Ulysses will the curse be lifted and the queen find peace, restored to her normal, loving self. In a hunt for the child who would be king, second-in-command Dante Di Paolo (Iftus) razes Germano Longo's village to the ground but his wife, Vira Silenti (Penope), escapes with their infant, the one that Alonso is after. Mitchell is assigned the task of protecting the toddler, involving the muscleman in a stream of bone-headed japes in and out of Alonso's Gothic retreat.

"Who are you," the Cuban H-bomb pants at Mitchell when he saves her from death by supporting a crumbling cavern ceiling, arching her luscious eyebrows and gazing at his pecs. "Maciste … I am born from the rock." Di Paolo, lusting after the queen, simmers with jealousy, using a magic potion concocted by giant black slave Paul Wynter (Mumba) to give to Mitchell in the hope that he'll reveal the whereabouts of the child and Silenti, hiding in a shepherd's mountain cave. The infant is captured, Silenti coming forward to save her son, the rightful heir to the throne. Di Paolo seizes the opportunity to take mother and child to the Cyclops' island; Alonso, in love with Mitchell, releases him and follows in a boat whose crew has been drugged. No problem—Mitchell grabs all the oars and rows by himself, putting those formidable biceps to good use. On the island, Silenti and child are flung into a cage and lowered into the monster's lair. Mitchell and Alonso arrive on the scene; Di Paolo accidentally stabs her to death and is hurled into the pit by Mitchell, where he's gobbled up. The mythical warrior then leaps into the pit, plunges his sword into the Cyclops' single eye and brings the cavern walls crashing down on the beast's body. The toddler is finally pronounced King of Sadok, Mitchell riding away to tend to the needs of others, who may in future require that legendary strength of his to win over their enemies.

There's no doubting Alonso's animalistic sex appeal, especially in the scene where Mitchell feeds her grapes at a feast, cooing, "I am a prisoner of your beauty." Who wouldn't be while in her presence. The actress steals the show, Mitchell reduced to the role of a hulking, rather dumb, savior; as mentioned, the granite-faced one would promote what latent acting skills he possessed later on. Wrecked by muddy color and pan and scan, a remastering job on Leonviola's cranky "Ancient World" sword and sandal opus would stop detractors from announcing this archetypal peplum as rubbish. What it represents is genre mytho-

Maciste Against the Vampire (aka *Goliath and the Vampires*) was rated "X" in England; this spooky American lobby card shows the Blue Men marching on the vampire's lair.

logical ideology taken to its cheesy extremes, where nothing seems real, nobody plays it straight but where one should say, "To hell with it. Let's just sit here with the popcorn and enjoy it all." And if one of pepla's top three composers, Carlo Innocenzi, can go to all the time and trouble in coming up with a knockout score to match the dafter-than-daft action, *Maciste in the Land of the Cyclops*, the first of six *Maciste* features churned out on the Cinecitta conveyor belt during 1961, must have something going for it, surely. (Keen-eyed buffs can spot Mitchell as an extra in Cecil B. DeMille's *The Ten Commandments*; 86 minutes in, he's the guard standing next to Charlton Heston in chains.)

Maciste Against the Vampire [*Maciste contro il vampiro*] aka *Goliath and the Vampires*

Ambrosiana (Italy); Totalscope/Technicolor; 92 (89) mins; Producer: Paolo Moffa; Directors: Giacomo Gentilomo, Sergio Corbucci ✝✝✝✝✝

Maciste (Goliath in U.S. prints) saves young fisherboy Ciro from drowning and returns to his village to find it razed to the ground, his mother dead, the women all gone, including sweetheart Julia. Kobrak, a vampire lord, is ruling the land of Salmanak with an army of faceless, undead human robots created from captured slaves and a group of masked pirate marauders who need female blood to survive. Maciste and Ciro travel to the city and meet the mysterious Kurtik, an alchemist bent on destroying Kobrak with his own army of the Blue Men. Devilish Amazon queen Astra is in league with Kobrak, murdering all those standing in the path of her twisted game plan to rule the land using the vampire's supernatural powers. After numerous scraps with the Sultan's militia, Maciste and a squadron of Blue Men slog through sinister, mist-shrouded woods and marshes toward Kobrak's lair; the vampire possesses a magic potion contained in a vial that can restore the dead to life, while Kurtik has concocted a chemical of his own that will destroy the monster. In Kobrak's cavern, Astra has taken Julia prisoner; Maciste's beloved is now one of the undead. Astra, who loves Maciste, sacrifices herself to save him, Kobrak taking on the form of Maciste and engaging in a fight to the death. Kurtiks's chemicals cause Kobrak to reveal himself as a hideous creature before he expires under tons of falling rock. Kobrak's vaporized liquid restores Julia to normality, the vampire's reign of terror is over, Kurtik is proclaimed the new Sultan of Salmanak, a giant statue of Maciste is erected and the well-built savior rides off with Julia, back to their coastal home to be wed.

Fresh from Paramount's *Tarzan the Magnificent* (1960), Gordon Scott's (born Gordon Merrill Werschkul) first of 14 peplum outings is a firm fan favorite, and deservedly so. Imaginative set designs, especially Kurtik's (Jacques Sernas) and Kobrak's (Guido Celano) splendid grotto habitats, are bathed in Alvaro Mancori's equally imaginative colors, an artful blend of creepy fantasy and Gothicism that, combined with the film's horror elements, caused the British censor to slap an "X" rating on the movie when it was released in England in 1962 (Dino De Laurentiis handled worldwide distribution). Ghostly visitations, wax effigies dripping blood, a pit full of giant, rubbery clawed crustaceans, throats ripped out, talk of witchcraft, black magic and sorcery, an arrow in the eye, Celano's *House of Wax*-type face when unmasked, cries of "Our master needs that blood at once!" and little boys dying (Rocco Vitolazzi, as Ciro, is injured under a falling tree and fails to recover) were deemed unsuitable for a family audience. Good-looking Scott proved himself to be in the same charismatic league as Steve Reeves: There's plenty of energetic beefcake action here for buffs to get their teeth into, as in the three-minute sequence where Scott takes on the Sultan's men-at-arms in the market square, bashing them with a pole, picking up a cart and tossing it in the air, demolishing a wall and chucking a bed of spikes at his adversaries. Twice during the movie, the muscular hero pulls down a pillar, causing the ceiling to collapse, and that's in addition to breaking his shackles, busting a yoke and sending soldiers reeling with two lengths of chain; he also survives the ringing of a gigantic bell placed over him by Kobrak's zombies. Jacques Sernas, head swathed in blue cloth, resembled Lawrence of Arabia in most of his scenes, and as for Gianna Maria Canale, the actress positively shimmered as Astra, one of the genre's undisputed aristocratic-looking beauties; beside her, Leonora Ruffo, playing Julia, didn't stand a chance, although herself blessed with ravishing looks. One jarring note was Les Baxter's jaunty guitar leitmotif, heard when a scantily attired wench dances in a tavern (inserted for Western audiences); thank goodness these anachronistic tones only lasted a couple of minutes and we returned to Angelo Francesco Lavagnino's more appropriate score (his evocative music in the earlier palace dance interlude is sublime, full of Eastern promise). Although Sergio Corbucci is listed as joint director, sources state that his input was minimal, Giacomo Gentilomo undertaking most of the spadework. A wonderfully bizarre mix of traditional peplum, 1950s horror and even a dash of sci-fi, *Maciste Against the Vampire* packs in the lurid set pieces, right from the very first moment Scott is framed up close, hoisting a massive boulder over his handsome head as he tills the land.

Kirk Morris in the "restraining the chariots" scene from *The Triumph of Maciste*

The Triumph of Maciste [*Il trionfo di Maciste*] aka ***Triumph of the Son of Hercules***

Jork Film/Panda Film (Italy); Totalscope/Eastmancolor; 88 mins; Producer: Roberto Capitani; Director: Tanio Boccia (Amerigo Anton) ✞✞✞

In the land of Memphis, Queen Tenefi sacrifices young virgins to the serpent-headed God of Fire on Thunder Mountain, if her oppressed people refuse to pay enough tribute. Maciste rescues a group of maidens in chains, among who is Antea. The mythic warrior then joins forces with Prince Iram, rightful heir to the throne, and infiltrates the city with the aid of Omnes, a silk merchant. On payment of 100 gold pieces, Omnes turns traitor, revealing to Prime Minister Agadon the whereabouts of Maciste; in an attack, Arsinoe, captain of Iram's men-at-arms, is wounded and Maciste taken prisoner. Tenefi falls in love with Maciste and releases him after he's restrained two chariots in a trial of strength; however, to ensure his loyalty, Maciste is injected with a drug from her scepter, making him lose his memory. Antea is given an antidote by the Sybil, administers the potion to Maciste via a dart and he regains his senses. During an ambush on Iram's troops, treacherous Omnes is stabbed in the back; Antea is captured, taken to the caverns in Thunder Mountain and laid on the altar to be sacrificed. Maciste follows, grapples with a lion, forces apart the Gates of Fire, slays an ogre, fights the Yuri men (a race of ugly troglodytes sporting talons) and rescues Antea. Denied its sacrifice, the giant idol disintegrates, a cataclysm bringing the roof down, killing Tenefi and Agadon under tons of rock. Iram's men storm Memphis, overthrowing the enemy and peace is restored. Iram, pronounced king, takes his place on the throne, while Maciste and Antea gallop off to savor the delights of each other's well-defined bodies.

A by-now typical *Maciste* adventure is directed with zip by Tanio Boccia, who obviously set out to promote Kirk Morris' physique after a movie producer had spotted the youngster as a gondolier and brought him to Boccia's attention. In the "restraining chariots" scene, his camera zooms up on the actor's bulging biceps, thighs and crotch area; no wonder exotic beauty Liuba Bodina (Queen Tenefi) licks her luscious lips in anticipation and later says to the sweating hunk: "Wouldn't you like a sip from my goblet?" And this isn't Morris' first tempting female offer; in reel one, Cathia Caro (Antea) whispers, after he has saved her, "I will be your slave or whatever else you want me to be." Strangely, Caro vanished without trace after making the picture (her sixth), as did Bodina with one additional movie after this (she only starred in three). The royal palace is a dreamy piece of art deco design and the subterranean sequences (seen in *Maciste in Hell*, made around the same time but not completed until some months later) were shot in the enchanting Castellana grottos near Bari. Carlo Innocenzi's score, augmented by Guido Robuschi and Gian Stellari's dramatic musical tones, works wonders; regrettably, current prints are in washed-out color; check online stills which display cinematographer Oberdan Troiani's vivid schemes as they *should* be seen. Cesare Fantoni (Agadon) and Giulio Donnini (Omnes) make a rascally pair of villains, and as for Kirk Morris (aka Adriano Bellini) in his first of 15 peplum features, he chucks the requisite number of boulders, roof supports, tables, gates and sundry stone objects at his antagonists with boyish glee, is corned by a circle of spears, the classic peplum pose, survives a landslide of rocks and emerges with a look of innocence and naivety, one of the younger of the slew of bodybuilder stars of his generation—he was 23 at the time of filming, a novice plucked from the canals of Venice, and it showed.

Maciste, the Strongest Man in the World [*Maciste, l'uomo piu forte del mondo*] aka ***Mole Men Against the Son of Hercules***

Leone Film (Italy); Totalscope/Eastmancolor; 91 mins; Producer: Elio Scardamaglia; Director: Antonio Leonviola ✞✞✞

Mark Forest's second crack of the *Maciste* whip is 91 minutes of cheesy schlock, a giggle from beginning to end and *not* to be taken all that seriously. The heroic strongman displays his bulging muscles from reel one, hauling in a whale by rope before white-robed, pasty-faced horsemen wearing shaggy-haired and horned fright masks ransack his village. Saving black bodybuilder Paul Wynter (Bango) from certain death at the hands of these twilight albinos (the ex-Mr. Universe's pecs are as impressive as the leading man's), Forest announces, "Let's go find the Mole Men," allowing him and his affable chum to be captured and escorted underground, where they meet Queen Halis Mojab (Moria Orfei) on the lookout for a husband to share her throne. Forest fits the bill nicely: He's strong, lovely to gaze upon and their children will be able to face the sunlight, unlike everyone else who has to scuttle beneath that grassy sliding entrance as soon as the sun's deadly rays appear. Gianni Garko (Kathar), the high priest's weedy son, desires Orfei, but she doesn't want to know, not after eyeing up Forest. What's more, Orfei isn't a *true* Mole Woman—she was abducted when only a child and brought up underground, so, without realizing it, she is quite able to step outside without melting into a skeleton, the fate that befalls those subjects who cross her path.

The producers manufactured some imaginative belowground set pieces, among the most striking in pepla, beauti-

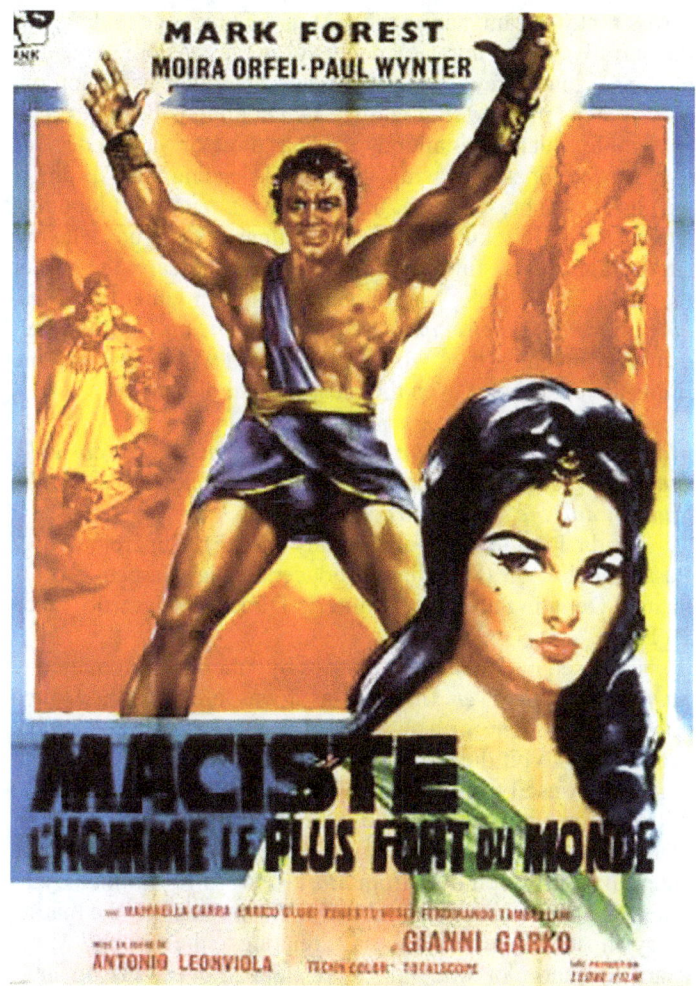

A French poster for *Maciste, The Strongest Man in the World*

Cinema's ropiest time machine sends two inventors back to Mycenae circa 3000 BC in *Maciste Against Hercules in the Vale of Woe*.

fully photographed by Alvaro Mancori: The gigantic wheel turned by scores of slaves looks incredible, rocks crushed into glittering diamonds by a massive stamping machine; Forest entwining a colossal chain around the wheel's base, jamming the mechanism, thus creating an underground collapse, is excitingly staged. The hunk has to take on a ferocious gorilla creature in a cage to prevent Princess Raffaella Carra from a mauling; and the lengthy interlude performed in near-silence, where the muscleman, chained to a wooden frame, has to withstand the weight of eight stone slabs in order to prevent curved blades from plunging into Wynter and Roberto Malli, will have audiences, like Forest, sweating with exertion. Orfei finally emerges into daylight after the Mole Men's domain is destroyed, Garko shriveling in the sunlight; standing by Italy's Marmore falls in ecstasy, she slips and tumbles into the raging waters, dying in Forest's arms. Wynter, meanwhile, has helped himself to a big bag of uncut diamonds, more than enough to build a new settlement for Forest and his freed people, and Malli is reunited with Carra.

Try to ignore that inappropriate, but infuriatingly catchy, "Sons of Hercules" ditty sung over the beginning and end credits of U.S. prints, with brief added intro. This was used in *The Sons of Hercules* televised repackaging of 14 peplum movies featuring various mythological heroes, none of which had *Son* (or *Sons*) *of Hercules* as their original Italian title: 1961's *Ursus*, part of the series (as *Ursus, Son of Hercules*), retained Roman Vlad's original title theme, heard on most DVD copies. The films were split into two halves for TV airing, the reason why, on low-budget DVDs, you'll get parts one and two. And after viewing *Maciste, the Strongest Man in the World*, sceptics will be forced to admit that Universal's *The Mole People* (1956) was, and still is, the best Mole Men picture ever made, something which diehard buffs knew all along!

Maciste Against Hercules in the Vale of Woe [*Maciste contro Ercole nella valle dei guai*] aka **Hercules in the Vale of Woe**

Cinesecolo (Italy); Totalscope/Technicolor; 90 mins; Producer: Italo Martinenghi; Director: Mario Mattoli ✞ for purists *and* spoof lovers

A couple of seedy, down-on-their-luck wrestling promoters (a solitary customer watching midget wrestlers in the ring) stumble across an inventor's time machine, head back to Mycenae circa 3000 BC and inadvertently end up staging a match between Maciste and Hercules. From the opening garish cartoon credits, backed by Gianni Ferrio's '60s pop score, you know with a sinking feeling that Mario Mattoli's dumb parody of peplum is going to match one of the picture's first lines of dialogue: "Find another act. This one stinks!" Raimondo Vianello and Mario Carotenuto are the pair of bumbling buffoons climbing aboard cinema's lousiest time machine (two red plastic swivel

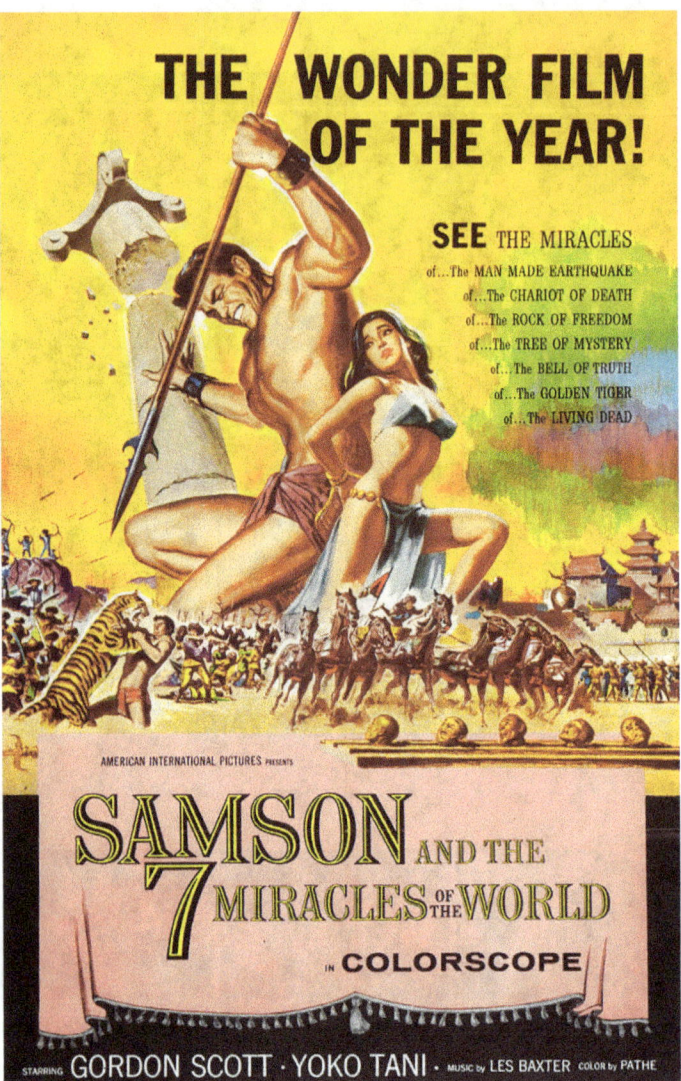

An International poster for *Samson and the 7 Miracles of the World* (aka *Maciste at the Court of the Great Khan*)

chairs and a few wires on a metal-painted cardboard base) and finding themselves in King Eurystheus' court, where every so often, a news bulletin is broadcast. Acrobatic dancing girls break into song like a second-rate revue act, the promoters joining in; the two clowns dress up in soldiers' uniforms and learn how to wield a sword; musclemen train and pose for the cameras; people wander around in animal masks (including the Minotaur); a mermaid siren warbles from a waterfall; Vianello and Carotenuto, imprisoned, snap their chains with ease; and the talents of genre beauty Liana Orfei are completely and utterly wasted.

Where, pray, do our mythical heroes fit into this farcical mickey-take? Hercules (Frank Gordon) gets the lion's share of the non-action, clashing with the Cyclops in his cavernous sanctum, while Maciste (Kirk Morris) doesn't put in an appearance until the 58th minute, a victim of prophetess Circe's (Bice Valori) lust—she places him under a deep hypnotic spell to have her wicked way with his muscle-packed body. Unfortunately, when Gordon flattens the one-eyed giant, he sets loose from captivity stupid slaves Franco Franchi and Ciccio Ingrassia, Italy's answer to Abbott and Costello (they made a huge number of films together), but they are nowhere near as funny. The duo's slapstick comedy routine consists of lugging Gordon's huge club across rocky terrain, acting the fool in the process and dragging the narrative down into new depths of inanity. After Carotenuto has undergone a few successful bouts grappling with Gordon, Morris steps into the ring and the two demigods begin a rough 'n' tumble which fades after a minute as director Mattoli decides to pan away for a quick wrap, sending his leading "star" promoters back to the present time. In downtown Lazio, a tart lounging against a wall, smoking, voices the feelings of everyone who has sat through this awful movie: "The bigger they are, the harder they fall!" If possible, Mattoli's effort is even lamer than *Hercules, Samson, Maciste and Ursus: The Invincibles*, with the accent very much on the "Woe" in the title. It will test to extreme limits the patience of even the most faithful of fans.

Maciste at the Court of the Great Khan [*Maciste alla corte del gran khan*] aka ***Samson and the Seven Miracles of the World***; ***Samson and the Seven Miracles***

Panda Film/Gallus Films (Italy/France); Supercinescope/Eastmancolor; 95 (80) mins; Producers: Luigi Carpentieri, Ermanno Donati, Salvatore Billitteri; Director: Riccardo Freda
♰♰♰♰

Released in Britain and America by American International, *Samson and the Seven Miracles*, as it was known in the United Kingdom, was one of a number of A-rated sword and sandal productions to hit the circuits in 1962, playing to perplexed audiences not used to watching dubbed, edited Italian mini-epics with foreign players and exotic settings (I caught it in September of that year). The picture, taking place in 13th-century China and utilizing sets left over from *Marco Polo*, was trimmed by 15 minutes, as are all English-dubbed DVD versions on the market today, most of the missing footage relating to the first half where characters and plot motivations are skipped over; scissors have also been at work during the final violent scrum in the city's main square. Fortunately, the movie's three main set pieces survive intact: Gordon Scott literally "wrecking the joint," bringing down a tavern's rafters and cutting a swathe through Mongol soldiers wielding a hefty roof support; the muscleman preventing an eight-horse-driven bladed chariot from lopping off the heads of five prisoners by using his feet as brakes (Scott performed all his own stunts); and China's eventual liberator, imprisoned in a narrow cleft (a sweaty scene), breaking his shackles, pushing the rock upwards and causing the palace courtyard to cave in, a destructive man-made earthquake.

Scott, looking mighty fabulous in a red loincloth, leaps into action in the 10th minute (20 minutes into the uncut print), uprooting a tree full of Mongols and rescuing Prince Tai Sung (Chu Lai Chit), tied up in a tiger pit. In Panyang (Peking in some prints), the Great Khan Garak (Leonardo Severini), aided by henchman Bayan (Dante Di Paolo) and cold-eyed consort Liu Tai (Hélène Chanel), covets the throne, the young prince and Princess Lei-ling (Yoko Tani) terrorized by this ugly-minded trio. Rebel leader Cho (Gabriele Antonini) is in love with Tani, his men gone to ground in a mountain Buddhist monastery and carrying out raids on Severini's barbarians, which they do in the opening few minutes, causing an avalanche to crush an enemy detachment in a rocky defile. To release the people from slavery and restore the prince and princess to the throne, someone has to ring the giant Bell of Freedom, and that someone is Maciste (or Samson in non-Italian versions). During the course of some pretty brutal events thrillingly orchestrated by Riccardo Freda (nuns butchered at a convent; villagers beheaded) and enlivened

An Italian poster for *Toto Against Maciste*

by Carlo Innocenzi's great score (Les Baxter augmented his own arrangements for Western audiences), the prince is killed, Chanel (a glare from those icy eyes would freeze any man dead in his tracks) swaps allegiances, there are *two* secret passages, Severini abducts Tani, proposing marriage to legitimize his unlawful claim to the seat of power, kindly Taoist priest Valéry Inkijinoff is murdered for aiding the insurgents and Scott, after ringing the sacred gong, performs his "seventh miracle," busting out of his entombment and demolishing the square and its pagodas just as Antonini and the rebels are about to be executed, a riveting finale. Chanel perishes under falling rubble, Severini bites the dust, a lance embedded in his ribs, as Tani weds Antonini, forming a new dynasty, while Scott is needed elsewhere, as ordained by the gods. Colorful (Riccardo Pallottini's photography is richly rewarding), exciting and a box-office hit, this film hoisted good-looking Scott a few rungs further up the peplum ladder, a serious contender to Steve Reeves' swift rise to fame and seat of power—coincidentally, both beefcake actors starred in 14 peplum films apiece.

1962

Toto Against Maciste [*Toto contro Maciste*]
Wanguard Film/Liber Film (Italy); Totalscope/Eastmancolor; 90 mins; Producer: Nino Battiferri; Director: Fernando Cerchio ††

Toto, otherwise known as Antonio De Curtis, was Italy's answer to Buster Keaton and Charlie Chaplin, starring in 138 films from 1937 to his death in 1967; the comic appeared in three pepla: This one, *Toto and Cleopatra* (1963) and *Toto Against the Black Pirate* (1964), all directed by Cerchio, who obviously had an affinity with the legendary droll-faced clown. The first of his three peplum spoofs was the worst of the trio, with *Toto and Cleopatra* and *Toto Against the Black Pirate* marginally better than this studio-bound farce. He plays Totokamen, a traveling performer dragging sidekick Nino Taranto (Tarantakamen) across studio deserts, mistaken for the Son of the God Amon and the Strongest Man in the World by the Egyptians. The diminutive charlatan is promptly tasked with heading the army against the Assyrians, who have enlisted Maciste (Samson Burke); the legendary hero, drugged by schemer Nadia Sanders (Faraona), is part of her wicked plans to rule Egypt over Nefertiti (Gabriella Andreini). Too much monkeying around in palace rooms, Toto scuttling from one daft situation to another, kitted out in a white nightgown, too much knockabout nonsense from Burke, toppling fake palm trees and sleeping under a bed of rock, and too much gabbling from Toto, Taranto, Sanders and Nerio Bernardi (as Ramses)—for non-Italians, this is almost depressingly unfunny, infantile fare, stock battle footage included to compound the cheapness of it all.

The (anticipated?) showdown between Toto, the fake simpleton/strongman, and Burke, the real deal (roaring his head off), brings the palace walls crumbling down after six minutes of shoddy slapstick; Burke, hit on the head, regains his senses and realizes he has been duped by Sanders, who goes into self-denial. The film ends with Toto and Taranto back where they started, a couple of useless vagabonds with nowhere to go on their donkey and cart, plus parasol. The art design in the interiors is fetching, as is Angelo Lotti's cinematography, but for Western audiences, *Toto Against Maciste* is attractive-to-look-at balderdash.

Maciste in Hell [*Maciste all'inferno*] aka The Witch's Curse
Panda Film (Italy); CinemaScope/Eastmancolor; 91 mins; Producers: Luigi Carpentieri, Ermanno Donati; Director: Riccardo Freda ††††

Hell was never quite as picturesque as represented in Riccardo Freda's peplum fantasy/horror opus, *Maciste in Hell*, with the possible exception of Mario Bava's *Hercules at the Center of the Earth* (some have voiced the opinion that Freda's adventure in Hades is superior to Bava's). For 60 minutes, a lone Kirk Morris (Maciste), in brown loincloth and quiff, worms his way through a strikingly photographed underworld (shot by Riccardo Pallottini in Bari's Castellana caverns) to battle supernatural forces and put pay to a 100-year-old witch's curse. Never mind that 17th-century Scotland looks distinctly Italian (Castello Piccolomini at Balsorano, built in 1470, stood in for the Scottish fortress) and that the opening scenes of villagers storming the castle holding torches were straight from a Hammer horror movie—this was a bravura piece of filmmaking by Freda, thin on plot, rich on visuals, a loose remake of the 1926 flick of the same title. Like Bava's excursion into Hades, it's a genre one-off, a weird and goofy blend of horror, kitsch, sensuality, camp and outlandishness that rises above its basic peplum roots to become something that little bit special.

First, let's mention Carlo Franci's terrific score. His title theme is one of the genre's finest, an all-out aural assault that

An Italian poster for *Maciste in Hell*

grabs you by the throat and refuses to let go; his incidental music is just as imaginative and atmospheric, perfectly complementing Freda's lurid concepts. In 1550, Martha Gaunt (a heavily made-up Hélène Chanel; grimy wig and broken teeth) is burned at the stake in Loch Laird for witchcraft, cursing the village and its witchfinder judge, Andrea Bosic, real "X" certificate stuff. 100 years later, her descendant Vira Silenti marries Angelo Zanolli but finds that on her wedding night in the castle, she carries the evil eye, seeing disturbing visions and hearing strange sounds. Alarmed villagers whose womenfolk act crazy on occasions (another result of the curse) grab the couple; Silenti is tried and sentenced to hang. In rides Morris from Ancient Greece, looking slightly out of place in loincloth and nothing else, he rescues the girl and embarks on a journey into hell to dispatch Silenti's wicked ancestress and lift the curse, the gateway lying beneath the roots of an accursed tree. (A few of the Hades segments were inserted into *The Triumph of Maciste*, both movies shot at the same time by Panda Productions.)

Apart from a couple of brief interludes of Silenti and Zanolli in a cell awaiting their fate, the next hour charts Morris' trek through Hades and the obstacles he encounters in his quest. Almost a silent film in places, with very little dialogue, only Franci's ominous tones rumbling in the background, Morris, observed by Chanel and Bosic, consigned to the dark regions, fights a lion and negotiates the Chamber of the Writhing Damned, with tortured souls preyed on by flesh-eating ghouls. Morris pushes open the Gates of Fire and meets Chanel, now transformed into beautiful seductress Fania (Chanel herself was absolutely stunning). She cures his scorched hands, makes love and casts a spell to make him forget his mission. Morris continues on his way, grappling a constrictive snake and fighting an ogre over a chasm of fire. He then uses a boulder for a shield to cross a cavern of showering embers and saves Remo De Angelis (Prometheus) from entrails-gorging vultures. In return, De Angelis shows him a pool depicting scenes from his past life, which jogs his memory back (in this sequence, footage from *Maciste in the Land of the Cyclops*, *Maciste in the Valley of the Kings* and *Maciste at the Court of the Great Khan* was used; no attempt was made to disguise the fact that what we viewed was not Morris in these clips but Gordon Mitchell, Mark Forest and Gordon Scott!). Next, Morris survives a rock avalanche and diverts a herd of rampaging bulls into a deep pit, a distressing moment that would have animal activists up in arms today (and the censor). Chanel, professing her love for Morris, claims his purity has overcome her evilness; she kisses him and crumbles into dust, Bosic plummeting to oblivion. As Silenti and Zanolli are about to be burned at the stake, rain extinguishes the flames, Morris clambers out of the pit, the accursed tree seals the gateway to Hades, and Chanel's ancient curse is finally lifted. Peace returns to Loch Laird as Morris, not a mark on his rippling torso (what happened to those deep red lion scratches?) and his well-groomed hair still neatly in place, gallops off to new adventures and new time zones! Note: Online sources state that the film was refused a certificate in Britain in 1969 and was never released—if it had been, it would undoubtedly have gone the rounds as an X-certified production.

Maciste Against the Sheik [*Maciste contro lo sceicco*] aka *Samson Against the Sheik*

Compagnia Italiani Grandi Film (Italy); Totalscope/Eastmancolor; 95 mins; Producer: Alberto Manca; Director: Domenico Paolella ††

Dull and lifeless, *Maciste Against the Sheik* placed the mythical hero, played by Ed Fury (born Edmund Holovchik), in 16th-century Spain where he becomes involved in an attempt to rescue the Duke of Malaga (Giuseppe Addobbati), his daughter, Lady Isabella (Gisella Arden), and her beau, Antonio (Massimo Carocci), from the clutches of Moorish sheik Abdul Khadar (Erno Crisa), ruler of Maleda. In Addobbati's enforced absence, Don Alfredo Alvarez (Adriano Micantoni) covets the position of Malaga's governor, and so does his brother, Don Ramiro (Piero Lulli). The sheik also desires to rule Malaga, "the land of my ancestors," threatening to murder Addobbati if Arden refuses to marry him. Throw in an eye-patched French assassin (Bruno Scipioni), a crusty old Irish convict (Carlo Pisacane) and a beautiful consort to the sheik (Mara Berni), plus plenty of daring escapes, both on the high seas and in Crisa's fortress prison, and what you should have is a thrilling *Maciste* adventure taking place out of the hero's usual ancient setting, but none the worse for it.

This isn't the case, as *Maciste Against the Sheik* is made even more unpalatable by the fact that as I write, rough-looking prints are only available in black-and-white pan and scan. Fury, spending at least a third of the picture draped in a variety of different-sized chains, smiles rather than hurls his way through

Ed Fury in chains, from *Maciste Against the Sheik*

Reg Lewis, in a Tarzan loincloth, uproots a tree in *Maciste Against the Monsters*

the leaden narrative, the only piece of excitement coming when he has to combat seven beefy warriors on orders from Crisa; he gets to take his shirt off, and Paolella finally gets to take his foot off the brakes. Elsewhere, Carlo Latimer lays claim to being one of the genre's least-effective sidemen; Lulli's villain could have done with a touch of the Livio Lorenzons to add zest to the character, a lackluster performance (bad guy Lorenzon only starred in a single *Maciste* movie, 1963's *Maciste, the World's Greatest Hero*, unusually cast against type on the side of good), while Arden as the main female interest is pretty but passively doll-like. Fury kills a lion (a feature of most *Maciste* outings), demolishes a scaffold, sticks his fingers through coconuts, shifts walls and, in the end, raises the fallen sacred Obelisk of Maleda, the Moors' symbol of power, earning the gratitude and pardon of the sheik. In Malaga Lulli topples backwards through a window to his death after a confrontation with the muscular infidel (and a pretty tame one), Addobbati resumes control, Arden and Carocci are wed and Fury, smooching with his peasant girlfriend, is called upon by the Chinese to come to the aid of their oppressed villagers. Full marks to composer Carlo Savina for a calamitous score that unfortunately fails to lift this tired actioner out of the rut.

Maciste Against the Monsters [*Maciste contro i mostri*] aka ***Colossus of the Stone Age***; ***Fire Monsters Against the Son of Hercules***

Euro Intl. Film/Caserbib (Italy/Yugoslavia); Totalscope/Eastmancolor; 82 (78) mins; Producers: Giorgio Marzelli, Alfio Quattrini; Director: Guido Malatesta ††

Mae West eyed up 18-year-old bodybuilder Reg Lewis' well-chiseled torso in a gym around 1954 and promptly added him to her retinue of strongmen admirers, featuring the soon-to-be Mr. Universe (1957) and Mr. America (1963) in her nightclub act. There's no two ways about it—Lewis couldn't act. Some unkind critics might suggest he was ideally suited to a film made by a man who couldn't direct, but, as with *Maciste Against the Headhunters*, Guido Malatesta proved he was quite at home with this type of schlocky claptrap to work on, if nobody else was (apart from peplum trash alumnus Emimmo Salvi). Lewis made only four films, this being his one and only peplum, and a shoddy one at that. Made back-to-back with *Headhunters*, Lewis, his mighty tanned, greased frame stomping all over brightly colored cardboard sets, made Kirk Morris look like a possible candidate in a William Shakespeare play. Mouthing his lines without a flicker of emotion, he hurled rock pillars at his enemies, slew three monsters and romanced, for want of a better word, red-haired, pouting Margaret Lee, her locks perfectly matching Lewis' orange/ginger crop. *One Million Years B.C. Meets The Land that Time Forget* would be an apt title for this dose of Stone Age twaddle, not quite as enjoyable as *Headhunters* but still mildly diverting.

A peaceful tribe of sun-worshippers (in white furs) sets up home near the Droods, a malevolent race (in black furs) glorifying the moon and inhabiting a system of caves sealed off by a secret, massive stone slab that only slides open if you yell like Tarzan. Stumbling around in a prehistoric version of Ugg boots, Demeter Bitenc's people treat the audience to some hilarious snippets of dumb dialogue before Lewis (as Maciste, or Maxus) appears on a ridge in his loincloth and throws a well-aimed spear fully 300 yards, straight into the eye of a huge menacing river lizard, conjured up by Carlo Rambaldi and his technicians; Birgit Bergen (Rhia) to Luciano Marin, her boyfriend Aydar: "When will you choose your woman?" Marin, busy fishing, responds, "I'll pick when it pleases me." Bergen: "I'm 18 and I'll be old soon." The pair's marriage ceremony is rudely interrupted by Andrea Aureli's Droods, attacking in force, all the girls herded off to be sacrificed by decapitation as virgins to the moon god, even though there's probably not a single virgin among the lot of

An Italian poster for *Maciste, the World's Strongest Gladiator*

them. Lewis lumbers to the sun-worshippers' defense, infiltrating the Droods' network of caves, slaying a pale-skinned Hydra and meeting Drood vixen Lee (Aureli's woman, Moah); the two, as expected, fall in lust. There's another odd dance number, followed by an eclipse of the moon; the Droods, terrified, stay rooted to the spot while the women escape to the outside, Lewis caught and buried up to his neck for torture, along with Lee for snubbing Aureli's brutish advances ("I'm leader and I'll take you anytime I want. I'll tame you yet!"). An eruption and earthquake enables Lewis and Lee to break out, the fugitives encountering a giant lizard in woods and another in a grotto—our beefy hero jams its jaws open with a stick and kills the beast. The final confrontation in the Valley of the Sun sees the Droods, headed by Aureli, Nello Pazzafini and Frank Leroy, defeated, Aureli crushed under a huge granite block after a savage fight

with Marin, both armed with stone axes. Lewis wanders off for fresh adventures (but not in peplum), followed by Lee, who smothers the one-dimensional Adonis in kisses; Marin, his father dead, is made head of the tribe. Guido Robuschi and Gian Stellari's score is a thumping winner, Giuseppe La Torre's color just about shines through the scum of current DVD releases and Malatesta, to his eternal credit, directs with pace and a pretty good visual eye. In the realm of undiluted hokey peplum for the less-perceptive punter, or for those not culturally minded, nobody could do this sort of scatty picture better than he could.

Maciste, the World's Strongest Gladiator [*Maciste, il gladiatore piu forte del mondo*] aka ***Colossus of the Arena***
Leone Film (Italy); Totalscope/Eastmancolor; 98 (89) mins; Producer: Elio Scardamaglia; Director: Michele Lupo ††††

Mark Forest's third stab at playing the monosyllabic strongman saw him pitted in opposition to seven champion gladiators, hired by crooked Vittorio Sanipoli to aid corrupt consul Erno Crisa in ousting Thalima (Scilla Gabel), Queen of Mersabad, capital of Asia Minor in 261 BC, from the throne and install him in her place. Gabel's sister, José Greci, Crisa's lover, is in on the cause, although wishing no harm should come to her sibling. Did Ridley Scott ever catch this movie before embarking on *Gladiator*? The opening sequences inside the amphitheater smack of incidents that cropped up in Scott's epic 40 years later; decapitation by double sword, chests and faces sliced open, terrific rough and tumble stuff. The same can be said of the chariot scene later on, one wheel breaking off, the rider clinging on to his horse for dear life. Forest, clad in a lime-green loincloth, comes into the fray after we're treated to a noisy seven-minute episode in which the seven intoxicated gladiators wreck a public house, pet giggling chimpanzee Cleopatra and comic actor John Chevron providing light relief where it's not really needed. In Mersabad, Forest enrolls in the gladiator school, enabling him to overhear the plot against the queen, but he is quickly found out, drugged and left to be murdered; however, the gladiator tasked with carrying out the deed was saved by Forest when his chariot crashed and draws the line at plunging a sword into his bulging chest, leaving the muscleman at liberty to rout the rogue gladiators and rescue Gabel, festering in a dungeon.

Director Lupo moves swiftly through the paces, including in the narrative a savage fight between gladiators and Romans (spear and sword rammed into throat; two men smothered in the dirt; bloody corpses littering the ground), villagers beaten, raped and tortured in a river, plus a trial of strength occurring in the picturesque wooded locations of Italy's Monte Gelato waterfalls where Forest and Dan Vadis (his debut peplum outing) slug it out, muscle on muscle; it takes Forest 23 blows to stun his opponent and even then Vadis returns for the finale! And that finale takes placed in the packed arena. Valorous Forest, after killing scarred brute Ciccio Barbi, dons his helmet, strides into the stadium, slays another, removes his helmet to reveal his true identity (*Gladiator* again!) and polishes off Vadis, slashing him to pieces. Queen's favorite Germano Longo, prefect of the guards, does away with Crisa and Gabel, back on the throne, forgives her sister's treachery. "Your name will become legend," she tells Forest as the crowd applauds the victor for his endeavors.

Spoiled in parts by Chevron's infantile mugging and clowning (he dresses up as a sheep at one point, and, for reasons unknown, a woman), the 12th *Maciste* entrant is among the best, featuring a stirring soundtrack from one of peplum's greatest

An Italian poster for *Maciste Against the Headhunters*

composers, Francesco De Masi (19 torch and toga scores under his belt, from 1959 to 1966), and Guglielmo Mancori's fine photography which fully enhances the Roman cityscapes. And Forest, acting-wise, puts increased effort into the part, making Maciste appear more alive as a person rather than just a walking, talking well-honed statue.

Maciste Against the Headhunters [*Maciste contro i cacciatori di teste*] aka *Colossus and the Headhunters*

RCM Prod./Alta Vista (Italy); Dyaliscope/Eastmancolor; 81 (79) mins; Producer: Giorgio Marzelli; Director: Guido Malatesta ☥☥

Ex-gondolier and Elvis Presley look-alike Kirk Morris (Adriano Bellini) was once more hired to take on the role of Maciste, the 13th entry in the franchise, for his boyish good looks and powerful physique—but not for his acting ability! It was his fourth crack at playing the mythical muscleman if you include *Maciste Against Hercules in the Vale of Woe* in the series (which I've done); sometimes, this movie is classed as a *Hercules* feature. *Maciste Against the Headhunters* was completed in 1962 by king of the comic book peplum Guido Malatesta; however, its release date was delayed by a few months, the film finally issued in Italy at the beginning of January 1963, giving the cult hack director time to tinker with his pet project *and* finish work on *Maciste Against the Monsters* (*Fire Monsters Against the Son of Hercules*), both productions made in tandem; he wrote the story and screenplay to the pair. The 5th of Morris' 15 peplum outings (1962's *Clash of Steel* came before this one) is as crazy as they come, not quite the nadir of bad filmmaking, but getting there. It's probably best not to dwell too deeply on a plot that's about as shallow as a dried-up riverbed—let's simply list the main points of interest as they occur.

Morris, Demeter Bitenc, Ines Holder (in a Dorothy Lamour sarong) and the nicer looking members of their tribe (the uglier, Neolithic ones are all killed) escape their island abode of Sandor following an earthquake and volcanic eruption, the footage lifted from *Maciste Against the Monsters* ("Hurry. It's the end of the world. You must do something," yells a caveman as he's swallowed whole in a crevasse). For a few brief seconds Reg Lewis, from *Monsters*, can be spotted running for his life. Drifting on their makeshift raft, Malatesta uses up several minutes of precious celluloid focusing on Morris' posing sculptured torso gleaming in the sun, and nothing else (yes, we agree he's body-beautiful—just get on with it!). The group lands in the domain of the Urias, quickly captured by Laura Brown (Queen Amoha) and her warriors; Morris, wounded, swiftly recovers, and Brown just as swiftly falls in love with him. Neighboring headhunters led by renegade betrayer Frank Leroy (Kermes), deputy Luigi Esposito (Aris) and chieftain Nello Pazzafini (Gunk!) threaten her tribe. Leroy wants to marry Brown so that he can rule the Urias, having blinded her father Alessio Pregara (King Olibauna) and incarcerated him behind a wall in the ruined City of Gold, along with his mummified friends. The headhunters attack Brown's village (check that guy having his head pushed into a fire) and take her plus dozens of hostages to their quarry stockade; Morris and Bitenc locate Pregara, the blind monarch hauled back to the headhunters' camp by Leroy, Brown's head placed on a chopping block, the old king issued with an ultimatum: "Give me your consent or she will suffer." To delay the sham wedding, maid Letizia Stephan (Moana) performs (to use the term loosely) a totally inept three-minute dance to the accompaniment of tom-toms, dressed like a provocative sugarplum fairy, wasting everyone's time (and ours); Bitenc leads an eight-minute assault on the headhunters (very bloody; arrows through eyes and necks; faces gashed open), Morris eventually joining the fray after wandering around the countryside like a lost soul. He gets stuck hurling logs, toppling a tower and bringing down six men at a time; in the City of Gold, Leroy is slain by Morris, expiring at the feet of the mummified kings. Pregara is proclaimed ruler again, Holder kisses Bitenc and Brown swims out to join Morris on his raft. "What have I got to offer you?" he asks the dripping wet lass as she eyes him up in his loincloth. Well, if he doesn't know, no one else does!

As lowbrow as peplum can possibly get, Malatesta's lame-brained rib-tickler, despite cardboard effects, corny dialogue and a hesitant performance from Morris (he would improve slightly over his next 10 movies) brings a smile to the face. Nobody could get away with dishing up stuff like this these days, could they? Yet way back in the early '60s, directors could, and did, as this film attests. It doesn't transpire to be anything but what it is, trash-laden sword and sandal hokum concocted to appease a popcorn and Coke audience. On a definite plus side, Guido Robuschi and Gian Stellari's ominous music (the two composers collaborated on several pepla) works wonders, solid proof that whatever the material, be it good, bad or ugly, the Italians knew how to score movies of this kind to maximum effect (sadly, ex-

An American half-sheet poster for *Goliath and the Sins of Babylon* (aka *Maciste, the World's Greatest Hero*)

isting tatty prints have sabotaged Domenico Scala's color photography, reducing it to a reddish hue).

1963

Maciste, the World's Greatest Hero [*Maciste, l'eroe piu grande del mondo*] aka *Goliath and the Sins of Babylon*

Leone Film (Italy); Techniscope/Technicolor; 92 (80) mins; Producer: Elio Scardamaglia; Director: Michele Lupo ✝✝✝✝✝

Michele Lupo was one of pepla's finest practitioners of the in-your-face combat scene, catapulting the audience amid the thick of the bruising action in a welter of savage, rapidly-edited sequences, forcing you to duck as those swords cut, swung and slashed. The man responsible for one of the genre's true classics, *The Revenge of Spartacus* (1964), breathed new life into the ailing *Maciste* series, his vigor behind the camera energizing a recycled torch and toga plot, producing a vibrant, breathless actioner of some note. Two hundred years before the birth of Christ, the city of Nefer pays a yearly tribute of 30 virgins to Babylon as part of a peace deal. In the opening minutes, Eleonora Bianchi, one of the 30, evades her guard detail, Mark Forest (Maciste, or Goliath in U.S. prints) coming to her rescue. Forest then joins a gang of rebels led by Livio Lorenzon (Evando), Mimmo Palmara (Alceas) and Giuliano Gemma (Xandros), who are planning to put a stop to the wasteful sacrifice of their young women and teach the Babylonians, ruled by King Cafaus (Paul Muller, resembling Vincent Price in a cowl), a lesson. It goes without saying that the squabbling hierarchy of Nefer, comprising Erno Crisa (Morakeb), Piero Lulli (Pergasos) and henchman Alfio Caltabiano (Meneas), refuse to take this lying down, determined to stamp out any insurrection. In between all the plotting and counterplotting, Gemma is romancing, beside the Monte Gelato falls, a mysterious woman called Chalima (José Greci), who happens to be Princess Resia, Nefer's champion chariot racer. She has never lost the annual chariot tournament; whoever can beat her will win her hand in marriage and share the throne. Gemma is up for it but can't compete due to a wound sustained in a fracas with Crisa's men; Forest steps into his sandals, thus precipitating a catalogue of turbulent events that ends with every villain slain and Greci and Gemma wed, the new rulers of a peaceful domain.

That five-minute chariot race, while not up to *Ben-Hur* standards (which it is obviously modeled on), is a fantastic, pulse-racing humdinger, one of pepla's greatest set pieces, enacted on a huge Cinecitta arena set (built for a world fair in 1943 but never used), the vehicles careering round corners in clouds of dust, riding over Lupo's floor-level camera, three crashing, Forest whipped by an opponent. Cleverly, Lupo constructed this sequence using footage from the chariot race in Riccardo Freda's *Theodora, Empress of Byzantium*; with added shots, it's even more of a thrill-ride than the original. But preceding that comes another exciting action scene orchestrated by the director, where Forest's galley rams a Babylonian vessel, an almighty clash resulting in the enemy ship going up in flames. Lupo also knows how to rack up

An Italian magazine preview for *Zorro Against Maciste*

the tension in more intimate moments. Midway through, Forest is chained to a bench, a number of spears above his body attached to ropes; Palmara, Gemma and comrades are ordered to take it in turns to cut a rope with an axe, the spears dropping from holes in the roof. One, and one only, will kill Forest—yes, it's a devilish peplum variation on Russian roulette, guaranteed to make audiences perspire as much as the mythical savior (he breaks his shackles and escapes). Many have been dismayed at the inclusion of midget Arnaldo Fabrizio (aka Little Goliath) in Lupo's scenario. In the first of six peplum appearances, Fabrizio is cute here rather than irritating, not overstaying his welcome, Lupo cutting back on the comical shenanigans (knocking guards on the head and feet with a club), which was a distinctly Italian thing anyway, perhaps never appreciated by audiences elsewhere. Even his final line, after Babylon has been torched and reduced to rubble, Crisa stabbed by Palmara in yet another macho close-quarters duel, is amusing. Parading an equally diminutive lass before the cast, Fabrizio proudly announces, "This is my wife. No flirting. You know how strong I am!" A fabulous score from Francesco De Masi; deep, rich photography via Guglielmo Mancori (decent, unedited widescreen prints can be found on the market); believable performances from all involved; and Lupo's cut-to-the-bone, no-frills direction make *Maciste, the World's Greatest Hero* one of the finest in the *Maciste* franchise, and a reminder of how great peplum was at its height.

Zorro Against Maciste [*Zorro contro Maciste*] aka *Samson and the Slave Queen*
Romana Film (Italy); Totalscope/Eastmancolor; 86 mins; Producer: Fortunato Misiano; Director: Umberto Lenzi †††

A masked avenger in black battles against the mythical loinclothed do-gooder in 17th-century Spain. King Philip IV of Nogara has died of the plague on the Island of Guadarrama, near Madrid. Which of his two nieces will inherit the throne—blonde Isabella, dressed in white, or brunette Malva, attired in black (no prizes for guessing who the evil one is). The rightful heir's name is written on a scroll, housed in a royal box. Bandit top-dog Rabek steals the box in a raid on a troop detachment in the Gorge of La Croces; Garcia, Malva's guard captain and paramour, engages the services of strongman Maciste to recover the scroll, hoodwinking him into thinking that it contains military secrets. Malva plans to replace it with a forged document, naming her as queen. Ramon, a poet in love with Isabella, advises her to contact Zorro so that he may retrieve the scroll, which will prove that she is the true heir. The two peplum superheroes come to blows over the missing vital document (rapier against pole) before Maciste realizes that duplicitous lovers Malva and Garcia have fooled him. A fake will signed by Zorro leads to Rabek's murder, with Maciste incarcerated in dungeons and Isabella imprisoned, sentenced to death for treason. During a forced ceremony to place the crown on Malva's head, the genuine scroll is read out to the court, proclaiming Isabella as queen. Zorro kills Garcia in a swordfight, Malva is exiled and Maciste rides off to set right more wrongs. Zorro reveals to Isabella that he is, in fact, Ramon, and the two are married.

Now available on a gleaming widescreen subtitled print, *Zorro Against Maciste* is a fairly harmless, bloodless cloak-and-dagger/strong-arm costumer, Angelo Francesco Lavagnino's jaunty trumpet/castanets music matching Umberto Lenzi's light touch on the camera. Alan Steel (Maciste), Pierre Brice (Ramon/Zorro), Massimo Serato (Garcia), Andrea Aureli (Rabek), Ma-

A French poster for *Maciste Against the Mongols*

ria Grazia Spina (Isabella) and Moira Orfei (Malva) go through the motions professionally enough without too much spirit; it's never boring but not all that exciting either; it's more for the kids than adults, leaving you with one thought in mind: Why does the quest for absolute power in these movies make those seeking it look so downright miserable? Haughty Orfei glares, scowls and barks orders throughout; doesn't the thought of becoming queen please the lady just one iota?

Maciste Against the Mongols [*Maciste contro i mongoli*] aka *Hercules Against the Mongols*
Alta Vista/Jonia Film (Italy); Totalscope/Eastmancolor; 90 mins; Producer: Jacopo Comi; Director: Domenico Paolella †††††

Domenico Paolella may have applied the brakes in *Maciste Against the Sheik*; here, he applies the accelerator in one of the best of all the many peplum barbarian movies, a gritty, helter-skelter opus that doesn't stop for 90 minutes, Carlo Savina's vibrant score driving the narrative from the very start. In 1227 AD, Genghis Khan dies, his final request to his three errant sons being that peace should remain throughout the land. But Ken Clark (Sayan), Howard Ross (Kie Han, billed as Renato Rossini) and Nadir Moretti (Susdal) have other ideas; they lust after conquest and, to kick things off, an arrow is fired into the Great Khan's counselor, the blame placed squarely on the Europeans. War is declared, the Mongols invading the Christian city of Judeyla, the king murdered, his daughter Bianca (José Greci) on the run with wily minister Tullio Altamura; the young heir to the

A peplum torture device par excellence from *Maciste at the Court of the Czar*

throne, Alexander (Loris Loddi), is also a wanted fugitive. Greci is eventually captured, arousing the jealousy of Maria Grazia Spina, Moretti's consort, the three siblings arguing over her charms. Mark "Maciste" Forest steps into the frame by fighting off a troop detail led by Clark with the aid of a large tree trunk and ingratiating himself into court by pretending to possess a free passage given to him by Genghis Khan, aware that he'll be imprisoned, his sole purpose to communicate with Greci. Not only is the lass at the mercy of Clark and his unruly brothers, but Altamura, the defector, sides with the Mongols, desiring to know the whereabouts of a stockpile of treasure hidden in the hollow of a gristmill, and Greci is the only person who knows where it is.

Don't pause for breath as Forest, in a series of cliffhangers, works the gristmill; raises a massive stone lintel and places it over two pillars; is forced to take on the squabbling brothers in arena combat, defeating all three; grapples with a lion; breaks free from a massive yoke and chains; causes a dam to burst, flooding the countryside and drowning the Mongol army in quicksand; and prevents Greci from being flattened under a slowly descending cell roof. A word about that hard-to-stomach lion scene—it's unnecessarily drawn out, the magnificent beast in obvious distress, and even today would offend many people as well as the censor (similarly, horses floundering in the quicksand sequence look absolutely terrified, as well they might). At the 72nd minute, Paolella pulls out all the stops, manufacturing a tremendous large-scale battle, Forest entering the fray and choking Moretti to death with a wooden beam. Ross perishes in the quicksand, Clark is run through by the heroic bodybuilder, Altamura, trying to sneak off, is brought down by a flight of arrows and little Loddi is seated on the throne, Forest and Greci riding away for some romantic light relief. The set design (remaining from 1961's *The Mongols*) looks just right for the period, as do the flamboyant pagan costumes, all dressed up in Raffaele Masciocchi's vivid colors. Persuasively acted by all concerned and directed with determination and flair by Paolella, *Maciste Against the Mongols* is pure popcorn peplum, one and a half hours of nonstop barbaric action-filled entertainment!

1964

Maciste at the Court of the Czar [*Maciste alla corte dello zar*] aka *Atlas Against the Czar*; *Giant of the Lost Tomb*; *Samson vs. the Giant King*

Cineluxor (Italy); Techniscope/Technicolor; 91 (84) mins; Producer: Luigi Rovere; Director: Tanio Boccia (Amerigo Anton) ✝✝

Tanio Boccia's yarn begins well in '50s fantasy/horror style, after a two-minute dance routine. In Russia, despotic Czar Nicholas (Massimo Serato) organizes an archaeological expedition to travel to a remote area in the Ural Valley and unearth a rumored fortune worth millions, valuable hidden treasure left from an ancient civilization. After 20 days, the team, headed by Tom Felleghy (Akim), discovers a labyrinth of freezing caverns adorned with archaic inscriptions—we are now firmly in B-movie *Mummy* territory, the steady pace and overall look nicely atmospheric. Chests of gold and jewels are found. Battering through a rock wall, the men come across a sarcophagus standing in an icy cavern; the lid is shifted and within the tomb lies the perfectly preserved body of Kirk Morris, complete with loincloth, studded belt and blond rinse. Outside by a warming fire, Morris comes to, wolfing down a meal, ravenous after being in a state of suspended animation for centuries, and a messenger is sent to inform Serato and Giulio Donnini (aptly named Igor) of the finds, the devious pair planning to purloin the riches for themselves and wipe out all traces of the expedition.

Up to this stage, the film intrigues; not only do we have the possibility of Morris joining in a revolt against Serato's brutal regime ("And if they're thirsty," he tells his torturers, viewing slaves in the dungeons, "give them a drink of blood. Their own, of course."), but three lovely women are on hand—sisters Gloria Milland (Nadia) and Ombretta Colli (Sonia), and Serato's mistress, Dada Gallotti (Katia) to amp up the action. Morris arrives in Russia after thwarting an ambush on Felleghy's caravan and the narrative flags, the pretty-boy muscleman and off-form Serato competing to see who can be the more wooden of the two. Even Milland's stunning dark-haired charms don't amount to much. Many scenes are stretched out to interminable lengths, as when Morris, in the arena, has to hold back two riders, each manning three horses, to prevent impalement on a circle of steel blades, the actor's trademark grimace of exertion overplayed. Slimy Gallotti, either in Serato's good books or threatened with decapitation, drugs Morris, Colli administering an antidote obtained from an old wizard, to bring him back to life, not that you will notice much difference. Felleghy becomes one of the rebel ringleaders. Morris, after freeing slaves from a labor camp, has to take on a deformed strongman in a secret tunnel to gain access to the palace courtyard, as the insurrection gets into full swing on public execution day, citizens versus Cossacks in baggy pants. Milland and Colli are saved from a spiking, Morris demolishing the roller on which the fiendish contraption works, and the limp finale sees Serato and Gallotti simply arrested, the movie not even closing with the obligatory pumped-up showdown (although Morris *does* hurl a massive urn at the guards). "Other lands are in serious danger and need help," Morris drawls, galloping away with Colli at his side. A monumental Russian-based score by Carlo Rustichelli thunders merrily in the background,

Mark Forest tangles with a man in a gorilla suit in the Danish poster for *Maciste, Gladiator of Sparta*.

but the director is unable to match the composer's exciting rhythms, the end result a flashy washout; if only it had kept up the pace and mood of that opening 30 minutes …

Maciste, Gladiator of Sparta [*Maciste, gladiatore di Sparta*] aka *Terror of Rome Against the Son of Hercules*

Prometeo Film/Sancro Film (Italy/France); Techniscope/Technicolor; 103 (96) mins; Producer: Albino Morandini; Director: Mario Caiano ✞✞✞✞

Mark Forest's sixth *Maciste* outing (he's called Poseidon of Sparta in non-Italian DVD issues) was a bouncy entrant in the series in which that classic line spoken from gladiators to emperor was given an airing: "Hail, Caesar! We who are about to die salute you." Forest, Emperor Vitellius' (Franco Cobianchi) invincible champion, trounces "four young butchers" in the arena, earning not only the ruler's respect but rousing the ardor of Marilù Tolo (Cobianchi's daughter), who can't keep her hands off him at a fancy feast, much to the chagrin of praetorian captain Claudio Undari; the ambitious commander desires marriage to the beauty and looks upon Forest as a threat. Stepping up to the gauntlet thrown down by Undari, Forest fights him blindfolded within a circle of rope (filmed minus Carlo Franci's music to heighten suspense), Undari cheating but still losing out to the muscleman. The scenario then focuses on the familiar Christendom versus Roman misunderstanding of its religious foundations: Forest rescues Elisabetta Fanti (Livia) from two praetorian soldiers, is introduced to her family in the catacombs and falls in love with the girl, having to fend off the advances of female predator Tolo back in Rome. As punishment for killing one of the soldiers, Forest is ordered to enter the arena and do battle with a giant gorilla. Flattening the man in the ape suit with several blows, he again finds himself in the emperor's good graces and told, "Ask for any reward. Even the death of a human being." Resisting the temptation to condemn glowering Undari, Forest requests the life of a Christian girl. "So be it," says Cobianchi, and Fanti is spared when Undari's platoon breaks into the hidden chamber, arresting everyone except her.

Caiano, for the remainder of this overlong but involving movie, takes us down the "victimized Christians" path, Undari making it his business to eliminate "these pests," Forest their knight in shining armor and Cobianchi, forever grumbling that he's hungry, not quite sure what to make of people who pray to only one god: Should he accede to this strange religion or abolish it? Forest teams up with a bunch of Spartan gladiators, imprisoned for upsetting the Romans, leading to a string of bone-crunching scrimmages (Forest wields a ball and chain to good effect), while poor Tolo, aiding Forest in his campaign to bring justice to the Christians but unable to share her love with him, has her throat slit by Undari. Taking refuge in a vast grotto, the Spartans are overcome in a seven-minute collision with the praetorians (one of their number has betrayed their whereabouts to Undari); the Christian brethren are led to safety, but Forest recaptured. In Rome, he survives trial by combat in the arena, dragged through the dirt by three horses; mounting one steed, he rides off, Undari in pursuit. The two pitch into a mud pool and, in the ensuing scuffle, Undari accidentally stabs himself to death when Forest ducks away from his lunge. The picture closes on an idyllic note, Fanti tending a flock of sheep in a sunlit meadow as Forest approaches, ready to play house with the heavenly blonde maiden.

In a solid, well-written story, Cobianchi scene-steals with unreserved glee, an out-and-out glutton constantly stuffing his face with food, always complaining of stomach pains and issuing death ultimatums on a whim, a semi-mad ruler to enjoy rather than despise. Elsewhere, Ferruccio Amendola turns in a nice performance as a bumbling Christian trying his hardest to emulate Forest's prowess in the field and paying with his life. And Forest himself showed remarkable progress since his first *Maciste* outing in 1960, proving in the long run to be one of pepla's most engaging strongman heroes, and certainly one of the more appealing of the bunch.

Maciste in Genghis Khan's Hell [*Maciste nell'inferno di Gengis Khan*] aka *Hercules Against the Barbarians*

Alta Vista/Jonia Film (Italy); Totalscope/Technicolor; 96 (84) mins; Producers: Jacopo Comi, Felice Felicioni; Director: Domenico Paolella ✞✞✞

Domenico Paolella's follow-up to *Maciste Against the Mongols*, utilizing the same cast and technicians, was lower in key, more studio-bound and very talkative, not up to the bulldozing pace set by its predecessor. Mark Forest pitted his wits against Genghis Khan (Roldano Lupi, who specialized in playing Mongol warlords), who was busy making inroads into Poland in 1227 AD. José Greci ("A peasant girl of some importance," state the Mongols) flees from a Krakow besieged by barbarians, hiding out with priest Tullio Altamura and informed by Gloria Milland, a supposed witch (Arias), that the star-shaped scar on her neck proclaims her as Princess Armina, heir to the Polish crown.

Mark Forest poses for a beefcake shot for *Maciste in Genghis Khan's Hell* (aka *Hercules Against the Barbarians*).

Greci's father has been festering in a dungeon for 20 years, refusing to tell Ken Clark (Kubilai) where his daughter is ("I'm going to burn your face. Then you can sleep forever," growls Clark to his recalcitrant captive). Word gets out that Maciste/Hercules is in the vicinity; Howard Ross and his troops trap the he-man in a pit where he fights a giant plastic snake, clambers out, wrestles a cardboard crocodile (one of celluloid's poorest croc props) and heads toward Tarnopol to confront Lupi in his opulent court, looking mighty handsome in a blue toga, the robe offsetting his gleaming torso to perfection. After demonstrating his great strength (bending bars and defeating strongman Harold Bradley inside a square of lances), Forest is lured into the dungeons by Milland and trapped. Clark stabs her to death, engages in a fistfight with Ross and Forest storms out of prison, scattering the guards. Clark, harboring thoughts of power, then decides to wed Greci and have Lupi murdered, his marriage proposal succinctly met with one word: "Pig!" On the road to Egypt, the Great Khan is assassinated by Bradley (pure conjecture, this; the cause of Genghis Khan's death has never been determined); Tarnopol is attacked by Polish forces commanded by Mirko Ellis (stock battle footage is used in these scenes), Forest rescues Greci from a cell shielded by a wall of fire and Bradley pulls a lever, a spiked gate skewering Clark to the floor. In disarray, the Mongols, led by Ross, retreat, swarming back to Mongolia; Forest and Greci ride away together; she doesn't want to be queen, only a woman nestling in the man of her dream's masculine arms.

Forest is in fine form, Milland (she also loves the mythical hero) emotes hot lust like crazy, Greci, as always, dazzles and both Clark and Lupi glower suitably as the Mongolian heathens. Paolella's second Mongol adventure in a row contains a deeper plot than the norm, the accent on intimate standoffs, but it could have done with a few more action bodybuilding set pieces added to liven it up a bit.

Maciste in King Solomon's Mines [*Maciste nelle miniere del re Salomone*] aka *Samson in King Solomon's Mines*

Panda Societa (Italy); Techniscope/Technicolor; 93 mins; Producers: Luigi Carpentieri, Ermanno Donati; Director: Piero Regnoli ††††

Reg Park was 36 when he starred in Piero Regnoli's solid, good-to-look-at *Maciste* outing, older than many of his contemporaries but still sporting a massive physique. Filmed mainly in South Africa, the movie had an unusual, compulsive 20-minute opening. The African city of Zimba lies on top of King Solomon's fabled gold mines, accessible only by a secret gallery hidden behind the sliding face of a stone idol. Benevolent King Namar refuses to work the mines, placing peace of mind before greed, but minister Elio Jotta (Riad) has other ideas; he desires the throne *and* the riches beneath his feet, plus he desires for his son to become eventual king. In a bloody coup, the old monarch is murdered, Wandisa Guida (rampant in a black wig as Queen Fazira) and her heathen warriors brought in by Jotta to take control of Zimba, Guida's lust for gold and rule equal to the crafty minister's ambitions. But during the fracas, Eleonora Bianchi (Samara) manages to smuggle the true heir to the throne, Loris Loddi (Vazma), out of the city, seeking the help of legendary Maciste to restore law and order and overthrow Guida's mad rise to power and crush her fanatical dream of founding a new empire built on gold.

Boasting an eye-boggling art deco city, careful, incisive direction and buildup from Regnoli, imaginative lighting courtesy of Mario Capriotti and Luciano Trasatti (especially in the underground mine passages; their work just about survives in current ragged prints) and a doom-laden Francesco De Masi score, *Maciste in King Solomon's Mines* is almost Gothic in

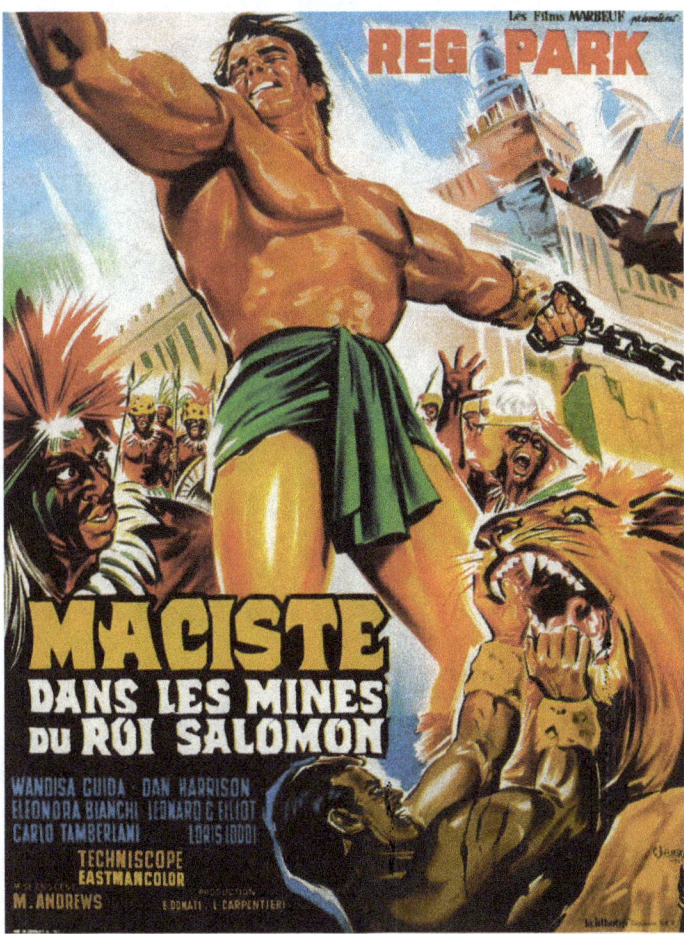

A French poster for *Maciste in King Solomon's Mines*

ing skewered in the face and back. Impressed by his immense strength (and those sweaty biceps), Guida offers a proposition, that they share the throne (and her bed); rejected, she drugs him with toxic flowers and he awakens in the mines, though in a trance. Meanwhile, Piergentili desperately searches for Bianchi and Loddi who are, in fact, among the slaves. Discovering this, Guida organizes the death of Bianchi—she's to be covered in molten gold ("You will be the first human statue in Zimba."). During the obligatory slave revolt, a magic bracelet is sawn off Park's ankle, restoring him to normal; the palace guards seal the mine by demolishing roof supports; the strongman shifts boulders and presses upwards on the tunnel ceiling, causing the huge idol face to collapse onto his foe, enabling everyone to escape. In the palace square, as a battle rages, Park rescues Bianchi and that molten gold pours over Guida and Jotta—they're the first human statues in Zimba! "My duty here is finished," states Park, young Loddi paraded before the cheering public as Zimba's new king, lovers Piergentili and Guida back in each other's arms.

Maciste and the Queen of Samar [*Maciste e la regina de Samar*] aka *Hercules Against the Moon Men*

Nike Cinematografica/Comptoir Francais CFPC (Italy/France); Cromoscope/Eastmancolor; 90 mins; Producer: Luigi Mondello; Director: Giacomo Gentilomo ✞✞✞✞✞

A fiery mass from space hits the Kingdom of Samar, invaders from the moon setting up home base inside the Mountain of Death. Every third full moon, youths are rounded up by Queen Samara's minions and ritually sacrificed to appease the invaders. The queen's half-sister, Billis, is earmarked for sacrifice as she bears an uncanny resemblance to Selena, the moon men's monarch; her blood will revive the comatose queen and she will rule a new Earth alongside Samara and Rudolphis, her guardian. The moon is to be drawn toward Earth, thus breaking the evil influence of the planet Uranus, cause a worldwide cataclysm, wipe out mankind and create a habitat for the lunar interlopers. Maciste joins rebels led by Prince Darix, the citizens determined

mood and atmosphere throughout its opening framework, Italian grand opera set in ancient times. Then, inexplicably, it slows down. The next 13 minutes bogs itself down in an over-reliance on extensive wildlife footage, tribal customs and Bianchi caring for Loddi, alone in the bush. Park enters the frame at the 25th minute, strangling a rampaging lion, while Loddi cuddles a lion club, the cutesy tone diminishing that initial 20-minute impact. Thankfully, the darker scenario recovers, picking itself up, shaking off the dust of the African outback and returning to Zimba where Solomon's mines have been reopened, elderly Carlo Tamberlani among the enslaved workforce. Rebel Bruno Piergentili (Abucar, billed as Dan Harrison) is graphically flayed, Guida and Jotta wanting to know where Loddi has been secreted; he's then tied to a contraption whereby a bed of spikes is hauled toward his face. In bursts Park through the city gates, frees Piergentili, but is netted, much to the pleasure of Guida who delights in slaughtering young children to ensure no infant heir ever reaches the throne ("The sword becomes you much more than a mirror," observes Jotta, gazing in unrequited passion at the evil monarch preening herself). In a seven-minute sequence, Park is placed in a cage, restraining two teams of horses to prevent him from be-

Head Moon Man Rudolphis tends to his comatose queen in an American lobby card for *Hercules Against the Moon Men* (aka *Maciste and the Queen of Samar*).

The Italian Peplum Phenomenon 1950-1967

to eliminate Samara and the moon people; Darix is betrothed to Billis, while Agar, daughter of Gladius who is murdered for assisting the insurgents, clings desperately to Maciste whom she adores. After many perilous cliffhangers, including a clash with the rock monsters, Maciste rescues Billis, Selena shrivels to dust, the rock creatures kill Samara, the Mountain of Death is destroyed, Darix weds Billis and Maciste rides off with Agar for fresh adventures.

You can't help but love *Maciste and the Queen of Samar*, Giacomo Gentilomo's final film before he quit the industry to take up a career in painting. Like a '50s B-movie sci-fi flick (it could have been directed by hack specialist Richard E. Cunha; those rubbery rock monsters are superior versions of *his* foam-rubber rock monsters in 1958's *Missile to the Moon*), it's corny, cardboard, fantasmagorical fun, the plot 10 percent ham, the hokey effects typical of those far-off, pre-CGI days when craftsmen, not computers, got their hands dirty. From the opening shot of chained captives being herded through the mouth of a statue radiating blue light, to the frenetic end sequence (photographed by Oberdan Troiani in monochrome and sepia to accentuate the moon men's subterranean abode), this is a peplum guilty pleasure of the highest order. Alan Steel (billed as Sergio Ciani) was never better, a muscle-bulging, handsome heroic figure utilizing martial arts moves in his vigorous fight scenes, a perpetual grin on his face—boy, was he enjoying himself! Whether pitting his mighty strength against a huge vicious "jaws of death" torture instrument (diced Maciste, anyone?), knocking down soldiers like bowling pins, picking up those seven-foot lumbering rock creatures, tussling a fanged, ape-like being, escaping a water-filling pit, bending bars or fending of the sexual advances of Jany Clair (Samara, a real vulpine beauty), Steel romps through the action superbly, a winning performance (but the director focuses on his nipples a little *too* frequently!). Anna Maria Polani (Agar) smolders as Steel's admirer ("Pleasant dreams," she simpers longingly, gazing at the rugged hunk with her big brown eyes), Nando Tamberlani (Gladius) is skewered to death after a few minutes' screen time, Jean-Pierre Honoré is adequate as Delia D'Alberti's beloved (she plays Billis/Selena), while Roberto "Rudolphis" Ceccacci's goggle-eyed alien helmet/mask is a hoot, straight out of the Ed Wood school of filmmaking.

Much of the picture was shot around Lazio's Lapilli quarries in the Fiora Valley, a very familiar location site in pepla and one used literally scores of times; the closing sequences, showing the moon approaching Earth, resulting in stock footage of tidal waves, volcanic eruptions, fierce winds and storms, work in this context, Steel bringing down a giant idol *and* a stone pillar on the heads of the rock creatures as the moon men's domain implodes dramatically. Carlo Franci's mesmerizing score from *Maciste in Hell* was used again (and why not; it's a great piece of music), the only downside to the whole surrealistic affair being the "rebels caught in a sandstorm" scene in the finale, overstretched to a certain degree. However, this is a minor quibble—*Maciste and the Queen of Samar* is peplum served with

Two attractive peplum stars: Hélène Chanel (Queen Farida) and Kirk Morris (Maciste) in *Valley of the Thundering Echo*

several layers of cheesecake, thoroughly entertaining nonsense; cinemagoers unable to appreciate the whole peplum deal would probably dismiss it as total tosh, while those in the know can appreciate Gentilomo's swansong as the pulp classic it truly is.

Valley of the Thundering Echo [*La valle dell'eco tonante*] aka *Hercules of the Desert*; *Desert Raiders*; *Maciste and the Women of the Valley*

Cineluxor (Italy); Techniscope/Technicolor; 95 (90) mins; Producer: Luigi Rovere; Director: Tanio Boccia (Amerigo Anton) ††

Made back-to-back with the far superior *The Ruler of the Desert* (aka *Desert Raiders*), Tanio Boccia's Arabian clunker flounders in fits and starts, the action stuck in the Lapilli quarries (where's the desert?), a case of too many sheiks spoiling the broth. Maciste (Hercules in dubbed prints), or "The Man of 1,000 Legends," materializes in a cloud of smoke inside the sacred Silver Temple after a high priest has invoked the gods; it's Kirk Morris, looking bemused in a black loincloth edged with gold. He's been summoned to help the nomadic Gameli tribe regain their fertile lands in the Emerald Valley, which lies on the other side of the forbidden Valley of the Thundering Echo. The snag is, wicked Hélène Chanel (Queen Farida) has convened a meeting of the heads of four warmongering tribes, led by Furio Meniconi, with one remit—get rid of the Gameli by enslavement and murder, and reclaim the fabled Emerald Valley, and goes without saying that an antidote is administered to Morris by rebel leader Dante Posani, enabling him to withstand being crushed between pit walls (his Herculean strength disables the capstan pulling the ropes); tossing a 20-foot statue at the guards, he rides off after archers slay two-timing Farnese. The climax has the entire cast assembled at the mouth of the dreaded Valley of the Thundering Echo. And what's causing that infernal racket? Bald-headed troglodytes in caverns bash sheets of metal with clubs. Morris gives *them* a bashing; Chanel, fleeing on horseback, is brought down by arrows on orders from Neri, and the Gameli reach their green and pleasant Promised Land, led by Morris like Moses of yore. Meniconi and his tribes depart, content to let the Gameli get on with it without interference.

Although Aldo Giordani's color bursts into radiance in the climactic grotto sequences, *Valley of the Thundering Echo* is a drab offering, with one notable exception—composer Carlo Rustichelli. The maestro's title music stirs the blood (unlike the film); his incidental cues are magic, and for the dance sequence, he conjures up two minutes' worth of sublime melodies. It's a testament to the weighty genius of composers like Rustichelli that they were able to rise above such mundane material and work their socks off to produce something special; they very rarely let the side down, and Rustichelli doesn't on this occasion. Rather messy in execution, with Morris, Farnese, Meniconi, Chanel and Neri listless and below form, this is one of the tackiest of all peplum "desert" movies, the lack of actual desert locations contributing toward the cheapness of it all.

The Invincible Brothers Maciste [*Gli invincibili fratelli Maciste*] aka *The Invincible Gladiators*

IFESA (Italy); Totalscope/Eastmancolor; 92 mins; Producers: Domenico Seymandi, Vincenzo Musolino; Director: Roberto Mauri ††

The penultimate *Maciste* movie came at a time when the genre was beginning to wind itself down, preparing to morph into the Spaghetti Western. As a result, the glorious soundtracks of Carlo Savina, Carlo Franci, Francesco De Masi, Carlo Innocenzi, Carlo Rustichelli et al. were no more, here replaced by Felice Di Stefano's shopping mall Muzak. Romolo Garroni's bland color schemes and tired performances from everyone except Iloosh Khoshabe, playing Maciste the Elder (billed as Richard Lloyd), compounded the "let's get it all over with" effect; the Iranian ex-bodybuilder put beef into the fight scenes, hurling his mighty bulk through the action with vim, a spirited turn. Shot around Italy's spectacular Cascata delle Marmore in Umbria (the Marmore waterfalls), the play-it-by-numbers plot had Claudie Lange as Queen Thaliade, ruler of an underground kingdom, abducting Ursula Davis (Princess Jana) as bait to lure her betrothed, Anthony Steffen (Prince Akim), to her lair in order to forge a possible queen/king partnership. Davis is drugged and, under Lange's spell, sent back to her city to pull the wool over Steffen's eyes by enticing him to enter Lange's domain. Khoshabe, ordered to locate Davis, tussles with the queen's minions (the leopard men), discovers the entrance to Lange's kingdom beside the foaming rapids (The Waterfall of the Gods), gains access through a massive stone doorway, engages in a fierce rough 'n' tumble with more grunting leopard men and gets trapped beneath a descending roof of spikes. The business end of one blade injects him with a potion and *he's* now drugged. Davis also drugs (that makes three) Khoshabe's brother Mario Novelli (Maciste the Younger, billed as Tony Freeman). She re-

An Italian poster for *The Invincible Brothers Maciste*

its rumored riches, for herself. Her second-in-command, Alberto Farnese, romancing Rosalba Neri (Ramhis), is after a place on the throne, while Gameli lass Spela Rozin (Selina) casts her eyes over Morris' oiled muscles, even though he doesn't utter a single word until 30 minutes have gone by.

What Morris does do is hurl peplum's biggest-ever polystyrene boulder at Meniconi's warriors from a ridge—it's the size of a house; you get a longshot view of the actor's legs protruding beneath the colossal "rock," a laughable sight. The numerous sheiks discuss this and that in tents, Boccia's camera pans over that quarry or remains static and women are rounded up, chained and forced to march to the city. "Send an army to capture that man," barks Chanel, and sure enough, Morris suffers the fate endured by Maciste that's figured in most of his other adventures—he's caught in a net and, in Chanel's boudoir, drugged to make him lose his will. "You don't understand women," she slyly remarks and, on this showing, he obviously doesn't! It

An Italian poster for *Maciste, Avenger of the Maya*

turns to the underground domain and the queen's sparse temple where Khoshabe is a puppy dog servant to the queen's demands (he fights her favored strongman and wins), slave mistress Gia Sandri also desiring the demigod to be her man. Steffen and his troops arrive on the scene, those drugged are given an antidote and restored to normal, the slaves are released, the massive wheel that works the life-support system for the subterranean world is disabled and the caverns collapse; Lange perishes under that roof of spikes. Steffen and Davis ride into their city in a frenzy of schmaltz, Khoshabe galloping off with Sandri for those new adventures, which never did materialize.

The film boasts a highly erotic male/female dance routine; an impressive capstan working the giant wheel; the somewhat terrifying, tumbling cascades of Marmore; imaginative underground shots; Lange stepping naked out of a bath; and Khoshabe, if not that great an actor, at least putting some energy into the part—*The Invincible Brothers Maciste* isn't all that awful, hampered by a slushy, soapy initial 10 minutes (Steffen and Davis kissing, panting, groping and whispering, "Darling, I love you"

ad nauseam) and an inappropriate score. But it fails to hark back to past glories, appearing to distance itself from the previous 22 films, a *Maciste* flick in name only. Yes, by the end of 1964, sword and sandal was heading for the exit door, and Roberto Mauri's picture proved it in more ways than one.

1965

Maciste, Avenger of the Maya [*Maciste il vendicatore dei Maya*] aka *Maciste, The Avenger of the Mayans*

Urias Film (Italy); Totalscope/Eastmancolor; 76 mins; Producer: Giorgio Marzelli; Director: Guido Malatesta ✝

Guido Malatesta, some might say, had the bared-faced affront in returning to his two bone-headed masterpieces, *Maciste Against the Headhunters* and *Maciste Against the Monsters*, chop them to pieces, film fresh footage starring Kirk Morris, mix it all altogether and issue the whole hare-brained package as *Maciste, Avenger of the Maya* in 1965, the last in the series of movies featuring the time-traveling superhero. It both helps and hinders if you've caught the first two: help in so much as you'll be able to just about follow the zigzagging plot; hinder because you'll soon come to realize how haphazard in execution the whole exercise was. Basically, the peaceful Savi, led by Queen Barbara Loy (Aloha), are under threat from Andrea Aureli's marauding Ulmas. Morris appears out of nowhere, helps defeat the baddies (with Demeter Bitenc) and wins the day; as the beefcake actor walks off at the end, it's not Laura Brown (from *Headhunters*) or Margaret Lee (from *Monsters*) that runs after him, but Loy, slobbering all over his pecs.

Reg Lewis, from *Monsters*, appears briefly, poised on a ridge, hurling a spear into the eye of a water dragon—we then switch to Morris (who seems bewildered throughout) for the remainder of this mishmash. And what a mishmash it is. Sequences from one movie are quickly followed by sequences from the other, everything out of order, a chaotic jumble that makes little or no sense, even to peplum fanatics. Minor actors and actresses can be spotted from *Headhunters* and *Monsters* that don't appear in the new footage, which rarely matches, in color tones and texture, the originals. For example, the decaying interior of the City of Gold (from *Headhunters*), in Malatesta's brand new shots, looks almost unsullied and the earthquake sequence (featured in *Headhunters* and *Monsters*) is bolstered by having dozens of polystyrene boulders falling on the heads of the cowering Ulmas (and bouncing off the floor!). To spice things up (and prevent boredom from setting in), the inclusion of six-foot-four-inch circus strongman Koloss, playing cave-dweller Goliath, who gets the hots for Loy, is an amusing diversion, but those with an eagle eye will spot so many irregularities and spend so much time fathoming out which scene belongs to which film (a couple of battles are flagrantly repeated to stretch the running length) that interest in what's actually occurring in *this* production will rapidly evaporate (and where, pray, are the Mayas?). *Maciste, Avenger of the Maya* was drummed up in double-quick time under Malatesta's own production company, named after the Urias in *Headhunters* and only released in Italy and France: It's nothing more than cheapskate fare and should be avoided by all except completists who must have every single *Maciste* outing in their collection; decent DVD prints in Spanish are available on the market. It's best sticking to *Headhunters* and *Monsters* for your viewing pleasure—at least you'll be able to understand what's going on.

7
Samson 1961-1964

The character of Samson appeared in five sword and sandal features, only three of which were released containing Samson as the lead title character. The other two were *Hercules Challenges Samson* and *Hercules, Samson, Maciste and Ursus: The Invincibles* (*Samson and His Mighty Challenge*). Because of the popularity of the Samson persona, synonymous in the public psyche with great strength, he manifested himself in six retitled and dubbed *Maciste* features as the name "Maciste," even though the famous Italian folk hero was deemed unmarketable to U.S. audiences, who could more readily associate themselves with "Samson": *Maciste in the Valley of the Kings* (*Son of Samson*), *Maciste at the Court of the Great Khan* (*Samson and the Seven Miracles of the World*), *Maciste Against the Sheik* (*Samson Against the Sheik*), *Zorro Against Maciste* (*Samson and the Slave Queen*), *Maciste in King Solomon's Mines* (*Samson in King Solomon's Mines*) and *Maciste at the Court of the Czar* (*Samson vs. the Giant King*). 1964's *Samson and the Treasure of the Incas*, directed by Piero Pierotti, was a Spaghetti Western in all but name only, straying into peplum territory, a bizarre tale of outlaws and good guys, led by Alan Steel (as Samson/William Smith/Hercules), searching for an Incan treasure in a remote valley. Extremely difficult to obtain, it doesn't really form a part of the *Samson* roster but nevertheless is included in this chapter.

1961

Samson [*Sansone*]

Cineproduzioni Associate (Italy); Totalscope/Eastmancolor; 100 (90) mins; Producers: Mario Maggi, Ernesto Gentili; Director: Gianfranco Parolini ††

Someone forgot to light the fuse when it was decided to introduce to the peplum role of honor the titular muscleman inspired by Cecil B. DeMille's double Oscar-winning *Samson and Delilah*; *Samson*, starring Brad Harris in the lead, fails to flare into life, lethargically presented by Gianfranco Parolini and acted without any real vigor by the cast. Francesco Izzarelli's pastel color photography is wonderful, but you can't leave it up to a cinematographer to carry a movie, which appeared to be the case here. What's more, Alan Steel (Sergio Ciani) as beefcake Millstone (Hercules in French prints) supported Harris, so you had two he-men for the price of one; more should have been made of this.

The first six minutes of *Samson* is given over to Harris and Steel in a cavern, punching the living daylights out of one another to determine who's the strongest, even playing tug of war with a dead boar. White-robed soldiers enter, Harris arrested and placed in a cell with his two comical buddies. A lengthy dance

An Italian poster for *Samson*

follows, performed by the Ballet of the Zagreb Operatic Society, and then the plot kicks in. Cold-eyed Mara Berni (Queen Romilda) and weasel-like counselor Serge Gainsbourg (Barcalla) rule the kingdom of Sulom; the pair are after a hoard of hidden treasure, and only Irena Prosen, Berni's sister, knows of its whereabouts but refuses to tell, hence her incarceration in a dungeon. Harris breaks out of jail with his pals, gate-crashes a feast literally, using a cell gate to force back the guards, fights strongman Igor in court, drinks drugged wine and falls through a trapdoor, straight back behind bars. Luisella Boni (Janine, billed as Brigitte Corey), Berni's handmaiden and Steel's sister, revives Harris; he escapes, meeting Steel and a band of rebels in a tavern, the aim being to overthrow Berni and Gainsbourg,

An Italian poster for *Samson Against the Pirates*

while deposed monarch Carlo Tamberlani in on the act. Prosen's son, shepherd boy Franco Gasparri (Azrai), happens to be the rightful heir to the throne; he's flung into prison and threatened with a throat slitting if his mother doesn't divulge the hiding place of the treasure. A protracted games tournament follows, Harris matching his mighty strength against an army of strongmen and, blindfolded, Steel; the two warriors clap each other on the shoulders, wrap a huge chain around a pillar and heave, bringing the palace roof crashing down (a homage to *Samson and Delilah*'s legendary final scene), all over in a flash. During the fracas, Gainsbourg stabs Berni to death and flees with the gold. He's brought to ground attempting to get away on a raft; Harris pushes the sniveling wretch overboard, straight into the jaws of an approaching crocodile. Back in the city, Gasparri and Prosen are pronounced the new rulers of Sulom, Steel is given a golden sword and Harris goes off to play house with Boni.

Harris is perfectly adequate as Samson, both in physique and acting capability, but certainly no Victor Mature (and Berni is no Hedy Lamarr), his on/off partnership with Steel fairly engaging in a "boys will be boys" kind of way. But the comedy elements involving Harris' tubby compatriot grate, and any audience would find it hard to swallow the fact that an ingratiating little runt like Gainsbourg could boss whole legions of hard-bitten soldiers around. The slow pace kills it; if beefed up, like its two main stars, it would have been much more fun to look at.

1963

Samson Against the Pirates [*Sansone contro i pirati*] aka ***Samson and the Sea Beast***
Romana Film (Italy); Totalscope/Eastmancolor; 89 (81) mins; Producer: Fortunato Misiano; Director: Tanio Boccia (Amerigo Anton) ††

"Someday, a man will come out of the sea and pass judgement on us all." So sayeth a prisoner in the year 1630, as he perishes in pirate chief Daniele Vargas' torture chamber on Devil's Island. And that man is Elvis Presley look-alike Kirk Morris, who is tall, muscular, handsome (in a sulky kind of way) and about as wooden as the skiff he rows backwards and forwards in. Morris, two cohorts and heavily made-up Margaret Lee (Amanda) join forces with rebel Aldo Bufi Landi (Manual) in an effort to kick the butt of Vargas and his piratical buddies, busy looting Spanish galleons and sending them to the bottom of the ocean in a barrage of cannon fire. Women, captured during a raid, have to be saved from slavery, so who better than the impassive hunk to carry out this mission, first by posing as a slave trader, then a leader of Landi's gang. ("You're the living symbol of our cause.")

Wearing next to nothing, a stark contrast to everyone else who is dressed to the nines, Morris prances here, there and everywhere, engaging in a round of uncustomary (for peplum) limp-wristed fights (including a tavern brawl) and featuring in two peculiar scenes. In one, he has to drag a boat packed with beefy oarsmen backwards to prevent him being impaled on a bank of spears, a sequence that goes on far too long (but at least the actor seems to be exerting himself); in the second, Morris grapples with peplum's (no, that should read cinema's) lousiest dummy crocodile (the sea beast of the title?), a tatty prop that wouldn't have looked out of place in a 1940s Hollywood B-jungle flick. Tullio Altamura and Nello Pazzafini posture and threaten as Vargas' lieutenants, while Vargas, intoxicated with liquor most of the time, overacts to the point of parody. In a damp squib of a climax, Morris pulls a massive chain and Vargas' retreat crashes to the ground; the three villainous corsairs meet their Maker, with the pirate boss falling backwards onto a sword aboard his ship. Morris, Lee and his two pals sail off in their little craft, back to their village and a life of leisure.

Angelo Francesco Lavagnino provided a decent score in a movie that didn't really warrant one, and the same goes for Augusto Tiezzi's sharp photography, wasted on this occasion.

An Italian poster for *Samson Against the Black Pirate*

A lame addition to the muscleman/mythological hero cycle that drifts merrily along without an ounce of impact or excitement—in its favor, current DVD prints are of fine, widescreen quality.

1964

Samson Against the Black Pirate [*Sansone contro il corsaro nero*] aka *Hercules and the Black Pirate*; *Hercules and the Pirates*

Romana Film (Italy); Totalscope/Eastmancolor; 93 (85) mins; Producer: Fortunato Misiano; Director: Luigi Capuano ✞✞✞

Any film that features Luigi Capuano, Fortunato Misiano, composer Angelo Francesco Lavagnino and cinematographer Augusto Tiezzi behind the scenes deserves some modicum of attention, even in a slice of piratical baloney such as dished up here. In U.S. prints, nice looking hunk Alan Steel (Sergio Ciani) became Hercules and the badly dubbed dialogue reached new depths of inanity (seven-year-old Cinzia Bruno to Steel: "Would you give me a little kiss, Hercules?"). The story treads old ground. Deputy Piero Lulli (Rodrigo Sanchez) wants to boot Nerio Bernardi, Governor of San Sebastion, out of office and seize the colony's treasure, linking up with Andrea Aureli, the feared Black Pirate. Hero of the seas Steel (introduced in a rapid montage of stock action footage) plays a brawny naval officer romancing Bernardi's tasty daughter Rosalba Neri (Rosita), honored, along with his troops, for eliminating piracy in the area. Although static and dialogue-driven in the early section, Capuano treats us to a prolonged acrobatic, juggling, dancing and firework display (audiences lapped up these big screen antics in the 1960s), a macho-charged, hand-to-hand grapple between Steel and a second strongman, glistening muscles shot full-frame (how those gay patrons must have loved this sequence!) and a rip-roaring sally on Steel's fishing village. Lulli (forever playing villains in pepla because of his sharp, menacing features) tries unsuccessfully to murder Bernardi and his wife, Elisa Mainardi, abducting Bruno instead; Steel, laid low by a poison-tipped dart, narrowly avoids drowning in the hold of Aureli's flagship, smashing his way to freedom through the bulwarks, a cannon used as a convenient battering ram. After delivering Bruno safely into the arms of her relieved parents (Lulli receives a dagger in the back from dying Aureli following a shipboard fracas), Bernardi reverses his haughty decision that his blue-blooded daughter shouldn't be deporting herself with the son of a fisherman, granting his blessing on Steel and Neri's union.

Samson Against the Black Pirate is colorful, wacky nonsense, just about steering clear of the path to flatness because of the expertise of the technicians involved—in lesser hands, it would have been a stinker. Steel, like so many other he-men of this period, let his commanding physique do all the talking (he lobs a tree trunk at his opponents in one scene), while female lead Neri was decorative but vacant. As was often the case, it was left to the bad guys to carry the picture and, in this respect, Aureli and Lulli came up trumps, a pair of rascally no-gooders who hold the attention throughout.

Samson and the Treasure of the Incas [*Sansone e il tesoro degli incas*] aka *Hercules and the Treasure of the Incas*; *The Lost Treasure of the Incas*; *The Lost Treasure of the Aztecs*

Romana Film/Ulysse Prod. (Italy/West Germany/France); Totalscope/Eastmancolor; 105 (90) mins; Producer: Fortunato Misiano; Director: Piero Pierotti ✞✞✞

It was during 1964 that peplum began to lose mass audience appeal, the overworked genre and its technicians gravitating toward the Spaghetti Western, hoping to cash in on the success generated by Sergio Leone's influential *A Fistful of Dollars*. As we shall see in chapter 18, many *Zorro* pictures of this period were an uneasy marriage of peplum and Spaghetti Western ideals, but hybrids would never come any more bizarre than Piero Pierotti's blend of *fusto* and cowboy actioner in which Alan Steel (Samson/William Smith/Arizona, billed as Sergio Ciani on Italian prints) starred as a musclebound cowpoke searching for Incan gold in a remote New Mexico valley. According to one source, Piero Pierotti's initial intention was to make a *Samson* sword and sandal opus but a short way into production, the team performed an artistic turnabout, togas and swords exchanged for shirts and guns, although the fantasy ending was kept intact.

Peplum meets the Spaghetti Western: Mario Petri is Jerry Darmon, on the search for Inca gold in an Italian photobusta for *Samson and the Treasure of the Incas*.

Even Angelo Francesco Lavagnino's score was altered to fit the bill—part rousing peplum, part Old West-cum-Ennio Morricone, an odd-sounding mix. Just as odd was seeing Steel stripping off to reveal his rippling torso, fighting the bad guys in a saloon, not a tavern or palace. We had a ribald, heel-kicking dance number (but not by writhing, scantily clad Roman maidens) and Mario Petri (Jerry Darmon), boss of the Silver Dollar saloon, dressed in smart duds; what the six-foot-three former opera singer, who discovered his métier in 18 pepla playing mostly villains, made of it all is anyone's guess. Very hard to lay hands on, widescreen DVD copies come in English dubbed over Spanish, "Incas" substituted with "Aztecs." However, twice during the movie, Italian replaces English dubbing, subtitles appearing (first, for eight minutes; second, for five minutes); "Aztecs" reverts to "Incas" and Steel, formerly William Smith/Arizona, is now Samson! All this is very confusing, but stick with it because you'll never experience anything like it again.

In Pioneer City, Petri and henchman Wolfgang Lukschy (El Puma) are rubbing their hands in glee, having organized the murder of a moneyed ranch owner, relieving him of $20,000. Toni Sailer, one of two sentries assigned to keep watch on the deceased land baron, is falsely accused of the crime and placed behind bars. Buddy Steel joins forces with the town sheriff (Harry Riebauer) and the baron's sister, Brigitte Heiberg, escorting the stagecoach carrying Sailer to Silver City, where he's to stand before a tribunal. They don't want Petri and his mob to waylay the coach and kill Sailer; his trial and subsequent court inquiry will expose the real culprits, and Petri will face the rope as a result, a much-favored plotline in many '50s Westerns. There's mention of an Aztec/Incan treasure in the 20th minute and a "Sacred City" 22 minutes later to keep us on our toes; card sharp Pierre Cressoy (Vince) warns a punter to, "Keep your paws off a lady, you lowdown half-breed" and a black-clad Jack Palance look-alike skulks in the shadows, his sharpshooter for hire. A couple of gunfights into the action, Steel meets pert Incan Anna Maria Polani (Queen Mysia, the Bride of the Sun God), dressed as a boy, who takes him to her temple in Buzzard Valley near Demon Pass, hidden behind a golden doorway set in the side of a cliff. Petri and company, anxious to grab the treasure as well as Sailer, converge on the Inca's domain after Polani has revealed her feminine assets to Steel (and her maid), his blond quiff remaining unruffled at such a gloriously tempting sight. Following a shoot-out inside picturesque caverns, Steel, Heiberg, Riebauer, Polani, Sailer and Petri are chained together: "You must perish with the others in the rivers of boiling fire," announces the high priest to the disgraced queen (well, you can't blame the girl for falling in love with Steel's magnificent body). A volcanic eruption causes an explosion: Molten lava spews from a statue's mouth, pillars topple and the temple roof caves in; everyone except Petri makes it out to the open where they head back to Pioneer City to play house.

A potty concoction that is weirdly enjoyable, *Samson and the Treasure of the Incas* must be the exact spot where pepla morphed into Western (Mario Caiano's 1963 *The Sign of the Coyote* also falls into this category); it's a one-off, an important constituent in Italian moviemaking where two differing genres collided head-on and resulted in cinematic fallout of a sort, sword and sandal giving way to guns and boots. An important film, then, despite its slightly skewed merits, even though it has gone unnoticed by the majority of fans.

8
Goliath and Ursus 1961-1964

In the wake of the global sensation of musclemen/sword and sandal features generated by Steve Reeves' two *Hercules* pictures, Italian moviemakers scouted around for alternative mythological heroes to broaden their filmic horizons. Reeves' *Terror of the Barbarians* (*Goliath and the Barbarians*) became a huge worldwide box-office smash in 1959/1960, leading to a further four movies featuring the mighty muscleman's exploits, none related to the other. The name "Goliath" also featured in the non-Italian versions of *Maciste Against the Vampire* (*Goliath and the Vampires*), *Maciste, the World's Greatest Hero* (*Goliath and the Sins of Babylon*), *The Revenge of Hercules* (*Goliath and the Dragon*) and *The Hero of Babylon* (*Goliath, King of the Slaves*). *David and Goliath* can be ruled out as this was a retelling of Biblical events.

Time-traveling Ursus, named after Buddy Baer's giant slave character in MGM's *Quo Vadis*, was referred to as a "Son of Hercules" in two movies, appearing in all manner of historical periods, from Roman times to the 17th century, spread over eight outings (nine when including *Hercules, Samson, Maciste and Ursus: The Invincibles*). The *Ursus* features are lively, extravagantly produced and violent, as good as any *Hercules* or *Maciste* offering, with Ed Fury coming out tops as the best Ursus of the crop. Within these 12 offerings can be found the very best (and in one case, the very worst) that peplum has to offer, often overlooked in preference to the *Hercules* and *Maciste* adventures. The *Goliath* movies are listed in the order that they were released in Italy, as are the *Ursus* pictures.

1961

Goliath Against the Giants [*Goliath contro i giganti*]
CI.AS./Procusa (Italy/Spain); Supertotalscope/Eastmancolor; 98 (87) mins; Producers: Manuel Pérez, Cesare Seccia; Directors: Guido Malatesta, Gianfranco Parolini ✞✞✞✞✞

It's got everything: sea monsters, giant dragon-type lizards, a tribe of Amazons, apemen, a Yeti-cum-gorilla, outlandish torture instruments, lions, a mad ruler and Gloria Milland in a blonde wig. *Goliath Against the Giants*' plot may be paper-thin, but Parolini and Malatesta manufactured a king-sized helping of peplum hokum to keep the fans happy, one of *the* archetypal genre movies of its day. Dressed up in Alejandro Ulloa's shimmering colors, Carlo Innocenzi's urgent score pumping away in the background, this is mindless entertainment for a good night in—there's nothing remotely cerebral on offer here.

After five long years of warfare, Brad Harris (Goliath) and his conquering heroes head for home, their beloved kingdom now ruled by fruitcake usurper Fernando Rey (Bokan) and his mistress, Carmen de Lirio (Diamira). Rey, justifiably terrified that Harris will kick him off the throne, orders Gloria Milland (Princess Elea) to intercept the strongman, turn on her seductive charms and kill him before he reaches the city; she only succeeds in falling for Harris who, after a string of adventures involving Amazon warriors, a huge sea serpent, a vicious typhoon and Milland's hesitant hand on the dagger, arrives at the city with the lady and lovers Pepe Rubio and Barbara Carroll, bent

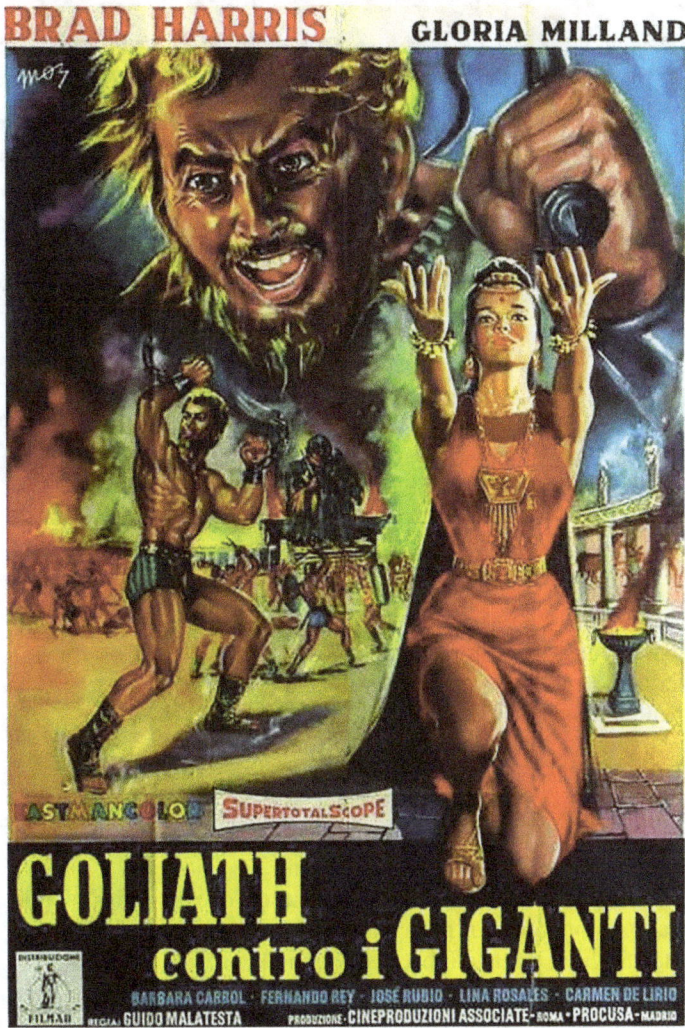

An Italian poster for *Goliath Against the Giants*

on inciting the population into open revolt against Rey's tyrannical regime. Everything *including* the kitchen sink gets tossed into the mix, ensuring not one second of boredom: a couple of ingenious torture devices straight out of the pages of an Edgar Allan Poe story; Harris grappling with a gorilla creature *and* lions; a brutal arena clash in which the bloodied victor receives for his efforts an arrow through the neck (much to the crowd's displeasure); and a tremendous 12-minute all-blazing skirmish, climaxing with Rey slumped on the throne, half a dozen arrows sticking out of his back. Harris then has to rescue Milland from the smoke-filled Valley of the Giants, causing a landslide that wipes out both apemen and overlarge horned lizards. Back in the city, the loving two-some find themselves trumpeted as the rightful heirs to the throne.

Square-jawed Harris had the muscles but not a great deal of screen charisma, but he does get to speak the film's one great line: "It's more difficult to understand women than to beat an army," referring to Milland's repeated deceptions. The sets are fantastic, as are the numerous landscape shots, composed with a

genuine taste for filmmaking craft and atmosphere. Colorful and daft, moving like an express train, *Goliath Against the Giants* is peplum cinema at its very best.

Ursus [*Ursus*] aka *Ursus, Son of Hercules*; *The Mighty Ursus*

Cine-Italia Film/Atenea Films/Acine (Italy/Spain); Totalscope/Eastmancolor; 95 (90) mins; Producer: Italo Zingarelli; Director: Carlo Campogalliani ✝✝✝✝✝

32-year-old American Ed Fury took on the duties of portraying mythological muscleman Ursus in the first of three outings for him, doing all that was required in a tremendous start to the series: wear the briefest of tunics, flex his impressive pecs, look mean and menacing, shout warnings to his protagonists and come to the aid of the damsel in distress, everything performed with the minimum of acting know-how but the maximum of muscle-packed energy. Carlo Campogalliani set out his stall with those recognizable components Italian audiences were fast becoming au fait with, addicted as they were to sword and sandal actioners, a sure-fire way to guarantee box-office success (the picture was a decent-sized hit in Europe): a powerfully built, handsome hero; a wicked queen; attractive female leads (three in this movie); black-hearted villains; a rowdy tavern; punishment on the gristmill; waterfalls; caverns; secret tunnels; a test of strength; sexy dances; a decadent banquet; floggings; an ornate temple; and a violent mass fight to round it all off. Shot in Totalscope and Eloy Mella's matchless Eastmancolor, with Roman Vlad's full orchestral score lifting the narrative to almost operatic heights (as it did in *Son of the Red Corsair*), *Ursus*, like its titular hero, is big and dumb but *not* so stupid, immensely entertaining, quintessential peplum that can still be enjoyed today with a bag of popcorn and a large Coke, 50 years after it graced the cinema screen.

Returning from the wars after a five-year absence, Fury picks up blind shepherdess Maria Luisa Merlo (turning in the movie's finest-tuned performance as Magali), saves her from bad guy Luis Prendes' predations and discovers that his betrothed, Moira Orfei (Attea), has been sold into slavery, her father murdered; Merlo heard that those who carried out the deed and also Prendes (as Setas), involved up to his neck, want the blonde lass out of the picture. The scenario hurtles along like an express train: Fury has a contest of chain-breaking strength with a hairy bodybuilder ("Hero of a hundred battles and the most powerful of all warriors," shouts Fury's friend Roberto Camardiel to the inn's clientele), tracks down those responsible for killing his prospective father-in-law, finds that Orfei was sold to a merchant (Mario Scaccia), who in turn sent her to a sacred island where virgins are sacrificed, and is drugged, forced to work two giant millstones while mercilessly flogged by Prendes. Cristina Gaioni (credited as Gajoni) helps Fury escape, joining him and Merlo on a sojourn through the desert where they encounter a Gypsy and his beautiful daughter, Mariangela Giordano. Prendes and his soldiers catch up, Fury lobs boulders at the attackers, Giordano knifes Gaioni and eventually, Fury, Merlo and Prendes reach the island, the action slipping into a higher gear as Fury discovers that the reigning queen of this verdant paradise is none other than Orfei, his intended bride, now a masked, raving megalomaniac. ("You are the queen of this cursed island! You are a monster!")

Fury and Merlo are tied to stakes, their execution suspended; he's ordered to slave in the mines; Merlo is condemned to die as a sacrificial virgin; Fury wrestles with a bull (full marks to the stunt double assigned to tackle this ferocious beast; oversensitive souls will recoil in horror) and Prendes is slain by Orfei. Yes, *Ursus* delivers the goods in spades, each overdramatic scene punctuated by Vlad's equally overdramatic music, hoisting the movie into the realms of a grand Italian opera. It concludes with a tremendous tussle within the temple's arena, Orfei stabbed to death, her men-at-arms joining in the slave revolt against the conniving council and its corrupt high priest, Rafael Luis Calvo. Merlo regains her sight and casts off in a skiff with her good-looking, brawny benefactor, leaving the island in the hands of the army, the priests crushed under the colossal gold statue of their perverse god; Fury pushes the effigy down on their heads in homage to Samson during the combat's endmost stages.

The Revenge of Ursus [*La vendetta di Ursus*] aka *The Vengeance of Ursus*; *The Mighty Warrior*

Jonia Film (Italy); Techniscope/Eastmancolor; 88 (85) mins; Producer: Ferdinand Felicioni; Director: Luigi Capuano ✝✝✝✝

Next in line for the role of Ursus, on the recommendation of fellow muscleman Gordon Mitchell, was Canadian bodybuilder/

An Italian poster for *The Revenge of Ursus*

athlete/swimming champion Samson (Samuel) Burke, he of the rough-hewn features whose colossal torso and biceps almost defied description. Kicking off in rousing style courtesy of Carlo Innocenzi's brash theme music (used in many other pepla, but that's no bad thing), Luigi Capuano's lively contribution to the series (and Burke's first film credit) was big, bold and brainless, the simplified plot as follows. Ursus, now a farmer, befriends former love Princess Sira (Wandisa Guida), off to marry King Zagro (Livio Lorenzon) for a political alliance only. He escorts her caravan to Zagro's palace, young brother Darius (Roberto Chevalier) in tow, and has a run-in with bandits and becomes embroiled in a rebellion to overthrow the king; the tyrant is loved by mistress Sabra (Nadia Sanders) and helped in his climb to power by Sira's devious advisor, Licurgo (Gianni Rizzo). Sira's father, King Alteo (Nerio Bernardi), is assassinated, Ursus is wrongly accused, there's an uprising, Zagro is killed and Sira announces to the applauding, liberated masses that her next husband will be none other than Ursus.

Granite-faced Burke, it must be said, put 100 percent physical effort into his action scenes, drop-kicking his opponents, scattering them like leaves in the wind, swatting bandits like flies with a hefty war club ("He's no man, he's a demon!" yells the chief in terror), hauling a stranded barge to a riverbank, breaking his bonds and escaping from the grindstone, busting out of his fetters, triumphing over seven musclemen on a huge pivot who attempt to push him into a bed of flames and pulling an elephant backwards to avoid impalement on a plank of spikes. In fact, the first 15 minutes concentrate on Burke strutting his stuff with enthusiastic bursts of energy and boundless aplomb, almost an advert to promote the beefcake's superhuman, animalistic strength; why he only made three peplum movies (you can discount Columbia's 1962 offering, *The Three Stooges Meet Hercules*) is a mystery. Lorenzon, as usual, spits, grimaces and conspires, Rizzo's trademark toadying confidant in collusion for his own greed. The bald-pated growler weds Sanders by mistake, the girl placing a mask over her face to pretend she's Guida; the marriage lasts all of five minutes, Lorenzon stabbing her to death for her deceitfulness. Delightful, red-haired Chevalier helps the outlaws where he can, perhaps the youngest-ever warrior in peplum to be hemmed in by a circle of blades, while Franco Fantasia (also billed as the movie's fencing coach) is Master of the Guards, leaping to Burke's cause when the giant feigns defeat in the arena. Fantasia and his men, disgraced at not capturing him earlier, are forced to fight him, forfeiting their heads if they lose; Burke takes pity, Fantasia offering him thanks and future assistance. Throw in a couple of over-the-top feasts, a dance performed by golden-masked maidens ("You want a woman? Take your pick of the dancers," grins Lorenzon to Burke who declines the offer posthaste), Chevalier cowering terrified in an urn, hiding from a prowling hungry leopard, and a thundering all-out climactic skirmish, Lorenzon sticking a knife into Rizzo's fat belly and succumbing to Burke's sword as the rebels, led by Fantasia, defeat the king's forces, and you have archetypal mythological *fusto* heroics, marred by a scratched, jumpy print on current DVD copies—but that, as we will discover throughout this book, is regrettably the norm in pepla.

Ursus in the Valley of the Lions [*Ursus nella valle dei leoni*] aka ***Valley of the Lions***

Cine-Italia Film/Les Films Marbeauf (Italy/France); Totalscope/Eastmancolor; 94 (82) mins; Producers: Fernando Cinquini, Giuseppe Fatigati; Director: Carlo Ludovico Bragaglia ✟✟✟✟

The third entry in 1961's quartet of *Ursus* movies saw Ed Fury returning to the role, displaying a violent energy in keeping with villain Alberto Lupo's violent disposition (and composer Riz Ortolani's rowdy score). As of 2015, Bragaglia's exuberant gem can only be viewed in pan and scan and monochrome, or atrocious color. Try to imagine the film as it was 56 years ago and you'll appreciate that top rating. Ursus is first seen as an infant, his father, King Annurius, and mother slaughtered by Lu-

Ed Fury demonstrates his ultimate strength in *Ursus in the Valley of the Lions*.

po's barbarians. Years later, the mythical muscleman is frolicking in a grotto with a pride of lions, having been brought up (like Tarzan) as one of their own; he knows very little of the outside world, not, that is, until a passing slave merchant's wagon from the Levant, carrying a bevy of delectable women, gets wedged in a trap. Fury hauls the wagon onto its wheels, befriends Mariangela Giordano (Annia) and her pooch Argo (soon, he's frolicking with *her* in Monte Gelato's pools, his hormones in overdrive) and gives trader Giacomo Furia (Simud) a gold medallion in payment for the girl. When Lupo (King Ayak) learns of the pendant, he realizes that Fury is baby Ursus, the rightful heir to the kingdom, and sets out to murder him ("The throne is mine and I'm going to keep it."); Fury, on discovering he's the rightful heir, turns nasty, determined to head a rebel group, kill the usurper and regain his position as ruler.

The whole cast is on top form, not an off-key performance in sight. Good-looking Fury steams into his opponents without hesitation, turning the tables on a bunch of soldiers as they try to net him in the pool; he nets them instead! Moira Orfei plays Attea, an over-ambitious slave girl who latches onto Lupo for personal gain (she fancies herself as queen) and winds up strangled when the tyrannical bully has no further use for her; Lupo's henchman, Gérard Herter (Lothar), radiates pure menace; and Lupo thunders around on set, barking orders and trying it on with Giordano after he's callously disposed of Orfei. A spectacular climax has Lupo's prisoners dragged toward a bed of flames by four elephants in a packed arena; Fury, after escaping from a collapsed cavern, then breaking his chains in a dungeon cell and surviving a pit of ravenous hyenas (he pushes Herter into the pack), forces each elephant onto its knees; Simba the lion, having followed his master to the city, pounces on Lupo and mauls him to death. "Long live Ursus!" roars the crowd as Fury and Giordano hug and kiss. A splendid sword and sandal actioner proved conclusively that the *Ursus* features were every bit as good, if not better in some instances, than the much-vaunted *Hercules* movies.

Ursus and the Tartar Girl [*Ursus e la ragazza tartara*] aka ***Ursus and the Tartar Princess***; ***The Tartar Invasion***; ***The Savage Hordes***

Explorer Film '58/Comptoir Francais CFFP (Italy/France); Techniscope/Eastmancolor; 100 (85) mins; Producer: Nino Battiferri; Director: Remigio Del Grosso ✝✝✝✝✝

They say that a great motion picture score can hold up a not-so-great movie. In the case of the fourth *Ursus* outing, Angelo Francesco Lavagnino's blistering soundtrack contributes immensely to one of pepla's more underrated muscleman/barbarian adventures. The composer's pounding, warlike tonalities, interrupted by a lilting, evocative leitmotif played on mandolin, makes for electrifying listening. Lavagnino was one of the genre's finest exponents of the now long-lost art at providing the right chords in all the right places; here, he excelled. Having listened to the musical output from all the main peplum composers spread over 300 Italian films, I can state unequivocally that the Genoese musical giant's music to *Ursus and the Tartar Girl* is right up there in the top five best pepla soundtracks of all time; it's that brilliant.

And the film overall is brilliant also. Scriptwriter Remigio Del Grosso's sole effort at directing is a hard-hitting, gritty, action-packed, thoughtful and intelligent entry in the series, acted every inch to the full by a strong cast. In fact, this is more of an Ettore Manni picture than a Joe Robinson picture. Robinson, playing bearded Ursus (now living in the second half of the 17th century), takes second place to Manni's center stage performance as Prince Stefan, a Polish knight who falls in love with Tartar princess Yoko Tani and convinces her that the way to peace and happiness is through his way, not the pagan way. In dealing with this part of the story and shooting in intimate close-up (highlighting Tani's delicate bone structure), Del Grosso brought a sense of weight and meaning to the lead characters, instead of the usual one-dimensional portrayal, allowing them to flesh the parts out. It's in his careful handling of the romantic side of the plot that makes *Ursus and the Tartar Girl* resemble an American mini-epic from the 1950s, rather than a standard Italian sword and sandal costume feature.

The Polish army is ordered to proceed to the frontier, capture as many Tartar prisoners as they can and gain information regarding their stratagem, under torture if necessary. Robinson joins the knights (wearing full body armor and winged helmets) when his young son Mikhail is abducted by Tom Felleghy's barbarian hordes, teaming up with Manni in the hope that the child can be located. Opening with a savage attack on Robinson's encampment (women butchered; men burned at the stake; faces slashed), the action swiftly moves to a Polish reprisal assault on Felleghy's camp, equally fast and ferocious, Robinson laying into the pagans, swinging a massive war axe. Riding through a deep ravine, Manni's troops find themselves surrounded. Making a stand at daybreak, Felleghy, under a flag of truce, offers a suggestion to prevent wholesale massacre: Manni will give himself up and will be offered to the Polish authorities for a ransom of 20,000 talents, his men spared but held prisoner. Manni agrees, and the narrative switches to the Tartar city, detailing

An Italian poster for *Ursus and the Tartar Girl*

willpower to turn down *that* offer), also aware that she has converted to his religion. He's already offered a leadership to Manni ("My daughter loves you. You will marry her and become a Tartar chieftain.") who, refusing, has wound up on the slave gang; he's even offered the position of head groom in Felleghy's stables to save his hide. The two love rivals viciously fight it out for her honor in the arena; Manni's the victor, fatally wounding Staccioli who later dies, resulting in bedlam. Felleghy is shot dead, Tani's trusted maid Maria Grazia Spina knifed and Tani sentenced to burn alive for treason (set on fire from the arms downwards, the Tartar method). Andrea Aureli's house is raided for weapons and Manni's men break out, taking Robinson's son and Tani, Tamiroff's army in hot pursuit of "those Polish dogs," the start of their "Great Offensive." Robinson, at long last, enters into the frame, pulling down a vital bridge, which does little to prevent the hordes from converging on the Polish capital. In a mighty battle, Tamiroff is slain by Manni; on learning of the death of their khan, the tribes retire from the field. In reward, Manni and Tani are given their own regiment on the frontier, riding off clasping hands to the swelling notes of that "Pomp and Circumstance"-type music, an uplifting closer, while Robinson, holding Mikhail close to his bulging chest, wants nothing: "I am happy … my family and my freedom, and my woods. That's all I need."

Try to root out French VHS copies, which are at least in color and widescreen; DVD releases are pan and scan, and monochrome, destroying Anchise Brizzi's expertly muted period color tones. And ignore unfavorable reviews elsewhere—this is classic peplum entertainment containing a classic peplum score, one of those actioners that can be reveled in time and time again. This is an enthralling, full-blooded drama with depth and fire in its belly.

1962

Manni's precarious relationship with Felleghy (both acknowledge the other's strengths), their discussions over Tartar beliefs ("The Tartar is a warrior in need of new land."), his growing love for warlord's daughter, Princess Ila (Tani, looking truly delectable), the ill-treatment of his fellow captives and Robinson's furtive operations in digging through a collapsed tunnel to escape the city (his son is being brought up in Felleghy's court), with Lavagnino punctuating each new scene with the crash of a gong. Akim Tamiroff (the Great Khan) arrives with lizard-eyed son Ivano Staccioli (the actor specialized in playing psychopathic gunslingers in many Spaghetti Westerns), promptly declaring that Tani is to wed Staccioli to cement the Tartar throne, thus presenting Felleghy with a dilemma; he knows of his daughter's passionate feelings for Manni ("I want to be your slave," she whispers huskily to the Polish knight; who would have the

Ursus, the Rebel Gladiator [*Ursus, il gladiatore ribelle*] aka ***The Rebel Gladiators***

Splendor Film (Italy); Techniscope/Eastmancolor; 95 mins; Producer: Ignazio Luceri; Director: Domenico Paolella ✞✞✞✞

Two musclemen for the price of one appear in Domenico Paolella's enthralling grade-A peplum production—Dan Vadis as Ursus and Alan Steel (aka Sergio Ciani) as Emperor Commodus. An educated script (the director was one of three writers), carefully paced direction, bombastic score (Carlo Savina), bold color photography (Carlo Bellero) and believable performances (even from Messrs. Vadis and Steel) contribute to one of the genre's best-ever, and most well-rounded, entries. Whether you're a fan of the sword and sandal programmer or not, one cannot dispute the fact that *Ursus, the Rebel Gladiator* is a darned fine piece of cinema in anyone's book. Like quite a few others included in these pages, it gives Ridley Scott's *Gladiator* a real run for its mega-bucks; maybe it was one of many that

Peplum beauty Gloria Milland in *Ursus, the Rebel Gladiator*

influenced Scott into putting his Roman epic onto the big screen. One can only surmise.

In 180 AD, on his deathbed, Emperor Marcus Aurelius bequeaths his title to his son, Marcus Commodus (Steel), with the one proviso: "Rule in peace and the empire will flourish." Does the ex-gladiator (first seen scrapping in the arena) take any notice of his father's dying words? No! Returning from Gaul, he embarks on a reign of terror, looting, burning and herding prisoners to the foot of a cliff. "Be merciful," pleads mistress Gloria Milland (Marzia). Ignoring her, he takes on the leader in a bone-crunching five-minute head-to-head, beats him to death, drags his body to the cliff's base and instructs his soldiers to bury it under an avalanche; the remaining captives are put to the sword. But when Steel's troops storm into a barbarian stockade, they're met by one-man war machine Dan Vadis. He topples a lookout tower, chucks logs and rocks and smashes his mighty fists into one soldier after another, Steel overawed by the giant's awesome fighting qualities and brute toughness, yet personally humiliated when Vadis overpowers him but demurs at delivering the *coup de grace*. In Rome (that oft-used painting of the city showing the Coliseum is inserted), Gianni Santuccio and a few select senators scheme to dispose of the emperor. He's too much of a loose cannon, his hotheaded, schizophrenic behavior threatening non-aggression pacts with their neighbors; a way to get rid of him must be found to enable Rome to be ruled by a more-noble emperor.

There's a great deal to sink your teeth into here as the narrative unravels slowly but grippingly. Milland, never looking lovelier, both adores Steel and despises his heartless nature; when José Greci (as Arminia, just as gorgeous; her U.S. pseudonym was Susan Paget), Vadis' fiancée, is abducted, Milland is on her side, even in a tense scene in which Greci steals into the palace, knife in hand, ready to kill Steel. Hovering above his sleeping figure, she prepares to administer the death thrust,

Milland on her knees, praying. At the last moment, Greci stays her hand, the two women consoling one another. As for Vadis, he's brought to Rome, shaved of his beard, trained in the arena by Andrea Aureli and informed: "Fight as a gladiator for three months and Arminia (Greci) will be liberated." The snag is, Vadis is a Christian and has principles, finding it difficult to involve himself in combat duties just for combat's sake. But Steel, determined to prove *he's* the strongest warrior in the city, enters the arena incognito with the strongman during which a lethal prong springs out of the huge ram's head club Vadis is wielding, wounding him in the chest. Ripping off his bandages ("I don't intend to wear this. It's a device of mortals."), the emperor smells a rat and *still* feels humiliated by his nemesis' prowess; uncovering the assassination plot, he strangles Santuccio barehanded. Vadis is chained to a dungeon wall but bursts out of his bonds, barging in on a feast and battering the guards senseless. He's spared by a drunken Steel, who tells him he will have to fight his emperor again; in the meantime, Santuccio's son, Carlo Delmi, is amassing his legions outside the city, ready to rebel against Steel's praetorians in a battle for justice ("Commodus has lost all sense of reason."). The second set-to between Vadis and Steel is a sweaty, dusty humdinger, real he-man stuff, putting a lot of modern-day fare firmly in the shade. Vadis has to run a gauntlet of 12 gladiators brandishing clubs, nets, tridents, balls on chains and swords to retrieve his armor and weapon, Greci watching, tied to a pillar; he defeats the lot, puts on his attire, rips a post out of the compound and engages in a titanic, bruising struggle with Steel, ending up the victor. "Don't kill me," squeals Steel, pinned under Vadis' massive frame. "Free Arminia!" cries Vadis. "Set her free," the cowering ruler orders his guards.

In the movie's final rousing chapter, Vadis and Aureli demolish a vital bridge the praetorians are using, Delmi's divisions clash with the emperor's corps in a stupendous battle sequence, Greci is recaptured ("I consider you the loveliest trophy of my victory.") but Steel finally outflanked, his praetorians in tatters, the survivors deserting him in droves. It's left to Aureli to heft a spear into Steel's back: "Have mercy on him," says Milland to her Roman god, standing over his body; Delmi is announced as the new emperor and Vadis and Greci walk off into the sunset to play house.

Vadis has been derided over the years for his perceived lack of acting ability, but within the world of peplum, he was one of the greatest; *Ursus, the Rebel Gladiator* serves as a reminder of his agility, animal strength, prodigious physique and a certain amount of innate good humor, plus he had that distinctive Vadis crouching pose: knees and elbows bent, a "take me on" attitude if ever there was one. Steel's mad Commodus, while not matching Joaquin Phoenix's finely tuned portrayal in *Gladiator*, is good enough in this setup, a setup that must have looked heavenly in a packed theater, up there on the big silver screen. Perhaps one day we'll be treated to a digitally restored wide-

Gordon Scott, one of peplum's greatest musclemen, in a typical "don't mess with me" pose from *Goliath and the Rebel Slave*

screen version, presenting Paolella's spectacular actioner as it was meant to be experienced—current DVD issues are pan and scan, cursed with uneven color balance.

1963

Goliath and the Rebel Slave [*Goliath e la schiava ribelle*] aka ***The Tyrant of Lydia Against the Son of Hercules***; ***Arrow of the Avenger***
CIRAC/FIA (Italy/France); Euroscope/Eastmancolor; 105 (86) mins; Producer: Giorgio Agliani; Director: Mario Caiano ✞✞✞✞✞

Quintessential peplum featuring a definitive quartet of genre stars: Gordon Scott, Massimo Serato (Marcius), Mimmo Palmara (Artafernes) and Gloria Milland (Zoé). Low on action but high on characterization and plot, Caiano's richly entertaining brew centers on regent Palmara's efforts to persuade his ruler (and cousin), Serato, to side with Darius, King of Persia, instead of Alexander the Great's Macedonians, who are marching on the Persians. Lydia is a neutral state and, although Alexander has deployed his troops along the country's borders, he has no plans to besiege the capital city. General Scott (in U.K./U.S. prints, he's Gordian, not Goliath) trusts Alexander (Gabriele Antonini) implicitly, viewing him as a man of honor, while Lydia remains neutral; however, devious Palmara, shifty mistress Milland and slimeball consul Giuseppe Fortis are after Serato's seat of power whatever it takes, even, if need be, sowing the seeds of discord between the Macedonians and Lydia. And Serato is no saint either, constructing a secret tunnel under the temple in which to stash his pile of treasure boxes, then putting to death all those who dug the labyrinth to prevent them from talking, except for black slave Serge Nubret. The beefy warrior later becomes an ally of Scott's.

Caiano changes course after 30 minutes, taking the scenario out of the confines of the court with all its intricacies, vitriolic exchanges and intrigues. Scott, en route to Antonini's camp, rescues a group of damsels under ambush from bandits, falling in love with Ombretta Colli (Princess Cori), Antonini's ward. When Antonini introduces Colli (a real stunner) to the Lydian court, Serato develops an almighty crush on the girl, letting it be known that she's to be his intended wife. Through Palmara's devious machinations, Scott is branded a liar and betrayer when a peace mission to welcome the Macedonian invader for further talks is wiped out by Bedouin traitors in Palmara's pocket; as for Colli, she's blamed for poisoning Serato at a feast (Milland is the culprit) and given a death sentence. Scott helps her to take flight, but she's captured by Arabs, dragged off to a slave market and brought to court, straight back into Palmara's hands. In a frenetic finale, Scott (who has broken out of prison) and Nubret gain entrance to the palace rooms via the unstable underground corridors, just as Colli is placing her blonde head on the executioner's block; Antonini's troops rush through the city gates, resulting in a colossal set-to with Palmara's guards. Fortis dies in the melee, Milland is brought down by an arrow and Palmara, scrapping with Scott, falls backwards onto an upturned axe. Calmness restored, Antonini guarantees his protection to Lydia, leaving Scott and Colli to marry and take up their positions on the throne.

Although Scott, by sheer physique alone, was a force that couldn't be ignored, it's Palmara who dominates. Star of 25 pepla movies, the tall, well-built actor throws his weight around, gobbling up the scenery with over-the-top gusto, an overripe display of menacing falseness that even overshadows Serato's guileful, slightly unhinged, ruler. Milland, decorous and bewitching, exudes sexual allure every time she appears, while Pier Ludovico Pavoni (photography) and Carlo Franci (music) add the finishing touches to Caiano's measured, well-crafted directorial strokes, becoming a peak of peplum perfection.

Goliath and the Masked Rider [*Golia e il cavaliere mascherato*] aka ***Hercules and the Masked Rider***
Romana Film (Italy); Totalscope/Eastmancolor; 86 mins; Producer: Fortunato Misiano; Director: Piero Pierotti ✞

Goliath, Hercules—or Zorro? Taking place in 16th-century Spain, *Goliath and the Masked Rider* was more costume swashbuckler than sword and sandal, with Alan Steel (as Goliath) appearing on screen for a total of around seven minutes, mouthing a handful of lines of inane dialogue. The peplum gifts of Mimmo Palmara, Ettore Manni, Arturo Dominici, Loris Gizzi, José Greci, plus producer Misiano, director Pierotti, composer Angelo Francesco Lavagnino and cinematographer Augusto Tiezzi were patently squandered on a tedious, comic book potboiler that is very difficult to be positive or enthusiastic about.

The plot, by 1963, had been tried and tested many times previously, so no excuses for this below-standard example. Domi-

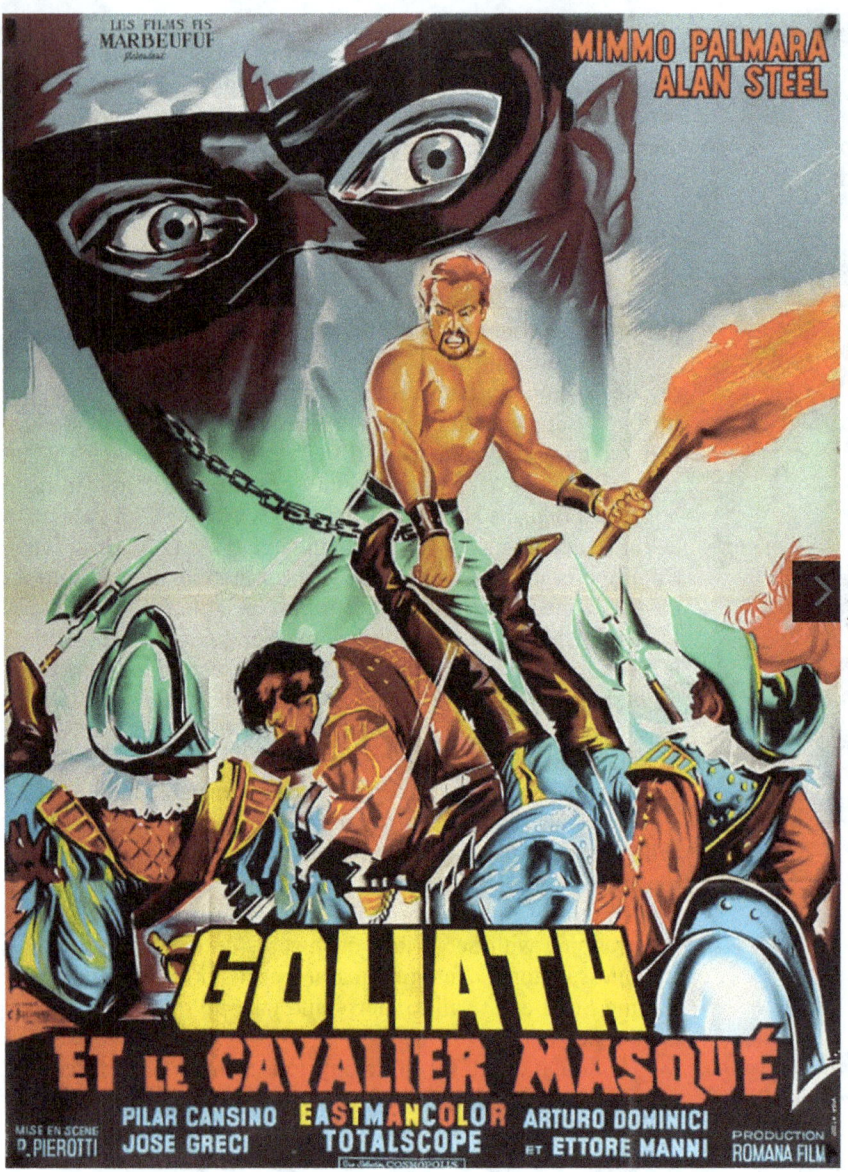

A French poster for *Goliath and the Masked Rider*

nici (Don Ramiro) and Manni (Captain Blasco) covet neighboring land owned by Renato Navarrini (Don Francisco); Dominici also coverts the Don's daughter, Greci (Dona Blanca), promised in matrimony to Palmara (Don Juan). Riding roughshod over the oppressed peasant population, Dominici murders Navarrini and sets himself up as lord of the manor, not accounting for the fact that Manni opposes his brutal tactics. The captain allies himself to a band of Gypsies, led by flame-haired Pilar Cansino (Estella), and falls in love with the vagabond queen; Palmara, wearing a red mask and cape, becomes the fearless Masked Rider, straight out of a *Zorro* flick, wading into Dominici's soldiers when they're occupied in robbing the peasants of their grain. The concluding showdown in Dominici's castle sees Palmara escape the hangman's noose and Dominici falling from a balcony to his death after a fight with his rival. In front of portly king's representative, Loris Gizzi, Palmara and Greci are wed, Manni and Cansino waiting their turn to tie the knot.

Where does Steel fit into all of this? Striding shirtless through the wooded scenery in the few scenes allotted to him, the big strong guy looks several centuries out-of-date, a square peg in a peplum round hole, contributing very little. Dominici sneers and snarls, acting like a Spanish pig, Manni appears listless, beefy Palmara tries to inject some vigor, Greci looks frozen in time (Cansino is a lot more animated), Piero Leri and Dina De Santis play giggling young newly-wed couple Felipe and Dolores, longing to consummate their marriage, while Lavagnino's bouncy music does its level best to keep things moving. Overall, *Goliath and the Masked Rider* is a tired, play-it-by-numbers affair that drags interminably over 86 minutes, perhaps the worst of any *fusto* actioner produced during this hallowed period in the genre's history. Everyone is entitled to an off day—in this instance, the entire company, who made far, far better pictures than this one, had an off day en masse. This becomes an unlikeable, instantly forgettable addition to the sword and sandal/swashbuckler roster.

Ursus in the Land of Fire [*Ursus nella terra di fuoco*] aka *Son of Hercules in the Land of Fire*

Cine-Italia Film/Splendor Film (Italy); Dyaliscope/Eastmancolor; 90 (87) mins; Producer: Giuseppe Fatigati; Director: Giorgio Simonelli
††††

Ed Fury's third and final *Ursus* outing (and the actor's last of six peplas) is a very violent affair, displaying a propensity toward the kind of bloody mayhem you might expect to witness in an X-rated Italian horror film. Ursus, leader of a settlement of shepherds inhabiting land near a hotly contested lake, takes on Adriano Micantoni (as General Hamilan, or Hamilkar), a venomous brute who slays King Lotar (three sword thrusts to the neck), butchers Nando Tamberlani's priests in the Temple of Ayat, the fire god, by blade and arrow (full-on savagery here) and raids Ursus' hutments, hacking to pieces all women and old men; he doesn't want to share that precious, money-making body of water with anyone, let alone "too ambitious" Ursus and his sheep farmers. Matching Micantoni's unbridled ferocity is mistress Claudia Mori (Mila), vindictive cousin to Luciana Gilli (Princess Diana); she's jealous of Gilli's regal position, laying into the girl with a lash a little too eagerly at one stage. We know that these two vipers will eventually meet their doom—what leads up to their demise makes for riveting viewing.

The action is shot mainly around Lazio's Lapilli quarries, the Salone caverns and a short spell at Monte Gelato's cascades. Micantoni murders Gilli's father following public outrage over the vicious slaughter of Tamberlani's priests, declares himself king and throws a tournament to prove to the masses that, although they may detest him and Mori sitting on the throne, he can demonstrate goodwill and hospitality if it suits him. ("The people we govern hate us.") Fury, almost trapped in a volcanic eruption and landslide in the sacred land of fire, arrives at the games with Gilli, both in disguise; the tournament's winner, as decreed by age-old law, will be granted one wish (this lengthy section lasts almost 20 minutes). Fury combats king's champion Pietro Ceccarelli plus five others, each hurled into a spit-filled pit (their gruesome deaths are shown in graphic close-up). He then reveals himself to the crowd, is captured and immediately

A Spanish poster for *Ursus in the Land of Fire*

set to work on a double gristmill, thrashed without mercy; Gilli is imprisoned, tormented by half-crazed Mori. But Micantoni has grown tired of Mori's whining ways, stabbing her in the chest in order that he may marry Gilli; with the popular princess at his side, the people might look more favorably on his leadership. Fury breaks free from the gristmill, cornered and fettered in a cell, holding a massive stone slab above his head, the weight of which will eventually embed him on rows of spikes. Spotting Gilli on the run from lustful Micantoni, he shatters his shackles, heaves the slab at the prison bars and escapes deep into the mountain with Gilli, meeting Tamberlani, the high priest, sole survivor of the massacre of his brother priests. The volcano erupts, Tamberlani dying on the point of Micantoni's sword; in a tussle with Fury, the evil king is pushed into a volcanic fissure, expiring in the flames and lava. Fury and Gilli walk through the cheering throngs to become new rulers of the kingdom.

Vivid photography by Luciano Trasatti, a high-decibel score courtesy of Carlo Savina and Giorgio Simonelli's incisive direction, combined with great performances from Fury, Micantoni, Gilli and Mori, ensures that *Ursus in the Land of Fire*, gritty and aggressive, makes for compelling peplum viewing on all levels.

1964

Goliath at the Conquest of Bagdad [*Golia alla conquista di Bagdad*] aka *Goliath at the Conquest of Damascus*

Romana Film (Italy); Totalscope/Eastmancolor; 95 (80) mins; Producer: Fortunato Misiano; Director: Domenico Paolella †††

Completed at the close of 1964 but not released in Italy until March 1965, *Goliath at the Conquest of Bagdad* (Damascus in Americanized prints) was produced toward the final stages of pepla's golden age (in conjunction with *Hercules Against the Tyrants of Babylon*) and shows marked signs of tiredness, both in plot and execution. Even a stalwart cast of regulars—Mario Petri, Helga Liné, Piero Lulli, Arturo Dominici, Andrea Aureli, Daniele Vargas, Mino Doro—are unable to prevent the movie slipping into boredom and sameness on occasions. A little over a year on, the peplum phenomenon would be all but finished; Paolella's beefcake romp harks back to better times when "hunk rescues princess and helps young prince regain right to throne by overthrowing tyrannical ruler" storylines hadn't stagnated in the public's minds.

So the oft-used narrative runs as follows. Skimpily clad Peter Lupus (billed as Rock Stevens) strolls into the town of El Koufa, indulges in tavern fisticuffs with hostile clientele and forms a partnership with Mario Petri (Yssour), in order to restore wimpy Marino Masé (Prince Phir) to the throne of Bagdad. Anna Maria Polani plays Myriam, the girl Masé is to wed, thus forming a peaceful union between their two states, while villains Lulli (Thor), Vargas (Saud) and Aureli (Bhalek), acting for usurper Dominici (Kaichev), try their hardest to put a halt to *any* kind of a peace deal. The bad guys wear red robes and sport a zigzag-shaped scar on their right cheek, while the two spiritless lovers end up in a gloomy torture chamber; Liné's seduction technique on Lupus falls flat on its face (she's Petri's wife, Fatma, ordered to test

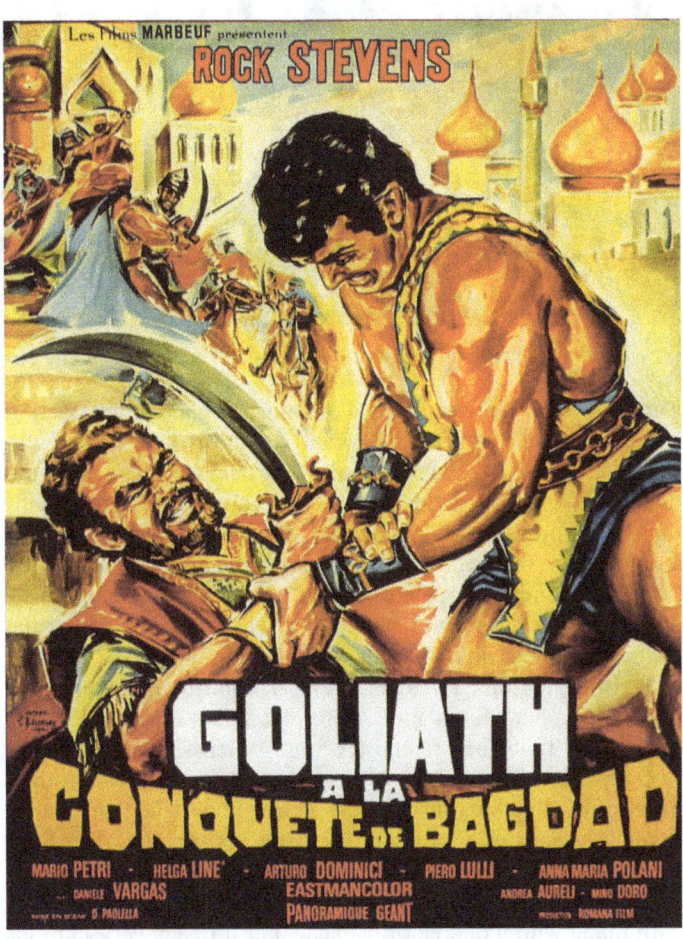

A French poster for *Goliath at the Conquest of Bagdad*

A French poster for *Ursus, the Terror of the Kirghiz*

Ursus, the Terror of the Kirghiz [*Ursus, il terrore dei Kirghisi*] aka *Hercules, Prisoner of Evil*

Adelphia/Ambrosiana (Italy); Totalscope/Eastmancolor; 100 (90) mins; Producer: Adelpho Ambrosiano; Directors: Antonio Margheriti, Ruggero Deodato (uncredited) ††

The glories of Ed Fury's classic trio of *Ursus* movies seem a long way off when viewing horror director Margheriti's variation on the *Ursus* theme, in which sorceress Mireille Granelli possesses the power to turn our titular hero into a deformed-faced monster for her own ends. Reg Park, in the fourth of his five peplum outings, starred as the mythical strongman (Hercules in American prints), an anonymous performance compared to Fury, Dan Vadis, Samson Burke, Alan Steel, Joe Robinson and Yann Larvor (from *Hercules, Samson, Maciste and Ursus: The Invincibles*) in the role. Shot mainly in three locations—woods, caverns and a stockade palace—*Ursus, the Terror of the Kirghiz* is laborious, drawn-out and messy; not even the presence of stalwarts Ettore Manni and Furio Meniconi can spice up this lumpy broth.

A furry-chested, grunting monster in a black cloak causes mayhem among the people of Sura. Meniconi (Prince Zereteli)—who assassinated the Great Khan 10 years previously—blames Park for the deaths and disturbances, wishing to rid the land of the muscleman's Circassians and gain overall control. In Park's settlement, blonde Maria Teresa Orsini (Katya) acts as his slave girl, suffering from amnesia. In fact, she's a bona fide princess, the true heir to the realm. Mireille Granelli (Amiko), Orsini's malicious cousin, has taken her place, residing both with Meniconi and in the Grotto of the Falcon, an alchemist's cave where she concocts a red liquid; whoever drinks it changes into a rampaging monster (there's even a brief transformation scene near the end). Ettore Manni himself gets to sup the potion, morphing into the beast and attacking his brother, Park, who, injured, has to recuperate in the Great Healer's cavern in the mountains. Meniconi's pugnacious attitude threatens a civil war between the Kirghiz and Circassians; he sets a spy onto Granelli, sealing her in the grotto with a big boulder. Following an assault on the Kirghiz palace, Meniconi is placed in chains; Park, fully recovered although still swathed in bandages, goes to Granelli's cave, pushes the rock to one side and confronts the witch: "You are not the true princess of Sura," he tells her. Feeling dizzy, he drinks the deadly liquid, changes into the cut-price wolf man, runs amok, torches a village and carries off Orsini, intending to throw her off a cliff. Manni tackles Granelli in her rocky chamber ("Ursus is a zombie at my command!"), she loses her footing and slips backwards into a pit, dies and the spilled liquid evaporates—the spell broken, Park returns to normal, pushes a huge boulder onto a dam to quench the raging fires and rides off with Orsini, who has since regained her memory. Manni knows the

Lupus' loyalty to the cause) and our muscular hero, after beating strongman Nello Pazzafini (Horval) senseless in a street fight, hires him and his squad of heavies to conquer Bagdad in the final reel (stock footage is used extensively here), thereby winning the approval of Sultan Selim (Mino Doro), as his daughter and Masé are married to much cheering and applause.

The money's up there on the silver screen (a fantastical grotto containing a giant gold statue is splendid, as is the flashy costume design), composer Angelo Francesco Lavagnino and cinematographer Augusto Tiezzi contributing their customary excellent foundation work, but this scenario had been done many times before and a certain staleness was beginning to creep in. As for Lupus, the handsome bodybuilder bulldozes his considerable bulk through the action, impassive features occasionally registering a flickering smile, especially when foxy Liné eyes him up. (Why wasn't she made the heroine instead of uncharismatic Polani?) It's still a flashy-looking Middle Eastern yarn made with a degree of panache, but it treads very familiar territory.

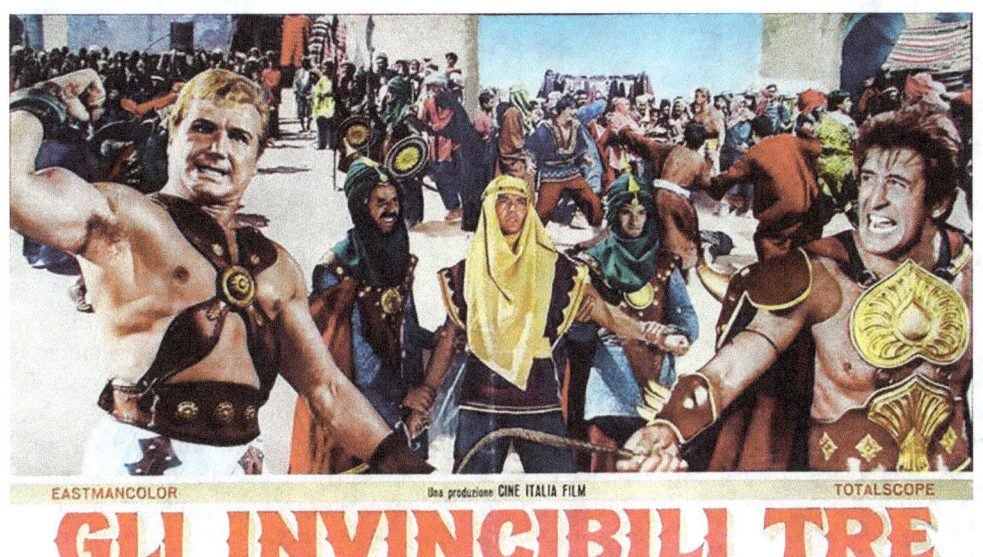

An Italian photobusta for *The Invincible Three*

truth about the monster ("His body was consumed in the forest fire.") but is saying nothing.

Perhaps Margheriti and novice director Deodato's intentions were to attempt something different within the sword and sandal/sorcery arena; in doing so, they left out the requisite action, spending too much footage on soldiers rummaging around in the woods (murkily photographed by Gabor Pogany), searching for the terrorizing monster at the expense of a cohesive narrative. This is without doubt the least interesting of the *Ursus* features, Park looking out of his depth and unwieldy in the movie's few combat scenes, the whole erratic package set to a limpid score from Franco Mannino.

The Invincible Three [*Gli invincibili tre*] aka *The Three Avengers*; *Ursus the Invincible*

Cine-Italia Film/Elios Film (Italy/Tunisia); Totalscope/Eastmancolor; 101 (96) mins; Producer: Giuseppe Fatigati; Director: Gianfranco Parolini †††

Ursus (Sergio Ciani, billed as Alan Steel) and his two buddies, Roebuck the Acrobat (Arnaldo Dell'Acqua) and Manina the Mute (Vincenzo Maggio), bowl into the Tunisian city of Atra, treat the crowds to an exhibition of fights and brawls and become entangled in Mimmo Palmara's scheming; the tyrant, dictating law and order over the head of King Igos (Carlo Tamberlani), has passed himself off as an imitation Ursus ("False Ursus"), bent on destroying the neighboring Hanussa tribe, kicking out Prince Dario (Vassili Karamesinis) and marrying Princess Alina (Lisa Gastoni) to gain control of the city.

The final *Ursus* feature is an occasionally strained blend of knockabout farce and gritty peplum action, tending to drag its sandals in the middle section. Scenes of Dell'Acqua and Maggio clowning, leaping around and constantly mugging furiously, dispel the mood sustained in the graver moments concerning Steel's clashes with Palmara and court intrigue; halfway through the movie, the blond beefcake (looking as though he's just stepped up from a Tunisian beach) is blinded by donning a helmet containing a corrosive liquid concocted by alchemist Gianni Rizzo, regaining his sight near the end, long enough for him to finish off Palmara after the despot's mercenaries have been overrun. Gastoni is murdered by Palmara midway through—he latches onto Hanussian beauty Rosalba Neri (as Demora, one of the genre's loveliest actresses) when she's brought to court, cruelly dispensing with the princess' services, even though Karamesinis loves the dark-haired barbarian. A prolonged flurry of semi-comical mayhem in the palace dungeons, an exotic, red-veiled dance and lovers Neri and Karamesinis tied to stakes, ready to be roasted (the prince has been wrongly accused of plunging a dagger into Tamberlani's back), plus a double-sworded duel between Steel and Palmara, carried out on a platform erected over a bed of sharpened stakes, enlivens a film that veers from silly humor to bloody aggression, Angelo Francesco Lavagnino's quirky soundtrack following the same haphazard course. Nello Pazzafini grumbles and growls, Neri's champion warrior unable to beat Steel in combat, while winsome Orchidea de Santis, Steel's female admirer, floats in the background, not doing a great deal. Photographed in bleached-out colors by Francesco Izzarelli to match the Tunisian glare, *The Invincible Three* is fine for the kids, but adults may find the mix of jocularity and rough 'n' tumble a bit hard to digest. Note: Dell'Acqua had two acting brothers who also performed in a couple of genre features: Alberto (*The Giants of Rome*, 1964) and Roberto (*Anthar the Invincible*, 1964).

9
Ancient Greece

Ancient Greece, the playground of the gods, is of course steeped in classical myth, providing a myriad of material for peplum filmmakers—Jason and his Argonauts, Achilles, the colossal statue of Rhodes, the Minotaur, Helen of Troy and the Trojan conflict and the gods on Mount Olympus. Surprisingly, not that many peplum movies were based on Ancient Greek mythology, but what few there were threw up a handful of genre classics: *The Giants of Thessaly*, *Theseus Against the Minotaur*, *The Bacchantes* and *Perseus the Invincible* are all essential must-haves, as is the gloriously outrageous camp *Queen of the Amazons*, while the trio of films based on the fall of Troy—*The Trojan War*, *The Fury of Achilles* and *The Legend of Aeneas*—are among the greatest pepla ever turned out from the Italian film industry, topping anything modern-day cinema, armed with its plethora of multi-million dollar CGI wizardry, can come up with. Number one acting honors in the Ancient Greece category go to craggy Gordon Mitchell for his in-your-face portrayal of Achilles in *The Fury of Achilles*, a demigod-cum-hero fearsome enough to make any enemy quake in his leather boots!

1960

The Giants of Thessaly [*I giganti della Tessaglia*] aka ***Jason and the Golden Fleece***; ***The Argonauts***

Alexandra Produzioni/Lyre (Italy/France); Totalscope/Eastmancolor; 97 (86) mins; Producer: Virgilio De Blasi; Director: Riccardo Freda ✞✞✞✞✞

In carrying out an assessment of Riccardo Freda's version of Greek mythology's most famous tale, that of Jason's search for the Golden Fleece to regain his throne, one cannot help but compare it to Columbia's *Jason and the Argonauts* (1963), still, after over 50 years, the definitive motion picture on the subject and one that has never been bettered. In fact, Don Chaffey's movie is one of the greatest peplum films ever made outside of Italy, and its attention to mythical detail and *feel* is unsurpassed. *Jason and the Argonauts*, as fans all know, contained Ray Harryhausen special effects almost as legendary as the fleece itself, while Hollywood composing maestro Bernard Herrmann provided one of fantasy/sword and sandal's most magnificent Ancient Greek soundtracks. Chaffey's direction was freeflowing and pacey, while Freda's approach was pretty static most of the time, more Italian opera in design than full-blooded English/American action. And it's doubtful whether *The Giants of Thessaly* would ever have been noticed on British cinema circuits if Columbia's blinder hadn't proved to be the huge smash it turned out to be; released in the United Kingdom in 1964 on the back of the latter's popularity as *Jason and the Golden Fleece*, it was screened at small independent venues specializing in continental fare, perplexing all those who had sat through Harryhausen's magical monsters a year earlier, leaving them wondering (as I did at the time): "What the hell is *this* all about?"

But *The Giants of Thessaly* remains a key peplum work, despite its shortcomings. The five-minute storm at sea segment is poorly handled—in one instance, a jet can be observed spraying water over the *Argo*'s deck which steadfastly refuses to rock, despite the dreadful weather conditions; the gorilla-cyclops monster, created by effects wizard Carlo Rambaldi, appears amateurish, although creepy; Raffaele Masciocchi's photography in the seagoing sequences is muddy in places; the pace flags occasionally; and Roland Carey, who took over the role of Jason from Mickey Hargitay, is big, blond, beautiful and bland. On the plus side, the fantastically ornate production design dazzles the senses (plenty of caverns on display for all cave-lovers); Carlo Rustichelli's melodious score ranks as one of peplum's most memorable; Alberto Farnese (Adrastus) and Raf Baldassarre (Artino) make a fine pair of villains; there's a couple of elaborate, saucy dance routines; and witch Nadia Sanders' startling horror transformation from alluring sex goddess to withered crone on the accursed Isle of Lemnos, where men are turned into sheep, trees and rocks, made you wonder how on earth this movie passed through the censor's office and emerged with a "U" rating (suitable for all age groups) in England. The highlight is the lengthy interlude in which Carey negotiates a titanic unstable wall and has to scale a colossal statue to retrieve the fleece, nesting in the palm of one gigantic hand, a sequence that manages to be both jawdropping and vertigo-inducing.

In 1250 BC, Carey, introspective companion Massimo Girotti (Orfeo) and their crew of Argonauts (all ex-bodybuilders) search for the Golden Fleece in the land of Colchis, while back in Iolco, the starving, famine-ridden populace are up in arms, on

An Italian photobusta for *The Giants of Thessaly*

148 Heroes Never Die!

Daniela Rocca tries unsuccessfully to ward off the advances of frisky Rod Taylor in the gloriously camp *Queen of the Amazons*.

the verge of revolt; angry Zeus is causing volcanoes to destroy the land and Carey's cousin, Farnese, won't lift a finger to help. All he desires is the throne, the riches of Thessaly and Carey's wife Ziva Rodann (Creusa) with it. After many adventures, Carey arrives in Iolco with his glittering prize, leading to a pitched battle within the palace walls (shudder at that bit when a soldier receives an arrow through his ears—in close-up!); the returning hero and his gang leap out of collapsible metal figures, Farnese, Baldassarre and Girotti are slain, Carey is reunited with wife and baby son and Zeus, placated by the Golden Fleece, ceases to annoy his subjects by putting a stop to further volcanic activity. A tad ponderous, perhaps, but glorious too look at, *The Giants of Thessaly* is firmly lodged in pepla's list of all-time greats and one of the few films of its type to receive a national airing in Britain; so many others remained out-of-bounds to U.K. audiences, as they do today.

Queen of the Amazons [*La regina delle Amazzoni*] aka *Colossus and the Amazon Queen*

Glomer Film (Italy); Dyaliscope/Eastmancolor; 98 (84) mins; Producer: Enzo Merolle; Director: Vittorio Sala ✝ or ✝✝✝✝✝

A gender-bender camp (as in CAMP) classic of the highest order—you've got to be a real sourpuss if Vittorio Sala's crazy, titillating and just plain *daft* romp doesn't at least bring a flicker of a smile to the face. "Let's just go ahead and be stupid," must have been the directive when all concerned embarked on the project, roping in, of all people, Australian Rod Taylor, to star as one of two Greek warriors returning from the Trojan wars who enlist on a merchant ship, are drugged along with the crew when they retrieve treasure from an unknown shore and find themselves in a land of man-hungry, full-figured '60s babes ruled by a sexually frustrated virgin queen. Yes, these are *real* women, not the skinny clothes pegs populating today's pictures, with enough bosoms, crotches, thighs, legs and pouting lips on show to have you heading for a cold shower after taking it all in. Taylor hated the movie, even though he surely must have enjoyed making it; diehards may despise it, while others will revel in the picture's unflagging silliness.

First, the score: Boogie-woogie piano morphs into jungle jazz, drums and tom-toms create an aural racket of the non-peplum variety, completely out of context. Second, the badly dubbed script (eight writers contributed toward the screenplay, or should that read screamplay?) is hilariously anachronistic, belonging to 20th-century New York, not Ancient Greece around 1100 BC, deserving a chapter all to itself. The plot? Devious merchants leave Taylor (Pirro), Ed Fury (Glauco) and crew to rot on a beach; recovering, they walk through a tunnel, spot a wondrous city and encounter busty maidens bathing in the waters of the Monte Gelato falls. "Don't get any funny ideas," says blonde Dorian Gray (Antiope) to Adonis-like Fury, his eyes bulging, just after a talking parrot has butted in (and the last thing this movie needed was a talking parrot). In the city, Queen Gianna Maria Canale, 33 and never been kissed, has two warriors vying for her throne: Gray and Daniela Rocca (Melitta). To become queen, you have to remain chaste, difficult when a bunch of hunks in short tunics appear in your midst. It's either a man or the throne … you can't have both. "A woman in uniform. Hey, what's going on here?" grins Taylor in prison. "If we're in the hands of women, who wants to escape, huh?" is followed by, "Hey cutie!" to a guard. The "inferior sex" gives rise to one unprecedented bout of heated bitchiness after another, the male of the species in this female domain slaving in a mine, cooking or dancing in thongs, as a four-minute routine midway through shows (plus we get to see semi-nude cavorting female archers). Cleaned and attired in fresh new outfits ("These men are so spectacular," coos Canale), the bemused crew are paired off, Taylor with Rocca ("Melitta, we can make beautiful music together."), who's not in the mood for hanky-panky, having just been ousted as the next monarch after losing a jousting duel with Gray (Fury is her suitor). "Let's be off, my babyeez. Y'all is my women now," chortles one skinny prisoner, not believing his luck as he waltzes away with two women on his bony arms. "How does a kiss affect you? Does it produce a flavor?" sighs the queen, as all around her indulge in unbridled lust, except Taylor. Rocca has one eye on that throne, and lifting her skirt to her piece of Greek beefcake won't further the girl's cause.

The film lurches from one piece of outlandishness to another. Masculine Taylor (he was as ruggedly built as any peplum muscleman), turning more effeminate by the minute, hides a sacred golden girdle in his quest to bed Rocca (it's required by any prospective monarch). Freebooters, led by Alberto Farnese, land on the shore and Gray finds herself increasingly attracted to Fury's tanned muscles. The rest of the Amazonians degenerate into promiscuous harpies; Farnese and his corsairs attack the city, the women encircled by wagons, firing arrows, but the

An American one-sheet for *The Warrior Express* (aka *Sappho—Venus of Lesbos*)

male slaves drive the pirates off ("The cavalry to the rescue!"). The girdle is returned to Canale, lovers Taylor, Rocca, Fury and Gray canoodling in the surrounds of the Monte Gelato waterfalls at the climax; poor Canale, forever a virgin, is still left wondering what a kiss feels like. Perhaps she should have given in to the two attractive male leads instead of trying to run a kingdom now full of debauched subjects. The last word in this utterly mad voyeuristic confection is left, naturally, to that pesky parrot, squawking, "Hooray for women, hooray for men!" from the city walls.

On a saner note, the arena set design looks a treat, as does the interior palace shots and costumes, while Adalberto "Bitto" Albertini's cinematography is luxurious in the extreme, given the content. But "sane" isn't what *Queen of the Amazons* is all about, and the one abiding impression it leaves is this: Whatever possessed an actor of Rod Taylor's repute to ever want to appear in something as downright bizarre as this? The answer lies in a fans' newsletter dated October 1964. Taylor admits to having a "lapse of sanity" and making this "fiasco" solely to enable him to travel to Italy and resume his affair with continental screen sex goddess Anita Ekberg. This "skeleton in my closet" became a source of embarrassment to him over the years.

Sappho—Venus of Lesbos [Saffo—venere di Lesbo] aka The Warrior Empress

Documento Film/Orsay Films (Italy/France); CinemaScope/Eastmancolor; 105 (89) mins; Producers: Marcello D'Amico, Gianni Hecht Lucari; Director: Pietro Francisci ✟✟✟✟

Kitsch with a capital "K" sums up *Sappho—Venus of Lesbos*, a sprightly mythical romp with enough female legs and thighs on display to have male members of the audience needing an ice-cold bath at the end of it all (like they did after watching *Queen of the Amazons*). And it's violent—edited prints don't include the complete, very graphic rape scene of a farm girl, which the British censor excised, and there's a savage "mauling by lions" moment at the end not shown in its entirety. Kerwin *The 7th Voyage of Sinbad* Mathews is Phaon, the leader of the poor and starving populace, slipping into the Greek court of King Melanchrus in the land of Mytilene under the guise of a soldier after falling in love with statuesque Tina Louise (Sappho, the "World's Boldest Beauty!"), whose home is the female-dominated Island of Lesbos. Here within the temple grounds, the bevy of lovelies in their tiny togas play music, race chariots, row sleek boats across blue waters and fantasize about men, apart from Susy Anderson (Actis, listed as Susy Goli)); she fantasizes about Louise, the one person on the isle to harbor lesbian feelings. ("Men bring only deceit, hatred and lies," she warns the object of her desires.) Into this hotbed of leggy female flesh comes Mathews, wounded by an arrow and on the run from Riccardo Garrone's troops. Tended to by Louise who happens to be promised to Garrone (as Hyperbius), Mathews recovers and goes undercover into the king's palace, determined to find a way to get rid of the lazy monarch (played like an overweight young Nero by Enrico Mario Salerno), bring justice to his people and wrest Louise away from the evil embrace of Garrone.

Pietro Francisci's energetic excursion into trumped-up Greek myth kicks off with Greek warriors hurling spears into a guerrilla camp, followed swiftly by an exhilarating female chariot race in the coliseum of Lesbos, like a mini-version of *Ben-Hur*'s legendary set piece, seguing into a dance performed in diaphanous costumes; it wraps up in fine style, the 2,000-strong rebel army, reeling from a hail of burning arrows, smashing down the city walls with their huge battering ram and riding into Salerno's palace; the ruler and his confidants are promptly banned from the kingdom. Sandwiched between these two stirring sequences is man-hating, treacherous Anderson walking into a lion's den to her doom, her lust for Louise not reciprocated; rampant soldiers killing and raping (these scenes were missing in the British "U" certificate release); Mathews, Garrone and Louise playing guessing games in the splendid Temple of Antiquity; a mutineers' ship ramming the galley on which Mathews is held prisoner (Garrone has issued the standard peplum ultimatum to Louise: "Marry me and I'll spare him."); and Mathews and Louise rolling around in the surf canoodling, like Burt Lancaster and Deborah Kerr from *From Here to Eternity*. Mathews and Garrone engage in mortal combat after Salerno's capitulation, the Greek captain tumbling into the lion pit and ripped to shreds. Francisci chooses to end his picture framed like a Greek holiday postcard, Mathews and Louise, on a chariot, smooching under a sunset, the ocean reflecting the golden rays. Imaginative, costly-looking set design, vulgar wardrobe, mermaids on rocks, a sorceress at work in an enchanting grotto, gleaming color (Carlo Carlini) and a bombastic score (Angelo Francesco Lavagnino) make for the kind of peplum guilty pleasure filmmakers just don't come up with anymore. A movie that's great fun for the undiscriminating!

Theseus Against the Minotaur [Teseo contro il minotauro] aka The Minotaur; Warlord of Crete

Illiria Film (Italy); Totalscope/Technicolor; 105 (98) mins; Producers: Giorgio Agliani, Gino Mordini, Rudolphe Solmesne; Director: Silvio Amadio ✝✝✝✝

In Ancient Crete, circa 2000 BC, King Minos rules the island from his palace at Knossos where virgins are sacrificed to a part-man/part-bull being known as the Minotaur, inhabiting a forbidding labyrinth. The king has twin daughters, Phaedra and Ariadne. Ariadne has been sent to Athens to escape sacrifice; when ambitious Phaedra, who covets the throne, finds out the truth about her sibling, she sends her lover, Chyrone, to murder the girl. Theseus, Prince of Athens, and friend Demetrius, foil Ariadne's assassination attempt and take the princess to the Greek capital. Chyrone turns up, threatening Demetrius with the death of his father and sacrifice of his sister if Ariadne isn't killed. Demetrius, unable to carry out the deed, returns to Knossos with Theseus, who pretends to love Phaedra in order to save the people from further needless sacrifice. In a struggle, as maidens are herded toward the opening to the labyrinth, Demetrius and his family are slain. Seriously wounded, Theseus falls off a cliff into the ocean, to be taken into care by the sea goddess Amphitrite, who falls in love with him, a love that can never be reciprocated. In a blue pool, the goddess shows Theseus that war has broken out between Crete and Athens; a mighty battle rages, with the Athenians losing heavily. Theseus goes back to Knossos, fully recovered, where he finds Ariadne shackled to the wall in a torture chamber. During a fracas, Phaedra is hit in the face by a red-hot brand and topples into a pit of ravenous dogs. Ariadne takes her place, Theseus entering the labyrinth where he exterminates the monster (a sword thrust, then a rock on its head); Ariadne, who has followed Theseus, trails a golden thread behind her to enable them to find the way out. In a palace skirmish, Chyrone is put to the sword six times as the citizens of Crete revolt against his regime. King Minos bestows his blessing on Theseus and Ariadne promises to outlaw human sacrifice now that peace has been restored.

Within the pantheon of movies that make up the pepla spectrum, *Theseus Against the Minotaur* is among the genre's most important works. Acting throughout is first rate: Classy-looking Rosanna Schiaffino plays both Phaedra and Ariadne, one a hard-faced schemer, the other the proverbial vestal virgin; Alberto Lupo scowls beautifully as Chyrone; ex-American athlete Bob Mathias acquits himself as Theseus (his one and only peplum); Rik Battaglia is personable as Demetrius; and Carlo Tamberlani (King Minos) and Nerio Bernardi (King Egeo of Athens) lend good support. Horror lovers will savor a rare appearance by Susanne Loret as Amphitrite, a blonde vision in a revealing aquamarine robe—Loret and Lupo had starred together the same year in Anton Giulio Majano's seminal X-rated shocker, *Seddok, Son of Satan*. Also appealing to horror fans will be the torture scene showing a tethered prisoner lowered face down onto a bed of hot coals. Six-foot-five ex-boxer Milo Malagoli played the Minotaur, wearing one of cinema's heaviest face-masks and a fearsome one at that. Three pulsating, sexy dance numbers, ornate marbled palace sets, two wonderfully visualized grottos (the Minotaur's and Loret's), a fabulous mythical monster, Aldo Giordani's sumptuous color tones, Carlo Rustichelli's Ancient

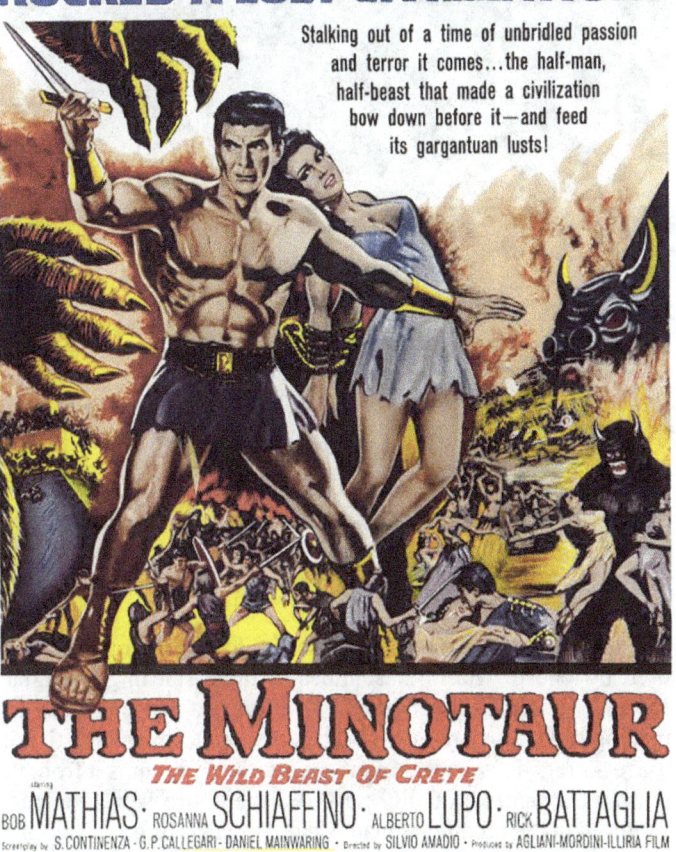

An American one-sheet for *The Minotaur* (aka *Theseus Against the Minotaur*)

Greek score and Loret a sleek, shimmering delight—all add up to a heady brew, filmed with stylish vim by Silvio Amadio, not a single boring second in sight. The movie is timeless.

1961

The Bacchantes [Le baccanti] aka Bondage Gladiator Sexy

Vic Film/Lyre Film (Italy/France); Techniscope/Technicolor; 100 (95) mins; Producers: Giampaolo Bigazzi, Gino Del Duca; Director: Giorgio Ferroni ✝✝✝✝✝

Greek tragedian Euripides wrote *The Bacchae* around 405 BC, toward the end of his life, a play centered on man's opposing natures, the civilized and the sensual. In Giorgio Ferroni's eye-catching blend of intellect and high camp, King Pentheus (Alberto Lupo) represented rational, civilized man, while the god of fertility and wine, Dionysus (Pierre Brice), stood for sensuality and instinctiveness, mirroring the dual characteristics of the drink he so favored: joy and ecstasy one moment, cold hard rage the next. The Bacchantae, a group of maidens blessed with flawless beauty who inhabit caverns on Mount Cithaeron, symbolize his spiritual power. Thebes is plagued by famine and drought through not bowing down to Dionysus' earthy rites and beliefs; only by acknowledging Dionysus as their one true god can the discontented citizens save themselves and release their souls to the joys of unrepressed living—in plain language, wine, women and song.

Lovers Raf Mattioli and Alessandra Panaro share an intimate moment in *The Bacchantes*; the film was released a few months after Mattioli's death from a heart attack at only 23 years old.

Lavishly photographed by Pier Ludovico Pavoni and honored by one of Mario Nascimbene's most startlingly original scores, *The Bacchantes* (ignore that crass American title, appealing to the dirty raincoat brigade) is one filmic adaptation of a Greek tragedy worth taking in, so utterly different is it from the norm. A dreamlike quality pervades the entire narrative, fully captured in the credits sequence, dancers cavorting in and out of the ruins of a Greek temple overlooking the bright blue ocean, Ferroni's camera then panning over parched, cracked wastes, bleached bones and dried-up wells. Lupo's venomous mother (Miranda Campa) convinces him that the only way to bring rain is for a virgin to be sacrificed to placate the goddess Demeter, Alessandra Panaro (Manto) the chosen victim. Moreover, it is foretold by the gods that Panaro, betrothed to Raf Mattioli (Lacdanos), a lowly slave, will give birth to a son who one day will take his place on the throne; Mattioli, in fact, is the true heir, so to get rid of Panaro is the best solution all round. Lupo's unhappy intended, Taina Elg (as Dirce: "All I want from you is a son," her proposed husband bluntly announces) opposes the sacrifice and so does Brice, appearing in mortal form and entering Thebes as a mysterious stranger where he finds blind Akim Tamiroff (Teiresias) stirring up trouble with the populace. Elg and a select band of maidens journey to the Temple of the Bacchantae for divine guidance, getting caught up in a fast and furious orgasmic dance routine choreographed by American Herbert Ross to the sound of pounding conga drums, pirouetting and shedding most of their clothes until they collapse from exhaustion. In Thebes, as the high priest (Nerio Bernardi) raises his sword to slay Panaro, a thunderbolt strikes him dead. A black cloud appears, the heavens open, Panaro is freed and the exultant crowds are drenched in rain, hailing Dionysus as their savior ("A song to Dionysus!")

End of the drought, and act one. Act two concerns Lupo's resolve to hunt down and enslave those "believers in a false god," culminating in one of pepla's most bizarre fight set-tos, Lupo's soldiers versus the Bacchantae maidens in their mystical grotto, the girls fronted by Elg, now one of them and hopelessly in love with Brice. Another frenzied dance session is followed by the troops wiped out by the maidens' magic staffs (wind, fire, falling rocks and, in one scene, the ground opening beneath their feet, swallowing them whole), their battered, bloody bodies viewed with dismay by Lupo who expires with Brice's blade stuck in his belly. "My human journey comes to an end," the god tells Elg, Nascimbene's haunting leitmotif adding to the emotion. "The man in me is dead. There is nothing left in me but the God. I am immortal. You, Dirce, will lead the Bacchantae." With that, in a flash of lightning, Brice disappears, the movie closing with Lupo's funeral, Panaro and Mattioli now joint rulers of Thebes.

Brice, sporting a peculiar gray wig, seems slightly out of his comfort zone playing a Greek god, but his despondent, edgy performance fits in with the film's offbeat, stagy histrionics; Gérard Landry appears briefly as a warlike shepherd. It's left to Alberto Lupo, one of the genre's most underrated actors, to hold center platform, his King Pentheus veering between forgiving and benevolent, and deviously underhand and cruel. The look, though, is the thing: *The Bacchantes* wallows in a cornucopia of fantastical cinematic lushness not experienced by today's younger generation of moviegoers, mythological peplum at its very finest. Note: The other tragedy connected to *The Bacchantes* is the untimely death from a heart attack at the age of 23 of Raf Mattioli, in October 1960; the film was released a few months after his death.

The Colossus of Rhodes [*Il colosso di Rodi*]

Cine-Produzioni Assoc./PAC/Procusa (Italy/France/Spain); Supertotalscope/Eastmancolor; 139 (123) mins; Producer: Michele Scaglione; Director: Sergio Leone ✝✝✝

In 280 BC, the Greeks erected a giant bronze/iron statue of the sun god Helios at the entrance to Rhodes harbor (legend gives it as being 105-feet high, standing on a 50-foot marble plinth); in 226 BC, it was destroyed in a cataclysmic earthquake, the remains never discovered to this day. Sergio Leone's first major feature rang tills in the United Kingdom when released in 1962 and rated "A," despite it being a dubbed foreign production, a novelty (and oddity) at the time, and overlong. Around this mythological colossus, Leone and his team drummed up a tale of Greek military advisor Rory Calhoun (Darios), holidaying on Rhodes just as the unveiling ceremony of the statue takes place, becoming drawn in to a plot by rebels to overthrow King

Serse, played by Roberto Camardiel, a tyrant who wants to form an unholy alliance with the Phoenicians. Second-in-command Conrado San Martin (as Thar) also has his eyes on the throne, assisted by two-timing mistress Lea Massari (Diala). Calhoun falls for Massari, is involved in numerous escapades with Georges Marchal and Angel Aranda's conspirators, and he finally escapes the earthquake that reduces Rhodes to ruins, riding off with Mabel Karr and the island's liberated people.

Pepla's normal running length of 90-95 minutes was exceeded by a further 40 minutes in Leone's visually attractive (cinematography by Antonio L. Ballesteros) but occasionally leaden Ancient Greek drama, enlivened by a couple of well-staged brutal action pieces, sumptuous set design and the statue itself, an imposing figure looming over the ant-like humans scurrying beneath its huge feet. When Marchal and his crew row like crazy under the statue (stop-motion wizard Ray Harryhausen copied this shot in *Jason and the Argonauts*, where the *Argo* sails under the legs of Talos), a compartment opens, raining burning oil onto their vessel; a graphic torture interlude has prisoners strapped to benches, acid burning into their flesh; there's a fight-in-the-arena section; and endless trysts between Calhoun and Massari, mostly in the fountain gardens of Villa d'Este, Tivoli. The final half hour takes place inside and outside Helios' statue, Calhoun a prisoner, the Phoenician fleet approaching on the horizon. As the wind gets up, the sea rises, the sky darkens and the ground trembles, Massari is crushed by a falling beam inside Helios' head; Calhoun manages to flee the statue (San Martin receives a spear in the guts during a tussle) and a 10-minute earthquake occurs, orchestrated with panache (a minute or so of footage from *The Last Days of Pompeii* was inserted). However, by that riveting concluding sequence, among the audience when I sat watching the movie way back in October 1962, there were more than a few restless bums on seats; the picture could have been a good 20 minutes shorter and still have worked as a more rewarding slice of sword and sandal spectacle. *The Colossus of Rhodes* is without doubt a famous name in pepla, one of those decisive movies of the period responsible in making the genre acceptable to mass Western audiences, but compared to others that came after, it's not as great as it should have been; a classic it isn't.

The Trojan War [*La guerra di Troia*] aka *The Trojan Horse*; *The Wooden Horse of Troy*

Europa/Les Films Modernes/CICC (Italy/France/Yugoslavia); Euroscope/Eastmancolor; 115 (105) mins; Producer: Giampaolo Bigazzi; Director: Giorgio Ferroni ✟✟✟✟✟

A top-notch production that dazzles the eye and senses, *The Trojan War* classifies as one of the greatest, most famous peplum movies of all time, featuring amazing scenes of battle carried out by a cast of thousands, a taut script that commendably adheres to Homer's *Iliad* (Ferroni, Vigo Liberatore, Giorgio Stegani, Federico Zardi) and believable acting from a fine cast. Although made a year before *The Fury of Achilles*, the events depicted follow on from the death of Hector, the Prince of Troy. Achilles, Agamemnon, Ulysses and Menelaus still figure in the plot, but the hero's role goes to Steve Reeves as Aeneas, holed up in Troy with the two people he loathes the most—weak, prissy Paris and Helen, classed, in his eyes, a "gravedigger."

Comparisons with Wolfgang Petersen's *Troy* are inevitable, yet Ferroni's peplum masterpiece comes out tops, made for around $1,000,000, small change compared to the $175,000,000 Petersen had at his disposal from Warner Bros. For starters, Pe-

An American insert poster for *The Trojan War* (aka *The Trojan Horse*)

tersen felt obliged to close his epic with a big climax to appease 21st-century audiences, Achilles (Brad Pitt) meeting his end during the fall of Troy by Paris' arrow. Achilles, in fact, took no part in the Trojan horse episode; he was slain outside the city walls *before* the horse was constructed. *Troy* led us to believe that the war lasted about a week, not 10 years, while Agamemnon, Menelaus and others survived the conflict; Petersen had them all exterminated in the name of bumper ticket receipts, allowing Paris to live. And no matter how hard you try, computerized armies are no match for the real thing; Ferroni used around 10,000 extras in his battle sequences and it shows. Likewise, the hands of men and not computer technology constructed Troy's walls, resembling long Bronze Age fortifications. So *The Trojan War* looks the business—no boring, talkative interludes to slow the pace and pad out the running time, a grand spectacle to revel in, to see how it was all done 50 years before CGI took over, and with it, blandness of product.

Ennio Girolami (left, as Patroclus) and Gordon Mitchell (as Achilles) discuss battle tactics in *The Fury of Achilles.*

Hedy Vessel portrays Helen of Troy as a narcissistic slut, ravishing but empty, now tired after nine long years of Warner Bentivegna (Paris) hanging around her skirts like a lovesick puppy dog. Besides, with hunk Reeves in and out of the palace, does she need a wimp like her lover turned out to be? Reeves has a less-than-flattering view of her: "No woman is worth the blood that has been shed in these nine years—least of all Helen." After King Priamos (Carlo Tamberlani) has collected the body of Hector, slain by Achilles, Reeves, who advocates an end to what he regards as a pointless power struggle, overcomes strongman Ajax (Mimmo Palmara) in a contest in front of the Greeks (much to Achilles' approval) and is then ordered by the Trojan council of elders to go and round up an army sourced from their allies. Vessel has been labeled an adulteress in front of the senate and, scared of Reeves' increasing influence, wants him out of the way. A truce is arranged: Nerio Bernardi (King Agamemnon) demands 10 chariots of silver, quantities of gold, a large supply of wood and 10 hostages, one of which must be of high rank, to hold fire; naturally, the high ranking captive just happens to be Reeves' pregnant wife Juliette Mayniel (Creusa). Ulysses (John Drew Barrymore) explains to Bernardi's bemused captains his sneaky plans for all that felled timber and, on the 43rd minute, Reeves' massive army approaches the Greek encampment, setting in motion a mammoth 12-minute confrontation as the Greek infantry file out to meet them head on. There's a short lull in pulsating action, then another large-scale assault, the Trojans pulling down the Greek stockade's walls with chains and piling into the compound. Bentivegna is livid, giving instructions for Reeves' troops to pull back; he wants to bask in all the glory, never mind his adversary. Riding out to the battleground on his chariot, he catches sight of Reeves and Arturo Dominici (Achilles) in hand-to-hand combat and lets fly with an arrow, striking the Greek hero in his most vulnerable spot, the heel. Reeves then upsets Bentivegna further by taking Dominici's body back to the Greeks for cremation; on his return to Troy, he's imprisoned for treason.

The actual wooden horse sequence trounces *Troy*'s version by a mile: It's longer, more detailed in concept and the horse itself is a fabulous creation, angular and slightly sinister in appearance. Dragged by several hundred slaves across the plain (a breathtaking sight), the "trophy to Poseidon" containing human cargo is deposited inside the city walls to a great fanfare ... and the rest is history, as prophesied by Cassandra (Lidia Alfonsi), Troy's resident Sybil. The city is burned to the ground, Reeves breaks Palmara's neck, Mayniel dies in childbirth, Nando Tamberlani (Menelaus) rams a blade into spineless Bentivegna and the Queen of Sparta, seemingly glad to be rid of her lover regardless of the huge cost in life the pair have caused by their illicit affair, is ordered back to the Greek camp by her black-as-thunder husband. Out on the plains, Reeves, his baby son and several hundred stragglers turn their backs on the smoking ruins of Troy, hoping to begin a new life elsewhere.

Recently available in widescreen/LBX and polished up, *The Trojan War* doesn't fall short of expectations. A rousing score (Mario Ammonini and Giovanni Fusco), glowing color (Rino Filippini) and Ferroni's expert eye for the sweeping spectacular add up to a peplum must-see. Watch this in conjunction with *The Fury of Achilles* (which should, in context, be viewed first) and you have a sword and sandal double bill of such intensity, majesty and grandeur that you will never bother with a modern-day "epic" ever again. This is essential and highly recommended viewing.

1962

The Fury of Achilles [*L'ira di Achille*] aka *Achilles*
Uneurop Film (Italy); Ultrascope/Technicolor; 118 (95) mins; Produced and Directed by Marino Girolami ✝✝✝✝✝

Out of the four big film productions to have detailed the 10-year Trojan war, who made the best Achilles? Discounting Arturo Dominici's relatively nondescript showing in *The Trojan War*, we have Stanley Baker in Robert Wise's *Helen of Troy*, Brad Pitt in Wolfgang Petersen's *Troy* and Gordon Mitchell in Marino Girolami's interpretation of the Greek legend. Baker, clad in black armor, presented us with a surly, arrogant Achilles, his quick fuse rubbing everyone up the wrong way; in *Troy*, Pitt came across like a musclebound blond beach boy, slightly effete in manner, obsessed that his name would forever be remembered; here, Mitchell is six-foot-three-inches of mean attitude, and blessed with those granite features, how could he not be otherwise, the ultimate Greek hero. Like the others, he knows his eventual destiny lies at the gates of Troy; it has been decreed by the gods. He has no time for King Agamemnon's ruthless ambitions to conquer all, calling him a "snarling dog" and quitting the conflict, only to return with his Myrmidons when bosom buddy Patroclus (in the *Iliad*, Homer hints that the pair were lovers) is killed by Hector, the Trojan's champion fighter and Prince of Troy. By defeating Hector in armed combat, Achilles is aware that his own death will shortly follow ("I know I will not return alive from Troy."), but how will not be disclosed to him, not even by his mother's spirit, which visits him at nightfall on a rocky shore. He has a solitary weak spot on his well-honed body—but where can it be? "Tell me where I'm vulnerable," he pleads with his mother's phantom. "I cannot. The gods forbid it," is her curt reply.

The Fury of Achilles may well be badass Mitchell's finest hour behind a sword and shield—it's certainly hack director Marino Girolami's one and only magnum opus. His intimidating persona and massive, thickset sinews command the attention for the entire duration of a robust, head-crunching exercise in macho heroics that places Petersen's vastly more expensive epic firmly in the shades of Hades. Incident piles upon incident, shot briskly without frills: In the 10th year of the Trojan war, Agamemnon (Mario Petri) and Ulysses (Piero Lulli), on a foraging expedition in the city of Lyrnessus to replenish stores (the film opens with Petri's army carrying out an assault on the city walls), leave their flanks wide open; Hector (Jacques Bergerac) takes full advantage, massacring a detachment of Greeks before leading his Trojans through a tunnel onto the shoreline where the enemy ships are beached. Achilles and his Myrmidons arrive to the war cry of "Hi-yah! Hi-yah!" and Bergerac is forced to flee. Petri returns with a bunch of beautiful female hostages; Mitchell ("Achilles. A fighting machine created to kill.") chooses Gloria Milland (Briseis), Ennio Girolami (the director's son, playing Patroclus) nabs Cristina Gaioni (Xenia) and Petri drags protesting Eleonora Bianchi (Criséide) off to his tent. A crucial interlude has Milland plunging a dagger into Mitchell's back (she was *always* plunging daggers into men's backs in her movies!); it doesn't even penetrate his skin, the tip disintegrating in flames, illustrating the hero's invincibility and the gods' divine intervention. Smiling, Mitchell takes the weapon, bends it and places it on Milland's wrist as a bracelet, allowing his caring nature to show through, just for a moment. Over at Petri's camp, Bianchi's outraged father, soothsayer Nando Tamberlani, invokes the wrath of Apollo and the Greek army is hit by 10 days of pestilence. To placate the insulted gods and lift the father's curse, his daughter is returned; in exchange, Petri demands that Milland be sent to his tent, thus arousing the wrath of Mitchell who walks out of the war, gets drunk and informs his detachment that they're heading back to their homeland. But when Girolami dresses in Mitchell's battle gear and is slain by Bergerac in a skirmish, Mitchell dons golden armor forged on Mount Olympus and rides out on his chariot to face Bergerac, as foretold by the gods. After defeating Troy's prince (a hard fought, sweaty five-minute combat to the death carried out to the sound of clashing swords, knocking spots off the Pitt/Eric Bana affair of honor in *Troy*) and allowing King Priamos (Fosso Giachetti) to collect his son's body for ceremonial burial, Mitchell is left alone looking out to sea at a setting sun in contemplation, wondering what fate the gods have in store for him now.

Gino De Santis' literate script stays pretty faithful to Homer's *Iliad* and bursts with succinct prose, Mitchell ably demonstrating his rough and ready style of acting chops, particularly in his frequent acidic altercations with Petri. "Agamemnon! Famous for his avidity and no less for his greed," sneers Mitchell, turning on his detested king when he learns that Milland is to be transported to his camp for *his* pleasure. "I am here, not for my hate for the Trojans but for your benefit and the honor of your brother. I, who bear the major burden of the war, do not see you taking equal shares of mine but a much larger part—always!" Later, Petri admits to Milland that "We are nothing without him (Achilles). Tell him I'll kneel before him and humbly beg his help. He can name his price as long as he returns to the battle," pinpointing the grudging respect he has for Greece's bravest, most feared, most confrontational, warrior. Helen of Troy, the "Face that Launched a Thousand Ships" and the chief instigator of this protracted war, is never glimpsed, only mentioned, while Roberto Risso, in his few appearances, makes a wan-looking Paris, leaving you wondering what on earth the Spartan goddess ever saw in him. Complementing the pithy dialogue and earthy, rampaging engagements is Mario Fioretti's harsh photography and Carlo Savina's pumping Greek Mythology-based score, a year before Bernard Herrmann did something similar in *Jason and the Argonauts*. Blessed with a ferocity both in direction and battle set pieces that modern-day fare cannot replicate, despite all their millions of dollars, *The Fury of Achilles* is barebones sword and sandal at its absolute pinnacle of perfection, suffused in Ancient Greek atmosphere—and yes, Gordon Mitchell *is* the screen's greatest (and certainly most formidable to look at) Achilles of them all! Tremendous, thrill-packed entertainment—thankfully, widescreen prints have recently become available on the market, dubbed in English.

The Legend of Aeneas [*La leggenda di Enea*] aka *The Avenger*; *War of the Trojans*; *The Last Glory of Troy*

Mercury Films/Films Sirius/CICC (Italy/France/Yugoslavia); Euroscope/Eastmancolor; 105 (95) mins; Produced and Directed by Giorgio Venturini ✝✝✝✝✝

What happened to Aeneas and the Trojan survivors following the destruction of Troy? In *The Legend of Aeneas*, we take up where *The Trojan War* left off, Steve Reeves (Aeneas) pitching camp on the banks of the River Tiber and immediately being ordered to pack up and get out by King Tourno and his renegades (a venomous performance from Gianni Garko). Venturini's movie (Albert Band gave himself a director's credit for the American release, but his input is negligible) is talkative for its initial 50 minutes but still manages to grip, due to assured direction and taut editing, imparting a higher degree of intelligent handling than is normal in this type of fare. The intrigues come thick and fast—you need to be concentrating 100 percent before the inevitable battle commences. Reeves visits affable Latino, King of Latium (Mario Ferrari), asking for refuge; the kindly monarch willingly grants the exiled Trojan leader sovereignty over his patch of ground near the Tiber (cue for footage from *The Trojan War*, telling us how Reeves arrived at this phase in his life). However, Ferrari's wife Amata (Lulla Selli, radiating pure malice) disagrees with this magnanimous offer; the harpy wants her aged husband to marry their daughter Lavinia (Carla Marlier) to Garko and kick Reeves all the way back to Troy, seeing him as a threat to her own goal in life, to rule over Ferrari, whom she regards as ineffectual. Warrior Queen of the Volsci, blonde Liana Orfei, doesn't know who to support in this battle of wills; Garko calls for war ("I'll fight the king's decision.") while Marlier swiftly falls in love with Reeves and his muscle-packed physique. The Trojans erect a substantial defensive stockade, are almost destroyed by a herd of stampeding bulls (Garko is behind this), Reeves and his men are framed for the murder of two of Ferrari's loyal subjects, there's a colorful games sequence and

A U.S. poster for *The Avenger* (aka *The Legend of Aeneas*)

Reeves, aware of impending hostilities, heads off to old allies the Etruscans to organize an army that will hopefully counteract the forces that Garko has assembled on the plains bordering the Trojan encampment.

On the hour, battle commences and it's a cracker, enlivened by vibrant color photography (Angelo Lotti) and a pounding, drum-laden soundtrack (Giovanni Fusco), Venturini expertly marshaling a cast of several thousand into various battle formations, a phalanx of archers first taking predominance. The air is thick with arrows in an Alamo-type confrontation that's violent, exhilarating and spectacular in equal measures (Giacomo Rossi-Stuart, a friend of Reeves, dies in agony, six arrows riddling his body; both women and children are brought down; and Orfei, riding at the head of her troop detail, gets an arrow in her left breast). What's more, Reeves emerges the victor, setting up a climactic encounter with Garko to determine which of them will rule the roost. The two meet on the plains (mirroring the famous Achilles/Hector head-to-head), Reeves riding a white chariot, Garko, fittingly, a black. Jousting, the wheels come off Garko's vehicle and Reeves pursues him through the woods and marshes; they tumble to the ground, a sunlit glade ringing to the clang of steel on steel, and lock horns on the Tiber's muddy banks. There, Reeves administers the mortal blow, Garko staggering into the river, clasping the hilt of Reeves' sword buried in his stomach. Reeves is united with his people (and Marlier), a voice-over informing us that the Trojan struggle culminated in the founding of Imperial Rome and its far-reaching empire.

With *The Trojan War*, *The Fury of Achilles* and *The Legend of Aeneas*, Rome's Cinecitta studios reached new levels of excellence, a classic trio centered on the downfall of Troy that, half a century on, resonates to the sound of the clash of sword on sword, the swish of arrows, the thud of javelins hitting shields, the tread of thousands on the march and the rumble of chariot wheels in battle. Rising above the popcorn and pulp culture, they remain key ingredients in that vast sword and sandal/torch and toga mix that only fans of this unappreciated area of cinema are aware. Others should be, too.

Mars, God of War [*Marte, dio della guerra*] aka *Venus Against the Son of Hercules*; *The Son of Hercules vs. Venus*

Galatea Film/Incei Film (Italy); Totalscope/Eastmancolor; 98 mins; Producer: Armando Morandi; Director: Marcello Baldi
††††

There's rubbish cinema—and there's entertaining rubbish cinema. *Mars, God of War* comes into the second category by sheer outlandishness of plot alone, plus imaginative, intricately detailed set design, rich inky color tones (Marcello Masciocchi), an exotic score (Gino Marinuzzi, Jr.) and Roger Browne as Mars, sporting pepla's largest-plumed helmet (Browne also played Mars in *Vulcan, Son of Jupiter*, released the same year). John Kitzmiller (King Afros of Africa) and his legions attack the walled city of Telbia in a thrilling 12-minute skirmish. Boiling pans of oil, smoke screens, warriors scaling the walls, hand-to-hand combats and a huge battering ram; Marcello Baldi piles it all on with gusto, a tremendous sequence by any standard. Massimo Serato (Antarus) and Renato Speziali, traitors aiding and abetting Kitzmiller, open the gates, the Africans swarm in and suddenly, in a flash of lightning and clap of thunder, a golden-armored soldier appears, cutting a swathe through the fleeing enemy ranks with his giant broadsword, killing their king. Browne has intervened from above to defeat the African army, but Jupiter, his father, isn't pleased that his son wishes to remain on Earth. He's head over heels in love with Jocelyn Lane (Daphne) and refuses to go back to Mount Olympus. In a cloud of blue smoke, furious Jupiter roars his disapproval and leaves Browne to it; soon, the God of War is up to his muscular neck in trouble. Lane is banished to the Temple of Venus to become a priestess, her punishment for upsetting King Giuseppe Addobbati and, more importantly, devious Linda Sini (Ecuba). The raven-haired queen wants her out of the way to pursue her entitlement to the throne with Serato and Speziali by her side. At the temple, Browne is seduced by glamorous Michele Bailly (Venus) in a misty cavern, after witnessing a surreal dance in-

An Italian poster for *Mars, God of War*

An American one-sheet for *My Son, The Hero*

volving streamers of different colored cloths, trying to secrete Lane away from the accursed place. In keeping with the Bavaesque fantasy aspect prevalent in the film's middle section, Lane enters a glorious mythological grotto and is shown, in a pool, a vision of Browne cavorting with Bailly to invoke jealousy; the high priestess has taken a fancy to the god herself.

Meanwhile, during a heated argument, Serato viciously stabs Sini twice in the chest; Lane's maid is blamed for the murder, undergoing a unique torture to disclose the whereabouts of Browne, walking barefoot across a narrow plank over a pit of boiling water, two spiked walls closing in. Serato finishes off Speziali, getting too big for his boots by demanding more than his fair share of their misbegotten pile of treasure, and he hightails it to the temple where he fights Browne in a clearing dominated by a monstrous, man-eating Triffid-type plant; the usurper is dragged backwards by tentacles into the thing's maw and gobbled up alive. Browne's sidekick, Dante Di Paolo (a likeable serio-comic turn), his features blackened after Serato has pushed a torch into his face, is reunited with Lane's maid, his true love; Lane, fatally wounded by an arrow, dies but the gods come to the rescue. She's restored to life and joins Browne on a white chariot drawn by three magnificent white steeds, the pair galloping skywards into the heavens toward Mount Olympus, leaving Addobbati to rule in peace. A good-to-look-at Italian peplum of the fantastical variety, cheesy, schlocky and campy in equal measures, but put across with professional zeal and acted commendably by a straight-faced cast—peplum toughie Livio Lorenzon is in it, relegated way down on the cast list to a walk-on part.

My Son, The Hero [*Arrivano i titani*] aka **The Titans**; **Sons of Thunder**

Vides/Les Films Ariane/Filmsonor (Italy/France); Technicolor; 120 (112) mins; Producers: Franco Cristaldi, Alexandre Mnouchkine; Director: Duccio Tessari ✟✟✟

King Cadmus of Crete has learned the power of immortality by murdering his wife and marrying his mistress, declaring himself a god; for this heinous act, the oracle informs the cruel tyrant that should his daughter Antiope find love, or he kills her, he will die instantly. Therefore, Cadmus proclaims that when Antiope reaches 18 years of age, she will become a vestal virgin. Jove, furious, releases one of the Titans from Hades, Krios, whose remit is to save the girl and deliver Cadmus to Hades for just punishment. If his mission is successful, the Titans will be set free from the infernal pit. After many adventures, Krios dispatches Cadmus with a thunderbolt, his brother Titans are returned to Earth and the golden-haired savior hitches his toga to Antiope.

As soon as Carlo Rustichelli's stomping title music gets underway against a backcloth of classical paintings (sounding similar to Malcolm Arnold's score from *The Bridge on the River Kwai*), you know deep down that *My Son, The Hero* is *not* going to be a scholarly piece of cinematic art, and therein lies its downfall. Pictorially, the film is splendid to look at, cinematographer Alfio Contini's rich colors imbuing the many crystalline cave sequences with an air of mythological fantasy mystery. But when Giuliano Gemma (Krios) appears on the scene complete with bleach-blond mop and toothy, ingratiating grin, the comic mood kicks in with a vengeance. A protracted fight interlude sees Gemma vaulting and somersaulting over rooftops to evade capture; in his cell, he glimpses Jacqueline Sassard (Antiope) in her palace room through bars, tangles with big black slave Serge Nubret (Rator) at a feast, is turned loose after winning, watches a bullfight, encounters a giant in a grotto, places Pluto's helmet on his head to render himself invisible and rescues Sassard from the clutches of the Gorgon. The Titans then arrive to assist, changing from clean-shaven blond (in the Hades scenes) to unshaven brunette. Weapons are purchased from a friendly Cyclops, more skirmishes follow, Cadmus (Pedro Armendariz plays the king) deciding to execute Nubret, who's saved from a rolling bed of spikes by the Titans bursting out of statues. The action finishes with Gemma and his gang in a fracas with the enemy, coated in dragon's blood, thus making them invincible; Gemma causes the caves to flood, the blood is washed off, the soldiers are defeated and Armendariz (he's previously done away with wife Antonella Lualdi) is eliminated in a flash of thunder and lightning. Sassard cuddles up to Gemma; the winsome lass will now govern Crete in her father's place.

My Son, The Hero would have worked better minus the constant backslapping bonhomie; some would argue that while a lot of pepla contained some form of humor, if allowed to take over to the extent it does here, the ambience could be irreparably damaged. After all, was *My Son, The Hero* meant to be a comedy? Director Tessari's attempt to amalgamate Greek Mythology and high camp histrionics doesn't always come off, hindered by Gemma's juvenile antics and periods of infantile shenanigans. A case of, "If only they had played it straight …"

The Tyrant of Syracuse** [Il tiranno di Siracusa] aka **Damon and Pythias

IMP Enterprises/MGM (Italy/US); Technicolor; 101 mins; Producer: Franco Riganti; Director: Curtis Bernhardt ♱♱♱

Distributed by MGM worldwide as *Damon and Pythias*, German-born Curtis Bernhardt's movie is literate, earnest, long, slow and ever so slightly dull, almost devoid of the type of action set pieces lovers of sword and sandal were used to being served. Set around 400 BC, the story tells of Pythias, a young liberal-minded Athenian, who travels to Syracuse in order to bring back Arcanos, a philosopher earmarked as the new senate leader. Dionysius, the city/state's tyrannical crowned head, finds "peace toward all men" views dangerous, a threat to his regime. When Pythias is captured, he allows the Athenian to return home with Arcanos to tend to his sick pregnant wife, holding thief Damon as collateral; Pythias and Damon have formed an unlikely friendship, and if Pythias doesn't arrive back in Syracuse on the appointed hour, Damon will be executed, a test of the Athenian's creed of honor and trust. Is he a man of his word as he says he is, especially as Damon's tainted view of life is that "to me, every man is my enemy." Pythias *does* return as promised, and Dionysius, in order to find favor with his rebellious subjects *and* listening to the pleas of his son, frees both men to tumultuous applause.

A peplum with depth rather than gladiatorial combat and mythical monsters, *Damon and Pythias* would have audiences fidgeting in their seats today—50 years ago, punters were con-

An International poster for *Damon and Pythias* (aka *The Tyrant of Syracuse*)

tent to pay good money to watch a decent story unfold in a darkened auditorium. On the acting front, Guy Williams makes an engaging roguish thief, a wastrel forever juggling his dishonest ways to keep mistress Liana Orfei happy; Don Burnett's Pythias is honorable but naïve, but not all that good in combat; Arnoldo Foà sneers wonderfully as Dionysius; Andrea Bosic (unrecognisable under a thick beard) spouts words of wisdom as Arcanos; and Carlo Giustini's Cariso, the dictator's argumentative commander, is your standard genre bad guy, torn to pieces by the angry crowd at the end. On the downside, Ilaria Occhini, playing Burnett's wife, is a whining, clinging, self-pitying bore, all over her husband one minute, spitting venom at him the next ("Let him be a hero. Let him die!" she screams when she learns that Burnett is going back to the city for his friend). She is terrified of being left out of the picture on his jaunts to Syracuse and demonstrates a bad case of histrionics, a pity when you consider her measured performance in *Pia of Ptolomey*. Partly shot inside Rome's ancient catacombs, cinematographer Aldo Tonti's lighting techniques enhanced those gloomy caverns to perfection, the only sequences to remain unblemished in current ragged prints, while Angelo Francesco Lavagnino's wonderful score underlined the nuances within the narrative without becoming intrusive. Peplum regular Franco Fantasia has a "now you see him, now you don't" part as fencing instructor to Foà's son—the

An Italian poster for *Vulcan, Son of Jupiter*

actor was, in fact, adept at the art of fencing and taught many of his co-stars the finer aspects of the sport on set.

Vulcan, Son of Jupiter [*Vulcano, figlio di Giove*] aka *Vulcan, God of Fire*; *Battle of the Titans*

Juno Produzione (Italy); Supercinescope/Eastmancolor; 80 mins; Producer: Spartaco Antonucci; Director: Emimmo Salvi ††††

Emimmo Salvi was undisputed master of the peplum camp/schlock classic and he didn't let the side down with *Vulcan, Son of Jupiter*, filmed in Iran and featuring Iranian Iloosh Khoshabe (aka Rod Flash; Richard Lloyd) in the title role. On mist-wreathed Mount Olympus, the Abode of the Gods, bellicose King Jupiter (Furio Meniconi) is fed up with Venus' (Annie Gorassini) wanton ways, and with blacksmith Vulcan (Khoshabe) and Mars (Roger Browne) squabbling over her enticing favors. "She needs discipline," he grumbles. "But who can tame her?" Yes, who indeed, the blonde hussy wandering into Khoshabe's workshop, running her well-manicured fingers over a sword and breathing huskily "Gigantic." Was she referring to the weapon, Vulcan's mighty frame or something else? All three are banished to Earth for two months to sort out their differences as mortal beings; Browne (who shouts his way through the action) and Gorassini find themselves in the camp of the Thracians, their king (Ugo Sabetta) soon salivating over Venus' lithe, sensuous figure.

"What are you thinking?" he asks her. "I can read your mind," she replies. "It's not a bad idea." Some miles distant, Khoshabe is dragged from the surf by water nymph Bella Cortez and her nubile babes, joining up with diminutive Salvatore Furnari in a campaign to set loose slaves imprisoned in a vast cavern by pug-ugly men dressed in rubber lizard suits.

This is one of those badly dubbed foreign quasi-mythological pictures where an English audience, catching it on a Saturday night during the 1960s, would have asked themselves, "What a crazy mixed-up load of twaddle," at the same time probably enjoying every scatterbrained minute of what they had paid to watch. As Browne and Sabetta formulate plans to construct a tower to Mount Olympus, thus enabling the Thracians to depose Jupiter (how tall would *that* have to be?), Khoshabe travels to the undersea domain of jovial King Neptune (Omero Gargano) and enrolls his warriors, the Tridents, to assist in overthrowing the lizard men. Mission accomplished (the lizard men's fanged leader is strangled by a chain), Cortez and Khoshabe return to Neptune's picturesque grotto where the nymph, wearing a jade bikini, performs a hip-gyrating, bottom-wiggling, breast-revealing dance of so much fervid sexuality (one of the actress' best), that it's a wonder Neptune's kingdom doesn't explode in clouds of steam; instead, Khoshabe's facial muscles don't move an inch, and that goes for the rest of the movie. Mercury (Isarco Ravaioli), Messenger of the Gods, turns up, a gay, effete youth, although not quite that gay as to prevent him from fondling Cortez's bikini bottoms! Khoshabe, Cortez and Furnari make tracks for the Thracian camp, are assailed by a bunch of cavemen in a ravine and it's here, on the hour, that Salvi's outlandish broth threatens to run out of steam, the director appearing to have put all his eggs in one basket and coming up short of ideas for a suitable finale to round off this slice of hooey. Thankfully, the pace gains momentum for the remaining 20 minutes, the trio arriving at Sabetta's camp, overlooked by cloud-capped Mount Olympus. "The God of War must fight the God of Fire," declares a soothsayer, Gorassini (who has spent the entire running time draped over sedans in a permanent state of orgasmic lust, straight from the pages of *Playboy* magazine), adding, "The victor will be my husband." Cortez and Gorassini engage in a cat-fight with bullwhips, the Thracian slaves are freed, their chief killing Sabetta, and Meniconi thunders down from above that the fighting must stop (that partly-built tower is only around 15 feet high). Mars and Venus are recalled to undergo further punishment, while "Vulcan will remain on Earth for as long as I wish," which suits Khoshabe just fine; at last the stone-faced big guy has woken up to the fact that busty Cortez is the girl for him, not Gorassini who, in modern-day vernacular, is anybody's for a glass of wine. Perhaps the hunk can now live up to that semi-porno pseudonym of his, "Rod Flash"!

Imaginative sets beautifully photographed by Mario Parapetti (Salvi's preferred cinematographer) and a choral fantasy score (Marcello Giombini) contribute to one of pepla's wackiest of all offerings. One major fault, though, is the casting of Gordon Mitchell as Pluto, the God of Darkness, a minor role. Mitchell would have made a terrific Vulcan; he was far more expressive than Khoshabe and possessed screen presence, as well as a packed physique *and* those trademark fearsome features, backed by his maniacal cackle. Here, the Mitchell trademark brusque forte was squandered, odd considering that he was one of the director's favorite musclemen, having little to do other than prowl Mount Olympus and roar his disapproval. A four-

A Belgian poster for *The Invincible Seven*

star rating for what many would describe (and have done) as undiluted trash? Yes—Emimmo Salvi's films in particular are one-off guilty pleasures and should be viewed as such. Corny, freaky, laughable and just downright goofy, all the while visually splendid and entertaining as only these Italian fantasy sword and sandal movies can be. Besides, Cortez and Gorassini alone are worth the price of a ticket, two utterly gorgeous females who set the screen on fire whenever they appear in all their seductive glory.

1963

The Invincible Seven [*Gli invincibili sette*] aka ***The Secret Seven***

Film Columbus/Atenea (Italy/Spain); Totalscope/Eastmancolor; 92 (81) mins; Producers: Anacleto Fontini, Italo Zingarelli; Director: Alberto De Martino ✞✞✞

Circa 400 BC: Greece is under the thumb of Sparta, Athens haven fallen. Massimo Serato (as Axel) sees his village of Tur ransacked by Spartan jackals. Hauled before Spartan supremo Gérard Tichy (Rabirio) for having the audacity to retaliate against being roughly handled, he's placed behind bars, awaiting slow death by starvation. To the rescue comes his brother, Tony Russel (Leslio), and five ex-galley slaves (Livio Lorenzon, Renato Baldini, Barta Barri, José Marco and Cris Huerta); freed from his cell, Serato and his six slaphappy comrades form a Grecian Band of Brothers, determined to right the wrongs imposed on the populace by Tichy's wicked regime.

A serviceable peplum offering, *The Invincible Seven* (originally released in Britain as *The Secret Seven*, double billed with Hammer's *The Devil-Ship Pirates*) is sabotaged in one department—Carlo Franci's inappropriately chirpy music. This is supposed to be pretty serious stuff. Serato and Russel's mother is killed and Serato's young son found in a state of shock when Tichy, incensed at the seven rebels having a go at his fortress, orders the total destruction of Tur and all its inhabitants; abducting an architect (Tichy's new villa is under construction), Russel takes on his persona, worming his way into the palace in search of a hoard of stolen treasure. There, he meets ex-girlfriend Helga Liné (Lydia), Tichy's mistress, and old passions are stirred, putting the pair in danger; numerous sorties are carried out, the Spartans losing men and gold shipments, soldiers stoned by angry villagers; and a heist is meticulously planned to relieve the Spartans of their riches. During these scenes, Franci's music burbles merrily away and, instead of nailing the narrative, becomes a distraction (it gets more warlike in the final reel). Yes, there are a few amusing sequences: Lorenzon invents a boomerang-type weapon that floors the Spartans without them realizing what's happening, the seven indulge in knockabout horseplay and after the gold coins are catapulted from the top of the fortress into the sea, the five who committed the crime follow suit at the risk of breaking their necks. A Gatling gun device that fires off spears adds to a terrifically high body count in the movie; in the closing moments, Liné, Serato's son, and an old man are saved from burning at the stake, Tichy receiving a well-aimed spear between his shoulder blades as a herd of stampeding horses trample his beleaguered troops to oblivion. *The Invincible Seven* is roisterous fun, Serato (a good guy for a change), Russel, Tichy and Lorenzon in rattling fine form and Liné looking as glamorous as always, but it would have been far better if Franci's soundtrack mirrored the rough-tough action set pieces instead of appearing, on the odd occasion, to belong to a lighthearted sword and sandal comedy.

Perseus the Invincible [*Perseo l'invincibile*] aka ***Medusa Against the Son of Hercules***; ***Perseus Against the Monsters***

Cineproduzione Emo Bistolfi/Cooperativa Cinematografica (Italy/Spain); Totalscope/Eastmancolor; 95 (82) mins; Producer: Emo Bistolfi; Director: Alberto De Martino ✞✞✞✞✞

Filmed on the outskirts of Madrid, *Perseus the Invincible* is what peplum is all about: an immortal heroic figure, a beautiful princess in distress, an evil usurper to the throne, exciting battles and exotic monsters. Carlo Rambaldi (*King Kong*, 1976; *E.T.*, 1982) designed the 10-foot-high Medusa, a tentacled Cyclopean walking tree with a single glowing red eye, a creation that could have leapt straight from Ray Harryhausen's *Clash of the Titans* (1981). Rambaldi worked with Amando de Ossorio on the huge water dragon, a hydraulically controlled creature living in a lake; this, too, was pretty impressive for pre-CGI times. Two great monsters, then, and a great movie too, Alberto De Martino acknowledging the laws of action fantasy by refusing to take his foot off the gas pedal, backed by Carlo Franci and Manuel Prada's thumping score, Eloy Mella's shiny bright cinematography, some truly imaginative matte painted backdrops conceived by Emilio Ruiz del Rio and another winning performance from Richard Harrison in the title role. Harrison rarely disappointed in a peplum—he doesn't disappoint here.

The Kingdom of Seriphos' trade routes to the sea are being blocked by neighboring Argus, whose warriors force its citizens to take dangerous diversions past a lake harboring a fearsome monster and the forbidden Valley of the Petrified Men where lurks the evil Medusa. Kicking off with an ambush on the king's son (Fernando Liger) and his men, which won't please horse lovers (blazing logs are thrown at the distressed steeds, resulting in much whinnying and snorting; this disturbing scene is repeated later on), the reptilian monstrosity emerges from its watery lair. Liger and company run off, unfortunately, into the realm of the waddling Medusa where they are turned to stone (Emilio Ruiz del Rio's surrealistic frameworks come into their own during these

A Spanish poster for *Perseus the Invincible*

sequences). In Argus, King Acristo (Arturo Dominici) sends his son Galenore (Leo Anchóriz in brutish form) to Seriphos to meet King Cefeo (Roberto Camardiel) and woo Andromeda (Anna Ranalli), but the flame-haired goddess has set her sights on Perseus (Harrison), secretly meeting him in the hills where he tends his deer. On a hunting party, Anchóriz slaughters Harrison's favorite fawn; the two viciously fight it out using whips; Harrison is driven back but swears Anchóriz will pay, so a tournament is arranged at Seriphos, a trial of arms. Ranalli stipulates that, "whoever wins will be my husband." Harrison is the ultimate victor but wants nothing, unaware that his mother (Elisa Cegani) resides at Dominici's palace. It is foretold by Jupiter that Perseus, thought long dead, will return as rightful king of Argus and destroy all those who have taken his throne. Dominici and Anchóriz murder Cegani and her mother, Harrison vowing retribution by stirring up the locals and inciting a revolt ("I'll return to avenge my mother. I'm the rightful king!"), after dispatching the monster in the lake. The final thrill-packed 20 minutes is given over to the spectacular siege on Seriphos by the armies of Argus, catapults and battering rams clearing a way for Dominici's troops to enter the city. In the Valley of the Petrified Men, Harrison plunges his sword into Medusa's eye and shouts, "You must come back to life!" several times; Liger, his commanders and hundreds of petrified soldiers plus their horses return to normal and charge off to Seriphos, overwhelming Dominici's army. "He must be immortal!" cries Anchóriz, spotting his foe Dominici dying with an arrow lodged in his chest; a bruising struggle ensues, Anchóriz falling on Harrison's sword. Restored as king, Harrison rides away on a splendid chariot with Ranalli at his side, both kingdoms united in peace at last, the climax to a marvelous piece of peplum myth/fantasy that rewards on repeated viewings.

1964

The Lion of Thebes [*Il Leone di Tebe*]

Filmes Rome/Films Sirius (Italy/France); Euroscope/Eastmancolor; 89 mins; Producer: Diego Alchimede; Director: Giorgio Ferroni ✝✝✝✝

Giorgio Ferroni reacquainted himself with Helen of Troy after the success of *The Trojan War*, Yvonne Furneaux (of Hammer's *The Mummy* fame) starring as the legendary head-turner, washed up on the arid Egyptian shores with Mark Forest (Aryan) following a shipwreck and finding herself fending off the advances of Thebes' Pharaoh Ramses (Pierre Cressoy), who desires the beauty as his new queen, much to the dismay of loyal mistress Rosalba Neri. Neri actually sides with the Spartan queen in this instance, the two gorgeous women attempting to ensure that Cressoy changes course and stays in her arms. The Italian muscleman cycle, by the time this film was released in Italy in June 1964, wasn't quite a spent force but probably on an artistic slide, with budgets growing smaller and smaller; *The Lion of Thebes* lacked the big action set pieces seen over the previous five years, acted mostly on elaborate stage sets (a battle *is* included, using extensive footage from *The Trojan War*) but made up for it by decent performances, an involved plot, Francesco De Masi's melodious score and Angelo Lotti's colorful cinematography. The movie also contained a harrowing torture sequence as part of its payoff, featuring one of the genre's foremost fiendish instruments of death, the director milking the scene for all its worth. Imprisoned in a dungeon, Furneaux is shackled to a slab and forced to stare up as a massive block of

An Italian photobusta for *The Lion of Thebes*

The Italian Peplum Phenomenon 1950–1967

granite slowly descends, ready to crush her exquisite body; Forest has to fight a stubborn Theban guard before finally dragging her off the contraption, just as the block crashes onto the slab.

Forest is then proclaimed "Lion of Thebes" and is given a coveted dagger after he's wrestled gladiator Nello Pazzafini during a banquet, throwing peplum's resident bit part heavy into a pool where he's bitten by a poisonous snake, meant for Forest. When Cressoy is found with that incriminating dagger between his shoulder blades, ambitious court advisor Massimo Serato (Tutmes) assumes control, Furneaux and Forest both charged with the crime and consigned to the dungeons; Forest escapes, meets up with Furneaux's husband, Alberto Lupo (Menelaus), and joins in the battle for Thebes, rescuing the woman he secretly loves from the Death Chamber. Lupo isn't concerned in getting back on husband/wife terms with Furneaux, gleefully running his hands through the pharaoh's riches after skewering Serato on the keen end of his sword. An arrow in the back brings him down, benevolent Carlo Tamberlani (as Menophis) is crowned the new pharaoh after hostilities have ended. "Oh, Aryan. I've longed for you as the blind long for the light," simpers Furneaux to Forest who, by and large, remains fairly anonymous throughout, content to hover in the background and allow Ferroni's camera to focus on those well-oiled, tanned muscles. The two go off together, Furneaux wanting to live life as a normal woman, not as the schemer who had cost so many lives in the past during that 10-year Trojan conflict.

An Italian photobusta for *Seven from Thebes*

Seven from Thebes [Sette a Tebe]

Avala Film/SNEG (Italy/France); Techniscope/Eastmancolor; 105 (88) mins; Producer: Moris Ergas; Director: Luigi Vanzi ✞✞✞✞

The cinematic glory that was once *Seven from Thebes* is, as of 2015, commercially unavailable. Ragged DVD issues taken (it appears) from 16mm film reels do scant justice to a movie that features, as its climax, a majestic 21-minute battle sequence (yes—21 minutes!) that positions itself as one of pepla's finest. Luigi Vanzi plunges us into the thick of the bloody action (as did Mel Gibson 30 years later in *Braveheart*) as thousands of Spartan and Theban cavalry and foot soldiers attired in elaborate battle gear come to blows on the plains and in the swamps, fighting, falling back, regrouping, setting up battle formations and repeatedly counterattacking, each trying to gain the advantage. A remarkable finale in size and scope that more than makes up for the occasionally stodgy narrative preceding it, not helped by judicious editing, worldwide distributors trimming 17 minutes off the running time for international screenings.

André Lawrence plays young Theban Diomedes, devastated by the loss of his father and sister in a particularly violent opening five minutes. Spartan warriors (looking swell in red capes and red-plumed helmets) led by psycho Raf Baldassarre (Leonidas) launch into a rampage of looting, murder and rape; Lawrence's father is stabbed, his young sister trampled underfoot. Grouping together six compatriots, Lawrence swears to "Free my people and avenge my blood" from Spartan military domination. Until that happens, he's caught, imprisoned in a subterranean dungeon, tortured with hot irons, unfettered, set his cap at Theban governor Viktor Starcic's daughter Lena von Martens (Doride), dressed as a woman and wiped out a Spartan banquet *and* found the time to form a vast army hiding among marshland. Burly Pavle Vuisic stars as the Spartan general tasked with bringing the Theban hordes to heel, and there's an informant in the Theban camp. Although punctuated by outbreaks of Spartan mayhem, too much of the first 50 minutes is spent in political skulduggery. Both sides constantly argue over who should rule Thebes; Starcic is hand in glove with Spartan councilors and von Martens makes an irresistible but vacuous heroine. The dialogue-driven narrative struggles at times to ignite passion for the subject in hand, but when that epic-scale battle gets underway, those buried passions are brought to the surface, in spades. Smashed and broken after repeated assaults (Baldassarre dies in a swordfight with Lawrence; Vuisic falls on his sword in disgrace), the Spartan divisions scatter like leaves in the wind, the Thebans embracing "like brothers" another huge armed force, serving the enemy cause, that has appeared just when you thought it was all over: "Lay down your arms. Spartan rule has ended." Leading the army of liberation, Lawrence and von Martens head toward Thebes to join in the celebrations of a city finally rid of Sparta's tyranny.

Try to look beyond those mutilated, less-than-pristine digital releases with their muddy color and visualize the film as it was originally presented in Techniscope and Eastmancolor, that spectacular collision between opposing armies electrifying a packed auditorium, Carlo Savina's thundering music adding to the excitement. For that reason alone, *Seven from Thebes* fully deserves a four-star rating in this writer's estimation.

10
The Gladiators

Perhaps today's cinema audiences aren't even remotely aware that decades before Ridley Scott's *Gladiator* caused a stir at the box-office and spearheaded a sword and sandal mini-revival, the Italians were unleashing gladiator movies by the arena-full onto the public, and pretty spectacular efforts at that. Filmed for the most part in real-life Roman amphitheaters stocked with hundreds of extras, peplum gladiator pictures were violent and bruising, as witnessed in the opening 17 minutes of *The Invincible Gladiator*; you were dragged into the action, directors of the caliber of Alberto De Martino, Michele Lupo, Nick Nostro and Mario Caiano making you run for cover as swords, spears, tridents and other vicious weapons flashed in the sunlight, raising the excitement factor to new levels. The *fusto* regulars had a ball in these actioners, Richard Harrison, Dan Vadis, Gordon Scott, Mark Forest, Gordon Mitchell, Roger Browne et al. up to their leather togas in stadium clashes, devious senators, mad emperors and beautiful ladies in distress. This was the heyday of the Italian gladiator flick and all concerned put their backs into the product, coming up with some incredibly marvelous stuff en route. A complete lack of computer effects makes them all seem so grittily realistic—what you saw is what you got, blood, dust, sweat, the lot. They make for great entertainment, even today; the progress of time hasn't lessened their power and impact, or their ability to thrill a viewer.

Isabelle Corey and Richard Harrison lead the charge in *The Invincible Gladiator*.

1961

The Invincible Gladiator [*Il gladiatore invincibile*]
Film Columbus/Atenea Films/Variety Film (Italy/Spain); Techniscope/Technicolor; 105 (92) mins; Producers: Alberto De Martino, Antonio Momplet, Anacleto Fontini, Italo Zingarelli; Directors: Alberto De Martino, Antonio Momplet ✝✝✝✝✝

Any film that kicks off with a 17-minute montage of fierce gladiatorial action and climaxes in a 16-minute bloody rebellion must have a lot going for it, and *The Invincible Gladiator* does, one of the peplum genre's finest gladiator moments. A full-bodied score from Carlo Franci (16 pepla, 1961-1965), vivid photography via Eloy Mella and enough in-your-face encounters to appease even the most bloodthirsty of addicts set the seal on a movie that delivers the goods by the bucketload, not letting up for a single second, making Stanley Kubrick's *Spartacus* seem tame by comparison. This is one unremitting actioner that will leave you breathless!

Set in the 3rd century AD, personable strongman Richard Harrison, in his first peplum, plays Rezius, head honcho in Livio Lorenzon's (Itus) gladiator school ("We live well. We die well."). The province of Acastus has a 12-year-old king (Edoardo Nevola) on the throne, but ambitious regent Leo Anchóriz (Rabirius) plans to rule the state by having Nevola and his older sister, Isabelle Corey (Sira), done away with. Following that mighty rough 'n' ready 17-minute opener, the camera homing in on the clang of steel swords, engraved metal breastplates, plumed helmets, decorative shields, flashy armor and sweaty, blood-smeared faces, Harrison saves Anchóriz from an assassination attempt and is recruited as a bodyguard in reward; the regent then commands him to take 200 men into the surrounding hills and rout those troublesome brigands and insurgents. He succeeds and in doing so uncovers Corey as the renegade mogul; she wants to rid Acastus of tyranny, remove the wily regent from office and restore her brother as rightful ruler. Harrison changes sides, partly because he's taken with her, partly because Anchóriz shows no mercy to the surviving rebels, burning them at the stake en masse and hanging dozens more in the hills. Corey is slung into prison with a statement of terms from Anchóriz: "Marriage or the scaffold." Harrison is almost killed (along with Nevola) in an exciting chariot race after Anchóriz tampers with the chariot's bolts, the vehicle careering over a cliff into the sea. Battered but alive, the gladiator returns to the city (Nevola is left with Ricardo Canales, as Semanthius, also plotting to dethrone the regent) and promptly locked up with Corey, Lorenzon and the gladiators; later, he's forced to fight his best friend, José Marco. The regent, thinking the boy king dead, forces Corey into a joint coronation and wedlock after she pleads with him not to blind Harrison under torture; Marco is slain by a whip-wielding brute assisted by a pack of malicious dwarfs, Anchóriz giving the thumbs down sign in the arena. On the day of the wedding ceremony, all hell breaks loose. Like Samson, Harrison pushes two pillars apart and the prison walls come tumbling down; Lorenzon and the gladiators burst forth from their confinement, attacking the guards and joining in on the riot; Nevola is presented to his adoring public; and there's a splendid fight to the finish between Harrison and Anchóriz, both armed with lances. Pinning the evil administrator to the ground by his throat, Harrison stands back, allowing Lorenzon to deliver the *coup de grace*, a well-aimed spear straight into his chest. Order restored, Harrison and Corey walk off hand-in-hand to begin a new life.

Visceral and fast-moving, *The Invincible Gladiator* (it went the rounds in England on a double bill with *The Giant of Metropolis*) showcased Harrison in his debut peplum outing, the first of 11; he was a touch more animated than other muscle-bound heroes, relying on his above-average acting skills as well as his strength, and it showed in his more intimate scenes with the delightful Corey. This is a gladiatorial spectacle par excellence!

1962

Gladiator of Rome [*Il gladiatore di Roma*] aka ***Battles of the Gladiators***

CIRAC (Italy); Euroscope/Eastmancolor; 100 (80) mins; Producer: Giorgio Agliani; Director: Mario Costa †††

You cannot discount any gladiator movie that stars Gordon Scott, Wandisa Guida, Piero Lulli, Roberto Risso, Alberto Farnese, Gianni Solaro, Charles Borromel, Andrea Aureli and Nando Tamberlani, and has director Mario Costa at the helm, even though the end result is low on action and high on talk. The plot is involving, perhaps *too* involving for a film of this nature, with a great deal of scheming going on at the expense of the usual bloodbath, fistfight and battle. There isn't even one gladiatorial contest in the arena to get your teeth into, although plenty of gladiator-training footage is on show. Perhaps Costa and his team decided on a more personalized approach to a much-favored storyline, that of Christians submitting under the yoke of Roman tyranny and a slave protecting his mistress, who happens to be part of Rome's nobility, a Royal personage whose family was massacred on orders from the emperor, scared that his reign would be under threat.

Scott plays Silesian servant Marcus, protector to Wandisa Guida's Nisa, and remains bare-chested throughout, displaying those pecs to perfection, as when hurling logs at soldiers, bending prison bars or pushing boulders over a cliff during a bout of road construction. Sharp-featured, steely eyed Piero Lulli is General Astarte; he's got a contract out on Guida, determined to have her murdered to prevent the girl from ruling Rome. When her boyfriend, legionnaire Roberto Risso, turns up at his villa to find his entire family wiped out in a brutal attempt to eliminate the princess, he vows vengeance on the perpetrators. Scott and Guida, captured during the assault, join slaves on the march; the muscleman prevents Prefect Gianni Solaro (Macrino) from drowning in a chariot accident. Solaro, grateful, suggests that he sign up for Charles Borromel's gladiator school, because of his superhuman strength. Meanwhile, Alberto Farnese (Magistrate Vezio Rufo) and Lulli are still trying to find out where Guida is, unaware that she's right under their noses. Scott's waitress girlfriend, Ombretta Colli, helps him escape but he's caught again and chained to a rock wall. About to be blinded, he's reprieved by a captain of the guard and begins combat duties with the gladiators (no one can match his prowess and power in a tussle), while Guida is assigned servant duties to Borromel's poisonous harridan of a wife, Eleonora Vargas (Prisca), who detests the girl because of her Christian leanings. Consequently, because of her beliefs, the bedraggled heroine ends up in prison with other Christian slaves. Scott bends the cell bars, as everyone runs into the woods, where they're attacked and Scott and Guida end up in fetters once more (much to Lulli's satisfaction). As Scott, Guida and Colli are about to be burned alive on makeshift crosses, in a gruesome Christian bonfire, Risso and his men charge in on the

An Italian poster for *Gladiator of Rome*

scene. Lulli and Borromel are both killed and kindly Solaro, the new emperor, orders all Christians to be freed and made citizens of Rome. The two happy couples are left to get wed and play house.

Scott was 35 at the time of filming but still possessed the physique and charm to pull this kind of thing off—Costa brought out the best in him, as he did when they worked together on *The Son of the Sheik* (1962); the good-looking bodybuilder certainly carried this picture on his broad shoulders, ably assisted by a professional cast. Carlo Franci's bulldozing theme music was

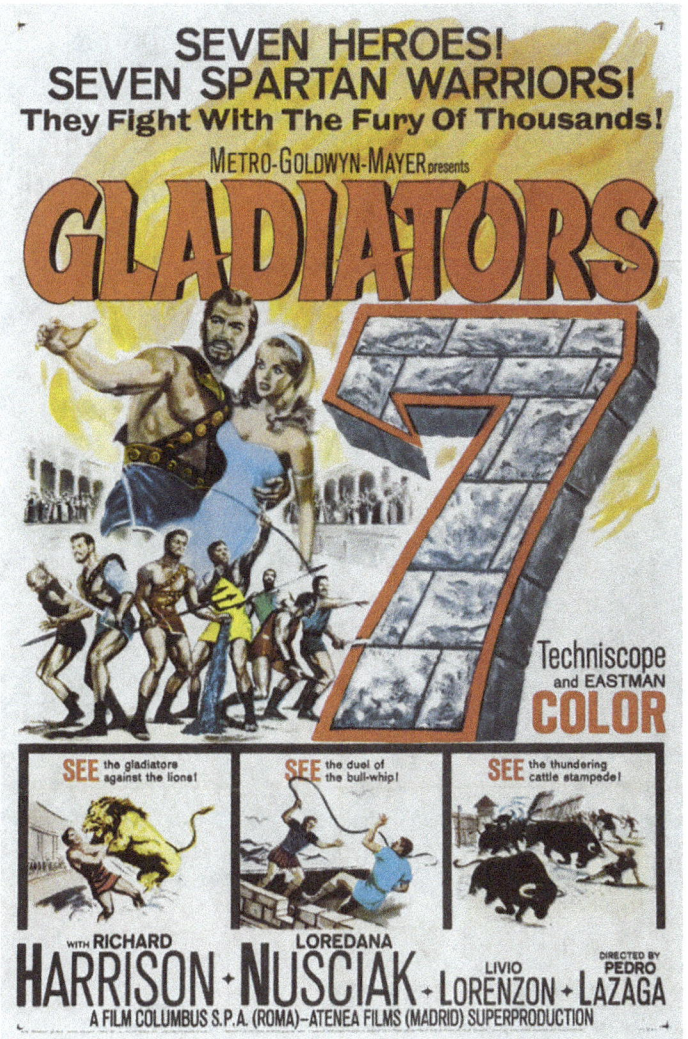

Clearly derived from John Sturges' *The Magnificent Seven* (MGM, 1960), Lazaga's MGM-distributed sword and sandal opus is one of the best from 1962, and that's saying something, with bags of forceful set pieces and incident. When Harrison is recruiting his six confederates one by one, Nazzareno Zamperia has to be rescued from Tichy's circus, fighting a bull (a real one, not a model) and a lion, while torch and toga regular Livio Lorenzon's gruff persona was always a snappy addition to these kind of action adventures. *Gladiators 7* tends to sag in the middle when the team relax and refresh themselves in their valley hideaway, flighty peasant lass Franca Badeschi mooning all over Harrison like a lovesick puppy dog, but the film picks up when a snooping patrol is decimated by the seven, including another of those "death by suffocation in the dirt" routines. The finishing onslaught on Tichy's stronghold is exciting stuff, Harrison and his men stampeding a herd of bulls which break into the fortress; Tichy, having already disposed of Rojo, fights Harrison on the lofty ramparts, tumbling to oblivion with a sword embedded in his abdomen, and the Ephors are overpowered. "Farewell till we meet again," cries Harrison to his friends at the end and rides off—strangely, his beloved Nusciak is nowhere in sight.

Harrison acquits himself well in this, his third peplum movie (*Executioner of the Seas* was his second), injecting some meaning into his character, not content to be just another bundle of muscle on a rampage, while Marcello Giombini's jaunty score carries the action along nicely. This is one of the worthier of the 20-odd gladiator films produced across the broad peplum spectrum in Italy during this heady period.

1963

The Ten Gladiators [*I dieci gladiatori*] aka *The Ten Desperate Men*

Cine-Produzioni Associate (Italy); Supertotalscope/Eastmancolor; 110 (104) mins; Producer: Armando Morandi; Director: Gianfranco Parolini †††

The Ten Gladiators was the first in a trilogy of adventures charting the exploits of 10 rogue gladiators battling against in-

another plus, as was Pier Ludovico Pavoni's color photography. This is a peplum more dialogue-driven than most, but worth a look all the same.

Gladiators 7 [*I sette gladiatori*]

Film Columbus/Atenea Films (Italy/Spain); Techniscope/Technicolor; 105 (93) mins; Producers: Anacleto Fontini, Italo Zingarelli; Director: Pedro Lazaga ††††

Darius (Richard Harrison), the son of an emperor, helps five Spartan gladiators break loose from prison; for his pains, he's punished in the arena, having to contend with 10 opponents while perched precariously on a high ramp surrounded by lethal sharpened staves. Killing six, Harrison is spared death by javelin and rides out to the country of the Ephors, only to find that whip-wielding tyrant Gérard Tichy (Hiarba) has murdered his father, the act disguised as suicide. Not content with this heinous crime, Tichy's slippery lieutenant, Antonio Molino Rojo (Macrobius), sticks Harrison's sword into the back of Loredana Nusciak's father; the girl is betrothed to Harrison, but Tichy desires her. Nusciak (Aglia) blames Harrison for her father's death, Tichy moves in to claim his prize ("My wedding gift to you will be the head of your father's murderer.") and Harrison avoids arrest, signing up six of his buddies to liberate the overtaxed, impoverished people from Tichy's rule and win back Nusciak.

Eight gladiators plus José Greci gather over the body of Dan Vadis in *The Ten Gladiators*; Vadis' character of Roccia was so popular that it was reprised in the two sequels.

justice and wrongdoing in Rome. Beefed-up Dan Vadis, playing Roccia or The Rock, joins the team after he and girlfriend José Greci (Livia) are mistakenly accused by the praetorian guard of being members of a black-hooded bandit gang causing Emperor Nero (Gianni Rizzo) bother. Ugo Sasso (Resius) is group leader/teacher, in cahoots with patrician Roger Browne (Glaucus Velarius); the nobleman, who can hold his own in a fight, wants to unseat ineffectual Nero and the praetorian's thuggish boss Mimmo Palmara (Tigelinus) and place sensible consul Mirko Ellis on the throne. Escapades galore happen before Ellis arrives in Rome from years of campaigning; Rizzo is stabbed to death by his boy-toy lover and the city is restored to some kind of (by Roman standards) law and order. Those 10 musclebound heroes fight in the arena, get mixed up with a bunch of Christians holding sermons in Rome's catacombs, break out of a dungeon, fool around with one another in displays of "Who's the strongest among us"; enter the stadium for a second time, fire arrows into the crowd instead of at the cowering Christian lion-bait, and save Greci from burning on the cross, all the time dodging smirking Palmara and his pack of vultures.

It's a fact that many peplum features had to include within their framework a comedy element; regrettably, those elements are present here, annoyingly in large doses. Salvatore Borghese, as Milo the Mute, horses around, eyes rolling, emitting hooting noises and, in one scene, impersonating a chicken; midget Arnaldo Fabrizio scuttles here, there and everywhere like a naughty child, stamping on people's feet and trying to chat up the girls. And why do we have to have the gladiators continually throwing back their heads and guffawing with laughter? These brief snatches of kindergarten-type high jinks contrast wildly with the violent, bloody set-tos and a couple of particularly nasty deaths: Vadis gets a lance in the stomach plus two fatal sword thrusts to the side and back, expiring in the dirt, shouting, "Good red wine for everybody," while Palmara's termination is truly spectacular, eight of the surviving gladiators (Sasso has been killed) plunging their swords into his body. They step back and he stands in full view, eight blades protruding from his breastplate, before slumping lifeless on the senate steps.

Several nice touches abound: slob Rizzo using the lithe form of a blonde concubine as a footrest during festivities; Franca Parisi's opulent villa containing an avenue of arched fountains; Vadis yelling gleefully, "I could eat a raw praetorian!"; and Angelo Francesco Lavagnino's score is exceptional, as is Francesco Izzarelli's bright color photography. Ever-grinning Vadis, oiled six-pack gleaming in the sunlight, steals the show in what turned out to be the weakest (but still fun-packed) of the three Ten Gladiator movies; he reprised his Roccia character in the next two, which thankfully were a distinct improvement on Parolini's rumbustious but vaguely dissatisfying rambling actioner, which was rather low on characterization (apart from Vadis). Having said all that, a digital remastered widescreen transfer of The Ten Gladiators would be much appreciated by fans.

Note: "Buddy-buddy" gladiatorial outings such as the three Ten Gladiators movies had, for a short time, a homoerotic stigma attached to them in some quarters, no doubt due to the amount of briefly clad male beefcake on display. This sexual connotation certainly wasn't the intention of the filmmakers! In mythological and documented records, what these actors wore (or didn't wear) mirrored the fashion of those times, however minimal that fashion may have been. In hindsight, persons of a certain sexual

A French poster for *Hercules Against the Mercenaries* (aka *The Last Gladiator*)

persuasion *could* view the films as such, while the rest of the audience sat back and enjoyed them for what they were, escapist entertainment featuring a bunch of muscular males clad in next to nothing who had *no* leanings toward each other in *that* direction whatsoever!

1964

The Last Gladiator [*L'ultimo gladiatore*] aka ***Messalina Against the Son of Hercules***

Sancro Film/Prometeo Film (Italy/France); Techniscope/Eastmancolor; 98 mins; Producer: Carlo Vassalle; Director: Umberto Lenzi ✝✝✝

Emperor Caligula (Charles Borromel), on a visit to Britain in 41 AD, spots Glaucus (Richard Harrison) almost single-handedly making mincemeat of his select troops and, impressed, ships him back to Rome, to be trained as a prize gladiator. After demolishing 10 opponents with a hefty axe in the arena and then, disregarding the thumbs down gesture, hurling the weapon at Caligula, he's jailed for his insolence but breaks out, becoming embroiled in two plots: one, to free slaves, the other to bring about the downfall of the mad ruler and restore Rome's Republican ideals. Harrison also has two women on his hands: slave girl Ena (Marilù Tolo, a blonde rinse disguising her normal dark locks), who toils in the mud and at a Roman laundry, and Messalina (Lisa Gastoni playing the infamous seductress). When Borromel is assassinated, Gastoni's ineffectual husband Claudius (Philippe Hersent) is ordained sovereign, but this isn't enough to satisfy Gastoni; she uses her wiles on Harrison to arrange meetings with a lover (Jean Claudio); if he fails to carry out her wishes, Tolo will be put to death.

Lenzi's Roman jaunt begins in serious mood, his camera panning over a field of corpses to the sound of Carlo Franci's doom-laden music, but as soon as Borromel appears, it descends into pure melodrama bordering on Roman soap opera. With midget lackey Arnaldo Fabrizio at his side, the loony one makes his horse a senator and rants and raves incessantly until polished off in the 32nd minute; thereafter, aloof Gastoni preens and pouts her captivating figure throughout the action (she looks lovely half-submerged in a milk bath!), impatient with everyone around her, while Harrison, not flaunting his muscular frame once (a grave omission by the makers, surely), engages in several arena duels, gets to grips with the palace guards, escapes, is recaptured, and prevents Tolo from being spiked to oblivion in a suspended animal cage.

There's one stupendous battle sequence showing the Roman army breaking into a stockade and razing it to the ground, and, against type, centurion Livio Lorenzon turns out to be a decent chap on the side of justice, acknowledging Harrison as his equal at the end after the hero and his girlfriend have narrowly avoided a roasting and routed the bad guys; Claudio dies from a sword thrust and Gastoni poisons herself. The fadeout has Harrison and Tolo walking off, presumably to take up their new roles as King and Queen of the Britons. It looks and sounds good (Franci scored 16 peplum movies, cinematographer Pier Ludovico Pavoni featured in 19) but lacks dynamism. Harrison, when you consider he received top billing, appears jaded, his acting just about managing to scrape through to the climax. Not one of his finest moments.

The Magnificent Gladiator [*Il magnifico gladiatore*]

Seven Film (Italy); Techniscope/Technicolor; 95 (82) mins; Producer: Anacleto Fontini; Director: Alfonso Brescia ††††

When a squad of Roman soldiers espies Dacian Mark Forest (as Attalus, or Hercules in American prints) demolishing an entire legion, they decide to capture, not kill, the hunk, take him to Rome and present him to Emperor Galienus (Franco Cobianchi). Cobianchi takes an unexpected liking to Forest and so does his daughter, Marilù Tolo (Velida), electing to utilize the warrior's awesome strength by allowing the man to train Roman infantry to his own high standards. Forest and his corps can then be posted to Rome's eastern frontier, under threat from invading Huns. On successful completion of the mission, all Dacian prisoners will be freed and Dacia made a Roman republic. Praetorian boss Paolo Gozlino (as Zullo; the actor specialized in playing out-and-out charlatans) burns with indignation and

An Italian photobusta for *The Magnificent Gladiator*

envy, not only at Forest's swift rise to power but the way Tolo salivates every time he swaggers into court. The reptile asks for (or demands) her hand in marriage, but she's not interested. Cobianchi, sick and tired of his lieutenant's constant bellyaching, sends him packing to the eastern front ("Go to Quintilius and satisfy your bloodlust.") where he sits and stews, scheming to rid himself of Forest and the emperor *and* marry Tolo, whether she likes it or not.

If a sense of déjà vu takes over while watching, it's because Forest, Cobianchi and Tolo all appeared in *Maciste, Gladiator of Sparta* (1964), as did many of the set pieces (Forest lifting a massive gate counterweight in the dungeons to free the prisoners) and design work (both arenas are identical). Alfonso Brescia's hugely enjoyable amalgamation of court intrigue, fights, escapes and strong-arm tactics is given added spice by the inclusion of a counterfeit emperor (also played by Cobianchi), a look-alike vagabond actor who's substituted in the imperial hot seat when Gozlino abducts the real article and imprisons him in a cave. Cobianchi Mark II (Gozlino's "secret weapon.") is under strict orders to counteract everything Cobianchi Mark I has done. Tolo is told to marry Gozlino, Forest is jailed as a conspirator while Jolanda Modio (Clea), Gozlino's mistress, has to suck up to the imposter to stop him running off at the mouth and giving the game away. Help for the Dacians comes in the form of sheep farmer Oreste Lionello, a garrulous bumpkin speaking in a Jerry Lewis screeching drawl; he arranges for the prison grate to be removed, thus freeing Forest and his comrades, who extricate the real emperor from his grotto hell. ("How many were there?" Forest asks Lionello, concerning the number of soldiers keeping an eye on the emperor. "I don't know," replies the farmer. "I can only count sheep."). At Gozlino's lavish nuptial festivities, all hell breaks loose in a riotous climax: Cobianchi Mark I is presented to an astonished audience; Cobianchi Mark II receives a spear in the back; Modio swallows poisoned wine by mistake; the praetorians clash with an up-for-it street mob who surge into the palace; the Dacians fire arrows tipped with lead weights; and

A German poster for *Revenge of the Gladiators*

A French poster for *Revolt of the Seven*

Gozlino, chased into the arena by Forest, falls onto Lionello's upturned sword, the well-meaning peasant having been killed by the treacherous swine. "You and your people are free citizens of Rome," announces Cobianchi to Forest at the end, as the muscleman ponders on the delights that Tolo (a real honey) has to offer. A rip-roaring, fun-filled gladiatorial peplum offering that which is amusing without resorting to silliness for a change. It will put a smile on your face.

Revenge of the Gladiators [*La vendetta dei gladiatori*]

Splendor Film (Italy); Euroscope/Eastmancolor; 98 (90) mins; Producer: Ferdinand Felicioni; Director: Luigi Capuano
†††

Standard thick-ear gladiator fodder set in 454 AD, starring Jayne Mansfield's then-husband Mickey Hargitay, playing Fabio, leader of a gang of gladiators known as the Invincible Six, who pit their brawn and wits against Livio Lorenzon's (Vandalo) barbarians and the corrupt court of Emperor Valentiniano III (Roldano Lupi in top form). Opening with a fearsome, full-on gladiatorial action sequence where the six combatants slay a dozen opponents, the story subsequently shifts to the return of Renato Baldini (General Ezio) to Rome, hailed as a hero for warding off heathen tribes from the empire's southern borders. But Baldini has a gripe. Supplies aren't getting through to his troops, the reason why he's returned from the battlefront posthaste to remedy this serious situation. Indolent Lupi, though, is too corroded by vice to pay much attention to his commander's grumblings, being more interested in wine, food, women and Greek dances than war ("Leave me in peace so I can watch the dancing," he complains), while wife Andreina Paul and her two conspirators are the felons behind those vital missing stores. The haughty diva is dead scared that Baldini will become admired to such an extent in the eyes of his adoring public that he'll take over as Caesar, shunting her and her cronies into obscurity ("We'll be so unpopular they'll want our heads.")

Baldini's son, Bruno Scipioni, appears on the scene, thought fallen in battle. He's concerned at Rome's weakness, the dangerous element in court and the underhanded way the citizens are being overtaxed and robbed, wanting justice to return to the province. Capuano's movie becomes rather politically orientated at this stage, a case of who's planning to oust who from power; it's only when Livio Lorenzon's barbarians arrive that we knuckle down to basics. Hargitay (he doesn't appear until 20 minutes have gone by) loves Lupi's daughter, José Greci (Priscilla), but later on, the girl finds herself promised in matrimony to Lorenzon's son, Mirko Ellis, consenting on condition that captured Hargitay is not harmed. "Is she pretty?" asks son to father. "As beautiful as an angel," replies one of the Roman traitors. "What does it matter," growls Lorenzon in the movie's one great line. "Whenever you get tired of her, you can throw her away—the way I got rid of your mother." Greci, though, is a Christian (yes, we have a Christian gathering in a grotto!), meaning Ellis will have to be converted if he wishes to wed the lass ("The only religion I believe in is this iron blade."). In an ensuing lengthy, exciting battle, the Romans are outnumbered, Baldini succumbing to a chest wound, his stockade burned and looted. Meanwhile, the Roman population is in turmoil, Lupi blundering around his empty palace in a blind panic ("They've all abandoned me!"); yes, this is one peplum outing where Rome *doesn't* get the upper hand. "Your women smell like sheep—but better than you do!" spits trussed-up Hargitay to Ellis, receiving several stings of the whip for his cheek; at the wedding ceremony, he's tied to a cross, Lorenzon giving orders for him to be peppered with arrows as soon as his son ties the knot; in jump the Invincible Six, cutting loose Hargitay (very fetching in a tiny pink loincloth). In a bloody tussle, Ellis is slain but Lorenzon's tribes are victorious, marching on Rome. The film ends on a downbeat note, the gladiators, Hargitay and Greci joining a procession of cross-bearing Christians and thousands of citizens in the setting sun, fleeing a city overrun by barbarians spreading death and destruction in their wake.

An American half-sheet for *Seven Slaves Against the World* (aka *The Strongest Slaves in the World*)

Revolt of the Seven [*La rivolta dei sette*] aka *The Spartan Gladiators*

Sanson Film (Italy); Techniscope/Eastmancolor; 90 (85) mins; Producer: Joseph Fryd; Director: Alberto De Martino ✝✝✝

Tony Russel (Keros), pals Massimo Serato (Baxo), Piero Lulli (Silone), Howard "Red" Ross (Croto, billed as Renato Rossini) plus Livio Lorenzon (Nemete) and his traveling band of performing players try every which way they can to steal the Athena statuette, secreted in a hidden alcove inside a Roman temple by Russel's mortally wounded brother. They're worried that with the inscribed artefact in his possession, corrupt proconsul Nando Gazzolo (Sar) can supposedly (it's never made clear) form an alliance with a neighboring province and force the local citizens into bondage. Russel happens to be carrying out an illicit affair with Helga Liné (Aspasia), Gazzolo's girlfriend, while blonde doe-eyed country lass Paola Pitti (Helea) wrings her delicate hands in the background, waiting to be caressed by the handsome rebel who joins in with the Spartans to take on Gazzolo's thugs.

Russel, Serato, Lulli, Lorenzon, Ross and the delectable Liné's combined experience and effort does its utmost to save De Martino's confusing "let's just chuck it all in" peplum potboiler from sinking without a trace, and admirably succeeds. A barrage of fights, both in the arena and out of it (Russel, a little on the slight side for a gladiator, forms a bond with Ross, the pair escaping together), makes up for a paucity of ideas in the plot department, the director content to let the fistfights and swordfights do all the talking. In one scene, Russel is blindfolded, a sack placed over his head and dragged around the arena tethered to a horse. It looks painful and probably was painful, the actor appearing distinctly the worse for wear afterwards. Similarly, horses in peplum actioners tended to come in for some unduly rough treatment and suffer greatly as a result (such treatment wouldn't be allowed today and sometimes makes for disturbing viewing), as in the climax when Russel and Gazzolo grapple in a muddy pool after the consul's chariot crashes off the road (a terrific piece of stuntwork), their distressed mounts having extreme difficulty in rising to their feet. The gold statuette is eventually retrieved by Russel and company attending a ceremony dressed as vestal virgins (cue for more buffoonery); the Spartans enlist in Lorenzon's ramshackle troupe, putting on plays in various towns; there are umpteen confrontations between the two factions (one involving a herd of stampeding bulls); Lorenzon, hamming it up to the hilt, is stabbed in the back during a dungeon skirmish; Gazzolo murders Liné; and Serato orders Russel to back off in that mud fight, hurling a spear into Gazzolo's belly. Pitti gets her man, Serato, Lulli and their group leaving the two lovers to get on with it. Not a thinking man's peplum, that's for sure, simply unrelenting, brainless, colorful entertainment, tailor-made for a good night in.

The Strongest Slaves in the World [*Gli schiavi piu forti del mondo*] aka *Seven Slaves Against the World*; *Seven Slaves Against Rome*

Leone Film (Italy); Techniscope/Technicolor; 96 (85) mins; Producer: Elio Scardamaglia; Director: Michele Lupo ✝✝✝✝

What an opener! A group of Romans rides up to Gordon Mitchell's farm, eyeing his corral of fine horses. Are they for sale, they ask? Mitchell (Balisten) says no, not really. They refuse to accept "no" for an answer, dismounting. Mitchell strips to the waist, displaying his impressive pecs, and takes them on, wielding a log. After a thumping set-to, he's overpowered and carted off to work as a slave on the construction of a colossal aqueduct stretching from Rome to an area of waterfalls. Under centurion Giacomo Rossi-Stuart's (Gaius) vicious rule, the men are constantly thrashed, bullied, stabbed and put on half rations until kindly tribune Roger Browne (Marcus) is placed in charge. He adopts a more lenient attitude toward the abused workforce, leaving Rossi-Stuart, busy embezzling Roman funds and in cahoots with wily Arab Calisto Calisti (Selim), fuming in anger. To get even for his perceived demotion, the unhinged centurion arranges for the slaves to be unshackled, inciting a revolt; a mass escape ensues, Browne finding himself the scapegoat and discredited. On the run, he meets up with Mitchell and five other men (most of the escapees are recaptured and crucified), deciding to enrol in Alfredo Rizzo's gladiatorial school as one of the seven Wolf's Head gladiators and return to Rome to prove his innocence, both with the council's procurator and his betrothed, the gorgeous Scilla Gabel (Claudia.)

Michele Lupo drives the narrative along at full-speed-ahead velocity for the first hour, real brutal in-your-face beefcake stuff, Rossi-Stuart terrific playing a hiss-boo Roman hoodlum, but with the introduction of pint-sized Arnaldo Fabrizio (Goliath) and his clownish sidekick, matters take a decidedly semi-comic turn, serving to spoil the mood of savagery built up in that initial 60 minutes. Following an interval of repose by the Monte Gelato cascades, the six strongmen plus Browne fight in Rizzo's gladiator arena, their true identities exposed; there's a five-minute heroes versus villains tavern ruckus (conducted on zany lines), Fabrizio joining in on the scrimmage, and Browne pursues Rossi-Stuart through the night streets, plunging a sword into his belly. The final shot sees Mitchell and his five pals riding off, having regained their freedom, while reinstated tribune Browne finds solace in the arms of Gabel. Francesco De Masi reprised his score from *Maciste, the World's Strongest Gladiator* to good effect, and if Lupo had opted for the serious approach throughout instead of featuring the infantile horseplay of Fabrizio, this would have been a barnstorming winner. Instead, it tends to peter out during the last 30 minutes, a pity as the mighty Mitchell is on top form from start to finish—but it's still great peplum cinema.

"Cornered!" Dan Vadis is surrounded by spears in *The Ten Invincible Gladiators*.

The Ten Invincible Gladiators [*Gli invincibili dieci gladiatori*] aka *Spartacus and the Ten Gladiators*; *Day of Vengeance*

Cine-Produzioni Associate/Balcazar/Copernic (Italy/Spain/France); Techniscope/Technicolor; 99 (88) mins; Producer: Armando Morandi; Director: Nick Nostro ††††

Made back-to-back with *The Triumph of the Ten Gladiators*, Nick Nostro's *Gladiator* outing was far livelier than its predecessor, *The Ten Gladiators*, reining in the comedy routines (even from mute Salvatore Borghese) by introducing a great deal more in the way of inventive action, Carlo Savina providing a thumping score to boost the narrative. Dan Vadis reprised the role of Roccia (the time is 71 BC) as did most of the cast with their characters from the first movie. An exciting sequence in a packed arena is the curtain raiser, the gladiators in combat with each other and armed horsemen, but no fatalities; these occur when 12 other gladiators are pitted man-against-man, a fight to the death using sword, trident and net. When Spartacus (Alfredo Varelli) protests at having to kill his own son, the 10 gladiators step in to prevent trouble with the guards; they're jailed but bought by trader Milton Reid (taking time off from playing heavies in British thrillers and Hammer horror movies). Out on the road, the group rescues Ursula Davis (Lydia) from a bandit attack and shown gratitude by her father, pudgy senator Gianni Rizzo (Sesto Vetulio), busy making plans to rout Spartacus and his growing band of vigilantes with the aid of psychopathic Reid. The sadistic trafficker in human flesh also runs a Roman concentration camp, his ill-treated workers constructing a giant aqueduct, whipped, tortured, their heads placed in yokes if they step out of line. When Varelli's camp is razed to the ground, Vadis and the gang decide to assist the rebel leader, but not before all 10 are drugged and slung into a dungeon by Rizzo, who was on the verge of hiring them in his crusade of hate against Varelli (Vadis has to prove his worth to Varelli by participating in a five-minute slugging match with him). Breaking out through the villa's garden, the gladiators, in their new livery of black, white-trimmed cloaks, raid Reid's camp, set loose the slaves and assist Varelli in his mission to conquer Roman villainy. (A blacksmith agrees to enter into the fray with the one proviso: "I'll join you, but you have the slaves. I want the iron!")

One-man battering ram Vadis, using his ham-sized fists more than his sword, proved to be one of pepla's more acrobatic, nimble-footed he-men in this roughhouse, high jinks caper, his expansive chest as wide as his engagingly cheeky grin. He even gets the tastiest girl, Helga Liné (Daliah), in the end after doing away with scar-faced Reid on the banks of a lake in a sweaty bout of no-holds-barred punching (including a head-butt!). Earlier, Vadis, caught by Reid's henchmen, has to endure a particularly harrowing torture with nine other slaves, hung by his right arm on a tree branch, awaiting an arrow in his chest; cut down, he wades in barehanded as Reid's camp is burned, the workforce spreading out to enlist with Varelli's forces. Commander Claudius' legions, sent to intercept Varelli, are decimated in a titanic struggle (catapults and flaming spears; stock footage is utilized effectively), the woods littered with Roman corpses, while a chariot flattens vicious Rizzo. Varelli is victorious, and Vadis leaves his nine comrades to go their own way, riding off with Liné for some post-battle treatment. Entertaining, knockabout peplum fun, not much depth to it maybe, but Vadis is at the top of his game, a joy to behold.

A Spanish poster for *The Triumph of the Ten Gladiators*

The Triumph of the Ten Gladiators [*Il trionfo dei dieci gladiatori*]

CI.AS. (Italy/Spain/France); Techniscope/Technicolor; 105 (91) mins; Producer: Armando Morandi; Director: Nick Nostro ✞✞✞✞✞

The final entry in the *Ten Gladiators* series is the best of the bunch, director Nostro focusing a lot more on the gang's camaraderie and incorporating several blistering gladiatorial sequences (over the course of the trilogy, eight actors cast as the gladiators featured in all three flicks). The plot is pretty straightforward (Nostro wrote the script), allowing action fans to wallow in numerous arena free-for-alls, brawls, battles and hand-to-hand tussles without pondering too much on what is taking place. Carlo Savina's military score is one that wedges itself into the brain and refuses to let go, while Tino (Clemente) Santoni's photography is as sharp as Dan Vadis' blade (when he gets to use it instead of those enormous fists).

In the opening shot, all 10 heroes run toward camera like excited schoolkids and emit a war cry, a neat ploy to establish their images in the mindset of the audience and to have you rooting for them. Rejected for a proposed round of gladiatorial spectacles to be held in Syria and Egypt (a tremendous opener in the arena, the gladiators, dressed in monogrammed black cloaks with white flashing, going all out to impress a snooty impresario with their skills), Vadis (Roccia, elected leader because elder warrior Ugo Sasso reckons he's past his prime) and his squad are offered a lucrative contract by Syrian proconsul Carlo Tamberlani—travel to Arbela in the Orient and entertain Queen Moluya (Helga Liné), who is in the process of forming a peace pact with neighboring Parthia. Halina Zalewska (Myrta), niece of one of the gladiators, tags along, as does wannabe gladiator-cum-spy Stelio Candelli (Glauco Marcio), aware of the true nature of the trip, to abduct the queen and smuggle her into Syria, to be held as a hostage for Rome. Her ambitions to unite with Parthia and form a giant army are too perilous for the empire, and she needs to be taught a sharp lesson to deter others from following in her footsteps. In Arbela, greedy Roman consul Gianni Rizzo (Sesto Vetullio), accepting gold for his treacherous allegiance, connives with Parthian Ivano Staccioli (Prince Arimandro) to march against Rome; Liné casts her kohl'd eyes at Vadis, thinking how nicely he fills his gladiatorial armor; wicked princess Leontine May (Selina) has her own hidden agendas; Zalewska falls for Candelli; and there's a balletic contest in the amphitheater in which the gladiators' opponents fight with poles containing hidden blades inside the ram's head butt. Vadis and company turn the tables on their assailants, killing eight and hurling all 10 weapons at the Queen's rostrum in defiance.

With barely a pause for breath, Nostro treats us to a tavern commotion, a lavish feast complete with dancing wenches; a skirmish in a cavern between rebels led by a masked man, slaves and Parthian soldiers (this sequence has been heavily cut in existing prints); Zalewska chained up in a torture chamber, flogged and burned by red-hot poker; Vadis pulling down a palace support pillar, crushing soldiers; a secret gallery in the Temple of Isis leading to a cavernous stone mine and umpteen fisticuffs where Vadis pummels, throttles, head-butts and uses a Roman form of martial arts to beat his components into submission with consummate ease. Liné, in fact, isn't planning to bring about the downfall of Rome; she's the mysterious masked man, coming to the aid of her maltreated populace, now being crucified in their droves by Staccioli and his Parthian dogs. A calamitous finale has the Roman army quashing Staccioli's forces (footage from other peplum actioners is inserted), May toppling into a pit harboring a giant python, Staccioli bashed to oblivion by Vadis wielding an eight-foot door bar and Rizzo asking his friend to put him out of his misery—the Eagles of Rome have entered the city and he knows his life isn't worth a single denari if the legionnaires get hold of him. "Long live the queen," shout the gladiators at the end, but Vadis isn't going to get to canoodle with Liné; she knows her job is to serve her citizens regally, not play house with a six-foot-four-inch ruffian who eats his enemies for breakfast. Arm-in-arm, the 10 gladiators leave the city walls and head off for pastures new to the sound of Savina's rousing music, the culmination of an equally rousing no-brainer that will appease all those looking for something a little less mind-taxing on their peplum menu.

The Two Gladiators [*I due gladiatori*]

Prometeo Film (Italy); Techniscope/Technicolor; 100 (93) mins; Producer: Carlo Vassalle; Director: Mario Caiano ✞✞✞

Borrowing heavily from the tried-and-tested "different brothers at loggerheads" centerpiece that made up the narrative thrust of *Ben-Hur*, Caiano cobbled together this cut-price *Fall of the Roman Empire* effort with minimal funds at his disposal, judging by the solitary arena wall on display in the film's latter stages and the barebones Roman streets. Where *The Two Gladiators* didn't skimp was on the cast, a veritable who's who of peplum: Richard Harrison (Lucius), Mimmo Palmara (Commodus), Moria Orfei (Marzia), Alberto Farnese (Lito), Piero Lulli (Cleandro), Gianni Solaro (Tarrunio), Mirko Ellis (Pertinance)

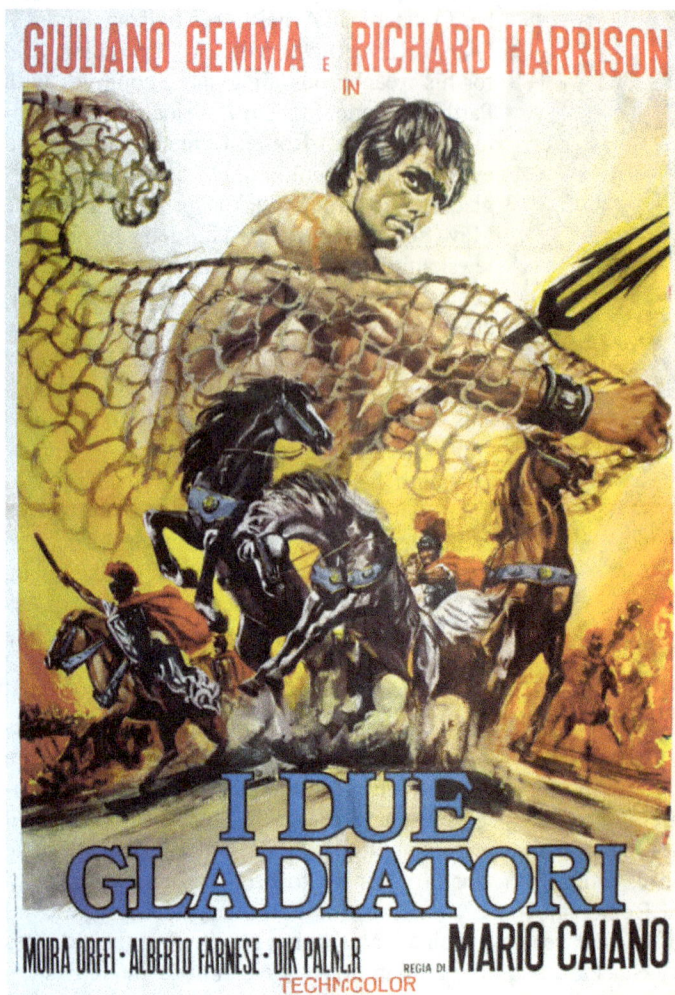

An Italian poster for *The Two Gladiators*

A Spanish poster for *Challenge of the Gladiator*

and Giuliano Gemma (Horatio). With that bunch on set, things were bound to happen despite the budget, and it's thanks to their proven experience within the genre that they did, although overall, the movie is formulaic and not overly exciting.

Upon the death of his father, Marcus Aurelius, Palmara is crowned emperor, unaware that he has a twin brother (Harrison) waiting in the wings, ready to take him on; the two were separated at birth 30 years back, and neither knew it. Palmara's blond-haired Commodus (with Caligula, Rome's favorite mad emperor) is a bullying libertine, discarding mistress Orfei in favor of ice maiden Ivy Holzer (Emilia), a pale-skinned Sabine beauty who steadfastly refuses to unthaw and yield to his constant groping. "By the precious girdle of Venus" and "By Zeus, you're a pretty witch" are just two of the more ridiculous sayings to spout from Palmara's lips, the complaining populace on the brink of famine due to his pitiless measures (in one scene, Caiano switches from the close-up of a rat, grabbed by a starving citizen, to a plate of goodies served up at Palmara's celebratory feast. Yes, even pepla could get arty at times!). When told of his blood ties by Senator Solaro ("You! Emperor of Rome!" laughs pal Gemma at the news), Harrison, busy fighting the barbarians ("The descendants of wild pigs.") alongside compatriots Gemma and Alvaro de Luna, heads for Rome, seeking shelter from prying praetorian eyes in Adriano Micantoni's tavern. From their base, they stage a revolution, leading to a confrontation between the siblings ("You're even worse than Caligula!" shouts Harrison), an uprising and a none-too-brotherly clash in the arena, filmed in brutal, head-on style, Harrison and Palmara attired in identical Thracian armor. Palmara is slain, Orfei is stabbed in the back and Lulli is fed to the crowd, while Farnese, who fancied Orfei all along ("You want her? You take her!" yells Palmara at him), is dispatched by sword and the ransacked palace overrun by the mob and General Enzo Fiermonte's legionnaires. Finally, when order has been restored, benign senator Ellis is hailed as the new emperor after Harrison has declined the crown ("One brother's blood has been shed for the common good."), choosing instead to carry on soldiering and getting to grips with breaking down Holzer's defenses (the two fall in love after one hour, when she's in prison). Gemma is made head of the praetorian guard, de Luna is promoted to commander of the legions in Gaul and Micantoni becomes Rome's new collector of taxes.

Alfonso Brescia worked on the cracking screenplay with Mario Amendola; he directed 1964's *Revolt of the Praetorians*, made in tandem with *The Two Gladiators* (same production team and cast). Carlo Franci's score moved the chaotic action when required and Caiano directed with purpose, especially in the fight/skirmish sequences. Not the greatest of all peplum *Gladiator* movies but an enjoyable one all the same, with Harrison and Palmara in good form, always worth catching.

1965

Challenge of the Gladiator [*Il gladiatore che sfidò l'impero*]
Jonia Film (Italy); Totalscope/Eastmancolor; 103 (90) mins; Producer: Ferdinand Felicioni; Director: Domenico Paolella ††

Produced during the tail end of the peplum boom period, *Challenge of the Gladiator* has a fatigued air about it; not even the combined presence of stalwarts Massimo Serato, Piero Lulli, Livio Lorenzon, Gloria Milland and Walter Barnes can drag the movie out of the gladiatorial quagmire, despite a few action highlights, one featuring a multiple spear thrower, and another Giuseppe Piccillo's fine score. In fact, this is Barnes' show, as he plays Terenzius, an ex-gladiator tasked with passing himself off as Nero, the "Divine One." The burly actor roars, giggles, acts the idiot, wields club, sword and trident and has a whale of a time, putting the rest of the cast almost to shame. His performance alone is worth the price of a ticket.

José Greci, one of peplum's loveliest of actresses, as Princess Assuer in *Seven Against All*

Peter Lupus (billed as Rock Stevens) stars as Spartacus (or his namesake), watching over a legendary Thracian treasure hoard secreted in a hidden cavern, which corrupt Senator Serato (Lucio Quintilio) covets. Emperor Nero is no more so Barnes is hired to impersonate the mad Roman ruler, leading Serato's forces who have twin objectives: subdue Lulli's (Consul Metello) companies and the Thracians and grab that fabulous treasure. Milland stars as Serato's daughter Livia, a regal beauty posing as a Christian slave who drifts in and out of the scenario with a look of serenity on her refined features, purring over Lupus' bulging biceps one minute, rejecting his advances the next; in the meantime, henchman Lorenzon (Commodio) goes through his usual psycho-Roman routine, snarling and spitting venom while Serato looks bored out of his mind. Lupus demonstrates that those muscles are not for show only, breaking his rope and chain bonds, tearing stone blocks from Lulli's prison cell (he's become a close friend of the wronged tribune) and wrecking a fiendish torture device involving spiked walls. He later takes on old foe Barnes in the arena but loses the contest, drugged by Milland—and the obligatory closing melee (padded out by stock footage), Romans versus Romans, sees Serato and Lorenzon killed, while loony imposter Barnes stumbles and falls into a fiery volcanic vent. Thrace is now independent of Roman rule, leaving Lupus and Milland to waltz off and play house. Current ragged DVD issues are shorn by 13 minutes from the original length, include one scene obviously inserted out of sequence (Lupus, drugged, *before* the arena interlude, showing Milland putting powder in his wine) and contain the title *Challenge of the Gladiators*, which it is not.

Seven Against All [*Sette contro tutti*] aka **Seven Rebel Gladiators**

Leone Film (Italy); Techniscope/Technicolor; 90 mins; Producer: Elio Scardamaglia; Director: Michele Lupo ✞✞✞

Seven rebel gladiators—plus Little Goliath! Arnaldo Fabrizio has as much to do in this slice of outrageous nonsense as Roger Browne, Pietro Ceccarelli, Harold Bradley, Pietro Torrisi, Nazzareno Zamperia, Jeff Cameron and Mario Novelli, playing the seven titular characters. An often jarring combination of in-your-face combat, breathlessly shot and edited by Michele Lupo, kitsch sets, backslapping tomfoolery and knockabout clowning, *Seven Against All* is entertaining but doesn't appear, or simply doesn't want to, place its cards on any one table. It veers from the sadistic to tough action to the semi-farcical in the blink of an eye, even closing on a bonkers note (Fabrizio winks at the camera, announcing, "And they all lived happily ever after!"). But the peplum phenomenon was in its final stages in 1965 and far less cultured, or at least heavyweight, than it once was, giving way to the Italian Spaghetti Western. The influences of Sergio Leone and Ennio Morricone can both be felt in Lupo's sequel to *The Strongest Slaves in the World*; the director shoots predominantly in close-up during the opening gladiatorial bouts, while Francesco De Masi's music gallops along on Western lines, a Morricone-type guitar leitmotif twanging in the slower segments.

Alfio Caltabiano plays Vadius, the psychopathic tribune of Aristea, in league with Erno Crisa (as Morakeb), dynastic ruler of the Kiva, a weird cult who dwells in a vast underground city (the Mole Men outfits from *Maciste, the Strongest Man in the World* were brought out of the wardrobe for this production). The Kiva require a constant supply of fresh slaves to work gigantic wheels that supply both air to the subterranean workings and energy to the city's machinery; Caltabiano can add to their workforce *if* they side with him in becoming king of Aristea, without Rome aware of it. Centurion Browne (Marcus Aulus) turns up, has a set-to with Caltabiano's soldiers and finds himself locked in the arena basement along with six other toughies and midget Fabrizio. Refusing to kill each other at the games, all seven are manacled and thrashed until set loose by Fabrizio; Browne and his small but deadly force then decide to put a well-oiled spanner in Caltabiano's crooked ambitions, which include marrying, against her wishes, Princess Assuer (José Greci, decoratively vacant and billed under her American pseudonym of Liz Havilland) and throwing her father, King Krontal (Carlo Tamberlani in his trademark role as an elderly monarch), into a dungeon. Their mission gives rise to a number of humorous rough and tumbles, the seven strapping gladiators ably assisted by diminutive deputy Fabrizio; in one scene, the gang (plus Fabrizio) dress as Kivas, rendering 106 guardsmen senseless; there's a boisterous tavern scuffle with much smashing of furniture; and the climactic ding-dong, the seven attired as dancing girls, lasts for a full 10 minutes, the sound of clashing swords ringing throughout the halls. Caltabiano receives the deathblow from Browne, Fabrizio rides on set astride a pony as a Kiva knight and the centurion winds up with grateful Greci in his arms.

The set design depicting the cavernous Kiva City is eye boggling (pristine prints are available in letterbox format with English subtitles), and that goes for the white, bushy fright masks the Kiva don when on the warpath. Browne was always one of the better-looking peplum musclemen and a reasonable actor with it, and together with his six comrades-in-arms plus undersized Fabrizio playing all kinds of tricks on the enemy, makes *Seven Against All* a worthwhile viewing experience, even if it is a little on the witless side.

11
Ancient Egypt and Biblical

Italian Egyptian and Biblical features may have lacked the polish and mammoth budgets of Hollywood Egyptian and Biblical spectacles but more than made up for it in flamboyancy, steel and evocative dramatics: *The Tomb of the Kings*, *Son of Cleopatra*, *The Pharaohs' Woman*, *A Queen for Caesar* and *Sodom and Gomorrah* are right up there with the best of Tinseltown, imaginative forays into life thousands of years before the coming of Christ. Thankfully, Italian movies based on the Bible tended to steer well clear of the ponderous sermonizing and sheer length that blighted other films made elsewhere; some, such as *Jacob, the Man Who Fought With God* and *Saul and David* are quite hard to come by today. And check the Noah's Ark sequence in *Jacob*: All that money spent by Paramount and Darren Aronofsky in *Noah* amounts to very little when compared to the effects on show in this modestly budgeted peplum, produced 54 years ago. Times in some areas of cinema have *not* changed for the better!

1960

David and Goliath [*David e Golia*]

Ansa Film (Italy); Totalscope/Eastmancolor; 113 (96) mins; Producer: Emimmo Salvi; Directors: Ferdinando Baldi, Richard Pottier, Orson Welles (uncredited) ✝✝✝

The story of how David slew Goliath and became King of the Israelites after the Philistines, who had stolen the hallowed Ark of the Covenant, were defeated in battle. A more-expensive-than-usual production all round: lavish, ornate sets and costume design, beautiful photography courtesy of Adalberto "Bitto" Albertini and Carlo Fiore, and a highly dramatic score from Carlo Innocenzi, plus Orson Welles in full flow. Welles (playing King Saul and slumming around Europe to finance his own projects) directed his scenes and it showed in his renowned theatrical fluidity behind the camera, framing his colorful robed bulk in odd angles and corners lit in varying degrees of light and shade, Innocenzi's music loudly punctuating each moment Welles appeared like a grand opera on stage. Placed beside an actor of Welles' stature and looming presence, the support cast fared from decent to middling: Ivica Pajer's David (the Croatian actor was billed as Ivo Payer) was a callow youth, muscular and wide-eyed innocent, having the mantle of kingship thrust upon his broad shoulders by God's will; Massimo Serato, excellent as always, played ambitious Abner, determined to assassinate Pajer following his victory over Goliath; Furio Meniconi made a fearsome Asrod, the Philistine ruler; British actor Hilton Edwards was the elderly prophet Samuel, hobbling into Welles' palace on two staffs and treating the audience to a 12-minute opening discourse on the reasons why the corpulent overlord should be dethroned; and Eleonora Rossi Drago and Giulia Rubini were Welles' two tantalizing daughters, emoting like crazy.

"The Lord has rejected thee from being king," shouts Edwards accusingly to a glowering Welles (there are a lot of "thees" and "thous" in this movie). The new king will apparently hail from Bethlehem and straight off, we espy young Pajer tending his flock of sheep in the hills, at the same time practicing his prowess with the slingshot. When his sweetheart is killed by a bolt of lightning, Pajer, doubting the word of the Lord, travels to Jerusalem, stirs up the people with propaganda, meets Welles and is seized upon by Rubini, Serato planning to rid the city of this troublesome usurper to further his own agenda. Welles is swayed by Pajer's charm and, instead of killing him, listens to what the young man has to say. In the meantime, Meniconi has witnessed first-hand Goliath's strength when the giant (six-foot-five ex-circus strongman Aldo Pedinotti, billed as Kronos) lifts the weight of a massive stone slab that would normally take 10 men to carry. To the statement of "My only god is gold. My only law is Goliath," Meniconi and his battalions converge on Pierre Cressoy's troops and, in the 80th minute, the much-anticipated David versus Goliath confrontation takes place, Pajer flooring the hairy behemoth with his slingshot and delivering the *coup de grace*, plunging Goliath's huge sword into his comatose body; the sequence is on the short side but effectively handled (Wolfgang Petersen's opening 10 minutes in *Troy*, which had Brad Pitt [as Achilles] putting his combat skills to good use against a lofty Thessalonian strongman while two opposing armies looked on, took its cue from this sequence). A ferocious humdinger of a battle ensues (faces slashed; spears in backs), Cressoy plunging a spear into Meniconi's neck; their king slain, the Philistines throw in the towel and take flight. In the court of King Welles, Serato's assassination attempt fails when the burly monarch brings him down with an arrow. Welles hands the crown to Pajer

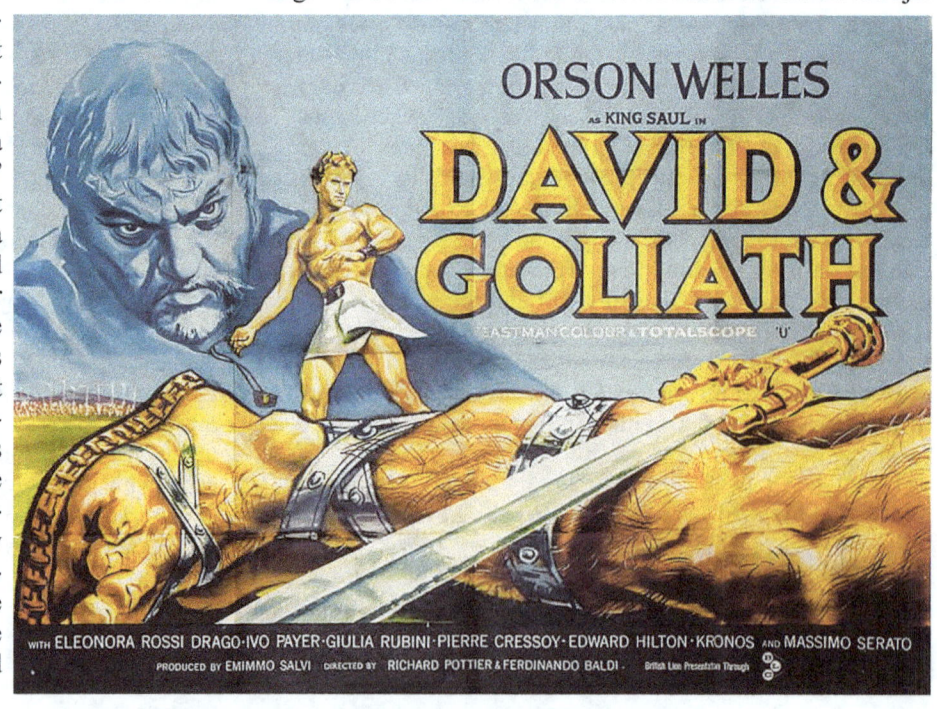

("I have sinned," he moans, convinced he's possessed by evil spirits) and daughter Rubini; Pajer is now the new King of the Israelites, Rubini at his side.

Two surrealistic scenes occur in *David and Goliath*: Meniconi's "human weapon" being enticed out of his grotto home by friend Dante Maggio, undertaken in freezing conditions judging by the amount of vapor issuing from the actor's mouths, and a bizarre ceremony held in the Philistine camp, in which an octopus is served up to the gods as an offering, held beneath the feet of an enormous statue. Half-naked dancing girls surround Goliath, one of the many delights offered to the humungous man-mountain if he falls in with the Philistines. Overall, the movie is ponderous to sit through, stately although visually arresting in the Welles' sequences (as one would expect), humdrum elsewhere, marred by Pajer's ineffectual central performance. The battle out on the plains is riveting stuff, raising the excitement level a few notches to relieve passages of wordy tedium. Welles and those fabulous sets are two good reasons to catch it.

Esther and the King [*Ester e il re*]

Galatea/Titanus/20th Century Fox (Italy/US); CinemaScope/Technicolor; 109 mins; Producers: John Twist, Raoul Walsh; Directors: Raoul Walsh, Mario Bava (uncredited) ††

British glamour queen Joan Collins took on the role of virtuous Esther, a Judaean maiden who weds King Ahasuerus of Persia (Richard Egan) for the sole purpose of using her influence to stop over-zealous tyrant Haman (Sergio Fantoni) from persecuting her people, ditching boyfriend Simon (Rik Battaglia) in the process. Despite the use of Mario Bava's renowned exaggerated color schemes, his favored reds and greens manifesting themselves in many of the interior shots, and a flowery score from Angelo Francesco Lavagnino, *Esther and the King* is a struggle to sit through, its air of pious melancholy palling long before the film finishes. The production fails to shift into a high gear, a genuine surprise when you consider veteran director Raoul Walsh's output from the previous two decades. This was the man responsible for three rousing classic 1940s Warner Bros. outings—*They Died With Their Boots On* (1941), *High Sierra* (1941) and *White Heat* (1949)—in addition to a clutch of great '50s Westerns. Walsh was an action director of some note, but there's little evidence of that here, what action there is filmed at night, and rather murkily.

Collins' Uncle Mordecai (Denis O'Dea) acts as Egan's conscience, especially when Fantoni and henchman Renato Baldini plant forged documents in the Hebrews' temple, giving details of the king's proposed battle plans for a forthcoming invasion of Greece, thus indicting the Judaeans in treason. This causes Egan to question his wife and the Judaeans' loyalties; she, and they, must renounce all faith in their strange god or die. Egan's former spouse, adulteress-cum-harlot Daniela Rocca (Queen Vashti), is strangled by Baldini acting on Fantoni's orders, the blame levied at the Hebrews to stoke the fires of unrest even further. Fantoni is out to rule Persia from the city of Shushan and wants Egan disposed of, ordering Baldini to bring back his head ("A thousand talents of gold for his head!") when the king and a platoon ride off on a scouting expedition. Instead, it's Baldini's head that's brought back, Battaglia organizing a mass revolt against Fantoni and his followers in Shushan—the tyrant is apprehended after a skirmish and hanged, Battaglia succumbing to a fatal wound, his death instituting the Jewish day of feasting called Purim. Collins is reunited with Egan as she still loves him.

Not really figuring in the narrative until the 43rd minute, Collins looks divine but is no match for the stunning Italian beauty of Rocca and co-star Rosalba Neri, content to drift around Egan in a white gown like a timid virgin (not so off-set!), calling him "dearest" when he's in a contradictory mood. Egan is weighty in a Hollywood Brylcreem-boy kind of fashion, not really cutting it as a Persian king, while Fantoni steals everyone's thunder as Haman, a thoroughly nasty piece of work. Too much sermonizing on God's will by O'Dea and protracted scenes of virgin maidens being taught court etiquette by the resident eunuch bog the pace down in a picture that comes under that cinematic category of "earnest and sincere, but very, very dull."

Joseph Sold By His Brothers [*Giuseppe venduto dai fratelli*] aka *Joseph and His Brethren*; *Sold into Egypt*

Jolly Film/Cosmopolis/Dubrava (Italy/Yugoslavia); Totalscope/Eastmancolor; 103 mins; Producers: Luigi Carpentieri, Ermanno Donati; Directors: Luciano Ricci, Irving Rapper ††

The Book of Genesis relates how Joseph, the 11th of Jacob's 12 sons, was despised by his siblings through jealousy and sold as a common slave into Egypt, thereafter becoming an eminent governor in the pharaoh's court, eventually reuniting with his family during the years of famine. Jumping onto the popular Biblical bandwagon of that time, the Italians brought in an English cast for the main leads in their version of events, while American Irving Rapper, an unlikely choice for this type

An International poster for *Joseph and His Brethren* (aka *Joseph Sold by His Brothers*)

of material, directed footage for international release. Labeled by many as a poor man's *Ten Commandments*, *Joseph and His Brethren* (its more familiar title) was critically lambasted when released in America in November 1962: "A film of no merit," commented *The New York Herald Tribune*. But does the picture *have* merit? Whether the film sticks closely to the Old Testament facts or not, let's examine the movie.

The production was spot-on. Beautifully designed Egyptian sets and accurate period costumes that positively dazzled the eye, saturated in Riccardo Pallottini's color photography, and a lilting score from Mario Nascimbene. Robert Morley chewed the scenery as Potiphar, the man who buys Joseph from the slave market after his life is saved by the youngster, while Belinda Lee as his sexually frustrated nymphomaniac wife Henet positively lit up the screen with lustful desire. Those are the positive aspects. The downside was in the pacing and Geoffrey Horne's underplaying of Joseph. Rapper, more so than Ricci, one suspects (Ricci was responsible for the brilliant *Alone Against Rome* which moved like a hurricane) seemed content to present us with a succession of static stage sets on which the actors came and went. There's little fluidity in the camerawork, leading to passages of near-inertness. As for Horne, he failed to capitalize on the promise he delivered to the public in *The Bridge on the River Kwai* (1957), becoming ever more morose and introverted as the film proceeded on its meandering course. He patently lacked the magnetism the role needed to carry the action, too restrained by far. What sexpot Lee ever saw in the sorrowful looking lad, heaven knows. After trying to seduce him in a steamy sauna interlude, she pounces on him during a feast; he backs off, she cries "Rape!" and he's sent back to work on the pyramid slave gangs. Morley, impotent, accidentally kills Lee in a struggle; unable to live without her, he sets fire to her boudoir, flaming embers providing instant cremation. Horne is restored to court, marries Vira Silenti (Asenath) and has to contend with crafty Arturo Dominici's ambitions; there's a war in which the enemy are defeated when a dam's floodgates are opened (a short, badly executed sequence) and famine strikes the land. At the end, Horne is reunited with his family, led by renowned Scottish thespian Finlay Currie (Jacob) and asks for his father's forgiveness, donning the by-now moth-eaten coat of many colors as a sign of repentance and releasing conniving brother Dante Di Paolo from the cells (Benjamin [Mario Girotti aka Terence Hill] was Joseph's only true brother, the rest having different mothers). *Joseph and His Brethren* looks the bee's knees in most instances (widescreen prints in Italian are knocking around the market) but is flatly handled and let down by a weak central performance. You would only want to sit through it once.

The Pharaohs' Woman [*La donna dei faraoni*] aka *The Princess of the Nile*

Vic/Faro Film (Italy); Techniscope/Technicolor; 87 mins; Producer: Giorgio Venturini; Director: Viktor Tourjansky ††††

"The little savage of the Nile who became Queen of Lower Egypt." Yes, from hitching a ride on a pharaoh's boat to placing her shapely butt on the throne at Bubastis, dark-haired screen goddess Linda Cristal (she played the title role in *The Legions of Cleopatra*) comes a very long way in a short space of time. Hard to lay hands on today, *The Pharaohs' Woman*, filmed

"The little savage of the Nile who became queen of Lower Egypt." Linda Cristal relaxes on the set of *The Pharaohs' Woman*.

An international poster for *Cleopatra's Daughter* (aka *The Tomb of the Kings*)

On the hour, a blistering six-minute battle is waged in the desert, the Assyrian vanguard falling into an ambush after collecting like greedy flies around a giant gold statue, caught like rats in a trap. The Bubastis army capitulates under the onslaught and Francioli's victorious warriors march on the city, sacking it. Barrymore receives an arrow while seated on his throne, the Theban pharaoh deciding to take Cristal, seated on *her* throne, as his personal slave. Later, in his field tent, Francioli confronts Cristal and Brice—the physician was apprehended attempting to make off with her to begin that new life. The pharaoh, livid at Brice's deception, lets them go, but on a spiteful condition; he dumps the lovers in the middle of the desert with no mounts, food or water, and, for good measure, Brice is laid low with an arrow wound. But hope is on the horizon in the form of a camel convoy; Cristal waves her arms frantically, shouting "We're saved," as the movie fades out, leaving us all wondering: Were they saved? We shall never know!

mainly in Egypt, perfectly captures through the use of dazzling color photography (Pier Ludovico Pavoni) the glare of those harsh Egyptian landscapes and the ostentatious costume designs of the period (1900 BC), a cut-price version of all those expensive Hollywood blockbusters but produced with real flair and pace. It's a treat for the eyes and ears (Giovanni Fusco's haunting, melodious title theme and incidental music packs a punch), while Cristal is gorgeousness personified as Akis, the ambitious dancer clawing her way up the ladder of success.

The girl first comes to notice on the banks of the Nile wearing a short yellow outfit, anxious to get away from her poverty-ridden existence by hailing a barge commanded by two pharaoh princes: Ramses, Prince of Thebes (Armando Francioli) and Sabuku, Prince of Bubastis (John Drew Barrymore). Pierre Brice is Amosis, Francioli's physician; it's he who dives in and prevents Cristal from becoming food for a crocodile. On board, the three men eye up her dripping wet curves and like what they see, gambling on who will bed her. All lose out, although it's as plain as daylight that Cristal has quickly set her sights on young Brice. In Bubastis, trouble flares between the two cousins. Notwithstanding the fact that Bubastis and Thebes have formed an uneasy pact to avoid war, Francioli refuses to put his differences aside; his chief objective is to become overall pharaoh of both provinces and wear the coveted crown of Lower Egypt, an idea violently opposed by the increasingly demented Barrymore, who kowtows to the Assyrian army in case of hostilities. More for her protection than anything else, Cristal is employed as a dancer in the city temple and is surrounded by a flock of catty, jealous lovelies. War breaks out after Francioli declares himself pharaoh following the sudden death of his father. His wife (Lilli Lembo) shunted to the sidelines, Barrymore, ever more insane, announces to his people that *he's* the new pharaoh, calls up the Assyrians and plans to confront his cousin's forces on the Plain of the Stone Lion. In the midst of all this turmoil, Brice departs from Thebes and heads for Bubastis, anxious to secrete Cristal away from Barrymore's dominance, thus enabling them to live peacefully together as man and wife.

The Tomb of the Kings [*Il sepolcro dei re*] aka ***Cleopatra's Daughter***; ***Daughter of Cleopatra***; ***The Tomb of the Pharaoh***
Explorer Film '58/Comptoir Francais CFPC (Italy/France); Ultrascope/Eastmancolor; 109 (100) mins; Producer: Giampaolo Bigazzi; Director: Fernando Cerchio ††††

Shila, Cleopatra's daughter by Marc Antony, has been raised in Assyria for 20 years following the death of her mother. To secure an alliance between Egypt and Assyria, it is ordered that the girl ("Daughter of a traitor") be wedded to Pharaoh Nemoret, who rules the land with his despotic mother, Tegi. Although the marriage goes ahead, Shila feels nothing but repugnance toward her mentally disturbed husband, recoiling at his touch ("You're as cold as marble," he cries, knocking her to the floor. "On your knees. I'm a god!"); it's no wonder that she falls for compassionate court physician Resi. When Nemoret is poisoned by ambitious courtier Kefren, Shila is blamed for his murder ("She's the one that killed me. Only words of hatred," he gasps with his dying breath) and incarcerated in a dungeon, to be buried alive with Nemoret's sarcophagus in the Tomb of the Kings at Cheops. Resi quickly concocts a cunning plan: Shila confesses to the crime, is placed into a death-like coma by swallowing a prepared potion and interred in a coffin ... but saved from eternal darkness by the physician (the tomb's architect) Inuni and a gang of tomb robbers. Kefren, revealed to be Nemoret's true killer, receives eight arrows in his torso on orders from Tegi, along with crooked tomb overseer Mana; Shila and Resi ride into the wilderness to begin a new life together.

Fernando Cerchio's slice of Egyptian hokum runs on similar lines to Warner Bros.' *Land of the Pharaohs* (1955), which cost $3,000,000. Cerchio's budget must have been a quarter of that sum but the result still looks like a million dollars and, out of the two, is marginally the better film. There's hardly any action, the movie centered on court subterfuge and intrigue, yet the sheer force of acting and the amazing art/set design and cinematography hold interest throughout. Debra Paget, of *The Ten*

A French poster for *Nefertiti, Queen of the Nile*

Commandments fame, emotes beautifully as Shila; Ettore Manni puts in one of his best performances as the love-struck physician out to rescue his beloved from a fate worse than death; Corrado Pani excels as the crazy young king cursed with schizophrenia (he played a similar part in *A Queen for Caesar*); Yvette Lebon's glacial Tegi resembles a black-attired witch, and behaves like one; Ivano Staccioli makes a sly tomb guardian; Pietro Caccarelli throws his bulk around as superintendent of the morgue ("I'm tired of slitting the bellies of dead bodies," he complains to Manni, offered a bribe to switch Paget with a real female corpse); Erno Crisa is suitably bombastic as the courtier/usurper to the Egyptian throne; and Robert Alda makes an engaging architect, forced to reveal the hidden pitfalls within the tomb and deciding to stay in his creation, sealed inside for all time. Set design, art direction and the multitude of costumes on show are faultless, an Egyptian tapestry unfolding before your very eyes, especially in the prolonged tomb scenes, Anchise Brizzi's gloriously rich color photography of a kind rarely encountered in today's digitally shot cinema. And Giovanni Fusco's score binds together each interlude in muted, tuneful tones.

Apart from Nemoret's grand burial ceremony, carried out to the sound of pounding drums, the 15-minute "breaking into the tomb" sequence is the film's highlight, one of peplum's most riveting and suspenseful moments. Manni, Alda (lashed and beaten, a sorry sight) and a team of treasure-hungry bandits force their way through rock walls and moveable slabs, while having to avoid concealed traps in order to gain entrance into Nemoret's burial chamber, a tension-racked spell where one false move means death. Once inside, Manni and Paget, reunited, make their escape into the outside world but Alda decides otherwise; he pulls on a rope to open the sarcophagus, setting off a succession of levers that bring the chamber crashing down on their heads, tons of sand, stone blocks, dust and rubble choking the passages, entombing those left inside. A mesmerizing chapter of events that contributes to a fabulous, enthralling picture produced during the genre's golden period, and another that needs an official release in widescreen to capture the splendor of it all.

1961

Nefertiti, Queen of the Nile [*Nefertite, regina del Nilo*] aka *Queen of the Nile*

Max Film (Italy); Supercinescope/Eastmancolor; 106 (98) mins; Producer: Ottavio Poggi; Director: Fernando Cerchio ††††

Americans Jeanne Crain and Vincent Price featured in Cerchio's slice of Ancient Theban hokum, as good as anything to have come out of the Hollywood studios in the 1950s, perhaps better in one aspect, that of the music—Carlo Rustichelli's beautifully evocative score rates as one of the finest from this noted Italian composer, and that's saying something. Lavish set and costume design was nigh on faultless, the Egyptian period ambience rounded off by Massimo Dallamano's plush color photography. As for the acting, leading man Edmund Purdom was upstaged by Price at every swish of the High Priest's robe: Price, as Benakon, was the real Queen of the Nile here, wearing enough eyeliner and beads to stock a beauty parlor and camping it up as only he could do, one of a select group of actors who was always worth the price of a ticket, whatever he starred in. Purdom's Tumos was similar to his physician character in Fox's *The Egyptian* (1954), only this time around he played a lowly sculptor caught up in a hopeless love situation with Price's daughter, Crain (first Tanit, then Queen Nefertiti), the girl betrothed to Pharaoh Amenophis IV (Amedeo Nazzari) counter to her wishes, but part of her destiny (Nazzari is also Purdom's friend). In a parallel storyline, Price, cohort Umberto Raho and their Amon Ra followers are dead set against a new religion being promoted by prophet Carlo D'Angelo to worship the God Aaton, endorsed by mentally unstable Nazzari. This leads to a religious war punctuated with outbreaks of violence and a final bloody confrontation in Thebes in which D'Angelo receives an arrow in the back, unhinged Nazzari commits suicide, harlot Liana Orfei murders Price and lovers Purdom and Crain are back in each other's arms, the camera closing on the famous bust of Nefertiti that Purdom sculpted.

Orfei, forever cast as a dark-haired seductress (and why not!), performed one of pepla's most daringly suggestive dance numbers in the confines of an army camp, successfully catching the eye of a drooling guard, thus enabling Purdom (whom she desires) to escape from his shackles. Crain looked stunning in Egyptian regal make-up. Price, as mentioned, dominated every scene he appeared in while Purdom, although energetic enough, was ever-so-slightly stilted, adding fuel to the suggestion that he never really fulfilled his true potential as a big-star attraction. Yes, he got offered a lot of juicy parts in his long career, but he failed to achieve the heights. He pales beside Price, but then, so would most actors of his generation. A feast for the senses (as was Cerchio's *The Tomb of the Kings*), *Nefertiti, Queen of the*

Sister and brother Pascale Petit (Queen Cleopatra) and Corrado Pani (Ptolemaio) sit on the throne of Egypt, each planning to oust the other, in a *A Queen for Caesar*.

Nile proved that whatever the Americans could do, in the heyday of peplum, the Italians could do just as well.

1962

A Queen for Caesar [*Una regina per Cesare*]

Filmes Cinematogrifica/Comptoir Francais CFPC (Italy/France); Euroscope/Eastmancolor; 100 (90) mins; Producers: Alberto Chimenz, Vico Pavoni, Giorgio Venturini; Directors: Piero Pierotti, Viktor Tourjansky ☥☥☥

It's a case of look but don't touch as 18-year-old Queen Cleopatra, played with oodles of dark allure by French actress Pascale Petit, uses her fabulous body to get her own way, rolled out of a Persian carpet to the astonishment of future lover Julius Caesar (Gordon Scott, who doesn't flex his pecs once in the picture) in the closing seconds (Fox's *Cleopatra* had this selfsame scene 19 minutes into their bank-busting four-hour epic). So the picture finishes at the very start of the infamous Cleopatra/Caesar relationship—what occurs up to then is a somewhat stilted production enlivened by Angelo Lotti's shimmering color and Petit's perky performance as the Egyptian minx, not averse to flashing her shapely thighs and enticing cleavage to achieve her goals.

"I'm the king and that throne is mine," pouts Petit's weakling brother Corrado Pani (Ptolemaio), as both he and his sister are crowned joint monarchs of Egypt. But straight off, Petit begins scheming to remove her petulant sibling from his throne, sucking up to Roman soldier Rik Battaglia (Lucio Settimo), poet Franco Volpi (Apollodoro) and loathsome Prime Minister Ennio Balbo (Theodoto). Rejecting Balbo's propositions and flung into prison, she's set free by guard George (Giorgio) Ardisson, the pair fleeing to Syria, just as Julius Caesar's battalions are amassing, waiting to do battle with rival commander Pompeio (veteran Akim Tamiroff hamming it up wonderfully). Throwing in her lot with Tamiroff, Petit promises a night of unbridled lust in exchange for a legion led by Battaglia to march on Alexandria and reinstate her as sole ruler. He falls asleep on the job, she pinches the battle orders and in the 60th minute the picture, up to then an Egyptian soap opera of sorts, turns a shade serious. The Romans enter Alexandria, Petit ousts her cowardly brother, sending him into exile, and Caesar's army overwhelms Tamiroff's divisions, the general murdered by treacherous Battaglia, who in turn is slain by love rival Ardisson in a swordfight. There follows a confrontation on the plains in which the Egyptians are wiped out ("Caesar is ruler of the world!"), Ardisson perishing on the battlefield. "A Queen for Caesar" announces a court ambassador, as Petit unfurls herself like a slinky cat on heat from the carpet in front of the drooling Roman commander ... and a legend is born. Juvenile and enjoyable, thanks to Petit putting her all into the role; she's no Elizabeth Taylor, but does well enough in this setup.

Sodom and Gomorrah [*Sodoma e Gomorra*] aka *The Last Days of Sodom and Gomorrah*

Titanus/Pathé/SGC (Italy/France/US); Technicolor; 154 mins; Producers: Goffredo Lombardo, Joseph E. Levine; Directors: Robert Aldrich, Sergio Leone (uncredited) ☥☥☥☥☥

Circa 2500 BC, the Hebrews, led by Lot, converge on the River Jordan near the twin cities of Sodom and Gomorrah. The Queen of Sodom, Bera, allows them to make their home on one side of the river ("Make this valley yours."), Lot issuing orders for his people not to enter the cities because of their iniquitous reputation. Lot marries Ildith, an ex-slave, and Astaroth, Prince of Sodom, ravishes his two daughters. The Hebrews' camp is attacked by the Helamites, a band of barbaric nomads, but a colossal flood caused by the bursting of a dam wipes out the tribe. Homeless, the Hebrews, against the wishes of the elders, take up residence in the fleshpots of Sodom, trading as salt merchants ("We will live in Sodom but apart from them."), eventually succumbing to the city's inherent wickedness and vice. In a duel over honor, Lot kills Astaroth, even though he's sprawled on the floor defenseless, realizing that by committing such an act, he has sunk to the sordid level of Sodom's infamous depravity. In a visitation by two wise old men, Lot is informed that Jehovah has decreed Sodom and Gomorrah be wiped off the face of the Earth and the Hebrews should leave forthwith; on no account should anyone look back. Lot takes his people away from the cities as they are engulfed in a cataclysm. On a ridge, Ildith, who steadfastly refuses to believe in the power of Jehovah, ignores the warnings and, staring in horror at the destruction, turns into a pillar of salt. Grief-stricken, Lot is comforted by his daughters, wandering into the desert wastes in search of a new Promised Land in which to settle.

Distributed worldwide by 20th Century Fox (J. Arthur Rank took over the U.K. rights, banking on Joseph E. Levine's prediction that the film would make a healthy profit), *Sodom and Gomorrah* was beset with production problems from the word go during its 18-month shoot in Morocco. Robert Aldrich, in contract disputes with Levine, walked off set at one stage, Sergio Leone directing some of the action sequences. Rocket-

Terrific art defines this Italian poster for *Sodom and Gomorrah*.

ing temperatures caused illnesses among the crew, particularly Rossana Podesta, who was laid off for several weeks, and Moroccan extras were called up by the army to help in the Algerian crisis. Costs also spiraled, from $1,000,000 to $5,000,000. Oscar-winner Miklos Rozsa, who had worked on a number of epics, including *Ben-Hur*, *King of Kings* and *El Cid*, replaced legendary Hollywood composer Dimitri Tiomkin; this was to be the last of Rozsa's epic scores. "Twin Cities of Sin and Unspeakable Wealth" screamed the posters and promotional ads when the movie hit U.K. circuits at the end of 1962, *Time* adding, "*Sodom and Gomorrah* is the first motion picture that ever tried to sell the story of sodomy to kiddies." But not in Britain! Viewing its content, which took in undisguised lesbianism, incest and sadistic cruelty, the British Board of Film Censors awarded the movie an "X" certificate, banning those "kiddies" from entering a cinema where it was being screened. Critics of the day were not kind to *Sodom and Gomorrah*, unfairly comparing it to more family-friendly Biblical blockbusters, not quite getting to grips with a predominantly Italian epic deemed suitable for an adult audience only. But ironically, it was *because* of that prohibitive rating that the film did brisk business in England, punters curious to find out what all the fuss was about; after all, *Ben-Hur* and others hadn't been classed as an "X"—why this one? At least the movie was screened in its original 154-minute length. On the Continent, it suffered savage cuts, down to 115 minutes in Norway and Denmark, whose cinematic tastes were more conservative than most.

Looked at 50 years on, *Sodom and Gomorrah* can be seen for what it is, or was, a meaty chunk of adult Biblical sword and sandal where the pace doesn't flag for an instant over two and a half hours. The cast is exceptional: Stewart Granger plays Lot as a God-fearing leader with attitude, not a weakling as so often is the case; British tough guy actor Stanley Baker (he was Achilles in *Helen of Troy*) stomps all over the set with menacing relish as skirt-chasing Astaroth, taking full advantage of Granger's two highly desirable daughters, Rossana Podesta and Claudia Mori, creating dissent among the ranks and getting all the best lines: "Leave me to my pleasure or die!" he barks at Granger when found *in flagrante delicto* with Podesta; Pier Angeli glows as Granger's wife, unable to believe in a god she cannot see; Anouk Aimée (Queen Bera) is like a viper on shapely legs, lusting after nubile female slaves and nibbling her brother Baker's fingers in a blatant display of incest ("It does no longer give you any pleasure?" she leers at him); and peplum regular Giacomo Rossi-Stuart makes the most of one of his few major roles as Ishmael, Granger's right-hand man. Peplum watchers will spot many familiar faces among the cast, including Rik Battaglia as Hebrew traitor Melchoir and Mimmo Palmara, a blind warrior wearing a deadly spiked breastplate. Unfortunately, those under-16s missed out on the main 15-minute set piece in which the Helamites, torching the Hebrew encampment, are deluged when Granger orders the dam his men are working on to be smashed, a thrilling sequence of events, one of the genre's finest. The momentous destruction of the twin cities (real Old Testament buildings of sun-baked clay and sandstone, not plush imperial palaces) by earthquake, tempest and fire is also well-executed, up there with the catastrophic upheavals depicted in *The Last Days of Pompeii* and *79 AD: The Destruction of Herculaneum*. There's no doubting the fact that a definite streak of perversion runs through *Sodom and Gomorrah*'s narrative flow. The tortures are more graphic, the dances more overtly lascivious, characters' hidden sexual agendas more openly conveyed. This gives the film a bite other major Hollywood Biblical actioners didn't possess, or didn't dare show because of adverse critical/audience reaction and possible loss of

A Spanish lobby card for *Jacob and Esau*

Mario Landi's excursion into Old Testament rivalries was given a far better, more expensive, treatment in *Jacob, The Man Who Fought With God* (see below), only Massimo Serato standing out as Ishmael; Edmund Hashim and Ken Clark are wooden in their roles of Jacob and Esau respectively. Glamour came in the form of Rossana Mace (Rachel) and Wandisa Guida (Judith), but in current ragged DVD prints, Anchise Brizzi's color photography is reduced to a faded blur in many sequences. Slow-moving and earnest, *Jacob and Esau* is not one of the worthier of the Biblical pepla, even though Carlo Savina's soundtrack tries its hardest to step the pace up a bit.

lucrative box-office returns. In this respect, *Sodom and Gomorrah* must be applauded for trying something different in portraying those bestial times as they actually existed. It has a breadth and sweep that sucks you into in its dark tale of sin, debauchery and violence, a one-off that pulls no punches and isn't afraid to lay its gaudy tackiness on the line.

1963

Jacob and Esau [*Giacobbe ed Esau*]

Arianne Film (Italy); Eastmancolor; 94 mins; Producers: Moraldo Rossi, Mario Landi; Director: Mario Landi ††

Twin brothers Jacob and Esau, the sons of Isaac and Rebecca, live in Beersheba. Jacob is the stronger-minded of the two, a ne'er-do-well out for his own interests, while Esau indulges in sporting activities. On learning of the exploits of their uncle Ishmael, a well-to-do wanderer, Esau decides to follow in his footsteps, eventually meeting with his uncle in the desert. Jacob then turns up like a bad penny, suspecting Esau of coveting their uncle's inheritance. The two siblings come to blows—Jacob, stealing Esau's birthright on the death of their father, flees to Haran to escape Esau's wrath, working seven years for his uncle Laban, where he marries Rachel and her sister Leah; Laban forces him to work another seven years for a pittance as part of an agreement. Jacob and his entourage finally make tracks for Canaan to take up residence on Esau's estates, but before the twins fight it out to the death, Ishmael intervenes, reconciling the two families to a life of peace.

Jacob, The Man Who Fought With God [*Giacobbe, l'uomo che lotto con Dio*] aka *The Patriarchs*

San Paolo Films (Italy); Techniscope/Technicolor; 122 mins; Producers: Toni Di Carlo, Agostino Ghilardi; Director: Marcello Baldi ††††

Before 1966's *The Bible: In the Beginning* ($18,000,000) and 2014's *Noah* ($125,000,000), there was 1963's *Jacob, The Man Who Fought With God* ($300,000). Yes, journeys through the Old Testament had been done before, on much lower budgets. Marcello Baldi's potted version of the Book of Genesis, long consigned to cinematic obscurity, is an object lesson in how to conjure up a mini-Biblical epic on medium funds and pull it off. Beginning with a five-minute narration on how God created the Heaven and the Earth, the Vatican's famous ceiling paintings (Raffaele's Bible) used to add to the description, we first have Adam and Eve's two offspring at loggerheads, blond innocent Abel bashed to death with a rock by jealous Neanderthal Cain. "What have you done?" roars God from above. "You shall be a fugitive, a wanderer over the Earth."

An Italian photobusta in the form of an open book for *Jacob, The Man Who Fought with God*

The Italian Peplum Phenomenon 1950-1967

Brad Harris (right) rides a chariot in *The Old Testament*.

The Noah's Ark/flood sequence is next, the best and longest in the picture (excellent special effects here), God deciding to wipe out the wicked human race except for a few deserving souls and their animals. The deluge's survivors erect the Tower of Babel, are scattered far and wide to procreate, and eventually God's chosen leader, Abraham (Fosco Giachetti), takes his people, after many incidents (including the destruction of Sodom and Gomorrah) throughout Hanan, Canaan and Egypt to the fertile Promised Land. God orders Abraham to climb a mountain and sacrifice Isaac, his infant son, as a burnt offering: Abraham is stayed at the last moment from committing the deed (another test of the wise man's beliefs) and Isaac grows into adulthood, begetting two sons, Esau and Jacob, who don't see eye-to-eye.

Up to this stage of the proceedings, Baldi's Old Testament essay commendably cuts down on the sermonizing, preaching and reverence usually associated with movies of this type, going all-out instead for pictorial splendor. Marcello Masciocchi's crystal clear cinematography is diamond-hard, outlining in sharp relief those arid Middle Eastern wilderness location shots (and giving prominence to the hundreds of authentic costumes), while joint composers Teo Usuelli and Gino Marinuzzi, Jr.'s symphonic score thunders in the background, kettle drums to the fore in announcing God's presence and bolstering the action scenes. The remaining 50 minutes concentrate on the precarious Jacob-Esau relationship and flounders in parts. The brothers split after Jacob (Giorgio Cerioni) steals Esau's birthright; Jacob goes to work for his conniving uncle, Laban, and marries two of his daughters, Rachel, the pretty one (Judy Parker), and Leah, the ugly one (Luisa Della Noce). Producing 12 children, Jacob falls out with Laban after years of toiling for him and, with his family and entourage, heads off, like Abraham of yore, for Canaan. To prove his undying faith, Jacob has to fight an indestructible stranger (God in human guise) and old enmities are put aside with Esau in the final reel. Each has learned the error of their ways and ready to bow to God's will; Jacob, now a divine prophet, leads his people into Canaan to at last settle in peace.

Steer clear of the German release entitled *Noah's Ark*; 38 minutes were edited from the original to produce a truncated concoction concentrating on the lengthy Ark sequence, and little else. The full-length version can be located on European sites as a download, in immaculate condition, the only way to view a lost Biblical minor masterpiece that is a whole lot more enjoyable than those three-hour plus elephantine epics that sprang from the Hollywood studios around this time.

The Old Testament [*Il vecchio testamento*]

CI.AS./Comptoir Francais CFFP (Italy/France); Supertotalscope/Eastmancolor; 112 (88) mins; Producers: Mario Maggi, Mario Damiani; Director: Gianfranco Parolini ✝✝✝

Or, to be more precise, events taken from the First and Second Books of the Maccabees, whose leaders staged a rebellion against the Seleucid dynasty, circa 150 BC. Hebrew Jews commanded by Djordje Nenadovic (as Judas Maccabaeus) clash with their Syrian masters in Jerusalem, flee into the desert wastes and eventually return to the city, triumphing over Jacques Berthier's (Apollonio) warriors and regaining Jerusalem as their own. That's the basic plot in a nutshell. *The Old Testament* may be historically suspect and riddled with inaccuracies, but that doesn't stop it from being a fast-moving Biblical feature that's well-suited to action fans, commencing with a violent 15-minute clash when priest Carlo Tamberlani attempts to stop Syrian soldiers from hauling a bulky statue of Zeus into his sacred temple. The Hebrews overwhelmed, Nenadovic takes them into the desert where they fall prey to repeated Syrian raids, prisoners whipped and massacred on the spot, many buried up to their shoulders, much to the delight of the wheeling hawks. Tamberlani expires on a makeshift cross and Nenadovic falls in battle, leaving Brad Harris (Simone) and Enzo Doria (Gionata) to take charge. Doria is also crucified; Harris and his men charge into the city just as Mara Lane, Harris' love interest, is about to be hanged for treason. Harris and adversary Berthier fight to the death on the scaffold, the Syrian chieftain receiving an arrow through his neck before he can deliver the *coup de grace* to Harris. The enemy defeated, Hebrew crowds march through the city rejoicing, Lane on Harris' arm, Syrian soldiers, instead of Jews, strung up on an avenue of crosses.

Current DVD/VHS issues are of lamentable image quality—pan and scan ruins the once-spectacular Supertotalscope format, color rendition is muddy and 24 minutes of edited footage means that players in minor roles such as Franca Parisi, Brigitte Corey (aka Luisella Boni), José Greci (billed as Susan Paget) and Alan Steel don't get a look-in. Unusually for a peplum movie, there are hardly any female goodies on display, only Lane simpering dewy-eyed over Harris' masculine (but wooden) charms. Best actor awards go to Berthier, a black-clad viper of the first order, and his roly-poly sidekick Vladimir Leib, who ends up the victim of a dozen sword thrusts. The set design of Old Jerusalem and Berthier's palace is fantastic, and once in a while, Francesco Izzarelli's superb color photography peeps through the murk, showing us how this neglected film must have

Would you allow this man to command your legions? Toto (alias Marc Antony) does just that in *Toto and Cleopatra*.

looked in a theater 50 years ago. Angelo Francesco Lavagnino provides a fine choral soundtrack to a pacey picture that isn't quite as awful as some people assert; a presentable widescreen print would perhaps cause those doubters to think again.

Toto and Cleopatra [*Toto e Cleopatra*]

Liber Film (Italy); Totalscope/Eastmancolor; 95 mins; Producer: Ottavio Scotti; Director: Fernando Cerchio ††

Toto was 65 when he starred in what must rank as the most expensive comedy spoof of all time, taking on the dual roles of Marc Antony and slave trader Totonno, strangely resembling in some shots a shorter, older version of Robert De Niro. Carlo Rustichelli's score mirrored the movie's erratic narrative—semi-serious one minute, vaudeville farce the next, even resorting to a soft-shoe shuffle when Cleopatra (Magali Noel) emerges from a giant clamshell in a burst of opalescent greens and reds. The Egyptian palace set design was superb, the same going for Alvaro Mancori's gorgeous cinematography, but was all this extravagance and money wasted on a farce such as this?

A flimsier than flimsy plot had the funnyman, as slave trader Totonno, infiltrating Cleopatra's court (where Marc Antony resides) and making a fool of himself via a number of sight gags, while outside, in the real world, war waged between Egypt and Rome. It's fairly mirthful fodder, even to non-Italians. Toto has a look-alike centurion buddy with the same big, crooked nose (Carlo Delle Piane) and he winds up with a goldfish bowl (complete with fish) stuck on his head, thrown by Noel. He actually kisses the queen in the 53rd minute (a chaste peck on the lips), sits on his bed with an orange hot water bottle and fends off the advances of a gay senator *and* two gay gladiators. But after an hour, the movie runs out of steam and falls flat on its face, Toto wandering from one ornately furnished room to another, his soldierly Marc Antony morphing into stupid Totonno and back again, thereby confusing every court official with his contradictory behavior. Moira Orfei (Octavia) and Lia Zoppelli (Fulvia) flit in and out, looking decorative if nothing else, and the comedian takes on celluloid's classic mirror sight gag, previously performed to utmost perfection by Groucho Marx (*Duck Soup*, 1933) and Bob Hope (*The Princess and the Pirate*, 1944). Battles are tagged on at the beginning and end, but this footage originates from other productions; it's highly unlikely that Cerchio and his team would have gone to all the time, expense and trouble of staging their own battle scenes in what was, after all, an extended comedy routine. Once really is enough for *Toto and Cleopatra*. Britain's *Carry On Cleo* (1964), made in a matter of weeks for a fraction of the cost, lampooned the whole Cleopatra shebang so much better and was funnier to boot, as witnessed by Kenneth Williams' (Julius Caesar) classic laugh-out-loud closing line when he's assassinated: "Infamy … Infamy … They've all got it in for me!"

1964

Saul and David [*Saul e David*]

San Paolo Films/San Pablo Films (Italy/Spain); Techniscope/Eastmancolor; 118 (109) mins; Producers: Emilio Cordero, Toni Di Carlo; Director: Marcello Baldi †††

Marcello Baldi's scholastic essay into the thorny relationship between King Saul (Norman Wooland) and David (Gianni Garko), circa 1100 BC, is okay fare for those into reading up on the Old Testament; others may find it overstretched to the point of tedium and too talkative. Following a lengthy discus-

A Spanish lobby card for *Saul and David*

A Spanish lobby card for *Son of Cleopatra*

Son of Cleopatra [*Il figlio di Cleopatra*]
Seven Film/Copro Film (Italy/Egypt); Techniscope/Technicolor; 128 (116) mins; Producer: Francesco Thellung; Director: Ferdinando Baldi
††††

American actor Mark Damon (*The Fall of the House of Usher*, 1960) was recruited to star as El Kabir, The Phantom of the Desert, in a joint Italian/Egyptian production high on thrills, spills and incident, boosted by a sterling cast of peplum regulars. The Egyptians and desert tribes are under the yoke of tribune Livio Lorenzon (Petronio), a snarling ruffian disobeying the edict of Emperor Octavian by persecuting the local populace (Alberto Lupo, famous as the mad surgeon in 1960's *Seddok, Son of Satan*, played Octavian). Opening with a mass flogging, broken up by Damon and his camel-mounted warriors, the plot-heavy action moves swiftly backwards and forwards from Lorenzon's scheming in Alexandria to Damon's determination in the sandy wastes to rid the region of all Romans. "Whose blood is in my veins?" asks Damon to the man who has reared him from birth. It's none other than Cleopatra's; Damon is the product of a liaison between the legendary Egyptian queen and Caesar, a secret kept all these years. As a scroll written by Caesar states that the people of Egypt have the right to rise up against oppression and slavery, Damon is even more resolved to drive the Romans back to Alexandria, especially when his brother, Hassan Youssef (Uro), is captured, tortured and murdered by Lorenzon's thuggish henchman, Mahmoud Farag. But Damon hasn't reckoned on falling for Scilla Gabel (Civia), Lorenzon's golden-haired daughter, when she's taken hostage by his troops, even though he's got a girl (Samira Ahmed) waiting in the wings. Which side will Gabel take in this battle of two nations, now that she's rather taken with hunky Damon herself?

Son of Cleopatra boasts a storming soundtrack by Carlo Rustichelli, responsible for scoring 34 sword and sandal/*cappa e spada* sagas between 1958 and 1965, while Adalberto "Bitto" Albertini's sharp photography brings to life those arid desert landscapes. Director Baldi piles on the torture with relish: 20 villagers are rounded up by legionnaires, their right hands chopped off, their daughters tied to stakes, at the mercy of chariots with axle blades, set in the pictorial splendor of Egypt's Valley of the Kings; and Damon, after refusing to kill best pal Shukry Sarhan (Akro) in a grudge match fought with double-bladed war axes, is graphically whiplashed by horsemen as penance. Two-timing Commander Paolo Gozlino (Furio), ordered by Lupo to check up on Lorenzon's avarice and shady activities, sides with the tribune, anxious to win Gabel's hand in marriage and the handsome dowry in gold coinage that goes with it. When Lupo decides to pay Alexandria a personal visit to find out what the oily governor is up to, Gozlino, on information supplied by a spy, falls upon Damon and his Lycinian allies at the oasis of Soutra—the rebel leader's head on a plate will appease Lupo's wrath and send him back to Rome a contented man. A robustly mounted finale sees Sarhan's hordes coming to the rescue of Damon; Gozlino is suffocated in the dirt by Damon (another gruesome scene) after throwing a knife into the back of Ahmed. At Lupo's camp, merchant Arnoldo Foà has wised up the em-

sion between Saul and Samuel (Carlos Casaravilla), in which Casaravilla tells the king that Israel is lost because of his disobedience to Jehovah, David and Goliath's legendary showdown is done and dusted after 21 minutes, the Philistines riding off in terror as Goliath's decapitated head is held high on a pole; young blond harpist David (Marco Paoloetti) becomes an instant hero and taken into Wooland's court, treated like one of his own sons. Years later, Garko (now the adult David) is the subject of court jealousy. Wooland's wife, Elisa Cegani (Akhinoam), is afraid that Garko will ascend the throne ahead of her own flesh and blood, Antonio Mayans (Jonathan), and spreads malicious gossip, hinting that Garko is plotting to usurp the king's seat of power. An assassination attempt on Garko by Virgilio Teixeira, Wooland's evil-hearted cousin Abner, fails—injured, he takes flight into the mountains, falling in with a band of thieves hiding out in caves. Wooland, increasingly verging on paranoia, slays 50 priests accused of siding with Garko (shot by arrows, one by one, a barbaric sequence), the act provoking an unofficial war between the Israelites and Garko's Philistine forces. The final battle at Mount Gilboa, magnificently staged over eight pulsating minutes, sees Wooland's Israelites defeated—mortally wounded, the king falls on his own sword after his servant refuses to finish him off, nominating Garko as his successor with his dying breath. Garko, victorious but downcast at the death of his old friend, becomes the new Israelite king.

A realistic telling of the decline of tormented King Saul and the rise of shepherd boy David, shot in desert regions, Baldi's dusty effort is an overlong, slackly directed and ultimately uninspiring Biblical drama, Wooland and Garko struggling to inject the necessary bravura into their roles. The climactic battle, though, is a humdinger, the director's camerawork at long last bursting into life, Wooland scything through ranks of soldiers on his bladed chariot until brought down with an arrow. A meatier score would have boosted the narrative; Teo Usuelli's theme music is fine, but then goes off the boil, much like the film does until that lively closing 10 minutes.

1965

The Great Leaders [*I grandi condottieri*]
aka **Gideon and Samson**

San Paolo Films/San Pablo Films (Italy/Spain);Techniscope/Eastmancolor; 101 mins; Producers: Emilio Cordero, Toni Di Carlo; Directors: Marcello Baldi, Francisco Pérez-Dolz ††

An Italian poster for *The Great Leaders*

A double bill within one picture—the first 50 minutes deals with Gideon's rise from humble farmer to leader of the oppressed Israelites, fighting neighboring warlike tribes in tandem with an archangel; the second is a potted version of the Samson and Delilah fable. Both stories are taken from chapters 6-8, and 13-16 of the Book of Judges.

Virtually the same team behind two other Biblical pepla of this period, *Jacob, The Man Who Fought With God* and *Saul and David*, concocted these simplified accounts of Old Testament events, filmed without too much in the way of frills, fine as a history lesson for the kids, but not so fine for others. The Gideon section has Ivo Garrani in the title role, spurred on by angel Fernando Rey to take up arms against the Midianites and Amalekites, his argumentative son (Giorgio Cerioni) and wife (Maruchi Fresno) dismayed over the brutal tactics employed in bringing their enemies to heel. To save face in front of his own people, Garrani is forced to behead the leaders of the two warring factions and share out their riches. Filmed largely outdoors in desert wastes, the 50 minutes shoots by, a couple of lightweight battles (one at night) quickening the pace in between Garrani's soul-searching diatribes with his family.

Section two was shot on stage sets, six-foot-six-inch Dutch television actor Anton Geesink playing Samson; Rosalba Neri was Delilah and veteran Spanish actress Ana Maria Noé starred as Samson's mother. Neri was her usual ravishing self

peror on Lorenzon's misdeeds; when the disgraced tribune goes to knife Lupo in the back, he receives three arrows piercing *his* back, ending his evil reign. The two armies face one another, as Damon rides into the Roman encampment and greets Lupo with the revelation that they are half-brothers, sharing the same father in Caesar. Peace is declared on this startling knowledge. ("There's only room for one son of Caesar.") "He belongs to the desert," states Lupo, as Damon gallops off into the shimmering wilderness with Gabel. "All I can offer you is the desert," El Kabir says to her, knowing full well that from the look in her eyes, Gabel will be offering him a lot more when they next pitch tent!

as the preening temptress, exuding buckets of sex appeal, while Noé put in a touching performance as Samson's elderly, distraught mother. Geesink's Samson resembled a shaggy-haired, shambling ape, not having the muscle-packed physique of your average peplum beefcake hero, although he brought some nuance to his scenes, especially when rendered blind and helpless after his locks have been shorn. The "pulling down the Temple of Dagon" sequence was excellently handled, considering the film's modest budget, but *not* in the Cecil B. DeMille class. Like section one, section two is all over in the blink of an eye. A curious, drab-looking pseudo-Biblical semi-epic is only worth viewing for its curiosity value, and not for any filmic qualities, which, by and large, are absent, the exception being Teo Usuelli's reverberating score.

12
Ancient Rome

On home ground as it were, Ancient Rome is one arena where the most traditional of pepla values outside of the *Hercules* and *Maciste* features can be discovered. The very finest endeavors of the genre's foremost directors, actors, composers, cinematographers and technicians hallmark the likes of *Messalina Venus Empress*, *Alone Against Rome*, *Salammbo*, *The Son of Spartacus*, *Romulus and Remus*, *Brennus Enemy of Rome*, *Constantine the Great*, *Amazons of Rome*, *Duel of the Champions*, *The Fall of Rome*, *The Giants of Rome*, *Slave of Rome*, *The Revenge of Spartacus*, *Revolt of the Praetorians*, *The Three Centurions*, *Revolt of the Slaves*, even *Julius Caesar Against the Pirates* … a roll call of classics, a fantastic body of near-flawless cinematic work largely neglected in these days of once seen but quickly forgotten fodder aimed at the video generation. For lovers of rich, not particularly deep, but *deeply* rewarding action sword and sandal cinema set around the time of Christ, look no further than the 31 titles listed in the following pages. Overall, you will not be disappointed.

1960

Carthage in Flames [***Cartagine in fiamme***]

Lux Film/Produzione Gallone (Italy/France); Super Technirama 70/Technicolor; 110 (93) mins; Producers: Guido Luzzatto, Marino Vacca; Director: Carmine Gallone ††

It may be shot in Super Technirama 70, have superlative (and expensive) production values and boast a full-blooded Mario Nascimbene soundtrack, but the fact remains that *Carthage in Flames* is labored to a level of annoying tedium for much of its running length. Director Gallone's camera remains rooted to the spot, content to dwell studiously on those amazing sets in a string of stately long-takes, simply allowing his characters to wander into shot, mouthing their lines. This approach worked a treat in the director's 1951 production of *Messalina*, but here, in what is supposed to be an action/disaster movie, it doesn't. Basically a love triangle with a villain on the sidelines, we have to wait 103 minutes before the tragic conflagration that reduced Carthage to ashes and cinders in 146 BC during the Third Punic War. The city's final hours is thrillingly executed; what a shame that the remainder of the picture couldn't match it for edge-of-the-seat excitement.

Washed ashore injured on a riverbank, exiled soldier Hiram (José Suarez) is cared for by the serene Ilaria Occhini, as Ophir (a sequence related in flashback), who loses her heart to him; in Carthage, under siege from the Roman army, sultry Fulvia (Anne Heywood) is rescued from sacrificial slaughter by Suarez and *she* falls in love with her gallant savior. Enraged at this sacrilegious act, forum badman Daniel Gélin (Phegor) pursues the pair in a war galley as they sail off in Aldo Silvani's ship. A fairly invigorating collision of crafts ensues, Gélin's vessel set on fire during the encounter. Back in Carthage, Suarez is alarmed to find Occhini about to be wed to young warrior Maro Girotti (Tsour; the actor was soon to star in a run of Spaghetti Westerns as Terence Hill). Bursting in on the ceremony, he grabs his beloved, Gélin nabs Heywood and slobbers all over her, Suarez *again* rescues Heywood, *again* boards the ship and is eventually, on his second return to the city, beaten unconscious and held captive in a dungeon.

It all borders on soap opera and the pace is leaden. To save Suarez's hide, Heywood gives in to Gélin's sexual demands; the soldier, now a free man, informs the grand forum that he will lead the army against the encroaching Romans. Girotti has a change of heart, agreeing to accompany his love rival Suarez on the battlefield. In the 84th minute, the two armies meet and at last we have a piece of action to sink our teeth into, although there are far better battle scenes to be had elsewhere within the pepla sphere. Suarez is wounded, Girotti dies and the Carthaginians turn tail in tatters, the Romans having won a decisive victory. As the enemy force nears the city walls, the director throws in a further dose of unnecessary plotting by Gélin who, losing his temper, stabs senior statesman Pierre Brasseur (Sidone) to death. Carrying brands, the Romans enter Carthage, torching buildings: Blazing roof beams crash over the screaming populace, villas and houses topple and lovers Gélin and Heywood perish in the inferno, the floor giving way beneath their feet as the imperial palace crumbles to rubble. On their ship, far out at sea, Suarez and Occhini gaze upon the flames lighting up the night sky, sailing away to an uncertain future.

Stagy and bogged down in sequences that have little movement, *Carthage in Flames* climaxes in spectacular style but by then, the game is up on this good-to-look-at but ultimately uninspiring epic—even English beauty Heywood manages to look tired and unglamorous for most of the time, a true waste of the actress' sex-charged virtuosity.

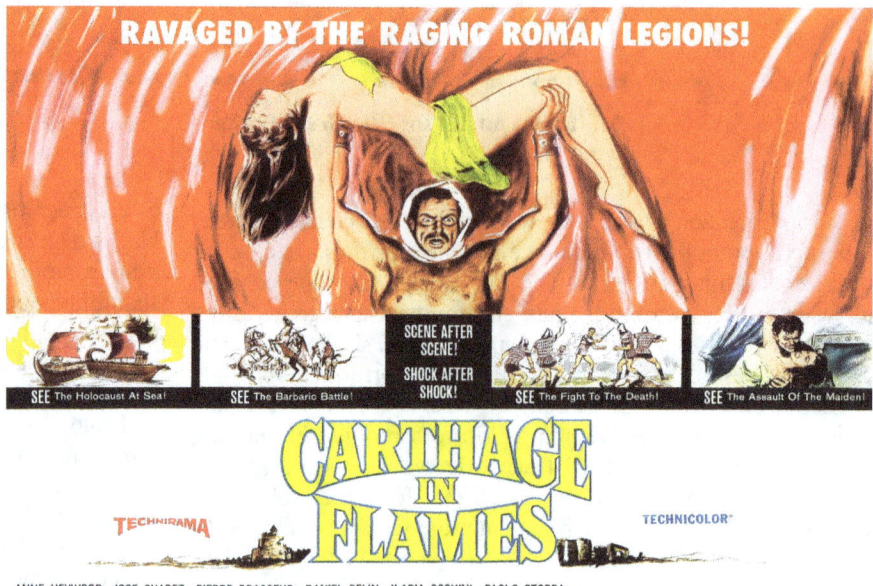

186   Heroes Never Die!

A Spanish poster for *Messalina Venus Empress*

Messalina Venus Empress [*Messalina venere imperatrice*] aka ***Messalina***

Cineproduzione Emo Bistolfi (Italy); Technirama/Technicolor; 96 (84) mins; Producer: Emo Bistolfi; Director: Vittorio Cottafavi ✞✞✞✞✞

This is a peplum movie for adults. Severely cut in Germany and France, Belinda Lee's third stab at playing a historical badass female would have received an "X" certificate if released in the United Kingdom. The calculating harlot, who became Emperor Claudius' third wife in 38 AD, shows no compunction whatsoever in stripping off to seduce anyone who takes her fancy, poisoning, stabbing and decapitating a lover (Giuliano Gemma) after a one-night stand, serving up his head on a platter, taking a would-be assassin between the sheets who's then dispatched by her guards and poisoning another (Carlo Giustini) who longs to caress that magnificent figure. Director Cottafavi dares to allow us a glimpse, through gossamer-thin drapes, of Lee stepping full-frontal nude out of a bath, opening her bathrobe to display her wares and shedding her top to stand naked; a hint of homosexuality, a senator and his young male boyfriend stroking each other's faces; a blood-drenched body sprawled on the floor, the throat gruesomely cut; several suggestive dance routines; graphic torture on a woman by poker; orgies; and the final mass slaughter at a banquet, bloody corpses draped over finery among the food and drink, is like a scene from Dante's Inferno. Yes, heady stuff, topped off by a magnificent battle sequence in which the praetorian guard, sent to eliminate Claudius on orders from his wife, are massacred to a man by the palace troops, their bodies clogging up the Monte Gelato falls. Presented in Marco Scarpelli's gorgeous color and Angelo Francesco Lavagnino's Roman military score, and further blessed with superlative set design, *Messalina Venus Empress* is peplum at its very highest level; thankfully, decent-quality DVD issues are available, a rarity in itself within the genre, to enable fans to wallow in 96 minutes of unadulterated Shakespearean-type Ancient Roman tragedy, with Lee at her bewitching best.

Caligula is dead—Claudius is crowned the new emperor at a spectacular coronation ceremony. In the Garden of Vesta, lined with statues, Valeria (Lee) meets tribune Spiros Focas (Lucio) and as quick as a flash, she's let her red locks tumble enticingly over her shoulders and taken off her white robe to roll on the ground with her handsome young lover ("Careful," she tells him, enticingly. "You'll tear my peplum."). In fact, Focos turns out to be about the only male that survives Lee's predatory urges; everyone else winds up dead. Firmly ensconced as Claudius' third wife (Marcello Giorda is the benign ruler), Lee, now called Messalina, rules the roost, her name proclaimed in the streets. But her cruel nature manifests itself in pressurizing the population to quit their homes and sell their hard-worked land for profit—her profit. The picture concentrates on Lee's manipulative way with men, her need to be "kissed and loved," Giulio Donnini, prissy court advisor Narciso, escaping her wrath by remaining loyal to the end. Focas, returning after a three-year campaign in Armenia, finds to his consternation that sweet vestal virgin Valeria is now domineering Empress Messalina, but that still doesn't prevent him loving her throughout all the intrigue and sex-induced murders. When the empress is stabbed to death at the climax in that horrific banquet bloodbath, gasping with her dying breath to Focas, "I loved only you," the tribune forgives her numerous crimes, shouting, "At this price, it would be better for Rome to die," his response to the cry of, "She had to die because Rome must live." He leaves Rome in the closing frame, hitching up with Christian Ida Galli (aka Evelyn Stewart) and her brethren, who are heading for pastures new, away from the debauchery of Rome. Without doubt, Lee's finest hour in an Italian peplum epic that, over 50 years on, still remains a feast for the eyes.

Revolt of the Slaves [*La rivolta degli schiavi*]

Ambrosiana/CB Film/Ultra Film (Italy/Spain/West Germany); Techniscope/Eastmancolor; 102 (90) mins; Producer: Paolo Moffa; Director: Nunzio Malasomma ✞✞✞✞

Film trivia: American screen goddess Rhonda Fleming, 37 at the time of filming, got wed to husband number three, 30-year-old Canadian-American Lang Jeffries, during the shoot (the marriage lasted two years); composer Angelo Francesco Lavagnino scored the British monster movie *Gorgo* in 1961; Jeffries' painful-to-watch full-frontal flogging ranks number two in Alvin Easter's *Lash! The Hundred Great Scenes of Men Being Whipped in the Movies*; Jeffries was whipped from behind in *Alone Against Rome*, making him one of a select bunch of peplum actors to get a tanning on both sides; and 32-year-old French crooner Serge Gainsbourg, playing inhuman police officer Corvino, unfortunately bore a strong resemblance to Alfred E. Neuman of *MAD* magazine fame. Overtly violent, *Revolt of the Slaves* was an opulently mounted Romans versus Christians yarn, a loose remake of 1949's *Fabiola* that chucked everything possible into the mix (the set design is fabulous), coming up with, of its type, a genuinely exciting, eye-catching platter of Ancient Roman hokum.

A French poster for *Revolt of the Slaves*

In the first few minutes, a disruptive slave has both hands cut off, thereby setting the movie's vicious tone; Jeffries (Vibio), thrashing the guards with his chains, nearly meets a similar fate but is bought by wealthy Gino Cervi (Fabio) and taken into his household as a slave. Daughter Fleming (a little too old for the part of Fabiola) orders Jeffries to be flogged after he declines to fight the court champion ("I want this coward lashed!"); afterwards, she perceives him in a different light, the man of her dreams. There's a lavish feast (to introduce leading members of the cast) and then Christianity raises its vexatious head. Fleming's cousin, pious-looking Wandisa Guida (Agnese), turns out to be a Christian, as does her beau, tribune Ettore Manni (San Sebastiano) *and* Jeffries; soon, power-mad Gainsbourg, looking like an overgrown schoolboy in Roman uniform (he keeps a pit full of ravenous dogs to dispose of his enemies), is engaged on a witch-hunt, the persecuted god-worshippers taking cover in the catacombs.

Along the way, Fleming gets into a torrid clinch with Jeffries, unsure of her true feelings toward this anti-Roman religion; she quickly changes her mind when Emperor Massimiano (Dario Moreno, spotty and plagued with a nervous itch) kills her father, cremating the body to hide any incriminating evidence and ransacking his estate. The Christians, including Guida, are rounded up and incarcerated in a dungeon ("If the Christians renounce their faith, they will be spared," announces Moreno); Jeffries and cohort Burt Nelson lever loose a stone, the river gushes in (one slave, chained to the wall, drowns after being baptized) and they take to their heels. Manni is the next to undergo a nasty end, roped to a tree and peppered with arrows; bleeding from his wounds, he staggers into Moreno's court and denounces him, only for Gainsbourg to plunge a sword into his guts. Mass oppression follows, the Christian dwellings burned, the occupants herded into the arena basement in preparation for the forthcoming circus. It's here that Gainsbourg meets his thoroughly deserved comeuppance, torn to ribbons by ferocious guard dogs. The games commence: Horsemen bearing lances, slaves whipping one another, the loser falling into flames and Christians burned on the cross, also having to run a gauntlet to avoid a javelin in the back. Most expire, including Guida. Meanwhile, Jeffries and his group have worked their way through a labyrinth of passages, emerging into the gladiator's basement; entering the arena, they overcome the men-at-arms but are cornered. On howls from the crowd and the praetorian guard, loyal to their murdered commander Servi, Morena, scratching like crazy, gives the thumbs up sign for Jeffries and the Christians to go free, which they do, marching toward camera and the fadeout to a satisfactory, all-action sword and sandal opus. The only minus points are a surprising lack of screen chemistry between Fleming and Jeffries, odd when you consider their offset romance, and the cloying nature of some aspects relating to the holier-than-thou religious preaching sequences held in the catacombs.

Salammbo [*Salambo*] aka *The Loves of Salammbo*
Stella Film/Fides Film (Italy/France); Totalscope/Eastmancolor; 110 (72) mins; Producer: Luigi Nannerini; Director: Sergio Grieco ††††

In the 3rd century BC, following the First Punic War, Carthage employs gangs of mercenaries to fight the legions of Rome, but when those mercenaries are not paid for five long years, heads roll—literally. Galloping past the city walls, hundreds of angry warriors show their displeasure by tossing poles adorned with severed heads into the dust. Black-clad chancellor Edmund Purdom (Narr Havas) gets the message loud and clear, opting to raid the Temple of Tanit for its gold and deliver the booty to the barbarians (as he terms them), camped 30 leagues from Carthage, as payment. High Priestess Jeanne Valérie (Salammbo) reluctantly agrees, unaware that Purdom, in his lust for power (and for her), plans to detain the shipment, fill the chests with rocks, have the gold returned to Carthage, murder everyone associated with the ruse and keep the riches for himself. When Purdom's scam is uncovered by the mercenaries, enraged commander Jacques Sernas (as Mathos, sporting a freakish headpiece) has a blue fit, crucifies five Carthaginian captives on the spot and declares war, first deciding to reconnoiter the palace, not only to gain inside information but to steal the sacred Veil of the Goddess Tanit, a religious artefact of huge significance to the people of Carthage; here, he meets Valérie in her bedchamber and the two fall in love, even though, by grabbing the blue glittering cloth, she has accused him of sacrilege. One kiss from those manly lips is enough for any girl to forget who she is, and whom she serves.

As at the time of writing (2015), *Salammbo*, adapted from Gustave Flaubert's 1862 novelette, is available in two versions: a dubbed, heavily cut, rough-looking 72-minute edit in widescreen; and a 94-minute edit in Italian, the color crisp and bright. The full-length original appears to be lost. To highlight the difference: Grieco's splendidly staged, sweeping battle sequence, mostly filmed in longshot on the open plains, begins at

Purdom, dressed to the nines, scowled wonderfully, peplum favorite Andrea Aureli could be glimpsed on occasions and Riccardo Garrone dominated, playing Valérie's warlord father who, at the end, takes over as Carthage's head of state and prevents Sernas, broken but unbowed, from being stoned to death because of his daughter's passion for him ("Kill me also. I love him."). Purdom is beaten and stoned, his bloody corpse dragged away in chains, a brutal sequence. Piero Portalupi's bright photography is bang up to "10 out of 10" pepla high standards, while Alexandre Derevitsky's ultra-loud military score is a little over-eager at times; the composer even throws in a piano leitmotif when Sernas, in the midst of battle, clambers over a rock and takes on two assassins. In a way, *Salammbo* is a one-off, steering clear of the usual peplum clichés, combining incident, court maneuvers, battles, palace clashes and potent romance, sprinkled with liberal doses of corn against a backdrop of magnificent set design and strong characters played to the hilt by an equally strong cast. Best line of the film? "Being in love makes you think you're invincible," spoken to Sernas by disgruntled Raf Baldassarre. Many would agree with that!

Siege of Syracuse [*L'assedio di Siracusa*] aka *Archimedes*

Glomer Film/Galatea Film/Lyre (Italy/France); Dyaliscope/Eastmancolor; 118 (97) mins; Producer: Enzo Merolle; Director: Pietro Francisci †††

Set during the Second Punic War (218-201 BC) at a period when mighty Rome was on a mission to conquer Carthage, *Siege of Syracuse* is glorious to watch, with fabulous sets photographed in pastel shades by Carlo Carlini and a beautiful, melodious score from Angelo Francesco Lavagnino. Action fans will be left disheartened in what is basically a romantic drama between the great mathematician and inventor, Archimedes, and the two women in his life: Clio, daughter of King Hieron, and Diana (also called Artemis), a dancer. The Roman fleet doesn't get to attack Syracuse until 100 minutes have passed, a marathon haul and one that has periods of *longueur*; the picture suffers from overlength, more of a character study than anything else, and in that respect, Rossano Brazzi, starring as Archime-

58 minutes in the shortened print; in the longer, it kicks off at 70 minutes and contains more footage. A few scenes are missing in their entirety or trimmed and secondary characters dropped; Sernas grappling with Purdom in a dungeon prior to execution by stoning is nowhere to be seen in the 72-minute cut, as is a raunchy, semi-nude clinch between the two lovers. For aficionados, view the dubbed print first and then switch to the more colorful Italian-only issue; *Salammbo* has a lot to recommend as an early '60s sword and sandal epic.

Sernas, for a change, was given his head to cut loose, playing a hotheaded grumbler: Too often cast as a wishy-washy romantic, and rather colorless lead, the actor throws his well-defined body around and gets the attention he deserves. French-born Valérie didn't possess the refined beauty of Gloria Milland, Rossana Podesta or Gianna Maria Canale, but her Parisian alley cat looks were more than acceptable for the role of a temple seductress—she certainly had sex appeal, in spades. Character actor Arnoldo Foà put in a nice turn as Sernas' philosophical muse,

des, carries the picture admirably, the former Italian heartthrob looking distinctly strange in his short tunic.

Rome is marching toward Carthage, neutral Syracuse in Sicily standing in her path. Alberto Farnese (General Marcellus) heads a deputation to meet with Alfredo Varelli (King Hieron of Syracuse), principally to check where Varelli's allegiances lie. Brazzi, spending time in his workshop/laboratory in the hills, is betrothed to Varelli's daughter, Clio (Sylva Koscina, wearing a *very* short blue skirt!), but when he spots Selinunte dancer Tina Louise (Diana) bathing naked in a pool (she's a member of Enrico Maria Salerno's retinue of good-time girls), he burns her clothes with magnifying mirrors reflecting the sun's rays, passes her a robe to spare her blushes and develops an almighty crush on the woman, shunting pretty, virginal Koscina to one side. In a twisty-turny change of events echoing MGM's unforgettable *Random Harvest* (1942), Louise, midway through the film, is herded on board a Roman galley with Salerno's bunch of promiscuous maidens (the Pleasure Girls, there for the crew's benefit). Pushed to the ground by an unfeeling guard, she bangs her head, loses her memory and marries doting Farnese (changing her name to Lucretia in the process), the consul raising Brazzi's lovechild as his own. As for the inventor, he weds Koscina; she miscarries and is unable to produce more heirs to Varelli's throne, an embittered woman wearing dark mauve dresses instead of short blue tunics. Ten years pass, and Brazzi's son is now a centurion (Luciano Marin), spearheading the assault on Syracuse. With the use of his reflecting mirrors, Brazzi sets fire to the invading Roman flotilla and is reunited with Louise; she regained her memory years ago (ironically, in a flash of sunlight) and has been leading a pretence marriage with Farnese, who dies when the Romans besiege Syracuse from the land (and so does traitor Salerno, by Brazzi's own hand). Marin, unaware that the inventor and savior of Syracuse is his real father, returns to Rome, leaving Brazzi and Louise alone in the Temple of Zeus to contemplate their future together, director Francisci, assisted by Lavagnino's wonderfully emotive music, ending on a note of sadness and loss.

A splendidly visualized Temple of Zeus; a steamy love scene when Brazzi rolls in the hay (literally) with a panting Louise; Roman pomp and ceremony as Farnese is appointed Consul of the Republic; and an excitingly conceived sea battle highlight the film. *Siege of Syracuse* has its highlights and moments of fatalistic mood but drags its feet in the water and has difficulty in maintaining interest over its two-hour running time.

1961

Amazons of Rome [*Le vergini di Roma*] aka ***Warrior Women***

Cine-Italia/Criterion Film/CFS Kosutnjak (Italy/France/Yugoslavia); Techniscope/Eastmancolor; 105 (93) mins; Producer: Arys Nissotti; Directors: Carlo Ludovico Bragaglia, Vittorio Cottafavi ††††

"A Thousand Tempting Beauties! They Fought Like Ten Thousand Unchained Tigers!" With a garish publicity poster screaming blurbs like that, how could you possibly take *Amazons of Rome* seriously? Bragaglia replaced Cottafavi after only three days, Cottafavi falling out with leading man Louis Jourdan, but whether his input made any difference to the end result is open to debate. What we have on offer is a fairly straightforward Romans versus Barbarians actioner, beautifully shot in pin-sharp color (Marc Fossard) and containing high production values (Marcel Landowski's score is a winner) that a third of the way in decides to replace gravitas and mayhem with male titillation, making for a quirky mix that just about comes off.

The film opens and closes with bloodthirsty engagements at Sublicius Bridge in 476 BC, the wooden structure presided over by one-eyed Ettore Manni (Horatio) and his hard-bitten troops. French suave guy Jourdan plays barbarian chief Drusco who, alongside the Etruscans and a squadron of Greek mercenaries, is marching on Rome. Nonchalantly munching fruit at the head of his cavalry, Jourdan gives the order to attack, the ensuing fight (javelins and swords, the bridge fortified by lethally sharpened stakes and a burning ditch) skillfully staged. Against mercenary Corrado Pani's wishes, Etruscan Jean Chevrier (King Porcenna) advocates a truce with Rome on condition that his camp receives 1,000 hostages. (A young Roman lad tries to assassinate Chevrier, backs down and burns his right hand in disgrace. This selfsame episode appeared in *The Colossus of Rome*.) In Rome, Jourdan takes an instant liking to beauty Clelia (Sylvia Syms), following her to a glade teeming with glamorous women on horseback ("And I thought I'd seen everything," muses Jourdan, eyes on stalks). The girls, all attired in short, low-cut tunics and red boots, are taken hostage along with others and escorted to the enemy camp ("Boy, this war's gonna be fun!" exclaims one soldier). Jourdan supervises the women's safety and welfare, allowing them a barn to rest in, and we are henceforth pitched

It's Greece combating the might of Imperial Rome circa 146 BC as the city of Corinth prepares for a Roman invasion, Gianni Santuccio (Governor Critolaus) demanding war, elder statesman Nando Tamberlani advocating peace. A Roman envoy sent by Julius Caesar requests that Greece breaks with the Aegean league, each province coming under Roman influence, but he's sent packing by the outraged assembly. The Greeks attack the visiting Romans. Centurion Jacques Sernas (Caius Vinicius) is wounded and cared for by blonde Genevieve Grad (as Hebe, Santuccio's virginal daughter); dark-haired, aristocratic-featured Gianna Maria Canale (Artemida), married to Tamberlani, a man twice her age, falls in lust with Sernas, Grad sighs every time she gazes at his bronzed, rippling torso, while John Drew Barrymore (Diaeus) skulks in the shadows, a Basil Rathbone-type ne'er-do-well who keeps in his apartments a pit full of poisonous snakes, very handy for putting paid to those who annoy him. Barrymore also longs for Grad's maidenly embrace, so when it's time for Sernas to be executed, Grad (yes, you've guessed right!) says she'll marry the creep on condition that the Roman will be spared.

With all this intrigue going on, plus some arresting battle sequences, you would have thought that the right ingredients were set firmly in place for the making of a peplum classic, but this isn't the case. Costa tackles the court/interior interludes indifferently, Grad emoting like crazy, mouthing laughable dialogue (courtesy of the English dubbing society) and sobbing uncontrollably throughout, particularly at the end when she's tied up in Barrymore's snake den. Gordon Mitchell (as General Metellus) has a guest appearance, but the actor's meaner-than-mean talents are wasted in his second peplum feature, while Sernas goes through the motions with the minimum of acting finesse. There are a few highlights including the collision between the Roman army (white-plumed helmets and red shields) and Corinthian foot soldiers on the scorched plains, featuring (literally) a cast of thousands, boosted by Carlo Innocenzi's bombastic score. Also impressive is the scene showing the Greek soldiers swarming to battle through the city gates, and the two leading ladies engage in a whip/dagger catfight, Canale falling on her own blade. Numerous jumps in continuity and a rushed climax are evidence of the savage editing job carried out for worldwide release, 28 minutes missing from the original print; in its full-length version, the movie would have been a lot more cohesive, and worthier. As it stands, *The Conqueror of Corinth* is so-so peplum, despite its lavish trappings. And yes, Barrymore *does* wind up in his own snake pit, and Sernas *does escort* Grad away from burning Corinth to begin a new life.

A French poster for *The Conqueror of Corinth*

straight into male fantasyland. Roman-hating Nicole Courcel (Lucilla) has Syms flogged naked, Jourdan steps up to save the lady's blushes and is immediately ordered off camp by Chevrier for "disturbing the discipline." During a drunken revelry engineered by Pani, Syms and her lasses break out of the stockade, afraid that their maidenly honor is in dire peril; after negotiating a cavernous sewer (a real one, judging by the noxious state of the water) and armed to the teeth, they join in the final offensive on the bridge, Jourdan's barbarians choosing to back the Romans, leaving Chevrier once more calling for peace terms. Back in Rome, Jourdan rushes through a wedding ceremony with Syms, anxious to discover what delights lie under her virginal white dress, on that note ending a hugely entertaining slice of torch and toga bunkum that veers from full-blooded action to girly-girly antics in the blink of an eye, put across with dexterity and zeal. Although slight in build, Jourdan makes a charismatic Barbarian chief, and it's a novelty to catch English rose Syms in a picture of this nature, when you consider that around this time the actress was up to her neck in drab, black-and-white X-rated British kitchen sink dramas, *Victim* (1961) and *The Quare Fellow* (1962) being two examples, the U.K.'s gray streets a far cry from Italy's sunny climes.

The Conqueror of Corinth [*Il conquistatore di Corinto*] aka The Centurion

Europa/Comptoir Francais CFPC (Italy/France); Euroscope/Eastmancolor; 105 (77) mins; Producer: Manlio Morelli; Director: Mario Costa ✝✝✝

Constantine the Great [*Constantino il grande*] aka Constantine and the Cross

Jonia Film/Jadran Film (Italy/Yugoslavia); Totalscope/Eastmancolor; 120 (109) mins; Producer: Ferdinand Felicioni; Director: Lionello De Felice ✝✝✝✝

This is a part factual/part fictional account of the reign of Flavius Valerius Aurelius Constantinus Augustus (306-337 AD), the first Roman emperor during the Byzantine era to advocate tolerance, compassion and religious amnesty toward Christianity, after overcoming opposition from the senate and fellow military officers. Cornel Wilde played Constantine, his part overshadowed by Massimo Serato's backstabbing Maxentius, brother of Wilde's wife, Fausta. (A few weeks after completion of filming, Belinda Lee died in a car accident while being

An American poster for *Constantine and the Cross* (aka *Constantine the Great*)

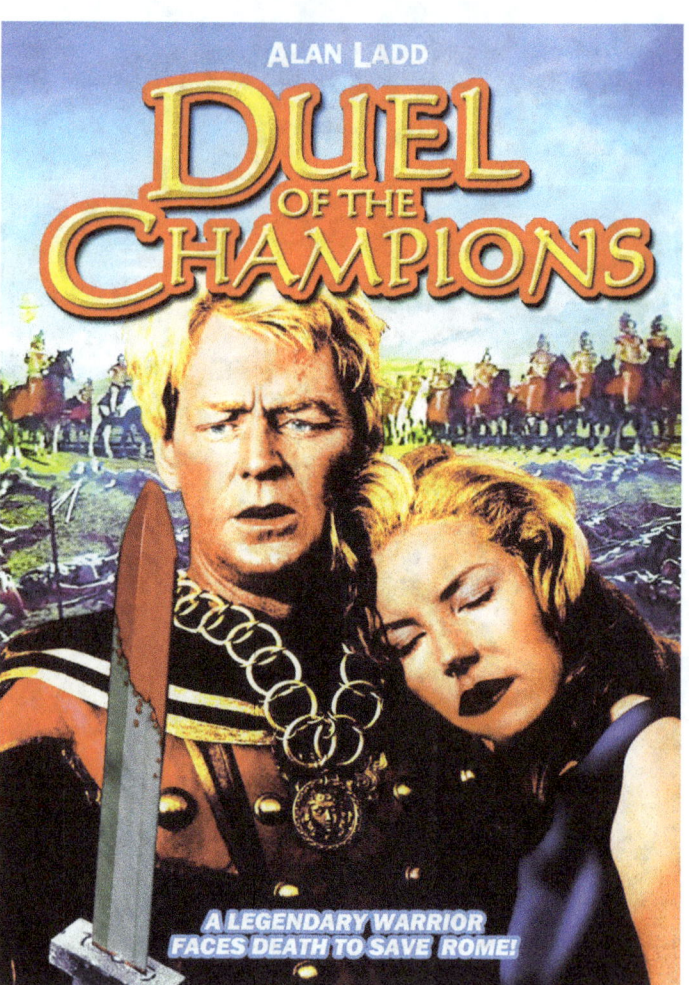

English language DVD cover for *Duel of the Champions*, featuring Alan Ladd and Franca Bettoia

driven to Los Angeles on a shoot.) Serato, a veteran of over 30 peplum features, would have brought a tad more gravitas and acting experience to the role; unfortunately, his wasn't the name producers banked on for overseas box-office takings and *Constantine and the Cross* was a big financial hit of its day, playing continuously in England (as *Constantine the Great*) throughout 1962/1963. Stunning production values dressed up in Massimo Dallamano's shimmering color photography, a thumping Mario Nascimbene score and the input from eight scriptwriters (including De Felice) contributed to a noticeable Roman extravaganza that held the attention for two hours, the movie climaxing with Constantine's decisive victory over his enemies at Milvian Bridge in 312 AD.

At the start, Wilde is stationed in Germany with the army of occupation, keeping tabs on the barbarian hordes. He's summoned to Rome, earmarked as the new emperor of the western provinces after the proposed abdication of emperors Diocletian and Maximianus. En route, his regiment is wiped out by bandits, sent on orders from consul Serato, who wants Wilde out of the way to further his own ambitions; Wilde and friend Hadrian (Fausto Tozzi) survive, cared for by Christians seeking refuge in caves. Tozzi falls in love with pious Christine Kaufmann (Livia), Wilde takes up residence in the city and courts Lee (in a black wig) prior to their marriage, while Serato and his praetorians hatch one plot after another in an effort to rid Rome of this Christian-loving emperor-in-waiting. Lionello De Felice's pace is unhurried (but never lags) during the first 70 minutes or so, the director content to let the complex series of events leading up to Wilde's accession unfold gradually, a sumptuous history lesson in motion picture guise. But he doesn't neglect to keep us on our toes. A nasty "Christians fed to the lions" scene, the mass rape of captive Christian women (earning the film, in Britain, an "A" certificate), a gruesome torture (eyes burned out with a poker) and a couple of barbarian raids, one of which sees Wilde's father slain, ensure that this particular cinematic pill remains bitter, not sugar-coated. Wilde's mother Elena (Elisa Cegani) turns out to be a follower of Christ; Kaufmann, brutalized and violated, dies in Tozzi's arms; and Serato arranges the capture of Lee *and* the murder of his own father, placing the blame on Wilde and electing himself emperor, appointing equally corrupt Nando Gazzolo commander of the praetorian guard. Wilde, on beholding the vision of a gigantic white cross emblazoned across a fiery red sky, organizes his legions for battle. The resulting clash at Milvian Bridge between cavalry and infantry is presented in the grand manner and won't let action addicts down; Wilde is reunited with his wife and mother, becoming the first Christian emperor to govern Rome. This is a lavish, opulent historical saga that deserves a full-blown digital makeover to restore the film to its former immaculate glory.

Duel of the Champions [*Orazi e Curiazi*] aka *Duel of Champions*

Tiberia Film/Lux Film/Lovcen Film (Italy/Yugoslavia); Totalscope/Eastmancolor; 105 (90) mins; Producer: Angelo Ferrara; Director: Ferdinando Baldi ††††

Hollywood legend Alan Ladd was 48 at the time his one and only peplum was released in October 1961; the five-foot-six-inch actor was to make only two more pictures (*13 West Street*, Columbia 1962; *The Carpetbaggers*, Paramount 1964) before dying from a cerebral edema in January 1964 at age 50. In Ferdinando Baldi's vibrant essay on the seven-year Roman-Alban conflict, which took place during the reign of King Tulio Hostilio (673-641 BC), Ladd looked tired and drawn, rarely smiling, the effects of alcoholism having taken its toll. Despite this, he still put in a measured performance as Horatio, one of three brothers ordered to fight three brothers from Alba in a final effort to end the war, which has cost so many lives; the king whose warriors win the contest gets to rule Rome and Alba. However, Commander Ladd has been branded a coward; in a thrilling 12-minute opening skirmish, the centurions of the 4th legion are attacked in a ravine, arrows and burning rocks raining down on their heads. Ladd is badly wounded, taken to Alba, thrown into a pit full of ravenous wolves and saved from a mauling by Alana Ladd (Ladd's real daughter as Scilla, a nice touch). Back in Rome, Jacques Sernas (Marcus), Ladd's younger brother, marries Ladd's sweetheart, Franca Bettoia (Marcia), King Tulio (Robert Keith) forced to surmise that his son, because of his absence, must have deserted his troops on the battlefield and is probably now dead. A month later, Ladd, fully recovered, trots into Rome, the coward tag removed, while Bettoia rues the day she ever married Sernas.

Assisted by Angelo Francesco Lavagnino's quality (and incredibly noisy) score, Baldi paints an evocative canvas of what life was like in bustling downtown Alba with its street dancers, taverns, beggars, jugglers, rowdy soldiers and loose women; the Albans are portrayed as illiterate, immoral and degenerate, the direct opposite to the savage, noble and intelligent Romans, a fact that Keith forcibly puts across to antagonistic Andrea Aureli (King of Alba) at the negotiating table. When a sorceress prophesizes that the only way to terminate this futile war and unite both nations is to have three brothers from each side battle it out to the death, a month's truce is announced, Ladd's sister Jacqueline Derval (Horatia) upsetting the applecart by falling in lust with Franco Fabrizi (Curazio) after he's abducted her; he happens to be one of the brothers *her* brother will have to fight. To the sound of a fanfare, the prolonged combat between the rival brothers gets underway (one side in red, the other in black), resulting in Ladd's two siblings slain and decapitated; he rides off into the forest where a cat-and-mouse hunt takes place, Ladd killing two of his pursuers and clashing with Fabrizi outside Rome's lofty walls. Fabrizi is run through; in anguish,

Ex-1950s knitwear model Roger Moore, years before he became James Bond, is on the hunt for Sabine females in *The Rape of the Sabine Women.*

Derval plunges a sword into her stomach to join her lover in the afterlife. Rome and Alba declare peace, Aureli falling in subservience at the feet of Keith, while Ladd and Bettoia ride off into the distance, the newly widowed lady having swiftly forgotten the one great line she shot at Ladd earlier on: "No man ever understands a woman."

This is another movie that deserves digital restoration. Amerigo Gengarelli's once glowing color photography is as battered-looking as Ladd's lined features, while jumps in continuity point to the missing 15 additional minutes directed by Terence Young for U.S./U.K. release—current issues are 90 minutes, dubbed, rough around the edges and pan and scan. For all peplum devotees, Hollywood tough guy Alan Ladd acquits himself well as a Roman commander, not as incongruous in the role as many fans might think.

The Rape of the Sabine Women [*Il ratto delle sabine*] aka *Romulus and the Sabines*

FICIT/CIPRA/Dubrava (Italy/France/Yugoslavia); Dyaliscope/Eastmancolor; 98 mins; Producers: Enrico Bomba, Carlo Infascelli; Director: Richard Pottier ††

Steve Reeves (left) as Romulus and Gordon Scott as Remus, two of peplum's most famous of all *fusto* stars, as they appeared in *Romulus and Remus*

Ex-1950s knitwear model Roger Moore, slumming around the Continent to pick up film work, starred in Richard Pottier's unofficial sequel to *Romulus and Remus*, taking on the Steve Reeves role of King Romulus, who presides over a Rome in its infancy, devoid, strange as it may seem, of the fairer sex. However, the neighboring Sabines have women a-plenty, so why not organize a raid, round up their young girls and bring them back to the city where they can be shared and hopefully put a stop to all this incessant grumbling about lack of womanly delights and female company.

The Rape of the Sabine Women, very loosely based on true events circa 750 BC, can be viewed as a comedy adventure, to be taken with a pinch of salt. Moore captures warrior Scilla Gabel (Dusia), busy evading his sex-mad soldiers, and they fall in lust. "Take me back to Rome," she pleads, stroking his face. "You'll be one against a thousand wolves with very sharp teeth," he warns her, hiding his prize in a cave den, very handy for the odd nightly bout of lovemaking. But as soon as Moore sets sights on Fulco Lulli's (King Titus Tazio) vestal virgin daughter, Mylene Demongeot (Rea), Gabel is rudely shoved to one side, the young monarch concentrating his efforts on inducing the blonde ice maiden to share his bed. Meanwhile, Walter Barnes, Marino Masé and their bumbling blind buddy chance upon a group of nubile maidens flashing their pins (and, horror of horrors, a breast!) in a pool (Croatia's beautiful Karst waterfalls were used for location). They immediately wade in and chat them up, Masé fastening onto Giorgia Moll (Lavinia), the sweetest of the bunch, like a leech. Back in Rome (depicted as a primitive hovel), Moore tells his complaining citizens to wash, look presentable and grab those women at harvest time. The abduction takes place during a games ceremony, Moore and his companions getting the Sabines drunk on wine; the captive women are corralled inside Rome's squalid walls with instructions that lots are to be drawn to see who gets who. The feisty prisoners are having none of it: "We'll select the men," they giggle, "and no manhandling," and they file off to choose a mate, only too eager to jump into the sack with this disagreeable bunch of scruffy menfolk who, in the words of Lulli, "lack good breeding." Pretty soon, a baby is born, probably the fastest pregnancy/birth on record; Moore gradually breaks down Demongeot's resistance and rejects Gabel's advances: "I don't want you anymore." "You'll pay for this insult," she snarls and arranges an attack, but not before Moore, asleep in a temple, has been visited and given a few words of much-needed wisdom by the gods Mars and Venus, played respectively by Jean Marais and Rosanna Schiaffino, two of Europe's most glamorous film stars of that period. In the course of the fight, Lulli is presented to the baby, has a change of heart and orders everyone to down weapons ("He is one of our sons."); Moore, feeling unworthy of kingship, hands the hot seat to advisor Claude Conty and, now "just a man," rides off with Demongeot, leaving the Romans and the Sabines united in peace.

To the background of a Carlo Rustichelli stock score, future James Bond star Moore carries the picture on his slim shoulders, boyishly handsome and exuding a certain amount of charisma, more so than Demongeot who appears strangely sulky and miserable in all her scenes until the dying seconds (Moore found his own Sabine woman in the shape of Luisa Mattioli while filming took place, the pair marrying in April 1969). It's his show, and his alone; without the curiosity value of Moore's presence, Pottier's quirky peplum battle of the sexes saga wouldn't warrant a second look.

Romulus and Remus [*Romolo e Remo*] aka ***Duel of the Titans***
Titanus/Ajace/SNP (Italy/France); CinemaScope/Technicolor; 108 (93) mins; Producers: Tonino Cervi, Alessandro Jacovoni; Director: Sergio Corbucci ✝✝✝✝✝

Within the pantheon of historical/mythological pepla, *Romulus and Remus* is in the top 10, a glorious throwback to pre-CGI days when thousands of extras filled the screen and huge sets were specially constructed with infinite attention to period detail, only to be razed to the ground by reel three! Orchestrated for maximum eye-arresting impact by Sergio Corbucci, we had "The Battle of the Beefcakes," Steve Reeves (Romulus, the good) at cross purposes with twin brother Gordon Scott (Remus, the bad), up against King Tazio's Sabine hordes and each other; vainglorious Scott wants to wrest leadership of their tribes from compassionate Reeves, the two parting company in their flight from Tazio (Massimo Girotti) but destined, as decreed by the gods, to eventually meet and fight it out. (Reeves was originally earmarked to play both parts but declined, bringing in his friend Scott, the two coincidentally born in the same year, 1926, but not twins!)

An American three-sheet poster for *Duel of the Titans* (aka *Romulus and Remus*)

Legend (and many archaeological finds) indicates that the twin babies, abandoned on the banks of the Tiber, spent the first year of their lives suckled by a she-wolf until cared for by a shepherd. Flash forward 20 years: Reeves and Scott attend the Feast of the god Pan, held in a vast cavern by dictator King Amulios of Alba Longa (Franco Volpi), the man responsible for murdering their father, their mother (Laura Solari) now in charge of the vestal virgins. During a debauched ceremony in which the congregation is whipped with a sheep's entrails, Reeves homes in on Girotti's daughter, bleach-blonde Virna Lisi (Julia). Scott also takes a fancy to the girl, anxious to rid himself of the leech-like attentions of infatuated Ornella Vanoni (Tarpeia). Thus are sown the seeds of mistrust and discontent, especially when the twins learn of their true origins. "I am the son of a god!" exclaims Scott. "I am the true king of Alba Longa. Amulios is a usurper." During the games (that horse riding sequence through burning hay bales would raise eyebrows today), thieves steal horses, Reeves is spread-eagled on a revolving wheel and flogged, and those opposing Volpi's iron rule start an incursion; Reeves kills the dictator and the revolt ends in the destruction of the city. "Stay together in harmony. Always," whispers Solari to her sons with her dying breath, but there's little chance of that happening. Moving out of their ravine sanctuary, argumentative Scott wants absolute control of the people (plus Lisi), prepared to fight his own brother for the privilege, but Reeves balks at drawing his sword. When the auguries proclaim Reeves as the true king, it signifies a divergence of the ways. Scott leads a splinter group over the forbidding mountain of fire, while his brother decides on a different route to their chosen destination, the Valley of the Seven Hills, where a new city will be established, as it was in 753 BC, the recorded date on which, it is said, Rome and its empire was founded.

Until that final tragic confrontation, Scott's entire group is decimated by a volcanic eruption, the exception being poor unwanted Vanoni, left scrabbling in the ashes as her disinterested lover rides off to join his brother, at mercy in the valley from Girotti's formidable Sabines, craven Jacques Sernas among their number (Sernas made a profession out of playing duplicitous characters, dating right back to 1956's *Helen of Troy*; here, he gets a war axe in the back for not showing Girotti enough guts in battle). Cunningly laying a battery of water-filled traps, they fend off the warriors with rocks, javelins, nets, stakes and arrows, winning the day. Girotti, suitably impressed, declares peace, even agreeing to the Reeves/Lisi relationship, but jealous Scott remains fuming; refusing to share in the glory with his brother, he demands that he alone is fit to be king. Reeves plows a furrow, Scott tramples all over it, there's the inevitable showdown and Scott lies dead from a sword thrust, the end of a legend but the beginning of the Roman Empire.

Sergio Leone was one of eight scriptwriters assigned to bring this absorbing tale to the screen. An intelligent script combined with Piero Piccioni's busy score and Enzo Barboni's just-right period photography (Corbucci, Piccioni and Barboni all worked together on another significant Reeves' picture, *The Son of Spartacus*), plus the pomp of the battle sequences (check that tremendous subjective shot of galloping horses carrying racks of spears mowing down enemy foot soldiers) ensures a first-rate peplum experience that has weathered well over the years, grounded by a cast of peplum dependables including Piero Lulli, Andrea Bosic, Germano Longo and José Greci. It counts as one of the best Reeves and Scott ever starred in.

Slave of Rome [*La schiava di Roma*]

Atlantica Cinematografica (Italy); Totalscope/Eastmancolor; 98 (91) mins; Producer: Marco Vicario; Directors: Sergio Grieco, Franco Prosperi (uncredited) ✝✝✝✝✝

A Walk in the Sun (Fox, 1945), Lewis Milestone's classic World War II drama, dealt with a small platoon contending with overwhelming enemy odds, voicing the thoughts, fears and longings of the men involved. While *Slave of Rome* doesn't pretend to reach the dizzy heights set by Milestone's seminal war drama, in its dealing with the innermost hopes and anxieties of Guy Madison's 70-strong group, it gets a whole lot closer to what made the average Roman soldier tick than many others managed

An Italian poster for Sergio Grieco's thoughtful *Slave of Rome*

to do. Thoughtfully scripted by Franco Prosperi, Silvano Reina and producer Marco Vicario, Sergio Grieco's taut little Roman thriller is an undiscovered gem; copies are as rare as they come, but thankfully English-dubbed.

The action takes place during the Roman-Gallic campaigns, circa 54 BC. Madison (Marco Velarius) and 70 battle-hardened legionnaires are ordered by Caesar to cross the river border and delay Mario Petri's Gauls from linking up with Gallic warlord Vercingetorix, thus creating a force strong enough to cause havoc among Rome's legions: diversionary tactics, ambushes, anything to put a spanner in Petri's plans. With the amount of wenching, carousing, orgasmic dancing, gorging on food, arguing over women and drinking going on in Petri's stockade, it's a wonder that any of his warriors will be fit enough for battle; Petri (as Lysircos) has designs on chief's daughter Rossana Podesta (Anthea), who fills out a pagan costume very nicely indeed. News comes through of Madison's men lurking in the woods; an attack results in Podesta captured. ("But he's a woman!" cries a soldier, almost disrobing her.) Podesta's father meets Madison under a flag of truce to reclaim his daughter by negotiation, but Roman-hating Petri organizes his own ambush, killing the chief who advocated peace. Pursuing the Romans, Petri's forces are halted by the collapse of a strategic bridge (a stupendous scenic longshot complete with matted painted backdrop), Madison badly wounded. Nursed by Podesta, the two fall in love in standard peplum double-quick time (only one day); recovered, the centurion and his handful of fighters take to the swamps, Podesta revealing her guilt feelings to Giacomo Rossi-Stuart (Claudius) over the death of Madison's father. She was the brains behind the raid that caused his death, Petri being the executioner (Madison later forgives her). Sergio Grieco wraps up this involving tale within the confines of a ravine, the Romans raining boulders and flaming arrows down on the heads of the Gauls. Madison dispatches Petri, slicing him across the stomach with a war axe, the Gauls retreating in disarray as Caesar's massed regiments approach. Madison and Podesta cling to each other, practically the only survivors left in the aftermath of the bloody skirmish.

Madison's weary compatriots express their opinions in the quieter interludes. They're sick of the enclosed forest and unending, pestilent swamps, yearning for sunnier, warmer climes back home and the comforts offered to them by their wives. They're also tired of the backbreaking march and lack of supplies. Rossi-Stuart's character is unusually complex; he's only ever loved once, inwardly jealous of Podesta's attraction for his commander, and sees no end to the war, dreaming of better times to come. The combat scenes are particularly savage, matching Petri's in-your-face Gallic leader, and as a bonus, we get to see a few precious seconds of Italian movie goddess Podesta swimming nude in the river. Scored with a throbbing undercurrent of menace by Armando Trovajoli and expertly paced by Grieco, *Slave of Rome* is a sharply observed minor classic, placing its protagonists in claustrophobic wooded locales instead of sun-baked, wide-open spaces, not a palace or any building in sight. Madison, Podesta and Petri shine (as do the support cast) in a memorable, pared-to-the-bone picture that's well worth seeking out.

1962

Alone Against Rome [*Solo contro Roma*] aka ***Vengeance of the Gladiator***

Atlantica Productions (Italy); Totalscope/Technicolor; 95 mins; Producer: Marco Vicario; Director: Luciano Ricci ✝✝✝✝✝

Question: Why is it that the Italians could produce magnificent mini-epics such as *Alone Against Rome* at under 100 minutes, when the likes of *Gladiator* ran an hour longer, yet contained far less incident? Agreed, Ridley Scott's mega-expensive homage to pepla contains nuances and subtleties that Ricci's torch and toga offering doesn't possess, but those computer-enhanced arena sequences don't hold a candle to the realistic arena scenes in Luciano Ricci's Roman Empire caper, a real coliseum to whet the appetite (Riccardo Freda directed these, using the lofty Pula amphitheater in Croatia for location authenticity, thousands of extras crowding the terraces and terrifying stunts performed without the aid of digital effects). The final 10 minutes is mighty exciting stuff, gladiator Brenno (Lang Jeffries) forced to contend with two scythed war chariots, one run by four black horses, the other by four white horses. Grabbing a charioteer's lash, he brings down the leading white steed, the chariot toppling, crashing and splintering right over the cameraman's head, a truly hair-raising moment; no wonder this violent form

of entertainment was so popular with the Roman public! Slaying the rider, our hero then issues an open challenge of trial by mortal combat to corrupt tribune Philippe Leroy (Silla), which the Roman, in front of a packed audience, can't turn down without losing face. A bruising encounter with lash and sword results in Leroy throttled to death in an armlock. Jeffries is reunited with his love, Rossana Podesta, and compassionate consul Franco Nonibasti lifts the yoke of persecution from the population imposed by Leroy and his squad of gorillas.

And that's just the main course. Side dishes include the graphic whipping of Jeffries (tied to a column), who later goes head-to-head with three gladiators at the games, dispatching all three, a provocative dance, a daring outbreak from prison through a tunnel and ancient catacombs, a Christian prophet tied to a cross in the arena and peppered with arrows, fierce gladiator training sessions in which Jeffries shows the teacher a thing or two, the sacking of a village and Podesta at her radiant best (the photogenic actress, once voted one of Italy's most beautiful women, was married to producer Vicario at the time). She's Fabiola, engaged to Jeffries, but not for long. Into her ransacked province marches Leroy, centurion Djordje Nenadovic and their legionnaires, subjecting the population to a regime of suppression, humiliation and greed, the Romans portrayed as merciless thugs who look upon the locals as "primitive clods." Podesta's home is commandeered by Leroy, as she herself is, while Jeffries and her brother Gabriele Tinti (Goruk) are left to rot in jail. Jeffries' combative prowess manifests itself and he's ordered to do battle in the stadium, continually under threat of being put to death if Podesta doesn't yield up her charms to the reptilian tribune ("Save him and I'll belong to you."). At a clandestine meeting in the forest, Jeffries fails to comprehend why Podesta is still under the same roof as the cold-hearted, ambitious official. "You live with him?" "Yes." "You did it to save me?" They kiss, then, "Go back to him and stay there." Leroy later announces to Podesta, after Jeffries has been apprehended for a second time, "Tomorrow, he'll be executed," to which she replies, "If you harm Brenno I'll commit suicide." In steps Nonibasti, enraged at Leroy's intolerant treatment of the populace. There's an uprising and, as we have seen, good triumphs over evil in the arena. What a pity smirking Nenadovic didn't receive a well-aimed spear thrust to top it all off.

Armando Trovajoli's fine score, splendid color photography (Silvano Ippoliti) and showy costume design plus slick direction from Ricci promote action-packed *Alone Against Rome* to essential peplum status. Ancient Roman pageants simply don't come any better served than this tasty platter which can only be fully appreciated in its original widescreen format, not too difficult to track down these days—the Greek Odeon issue presents the film in letterbox, lacking subtitles, while German widescreen DVDs are English-dubbed.

Julius Caesar Against the Pirates [*Giulio Cesare contro i pirati*] aka ***Caesar and the Pirates***; ***Julius Caesar and the Pirates***
C.A.P.R.I./Dubrava (Italy/France/Yugoslavia); Dyaliscope/Eastmancolor; 99 (90) mins; Producer: Gastone Guglielmetti; Director: Sergio Grieco ✝✝✝

Gustavo Rojo (as a young Caesar) goes on the run when Roman dictator Erno Crisa (Silla) orders the guards to ransack his villa. Leaving wife Franca Parisi (Cornelia) behind, Rojo, bosom buddy Massimo Carocci (Publio) and lackey Ignazio Le-

An Italian poster for *Julius Caesar Against the Pirates*

A French poster for *Julius Caesar the Conqueror of Gaul*

one (Frontane, the film's comedic element) head for the coast. Rojo is badly injured in the thigh during a skirmish, and is then picked up from a makeshift raft by Mario Petri's Cilician pirates. In Petri's court (he's King Nicomedes of Bitinia), Rojo is looked upon as a rich prize, because of his gifts in war strategy. Petri's rival, Gordon Mitchell (Hamar), holed up on the island of Formacusa, is on Petri's tail because he's abducted his mistress, Abbe Lane (as Plauzia), as bait; the king wants Mitchell put out of the picture. Lane, Rojo and his pals find themselves in Mitchell's stronghold after the pirate chief's men successfully raid the vessel on which Petri has allowed them to sail to Maletto in order to negotiate a deal to get rid of his arch enemy. Lane falls for Rojo, and Mitchell, fuming with jealousy, orders Carocci to go to Rome and return with 50 talents of gold; only then will he release the 25-year-old Roman commander.

Filmed among the impressive cliffs, coves and promontories along Yugoslavia's Dalmatian coast, Sergio Grieco's Romans versus Pirates saga, founded on factual events that occurred around 75 BC, is a colorful adventure that needed a few loose ends tied up. It's not made clear exactly whose ship Rojo boards from his raft, the sequence suffering from lack of continuity or minor editing; likewise, Piero Lulli's scenes (he plays Petri's second-in-command) are disjointed, the actor coming and going, then disappearing altogether, his character left hanging in the air; the same goes for Petri, confusingly there one minute, gone the next. It's left for Mitchell to level out the story inconsistences and carry the action on his broader-than-broad shoulders, which he does in true Mitchell style. Okay, it's a style that barely differed from one movie to the next, but it never fails to work: The macho big guy, complete with blond mop and scraggy beard, scowls, shouts, bullies, roars with maniacal laughter, throws his brutish weight around and treats his woman like a common whore, not a lady: "Kiss me!" he barks, grabbing Lane by the throat and roughly groping her breast, testing her allegiance; does she still find him desirable, or do her sexual interests lie in Rojo's direction? In Rome, Crisa has been assassinated. Carocci, on his way back with the gold, is one of the few survivors left when Lulli attacks his vessel and pinches the bullion, betraying Petri (another plot thread left dangling). Fedele Gentile (Valerio), a Caesar sympathizer, sets course for Formacusa with two warships to rid the seas of Mitchell and his corsairs (who resemble South American natives) and, to rescue his daughter, since Silvano Jachino is in love with Carocci.

Grieco wraps things up nicely in a rousing 13-minute climax where Rojo, Carocci, Leone and Jachino are chained to a wall in a grotto and face a moving bed of spikes, but Lane frees them and then finds herself in an identical position. Gaining access through a sea cave, Gentile's legionnaires wipe out the pirates en masse; Rojo wrestles with Mitchell, unshackles Lane, who dies in his arms and pushes the corsair leader onto the bed of spikes. Grieco treats us to a striking final shot of Gentile's ships sailing out of the pirates' sheer-sided rocky enclave as the sun sets, Rojo to be pronounced Rome's new governor. As was the norm in the majority of Italian peplum, the bright cinematography is superb (Vincenzo Seratrice), ace composer Carlo Innocenzi providing an appropriately exhilarating soundtrack to match the narrative and Mitchell's habitual in-your-face performance.

Julius Caesar the Conqueror of Gaul [*Giulio Cesare il conquistatore delle Gallie*] aka *Caesar the Conqueror*
Metheus Film (Italy); Totalscope/Eastmancolor; 104 (91) mins; Producers: Roberto Capitani, Luigi Mondello; Director: Tanio Boccia (Amerigo Anton) ††

Less an action movie, more of a reflective portrait of one of Rome's greatest military commanders during the Gaul campaign, circa 54 BC, culminating in the Siege of Alesia, in which Vercingetorix's forces were finally defeated in a bloody confrontation. Cameron Mitchell starred as Julius Caesar, a brooding, war-weary figure mulling over the vagaries of life as a leader of men, attempting to quell the Gauls *and* combat the Roman senate, most of who resent his power and ambition, refusing to send him much-required reinforcements to re-energize his campaign. Carlo Tamberlani and his fellow senators also oppose a suggested invasion of Britain on the grounds of cost. Brawny Rik Battaglia (Vercingetorix), released by Mitchell during a bare knuckle fight with a German, goes on to become a fearsome opponent, rallying various tribes in his bid to overrun the Roman legions. Young Ivica Pajer (aka Ivo Payer), a centurion in Mitchell's legion, loves noble lady Raffaella Carra (Publia) but she's been ordered to wed a rival captain ("It's a political necessity"); when the captain dies, she becomes Battaglia's center of attention after being captured, much to the hatred of his jealous mistress, Dominique Wilms (as Queen Astrid, a blonde Amazonian). Wilms eventually arranges the flight from captivity of Carra and Pajer (also caught and flogged); an arrow on the battlefield brings down the strapping female warrior when Mitchell's battalions overwhelm Battaglia's armies at his Alesia fortress, despite a betrayal by the Aedui tribes, a stirring sequence. Mitchell shows

A Spanish poster for *Pontius Pilate*

clemency to the Gaul chieftain in victory, allowing him to walk free as long as he doesn't stir up any further trouble.

Tanio Boccia presents us with a rash of stage-bound vignettes that tends to drag the conservative pace ever further downwards, the movie refusing to flow smoothly, relying on far too many close-ups of Mitchell's worried features and a wordy script. Place references and character's names are rattled off by rote, confusing the narrative, the only real slice of action appearing in the closing 10 minutes. Good points include the graphic aftermath of battle, casualties sprawled among undergrowth, with Mitchell demonstrating tenderness and grief by consoling dying soldiers with a few thoughtful words, to send them on the way to their god. A panoramic shot of Battaglia's smoking, ruined fortress, hundreds of bodies littering the ground, is also impressive. Mitchell's unalloyed gravitas carries a picture, which is a bit of a long haul, running out of steam well before that final skirmish takes place.

Pontius Pilate [*Ponzio Pilato*]

Glomer Film/Lux/CCF (Italy/France); Super Technirama 70/Technicolor; 103 (93) mins; Producer: Enzo Merolle; Directors: Irving Rapper, Gian Paolo Callegari ✝✝✝

Being an account of the events leading up to Christ's crucifixion on orders from Pontius Pilate, the Procurator of Judaea. Jean Marais starred as the ambitious Roman official with a perpetual look of harassment creasing those renowned chiseled features and sculptured profile, and who could blame him. Sent to oversee one of the empire's most troublesome hot spots, everything the magistrate does to appease the fractious crowds backfires. Workers rebel on construction of a giant aqueduct because it crosses holy burial ground; the mob bay in horror when the Roman eagle is hoisted above a Hebrew temple; zealots mumble, complain and conspire; there's a foiled assassination attempt by massed ranks of bowmen; his wife Claudia (Jeanne Crain) acts as his conscience, questioning his tactics and pleading with him to show compassion; and bearded rabbi Basil Rathbone (Caiaphas) makes it quite clear that his presence isn't welcomed (Rathbone played Pontius Pilate in RKO-Radio's 1935 production *The Last Days of Pompeii*). In addition, Barabbas (Livio Lorenzon) and his unruly bandits are busy pillaging and looting the surrounding villages, a thorn in the Romans' side.

Primarily, peplum movies were all about action—*Pontius Pilate*'s few action scenes took place in the first half of the movie, the main sequences showing catapults raining fiery death and destruction on the fleeing populace, with crows wheeling over hundreds of corpses; two galleys racing during a games tournament, the crew prey to prowling crocodiles. The second half concentrated on the appearance among the multitudes of Christ and Judas' betrayal for 30 pieces of silver, becoming bogged down in an unending spate of sermonizing vignettes and culminating in the crucifixion scene, filmed in longshot: Three crosses are highlighted against a stormy blue sky; a huge thunderstorm occurs, causing a cataclysm, Crain perishing under falling masonry as punishment for her husband condemning Jesus to death.

The events are told in flashback, Marais before a tribunal, having to explain his decisions to a demented Caesar (Charles Borromel). Rathbone played the high priest with reserved dignity, fighting for the spiritual rights of his people against what he regards as Roman tyranny, while John Drew Barrymore starred as both Judas and the Messiah, who is only seen from the rear in his white robe. Barrymore presented Judas as a tortured, wild-eyed maniac, aware that his betrayal has cursed him in God's eyes, a juicy, over-the-top turn, shot at odd angles to emphasize the man's craziness, which was somewhat at odds with the movie's staid political/religious remit. On a more sensitive note, a short scene where three naked boys romp in a river would *not* be allowed in today's cinema. Marais portrayed a man in mental conflict with the nigh-on impossible situation he found himself in, up to his neck in trying to cope with complex Hebrew ideals, sensitive but rather dour, while peplum regulars Lorenzon, Massimo Serato, Riccardo Garrone and Gianni Garko lent good support. A peplum Passion Play not without merit, although a little on the lengthy side—Angelo Francesco Lavagnino's rich score is a definite bonus.

79 AD: The Destruction of Herculaneum [*Anno 79: La distruzione di Ercolana*] aka *79 AD*

CI.AS./Comptoir Francais CFFP (Italy/France); Totalscope/Eastmancolor; 113 (95) mins; Producers: Mario Maggi, Mario Damiani; Director: Gianfranco Parolini ✝✝✝

The same team behind 1963's *The Old Testament* treated audiences to a beautifully photographed but aimless tale centered around the persecution of Christians by a despotic ruler, topped off with the eruption of Vesuvius and the destruction of Herculaneum, neighbor to Pompeii. Brad Harris was returning war hero Marcus Tiberius, who with pals Carlo Tamberlani (as Furius, playing, for a change, a veteran eye-patched soldier, not final 20 minutes, Harris and his buddies, plus hundreds of Christians, on an avenue of crosses, waiting to be burned alive, the air blue with smoke, an imaginative scene. Vesuvius erupts, everyone clambers down from their cross and Herculaneum crumbles in the cataclysm, a seven-minute sequence utilizing a couple of minutes' stock footage borrowed from *The Last Days of Pompeii* and quite well-executed. Berthier and Lane perish under tons of falling rubble, while Harris, Greci, Tamberlani and Holzer ride off to play house after receiving a full pardon from Hersent. Berthier takes the acting honors as the slimeball you wouldn't want to touch, let alone cross swords with, while Harris isn't too bad as the obligatory beefcake hero, making one wonder why he only starred in five peplum movies, four directed by Parolini, who also jointly directed *Goliath Against the Giants*. A full-blooded score would have made all the difference to this lovely-to-look-at but ultimately empty movie.

The Son of Spartacus [Il figlio di Spartacus] aka The Slave

Titanus (Italy); CinemaScope/Eastmancolor; 104 (92) mins; Producer: Franco Palaggi; Director: Sergio Corbucci †††††

Benefiting from gleaming Egyptian location work and a thoughtful script from Adriano Bolzoni, Giovanni Grimaldi and Bruno Corbucci (the events are wholly fictitious), *The Son of Spartacus* gives Stanley Kubrick's *Spartacus* a run for its money and in many ways betters it; Claudio Gora's devilish Crassus is the equal of Laurence Olivier's odious Crassus, the action sequences are bold and brutal and Steve Reeves (as Randus, beardless on this outing) towers over the production like the pyramids that dominate Julius Caesar's camp at Alexandria, where we kick off in 48 BC. Spartacus' rebellion having been crushed, Caesar (Ivo Garrani) sends centurion Reeves to Zeugma to winkle out what exactly Gora is playing at; Garrani doesn't trust him, aware of the man's dubious ambitions. But why does Reeves feel uneasy at the sight of crucified slaves and the way they are continually abused by their taskmasters? What is the significance of that amulet he has worn around his neck from childhood, especially when Garrani tells him that Spartacus had one just like it. With pals Franco Balducci (Verus) and Roland Bartrop (Lumonius), plus rescued Egyptian slave beauty Ombretta Colli (Saide), Reeves boards a galley bound for Zeugma, mixing with passengers Jacques Sernas (Vetius) and Gianna Maria Canale (runner-up in 1947's Miss Italia beauty contest); Canale (Claudia), a cougar of the first order, takes on Colli as her personal slave, while casting her dark, almond eyes over Reeves in his short tunic. In dense fog, the ship hits a reef; Reeves and Colli are washed overboard, land up on a desert shore, trek into the wastes and are captured by a slave train. "How can a Roman centurion be the son of a slave?" queries Reeves, when it's drawn to his attention by his fellow captives that his amulet was placed on the breast of Spartacus' infant ("What your father couldn't finish, you must finish."). Breaking loose, the slaves make for the ruined City of the Sun; there, down a stone-lined walkway, Reeves finds his father's sword, helmet and arm plate resting on a slab over Spartacus' sarcophagus. Aware of his true identity and destiny, he leads a fresh revolt against Rome, switching from resistance fighter to Roman commander, right under the noses of Sernas and Gora without either noticing that their number one soldier is leading a double life.

Corbucci lays on the excitement with a trowel (there's a tremendous avalanche episode in a gulch and numerous bruising clashes), never forgetting to frame his shots for maximum effect

A striking movie poster for *79 AD: The Destruction of Herculaneum*

an elderly senator, orator or religious fatherly figure) and Niksa Stefanini (Valerius), finds that Herculaneum is being lorded over by lizard-like Jacques Berthier (Tercius); the reed-thin narcissistic consul has ambitions to become emperor over Philippe Hersent's (Titus Flavius) dead body and busies himself stirring up unrest among the Christians, artful bitch Mara Lane (Diomara), hovering at his side.

The pace is deadly slow, Carlo Franci's score muted or entirely absent, an oddity in a peplum movie where usually the soundtrack bellows away like mad. Harris and company engage in brawls (Djordje Nenadovic as Sansom [*not* Samson!] slugs it out with Harris in two prolonged tussles, but they become firm allies), are introduced to Christian ethics, become involved in senate intrigue and clash with Berthier's guards. Apart from Lane, the other two damsels on show are José Greci (aka Susan Paget) as Livia, Harris' love interest) and Ivy Holzer (Tamberlani's girl, Claudia), while Berthier seems to favor the male of the species, judging by his nipple-revealing robe, skimpy bath towels and leering smirk when in the company of his officers. There's a fairly exciting games contest on rafts surrounded by a circle of flame, crocodiles encircling the participants, and the opulent set design is adorned to perfection courtesy of Francesco Izzarelli's gloriously bright color schemes. But the narrative is slackly handled by Parolini, who seems quite happy to let the grand palace interiors do all the talking; things pick up in the

1963

Brennus Enemy of Rome [*Brenno il nemico di Roma*] aka *Battle of the Spartans*; *Battle of the Valiant*

Alta Vista (Italy); Totalscope/Technicolor; 95 (90) mins; Producer: Luigi Mondello; Director: Giacomo Gentilomo ††††

In typical unsubtle fashion, Gordon Mitchell glowers, yells and slashes his way through Rome's legions in 391 BC, playing Brennus, leader of the Gauls, whose idea of a good time is to wed Roman lovely Ursula Davis (Nysia), ravish her for one night only and then present her beautiful head impaled on his war lance to the Roman senate the next day. The only man who can stop wild man Mitchell and his rampaging hordes from ransacking Rome is Massimo Serato (General Commilus), but he's quit his post in anger, falsely accused of appropriating a large amount of gold due to replenish the treasury coffers (this time around, Serato was on the side of good, not, as usual, cast as a traitorous commander or slippery court advisor/appropriator). Duplicitous senator Vassili Karis is the culprit, attempting to align himself with Mitchell so that he can help himself to as much gold as possible. Soldier Tony Kendall (Quintus) has the job of persuading Serato to assist Rome in crushing the Gauls who are encamped at the foot of Catalina Hill, preparing for a final blitz. When Kendall presents Serato with the body of his foster son, slain by an accomplice of Karis, the commander unsheathes his hefty sword from its scabbard, mobilizes his troops and gallops off to Rome's aid.

Brennus Enemy of Rome is a bit rough around the edges, concentrating on Mitchell's barbaric savagery in the first half—executions by arrow (the victims herded into a mass grave), torture by red-hot poker and an order to amputate thumbs and

by utilizing Enzo Barboni's stunning color wash: a beautifully composed sunset over the Nile; the glare of the desert; the deep rich hues in the nightfall scenes; and the grand opulence of Gora's palace. It's this painstaking care and attention to detail that lifts Corbucci's movie out of the peplum rut, onto a much higher plain. Scrawling the mark of an "S" a là Zorro as his calling card, Reeves, after several thrilling set-tos, is unmasked, shoved in a cage and then let loose, leading to a head-on scrum in Gora's rooms. Sernas, a Judas to Garrani's cause, is killed and Canale spared, left to wander in the desert; Gora pays for his love of gold by having a vat of the melted metal poured over his face. When Reeves visits his old boss, he's informed that although his people will be left to get on with their lives, he himself must be sacrificed "like your father" as Rome cannot allow another guerrilla figurehead to live. Out on the sun-baked desert plains, the entire population of Zeugma congregates in the thousands at the crucifixion site in open protest at Reeves' harsh treatment; showing clemency, his detachments vastly outnumbered, Garrani gives the order for the son of the most notorious rebel warrior of them all to be taken down from the cross, then marches off. The curtain closer is of Reeves and Colli standing over his father's tomb, contemplating what the future will hold.

Another bonus to be found in this riveting saga is the soundtrack. Original composer Carlo Innocenzi died during filming (in March 1962), so the producers brought in Piero Piccioni to work on the incidental music. Innocenzi's title theme is fabulous, as is Piccioni's score, augmented by Angelo Francesco Lavagnino's input. Soundtracks in peplum movies were uniformly outstanding, right across the board, and the music here is no exception. From the golden age of sword and sandal, *The Son of Spartacus* is an absolute blast, one of the greatest Reeves ever participated in.

An American half-sheet poster for *Battle of the Spartans* (aka *Brennus Enemy of Rome*)

An Italian poster for *The Fall of Rome*

forefingers of those still alive to prevent them from drawing a bow. When Mitchell tells captive Davis, "The man commands. The woman gives birth. The slave works. This is the order of things," later adding, "Tomorrow, you will be mine," you know the unfortunate woman is in for a very rough ride indeed. Kendall survives a Gallic massacre and the last third of the movie concentrates on the battle of Catalina Hill, in which the Gauls are wiped out in a pulsating confrontation, the Romans unleashing a volley of arrows and spears onto the disorganized opposition and razing their camp to the ground. Mitchell, who has little time for those who rat on their comrades ("Drink up, dog! If Rome produces only animals like you, it's not worth destroying," he sneers at double-crossing Karis), sinks a blade into the senator's midriff and winds up with a sword in his back after a fistfight with Kendall on the banks of the Tiber. Score (Carlo Franci) and photography (Oberdan Troiani) are both top-notch, and Gentilomo keeps things moving at a cracking velocity. But this is Mitchell's show, the one above all others that demonstrates his hard-edged persona to the full—not the most conventionally handsome of the pepla he-men, more rugged than matinee idol, he put his fearsome visage to effective use here, that quick-as-a-flash shark-like grin (perfectly captured in widescreen DVD releases) and those piercing blue/gray eyes guaranteed to frighten not only damsel in distress Davis but any Roman unlucky enough to get too close to him. No one in pepla could play the dyed-in-the-wool bastard better than Mitchell on his day, a tremendous headlining performance that holds the attention from beginning to end. As an amusing sidepiece, some Italians thought that Mitchell was gay because he didn't smoke or drink, and never chased after producers' girlfriends (*sic*). In an interview, Mitchell stated that he took acting seriously, kept himself to himself and didn't socialize all that much away from the cameras. It would have taken a very brave soul indeed to level that gay accusation to the six-foot-three actor in front of his face!

The Fall of Rome [*Il crollo di Roma*]

Atlantica Prods./Cosmopolis Film (Italy); Totalscope/Eastmancolor; 89 mins; Producer: Marco Vicario; Director: Antonio Margheriti ††††

It may lack the depth and intelligence of *Constantine the Great*, similar in fact to a cowboy versus Indians flick in presentation, but *The Fall of Rome* speeds through its 89-minute running time, throwing in an opening conflagration, scraps between Romans and barbarians, fights in the arena and a climactic earthquake. This picture moves! Barrel-chested Carl Mohner plays Marcus, a Christian tribune at odds with Giancarlo Sbragia's oily Christian-hating proconsul Giunio. Emperor Constantine is dead, and with his passing, so is Roman tolerance toward Christianity; Sbragia wants the old order restored and instructs his men to burn those gentle, God-fearing vermin's homes, slinging Mohner into a dungeon for his beliefs in a non-Roman god; "Welcome, Christian dog!" he sneers. Mohner manages to slip away with a few allies, shakes off Piero Palermini's soldiers by causing a dam to flood the surrounding countryside and is escorted into barbarian Andrea Aureli's (Rako) camp; the outlaw admires anyone who hates Rome (as Mohner does at that precise moment in time) and tends to Mohner's wounded beloved, Ida Galli (Licia), who later dies, leaving the door open for dark-haired pagan goddess Loredana Nusciak (Svetla) to make her move on the grieving Roman.

Jim Dolen (Caius), Mohner's old commander-in-chief, arrives in Rome and sends a message to his former compatriot. Attend the forthcoming games and, if you survive the ordeal of combat in the coliseum, the Christians will be set free from imprisonment and a law passed stipulating that it will become a criminal offence to victimize them, totally against Sbragia's concerns that "the Christians' strengths are founded on martyrdom." The tribune does just that, wiping the floor with three gladiators in a scrimmage. Sbragia and Palermini are placed under house arrest and Dolen rides out with Mohner at his side to vanquish the barbarian tribes, who are getting too big for their boots ("I need you and your Christian soldiers."). On the waterlogged battlefield, the Romans are cut to pieces, Dolen meeting his Maker ("We're finished and so is Rome."); Mohner, pinned down in a canyon, has to face his one-time friend Aureli, creating an avalanche to prevent a massacre, saved in the nick of time by a regiment of legionnaires. In Rome, news of Dolen's death has reached the ears of Sbragia and Palermini; seizing the advantage, they round up the Christians and hold a second contest, intending to feed their captives to the lions. A Christian prophet is tied to a stake and riddled with arrows (footage from *Alone Against Rome* is inserted here), Mohner finding himself arrested again while Palermini makes a play for "barbaric beauty" Nusciak. But no one has taken into account the wrath of God. In the darkened amphitheater, the aged prophet meets his Creator bearing a smile, the heavens rumble ominously and a colossal earthquake hits the city. Buildings crumble, the massive stadium topples, fire breaks out, Sbraglia and his mistress die under a falling pillar and Mohner and Nusciak leave the smoking ruins behind: Rome has got her just deserts.

One question: Was filming carried out during the winter months? Several sequences show vapor issuing from the actors' (and horses') mouths. Riz Ortolani (Margheriti's favored composer) provides a strident, trumpet-based score and Riccardo Pallottini's color tones bring out the best in all those Roman and barbarian costumes. Austrian-born Mohner looks a bit awkward at times—peplum was not his particular forte (he starred in one other, 1965's *Captain from Toledo*) and it shows. But Shakespearean delivery wasn't called for here (as Sbragia's one-dimensional villain proved); action was the name of the game and, in this respect, *The Fall of Rome* scores highly.

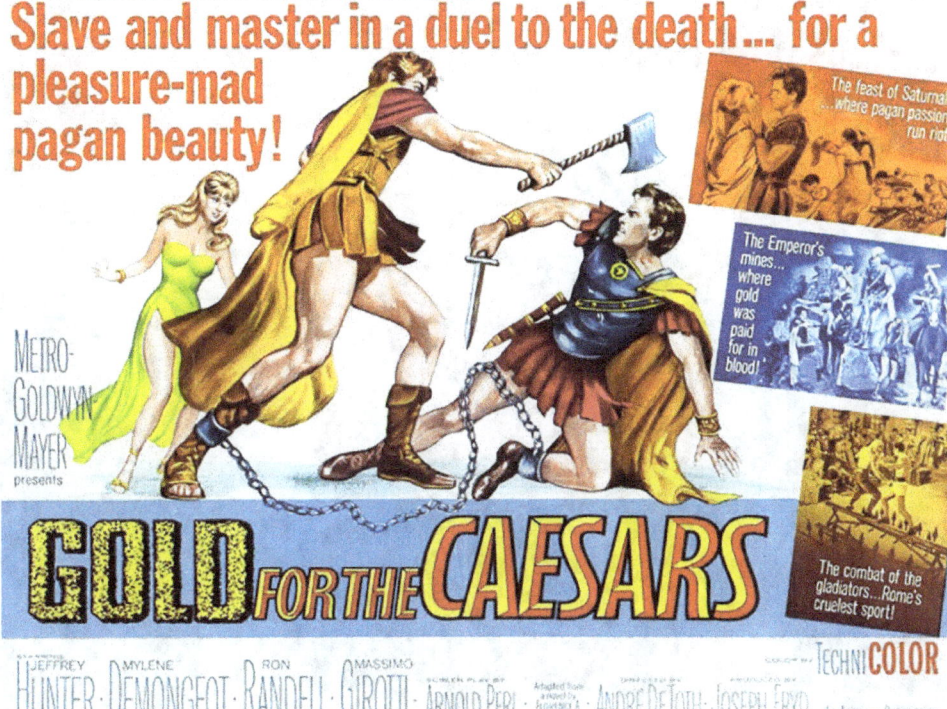

Gold for the Caesars [*Oro per i Cesari*]

Adelphia/CICC/Films Borderie (Italy/France); Technicolor; 98 (86) mins; Producer: Joseph Fryd; Directors: André De Toth, Sabatino Ciuffini, Riccardo Freda (uncredited) ♱♱♱

Spain 96 AD: Jeffrey Hunter stars as Lacer, architect and leader of a slave gang first seen putting the final touches to a Roman bridge, the hierarchy looking on in admiration as he clambers down a rope pulley, maneuvering the final stone block in place, a riveting, well-shot sequence. Also watching from a ridge is Georges Lycan (Malendi) and his Celts, who rain boulders down onto the construction but decide not to attack; his son, Ettore Manni (Luna), has other ideas, charging into the Roman camp brandishing a war axe, captured but released. Massimo Girotti (Proconsul Caius Maximus Cornelius) wants harmonious relations with Lycan, for the time being, that is; the coffers in Rome are empty, and he will shortly receive orders to take a detachment into the mountains, wipe out the Celts and look for gold. Hunter knows where that gold is, hidden away in the Sil Valley, so he's promoted, giving him a chance to romance Mylene Demongeot (Penelope), Girotti's sex kitten of a mistress.

Riccardo Freda collaborated with De Toth on *The Mongols* (1961), and for the first 50 minutes or so, *Gold for the Caesars* involves, all three directors manufacturing a tight scenario gleaming in Raffaele Masciocchi's dazzling photography. Hunter makes a good-looking slave with principles; Girotti chews the scenery; Ron Randell plays a vicious, whip-wielding centurion; peplum regular Furio Meniconi is Hunter's likeable, grizzled pal and Demongeot looks simply ravishing. Location work included the fabulous Cascata delle Marmore waterfalls in Umbria, actually begun by the Romans themselves, and there's a pagan Saturnalia festival included to whet the appetite. However, once Hunter, Girotti and their slave troops are in the hills looking for gold (located in a cavern behind a waterfall), the movie becomes heavy-handed, not helped by a studio mock-up stockade, a poor piece of set design lumbered with fake painted backdrops. Things liven up when Hunter erects a dam to gain easier entry into the caves. He fights Girotti to the death atop a sluice gate as the Celts rush in, the dam collapses, killing Girotti and drowning the Celts, and the slaves are freed and Hunter waltzes off with Demongeot, as Giulio Bosetti (Scipio) is proclaimed the new emperor. The camera closes on those magnificent waterfalls framed in the setting sun.

1964

The Colossus of Rome [*Il colosso di Roma*] aka ***Hero of Rome***; ***Arm of Fire***

Dorica/PEA/Unicité (Italy/France); Totalscope/Eastmancolor; 90 mins; Producer: Diego Alchimede; Director: Giorgio Ferroni ♱♱

Giorgio Ferroni, the man behind one of Italian cinema's most elegantly Gothic horror oeuvres, *The Mill of the Stone Women* (Galatea Film, 1960), came up with a bit of a dud in *The Colossus of Rome*, not one of Gordon Scott's better efforts. Playing he-man legion commander Caius Mucius, Scott spends the first few minutes foiling an Etruscan raid on a small caravan bearing vital food supplies to Rome. A one-man force, he slays around 20 men and lobs a 15-foot tree trunk at seven others—the antagonists retreat and the convoy reaches its destination safely. A sprightly beginning, then, but what follows is a turgid exercise in double-dealing and treachery, hindered by Antonio Visone's wordy script and a singular lack of thrills. Scott spends most of what little action there is fighting left-handed; as penance for not killing Etruscan king Porsenna (Roldano Lupi), he plunged his right hand into a brazier, rendering it useless (hence the film's U.K. title *Arm of Fire*). Because of this unselfish act, Lupi calls on a truce to end hostilities, but captain of his army, disposed Roman king Tarquin (Massimo Serato in the movie's top performance), agrees on one condition: 10 Roman girls are to be held as collateral in case the treaty doesn't work, and among those 10 is Gabriella Pallotta (Clelia), Scott's intended and, many moons ago, Serato's intended (a plot device lifted from *The Trojan*

A French poster for *The Colossus of Rome*

A Spanish poster for *Coriolanus: Hero Without a Country*

War). With Scott out of the way, Serato can claim Pallotta as his *and* scheme behind Lupi's back to overthrow the Romans.

The story is partly based on factual events. From 535-509 BC, a King Tarquinius, the seventh regent of Rome, ruled with a tyrannical hand and was eventually sent into exile. Lupi's son, Gabriele Antonini, falls for a Roman damsel, Maria Pia Conte; when she dies from an arrow wound after trying to escape Serato's camp, the prince sides with Scott, realizing that Serato has no intention of sticking to the peace terms. The picture drags in places and is no big epic, climaxing in a battle between Roman and Etruscan infantry, marred by utilizing stock footage from at least two other peplum productions and muddy photography; moreover, noted Italian composer Angelo Francesco Lavagnino (he scored an incredible 41 peplum movies between 1959-1966) provides a choral-laden aural cacophony, which is too discordant on the ear. Scott disposes of Serato, lobbing a sword into his chest, and Antonini finishes off the despot's lieutenant, Franco Fantasia, in similar fashion, the end to a rather dull sword and sandal offering that might have you fidgeting in your seat.

Coriolanus: Hero Without a Country [*Coriolano eroe senza patria*] aka **Thunder of Battle**

Dorica/Explorer Film '58/CFFP (Italy/France); Euroscope/Eastmancolor; 96 (88) mins; Producer: Diego Alchimede; Director: Giorgio Ferroni ††

Judiciously using stock footage from *The Trojan War* and *Hannibal* to pad out its running time, *Coriolanus: Hero Without a Country* is earnest and dull, despite a half-decent star turn from Gordon Scott, playing war hero Caius Marcius who, thanks to the machinations of perfidious senator Alberto Lupo (Sicinius), finds himself at war with Rome after falsely accused of treason. Republican Rome is in a state of conflict, not only with neighboring Volsci, but suffering internal strife within her own class system; the upper class (patricians) facing up to the lower class (plebeians). Naturally, devious Lupo sides with the patricians in order to feather his own nest, while upstanding Scott bats for the plebeians, especially when their grain is continually being stolen by bandits acting on behalf of Lupo. When Scott and his forces defeat the Volscian fortress at Corioli, Scott is renamed Coriolanus in honor of his resounding victory. Campaigning for the oppressed plebeians, he then takes on the role of senator at the insistence of politicians Philippe Hersent and Nerio Bernardi in order to expose Lupo's dirty tricks, but he is charged with the murder of a cowardly soldier, who was executed for desertion of duty. Kicked out of the city, Scott joins up with Pierre Cressoy (as Aufidius, leader of the Volsci), carrying out one successful raid after another on his native soil, his triumphant legions converging on Rome. Scott advocates a 30-year non-aggression deal with the Volsci, the senate agreeing: Lupo is unmasked as a treacherous rat (Scott produces incriminating messages sent by Lupo to Cressoy) and receives an assassin's arrow (meant for

An Italian poster for *The Giants of Rome*

Scott) in the back, the Roman hero riding off with his wife and child, peace and harmony having been restored to the Republic.

Excessive wordy interludes, stagy studio sets and the insertion of too much battle footage from elsewhere makes for a worthy but monotonous exercise in Roman history; even Carlo Rustichelli's score is below his usual high standard. Scott never once displays his well-honed physique, and hardly ever smiles; he appears ill-suited for the role, with villainous Lupo stealing the acting awards. As for resident peplum beauty Rosalba Neri (as Virgilia), she has very little to do other than plead with husband Scott not to take up arms against his own kind, her radiant charms not put to better use; Angela Minervini and Aldo Bufi Landi's romance is also forced and uninvolving, matching the overall mood of the picture.

The Giants of Rome [*I giganti di Roma*]

Devon Film/Radius Prod. (Italy/France); Totalscope/Eastmancolor; 95 mins; Producers: Mino Loy, Luciano Martino; Director: Antonio Margheriti ††††

Toward the latter stages of the sword and sandal craze, Antonio Margheriti concocted this "men on a deadly mission" opus which had its roots firmly in 1961's *The Guns of Navarone*. It's 52 BC and the Gauls and Druids, led by Vercingetorix, are fighting Julius Caesar's legions in the north and inflicting heavy losses on the Roman army, particularly in the siege of Gergorvia. Caesar (Alessandro Sperli) asks the Roman assembly for three additional brigades, from which he handpicks four of the bravest, strongest and toughest soldiers: Richard Harrison (Claudius Marcellus), Ettore Manni (Castor), Ralph Hudson (Germanicus) and Goffredo Unger (Varo). Their objective is to seek out and destroy, in three days, a Druid super-catapult protecting a vital pass, the weapon wreaking havoc on the Roman army. Joining the four hardmen is novice Alberto Dell'Acqua (as Valerius, renamed Robert Widmark in his subsequent film roles) and later, after a series of encounters with the Druids, Roman lady Wandisa Guida (Livilla), and her cowardly companion, soldier Philippe Hersent (Drusus), found manacled in a gloomy underground prison.

A promising beginning has five horse soldiers sacrificing themselves to the Druids, thereby enabling Harrison and his squad to sneak behind enemy lines. From then on, Margheriti lays on the aggressive incident with a trowel to keep things moving, the mercenaries extricating themselves out of one tricky situation after another; however, unlike most other peplum heroes, these men are not invulnerable. Harrison is branded with a white-hot iron, there's a getaway from a cavern during a fierce storm, requiring the crossing of a raging torrent, and Dell'Acqua is snared after squeezing through a narrow cave passage. "Caesar doesn't need dead heroes," growls Harrison, as the youngster is crucified on a tree; Dell'Acqua's final words uttered to his leader are, "I died as a Roman soldier." Down to four, the warriors swoop on two Druid rafts, taking captive a Druid woman and her fellow traveler. Hersent, wanting to save his own neck, cuts her bonds and runs off but is waylaid by Druid horsemen; dragged behind a horse, he expires in the dust. Next to go is muscular Hudson, plunging a sword into his abdomen rather than risk torture from the enemy. Then it's Unger's turn to fall before Manni, and Harrison locates the catapult, hidden on a mountain ledge stronghold. Manni is cut down by Druid chief Renato Baldini (Vercingetorix) as Caesar's army approaches; the weapon fires off one huge boulder coated in burning pitch and Harrison, lodged underneath the contraption, breaks the links of the massive chains holding it to the rock. Trundling forward, it topples over the cliff edge, crashing into the pass in a mass of timber and flame, leaving Caesar's legions in a position to overrun the Druid and Gallic hordes. Just for good measure, Harrison chokes Baldini to death with a length of wood.

Once again, Carlo Rustichelli provides a melodramatic score to underline the helter-skelter action, while Harrison shows that he wasn't just a musclebound ignoramus by giving his character Claudius some depth. Naturally, he gets the girl—victorious Sperli promises Harrison and Guida a wedding in the Temple of Venus on their return to Rome. And after all Harrison's been through, he deserves it!

The Revenge of Spartacus [*La vendetta di Spartacus*] aka *Revenge of the Gladiators*

Leone Film (Italy); Techniscope/Technicolor; 105 (93) mins; Producer: Elio Scardamaglia; Director: Michele Lupo ††††

In 73 BC, homeward bound, a soldier walks slowly down a farm track, right hand brushing ears of corn; at the house, his family lie slaughtered by corrupt Romans, his brother missing; swearing retribution on those who have perpetrated this crime, he joins a slave uprising, led by a man he will later come to hate. Yes, yet another contender for "movie that influenced *Gladiator*" (Ridley Scott must have sat through an awful lot of pepla before deciding on his own Roman epic) and a memorable one

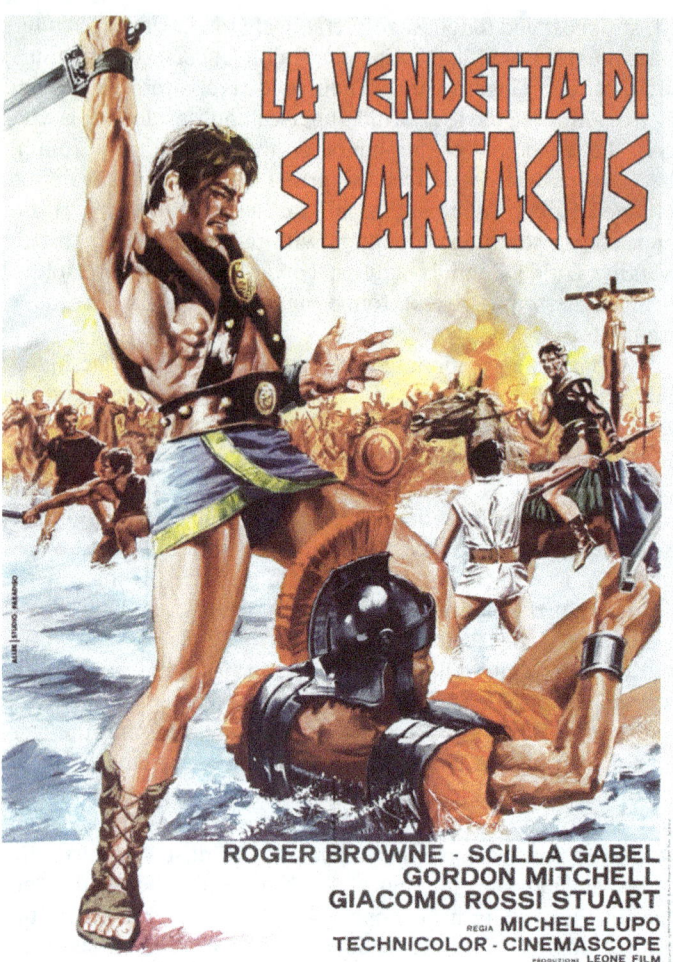

An Italian poster for *The Revenge of Spartacus*

to boot. It wasn't often you got a sword and sandal offering that had depth of character, moments of intimacy, stirred the soul and set the pulses racing for its entire length. Michele Lupo achieved precisely that here, with expertise and fervor—made back-to-back with *The Strongest Slaves in the World*, *The Revenge of Spartacus* is peplum cinema at its finest, featuring a fabulous Francesco De Masi score, bold cinematography from Guglielmo Mancori, a lucid script (Lupo co-wrote with Roberto Gianviti) and bruiser Gordon Mitchell at the peak of his game.

Mitchell, oddly listed in the credits as "guest star," is in fact one of the main stars, dominating the roller-coaster action from beginning to end. He's good guy turned bad guy Arminius, retrieving slave leader Spartacus from the cross and embarking on an agenda of pillage and destruction. In Rome, power-hungry senator Daniele Vargas (Lucius) appoints a commander over his hot-tempered son, Giacomo Rossi-Stuart (Fulvius), to quell the revolt and not show favoritism, but only to appease the senate; secretly harboring ambitions to rule the roost, he arranges for Rossi-Stuart to front the legions when the slaves continue to run riot. Roger Browne (Valerio), on leave from Spain, returns to find his mother, father and baby brother sprawled in the dust, his brother Germano Longo (Marcellus) absent. Killing five Romans still ransacking the homestead, Browne meets lovely Scilla Gabel (Cinzia), Longo's girlfriend, deciding to enlist with Mitchell's insurgents (Gabel quickly falls in love with Browne, and vice versa). However, although Spartacus is mentioned as a rallying cry to stoke the embers of unrest and spur the slaves on, why no sight of the man? Is there a mystery to be solved regarding his non-appearance?

The action, driven by Lupo's forceful direction, comes thick and fast before Mitchell shows his true colors. A Roman troop detachment is ambushed by the resistance fighters and decimated, Rossi-Stuart captured but then untied at the victory feast by persons unknown; Mitchell, Browne, Gabel and their compatriots have to up stakes and move, sure that Rossi-Stuart will lead his jackals to their cave sanctum; and Longo is discovered hurt and injured in a bog by the group's youngest member, Franco Di Trocchio. On his deathbed, he relates to Browne (shown in flashback) how Spartacus was dead when they hauled him off the cross ("We liberated a corpse."), how Mitchell arranged for all those present at the burial to be exterminated and how he alone escaped, only to bring destruction on the family. "You must avenge them," he gasps, dying in his brother's arms. So Mitchell is a backstabber, perpetuating the myth of Spartacus to keep the revolt flowing, while in cahoots with the Roman senate, his intention simple—exterminate the slaves and line his own pockets with gold in payment of his betrayal.

"Go rot in a ditch. I'm the boss here," snarls Mitchell to Gabel, eyes blazing (how Lupo loved to focus his camera on Mitchell's distinctive eyes!), before riding off to his Roman buddies. The refugees break into two sections; old men, women and children to go to the Bay of Circe, the warriors to make for the Bay of Vulci, where the final chapter of this tempestuous saga will take place. But Mitchell is on to them, planning a massacre. Browne and his splinter group arrive at Vulci to find the shoreline littered with thousands of speared and arrowed bodies, a spellbinding sight rarely experienced in epics costing 100 times as much, complemented by De Masi's beautifully judged score. Vargas, Mitchell, Rossi-Stuart and their men appear, galloping through the surf, laughing at the corpse-strewn beach. But not all those corpses *are* corpses. Up rise several hundred who have feigned death and battle commences. Vargas is speared, Rossi-Stuart slashed and Mitchell knifed in the back, the legionnaires annihilated. In a moving finale pumped up by De Masi's swelling music, Browne and his people rush across the headland to unite with Gabel and her lot, a vessel approaching to take them to a life unencumbered by Roman tyranny. "Our ship! We're free! Peace at last!" they cry. And if that wasn't enough to bring the emotions boiling to the surface, Di Trocchio, wiping away tears, bids a sad farewell to his faithful horse, Scipio. "You're also free. Goodbye." As the ship sails into the distance, Scipio stands on the foreshore, watching its departure; like the slaves, he's now able to wander at will, the end to a riveting slice of Roman mayhem that puts a lot of similar epics made before or since very firmly in the shade.

Revolt of the Praetorians [*La rivolta dei pretoriani*]

Prometeo Film (Italy); Techniscope/Technicolor; 100 (95) mins; Producer: Carlo Vassalle; Director: Alfonso Brescia ††††

In Rome, 96 AD, a marble bust on a plinth of Caesar Divas Domitianus (Piero Lulli) stands in the street; those not acknowledging their lunatic of a leader receive a sword in the guts from watchful henchman Aldo Cecconi. Praetorian Richard Harrison (Velerius Rufio), sick of the ill-treatment Lulli hands out to his downtrodden people, joins forces with young consul Giuliano Gemma (Cocceio Nerva) and takes on the guise of the "Red Wolf," leaping into the fray wearing a red wolf mask, cross-

Piero Lulli threatens Richard Harrison in *Revolt of the Praetorians*.

ing swords with Lulli and upsetting his preening Egyptian wife Moira Orfei (Artamne) at their numerous soirées. The troublesome rebel goes on to organize a mass revolt at his slave camp hideout, which proves to be successful after several clashes due to the intervention of the praetorian guards, also tired of Lulli's brutal chain of command.

Made back-to-back with *The Two Gladiators*, Alfonso Brescia's first feature film is 100 minutes of action-packed pleasure. Marvel at the sight of Orfei's swift change of colored wigs, commencing in silver, then green, on to blue, then black, then red and finally back to black; smile as Harrison's rather threadbare "Red Wolf" garb morphs into pink in some shots; hiss and boo every time Lulli sneers and pushes his weight around; laugh as diminutive court jester Salvatore Furnari (perhaps his biggest-ever role) constantly swaps sides, thwarting Lulli's gorillas at every turn of those underground galleries the cast spends so much time wandering around in; and take careful note of Carlo Franci's brilliant music, coming across like a Universal '50s horror soundtrack rather than your standard sword and sandal score. Luscious blonde babe Paola Pitti (Lucilla) plays Harrison's doll-like damsel in distress, ace photographer Pier Ludovico Pavoni lights those cavern scenes to perfection and Brescia brings a different kind of feel to his peplum outing, using a variety of artful camera angles not normally associated with these pictures. True to form, Furnari finishes off Orfei with an arrow while Lulli is speared in the abdomen following a well-staged fight with Harrison, who only displays his well-honed torso during the final 20 minutes. *Revolt of the Praetorians* is a little seen, efficiently made barnstormer, not a dull second in sight, and very difficult to obtain on DVD today.

Rome Against Rome [*Roma contro Roma*] aka *War of the Zombies*

Galatea Film (Italy); Totalscope/Eastmancolor; 98 (83) mins; Producer: Paolo Mercuri; Director: Giuseppe Vari
✝✝✝

Peplum was no stranger to *cinéma fantastique* as *Rome Against Rome* showed, a hokum-filled tale concerning a warlock, Aderbad (John Drew Barrymore in signature eye-rolling form), who plunders the battlefields for the bodies of dead soldiers, reanimating them through sorcery and the unholy worship of a mythical Cyclopean goddess, to be used against Rome's legions. Mario Bava or Riccardo Freda would have been in their element with this kind of pseudo-horror material to work on: Director Vari does a fair job of fusing sword and sandal with the undead, even though the pace crawls to a standstill on occasions and heroine Ida Galli (Rhama) switches from normal, to half-dead, to normal again so many times that we begin to lose count, wondering what state she's in from one scene to the next. Gabor Pogany's lush photography is a little too dark in some instances, while Roberto Nicolosi's weirder-than-weird score is straight out of a 1960s spookfest. The whole shebang is loose around the seams, leading man Ettore Manni looking as though he's totally bemused at what's taking place around him—probably being as mad as Barrymore's Aderbad helped!

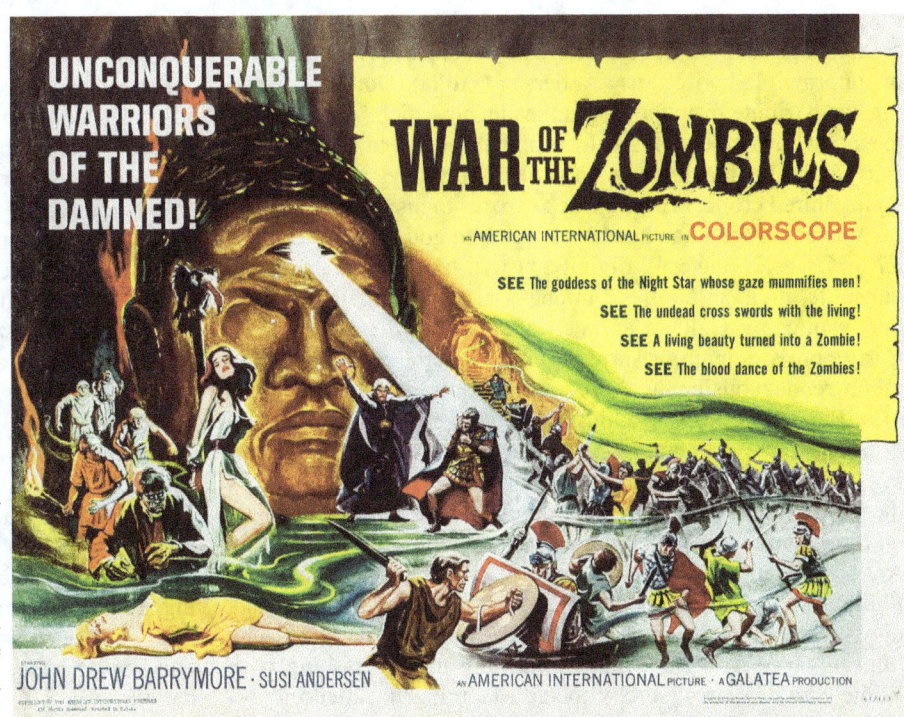

A U.S. half-sheet poster for *War of the Zombies* (aka *Rome Against Rome*)

The Italian Peplum Phenomenon 1950-1967

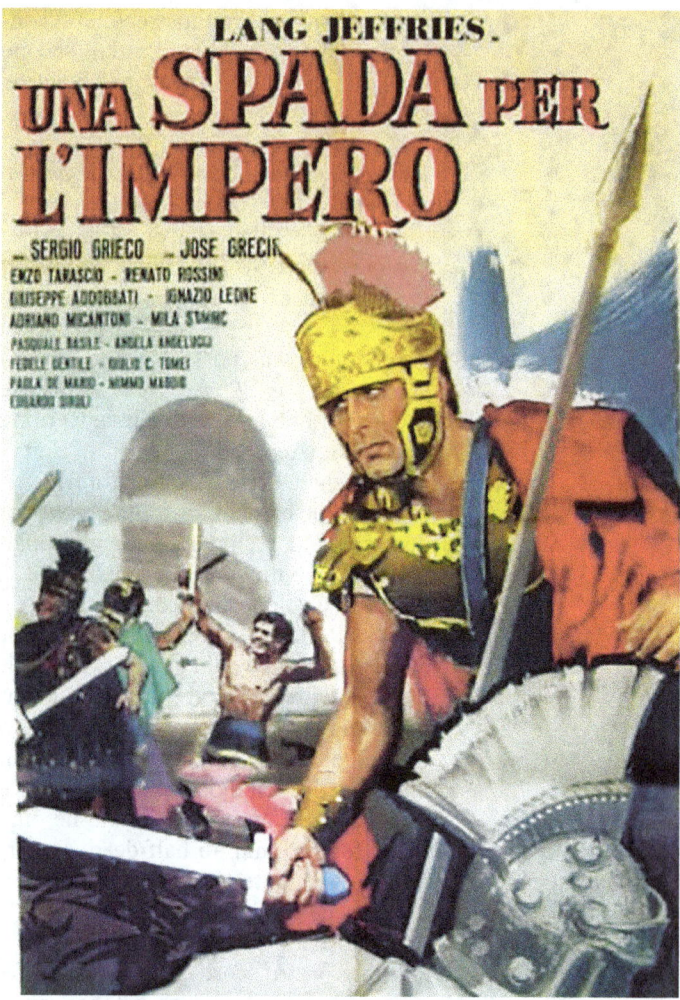

An Italian poster for *Sword of the Empire*

Manni (Gaius) is ordered by the senate to travel to Sarmatia on a secret mission and find out why a shipment of gold destined for Rome from the province has been hijacked, its guards massacred, liaising with ill-mannered legate Mino Doro (Lutetius) and his unprincipled wife, Susy Anderson (Tullia). Doro is squeezing harsh tribute from the disgruntled locals which Manni means to stop, while Anderson is a closet high priestess, in cahoots with Barrymore, the black magician's tribe of ugly pygmies, led by a white-haired crone, bringing back corpses to his misty chamber, dominated by the huge head of a one-eyed goddess, the Daughter of Osiris, a powerful divinity. "I will transfer the dead into our mute, invincible allies," intones Barrymore, Manni and his buddy tracking Galli to an enchanted forest where she enters Barrymore's domain, a slave to his mesmeric will, leading to much rendezvousing in those impenetrable, pitch-black grottoes, Barrymore (Vari's camera plays over that famous profile) grinning like a demented wolf as the sorcerer sets about creating his "soldiers of death." Anderson murders Doro and places the crime on Manni's doorstep (even though she has designs on him), and a Manni voodoo doll enters the frame, stabbed by Anderson, rendering the centurion helpless during a struggle; Philippe Hersent (Azir, chief of the Sarmatians) eventually links up with Manni to crush Barrymore's devilish shenanigans. The film climaxes with Barrymore's phantom troops clashing with Rome's legionnaires; stock footage was utilized, tinted in psychedelic, swirling blues, pinks and reds to lend an air of surrealism, but the sequences drag length-wise. In Barrymore's lair, Manni smashes the eye of the goddess which spurts molten liquid; the warlock goes blind, although still managing to plunge a sword into Anderson; the temple walls crumble, crushing the evil-doer, and the ghostly army disappears. Manni is last seen canoodling with Galli beside one of Monte Gelato's old mill buildings.

It's a bit hit and miss in some departments but idiosyncratic enough to entertain—Barrymore's deranged performance and Pogany's artistic color schemes make it worthwhile as a piece of oddball peplum cinema that was a veritable one-off, never to be repeated.

Sword of the Empire [*Una spada per l'impero*]

Assia Intl. Film (Italy); Cinemascope/Eastmancolor; 83 mins; Producer: Giorgio Marzelli; Director: Sergio Grieco ††

A distinctly below par tale of Romans in defiance of Christians/barbarians outing, the normally excellent Sergio Grieco seemingly going through the motions in yet another movie featuring mad emperor Commodus, played on this occasion by Enzo Tarascio. In 190 AD, the emperor has sent Consul Lang Jeffries (Quintus Marcus) to sort out the barbarian nuisance. Infiltrating barbarian warlord Adriano Micantoni's (Avalo/Artale) camp on perfidious friendly terms to gain information as to the chieftain's invasion tactics, he returns to Rome with abused slave girl José Greci (Nissia), a big mistake. Woman-crazy Tarascio gets the hots for her as well as Christian waif Mila Stanic (Marcia), a member of his household; both suffer continual sexual harassment from his grubby predations. Jeffries, beefy cohort Howard Ross (Leto) and their followers revolt against the emperor's depraved regime, rescuing the Christians and Greci in the final 10 minutes from burning on the cross; Jeffries stabs to death the hateful ruler in a swordfight, the consul assuming control of Rome's legions and the praetorians, with Greci resplendent in her aquamarine gown. The twosome is last spotted in a chariot, riding down an avenue of trees to set up house.

The pieces are all there, but somehow fail to fuse into a smooth flowing whole. Grieco stages two sequences of arena gladiator training, a bawdy pagan camp where female behavior is worse than the men's and the women are abused by lust-filled ruffians, senate in-fighting, Christians gone to earth in the gloomy catacombs and skirmishes between Jeffries' men and the praetorians. Jeffries and Ross are adequate as the buddies-in-arms, Greci is as radiant as ever but Tarascio's Commodus is the weakest portrayal of the deranged emperor ever committed to celluloid, acting more wimp than ruler of Rome, however insane he was. An average peplum score from Guido Robuschi and Gian Stellari fails to liven up a hastily put together Ancient Rome opus that's a little on the matter-of-fact side, nowhere near among the best this subgenre had to offer.

The Three Centurions [*I tre centurioni*] aka *Three Swords for Rome*

Capi Film/Radius (Italy/France); Totalscope/Eastmancolor; 95 (86) mins; Produced and Directed by Roberto Mauri ††††

When you have around 30 minutes of face-to-face fighting in an 86-minute movie (the edited version is the one currently on the market), you know you're in for a good time. And that's what happens when, due to budget cuts (yes, they even had those in 836 AD), three centurions who like nothing better than to enjoy a rough and tumble at every bend of the road are

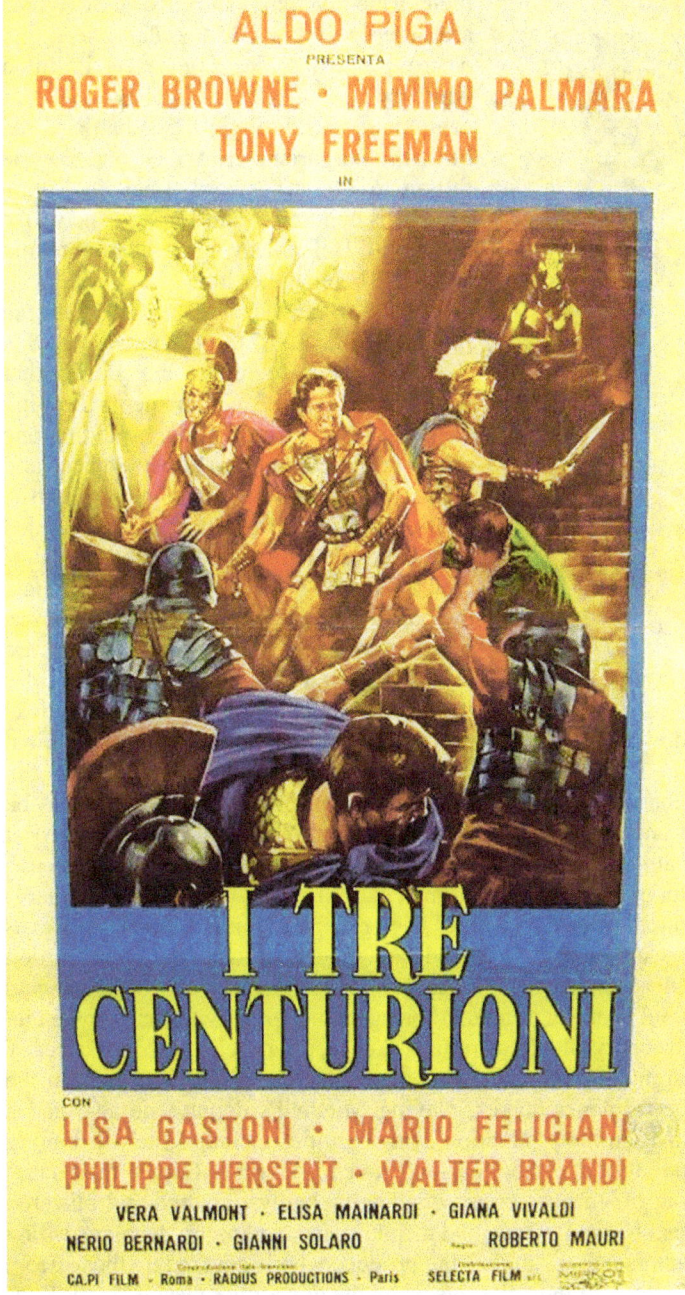

An Italian poster for *The Three Centurians*

demobilized from their legion, becoming embroiled in a plot to overthrow the King of Mousta, engineered by Queen Vera Valmont. One of pepla's lost treasures, *The Three Centurions*, as I write, is only available on scarce French VHS tapes, meaning that in the United Kingdom, due to France's SECAM broadcast system, color transference will be lost, Vitaliano Natalucci's photography reduced to black-and-white imagery. At least the tape is a high definition widescreen print with clear sound, a real bonus because Aldo Piga's Roman marching soundtrack is as thrill-packed as the action.

Buddies Roger Browne (Fabio), Mimmo Palmara (Maximo) and Mario Novelli (Julio, billed as Tony Freeman) quit their regiment, scrap with masked bandits, sample a bazaar's delights and get involved in a tavern brawl-of-brawls when they're swindled out of their winnings during a game of dice. The trio spills into the street; Valmont, in a sedan, admires them for their fancy fighting skills, and so does Mario Feliciani, King of Mousta, deciding to hire the beefy ex-soldiers as instructors, hoping their martial arts skills will rub off onto his useless guards. In the meantime, deep within a cavern under the palace, the bull-headed goddess Taishi is worshipped by a hooded sect presided over by Lisa Gastoni (Elena), cutting the throats of young virgins on the altar stone. Mauri's rapid-paced actioner squeezes its storyline between a series of bulldozing punch-ups, expertly choreographed: Valmont falls for Browne's boyish looks, counselor Philippe Hersent is in cahoots with her regarding who should be overlord and both want to defy Rome's authority by inciting a rebellion, preferably with the assistance of a rival state whose leaders arrive to back them up. Feliciani is murdered and Browne rescues the legitimate owner of the throne, 10-year-old Princess Eleanor, in a terrifying chase on a dilapidated chariot, crashing over a cliff but surviving. (The girl is hidden away in the woods by peasants.)

Nine minutes trimmed from the original print means matters get a tad fractured in the movie's latter half (and who is that crazy juvenile king briefly caught sight of at the beginning, never to reappear?), but the director rounds things off in furious style. The three comrades avoid being sacrificed by the hooded brethren, citizens riot, a Roman division enters the city and practically everyone bar Messrs. Browne, Palmara and Novelli, plus the child princess, is slain. The film becomes a barnstorming joy that shouldn't be taken too seriously (judging by their constant grins, the three lead actors didn't!). What a shame that in the United Kingdom it can't be viewed in color, *if* you are lucky enough to lay your hands on a VHS copy. (For an additional cost, professional transference to disc, using the correct software, *will* produce a color rendition.)

1965

The Fire of Rome [*L'incendio di Roma*] aka ***Fire Over Rome***; ***Revenge of the Gladiators***

GMC/Jadran Film (Italy/Yugoslavia); Totalscope/Eastmancolor; 94 (80) mins; Producer: Giorgio Marzelli; Director: Guido Malatesta ✝✝✝

"An unforgettable sight. Rome illuminated by the Christians!" So cackles mad emperor Nero (Vladimir Medar) as the city goes up in flames, God's retribution for burning all those Christians at the stake. Lang Jeffries is young Roman consul Marcus Valerius, returning from Gaul after a seven-year spell to find Rome led by a megalomaniac fruitcake and brutish Demeter Bitenc, head of the praetorian guard, who likes nothing better than to round up all those pesky God-worshippers, tie them to a cross and burn them alive. Unfortunately, both Jeffries' mother and girlfriend Cristina Gaioni (Giulia) are also followers of the new faith, so it's not long before they find themselves defenceless, under the heels of Bitenc's sandaled feet (his mother perishes; Gaioni survives). Sick of the way his once proud city has degenerated and intrigued by the words of the Christian disciples who hold closet gatherings in the catacombs (as in other pepla Christian-themed actioners, these solemn meetings can be rather over-sentimental in presentation), Jeffries, friend Franco Fantasia (Clodius) and the remnants of the 10th legion band together to come to the aid of the discriminated Christians and put an end to Bitenc's strong-arm tactics.

Like so many peplum movies made during this period, Malatesta's partially authentic take on Rome's downfall, coming

An Italian photobusta for *The Fire of Rome*

across like a watered-down *Quo Vadis*, has never been given the digital makeover it deserves; current hard-to-come-by issues lack the vibrancy of the original Eastmancolor print (Aldo Greci's photography is all but lost in the murk), while irritating jumps in the narrative indicate clumsy editing. Nevertheless, there's much to admire: a grand procession through the streets to mark the homecoming of a noted Roman general, milling crowds thronging the thoroughfares; Malatesta's thoughtful script; Medar's decadent festivities, mistress Moira Orfei oozing sex appeal; an energetic gladiatorial contest, Jeffries polishing off the head warrior; a mass execution of Christians; and a concluding tussle between Jeffries' men and Bitenc's guards, while all around them the conflagration rages and crowds stampede in terror. "If your God exists, he'll pardon us," shouts Jeffries to disciple Peter above the uproar, as he wades into the praetorians, killing their leader on the temple steps. The closing shot sees Jesus at sunset instructing Peter and Paul to help the suffering in Rome, even though, in the eyes of God, many had sinned. One interesting thing to note: In some scenes, vapor can clearly be spotted issuing from the actors' mouths. Were those Italian sound stages *really* that cold during filming?

1966

Shadow of Eagles [*All'ombra delle acquile*] aka ***In the Shadow of the Eagles***

Debora Film/Avala Film (Italy/West Germany/Yugoslavia); Totalscope/Technicolor; 88 (83) mins; Producer: Moris Ergas; Director: Ferdinando Baldi ††

Following the death of Emperor Gaius Octavius in 14 AD, the provinces of Illyria and Pannonia waged a bloody war of attrition against their Roman masters. In the 4th century AD, tribune Marcus Ventidius is sent to quell yet another uprising, capturing barbarian chief Magdus and his daughter Helen and placing them behind bars. Helen is betrothed to fearsome Illyrian warrior Batone but falls in love with Marcus, who in turn is loved by Roman noblewoman Julia. Out of jealousy, Julia arranges the escape of Helen and her father, who reunite with their tribe. Marcus and his legionnaires are ordered by consul Messala to seek and destroy; Magdus, desiring peace, is killed while trying to take flight from Batone's encampment, and during a fierce battle in the hills, the barbarians are wiped out, Batone falling to Marcus' sword. Back in Rome, Marcus is honored for his bravery and walks away with Helen, leaving a distraught Julia behind to bemoan her loss.

Made in tandem with *Massacre in the Black Forest* (1967), Ferdinando Baldi's last-ditch effort to revive the glories that were once Rome, within pepla's dying stages, is a sorry affair, notwithstanding one ornate set, decent color (Lucky Satson) and a fairly lively 80-minute climactic battle. Half-empty senate meetings, a feast attended by a handful of dignitaries and glum Cameron Mitchell (Marcus) riding off to defeat the pagan hordes with around 20 soldiers, a sequence repeated in its entirety later on, are indications of hasty production timetables and cost-cutting. Mitchell, aged 48, looks downright miserable most of the time, huddled in furs to combat the icy Yugoslavian weather (most outdoor scenes were shot in the snow), an indifferent performance, while love interests Beba Loncar (Helen) and Gabriella Pallotta (Julia) simply stare at camera and smile wanly (Loncar, attired in yellow, features in a loopy, otherwise men-only, dance routine, but even then remains impassive). Elsewhere, Dieter Eppler (Batone) screws his eyes up and glowers in a third-rate impersonation of the great Gordon Mitchell (or Jack Palance), Aleksander Gavric (Magdus) and Paul Windsor (Messala) bring a touch of gravitas to a movie that probably didn't warrant it and German Peter Carsten, a heavy in many 1960s war dramas, comes out better than most in the performance stakes, playing Mitchell's deputy (he also had a hand in the production). Incongruities include Mitchell running barefoot over hot coals to prove his worth to Eppler, then heading off to his troops with feet so badly scorched and blistered that he would have had difficulty in standing up, let alone riding a horse; and couldn't the producers have covered up those deep, far too obvious, tire ruts when the two armies clashed in the finale? As a nod in the direction of peplum's golden period, Mitchell meets Loncar in a fantastical grotto; there's a vicious whipping outside in the snow; and Gavric is cut off by a ring of lances in that classic peplum shot. Carlo Savina's score doesn't help matters; his theme music may be fine, but the incidental soundtrack is as funereal as the sluggish pace, adding to the air of gloom.

Shadow of Eagles showed, in many ways, a lack of fire in its belly, as though, like Mitchell's countenance, it had lost its fighting spirit. Like an end-of-season resort, Baldi's opus, lacking vitality and inventiveness, was there in name only, Italian film technicians and personnel connected with the genre having gone on to other things—*Shadow* in the title just about summed it all up. But, in parts, the picture looks attractive, enriched by Yugoslavia's bleak wooded scenery, hence the two-star rating.

13
Babylon and the Middle East

The Lost City of Atlantis, Old Bagdad, Aladdin, Ali Baba, rampaging sheiks, Ancient Babylon, Sinbad and Old Damascus—these were just some of the wonders encountered on pepla's journey through Middle Eastern fantasy, where directors' flights of imaginations knew no bounds and quite often disappeared altogether off the map of sensibility, entering into the realms of the quirkily absurd. Columbia's *The 7th Voyage of Sinbad* (1958) remains the ultimate in Middle Eastern fantasy, containing some of Ray Harryhausen's most exotic monsters and a tremendous Bernard Herrmann soundtrack, a movie soaked in Old Bagdad ambience, but the Italians, on occasions, tried to match it in Eastern promise, minus the stop-motion effects. So five years of camp, hokum and kitsch brought us Atlantis and its evil queen under the threat of the A-bomb, Gordon Mitchell thwarting the brain-transplanting, science-mad overlords of Metropolis, who plan to conquer the world, Steve Reeves stepping into the curly pointed shoes of Douglas Fairbanks, Ali Baba in the Valley of the Spirits, Babylon destroyed in a cataclysm, American teen heartthrob Tab Hunter's chiseled profile vying with that of Italian glamour girl Rossana Podesta's, a race of female gladiators clad in bondage leather, Kirk Morris charging across desert wastes in the name of freedom, lumbering Joe Robinson at large in Slovenia's striking Postojna cave system, Bella Cortez flaunting her considerable assets, Kirk Morris (again) defeating an evil Atlantean queen (again), Donald O'Connor on a magic flying carpet, Yvonne Furneaux's Queen Bitch of a temptress and a genre great in *The Hero of Babylon*. Elaborate sets, fabulous scores, dazzling photography and performances ranging from the believable to the corny; it would be a real sourpuss indeed not to enjoy every single one of the 21 guilty pleasures reviewed in this chapter!

An Italian poster for *The Giant of Metropolis*

1961

The Giant of Metropolis [*Il gigante di Metropolis*]

Centroproduzione SPA (Italy); Totalscope/Eastmancolor; 98 (85) mins; Producer: Emimmo Salvi; Director: Umberto Scarpelli ✝✝✝✝✝

The Giant of Metropolis receives a top rating because of its sheer uniqueness, if nothing else. A weird fusion of peplum, fantasy, science fiction and Atlantis myth, the production is adorned with outlandish art deco sets, garish colors spilling into every surrealistic nook and cranny (Oberdan Troiani), Armando Trovajoli's quirky organ-based leitmotifs ever-present in the background and a plot that takes in brain transplants, immortality, the creation of the perfect human being without the need for sexual intimacy and the conquest of Earth, adding for good measure a touch of bondage and S&M. The whole eccentric flight of fancy resembles a colorized 1930s *Buck Rogers/Flash Gordon* serial, representing hokey fun for enthusiasts; it's certainly not high art but is so utterly different as to be hugely entertaining.

Set in 20,000 BC (some film guides place the time in a different period, or even in the future), Gordon Mitchell (Obro) is the only member of his group to survive a magnetic storm (the "Whirlwinds of Death") on a volcanic rim outside the arcane city of Metropolis, dragged into the futuristic domain where every form of punishment is thrown at him by King Yotar (Roldano Lupi): heat rays, freezing rays, a lumbering giant caveman and five squawking, biting midgets. Lupi, taking advice from a 200-year-old prophet, acknowledges that Mitchell is nigh on invincible, deciding to transfuse his blood into his young son Elmos to make him immortal, even though the only thing the unhappy lad yearns for is fresh air, blue skies and the wind on his cheeks. Mitchell has arrived in Metropolis (another Atlantis) on a mission to bring death and destruction to the place, envisaging the city as a threat to civilization, shouting at Lupi, "Your power is based on a criminal form of science." Queen Texen (Liana Orfei) is bitterly opposed to Lupi's iron resolve and his experiments on their son, as is daughter Bella Cortez (Princess Mecede) and courtier Furio Meniconi. Cortez falls in love with Mitchell and Meniconi joins forces with the he-man to put paid to Lupi's rigid regime and crazy pseudo-scientific ideals, using a passage hidden under a giant statue's foot to come and go and scheme; Orfei eventually poisons herself rather than continue living with a tyrant for a husband. A violent volcanic eruption, brewing for centuries, causes a tsunami to deluge mist-filled Metropolis in the closing 10 minutes (excellent special effects

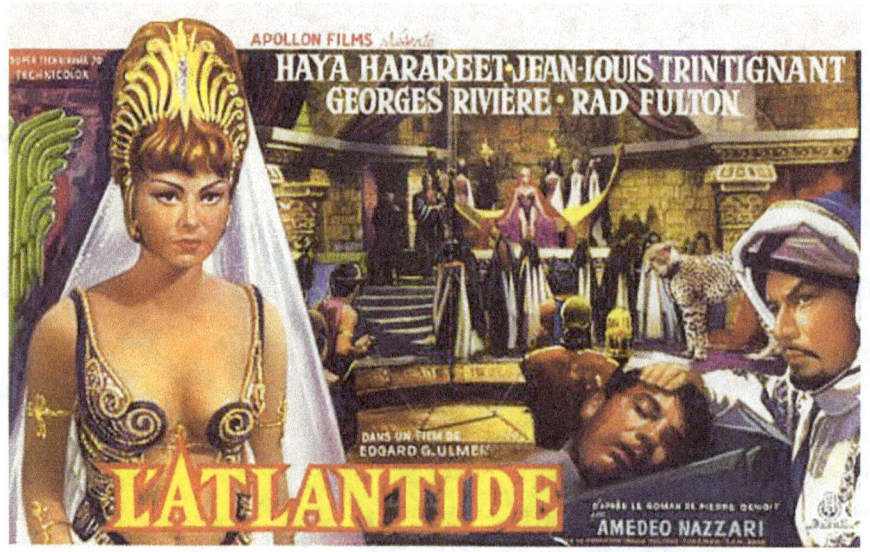

A Belgian poster for *Journey Beneath the Desert*

in this segment); the crowd, fleeing in panic, roar "Down with science!" and Lupi perishes under falling masonry in the ensuing cataclysm; Mitchell, Cortez and her brother escape into the outside world to begin a new life together.

Most genre productions include a dance routine. Here, lithesome Cortez and two loinclothed males perform a somewhat lewd robotic number in keeping with the film's sci-fi/sexually repressed fetish ambience. If the English dubbing doesn't match Mitchell's lip movements, it's because the beefcake actor only spoke a smattering of Italian, mouthing bawdy ditties instead of dialogue; it's a typical performance from the man, growling, snarling, making mincemeat of Lupi's ineffectual guards and stomping over the set, grinning like a wolf. Cortez and Orfei both look lovely, while Lupi chews the idiosyncratic, sharply angled scenery with relish. Kitsch with a capital "K" and the type of picture that will never be made again sums up Umberto Scarpelli's wonderful slice of Atlantis-themed schlock.

Journey Beneath the Desert [*Antinea, l'amante della citta sepolta*] aka *L'Atlantide*; *Siren of Atlantis*; *The Lost Kingdom*

Transmonde Film/Fides Film/CCM (Italy/France); Technirama/Technicolor; 105 mins; Producer: Luigi Nannerini; Directors: Edgar G. Ulmer, Giuseppe Masini, Frank Borzage ††††

Peplum meets sci-fi fantasy in a fourth adaptation of Pierre Benoit's famous 1919 novel *L'Atlantide*; unfortunately, current DVD issues are in pan and scan with deplorable color hues, rendering Enzo Serafini's cinematography to a sea of blues, reds, greens and, in several short spells, monochrome. Frank Borzage was taken off the project due to ill health and replaced by Masini; he died in June 1962 (Ulmer directed scenes for American consumption). Three guys in a helicopter (mouthy Jean-Louis Trintignant as Pierre, thoughtful Georges Riviere as John and handsome James Westmoreland as Robert [billed as Rad Fulton]) fly over a Saharan atomic bomb test site, crash on a mountaintop during a storm and find themselves in Atlantis, utterly bewitched by Queen Antinea (Haya Harareet, who played Esther in *Ben-Hur*). Israeli beauty Harareet, wearing a succession of outlandish headgear, simmers and stares through her slanted eyes, tying men up in knots; everybody loves her to death. High priest Amedeo Nazzari (Tamal) yearns for her favors, as does Gian Maria Volonté (Tarath), both jealous of the attentions Westmoreland, in particular, is receiving from the busty, predatory monarch. Which of the three non-Atlanteans can escape from the fabled underground metropolis before the A-bomb is detonated, consigning Atlantis to dust?

Is this a one-off weirder-than-weird gem or pure moonshine? The kitsch set design and art direction is flawless for a relatively low-budget offering such as this, while composer Carlo Rustichelli's score verges on the beautiful, especially his leitmotifs during Harareet's numerous seduction scenes. Never mind the so-so acting—Harareet glides impassively from set to set, Trintignant is fair-to-woeful, his two comrades almost as bad, Nazzari appears stiff, while notorious Italian hellraiser Volonté gives no indication that he would eventually become famous for his memorable psychopathic bandit chief, Indio, in Sergio Leone's influential *For a Few Dollars More*. It's the effect that counts here, and the overall effect is incredible, a merging of classic myth/fantasy ideals and Gothic grandeur. Bodies are submerged in liquid gold, emerging as golden statues, slaves work a giant grindstone to operate the subterranean mines, Westmoreland, in a cell, half-strangles Harareet in lust and self-loathing, calling her "a filthy beast," and Trintignant finds solace in another maiden, Giulia Rubini (Zinah), the girl massaging his fractured ego following one more rejection by the queen. In the closing minutes, the atomic bomb blast destroys Atlantis in a spectacular destruction

scene, ornate masonry tumbling down upon the Atlanteans and their ruler; Trintignant and Rubini take flight, out into the desert night, highlighted on a ridge as Rustichelli's powerful music wells up, leaving one to ask—couldn't Westmoreland or Riviere have made it out instead? And watch out for Harareet's nude dip in a pool, daring for early '60s fantasy cinema.

The Thief of Baghdad [*Il ladro di Bagdad*]

Titanus/Lux Film (Italy/France); CinemaScope/Eastmancolor; 100 (90) mins; Producer: Bruno Vailati; Directors: Arthur Lubin, Bruno Vailati ††††

Not quite able to reach the legendary heights set by Alexander Korda's 1940 production (what film ever could), *The Thief of Baghdad* nevertheless managed to raise the public perception of the whole peplum deal, plus what the Italian cinema industry was all about and had to offer a mass audience, just a few more notches above normal. The movie went on to become a sizeable hit in the United Kingdom when released with *The Giant of Marathon* in the latter part of 1961. Steve Reeves (as Karim, the thief) put in a winning, charismatic performance as the hero traveling to the land of the Seven Gates in search of an enchanted blue rose and encountering various weird and wonderful obstacles blocking his path. Backing up Reeves was Giorgia Moll's lovely Princess Amina, Arturo Dominici's cruel Prince Osman, Daniele Vargas' two-timing court advisor and Georges Chamarat's sprightly, diminutive magician. Reeves has to undergo this hazardous quest as the blue rose is the only object that can restore vitality to his poisoned beloved (Moll). Dominici is responsible for her condition, wishing to marry the girl by forcing her to drink a magic potion so that she may desire him; his plan has backfired—she loves the thief, hence the potion having an adverse effect. The tribal chieftain also wants to take over as sultan from Moll's father, Antonio Battistella.

The Thief of Baghdad, filmed in Tunisia, is a tad slow getting into gear, although to compensate for the methodical buildup, we are treated to some glorious set design and period costumes, drenched in Tonino Delli Colli's imaginative color tones, plus tracking shots of the hustle and bustle of street life in Old Baghdad. Once the journey begins, we are in true Arabian Nights' territory, the action steeped in the aura and spicy fragrances of those fabled mythological times. On the road, Dominici rips the water flasks belonging to Moll's several suitors and rides away sneering, leaving Reeves and the others to continue without him. Approaching a strangely carved line of cliffs, they tramp through an arch and camp in a grove of trees, whose branches become deadly serpents when the sun sets; when the sun rises, they revert back to branches. It's here that Reeves sets off alone, following the sign of the rose etched into rock faces. Crossing a field of molten lava, he enters an immense misty grotto full of gyrating dancing vixens, the realm of Kadeejah (slinky Hedy Vessel, billed as Edy Vessel), a seductive sorceress whose idea of fulfilling lovemaking is to turn her male admirers into stone statues. Italy's famed Monte Gelato waterfalls are supplemented by matte paintings of lofty caverns, rocky pinnacles and purple skies, lending the vistas the appearance of a Gustave Doré masterwork, a wondrously arcane image. Reeves turns the tables on Vessel, changing *her* into a stone figure, thus provoking the gods' fury; her temple is destroyed in a savage storm of retribution. Reeves struggles through an ensuing flood, scrambles onto dry land, scraps with a toothless pug-ugly wrestler on a precarious bridge, high above a sheer-sided ravine and spots a

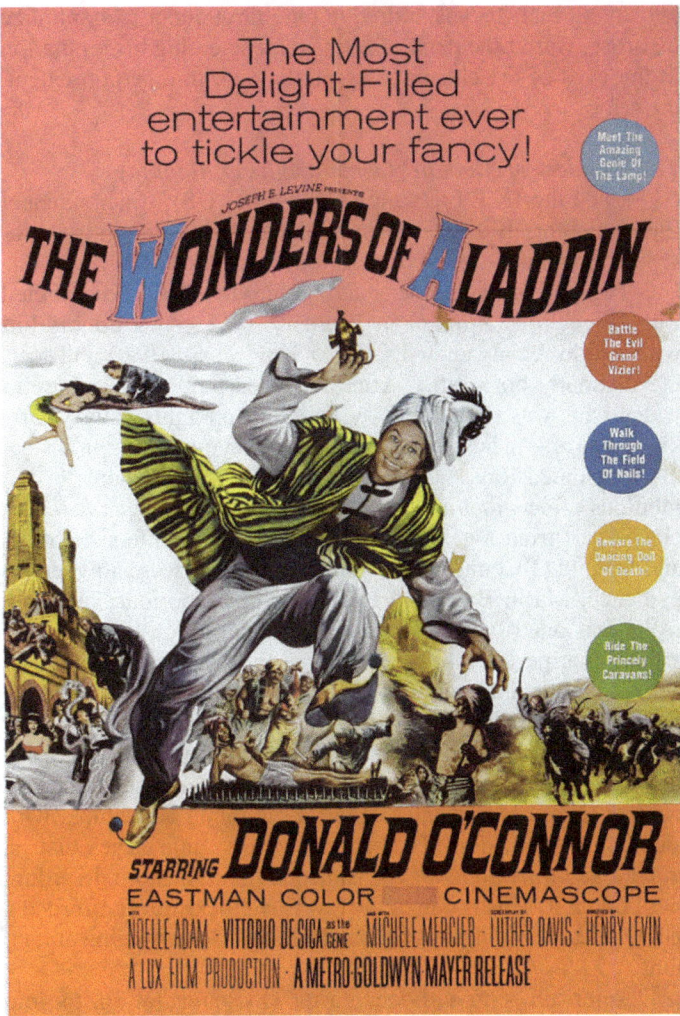

majestic castle in the far distance. Meanwhile, in Baghdad, Dominici has abducted Moll and has his men lined up outside the city walls, issuing the Sultan an ultimatum: "She dies if we can't have Baghdad to ourselves."

Within that baroque edifice, Reeves fights an army of egg-headed warriors, jumps on the back of a winged horse and nears a towering city, gleaming spires reaching up to the heavens. Inside the city's columnar opulence lies the rose; Reeves retrieves it, is given a magic ring by Chamarat, returns to Baghdad and replicates himself a hundredfold, sending Dominici's forces packing—this rowdy battle is played strictly for laughs, all 100 Reeves' wielding clubs, not a casualty in sight; it's not that kind of film (Carlo Rustichelli's bubbly score adds to the fun and games). During the fracas, the sacred blue rose is crushed; however, Reeves presents Moll with a white rose, it changes to blue and she's at last fit enough to whisper "I do" into the hunk's ear, a grateful Battistella handing over the sultanate to the now former Thief of Baghdad.

A top-notch production team hired ace British special effects technician Tom Howard, winner of two Academy Awards (*Blithe Spirit*, 1945; *tom thumb*, 1958), to supervise the astonishing fantastical backdrops that impart to the film its essential Arabian Nights mystical flavor; primitive by today's standards perhaps, but beguiling back then (Howard worked on the Korda picture but didn't receive a credit). There's an obvious feeling of care and attention to detail in an idiosyncratic Italian fantasy adventure, which can be enjoyed over and over again. It goes without saying that Reeves, attired in blue throughout to symbolize that rose, was at the peak of his game, cementing his reputation in the eyes of the cinemagoing public and, to a certain extent, the critics.

The Wonders of Aladdin [Le meraviglie di Aladino]

Lux Film/CCF/Embassy (Italy/France/US); CinemaScope/Eastmancolor; 100 (92) mins; Producers: Massimo Patrizi, Joseph E. Levine; Directors: Mario Bava, Henry Levin ††

The author remembers sitting through MGM-distributed *The Wonders of Aladdin* in February 1963 (on a double bill with Anglo Amalgamated's *Watch Your Stern*, 1960) and feeling distinctly bored stiff. After all, I had paid good money to watch what was supposed to be an Arabian Nights fantasy (of a kind, that is)—where were those exotic, eye-catching monsters that populated Ray Harryhausen's thrilling productions, or the fabulous effects that made 1940's *The Thief of Bagdad* so special? Apart from a genie, a couple of malicious life-sized dolls and Donald O'Connor on a flying carpet, they were nowhere in evidence. Mario Bava and Henry Levin's laborious, overlong frolic was one of several such films appearing on U.K. circuits around that period that fitted awkwardly between two slots, an adult's picture and a child's. Bava and cinematographer Tonino Delli Colli brought vivid color schemes to the production and there was a smidgen of Arabian Nights atmosphere in the opening 20 minutes, but the story, concerning a usurped prince, a wicked Grand Vizier and Aladdin's bumbling adventures with sidekick Omar, dragged interminably, to younger eyes that is; maybe adult members of the audience found it more diverting, but I doubt it. This is one of the few Bava flicks never afforded a DVD release, which says a great deal for its low standing among fans.

American song-and-dance actor O'Connor (at 36, too old for the part of "young Aladdin"), given a tiny oil lamp by his mother, conjures up a genial genie (four-time Academy Award winner Vittorio De Sica) and embarks on a trip with servile slave Milton Reid (Omar) to experience a prince getting wed. Sultan Aldo Fabrizi's daughter Michele Mercier (Zania) is due to marry Prince Terence Hill (Moluk, billed as Mario Girotti), but Grand Vizier Fausto Tozzi has designs on the damsel and the Sultan's throne, utilizing the services of a wily magician (Raymond Bussieres), who constructs two sinister dolls, one a male flute player, the other a female that can crush those caught in her murderous embrace. O'Connor and Reid, stranded like a pair of idiots in the desert on their enforced march to the palace, glimpse mirages (Bob Hope and Bing Crosby did this so much better in Paramount's *Road to Morocco*, 1942) and get buttonholed by a group of lofty, sex-starved Amazons. Like the praying mantis, the women want to mate with the pair (*this* pair?) and kill them afterwards ("Her Majesty has chosen the little one—the big one is ours."). De Sica emerges from the lamp in a plume of purple smoke, saves their necks (and probably their blushes through lack of sexual prowess) and dumps them in a line of prisoners on the march, O'Connor's delightful girlfriend Noelle Adam (Djalma) among them. The slave caravan reaches the palace and following one lame semi-madcap situation after another, Mercier marries Hill, Tozzi is vanquished and O'Connor and Adam fly off on a magic carpet.

Poor optical effects (the traveling mattes look obvious and amateurish), a lukewarm score from Angelo Francesco Lavagnino and umpteen shots of O'Connor tripping, tumbling, jumping

and vaulting over objects, forever acting the fool, do nothing to enliven a tiresome fantasy that fails to hold the interest. We are left waiting for things to happen; unlike the genie, they fail to materialize (although he fails at one point!). The movie may be pantomime-picturesque in some sequences, but its comedic elements come across as forced and unfunny; *The Wonders of Aladdin* lacks wonder and is far from enjoyable.

1962

The Golden Arrow [La freccia d'oro]

Titanus (Italy); Technirama/Technicolor; 91 mins; Producer: Goffredo Lombardo; Director: Antonio Margheriti †††

One-time teen heartthrob Tab Hunter donned blue turban and curly pointed shoes to star as Prince Hassan in this occasionally absurd, always entertaining Arabian Nights confection, aided and abetted by Rossana Podesta's statuesque Princess Jamila, her finely chiseled features perfectly matching those of Hunter's. A clutch of suitors are after her hand in marriage, including arch villain Mario Feliciani as Baktiar, a courtier who plans to become Grand Vizier of Dasmascus once Podesta is his. Present vizier Renato Baldini (the Prince of Bassora) is in on his plans, being responsible, alongside Feliciani, for the murder of Hunter's father, condemning the young prince to the life of a thieving bandit leader. To prove his true credentials and usurp

Club-wielding Iloosh "Rod Flash" Khoshabe as Ali Baba swings into action in *The 7 Tasks of Ali Baba*.

the dastardly duo, Hunter, with the aid (and hindrance!) of three crackpot genies (his "liberators"), has to travel over half of the Middle East in search of the magical golden arrow, a kind of Arabian Nights version of the legendary Golden Fleece minus the monsters.

Judging by the amount of picturesque location work involved, Margheriti had a larger-than-usual budget to work on— Hunter and his three loopy pals hop from an oasis to a ruined city; there's a gloomy cave system inhabited by an evil queen and fire monsters; and a temple in the abandoned metropolis of Thebes presided over by a mad magician (who can turn people to stone), where another regent and her subjects are held captive, all filmed in hard color hues to capture that intense quality of light prevalent in the Middle East. We are treated to dances, boxes of treasure, sexy queens, rooftop and dungeon escapes, the water of life that restores the dead, mystical trickery and a lengthy finale in which Hunter and the three affable genies, on flying carpets, hammer Feliciani's massed forces on the outskirts of Damascus by bombing them with jugs and urns. Hunter is the only one who can bend the bow to fire the golden arrow, which returns to him like a boomerang; Baldini and Feliciani fall off their shredded carpet into a bog, leaving Hunter to marry Podesta. *The Golden Arrow*, tongue set firmly in cheek, veers all over the place, serious one minute, ridiculously infantile the next (composer Mario Nascimbene's constant use of a twee leitmotif when the three genies are on screen becomes plain irritating), but it's lighthearted nonsense in a corny, fun-packed kind of way (peplum dazzler Gloria Milland is briefly in it), similar in tone to Donald O'Connor's inferior *The Wonders of Aladdin* and MGM, who distributed the film outside of Italy, made quite a profit out of it. Best line in the picture? "Women never admit their real weight or their age."

The 7 Tasks of Ali Baba [*Le 7 fatiche di Ali Baba*] aka **Ali Baba and the Sacred Crown**
   Avis Film (Italy); Totalscope/Eastmancolor; 96 (90) mins; Produced and Directed by Emimmo Salvi ✝✝✝✝✝

A turbaned turkey? Not one bit of it. Emimmo Salvi's Arabian Nights brew is one of peplum's rarest, most enjoyable productions; one day, it's to be hoped that a decent widescreen print will become available to fans. Cinematographer Mario Parapetti paints the picture, in particular the numerous underground sets, in bold color strokes straight from the artist's palette as befits a fantasy adventure of this type, while Marcello Giombini's Middle Eastern score is nothing short of fabulous. Monstrous torture devices, Bella Cortez (as Lota) looking stunning, Furio Meniconi looking just plain evil and strongman Iloosh "Rod Flash" Khoshabe in perhaps his best genre performance, all knitted seamlessly together by Salvi's taut direction; it only needed a Ray Harryhausen mythological being to stride into camera to make it a classic—but, in its own flamboyant way, it's a peplum classic. They really don't produce movies like this anymore.

In the city of Sheraz, "Black Dog" Mustapha Bey (Meniconi) is desperate to lay his hands on a sacred gold crown that, when worn, will promote him to almost Godlike status. Amedeo Trilli, a politician under Meniconi's thumb, sends word to Ali Baba (Khoshabe) to collect the artefact with its associated treasure and bring it to Sheraz as soon as possible, to placate the tyrant who's on a vendetta of torture and death, screaming, "Those who disobey my commands must be killed," adding to Trilli that if he isn't allowed to marry his daughter (Cortez) on her 18th birthday, he'll slaughter every young female in Sheraz out of pure spite. Meniconi's speciality is a frightening device fronting the city gates, a spiked pendulum that rocks back and forth, eventually pushing its victim into a bed of flames. Khoshabe collects the coveted chest from an age-old wizard residing in a secret grotto ("Open Sesame!"), delivers it to Meniconi and strings him along, telling him that the chest shouldn't be opened before the conjunction of the moon with Venus takes place. This doesn't fool the subjugator. Cortez performs a risqué dance involving ropes, while the chest is opened and sand, not treasure, spills out. Khoshabe, friends Omero Gargano and midget Salvatore Furnari are imprisoned and tortured, twice. First, they are lashed to a pole, slaves turning a screw, almost throttling Gargano and Furnari, while pushing Khoshabe up toward a row of blades; second, they are hauled toward a line of fire by two horses. Cortez, chanting magic mumbo jumbo, reveals a hidden gateway in the trio's cell and they escape to the enchanted Valley of the Spirits, inhabited by Sinbad's spirit; there, with brother Mario Polletin and his girl, Liliana Zagra, they hatch plans to depose Meniconi and bring peace to Sheraz. During a fracas with Meniconi's soldiers, Khoshabe is gravely injured; Cortez cauterizes the wound, he recovers and they fall in love. Salvi pulls out all the stops in the last 15 minutes to create a thrilling payoff. Cortez, Trilli and Zagra are tied up on that infernal torture instrument and, even with the crown now in his grasp, Meniconi denies their release; agitators lurking in the crowd get to grips with the enemy, Khoshabe's 40 men charge through the gates, the guards are overrun, our muscular hero prevents the pendulum from achieving its gruesome duty and Meniconi, knocked unconscious, is thrown into the flames like a rag doll. "I'm from the desert, and freedom is my life," states Ali Baba

A French poster for *The Seven Thunderbolts of Assur*

hitching up with Jocelyn Lane as Mirra ("You are a gift from the gods. Come with me to Babylon."), a dark-haired peasant girl who survived a village massacre and was brought to Duff's court by prophet Arnoldo Foà (Zoroastro)—the holy man forecasts doom and destruction if Duff doesn't adopt a more compassionate attitude toward his people, but is accused of blasphemy. "No man is as lonely as a king," intones Duff, having fallen in love/lust with Lane after viewing her asleep in her bedchamber; Marin spots the pair canoodling, bristles with jealousy, whisks her off to the Babylonian encampment (palace walls for tents? Not the best of exchanges for a young queen-to-be!) and goaded into hostilities against Duff by Giancarlo Sbragia (Arbace) and his generals, who are scheming to put paid to Marin anyway. He's failed to impress them; they regard the new king as being not tough enough for the job. By all that's holy, he even relied on Duff to slay the lion that leapt on him during a hunt and then claimed credit for the kill. On his way to Ninive to confront his brother, Sbragia's confederates murder Marin, his head stuck on a pole and positioned outside the city walls. War is immediately declared. In the 64th minute, the first battle commences and it's a thriller, ending with the Assyrian army in tatters and on the run. "Only the forces of nature can defeat me," howls Duff, tearing down the statue of Assur in anger, thus provoking the wrath of the gods. Storm clouds gather, lightning forks the night sky, the rain lashes down, river levels rise and a successful sortie on the Babylonian camp (Sbragia is pushed to his death onto metal chariot spikes) is followed by a celebratory banquet. However, the king should have heeded the warning of the prophet. A huge

to Trilli, turning down the chance to rule Sheraz; Cortez grabs *her* chance, waltzing off with her hefty suitor down an avenue of raised flags, aiming to return the holy crown to the ghostly wizard in that remote cave. Magical escapist stuff right up to the last second that director Salvi failed to improve on in his second *Ali Baba* outing two years later, *Sinbad* (or *Ali Baba*) *Against the Seven Saracens*.

The Seven Thunderbolts of Assur [*Le sette folgori di Assur*] aka *War Gods of Babylon*; *7th Thunderbolt*

Apo Film (Italy); Totalscope/Eastmancolor; 90 mins; Producer: Alessandro Tasca; Director: Silvio Amadio ††††

It's brother versus brother in this opulent Babylonian variation of *The Last Days of Pompeii*, featuring outstanding set design and art direction highlighted in glorious color tones by courtesy of photographer Tino (Clemente) Santoni, a real feast for the eyes. In the exciting climax, King Howard Duff's city is virtually wiped out by a cataclysmic tsunami-type flood, a riveting five-minute sequences that shows precisely what could be achieved in cinematic effects 50 years ago without computer technology. Before that, we are plunged into a talkative plot centering on court intrigue that allows for more character complexity than is usual in your standard peplum picture. In 630 BC, King Sardanapolo (Duff), potentate of the Assyrian city of Ninive (Nineveh), has Babylon firmly under his thumb, exacting unreasonable tribute from the country's legislators year-by-year. Weaker brother Luciano Marin (Sammash) is crowned King of Babylon to seal the fragile relationship between the two realms,

A French poster for *The Son of the Sheik*

flood obliterates the city and Duff, realizing his time has come, sets fire to the great hall, himself, his followers and Lane by his side, perishing in the flames and falling masonry, the ultimate sacrifice for spurning the gods and the words of holy man Foà. Yes, there's no happy ending in this picture!

Dialogue-driven for its first hour, *The Seven Thunderbolts of Assur* holds the attention mainly through those magnificent sets lit in deep rich color, the kind of attention to detail found in many other more expensive, and much longer, epics. Condensed to 90 minutes it may be, but this is one picture that crams an awful lot into its running time and manages to look fantastic in the process.

The Son of the Sheik [*Il figlio dello sceicco*] aka *Kerim, the Son of the Sheik*

Mercury Films/CFFF (Italy/France); Euroscope/Technicolor; 85 mins; Producer: Jean-Philippe Mérand; Director: Mario Costa ††††

Most of pepla's plot clichés figure heavily in Costa's blood and sand mini-epic, a virtual remake of 1957's *Desert Warrior*: a hero taking up arms on behalf of his victimized people (Gordon Scott); an evil oppressor (Alberto Farnese); the oppressor's equally evil henchman (Gordon Mitchell); a princess in dire distress (Cristina Gaioni); a spurned, devious mistress (Moira Orfei); a jealous eavesdropper (Lulla Selli); exotic dance routines; bad guys wearing red robes; public floggings; a climactic good versus evil battle sequence; and that oft-used peplum ultimatum: "Marry me and I'll spare him." But notwithstanding the familiarities, this is one hell of an action movie, packing more into its 85 minutes than many films twice that length. Costa dispenses with intimate, meaningful close-ups, going top speed for exciting set pieces framed against sparse desert vistas stunningly shot by Angelo Lotti. Add to this a thundering Francesco De Masi score and you have all the right elements in place for a rousing Middle Eastern romp. Fair enough, it's not *Lawrence of Arabia*, and Costa is no David Lean, but for out and out desert action, *The Son of the Sheik* takes some beating. And it's possible, with perseverance, to track down reasonable prints in widescreen, untainted by the dreaded pan and scan process.

In the 1860s, Farnese (Omar) is busy persecuting the nomadic Bedouin tribes, running them off their oasis homes to prove the point that he is the ruler of the Khedive nation, and no one else. Abducting Scott's sister, Maria Grazia Spina (Laila), in a raid ("I've heard so much of this little jewel of the desert, I've decided I want her."), the mountebank takes her to his fortress, forcing himself on the "Bedouin savage." In a struggle, the girl dies from a fatal knife wound. Seething with rage, Scott transforms himself into The Black Sheik, the leader of, at first, a gang of vigilantes whose sole aim is to be a thorn in Farnese's side. Then court advisor Nando Tamberlani's daughter Gaioni (Fauzia) becomes the object of Farnese's desires; jailing her father, he promises to save him from a beheading if she agrees to marry him. Scott is already in love with the girl, so when he learns of the despot's latest despicable act, he rallies the numerous tribes faithful to his cause in an attempt to depose the desert dictator, holed up in an impregnable fortress.

In the 48th minute, Gordon Mitchell (Yussuf) rides over a ridge, attired in black, his soldiers swooping on Luciano Benetti's caravan; annoyingly, old stone face only features in the

A Spanish lobby card for *The Green Flags of Allah*

movie for the next nine minutes, Scott's warriors soon entering the melee, the two bodybuilders coming to blows; Mitchell is killed, sprawled in the dust (he was always worth more than nine minutes of any buff's time). In the 69th minute, the major charge to capture Farnese's stronghold takes place, a 10-minute barnstormer that sets the pulses racing. Orfei (Zahira, Farnese's hateful mistress) is slain by Selli and Farnese, realizing his time is up, he gallops off into the sandy wastes, Scott on his heels, a mesmerizing panoramic sequence, both men black dots on a shimmering horizon (as was Omar Sharif in Lean's classic). Farnese is stabbed to death and, in the closing shot, Scott and Gaioni ride away to a fusillade from the grateful tribes now purged of the yoke of humiliation.

1963

The Green Flags of Allah [*Le verdi bandiere di Allah*] aka *The Slave Girls of Sheba*

Italia Produzione/Dubrava Film (Italy/Yugoslavia); Colorscope/Eastmancolor; 100 mins; Producer: Giacomo Gentilomo; Directors: Giacomo Gentilomo, Guido Zurli †††

Look beyond the current ragged pan and scan, black-and-white prints and try to visualize *The Green Flags of Allah* as it was, in widescreen and Eastmancolor; lobby cards, photobustas and posters for sale on the Internet help in this respect, but as at the time of writing (2015), that poor-quality issue is the only item available for diehard collectors. Not that the movie is great—it begins well, the Sultan of Constantinople drawing up plans to raid infidel Vittorio Sanipoli's impregnable fortress, then sags in the middle before picking up in the final 30 minutes. But experiencing it in its original format would have greatly amplified the viewing experience.

Sultan's favorite Mimmo Palmara (as Hibrahim, sporting an eye patch) enlists José Suarez (Omar) to help bring about the downfall of Sanipoli (Sheik Selim), who's determined to break the peace treaty between the Sultan's dominions and Spain; he's siding with Spain's enemies, the French. The anarchist abducts Suarez's girlfriend, Cristina Gaioni (Ursula), Suarez's father captured and hanged, so he's only too willing to join in the fight.

Gordon Scott is held at bay in *The Hero of Babylon*.

Suarez, with the aid of grappling irons, scales the castle walls but fails to rescue Gaioni, leaping into the sea to evade capture. Boarding Palmara's boat, the *Black Eagle*, the crew stop off at Sheba, pick up a couple of slave girls and drop anchor at Constantinople, and it's at this 40th minute juncture that the narrative falls apart, straying dangerously close to *Road to Morocco* territory. Another reprobate is thrown into the mix, a poisoner bent on pinching the Sultan's throne; slave girl Linda Cristal (Olivia; she's in love with Suarez) has the soles of her feet flayed in a torture chamber, a cryptic document is somehow tied up with a harem of 400 women (Hélène Chanel is the Sultan's number one choice) and Suarez and friar Walter Barnes flit from one room to another dressed as Arabs, a peplum variation on Bob Hope and Bing Crosby's skit from the duo's 1942 comedy classic; where's Dorothy Lamour in their hour of need? Guido Robuschi and Gian Stellari's up-to-then stomping soundtrack gives way to twee leitmotifs and everything and everyone becomes rather silly. Barnes (the American actor starred in 10 pepla adventures, mostly as a pirate) mouths one funny line, "What a place! Women! Poison!" before the poisoner/usurper receives four crossbow bolts in his chest and Palmara plus the shipmates head off for San Antioch, the home of Sanipoli's fortress. Entering the castle, Suarez discovers that two-timing Gaioni has married Sanipoli for financial stability; he's captured, tied to an enormous anchor and left to be lowered slowly into the ocean. Gaioni, in a fit of conscience, blows the cannon room to smithereens (and herself), while Palmara's vessel opens fire, Suarez is saved from a watery grave and delivers the death thrust to Sanipoli in a face-off, and fiery Cristal finally has her man all to herself.

Director Sergio Leone was one of five scriptwriters hired to bring this cheesy slice of Far Eastern promise to the big screen, and it's to be hoped that one day, peplum fans will be presented with the picture as originally intended to be seen. Not altogether 100 percent successful, perhaps, but entertaining all the same.

The Hero of Babylon [***L'eroe di Babilonia***] aka ***The Beast of Babylon Against the Son of Hercules***; ***Goliath, King of the Slaves***
Gladiator Film/CIRAC/FIA (Italy/France); Euroscope/Eastmancolor; 98 (93) mins; Producer: Albino Morandini; Director: Siro Marcellini ✟✟✟✟✟

It may indeed rank as one of the foremost of all peplum productions, embodying within its framework the ideals, if they can be termed thus, that made the genre so noteworthy at the time and so revered by fans today, but *The Hero of Babylon* is also notorious in another aspect—the depiction of unrelenting violence toward women. They're flogged, crucified, strangled, tortured and pitched into a pit of flames as sacrifices to the God of Fire, Ishtar, all to appease the bloodlust of King Balthazar of Babylon (Piero Lulli) and ice-cold High Priestess Ura (Moira Orfei). This misogynous streak is overplayed at times and slightly disturbing to watch, but it fits in well with the sadistic scenario (a scenario that Italian horror movies of the period wallowed in) and Lulli's terrifying performance as the malignant monarch, a man who radiates pure viciousness.

A fiery comet strikes the Earth, the signal for Lulli's vipers to raid an enslaved village, select a handful of beauties and drag them to the palace, there to be sacrificed. Genevieve Grad (Tamira) gets loose, saved from being hunted down by Gordon Scott, playing Nippur, the legitimate heir to the Babylonian throne. "You're my lord and master," she coos, instantly attracted to Scott's heroic ways and well-proportioned physique. In the city, Lulli's henchman graphically throttle one unfortunate girl, accompanied by a titillating dance heralding a batch of sacrificial lambs ("The first one!" shouts Lulli as the petrified creatures are hurled into the pit like rag dolls). Although the King of Persia (Mario Petri) has no immediate plans for a push on Babylon, he's appalled at the stories of atrocities coming out of the state; meanwhile, Scott ingratiates himself into court and offered a female slave as a gift. He chooses Célina Cély (Agar), who happens to be the girl of best friend Andrea Scotti (Namar). Orfei demands intimacy with Scott, suspicious of his real motives (is he going to kill Lulli at the next ritual, she wonders?), and Persian diplomats are told not to interfere in Lulli's affairs. "Ascend the throne with me and I'll not give away the secret location of your friends," demands Orfei to Scott; more sacrifices follow, Scott wades in, is shocked at the slaughter, rides off, is wounded and finds himself cared for in Petri's encampment. The Persian has decided to parley with Lulli and thrash matters out. Acts of barbarity increase ("Why can't those miserable idiots just die quietly without disturbing our pleasure?" queries Lulli callously at a banquet), hundreds of prisoners fill the cells to capacity and Babylon's enraged citizens are crying out for a rebellion masterminded by Giuseppe Addobbati (Licardio). Scott is imprisoned and chained to a dungeon wall, as Grad is on the brink of being barbecued, Orfei maliciously shrieking, "The last one!" Petri, pondering whether or not to break camp and pull his troops out, has a change of heart, attacking the city in force. Scott, tearing his metal restraints from their bolts, snatches Grad from the jaws of death, Orfei, in black glittering headpiece, taking her place in the hellish cauldron; repellent Lulli receives several inches of steel in his guts. Scott is now crowned the true King of Babylon, with Grad by his side.

The accent in Marcellini's style-packed offering is firmly on cliffhanging action, throwing in an exhilarating Babylonians versus Persians clash on the plains plus all those scenes of

A Spanish poster for *The Red Sheik*

downright female cruelty. Scott, complete with smartly trimmed goatee beard and flamboyant tunic, exudes charismatic machismo, the perfect foil to sneering Lulli's diabolical Balthazar, while Orfei drifts across the set like a Babylonian version of the Wicked Witch of the West (but far more attractive!). Composer Carlo Franci and cinematographer Pier Ludovico Pavoni do this sizzling picture proud (they collaborated on seven pepla), an exciting, operatic show that in some areas is a bit hard to stomach.

The Red Sheik [*Il rosso sceicco*]

Explorer Film '58/Comptoir Francais CFPC (Italy/France); Euroscope/Eastmancolor; 90 mins; Producer: Bruno Turchetto; Director: Fernando Cerchio †††

Great to look at (Angelo Lotti and Elio Polacchi's photography is akin to opening a chest of jewels, especially in the glittering interior palace shots), marvelous to listen to (Francesco De Masi's old-time Hollywood oriental soundtrack is a beauty), *The Red Sheik* comes unstuck due to Channing Pollock's stilted portrayal of desert campaigner Ruiz da Silva, out to avenge the death of his father at the hands of usurper Mel Welles (Hassan). The American actor/magician drifts through the scenario refusing to take it by the scruff of the neck, a rather lame turn instead of a requisite full-blooded one. In 19th-century Morocco, Welles has evicted the Sultan from his throne, lording it over the peasant population, mistress Rosalba Neri (Hammel) at his beck and call. Pollock is first seen in rebel leader Ahmad Amer's camp, forming an instant bond with his wayward daughter, Luciana Gilli (Amina); he later appears in Welles' palace, posing as a Spanish architect, demonstrating his sleight of hand skills at court while keeping one eye on the movements of Welles' men and figuring out a way to set free dozens of prisoners clogging up the cells. Leisurely paced, Pollock comes and goes as The Red Sheik (he also dons a black eye mask), his signature calling card a scrap of crimson cloth, inciting unrest among the people and skirmishing with the palace sentries. Ettore Manni (Mohammad) is completely wasted in the minor role of Amer's lieutenant, killed off in the 45th minute after his men are ambushed in an abandoned ghost town—a more substantial part should have been offered to this excellent actor. Cerchio throws in a Red Sheik imposter who dumps Gilli in the middle of the desert with no water; she's rescued by the real article who then gallops to Welles' imposing fort, determined to ignite the gunpowder store and send Welles to meet Allah (an old French fort in the Sahara was used for this sequence). The final 10 minutes blow away the cobwebs of the preceding 78, the rebel army charging toward the fort, guns blazing: Gilli is held aloft by Welles on the parapets, Pollock detonates the gunpowder, the walls come tumbling down, in swarm the insurgents and Welles' throat feels the keen edge of Pollock's blade after the crusader has revealed his true identity. Pollock marries Gilli, the pair now the new masters of the territory.

Worth a look because of the cinematography and score alone, steer clear of shabby pan and scan, badly dubbed copies and seek out the widescreen version in Italian with Greek subtitles. This presents *The Red Sheik* as it should be seen, bringing alive the desert scenery and Welles' palace, adorned with gold trappings; it will also make you forget the plodding narrative that matches Pollock's plodding performance.

I, Semiramis [*Io Semiramide*] aka *Slave Queen of Babylon*

Apo/Globe Film Intl. (Italy); CinemaScope/Eastmancolor; 101 (89) mins; Producer: Aldo Pomilia; Director: Primo Zeglio ††††

Semiramis was the legendary Queen of Assyria who, around 810 BC, restored Ancient Babylon to something of its former glory. Variously described as a homewrecker and harlot (and inventor of the chastity belt; she also castrated her male slaves), she had men falling at her feet and manipulated every one of them in her bloody rise to power. Yvonne Furneaux turned in a career-best performance as the devious temptress, ice-cold eyes staring from an unsmiling visage, two main suitors in her life battling for her honors—Germano Longo (General Omnos) and John Ericson (King Kir of the Dardanians). Semiramis lived in an age of idolatry, where human sacrifice to the gods was practiced on a daily basis, and Primo Zeglio presents us with a vivid canvas of those brutal, decadent times; in the opening minutes, a suggestive, vampish dance is followed by a servant having both arms set on fire for accidentally smashing a flagon of wine, thus angering the gods. The ornate art deco set design is fabulous, embellished by Alvaro Mancori's vibrant color tones, while Carlo Savina's Middle Eastern soundtrack underlies the action to perfection. And action is what Zeglio was extremely good at. There's not a great deal of it here, but he shoots what little there is in a stream of rapid edits, hauling you into the fray, making you duck for cover when those keen-edged broadswords come swinging toward the camera.

Sitting beside Renzo Ricci (King Minurte of Assyria) in the city of Nineveh, Furneaux in her finery harbors ambitions of becoming queen and finding the man of her dreams. Courtier Gianni Rizzo (Ghelas), who loves her from afar, murders Ricci to enable her to ascend to the throne. Longo, her on/off lover, is brushed to one side and Ericson, whom she adores, escapes from an execution squad, working with slaves on Furneaux's pet project, the rebuilding of Babylon: "The key to the Orient. I want it finished in a year," she barks at her harassed architects. The lovers are reunited in the final 20 minutes when Furneaux liberates the slaves and Ericson, cleaned up, escorts her to Nineveh. But he doesn't trust his beloved a single inch ("You're the cruelest woman I've ever met. Also the most beautiful," he had told her when they first clinched) and has organized his armies to lay siege to the city ("The Dardanians shall rule Assyria!"). Fully aware of this, she poisons his wine; as his body lies on a funeral pyre, a rebellious slave fires an arrow at the queen, who falls dead. Young Nino Di Napoli is pronounced child king as Furneaux and Ericson journey together to the afterlife in a sheet of flame.

Tortures (Ericson is tied to a waterwheel and savagely whiplashed), court intrigue, lavish temples and torrid love scenes, plus Furneaux's conniving, haughty and lascivious Semiramis, ensure that Zeglio's slice of Babylonian cheesecake entertains from start to finish, even in mutilated prints 12 minutes shorter than the original cut. The film's one distraction is

An Italian poster for *Taur, The King of Brute Force*

youthful, highly strung Ericson, looking somewhat undernourished. He doesn't cut it as King of the Dardanians; in all probability, Furneaux would have eaten him for dinner and still left room for seconds. Someone of Gordon Mitchell's muscularity and hardness of demeanor would have suited the role far better. In hindsight, Longo might have made a more believable Dardanian ruler, although not quite as nice looking as Ericson. A small niggle in an otherwise excellent production.

Taur, The King of Brute Force [*Taur, il re della forza bruta*] aka *Taur the Mighty*; *Tor: Mighty Warrior*

Coronet/Italia Film/Dubrava (Italy/Yugoslavia); Totalscope/Eastmancolor; 95 (89) mins; Producer: Alfredo Guarini; Director: Antonio Leonviola ✝ or ✝✝✝

Not quite a one-star stinker, but almost. "Goofy nonsense" sums up a movie that's the Italian equivalent to a 1930s *Buck Rogers* or *Flash Gordon* serial—evil-doer Antonio Leonviola (the director gave himself a major role, as well as participating in the script) is even made up to look like Ming the Merciless! Ninety percent of the picture takes place within a subterranean setting, which is no bad thing as Slovenia's (at the time of shooting, Yugoslavia) magnificent Postojna cave system became the star of this particular wacky show. And the accent is firmly on wackiness, with British actor Joe Robinson, all brawn and very little brain, cavorting about in a white microskirt, taking on Leonviola (buried under layers of greasepaint), King of the Kixos, a witchcraft-practicing tyrant who keeps hundreds of slaves toil-

An Italian poster for *I, Semiramis*

ing day and night on a gigantic treadmill, extracting precious ore from the Earth's center and piping hot interior waters to a cistern. Years ago (the action is set in 1500 BC) his minions murdered the King of Surupak, abducted two princesses and planted him on the throne. The rightful heir happens to be Alberto Cevenini (Syros sports a curious birthmark to prove his royal lineage) and he's in love with Isabella Biancini, the blonde princess (Illa, billed as Thea Fleming); Claudia Capone is the brunette, Tuja. Cevenini's old nurse, Janine Hendy (Afer), has spent 18 long years chained to a cave wall, bemoaning her fate, and relates this tale to all those who stumble across her. Seductive Bella Cortez smolders beautifully as the bogus queen Akiba and Carla Foscari plays the king's just-as-attractive consul, Ararut. In fact, all the women in *Taur* are enchanting, as is Guglielmo Mancori's vivid color photography, highlighting Postojna's wonderful grottos and caverns. And if, during the movie, you wonder whether you have seen any of this before, well maybe you have. Leonviola directed the equally half-baked *Maciste, the Strongest Man in the World*, whereby Mark Forest was teamed with a black comrade (Paul Wynter), undertaking similar escapades to what's on offer here.

Robinson, black buddy Harry Baird (Ubaratutu) in tow, goes through the motions with energy if nothing else. He shakes off Leonviola's guards, bends steel bars, breaks chains, survives being torn in half by two teams of horses, plonks a huge rock on a casket containing Cortez, wriggles off a conveyor belt (worked by colossal bellows) transporting ore to a vast melting pot, dresses as a soldier (complete with bizarre hooded headgear) and *almost* has his wicked way with Cortez, the brazen hussy revealing acres of shapely leg, her seduction rudely interrupted by Baird snoring underneath her bed. We even have a primitive arena where female prisoners in short green tunics strut their stuff; sisters Biancini and Capone are ordered to fight to the finish, surrounded by a ring of fire; refusing to do so, Capone commits hara-kiri rather than kill her own sister. "Master, what a mess we're in," complains Baird to Robinson, as they battle their way through one calamitous incident after another, the director rounding off matters in fine style with a truly spectacular volcanic eruption, smoke, ash and fireballs raining down on the masses, fleeing in terror. Biancini tracks Cortez underground, dispatching the usurper by sword, her body spiraling into a bottomless crevice, while Robinson pushes a massive rock pillar onto a wooden bridge that Leonviola is crossing, sending the slimy monarch crashing to his death. "Taur, I'm surely glad that's over," says Baird at the end, but Robinson hints at more adventures to come. Many will say, after sitting through *Taur*, "Thank goodness those further adventures never made it to film. Once is enough." But they did, in *Women Gladiators*! However, guilty pleasures are purposely made for multiple indulgence and in that respect, one of pepla's scattiest, more outlandish, offerings scores highly—it *is* so bad that it's good! (Note: Taur was originally to be named Tarzan, but Edgar Rice Burroughs' estate issued a lawsuit to prevent this from happening.)

Women Gladiators [*I gladiatori donne*] aka *Thor and the Amazon Women*

Coronet/Italia Film/Dubrava (Italy/Yugoslavia); Totalscope/Eastmancolor; 95 (85) mins; Producers: Alfredo Guarini, Ennio De Concini; Director: Antonio Leonviola ☦ or ☦☦☦

Hot on the heels of *Taur, The King of Brute Force* came another slab of Antonio Leonviola schlock—same team, same

A French poster for *Women Gladiators*

location (Slovenia's Postojna caves, icy cold judging by the vapor issuing from the cast's lips), same crazy ideas. Joe Robinson (Thor), one of the genre's less memorable musclemen, and dopey black servant Harry Baird (Ubaratutu) were once again thrown together in a crusade to bring the curtain down on the Black Queen (Eartha Kitt look-alike Janine Hendy), who rules the matriarchal kingdom of Babylos with a tribe of warlike Caucasian women; men, and pretty weak men at that, are the slaves under her command, inferior beings working in salt mines. From the opening moment a sorceress materializes in a red-lit grotto wearing pink lipstick, platinum hair, silver eye shadow and a see-through nightie, prophesizing gloom and doom if an invincible stranger, who is due among them, is not defeated (footage from *Maciste, the Strongest Man in the World* is inserted, showing Mark Forest wrestling with a gorilla) we know what to expect—pantomime theatrics on a massive, hokey scale. Hendy dispatches a squadron of butch female troops to the Mountains of Har to capture Robinson ("Elt! Elt! Elt! Elt! Elt!" is their ludicrous war cry), but all they return with is Susy Anderson (Princess Tamar) and her young brother. Robinson finally gets his act together after loping around on set doing nothing for 20 minutes, and sets off with scaredy-cat Baird to rescue Anderson from Hendy's domain and liberate the slaves.

There *are* plus points in this fantastically brainless, just plain silly, caper: The freakish costumes and pulp fiction set design is super, especially the gladiatorial compound, where the contests are held, ferociously bloody, fight-or-die stuff, the losers' bodies flung in a heap like rag dolls to the side of the arena;

A German poster for *Anthar the Invincible*

Guglielmo Mancori's photography dazzles the eye; Roberto Nicolosi's drum-thumping score is a winner; and despite the outlandish material, Leonviola directs with purpose, as though he had a real belief in what he was trying to achieve. Best of all is the script (the director was one of four writers involved), hilariously deadpan and stupid in the same breath.

"You will come with me," monosyllabic Robinson informs Baird.

"Why?"

"Perhaps to fight."

"Women?" is Baird's open-mouthed response.

On the outskirts of Babylos, the duo stumbles across several male corpses. "All the men are worms," sneers Baird, and then they spot a man being burned at the stake. "He's the queen's husband," states Robinson, without a flicker of emotion. "She doesn't want him anymore."

Baird, it turns out, is earmarked as the queen's new spouse. He's caught, ordered to pose on a revolving pedestal in front of an admiring Hendy. "Raise your arms, flex your muscles and now your chest," she orders, licking her lips, before leading the bemused musclebound sap to her bedchamber and announcing, "I've chosen you as my husband." "Me?" he splutters in confusion. When Robinson eyes them together, Baird in royal regalia and being fed grapes, he's just as confused. His pal puts him straight: "I'm her husband. Tell him I've become the king." "She will have you killed," Robinson warns. Baird turns to Hendy for backup, but she remains silent. "Don't just stand there looking like a mummy." The two slug it out, Baird is knocked unconscious and Hendy changes her mind: "Arrest that worm of a man," she instructs her guards. "You are no longer king." "You're a wicked woman," Robinson glares, stating the obvious: "Always changing husbands." True to form, there's an uprising against the "false queen" led by gladiator master Maria Fiore ("It was when I realized that the rule of women was the most frightful and horrible form of government.") who, in one scene, leads you to believe she's a closet lesbian, caressing Anderson's shoulders just a little *too* intimately and espying the mark of the royal family of Babylos on her pale skin. The male slaves revolt but the ringleaders are captured. Robinson goes tug of war with 101 warriors, the girls, heels of their boots dug in, attempting to drag him into a fiery pit, halted when the rope snaps; Anderson has to combat number one gladiatrix Carla Foscari in the "Triangle of Death." Foscari topples onto a bed of spikes, Fiore expires in agony on the rack, Hendy receives a lance in the stomach and Anderson, swiftly recovered from a near-fatal chest wound, transpires to be the true heir to this weird and wonderful realm; she promptly torches the fortress to the ground as her brother and his child bride are crowned king and queen of Babylos.

Remember when scoffing at fare like *Women Gladiators*—pictures such as these this aren't even thought about these days in the minds of filmmakers, let alone conceived, so treasure them as the guilty pleasures they purport to be. Dotty, ridiculous and enough camp to be found in a field full of tents, Leonviola's enjoyably garish romp brings a smile to the face, pitfalls, gaffes and all; you can even forgive and forget a monumentally wooden performance from leading man Robinson in the last of his five pepla: The six-foot-two-inch ex-champion wrestler and judo expert quit the movie business in 1971 after appearing in the *Bond* picture, *Diamonds are Forever*.

1964

Anthar the Invincible [*Anthar l'invincibile*] aka ***Devil of the Desert Against the Son of Hercules***; ***The Slave Merchants***; ***Soraya, Queen of the Desert***

Antares Produzione/CCM/Fides Film (Italy/Spain/France); Techniscope/Technicolor; 114 (93) mins; Producer: Luigi Nannerini; Director: Antonio Margheriti ††

Salvaged in the final reel by having Kirk Morris (Anthar) fight Mario Feliciani (Ganor) in the Chamber of Death, a room full of mirrors (memories of Bruce Lee versus Kien Shih in the famous climax to *Enter the Dragon* [Warner Bros., 1973] will come flooding back), *Anthar the Invincible* just about passes muster as yet another slice of sub-Arabian Nights' hokum, average and forgettable.

Morris plays a muscular desert nomad who restores Michele Girardon (Princess Soraya) to the throne after her father is murdered; she jumps out of a palace window, only to be caught and sold into slavery, auctioned for 50,000 piastres. With lanky mute lad Roberto Dell'Acqua in tow, Morris extricates the desert flower from her new master, reunites her with Manuel Gallardo (Prince Daikor) and joins in the revolt against Feliciani and henchman Renato Baldini (Feliciani and Baldini played virtually the same two villains in Margheriti's *The Golden Arrow*, 1962): the hustle and bustle of street vendors in the bazaar; a secret passage under the foundations of a pool; Morris grappling a savage rhinoceros in a pit; and an all-out blitz on the city by Gallardo's warriors, all backed up by Georges Garvarentz's

An Italian poster for *The Ruler of the Desert*

cacophonous score. *Anthar the Invincible* had all the right components but appears sluggish and derivative, one of the lesser of the many desert actioners made around this period. The first of a run of four desert-based movies for Morris was the least involving of the bunch, the actor faring much better in *The Ruler of the Desert* (see below), *The Conqueror of Atlantis* (1965) and *The Magnificent Challenge* (1965); as Anthar, he shouts, flails and leaps around on set in a revealing white loincloth with very little conviction, one of his poorest performances. Girardon is attractive but fails to emote like Gloria Milland or Chelo Alonso, while the Feliciani and Baldini double act is one we've all seen before, and done better. Appalling color rendition on a scrappy, badly edited pan and scan print doesn't help, but even so, despite that unique mirror tussle (Feliciani falls backwards from a window to his death), Margheriti's blood and sand opus is as dry as the Algerian desert wastes (where it was filmed), and just as interesting.

The Ruler of the Desert [*Il dominatore del deserto*] aka *Desert Raiders*

Cineluxor (Italy); Techniscope/Technicolor; 105 (98) mins; Producer: Luigi Rovere; Director: Tanio Boccia (Amerigo Anton) ††††

Made back-to-back with *Valley of the Thundering Echo* (virtually the same cast and production team and also entitled *Desert Raiders*), Kirk Morris' blood and sand actioner is a splendid no-brainer in which Aldo Giordani's rich photography paints the desert landscape in an unusual (but effective) ice-blue wash, a cold-looking desert as opposed to a scorching hot one. Combined with Carlo Rustichelli's melodic Arabian music, complete with full orchestral chorus in the romantic interludes, Tanio Boccia's yarn entertains from opening to final curtain, even though the story is stock goodies versus baddies stuff. It's how to present material like this that matters, and Boccia doesn't let the side down.

Thoroughly evil Sheik Yussuf (Paul Muller) kidnaps women for his overflowing harem if people refuse to pay tribute to his soldiers, commanded by thuggish heathen Ugo Sasso (Omar). Rosalba Neri (Fatima) is abducted with several other girls, her father killed in the affray, and Muller, struck by her alluring dark-skinned beauty, decides on marriage, much to Hélène Chanel's (Zaira, his long-term mistress) displeasure. Hunk Morris plays Nadir of Malek, raising an army from disparate tribes, including the Kadai and El-Krim Bedouins, to terminate Muller and his red-cloaked battalions in the city of Nemec, after his father is slain in a successful sortie to snatch back Neri; she escaped Muller's opulent palace, wandered into the wastes and was found by Morris at an oasis; unwisely, Neri's "handsome knight" took her to his house to recover. Needless to say, the two have fallen head-over-heels in love. "I swear by Allah I will have my revenge," steams Morris, infiltrating Muller's Palace with a friend, posing as jugglers, and giving Muller's soldiers the slip in a sandstorm. He then organizes guerrilla strikes on Muller's caravans, offloading the sheik's gold and supplies. Chanel, heartily sick of her dominant master trampling all over her feminine pride, finally does the dirty on him by disclosing his battle plans to Morris. With manpower now up to scratch, the combined task force storms Nemec and smashes Muller's troops; Morris, for only the second time in the movie, removes his Arab headgear, rams a dagger into the sheik's heart and is reunited with Neri, his brother and the Bedouin chieftain both having perished in the assault.

Muller's murderous scowling sheik is a memorable one: "Bring me Nadir's head—otherwise, I'll take yours," he spits at Sasso; the maniac also tortures a girl to death and lowers a bound woman by rope into a crocodile pit for helping Neri to get free. Swiss-born Muller was adept at playing repellent peplum heavies and he excels here. Morris is slightly wooden but nicely heroic, his normal "just about scraped through it to the closing shot" performance, but this picture really belongs to cinematographer Giordani. In an age of shooting straight to disc/tape, often resulting in dingy, bland color, his shimmering tones truly light up the screen, accentuating the desert scenery, the sumptuous sets, the gaudy dance routines and the ostentatious costume design to spot-on perfection. His is a filmic art that goes unrecognized by many cinemagoers and one that should never be forgotten; nowadays, color photography of this quality is so very hard to experience in a cinema.

Sinbad Against the Seven Saracens [*Sinbad contro i sette saraceni*] aka *Ali Baba and the Seven Saracens*; *Hawk of Bagdad*

Avis Film (Italy); Aviscope/Eastmancolor; 94 (81) mins; Producers: Alberto Puccini, Emimmo Salvi; Director: Emimmo Salvi † or †††††

Is this a one-star disaster? Or so utterly bad it warrants five stars for complete and utter nerve. Salvi's corniest of corny Ara-

An Italian poster for *Sinbad Against the Seven Saracens*

bian Nights lark has three things going for it: Gordon Mitchell at his ferocious best, big-busted Bella Cortez and multicolored Eastern stage sets. The drawbacks are a narrative as dense as treacle, requiring a deciphering machine to unravel (the shortened American version doesn't help), cheesy dialogue that will make audiences cringe and, in Bruno Piergentili (aka Dan Harrison), cinema's wimpiest, most anonymous Sinbad/Ali Baba (depending on which print you're viewing). You can revel in every single minute of its mind-numbingly awful running length or simply dismiss it as Italian peplum trash. Yes, *Sinbad Against the Seven Saracens* is a guilty pleasure of the first degree; it will certainly bring a smile to the face, whatever your thoughts may be as regarding its cinematic credentials!

Mitchell plays Omar, anxious to place his well-honed butt on the Golden Throne by rubbing his enemies the wrong way. His idea—to hold a tournament where the ultimate winner will be king; after all, where is the warrior who's strong enough to defeat *him* in combat! Not Ali Baba, that's for sure (we'll call him that; Italian prints are rarer than rare): "I want to see the terror of death in his eyes," growls Mitchell on hearing his name mentioned. First spotted on a studio beach, Piergentili (resembling a teenage '50s pop idol; his American pseudonym was Dan Harrison, blatantly filched from popular peplum star Richard Harrison) and his men are involved in a skirmish with soldiers; he hotfoots it out of the fracas, seeking refuge in a quarry cave where Chelo Alonso look-alike Bella Cortez (Princess Fatima) finds him. In no time at all, she's screaming, "Oh Ali Baba, I love you," pressing her well-proportioned breasts against his tunic, and he hasn't even demonstrated his prowess in battle yet. Cortez's uncle, Amedeo Trilli (Haswan), promises Mitchell he'll bring her back to the palace for punishment; Carla Calò (Farida), Mitchell's haughty mistress, seethes with jealousy every time Cortez walks on set, but the prisoners have an ally in diminutive Franco Doria (as Jukki), spending 99 percent of his screen time worming his small body through the palace walls, passing on messages and trying to locate the mechanism that opens the Great Stone Gate. Cortez increases the harem quota by one, Mitchell's lieutenant, Tony Di Mitri, hovers Dracula-like in the background and Piergentili summons up enough courage to spit at Mitchell, "You're the scum of the earth! A coward!" before being flung into a dungeon. "It's beautiful to love and die together," sneers Mitchell at the two lovers with his trademark wolf's grin (we get to inspect his rock-hard physique in the 23rd minute), and once in a while, the harem eunuch appears, suffering from a severe facial tic. And no glamorous dancing girls are on display either; on two occasions (two too many!) a plug-ugly male dancer gyrates obscenely before whirling off camera. What a crashing disappointment! On the hour, you might be forgiven for throwing in the towel by deciding to give up on seeing Cortez continually consigned to the harem, counting how many times soldiers and Cortez congregate in that drab quarry, wondering what exactly Ali Baba is proposing with fellow captive Alberto Conversi and tired of the umpteen shots of Doria squeezing through passages, all the while figuring out which tribal nationalities are attending the games (what happened to those seven Saracens after the eighth minute?). Just wait for the action to wrap things up and deliberate on how Mitchell will meet his end (he's run over by a chariot). Although Piergentili receives an arrow in the shoulder, he grapples with an opponent using a giant sword as though nothing has happened, even lumbered with a huge white-plumed helmet. "Ali Baba, save me!" shrieks Cortez as the gates are opened; the eunuch dies, croaking between twitches, "Tell Jukki I did my duty," Cortez and Calò indulge in a catfight, in gallops Conversi and Trilli's troop (all 14 of them!) and Mitchell's mob are quickly in disarray. Calò is condemned to slavery, Doria pops up in the middle of the courtyard through a grate and Trilli announces to the cheering crowd that "Tyranny is over! This is liberty!" Cue for Piergentili and Cortez to slobber all over each other, making you wonder why the voluptuous lass rejected Mitchell's far more masculine, testosterone-charged overtures than Ali Baba's less-than-manly arms around her curvaceous figure.

All credit to the producers for cutting down on the histrionics normally associated with midgets in peplum movies (Doria plays it mostly straight); Mario Parapetti's color work is also garishly apt for such hare-brained material. Piergentili's charisma bypass is just one of many ingredients in this hard-to-dislike mishmash that contributes to a Sinbad/Ali Baba Middle Eastern confection that isn't easily forgotten, however comically woeful it comes across as—besides, Gordon Mitchell is in it, reason enough to watch.

The Thief of Damascus [*Il ladro di Damasco*] aka ***Sword of Damascus***

Rodes Cinematografica (Italy); Dyaliscope/Eastmancolor; 105 (93) mins; Producer: Tullio Bruschi; Director: Mario Amendola ††

An Italian poster for *The Thief of Damascus*

Great-looking but juvenile—that's the verdict on *The Thief of Damascus*, a pseudo-comical romp through Old Syria starring Tony Russel (Jesen) and Ferruccio Amendola (as Tisba; he was the director's nephew) as a pair of happy-go-lucky thieves, who get embroiled in a plot by slippery merchant Giuseppe Fortis (Mannae) to become the new potentate of the kingdom in tandem with corrupt Gianni Solaro (Tibullo), the Roman legate. Luciana Gilli (Miriam), a potter's daughter, becomes the focus of Fortis' lustful desires, but Russel has his eyes on her as well as organizing a revolt among the people, dealing with a spy (Renato Baldini as Uria) and still finding time to pick the pocket of every coat and tunic that brushes past him. In fact, the first 15 minutes is given over to Russel and his reprobate buddy thieving without a care in the world and being chased all over town by a pack of useless soldiers, before Amendola introduces the audience to a flimsier-than-normal plot, incorporating a tavern brawl, Gilli's abduction, more thieving and the pickpockets, masquerading as dark-skinned acrobats and spouting gibberish, turning up in Solaro's palace to rescue Gilli. She stands on one end of a seesaw, Russel jumps on the other end and she's catapulted through a window, landing safely on a hay wagon and whisked off to the outlaws' cavern haven.

The picture at this juncture falls between two slots, Amendola changing tack, from loony antics to full-on bloodshed. Led to the secret caverns by spy Baldini, Bruno Ukmar's squadrons slaughter the insurgents in a 10-minute scene of rampant ferocity; Russel and Gilli are arrested, Amendola, dressed in legionnaire's uniform, scuttles off, leaving behind a cavern crammed full of corpses. Back in the city, Russel stands on the scaffold, awaiting the axe; his irrepressible friend and the rebels save the day in a second mighty scrimmage, Baldini dispatching Fortis before a guard plunges his blade into the traitor's back. During the fight, Russel's shirt is torn, revealing a scar on his left shoulder. Solaro spots it and, hey presto, it turns out that Russel is his long-lost son, heir to the patrician lineage! In the closing minutes, the camera pans across Ukmar cozying up to Solaro, Amendola smooching with Adriana Limiti and Russel getting to grips with Gilli. Yes, folks, it's happy families time!

And that's the problem with the movie: It's neither one thing nor the other, veering from farcical one moment to pretty savage the next, an uncomfortable mix that refuses to gel. Luciano Trasatti's cinematography is pin-sharp, the set design exemplary, but when Russel and Amendola are fooling around, up to no good, their pranks detract from Solaro and Fortis' villainous double act, which is far more interesting. Despite what some writers state, the picture has little in common with Columbia's *Thief of Damascus* (1952), described in chapter two. Harmless, lukewarm fun for the undiscriminating punter, light-fingered Russel cavorting amiably through the narrative, a perpetual grin creasing his boyish features (Ferruccio Amendola is the real star of this show)—an Arabian Nights scenario transposed none too successfully to Ancient Rome.

1965

The Conqueror of Atlantis [*Il conquistatore di Atlantide*] aka *The Kingdom in the Sand*
 PCA Produzione/Copra/Doina Cine (Italy/Egypt); Techniscope/Technicolor; 93 (84) mins; Producers: Giorgio Agliani, Alberto Chimenz, Pier Ludovico Pavoni; Director: Alfonso Brescia ✝✝✝✝✝

A classic mix of sword and sandal, myth and legend, alchemy and science fiction, *The Conqueror of Atlantis* is 100 percent unadulterated camp, kicking off in *Lawrence of Arabia* style and ending in a crescendo of absurdity. Where else would you get an army of gold-faced metal zombies dressed in blue one-piece outfits, gold boots and black outside pants fighting a tribe of nomads in a desert ravine, while superhero Kirk Morris grapples with their creator, Piero Lulli, in an Atlantean laboratory built over an active volcano. Suspend all disbelief and revel in the sheer craziness of it all.

Morris (called Heracules in U.S. prints), shipwrecked, is washed up on a beach and cared for by Luciana Gilli's (Princess Virna) caravan, soon finding himself caught in the crossfire between two warring tribes ruled by Mahmoud El-Sabba (Assur), Gilli's father, and Andrea Scotti (Karr). Fausto Rossi brilliantly photographs the opening section of the movie, the burning desert wastes radiating heat and scorching the eyeballs; Ugo Filippini's score is busy and memorable. But someone, or something, else is responsible for the death raids on villages, not the two tribes forced into hostilities with each other. The true culprits are The Phantoms of the Desert, whose murderous activities are heralded by weird howling sounds, and when those feared evil figures in black cloaks abduct Gilli, Morris and Scotti make tracks for the Mountain of the Dead Ones, behind which lies the City of the Phantoms. In the archaic city, they pass through a

Rosalba Neri, another in a long line of attractive peplum actresses, from *Kindar, the Invulnerable*

gaseous portal, discovering the remnants of another antediluvian metropolis erected in a volcanic crater, the last traces left of the once mighty empire of Atlantis. Hélène Chanel (Queen Ming), thousands of years old, is fed up with eternal life, so Gilli has been chosen to be her successor because of her strong resemblance. In his futuristic laboratory, Piero Lulli (Ramir) is busy transforming corpses into an army of "Golden Phantoms," by immersing the bodies in three different vats of liquid. When they emerge, the robots obey his commands, and no one else's; like all madmen, his ultimate dream is to conquer the world. Mario Giorsi's set design in the Atlantean underground sequences is fabulous, golden dragon statues containing an all-seeing red eye omnipresent, even though his costume design for the phantoms is not-so fabulous (Giorsi redeems himself with the luridly attired female spear-carriers and archers). Both Gilli and Scotti are turned into zombies but recover, fleeing the city while Morris, with the use of a fancy ray gun and his trademark overarm throw, decides to bring Atlantis, or what remains of it, to its knees. Meanwhile, in a desert ravine, dozens of blue-clad warriors battle with El-Sabba's men, who toss giant ball and chains at their attackers (note the instance when the tribes approach the ravine and one actor is ejected off his camel); when the Atlantean palace is reduced to rubble, Chanel and Lulli both dead, the sorcerer's power is broken and the golden phantoms collapse in the sand, reverting to remarkably fresh-faced corpses. As that smoldering volcano begins to erupt, Morris, Gilli, Scotti and El-Sabba gallop off to pastures new, thus bringing to a close one of the best of the fantasy pepla produced toward the end of the genre's heyday, a real hoot from start to finish, if you don't take the flick for what it is, pure cinematic corn.

Kindar, the Invulnerable [*Kindar, l'invulnerabile*]

Wonder Films (Italy/Egypt); Techniscope/Technicolor; 96 mins; Produced and Directed by Osvaldo Civirani ✝✝✝

A queen is struck by a bolt of lightning as she gives birth and dies; the baby's skin is impervious to the point of a dagger and, as prophesied, the child will grow up to be "an invincible savior" whose skin "no weapon made by man can penetrate." Only the mysterious "Red Flower" will be his Achilles heel. A treacherous slave girl overhears this furtive conversation between King Eman of Utor (Giulio Tomasini) and his soothsayer and abducts the infant, placing him in the hands of bandit chief Mimmo Palmara (Seymuth), who tests the boy's skin on the business end of *his* blade (a fairly alarming scene). Twenty years later, the infant is now strapping Mark Forest, unaware of his true origins and joining in on Palmara's repeated raids on Tomasini's caravans and camel trains. Palmara also wants to set up home in Tomasini's fortified city, constructed over a vast eternal spring of water, of immeasurable value in these desert regions.

Forest's final motion picture before he took up a career in opera is not as catastrophic as some people suggest: preposterous, yes; catastrophic, no. Osvaldo Civirani had a long pedigree in Italian cinema stretching back to the early 1940s, his various duties including director, producer, writer and cinematographer. Here, he produced, directed and took charge of photography in and around Luxor, Egypt, framing the pyramids at Giza and the muddy Nile waters in many of his shots to good effect. When Palmara's brigands swoop on a caravan, Princess Nefer (enchanting Dea Flowers in her solitary film appearance) is held captive and, in true peplum fashion, falls for Forest after one day in his company. The trouble is, pepla's first superhero has a brother (Howard Ross as Siro) in Tomasini's court, and Flowers is promised to him. To add fuel to the fire, utterly gorgeous Rosalba Neri (Kira), Palmara's mistress, longs to be Forest's slave, drooping her lithe limbs all over his oiled pecs in a display of undisguised lust. Caught sneaking into Palmara's oasis, Ross is ordered to fight Forest in a desert gulch littered with ruins, a striking five-minute interlude. Forest is the victor (not a mark on his bulging torso), but frees Ross and Flowers, deciding to show clemency. As a demonstration of his invulnerability, Palmara then instructs eight archers to let fly their arrows at Forest—all eight flights bounce off his broad, tanned chest! Forest finally gets to discover his true identity when he breaks into Flowers' boudoir on a reconnaissance assignment; trapped, he's placed in an iron maiden (the Bride of Horus) and emerges unscathed; it's then that Tomasini realizes who the superman is, reunited at last with his long-departed infant. To prove his new allegiance, Forest overturns Palmara's battering ram outside the city gates and the rebel leader, injured during the battle, scurries back to his oasis to lick his wounds. Flowers is abducted and imprisoned in the Temple of Horus, surrounded by flames, the Red Flower of prophecy; the fires don't seem to have much effect on Forest—he strides through the flames, rescues the girl (Neri, in on the action, is crushed to death by a falling beam) and fights Palmara bare-knuckled ("You fiend from hell!" cries his bogus father); the bandit is dispatched with a scimitar through his neck, thrown by Ross. Forest and Flowers go on to lead the peaceful, nomadic life, frolicking in the Nile with the crocodiles, Ross taking up the reins of new ruler of the Arabian kingdom.

Kindar, the Invulnerable has its moments: Palmara, as beefy as most peplum musclemen, chews the sparse desert scenery with evil relish, Flowers and Neri make a pair of dark-haired, bewitching lovelies (both possess striking Egyptian profiles) and Civirani rises above the hack material in his careful use of framing. One scene, showing Forest and Flowers conversing in an oasis glade, overshadowed by palms and cacti, is truly beguiling, like a Middle Eastern postcard of days gone by, bathed

A Spanish poster for *The Magnificent Challenge*

in muted colors. Coriolano Gori's music pushes the narrative along (there are no dull spots in *this* movie), marred slightly by an all-male chanting chorus when Palmara's troops embark on a rampage. As for Forest, he was the same in *Kindar* as he had been in *The Revenge of Hercules* five years earlier, but it mattered not; he had used his 12 peplum features (he starred in nothing else) to finance his interest in opera, and bowed out of the genre (and the movie industry per se) on an amusing, campy note. *Kindar, the Invulnerable*, considering it was produced in pepla's closing years, still remains surprisingly fresh, helped by incisive direction and photography, the schlocky brainchild of one Osvaldo Civirani.

The Magnificent Challenge [*La magnifica sfida*] aka *Falcon of the Desert*

Wonder Films/Hispamer (Italy/Spain); Techniscope/Technicolor; 98 (92) mins; Producers: Osvaldo Civirani, Maria Angel Borras; Director: Miguel Lluch ✝✝✝

Bearded Kirk Morris (as Kadir), trekking across the desert wastes toward his home at Semares, comes to the rescue of a camel train under attack from bandits (an eight-minute segment), saving Dina Loy (Princess Amar) and shifty-eyed Aldo Sambrell (Kames); he's then enrolled in tyrant Atatur's army as a reward—Loy is a king's daughter, Sambrell Atatur's trusted general, Kames. But Atatur (a splendid piece of sly villainy from Franco Fantasia) is the man responsible for the death of Morris' father; he desires marriage to Loy (counter to her wishes) and has usurped the throne to the kingdom, waging a war of sedition against the Bedouin tribes of King Hussein and King Keveren. Fifty-eight minutes into the picture, a blind beggar informs Morris of his true identity, leading to an uprising to vanquish Fantasia and his warriors, which culminates in a mammoth scimitar-rattling desert skirmish, Sambrell having changed allegiance. Fantasia's troops are defeated and he's beheaded, Morris taking up his rightful position on the throne with Loy at his side.

Fair enough, there's nothing new on offer in this latter-day peplum desert opus, but it's all put across with style, vigor and an expert eye for the arid sandy landscapes, Ugo Filippini's pumping score supplemented by an Italian stock soundtrack, which peplum music buffs will easily detect. A six-minute tavern brawl goes on far too long, but Morris looks hunky in Arab dress, whiskers disguising his boyish features, but he is less animated than usual (his final peplum). Erika Jones is a darkly-alluring dancer and, in some instances, Fantasia bears a strange likeness to Alec Guinness in *Lawrence of Arabia*. Among a retinue of bit part heavies, Howard Ross (Jafar) does little but look menacing astride his horse, while Sambrell, José Riesgo and Claudio Scarchelli are featured as resident tough guys in Sergio Leone's *Dollars* trilogy (Sambrell starred in all three). *The Magnificent Challenge*, as of 2015, is only available on old, scarce French VHS tapes, meaning that in the United Kingdom, viewing will be in monochrome, not color (producer Osvaldo Civirani handled the photography), unless transferred to disc by a specialist.

14
The Barbarians and the Pagans

Italian filmmakers had a field day on the gore front in their depiction of the savagery and brutality of pagan hordes rampaging across the undefended countryside, or simply warring with each other. Jack Palance starred in three of the better films, his Asiatic looks and bulldozing screen presence suiting the role of barbarian warlord to a tee, while Hollywood heavyweight Victor Mature cropped up in *The Tartars*. It's ironic that the finest of the crop of barbarian flicks—*The Black Lancers*, *Revenge of the Barbarians* and *The Seven Challenges*—are all extremely difficult to lay hands on these days, a fate, as we have seen, that has befallen so many peplum features over the years. Who is the most alluring female pagan? It has to be Chelo Alonso, in a figure-hugging bodice that displays the hot tamale's glorious figure to its best advantage. Who wouldn't want her as leader of *your* tribe?

1960

Fury of the Barbarians [*Furia dei barbari*] aka ***Fury of the Pagans***

L'Arion (Italy); Dyaliscope/Eastmancolor; 85 mins; Producers: Mario Bartoloni, Giuliano Simonetti; Director: Guido Malatesta ✝✝✝

Bloody but not all that inventive, *Fury of the Barbarians* starred poker-faced Edmund Purdom as Toryok, head of the village of Nyssia, vowing retribution on rival chieftain Livio Lorenzon (Kovo) for raping and strangling his bride-to-be following a raid on his settlement. Set in 570 AD, shaven-headed Lorenzon, thuggish boss of neighboring Rutar, joins forces with the Longobard hordes after taking Veronese beauty Rossana Podesta (Leonora) hostage (he wants her to become Queen of Rutar), determined to remove from power Purdom and his ragtag outfit who look as though they've just stepped out of the Stone Age (apart from two studded leather-clad musclemen transported straight from a *fusto* outing.)

A basic peplum storyline given the lively treatment, hack-of-all trades director Malatesta conjures up some bloodthirsty savagery in the numerous counterattacks—axes and spears sunk up to their hafts in chests, throats cut, arrows in back—while the female body count is disturbingly high, even for a film of this nature. But Vincenzo Seratrice's photography is as muddy as the ditches surrounding Purdom's stockade, doing little justice to the wooded Central European locales or Podesta's shimmering wardrobe. Three fairly orgasmic dance routines, backed by Guido Robuschi and Gian Stellari's Greek-style notes, lighten the tone and there's a touching scene when couple Ljubica Jovic and Luciano Marin die clasping each other's blood-soaked hands following a prolonged battle within the compound's walls. Purdom hacks his way through 20 adversaries, clashing with Lorenzon, who turns tail and flees. However, to save face in front of his own people, he returns in the climax for a hand-to-hand contest with Purdom after Rutar is burned to the ground, a bruising rough and tumble fought with double-bladed axes, the Nyssian chief finally plunging a dagger into his protagonist's rib cage. On that note, the red-cloaked Longobards retreat, leaving

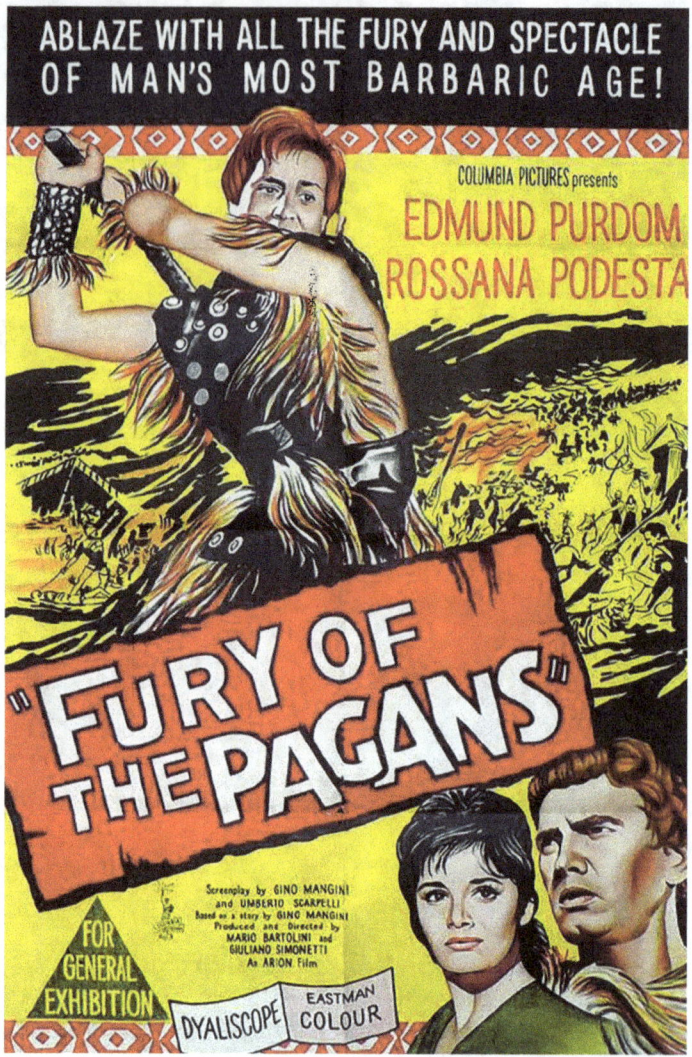

A British poster for *Fury of the Pagans* (aka *Fury of the Barbarians*)

Purdom to waltz Podesta (sensational in a variety of revealing gowns) off to his tent for some much-needed post-battle therapy—no doubt, she will soon become the next Queen of Nyssia!

The Queen of the Tartars [*La regina dei tartari*] aka ***The Huns***

Film Columbus/Comptoir Francais CFPC (Italy/France); Totalscope/Eastmancolor; 102 (85) mins; Producer: Carlo Lombardi; Director: Sergio Grieco ✝✝✝✝

In her sixth peplum outing, Cuban bombshell Chelo Alonso, playing Tanya (she received top billing), is brought up by Tartar chieftain Folco Lulli (Igor) following a raid on her village, in which she is orphaned and becomes queen of the tribe. *The Queen of the Tartars*' opening five minutes is a nihilistic, bloodthirsty overture crammed with plunder, pillage and rape that heralds an eventful romp featuring fine outdoor photography from Alfio Contini and a noisy score via Bruno Canfora. There's plenty of incident in Grieco's colorful Tartar adventure. Alonso, very fetching in a variety of outlandish headpieces and wearing a figure-hugging green bikini tunic that shows off her busty curves to perfection, is admired by Jacques Sernas (Malok), head of the Black Tartars, a rival tribe that combines manpower with Lulli's warriors in an attempt to topple the forbidding city of Quaroteem ("10,000 evil spirits hidden there within the city's walls."). Those brave souls who venture too near the fortress are bombarded by weird howling noises and either slain or return defeated; Tartar custom decrees that men wounded or mutilated in the field are dispatched by their fellow warriors, burdens deemed to be of no value (Lulli actually kills his own brother, Andrea Scotti, when he loses his right arm in battle); there are savage duels and sexy scraps between the women prisoners; Sernas harbors ambitions to become overall chief after Lulli's death, but haughty Alonso, elected leader, is having none of it; a captive tribesman is torn to ribbons by a man in a bear suit; and Lulli's second brother, Mario Petri (Timur), nursing a grudge against Alonso, swears that *he'll* be head honcho, then changes his mind and joins in the fray ransacking the city, led by the self-proclaimed Queen of the Tartars and Sernas, the barbarian mobs putting wax in their ears to keep out those harmful wailing sounds.

An Italian photobusta for *The Queen of the Tartars*

The Queen of the Tartars ends on a fantasy note of sorts, the warriors entering the mysterious art deco-type city after a confrontation with flaming chariots and being told by the priests in their temple that yonder is a fertile land of plenty fit for everyone, a haven for all people to live in friendship and harmony—the closing shot is of lovers Alonso and Sernas on a terrace, gazing out over the green sweep of the steppes to the sound of Canfora's rising notes, strangely uplifting after all the blood and thunder that has taken place. And Alonso, delicious when wielding her whip, smoldering wonderfully at camera, finally gets to smile for about the first time in an hour!

Revak, the Slave of Carthage [*Revak, lo schiavo di Cartagine*] aka **Revolt of the Barbarians**; **Revak the Rebel**; **The Barbarians**; **Rivak the Barbarian**

Galatea Film/NBC (Italy/US); Technicolor; 90 (84) mins; Producers: John Lee Mahin, Martin Racken; Director: Rudolph Maté ✝✝✝

Jack Palance's Asiatic features perfectly suited the peplum genre; combined with his beefed-up body (check the width of those thighs!), he looks the business in uniform, playing Revak, the Prince of Penda, a small Iberian island controlled by Rome. In storm the Carthaginians, led by Guy Rolfe (Kainus), to claim the island for themselves ("It has been a month since my sword tasted blood!" he scowls); Penda's palace is ransacked, one captive press-ganged into drinking molten gold, and Palance, his sister and father are taken into bondage for two years, royal collateral for Penda's citizens behaving themselves under Carthage's, not Rome's, governing. On board ship, galley slave Palance feels the sting of the lash and is beaten for his insolence; in Carthage, his belligerence and strength (and physique) comes to the notice of Milly Vitale (Princess Cherata), carried through the streets in a multi-colored sedan, a "Carthaginian cat," Palance calls her when he refuses to kiss her jeweled foot. Palance soon becomes embroiled in a scheme to give Carthage's slaves their independence, involving disgraced Roman exile Austin Willis (Varro) and a group of Spartan mercenaries commanded by Richard Wyler (Lycursus). But Vitale, as vain as they come, has other plans for Palance. Within the walls of her decadent court, the deposed prince drowns the local champion, a former gladiator, in a pool after a bruising, muscle-versus-muscle, knuckle scrimmage ("He's broken the backs of his last 20 opponents," brags an official); liking what she sees, Vitale gives orders for the victor to be sent to her chamber for a tryst. "You're right now looking at more man than you shall ever know," she says to her aid, licking her lips in anticipation. "Have the barbarian made presentable and brought to my quarters at midnight." Following a *very* racy dance routine, Palance is accosted in the corridor by Roman Deirdre Sullivan (Valeria), who has also fallen in lust (it's amazing what winning a fight can do to a woman's libido!); after declaring her feelings and informing him that preparations are set in place for a revolt, Palance, ensconced in Vitale's boudoir, succumbs to temptation, unable to resist the girl's irresistible charms; making *her* feelings crystal clear, she runs her painted claws all over that muscle-packed torso and drags the unprotesting Celt off to bed.

Up to this stage, the movie holds the attention on a purely camp fashion level, Carl Guthrie's lush color tones a delight and Palance, a contender alongside Gordon Mitchell for the title of peplum's strangest, most scary-looking hero, gobbling up the kitsch scenery with sneering relish. Vitale, bedecked in enough gold bangles to sink a ship, also ladles on the schmaltz in fine, overdramatic style. However, the final 20 minutes fizzle out. Palance has a fit of conscience over his passion for Vitale's desirability, especially on discovering that her brother is none other than the hated Rolfe, due to disembark at any moment. Deliberating over this dilemma to his comrades in, for him, a

An Italian poster for *Revak, the Slave of Carthage*

speech of Shakespearean proportions, Palance then heads the rebellion, Maté quickly wrapping up the picture by having the slaves sneak through a concealed gallery onto the quayside, clashing with the Carthaginian soldiers (one of Hannibal's elephants joins in the fray) and boarding Rolfe's galley where Palance sticks a sword into that "vilest of dogs" and dumps his corpse into the ocean. Off they sail to Penda, Sullivan (homely, but nowhere near as alluring as Vitale, who watches the ship depart) no doubt hoping that she will be the princess of this rocky kingdom. A clear-cut case of a film being too short—another 10 minutes would have added greatly to the entertainment factor and boosted that rather disappointing climax. But Palance was always worth a look whatever he starred in, and his meaty role in Maté's $700,000-budgeted contribution to pepla is no exception to the rule.

Revenge of the Barbarians [*La vendetta dei barbari*]
Oriental Film (Italy); Dyaliscope/Eastmancolor; 105 mins; Producer: Alessando Santini; Director: Giuseppe Vari ✝✝✝✝✝

In 408 AD, King Alaric of the Visigoths, sick of one defeat after another, is leading his hordes toward Rome in a final effort to take the city and overcome his hated enemy—but he hasn't reckoned on the wiles of Emperor Honorius' scheming sister, Galla Placidia, who plans a cunning stratagem in order to put a spanner in his works.

Revenge of the Barbarians is a hard-to-come-by peplum gem that has a rather kinky fragrance attached to it (and a fairly accurate telling of the historical events depicted), worth ferreting out mainly due to 23-year-old Daniela Rocca's playing of Queen Bitch Placidia. The scandalous vixen toys with men's emotions, double-crosses at will, finds sexual pleasure in being roughed-up and (it is hinted) harbors lesbian feelings toward her maid, José Greci (Sabina), especially after laying into the poor girl with a whip ("I do it because I like to."). Anthony Steel (Olympius), her on/off beau (he's the Consul of Rome), is ordered by Rocca to marry Greci midway through for political purposes, but only on condition that she can snap her fingers and have him back anytime she desires, whether Greci likes it or not. Yes, this is one female of the species you would *not* want to mess with and perhaps in her portrayal of this slightly unhinged character, Rocca was mirroring her own deeply troubled personality. Following a torrid romance with director Pietro Germi on the set of the highly successful *Divorce, Italian Style* (1961), she suffered a number of mental breakdowns and suicide attempts after he publicly rejected her, at one time certified as insane and committed to an institution. In May 1995, she died alone in a nursing home, at the age of only 57, a tragic end to a life that once held so much promise. In *Revenge of the Barbarians* (one of the actress' seven peplum films) she grabbed center stage and made the most of it, a riveting performance that holds the attention from start to finish.

Almost on a par with Rocca in the over-dramatic stakes was Mario Scaccia, hilarious as Honorius, a scatty, indecisive, simpering fool holding long conversations with his pet rooster in his palace at Ravenna. When told of the heathens entering Rome, he giggles to his court, "Don't be silly. I fed him (the rooster) just a quarter of an hour ago and he thanked me with a really splendid cock-a-doodle-doo." In fact, Gastone Ramazzotti's razor-sharp script bristles with acidic and droll asides, as when Rocca snarls to Alaric's son, Ataulf (Robert Alda), that it's no good marrying a man who takes a woman by force, you simply end up becoming his slave. As peplum entertainment goes, this movie has it all: a *very* erotic male/female dance routine; scantily dressed maidens cavorting in the waters of the lovely Monte Gelato falls; a "Wooden Horse of Troy" sequence whereby Rocca poses as a dancer (in skimpy red underwear), her troupe entering Alaric's (Cesare Fantoni) stockade in two wagons containing armed soldiers; racy (for 1960) bedroom scenes; a duel between Steel (his first peplum outing) and a seven-foot giant; the sacking of Rome; Evi Marandi's leggy, bosomy slave girl, continually lashed and abused by Alda (he beds her, then ties the lass up afterwards); Arturo Dominici's two-timing counselor; and, finally, what could be classed as a happy ending. To ensure peace, Rocca agrees to wed Alda (no doubt turned on by his warlike demeanor; Englishman Steel looks uncomfortable in Roman uniform) on condition the barbarians leave Rome and head south to Gaul, which they do, enabling Steel and Greci to get on

An Italian poster for *Revenge of the Barbarians*

with their lives without any further outside interference from his ex-mistress. Talkative, maybe, more personal drama than all-out action, but it's different from the norm, a rewarding, sexually charged frolic thanks to solid role playing from the entire cast, a great script, Sergio Pesce's glorious color tones and Rocca's dominating, lustful, strangely fanciable Galla Placidia. What a woman!

1961

The Mongols [*I mongoli*]
Royal Film/France Cinéma Prod. (Italy/France); CinemaScope/Eastmancolor; 115 mins; Producer: Guido Giambartolomei; Directors: André De Toth, Leopoldo Savona, Riccardo Freda ††††

Nobody could play barbaric pagans like six-foot-four-inch Jack Palance. He had the looks and the attitude—and here, starring as Ogatai, Genghis Khan's elder son, his eye-rolling and overripe performance hit new heights, even by his own standards. Factually suspect (Genghis Khan's death in 1227 remains unclear; he was *not* stabbed in the back by Anita Ekberg!), *The Mongols* does away with any pretence at a history lesson and presents us with the Jack Palance show, and boy, does he make a meal of it.

Blazing their way across Europe around 1200 AD, the Mongol hordes set their narrow eyes on Krakow as their next glittering coup d'état. The Polish king desires peace, not war, sending a delegation hosted by Franco Silva (Stepen) to Palance's inner sanctum in an attempt to pacify the heathen and prevent wholesale bloodshed of the Polish people. As Silva, companion Gianni Garko (Henry, the French regent) and their contingent ride across the flatlands (filmed in Yugoslavia), encountering refugees in their multitudes, the Mongols are gleefully tying hostages to cartwheels, raping women and whipping prisoners into servitude. De Toth's leisurely direction focuses on Silva's futile solicitations to Palance over peace being the best solution for all parties concerned; in addition, the Pole has to fend off Anita Ekberg's (Hulina) advances (she's Palance's woman and has a go at poisoning him) and falls for Antonella Lualdi (Amina), a peasant girl in league with rebels (the girl receives several strokes of the lash from Ekberg, stripped to the waist). The Great Khan (Roldano Lupi) arrives with youngest son Gabriele Antonini (Lutezia) and, after conferring with the spirits, decides he also wants a cessation of hostilities, sending Silva back to Krakow with an olive branch ("The war of the Mongols has finished. There will be peace."). But Palance is having none of it. "Our life is war. I won't stop fighting," he rants. "What will the Mongols do?" he asks his father. "Become shepherds again?" The ceasefire mission is sabotaged by Palance, who places the blame on Silva, labeling him a betrayer. Garko is tortured, a flaming torch thrust into his face, but survives long enough to free Silva and the hostages, and war is declared, Lupi stating to his overjoyed son, "One day there will be no land left. Who will you fight then?" However, Lupi learns the truth about Palance wrecking the armistice, stripping him of his sword and command. Then ice maiden Ekberg delivers that deathblow to Lupi's broad back. "You will be buried alive," Palance warns his mur-

An American lobby card shows Jack Palance as Ogatai.

derous other half before resuming command of his warriors; De Toth now vacates the director's chair, making way for Leopoldo Savona and Riccardo Freda to fashion a spectacular, rip-roaring 15-minute battle sequence, thousands of Polish troops marching on the Mongol fortress, towing huge war machines, only to be routed and massacred (Mario Nascimbene's tub-thumping music really comes into its own). The Polish monarch orders a withdrawal but Silva hatches a plan; he lures the Mongols into an area of treacherous swampland where they're wiped out, Ekberg drowning in a muddy bog, Antonini looking on as his father's hated killer sinks to her death. As for Palance, he realizes the game is up and decides that, as he lived by the sword, he must die by the sword; plunging a dagger into his midriff, he collapses beside the great chieftain's funeral pyre. Silva unbinds Lualdi from the cross and the hostages, rebels and villagers are last seen heading off into the sunset, the Mongolian reign of terror, for the moment, at a standstill.

Rosamund and Alboino [*Rosmunda e Alboino*] aka *Sword of the Conqueror*

Titanus (Italy); CinemaScope/Eastmancolor; 96 (85) mins; Producer: Gilberto Carbone; Director: Carlo Campogalliani
††††

Jack Palance is perfectly cast in the role of Alboino, leader of the Lombards, waging war with the neighboring Gepidae, who is offered the hand of king's daughter Eleonora Rossi Drago (Rosmunda), the main condition to an alliance. Guy Madison (Amalchi), Rossi Drago's clandestine lover, waits in the wings, ready to reclaim his woman and the "bastard son" they've conceived. Sucking up to the victors, conniving minister Carlo D'Angelo changes from one side to the other with rapidity, his eyes on the riches of the Byzantine Empire that Palance eventually wants to rule.

Carlo Campogalliani's energetic pagan broth is a cut above average thanks to Carlo Rustichelli's vibrant score, Palance in full flow (he could walk through a part like this in his sleep) and incisive dialogue (the director was one of five scriptwriters) that flits effortlessly between full-on action and the precarious Palance-Rossi Drago relationship, one built on hatred and mistrust. After all, would any future queen seriously want to marry a barbarian who orders her to drink wine from the upturned, hollowed-out skull of her murdered father? But the girl uses her feminine wiles, fooling Palance into thinking that he is the man for her and slowly but surely breaking down his resistance, waiting for the right moment to pounce; in the closing minutes, she plunges a dagger into her brand new husband's back after Madison lies at the barbarian's feet, awaiting decapitation.

The Lombards repulse the Gepidae, and Palance's brother Ulderico (Ivan Palance, Jack's real-life brother) meets Andrea Bosic (King Cunimond) to talk peace, but on *their* terms. Crestfallen Rossi Drago consents to marrying Palance for the good of the people and to broker the deal, and there's a tournament held to cement the uneasy pact. Ulderico crosses lances with Madison, whose weapon has been tampered with by D'Angelo's henchman. Result? The Lombard second-in-command tumbles from his horse, mortally wounded; Madison is branded a cowardly traitor and imprisoned and Palance, out of his mind with rage, declares war, vowing to avenge his brother's death. On the blood-spattered battleground (arrows through neck and eyes; faces split open), Palance decapitates Bosic, takes up residence in the Gepidae palace, snatches Rossi Drago's infant and tries

An American poster for *Sword of the Conqueror* (aka *Rosamund and Alboino*)

to work his manly charms on her, to no avail. There's effective interplay and acting nuance from Palance and Rossi Drago in their joint scenes, the Lombard chief harnessing his pagan urges, up against the lady's chilly, unresponsive stance. "Possession is what counts. I want no one's heart," he storms. Pulse racing and embracing her, she pushes him off in disgust. "Cold. Like ice! I'm not a jackal. I'm a man!" To show his softer side and gain her affections, he prevents lions from eating the prisoners and allows her to take on three maids, Madison's sister (Hedy Vessel) among them, the four soon busy hatching escape plans.

In the meantime, Madison, having fled the castle and thought drowned, recruits a friendly tribe after undergoing a totally unnecessary trial, swinging hand-by-hand across a frayed spiked rope above a bed of upturned spears; he proves his worth,

An Italian poster for *The Seven Challenges*

The Seven Challenges [*Le sette sfide*] aka *The Seven Revenges*; *Ivan the Conqueror*

Adelphia/Dubrava Film (Italy/Yugoslavia); Totalscope/Eastmancolor; 92 mins; Producer: Emimmo Salvi; Director: Primo Zeglio ☦☦☦☦☦

Great Khan Roldano Lupi is sick to the back teeth of two Mongol tribes, the Circassians and the Kyrgyz, led by Ed Fury (Ivan the good, the actor's best role) and Furio Meniconi (Amok the bad), continually at each other's throats, causing unrest among the population. His solution to the problem is to hold a contest of "fight to the death" challenges between the two cabals, the winner's chief to be crowned leader of both tribes. The contest will consist of seven trials of strength utilizing chains, axes and horses, all involving termination from strategically placed spikes, no quarter given. The 14-minute tournament appears in the 37th minute; until then, we have Fury and Meniconi squabbling in Lupi's grand court, lovers Gabriele Antonini (Kir) and Bella Cortez (Suani) romping in the woods, Fury killing one of five assassins, a male Cossack dance, the two lovers rolling in the leaves in a second spell of smooching, a slinky Cortez belly dance and the two Mongol chieftains dripping their blood over flames, prior to the contest beginning. As this murderous competition ends, broken bodies littering the arena, there's a mass fight involving all parties; Lupi joins in and is stabbed by Meniconi, who immediately announces that he's the new khan. Fury and his clan flee to the woods; in a skirmish, he's badly wounded in the face and takes refuge inside a vast mountain cavern barred by a massive stone door. Cortez and Antonini are taken prisoner, Fury's friend, Renato Terra, is tortured and Meniconi threatens to butcher trussed-up Antonini if Cortez doesn't relinquish her ample charms to him. Back in the cave, Fury reveals his hideous new X-rated features, looking as though he's just stepped off the set of an Italian horror movie; donning a mask, he sets out to terrorize Meniconi, first by luring his troops into an ambush (one gets trapped inside the cave, catches sight of Fury's visage, screams in terror and is strangled), then by tackling them out in the open. On returning to the cave, Fury finds everyone slaughtered; Elaine Stewart, his one true love (Tamara), receives a dagger in the back, dying in his arms. Enraged with grief, Fury gathers together his tribe and storms into Meniconi's palace. The guards crumble before the attack; equipped with a huge curved serrated scimitar, Fury hunts down his quarry and slays him with a savage blow to the head, splitting his skull, but he succumbs to an arrow wound on the palace steps, while mourning the death of Stewart. The crowds kneel in revered silence before his broken body; Antonini and Cortez are reunited, no doubt to be crowned joint monarchs of the realm.

Action specialist Primo Zeglio pulled out all the stops to create a barbarian flick that stands head and shoulders above the rest. The oriental set design is impeccable and intricate, the varied costumes eye-catching, the complete package augmented by Adalberto "Bitto" Albertini's beautifully vibrant color schemes, while Carlo Innocenzi's military score reverberates throughout. Great acting (even Fury displays emotion), incisive direction, gorgeous women, thumping set pieces, impressive scenery— *The Seven Challenges*, even in its present pan and scan format (Albertini's photography hangs on in there) is a peplum treat for the eyes, if you can lay your hands on a copy; availability is limited to one or two obscure outlets. (Note: It must have been extremely cold location filming in Yugoslavia. The "vapor issuing from mouths" quota is particularly high in this picture.)

the men entering the fortification by not one but two secret passageways. D'Angelo ends up in an iron maiden, unable to pull the wool over all-knowing Palance's eyes any longer, while the Lombards are annihilated (most of the soldiers are suffering hangovers from the previous night's festivities) and there follows that dramatic finale. At a palace gathering after the triumphant fight (and Palance's downfall), Palance staggers into the hall where Rossi Drago and Madison are, side-by-side, reunited with their child; lurching over to the couple, he stares into her porcelain features, hands her a glove and collapses, next to the goblet skull of her father. In disdain, she drops the glove onto his prone body, her thirst for revenge quenched at last.

The Tartars [*I tartari*]

Lux Film/Dubrava Film (Italy/Yugoslavia); Totalscope/Technicolor; 83 mins; Producer: Riccardo Gualino; Directors: Ferdinando Baldi, Richard Thorpe ††

"I'm no actor, and I've got 64 films to prove it." So said Victor Mature in an interview, and judging by the evidence on show in *The Tartars*, he wasn't far wrong. Mature, jet-black hair greased back and wearing a ridiculously short tunic, looks nothing like a Viking warrior but that is precisely what he's supposed to be, playing Oleg, leader of a Viking encampment at loggerheads with Orson Welles' Tartar hordes, circa 900 AD. An actor of Welles' legendary standing must surely have taken on this schlock-filled addition to the early '60s Tartar movie cycle for the money alone; as Burandai, he maneuvers his considerable bulk slowly across ornate sets, a flicker of the eyes here, a hand gesture there, but he does very little else, content to drift through the motions. The simplistic plot (six writers contributed toward the story/screenplay) goes like this. Mature sinks an axe into the back of Welles' brother, Folco Lulli (Togrul), after an argument about the bothersome Slavic tribes (Mature's brethren) and abducts his daughter, Bella Cortez (Samia), who's betrothed to the Great Khan; Welles, the local khan, vows revenge ("I will destroy Oleg. I swear it.") and, in retaliation, kidnaps Mature's wife, Liana Orfei (Helga). Mature's brother, Luciano Marin (Eric), falls for Cortez, getting her pregnant in the wink of an eye. Time for a hostage swap, but who will emerge the winner in this cutthroat struggle for supremacy on the Russian steppes?

The Tartars, distributed worldwide by MGM, has its good moments. The battle sequences are well-staged; Amerigo Gengarelli's period photography is nicely balanced in pastel browns, creams and greens. Peplum stalwart Arnoldo Foà stars as wily Tartar ambassador Chu-Lung, objecting to Welles' barbaric ways; Marin is tried for romancing Cortez (five axes in one post, five in the other; Mature has the casting vote) and Renzo Rossellini's music stirs the blood, which is just as well because Mature and Welles unreservedly fail to do so. Welles turns in a halting performance, while Mature appears out of context in the part of a Viking chief, smirking one minute, weak and soppy the next. And there is no happy ending—Orfei is returned to Mature after being drugged, beaten up and gang-raped by Welles' bully boys *and* falls from the battlements, dying in his arms. In the finishing nine-minute engagement, Mature gets an assassin's arrow in the back after drowning the corpulent khan in a river. The picture ends with the skirmish still in progress, the Viking fortress ablaze, Marin and Cortez sailing away in a Viking longship to a more harmonious future than can be found on those bleak Central Asian wastelands.

1962

The Black Lancers [*I lancieri neri*] aka The Charge of the Black Lancers

Royal Film/CFS Kosutnjak/France Cinéma Prod. (Italy/Yugoslavia/France); Cinescope/Eastmancolor; 97 mins; Producers: Jone Tuzi, Guido Giambartolomei; Director: Giacomo Gentilomo †††††

In giving *The Black Lancers* a five-star rating, one has to try to envision the movie at the time of its release 55 years ago, not as it appears at present on obscure DVD issues, rough around the edges, the sound quality uneven, the color fading in and out in many of the exterior shots (the interior scenes seem to have retained their original hues). A handsomely mounted (very expensive by the look of it), somewhat erroneous account of the Battle of Legnica in 1241, whereby combined Polish, Czech and German forces met with warlike hordes from the Central Asian Mongolian Empire. *The Black Lancers* benefits from a surging racket of a score from Mario Nascimbene, using pounding drums and crashing cymbals to the fore, while Raffaele Masciocchi's photography is positively Mario Bava-esque in its use of sumptuous tones. The master Italian cinematographer's expertise mirrored his work in *The Revenge of the Iron Mask*, especially in the wondrously backlit subterranean dungeon sequences; Italian Gothic horror within a peplum setting, complete with a shuffling, Lon Chaney-type jailor On the acting front, Yvonne Furneaux, playing Queen Jassa, made a bewitching Kyrgyz barbarian goddess, intent on bringing her squabbling tribes to order, thus enabling them to march on Krakow and conquer the Poles; Mel Ferrer (Andrea, in a blond wig) and Jean Claudio (Sergio) starred as two brothers hating one another, Ferrer (the good)

A French poster for *The Black Lancers*

vote. Roman is kidnapped; on his way to Furneaux's city to bargain for Roman's life, Claudio callously kills two shepherd boys, bringing the wrath of Tamberlani's council down upon his head; at the barbarian city, following a lengthy exotic dance routine, Claudio learns of Ferrer's appointment as commander and goes berserk ("I'll return to Krakow to destroy them all!"). He and his black lancers change sides ("Together we will march to war. I will betray my country but return as king!"); Claudio kills a Kyrgyz chieftain with a dagger poisoned by Furneaux, who gives her lover a golden sword and shows him where her treasure is hidden; Ferrer rides out to meet his brother and the queen to have a crack at staving off hostilities, but he is imprisoned, escaping through a secret passageway after encountering brutalized Roman, chained to a cell wall; Claudio disdains from killing Ferrer despite Furneaux's demand that the act will "prove to the chiefs your loyalty." The battle commences in the 79th minute, the Poles hauling huge towers, toppling them in front of the barbarians, wiping out the enemy and burning the city; Furneaux expires from an arrow wound; Roman is rescued; and the two brothers engage in single combat amid the conflagration, a burning rafter crushing traitor Claudio to death. The movie closes with Ferrer, Roman and the victorious Poles departing from Furneaux's city, now a smoking ruin, to take up a new life in Krakow.

It's a pity that motion pictures of this quality have been allowed to rot in the vaults and gone unnoticed for decades, a sad testament to all those technicians who worked long and hard to get their project onto the big silver screen. Director Gentilomo made seven peplum actioners, bowing out of the movie business in 1964 with *Maciste and the Queen of Samar* to devote his life to painting. His fourth feature film is a little-known masterwork that will regrettably never be seen in its original format, the one presented to the paying public all those years ago.

Taras Bulba the Cossack [*Taras Bulba il cosacco*] aka *Plains of Battle*; *The Tartars*

I.A.C.EI.D.C. (Italy); Totalscope/Eastmancolor; 93 mins; Producer: Henri Zaphiratos; Director: Ferdinando Baldi

Determined to conquer Poland, Chieftain Taras Bulba sends his sons Andrei and Ostapi to Dubno to gain information on the Polish army, and its strengths and weaknesses. Andrei falls in

obliged to go into combat against Claudio (the bad) when his sibling defects to the enemy, Claudio's eagerness to sample Furneaux's charms making his heart rule his head. Mutual love interest Leticia Roman (Mascia) had little more to do than to moan her plight, fettered in an underground cell reached by a flimsy rope bridge suspended over a bottomless chasm. Costume and set design, both in King Nando Tamberlani's Polish residence and Furneaux's frontier outpost, was impeccable, and to top it all off, we were treated to a full-scale 11-minute battle to end all battles, the Polish army versus Furneaux's Tartar warriors and Claudio's treacherous black lancers. All of the aforementioned points have to be taken into consideration if a sensible evaluation (and critique) of Gentilomo's expertly constructed adventure is to be undertaken; look beyond that tatty DVD copy and you'll experience a stirring semi-historical saga of the old school that, like scores of other peplum features, urgently requires a 21st-century makeover job to restore its finery.

Ambitious, swine-hearted Claudio is romancing Roman but treats her like dirt. He's more interested in taking on the role of military commander; Ferrer loves Roman, the pair spending a romantic interlude beside the Monte Gelato falls; Furneaux, ruler of "the people of the steppes," lays down the law to her bickering, wolfskin-clad Kyrgyz tribal chiefs; a court tournament fought with various weapons (large swords, flaming maces, shields-cum-daggers) decides on the new Polish commander, Ferrer unexpectedly crowned champion after a council

An Italian photobusta for *Taras Bulba the Cossack*

An Italian poster for *Tharus Son of Attila*

love with Natalia, the governor's daughter. When Taras Bulba's Cossacks march on the city, Andrei is classed as a traitor and imprisoned, but escapes to his father's encampment. Peace terms are thrashed out between the two factions, Taras Bulba decreeing that Natalia be held hostage in case the delicately balanced negotiations turn sour. Natalia reluctantly agrees but Andrei, furious, rebels against his father, taking Natalia back to Dubno. In a fierce battle, the two lovers are killed, forcing Taras Bulba to declare peace with the governor.

Starring Vladimir Medar as Taras Bulba, Jean-Francois Poron as Andrei, George Reich as Ostapi and Lorella De Luca as Natalia, Ferdinando Baldi's long-forgotten Cossack adventure was distributed in America by Universal under the title *Plains of Battle* but stood little chance of success at the box-office, competing alongside United Artists' heavily promoted $7,000,000 *Taras Bulba*, starring Yul Brynner and Tony Curtis, released in December 1962. The film remains unavailable; it was issued on German VHS in 1978, but copies cannot be traced.

Tharus Son of Attila [*Tharus figlio di Attila*] aka *Colossus and the Huns*

P.T. Cinematografica (Italy); Techniscope/Technicolor; 89 mins; Producer: Michelangelo Ciafré; Director: Roberto Bianchi Montero ††

It's the mid-fifth century AD and Attila the Hun is dead. The infamous barbarian's brother sends his own son Rik Van Nutter (Otto) and nephew Jerome Courtland (Tharus, Attila's offspring) to Livio Lorenzon's headquarters in the fertile, sunny south to form an alliance, thus enabling everyone to live in peaceful harmony. Also rubbing up to Lorenzo (King Haadem) is beefy Mimmo Palmara (Prince Kudrum); he too requests an alliance, but with the hidden aim of eventually ruling the roost. Lorenzon rashly yields to a marriage between Palmara and daughter Lisa Gastoni (Princess Tamall), but she desires a more caring soul, not a hairy ruffian, so when Courtland and Van Nutter arrive on the scene, Gastoni (reluctantly at first) takes a fancy to Attila's son (and his nonstop stream of sickly platitudes). Palmara boils with hatred and jealousy, thereby setting the scene for a talkative pagan soap opera firmly rooted in Lorenzon's camp.

A desultory raid on a settlement and a short (by peplum standards) battle bookend a movie suffering from lackluster performances all round, twee dialogue (the dubbing leaves a lot to be desired) and a Courtland/Gastoni/Palmara love triangle that quickly palls. Courtland (more of a barbarian dandy than the son of a notorious pillager) is arrested for dallying with "I can't make up my mind" Gastoni; Lorenzon is murdered by Palmara's chief assassin, Courtland blamed for the killing; Gastoni's trio of handmaidens indulge in endless rounds of gossip; director Montero throws in a near-nude bathing sequence to stop us from all falling asleep; a token dance is included, but with male dancers, not (as we would expect) scantily dressed females; and in the final skirmish between opposing factions, Van Nutter is slain, Courtland putting paid to Palmara. The curtain falls on Courtland and Gastoni, the new overlords of the dynasty, seated on their thrones in front of an adoring crowd of peasants; in all honesty, this weak-kneed couple thoroughly deserve one another in a production that has "damp squib" written all over it.

1964

The Plunderers of the Steppe [*I predoni della steppa*] aka *Terror of the Steppes*; *The Mighty Khan*

Cineluxor (Italy); Techniscope/Technicolor; 97 (87) mins; Producer: Luigi Rovere; Director: Tanio Boccia (Amerigo Anton) †††

There are two good reasons for catching Tanio Boccia's khan versus khan versus khan actioner—Carlo Rustichelli's score and large helpings of ludicrously dubbed English dialogue. Rustichelli's music thunders, crashes, pounds and booms in the background (even including a heavenly choir), propelling the narrative along to new heights, even when things begin to flag; never has the kettle drum been used to so much effect as here! Full marks, then, to the composer for keeping things on the move. The second reason is a dumb script doing its utmost to cripple the movie, excruciatingly awful in the translation from Italian to English. "I've had quite enough of your silly female chatter," barks Kirk Morris to Moira Orfei, just one example of the distributors reducing the script to the level of a reading primer for 10-year-olds. More snippets will follow!

Three potentates are locking horns for supremacy of the steppes: Morris (Sandar Khan), Franco Cobianchi (Yesen Khan) and Daniele Vargas (Altan Khan). Morris has abducted Cobianchi's daughter Ombretta Colli (Samira), who is betrothed to Vargas, a bullish thug wanting to lord it over his two rivals. Orfei plays dark-haired Malina, a busty guttersnipe lusting after Morris, while court advisor Giulo Donnini lurks in the background, looking for all the world like, in his black cape and Bela Lugosi peak, Count Dracula. It's a bustling mix, Furio Meniconi putting

Kirk Morris and Ombretta Colli pose beside the Monte Gelato falls in a publicity shot from *The Plunderers of the Steppe*.

in a likeable turn as Morris' oafish sidekick Kublai, the action flowing from Morris' ragtag camp to Cobianchi's city and Vargas' ornate palace, shot in rich Technicolor and displaying eye-popping set design; Boccia also shows an empathy with wide open spaces, the treeless steppes stretching endlessly under steel-gray skies. But the terrible dialogue continues unabated. "It's horrible, but they asked for it," chortles Meniconi, after blowing up a dozen of the enemy. "What are you hanging around for?" shouts Morris to love-struck Orfei. "You get on my nerves." Orfei has a tussle with Colli, threateningly drawing a knife. "You shameless hussy," she cries. "I shall have my revenge." A short interlude by the scenic Monte Gelato falls has Morris declaring to Colli, "You know I love you, my dear," before releasing her to her father who, in turn, immediately sends the poor girl to glowering Vargas as his bride-to-be. "I'm here against my will," she begs, but her pleas fall on deaf ears. "I want your beauty, not your brains," is the warlord's curt response. Morris, at one stage, has to grapple with two sweaty heavyweight wrestlers in front of Cobianchi, a curiously lethargic scene given the ex-gondolier's impressive physique. He triumphs, but is sent to work on that standard peplum instrument of torture, the millstone.

A sprightly finale sees Morris the winner in love and war; the city is stormed and taken; Morris gets the better of Vargas in a weird head-to-head contest, the two carrying giant spear-like logs on their backs that resemble oversized pencils; Donnini is brought down by an arrow; treacherous Orfei slumps to the ground, three arrows piercing her ample chest; and Cobianchi buys it from a sword wound. "He's gone to live in the land of the kings. I hope he'll be happy," sobs Colli, keeping those ridiculous lines going right to the very end. Morris is declared king and, as reward for his bravery, Meniconi becomes ruler of the nomads. Unadulterated tosh, with bleach-blond Morris wooden throughout, but enjoyable enough thanks to that score and dialogue!

A Spanish poster for *Revolt of the Barbarians*

Revolt of the Barbarians [*La rivolta dei barbari*]

Protor Film (Italy); CinemaScope/Eastmancolor; 99 (80) mins; Producer: Pier Luigi Torri; Director: Guido Malatesta ✝✝✝

Guido Malatesta tended to adopt a basic comic book/pulp approach to his movies, concentrating on brainless action and little else, and *Revolt of the Barbarians* doesn't buck the trend. It's set in 300 AD, the opening scenes showing barbarians carousing, wenching, feasting and rampaging through Gaul, taken from at least three other productions. When a shipment of gold is stolen in a convoy raid, Roland Carey (Darius) and his 10th legion, returning to Rome for a well-earned rest after six long years on the northern frontier, are instructed to go to Trivero and liaise with the governor, oily Mario Feliciani. The coinage, marked with a distinctive cross, was due to be paid to Roman troops in wages, and needs to be recovered fast, to prevent unrest among the battle-weary legions. To set a trap, a fictitious shipment of gold is arranged; the barbarians attack, their chief killed, and with a cry of "You're gonna pay for this," they gallop off, back to Andrea Aureli and Feliciani, the two ringleaders behind this scam, in league with the heathens to feather their own nests; the missing coins are stashed inside barrels, deep in the palace's cellar.

Much of *Revolt of the Barbarians* consists of Carey's men clashing with Aureli's praetorians and the barbarians at night, very darkly shot; sandwiched between is young Gabriele Antonini (Marcus) romancing Susan Sullivan, while Carey eyes

An Italian poster for *Zorikan the Barbarian*

up Maria Grazia Spina (Livia). In a protracted finale, almost 10 minutes in length, a mighty free-for-all results in Aureli and Feliciani both dead, and the governor's sly, artful mistress, Augusta (Spina's aunt), exiled. The Roman divisions march through the city and, for his gallant services to the empire, Carey is handed a golden sword, appointed the new administrator of Trivero; he also wins Spina into the bargain: "I too am at your service, Governor," she smiles at him enticingly. Carlo Franci's soundtrack helps things fizz along, and watch for the moment when an extra gets into a tangle, falling off his horse as his regiment rides through swamp waters.

Zorikan the Barbarian [***Zorikan lo sterminatore***] aka ***Zorikan***
Walmar Cinematografica/Triglav Film (Italy/Yugoslavia); Pancrorama/Eastmancolor; 92 (88) mins; Producers: Aldo Piga, Walter Brandi, Roberto Mauri; Director: Roberto Mauri ††

Hulking Dan Vadis plays Zorikan, a murderous black-clad Saracen ("Kill! Torture!") given orders by his vizier to conquer the Christian city of Postojna and retrieve, not only a fortune in treasure, but a holy relic contained in a golden casket that the people bow down to. Filmed in the short-lived Pancrorama process (Panorama by any other name) and shot in dingy color, Roberto Mauri's addition to the barbarian peplum cycle is not one of the better of its kind. The opening castle battlements scenes and the assault on the city's garrison take place around Slovenia's unusual Predjama Castle (positioned beside a mighty rock cleft), the acting is hammy, producer/composer Aldo Piga's score deafens throughout, a brave attempt to keep the momentum going (his title theme is, however, a thumper) and the awful English dubbing reduces the dialogue to ABC level, as in this twee aside from Walter Brandi (Ramperti) to Eleonora Bianchi (Julia), who queries why her hero isn't on garrison duty:

"Postojna's always as peaceful and quiet as a little village and besides, I wanted to be here to give my beloved her present personally on her 20th birthday. Nothing in the whole world could have kept me away from you."

Brandi and Bianchi are the Romeo and Juliet-type lovers leading an uprising against the white-cloaked heathen hordes with the help of Vincenzo Musolino and his fishermen, who live in stilted dwellings on the edge of a vast muddy lake. Zorikan, pretty gullible for a commander (Brandi has a parley with him wearing a false mustache, the Saracen failing to spot the disguise), has double-crossed his own men, including jealous rival Gino Marturano and brother Luigi Batzella, in order to lay his greedy hands on the entire treasure, but he's left red-faced in the process and ends up with the relic, but no treasure, which lies hidden in a cave (Postojna's caverns were utilized), and only Bianchi and her father know the whereabouts of that cave.

There's a fair amount of scimitar-rattling, charging around on horseback and torture; cartoon villain Vadis, resplendent in a silver turban, snarls, scowls and shouts clichéd lines; a couple of interludes in the striking surroundings of a waterfall provide a welcome change of tempo; and a snappy sequence occurs toward the end when Brandi's warriors bombard Vadis' camp with cannon fire. The climax is a battle to the death in the watery fishermen's village, Brandi dealing the death blow to the Saracen leader with two customary sword thrusts, while Musolino drives a pitchfork into Vadis' second-in-command; the Christians are reunited with their revered relic and the treasure, and Brandi and Bianchi ride off to play house. This becomes another sword and sandal rarity to single out, chiefly because of Vadis' over-the-top performance, if nothing else.

15
The Pirates

The Italians, it has to be said, excelled in the realm of the pirate movie, previously thought to be the sole provenance of Hollywood, and even Britain. This is not the case. Filmed on real galleons and disregarding the dreaded back-projected shot, movies such as *Morgan, the Pirate*, *Pirates of the Coast*, *The Adventures of Mary Read*, *The Terror of the Seas*, *Hawk of the Caribbean*, *The Devil Pirate* and even *Robin Hood and the Pirates* embodied the spirit of swashbuckling on the high seas, whose standards were set by Tinseltown way back in the 1920s. Action directors Primo Zeglio, Domenico Paolella, Umberto Lenzi, Mario Costa, Luigi Capuano, Piero Regnoli and others remain unheard of outside of their native country, yet they brought a boundless energy and hard-graft expertise to their work, perhaps unsurpassed when you think of the short time period involved, 1960 to 1966. Added to this were the riveting scores of Michele Cozzoli, Carlo Rustichelli, Gino Filippini, Egisto Macchi and Aldo Piga, while cinematographers of the caliber of Aldo Greci, Alvaro Mancori, Augusto Tiezzi and Raffaele Masciocchi embroidered the productions in deep, rich colors. Even *Toto Against the Black Pirate* is enjoyable in its own daft fashion, thanks to the skills of director Fernando Cerchio. So sit back, taste the salt in the air, prepare to be deafened by the thundering roar of cannons and duck at those swinging cutlasses as Steve Reeves, Lex Barker, Gianna Maria Canale, Lisa Gastoni, Livio Lorenzon (a goodie), Don Megowan, Richard Harrison et al. come to grips with pirate chiefs Walter Barnes, Livio Lorenzon (a baddie), Carlos Casaravilla, Carlo Ninchi and Nello Pazzafini, among others. Pleasing locations, beautiful damsels in distress, stirring, full-blooded action sequences (check the 14-minute siege in *Conqueror of Maracaibo*) and non-computerized galleons—the majority of the following 19 pictures are what pirate movies should be all about, entertainment on a grand scale, executed with aplomb by all concerned.

1960

Morgan, the Pirate [*Morgan il pirata*]

Adelphia/Lux Film/CCF (Italy/France); CinemaScope/Technicolor; 95 mins; Producers: Joseph E. Levine, Aldo Pomilia; Directors: André De Toth, Primo Zeglio (uncredited) †††††

Harking back to the Hollywood swashbucklers of the 1940s, *Morgan, the Pirate* remains one of pepla's finest piratical hours, filmed on real galleons and sun-drenched, exotic locations, Steve Reeves (discarding loincloth, sandals and, for most of the movie, his beard) putting in an honest performance as the English privateer-turned-slave, who takes to the life of a pirate, waging a war against the Spanish. Based partly on the exploits of Henry Morgan, an infamous corsair who was the scourge of the high seas between 1635 and 1674, the movie was shot in and around the charming hill-side resort of Procida Island, Naples, standing in for Tortuga and Panama City, beautifully photographed by Tonino Delli Colli. Franco Mannino's glorious score was music to the ears, while De Toth and an uncredited Primo Zeglio kept the rhythm going, ensuring there were very few lulls to hold up the action.

Chelo Alonso and pirate boss Steve Reeves survey their captured Spanish loot in *Morgan, the Pirate*.

Reeves is bought in the slave market by governor's daughter Valérie Lagrange (Dona Inez), the lady soon beginning to meet the handsome hunk in private for some after-dinner smooching. Father Ivo Garrani (Governor Don José Guzman) finds out and, fuming, orders his execution with five others, by lottery; one to die, five sentenced to hard labor on board a frigate. Reeves escapes quartering, winding up in the hold of a ship, where the prisoners overpower the Spaniards; Reeves takes command, hoists the black pirate flag and sails to Tortuga to replenish supplies. Pirate boss Armand Mestral (Francois L'Olonnais) is none too pleased to welcome him (a great standoff scene between the two in a tavern, Mestral viewing Reeves' muscular bronzed torso with unease and wisely deciding *not* to engage in a fistfight), resulting in a pulsating duel, Reeves emerging the victor. On Tortuga, Lagrange and her companion (Lidia Alfonsi) are being held captive following a raid on their vessel, but Reeves has no intention of escorting the pair back to Panama, electing to plunder yet another Spanish galleon for booty, his men dressed as women to set a trap.

In the 34th minute, Chelo Alonso (Consuela) writhes in untamed, wanton abandon to an Afro-Cuban beat, announcing her lust for Reeves, who's still hung-up on unresponsive Lagrange, stating the blindingly obvious at one point: "I am a woman!" In Panama, the bounty on Reeves' head rises to 50,000 ducats as, in a montage of action sequences, we see the privateer stocking up his coffers with looted Spanish gold. The English, headed by Giulio Bosetti (Sir Thomas Modyford, Governor of Jamaica), enter the frame; Reeves' notoriety, and the riches he has reaped, have caught the attention of King Charles II. The monarch, engaged in an uneasy truce with the Spanish, has the idea of offering him

An Italian poster for *Pirates of the Coast*

a knighthood and making him admiral of a large fleet to upset the enemy even further, while demanding a third of the treasure for his personal coffers. With this in mind, Reeves decides to carry out an attack on Panama and relieve the city of its gold; the first attempt fails, Reeves' vessel ablaze from a barrage of cannon fire, the pirate chief thought dead by Garrani and his minions. Unperturbed at their initial setback, Reeves, Mestral and hundreds of buccaneers cross the Isthmus of Panama on foot for a rearguard assault, clashing with the Spanish outside the city walls in a thunderous, Alamo-type siege. Demolishing the gates, they swarm in, overcoming Garrani's troops in ferocious street-to-street combat and winning the day ("The city is in your hands."). Reeves is reunited with Lagrange, who professes her love for him, and the movie closes with a galleon sailing off into the wide blue yonder, the ending to a rousing seafaring yarn

that was a big hit in the United Kingdom when released in early 1962.

Pirates of the Coast [*I pirati della costa*] aka ***Pirates of the Barbary Coast***

Romana Film/SNC (Italy/France); Totalscope/Eastmancolor; 104 mins; Producer: Fortunato Misiano; Director: Domenico Paolella ✝✝✝✝

The third of Lex Barker's five pirate peplum outings and the best, *Pirates of the Coast* is a terrific swashbuckler of the old school, as good as anything to have come out of Hollywood in the 1950s, containing a tremendous score (Michele Cozzoli), colorful photography (Augusto Tiezzi) and fine, all-round performances from the cast. Barker plays Luis Monterrey, captain of 40-gun man-o'-war flagship *Victoria*, cruising the pirate-infested Spanish Main, ensuring trade routes are cleared of these ocean-going robbers. Wrongly accused of allowing pirates, led by Livio Lorenzon (Olonese), to steal Loris Gizzi's (Governor Don Fernando Linares) silver, bound for Spain (Gérard Landry has a bit part as the prosecutor), the mariner is made a scapegoat, found guilty of negligence, stripped of his rank and sentenced to life in a penal colony. Soon he becomes a pirate himself (complete with eye patch) after busting out of the hold of the *Tortugas* and commandeering the ship, determined to clear his name ("We are men without a country—but not without honor!" Barker roars to his fellow mutineers). It's a put-up job, naturally, oily Gizzi in league with barking mad Lorenzon, both involved in stealing Spain's riches and selling out to the British, when war is declared between their home country and England; Barker and his buccaneers eventually come to the rescue of the Spanish convoy as it sails into a trap set by the conniving duo, and he and his men are pronounced by the Viceroy of New Spain as heroes of the hour.

An abundance of exciting piratical action abounds in Paolella's salty yarn, including galleons locking horns, a cannon bombardment on Santa Cruz and shipboard swordfights. Lorenzon and Gizzi camp it up nicely, a fine couple of reptilian villains, Lorenzon stabbed to death by Barker, Gizzi receiving a pike in his rotund midriff. Of the two female leads, Estella Blain (Isabella), Gizzi's niece, comes off second-best to Lorenzon's long-suffering mistress Liana Orfei (Ana), who the pirate chief callously murders in anger; Blain is rather wishy-washy compared to fiery Orfei and doesn't really deserve Barker's manly arms around her, when he's reinstated as captain of the *Victoria*. Costume and production design is right on the button, especially in the lavish ball sequence, and Barker makes a sinewy wronged sea captain, going through the umpteen incidents and intrigues (there are a lot of them) with aplomb. This is a seafaring adventure that would still appeal to most youngsters today if decent widescreen copies were more readily available.

The Queen of the Pirates [*La venere dei pirati*]

Max Film (Italy); Supercinescope/Eastmancolor; 80 mins; Producer: Ottavio Poggi; Director: Mario Costa ✝✝

A who's who peplum lineup highlights this underwhelming, mundane pirate flick set in the 1500s: Massimo Serato, Gianna Maria Canale, Scilla Gabel, Livio Lorenzon, Paul Muller, Moira Orfei, José Jaspe, Andrea Aureli, Franco Fantasia and Nando Tamberlani. You would have thought that with this laudable cast and experienced director Mario Costa at the helm, *The Queen of the Pirates* would have turned out to be something rather spe-

An Italian poster for *Robin Hood and the Pirates*

cial. It's far from it, with what little action there is whittled down to a miserly 80-minute running time. The wobbly plot goes as follows: The tyrannical Duke Zulian of Doruzza (Muller), who's main pastime is pinching grain from the poor, wishes his daughter Isabella (Gabel) to be wed to Count Cesare (Serato). Captain Mirko (Jaspe) and daughter Sandra (Canale) are imprisoned for roughing up Muller's soldiers, when they nose around his ship; Serato, arriving at the Duke's castle after stopping off at the Monte Gelato falls, prevents Jaspe from being strung up and Canale from being sent to a Turkish harem (Gabel's jealous of her beauty, although no mean beauty herself), seeing it as an injustice, leaving the pair to hoist the skull and crossbones and resort to a life of piracy on the Adriatic coast. Bald-headed tough guy Lorenzon makes an all-too-brief appearance as a pirate chief, with Orfei playing his mistress Jana (also wasted), and there's a solitary confrontation between two galleons at sea, Canale resplendent in the latest fashionable women's pirate costume (the booty is shared among the peasants), and in the end, the pirates storm Muller's stronghold. The oppressor is killed, but not before admitting that Canale is the constitutional successor to the Duchy. Serato opts to slink off with the new Duchess of Doruzza, while Gabel retires in sorrow to a convent.

Carlo Rustichelli provides a jaunty Jolly Roger score (used again in *Tiger of the Seven Seas* and *The Adventurer of Tortuga*; you can also detect refrains in the opening scenes of *Genoveffa of Brabant* [*The Revenge of the Crusader*]), which sticks in the mind, while Raffaele Masciocchi's cinematography is as sunny as the locations. *The Queen of the Pirates* must have looked tremendous on the big wide screen in a darkened theater 50 years ago; it's the underdeveloped narrative thrust and a rushed air that really lets the movie down. Extra footage should have been allocated to Canale and Lorenzon's pirate exploits; it could have been so much better if extended by a further 10 minutes or so, making the movie a more complete affair.

Robin Hood and the Pirates [*Robin Hood e i pirati*]

Finanziaria (Italy); Totalscope/Eastmancolor; 88 (82) mins; Producers: Leo Bomba, Carlo Infascelli; Director: Giorgio Simonelli ✝ or ✝✝✝✝✝

Suspend all disbelief, all sense of logic and rhyme or reason, as Italian moviemakers ask you to accept that legendary Englishman Robin Hood enlisted the aid of a pirate gang, plus a group of Creole gospel singers, to overthrow the dastardly Lord Jonathan Brooks in sunny Sherwood Forest-by-the-sea, with nary a greenwood tree in sight. It's a scatterbrained production that plumbs new depths in historical/location inaccuracy, deserving of one-star status, *or five-star* if you're in the mood for 88 minutes of no-holds-barred lunacy. *Robin Hood and the Pirates*, quite literally, must be seen to be believed!

Lisa Gastoni swashes her buckle under the alias of Captain Poof in *The Adventures of Mary Read*.

Washed up on a beach after Walter Barnes' pirate ship has sunk in a storm, Lex Barker (as Robin Hood: Yes, he wears Lincoln green tights!) scrambles up a cliff and begins a campaign to oust toad-like Mario Scaccia (as Brooks) from his murdered father's seat of power. Never mind the fact that Sherwood Forest in Nottingham happens to be over 60 miles from the sea; here, it's a stone's throw away, under a blazing Mediterranean sun in the Lapilli quarries, and there's very little in the way of forest. When Barnes (Guercio, sporting a black eye patch) and his rabble are also deposited ashore (including gospel singer Edith Peters and her troupe of wildcats), Barker signs them up on a promise of gold if Scaccia is usurped. In the despot's castle, his daughter Rossana Rory (Lizbeth) disapproves of her father's lustful interest in Maid Marian clone Jocelyn Lane ("Do I have to have her as a stepmother?"), coercing hunchback Giulio Donnini (Golia), dressed like court fool, into carrying out her dirty work. When she eventually meets Barker, *she* decides to marry him and have Lane strung up for treason; the girl is saved in the climactic skirmish between Scaccia's mob and the combined corps of peasant outlaws, Barker, Barnes' corsairs and a green talking parrot. Rory takes an arrow meant for Barker, Scaccia toppling onto rocks from the battlements after a duel with the hero in the feathered cap and fetching tights.

"Murder. What an ugly expression for lips that are so lovely," drools Scaccia, as Lane accuses him of just that as an innocent peasant approaches the gallows. Down at the beach, a cry of "Robin Hood! He's come back!" signifies the return of the savior, Peters hollering a calypso ditty that is definitely *not* 13th century in origin! Barnes (named One-Eye, even though he can see out of both) calls Peters Butterball. She objects. "I'll call you Sweet Pea if you want." "Oh yeah, well that's more like it," says Peters in a thick American drawl. "Hooray for Robin Hood! We'll all be rich," yell the salty seadogs as they start on their plan of attack. "I love fear in the eyes of a beautiful woman," leers Scaccio, threatening Lane with the gallows if she refuses his hand in wedded bliss. Lane and Rory engage in a catfight on the beach, and Barnes has set his sights on a plumed helmet worn by an enemy knight, a "Bird of Paradise" he covets, and Guido Robuschi and Gian Stellari's joint score throws in the lot: flutes, drums, trumpets and piccolos, an unceasing medieval mishmash that makes the eardrums ring. Scaccio states that he'll be magnanimous if Barker gives himself up, then opts to imprison Lane, informing her, "You're the bait in my trap." "You beast!" she retorts. Another 20th-century colloquialism, "It's all over but the shouting," worms itself into the goofy dialogue as Barnes, trying his hardest to take on the mantle of the great Robert Newton in *Treasure Island*, urges his "scum of the ocean" to storm the castle, shouting, "Throw the rascals overboard," even though he's on dry land. After the victory, the pirate chief is offered a new ship as just reward; the parrot squawks, "Man overboard! Man overboard!" and Barker the valiant canoodles with Lane. An absolute riot from beginning to end (full marks to Raffaele Masciocchi's gloriously rich color overtones) that you can't help laughing at. Whether that was the intention of director Simonelli and his team will never be known; at least the entire cast seemed to be enjoying the fun!

1961

The Adventures of Mary Read [*Le avventure di Mary Read*] aka ***Queen of the Seas***; ***Hell Below Deck***
  Romana Film/SNC (Italy/France); Totalscope/Eastmancolor; 87 mins; Producer: Fortunato Misiano; Director: Umberto Lenzi ✝✝✝✝✝

Well, if Jean Peters could successfully play a sexy female pirate in Fox's *Anne of the Indies* (1951), so could buxom Lisa Gastoni in Umberto Lenzi's rollicking actioner (his first peplum), not seen for many years. Sunny Italy stands in for gray old 18th-century England, the scenery and signs distinctly un-English in appearance, and would the commander of one of His Majesty's naval cruisers really be called Captain Poof? Quirkiness aside, Lenzi's high seas adventure rattles through its 87 minutes with dash, seemingly twice as long but never boring. Gino Filippini's symphonic, semi-classical score, pin-sharp photography courtesy of Augusto Tiezzi, Lenzi's "let's not pause for a second" direction and the ensemble cast putting their all into every scene makes for an enjoyable, old-fashioned and expertly constructed thrill-ride.

Gastoni stars as Mary Read, a notorious thief, first espied dressed as a man robbing jewels from a high-class lady in a carriage. Caught red-handed, she's put under lock and key in a dank London jail cell with Jerome Courtland (Peter Goodwin), a womanizing philanderer, but an appealing one; it doesn't take the pair long to indulge in a bit of frenzied lip action once Gastoni's male guise is dropped. Courtland, son of a lord, is released (he was only imprisoned because of a prank that backfired),

An Italian poster for *Conqueror of Maracaibo*

Gastoni ingeniously breaks out and, with grandfather Agostino Salvietti in tow, joins up as a sailor with Captain Poof (Walter Barnes), his ship en route to the Americas. Barnes slobbers all over her, is killed in a skirmish with a Spanish frigate ("A flower hidden among all this scum," remarks the Spanish captain, observing Gastoni's figure) and the feisty lady, after setting free the English sea dogs and clearing the decks of Spaniards, takes command, becoming the most feared corsair on the high seas, kitted out in a very fetching red pirate's outfit. Meanwhile, in Merry Olde England, serial seducer Courtland is forced into the military academy by his impatient father and emerges a captain, given the task of ridding the seas of that brigand Captain Poof, completely unaware that Poof is in fact the one woman he honestly loves, Gastoni.

It all sounds like pure bunkum and maybe it is as Gastoni abducts a dancer on a second raid and impersonates the girl, stripping down to her underwear, robbing the shocked guests at a soirée held in honor of Louis X1V and outsmarting Courtland, hoodwinking him into giving away his plans on capturing Poof. The novice captain then orders his privateers to inadvertently destroy a king's vessel of the fleet and is cashiered. But it's hugely entertaining bunkum of the type moviemakers are simply unable to produce anymore (Renny Harlin's 1995 female pirate flop, *Cutthroat Island*, proves it). In the end, true love conquers all—a 60-cannon man-o'-war blitzes the pirate stronghold of San Salvador; Gastoni's ship is taken and set on fire by Courtland (given one last chance to redeem himself) who, dumbfounded, then realizes the true identity of this tigress of the seven seas, alias Captain Poof, after partaking in a swordfight with the lass ("I was tricked! Mary!"). However, he doesn't let on to the authorities; this is one prize that he isn't going to let slip through his fingers twice. Six months later, they're a married couple, living in London's High Society, crusty old Salvietti relating his lurid adventures to a bevy of beauties. A long-forgotten treasure *and* a guilty pleasure from start to finish, even though the Italian interpretation of English prose in the subtitles shown on crisp DVD copies (difficult to obtain) is unintentionally hilarious.

Conqueror of Maracaibo [*Il conquistatore di Maracaibo*]

Produzioni Associate/Procusa/Epoca (Italy/Spain); Supertotalscope/Eastmancolor; 101 mins; Producer: Leonardo Martin; Director: Eugenio Martin ††††

In 1630 freebooters led by Carlos Casaravilla (Brasseur) and a mysterious masked figure known only as El Valiente are plundering Spanish galleons for their gold. Rival buccaneer Hans von Borsody (Alan Drake) also hungers after the booty, peeved when Casaravilla raids a rich Spanish vessel, dumps her crew overboard and lays his hands on treasure worth a million pieces-of-eight gold coin. Hiding the treasure from his men in an abandoned mine on a deserted island, Casaravilla blows up his own ship and makes for the island of Tortuga, where he resumes hostilities with staunch enemy von Borsody, blaming him for scuttling his vessel. Several uproarious swordfights and tavern free-for-alls later, "wharf rat" von Borsody, Lieutenant Luis Induni, diminutive nuisance Salvatore Furnari, a mischievous pet chimp and assorted shipmates manage to board their ship *Thundercloud*, raven-haired slave girl Luisella Boni (Altagracia, billed as Brigitte Corey) in tow. Von Borsody then comes to the aid of a galleon under bombardment from corsairs. Posing as a Spanish botanist, he meets Countess Jany Clair (Dona Isabella), escorting her ship to Maracaibo and safety. Invited as a guest at His Excellency's reception, von Borsody is dismayed to find that flighty Clair is promised to priggish officer Luis Sanchez Polack (Don Miguel Ortega); however, in compensation, Governor Carlo Tamberlani's lady, regal-looking Helga Liné (Moira), shows an unhealthy interest in von Borsody and his future plans for stealing more gold from the Spanish coffers. Casaravilla, in the meantime, is arranging for Maracaibo to be invaded and stripped of its entire stock of gold and treasure. Von Borsody is exposed as the pirate captain he really is and chucked into a dungeon; El Valiente helps him make off through a concealed passage and three pirate ships under the supervision of Casaravilla line up outside Maracaibo's harbor, ready to open fire.

Strikingly filmed at Peniscola, the fortified seaport termed The Gibraltar of Valencia, Eugenio Martin's rumbustious seafaring saga is a little on the complicated side plot-wise, an over-abundance of characters up to no good, involved in furtive operations and shady practices. But all hell breaks loose when Casaravilla's naval force begins their cannonade; the pirate gangs wade ashore, storm the beach, plant the skull and crossbones in the sand and ascend the steep rocky slopes to take on Maracaibo's heavily armed fortress. The director must have studied the climactic skirmish in John Wayne's *The Alamo* (United Artists, 1960) in minute detail; his 14-minute battle sequence is an extraordinarily noisy, smoke-filled blinder, a strong contender for one of the pirate subgenre's most rousing slices of full-blooded action, pirates and soldiers engaged in swordfights, gunfights, hand-to-hand tussles, explosions and a battery of fire,

A German still showing José Jaspe on the end of Ricardo Montalban's sword in *Gordon, the Black Pirate*

fought out among the castle's craggy stone walls. It will leave you open-mouthed in excitement (to his credit, Martin eschews Miguel Asins Arbo's score; the sound of battle speaks louder than music) and finishes with a flourish, all three pirate ships blown out of the water. Liné is revealed to be the elusive masked "man," Casaravilla hurling a dagger into her back before von Borsody runs the marauder through. "I have to die like a pirate," she gasps. "The sea will guard your secret," promises von Borsody, consigning her body beneath the waves, as seafaring tradition decrees. The buccaneer receives both the Knighthood of Maracaibo and title of Superintendent of the Caribbean seas for his endeavors in routing the pirates and heads off for a new life in Virginia, slave girl Boni cradled in his arms. A DVD release including subtitles (current issues are in Spanish only) would be very much welcomed.

Gordon, the Black Pirate [*Gordon, il pirata nero*] aka ***Rage of the Buccaneers***; ***The Black Pirate***

Max Production (Italy); Totalscope/Eastmancolor; 88 mins; Producer: Ottavio Poggi; Director: Mario Costa ✝✝✝

Even boosted by the appearance of horror star Vincent Price as Romero, *Gordon, the Black Pirate* is standard swashbuckling fare, colorful enough (thanks to Carlo Bellero's sunny photography) and directed with zest by Mario Costa, but dragging in the middle; the director focuses on the Ricardo Montalban/Giulia Rubini/Price love triangle to the detriment of rousing piratical action. Montalban, doing a passable impersonation of Douglas Fairbanks in his '20s heyday (in 1926, Douglas himself starred as *The Black Pirate*), is slave-turned-pirate Captain Gordon, the Black Buccaneer, his ship the *Indomitable* homing in on any vessel caught up in slave trafficking; once overpowered, he releases the poor unfortunates held captive. José Jaspe plays Tortuga, Montalban's arch-enemy, the pair initially introduced fighting on a beach. At the sharp end of the pirate's sword, Jaspe promises to leave the slave traffic be, a promise broken as soon as Montalban boards his frigate and sails to San Salvador. There, disguised as a Cuban plantation owner in need of cheap labor, Montalban attends the annual fiesta and ball, uncovering Price's intentions to oust Governor Mario Feliciani from power, marry his daughter Rubini (Manuela) and carry on in the slave business with Jaspe, to fund his ambitions, regardless of the human misery involved. Needless to say, Montalban falls in lust with Rubini right under Price's nose, poor pirate-wannabe Liana Orfei (Luana) left pining for a black-clad hero she knows she will never have all to herself.

An excitingly orchestrated clash of vessels, each firing broadsides, and a thundering showpiece, the buccaneers raiding the governor's hilltop fortress under a blanket of shellfire on the day of Price's pretence wedding (location filming was carried out in Valencia's seaport) drag the movie out of the "will Montalban win the love of hard-to-get Rubini" treadmill it finds itself on, although any movie featuring three lovely females—Rubini, maid Gisella Sofio and Orfei—must be worth a look. Price, after imprisoning Feliciani, has to reluctantly go along with Jaspe's grand vision of invading San Salvador with an army of slaves, but it leads nowhere; the Black Pirate and his men board the slaver's ship, the energetic corsair clambers up rigging and shims down sails, ripping them to shreds. Jaspe, the brigand of the seas, is run through, dropping lifeless into the blue ocean, and Price, after threatening to ignite kegs of dynamite, is knocked senseless, Rubini wrested from his clutches. The reformed pirate weds his prize trophy in the end, unconditionally pardoned by the Spanish court for all past misdemeanors. Carlo Rustichelli provides a tuneful score, heard in other peplum pirate films he worked on, and as for Price—well, he's nowhere near the hammy villain up to all kinds of mischief in countless X-rated (in the U.K.) Hollywood horror pictures, but here his very presence dominates every scene he's in, and that's good enough for any Price fan.

The Secret of the Black Falcon [*Il segreto dello sparviero nero*] aka ***The Black Brigand***

Romana Film (Italy); Totalscope/Eastmancolor; 92 mins; Producer: Fortunato Misiano; Director: Domenico Paolella ✝✝✝

In 1700, Spaniard Lex Barker (Captain Carlos de Herrera) and Englishman Livio Lorenzon (Sergeant Rodriguez) are after

An Italian photobusta for *The Secret of the Black Falcon*

The U.S. half-sheet poster for *Guns of the Black Witch* (aka *The Terror of the Seas*)

The Terror of the Seas [*Il terrore dei mari*] aka *Guns of the Black Witch*

Romana Film/SNC (Italy/France); Totalscope/Eastmancolor; 98 (84) mins; Producer: Fortunato Misiano; Director: Domenico Paolella ✞✞✞✞✞

Young buccaneer Jean saves a maiden from sinking in a quagmire; Livio Lorenzon's (Guzman) Spanish guards ride up, surround the lad, push him around a bit and let him go. He returns to a village razed to the ground, every person massacred, including his father. Lorenzon's responsible, ignoring the wishes of Maracaibo's warden, Loris Gizzi, and the Spanish court to treat the natives with respect. Along with two survivors, Jean rows away from his shattered home, boards Captain Franco Jamonte's pirate ship and enlists as a junior corsair, vowing to kill the person behind his father's death. Twelve years later, following the demise of Jamonte in a sea battle, Jean (Don Megowan) commands the *Black Witch*, waging a bitter war of attrition against the Spaniards and hunting still the murderer of his father.

Domenico Paolella was no stranger to the sea. This was one of five nautical-themed movies the director made (if you include *The Prisoners of Devil's Island*), the man behind one of the best-ever peplum pirate actioners, *Pirates of the Coast*. He knew how to maximize those exciting sea skirmishes carried out on real galleons, positioning his camera directly behind thundering cannons, or shooting them full-frame, to blast the audience out of their seats. And there are plenty of such incidents in *The Terror of the Seas*, as six-foot-six-inch Megowan (famous for playing the humanized gill-man in Universal's 1956 monster-romp, *The Creature Walks Among Us*) kicks Spanish ass to such an extent that a 60-cannon super ship ("A fortress of the sea.") is commissioned to put a stop to his shenanigans throughout the Spanish Main. It doesn't work, as the huge vessel is taken in battle, all officers hanged and the ship, listing to portside, limps into Maracaibo's harbor, much to the horror of Lorenzon, Gizzi and Gizzi's daughter, Emma Danieli (Elisa)—Megowan has triumphed again.

Back at the pirates' island stronghold, dancing tavern strumpet Silvana Pampanini (Delores), rudely rejected by Megowan, throws in her lot with Germano Longo (Michel) who, jealous of Megowan, throws in *his* lot with Lorenzon, betraying the buccaneers for gold. Megowan is wounded while attempting to sneak into Maracaibo undetected, cared for in a cave by Danieli, who melts in his arms. "I love you," declares Megowan after only knowing the lass for two days, but on learning of her liaison, Gizzi ("This is high treason!") decides to whisk her off to Portobello, unaware that Longo and Lorenzon are hatching a fiendish plan to eliminate the pirates: Round up a bunch of women, deposit them on the island among the sex-starved corsairs, let nature take its course and, while everybody is otherwise engaged, shell the place to oblivion. An all-cannon blazing final 15 minutes delivers the goods in blood and thunder style. Megowan waylays Gizzi's galleon and finishes off the crew by tying them to a main brace and letting a barrage of cannon balls do their work. The island is flattened and given to Longo as a gift

vital war documents held by pirate Walter Barnes (Calico Jack); only by infiltrating his gang of filibusters can the papers be retrieved by either party. But who is the mysterious figure clothed from head to toe in black that appears at inopportune moments, crawls through window openings, engages in duels and disappears in a flash? Spanish governor Loris Gizzi instructs Barker to enlist on the *Santa Maria* and grab those documents, while Lorenzon conveniently bumps into Barker near some ruins, the pair boarding Barnes' vessel after fending off bandits, chatting up the local trollops and engaging in a customary peplum tavern rumpus.

The Secret of the Black Falcon looks good, embellished by Carlo Bellero's fine Eastmancolor photography (pristine letterbox, German-dubbed DVDs are on the market), and both Lorenzon and Barnes (born to play a pirate chief, a sword and sash encircling his wider-than-wide girth) ham it up gleefully. Barker, in comparison, seems less active as a good guy-cum-pirate than he was in *The Scimitar of the Saracen* and *Pirates of the Coast*, much of the action taking place in the one location, Barnes' picturesque pirate village. A Spanish galleon is commandeered, the female captives herded ashore and ordered about by Barnes' lieutenant, Germano Longo (Zampa di Gatto); among the hostages is Nadia Marlowa (Leonora), Barker's royalty-connected girlfriend. A ransom note sent to Gizzi by Barker contains a craftily coded message, asking that the Spanish fleet comes to the rescue of the prisoners and retrieves those precious papers. Lorenzon fools around with the corsair captain's woman, Pina Cornel (Yvette), tied to a wheel in the glaring sun as punishment, and Chinese accomplice Ho Fung Ling, who wants to murder the females, betrays Barnes. Lorenzon turns out to be the black-clad Falcon; beating and stabbing Barnes to death (an out-of-context brutal scene), he's felled by a cannon blast when the Spanish arrive and attack in large numbers from the beach. Following the aftermath of battle, Barker and Marlowa are free to rekindle their relationship.

A French poster for *Executioner of the Seas*

ing forced by British marines to work day and night to satisfy the greed of their naval commanding officer, to the final fracas in Brensville. Pirate blockbusters didn't begin with the *Pirates of the Caribbean* franchise—they were around long before that and far punchier in delivery, as *Executioner of the Seas* admirably proves.

In 1790 deportees in Freeland cower under the iron heel of Roldano Lupi (Commander Redway), an uncouth naval officer who makes Captain Bligh look like a Sunday school teacher. The bulky oaf with the manners of a pig demands his monthly tribute in pearls and, if it isn't forthcoming, the poor devils must slave 24 hours a day to make sure that his coffers are full. Officer Richard Harrison (David Robinson), whose brother and father are among those who spend all day submerged in water avoiding sharks, objects to Lupi's heartless methods, retaliates too strongly when his brother is whipped and forced to work in an underground stone quarry; he's then shackled to rocks to await a slow death by drowning. Entering the scene comes jovial pirate chief Walter Barnes (Van Artz) and sidekick Paul Muller (Hornblut); his ship opens fire on the British garrison, the slaves revolt, Lupi and his marines run for cover and Harrison is unchained. On board ship, the brigands disembark at Barnes' sheltered bolt-hole after negotiating a dangerous reef; Barnes' daughter, Michele Mercier (Jennifer), takes a shine to Harrison, who comes to an arrangement with the pirate: He'll lead the way to Lupi's vessel on condition that he receives 50 percent of the pearls Barnes is after.

Director Paolella (he also directed another Walter Barnes pirate flick, *The Secret of the Black Falcon*) doesn't let up for a second, piling on the incident and set pieces with a commendable lack of restraint. Harrison disables the British ship's rudder, Barnes rams the floundering vessel, a furious engagement ensues to the ear-splitting sound of Egisto Macchi's musical tonalities and the marines abandon ship. Ashore at Freeland, Harrison's father has been murdered and the officer once more finds himself in irons, tortured by swinging upside down against a wall of lethal spikes. Lupi's long-suffering half-caste mistress, Marisa Belli (Nike), drugs Harrison's wine so that he'll disclose the exact spot where the pirates' village lies; the woman clings to the bully like a leech, dreaming of a ladies' life in far-away London. The narrative maintains the momentum right to the very end, including a bizarre semi-horror sequence in which Mercier and nine other captives, tied to stakes in a misty marsh, due for sacrifice in exchange for those cursed pearls, are almost gobbled to bits and pieces by man-sized carnivorous plants resembling giant Venus flytraps. Barnes and Muller wind up killed, Belli dies dreaming of London, a pike in her back, and that villainous swine Lupi meets a very satisfactory end, skewered by a falling portcullis in a hidden grotto. The pirates are given a royal pardon, allowed to live their lives unmolested by the British navy, and Harrison gets to play house with Mercier. Noisy, colorful and tremendous fun, even though current pan and scan prints render much of the original widescreen photography redundant.

instead of gold ("You're the new governor," sneers Lorenzon); women who escaped the slaughter gather together and stone the defector plus Pampanini to death. Wading ashore, Megowan is snared ("I intend to put a foot of steel through your stomach," he spits at Lorenzon), taken aboard a Spanish vessel and roped to the prow like a figurehead. His men hone in on the Spaniards, and there's yet another thrilling clash, as Gizzi perishes under a falling beam and Lorenzon, as promised by Megowan, gets that well-deserved foot of steel in his guts. With Danieli at his side, Megowan sets a course for the *Black Witch* and off they sail for more adventures.

Unfortunately, while Michele Cozzoli's fine score remains unscathed (augmented by Les Baxter and Ronald Stein for U.S./U.K. release), Carlo Bellero's color photography has suffered over the years in the faded, ragged-around-the-edges DVD issues currently available from independent sources. But enough is there to showcase Paolella's proven skill behind the lens, presenting us with a thumping good pirate yarn of the old school, one that might even keep the youngsters amused today.

1962

Executioner of the Seas [*Il giustiziere dei mari*] aka *Avenger of the Seven Seas*

Documento Film/Le Louvre Film (Italy/France); Totalscope/Eastmancolor; 90 mins; Producer: Gianni Hecht Lucari; Director: Domenico Paolella ✠✠✠✠

There's wall-to-wall action in Richard Harrison's frolicsome pirate flick, from the opening shots of pearl fishermen be-

Hawk of the Caribbean [*Lo sparviero dei Caraibi*] aka *Caribbean Hawk*

Nord Film (Italy); Totalscope/Eastmancolor; 115 (87) mins; Producers: Alfonso Donati, Umberto Borsato; Director: Piero Regnoli ✠✠✠✠✠

A popular singer during World War II, both with Gene Krupa's band and Glenn Miller's Army Air Forces Orchestra,

An Italian photobusta for *Hawk of the Caribbean*

Johnny Desmond also dabbled in acting; here, he took on the unusual (for him) role of Juan Rodrigo Olivares, a pirate chief who comes to the aid of the Spanish in 1648, when English forces threaten to invade the port of Santa Cruz. What Desmond lacked in height and stature he more than made up for in vocalization, spending practically the entire length of Regnoli's thrilling seafaring adventure movie shouting at the top of his voice. Desmond, first mate Piero Lulli (Manuel) and several other convicts are washed ashore following the sinking of Spanish cargo boat *Conception*. Swiftly taking command of Spanish-held Fort Esperanza, they equip themselves with provisions, Lulli takes wench Graziella Granata (Flora) for his own pleasure and the wanted criminals seize a well-armed vessel, the *Santa Madalena*, retaining the ladies but jettisoning the crew. Hoisting the Jolly Roger, Desmond, voted captain over glowering Lulli, embarks on a life of piracy, the women complaining that they're being treated "like common prostitutes," while one of their number, Yvonne Monlaur (Arica), devotes herself to Desmond ("I'm your slave. You're my master.") after he saves her from 20 lashes of the whip.

Following a furious clash with a Spanish warship, an enticing proposition is put forward to Desmond and his rowdy corsairs by the Viceroy of Santa Cruz: Make your way through the jungle, destroy the English and each man will receive 10,000 silver coins plus a barrel of rum. Loose cannon Lulli, forever arguing with Desmond as to who should be in charge, smells a rat but the deal is sealed. Trouble is, Desmond's got the manners of a pig. At a palace reception, where Lady Franca Parisi (Donna Maria) flutters her lashes at him, he shows himself to be an uncouth oaf among the posh gentry; storming out in embarrassment after cracking a tasteless joke, he returns to his ship, orders the men to clean up, returns to Santa Cruz in a better frame of mind and, with his marauders, eliminates the English. Lulli, simmering with hatred, turns the tables on his chief with the help of two-timing Claudio Undari (Don Pedro). Monlaur is imprisoned and tortured on the rack, Desmond leaps to her rescue, killing Lulli, and is then cornered in that classic oft-used peplum shot—the hero encircled by lances and spears. But friendly Spanish military supremo Armando Francioli has one more proposition to make to Desmond: Blast that pesky British frigate out of the water before it bombards Santa Cruz, and you and your men will be pardoned, given 1,000 doubloons each and found jobs in the Spanish army. Bucking the genre trend in an unexpected finale, Desmond leaves his crew behind (and Parisi); together with Monlaur, whom he has wedded in jail, the pair of doomed lovers steer their ship, under heavy fire, straight into the British man-o'-war, both vessels exploding in a fireball, the dejected pirates looking on in horror from the shore as their boss makes the ultimate sacrifice.

Another peplum hard-to-come-by, *Hawk of the Caribbean* comes today (if you can locate a copy) in a ragged-looking print, but it's good enough for buffs to appreciate Aldo Greci's deep, rich colors and Aldo Piga's belter of a score. Long, maybe, but crammed with incident and plot twists, Piero Regnoli's swashbuckler still excites after 55 years, a testimony to all involved, especially as Monlaur was once quoted as saying that the production was plagued with delays and labor disputes due to lack of funds, several sequences remaining unfinished.

Musketeers of the Sea [*I moschettieri del mare*]

Morino Film/France Cinéma Prod. (Italy/France); CinemaScope/Eastmancolor; 116 (97) mins; Producers: Robert Chabert, Alfredo Mirabile, Orlando Orsini; Directors: Massimo Patrizi, Stefano (Steno) Vanzina †††

Three pirates/musketeers (Channing Pollock as Pierre, Aldo Ray as Moreau and Philippe Clay as Gosselin) survive the sinking of their ship by taking refuge in a large barrel; taken aboard the Spanish galleon *Santa Maria*, they hijack the vessel and assume command, discovering a document that informs them where the ship is headed, and for what purpose. Sailing first to Tortuga to recruit a crew, including Gino Buzzanca (Captain Ciurma Gutiérrez), and then to Maracaibo, the three rogues, using assumed identities, become embroiled in a conspiracy by Vice Governor Robert Alda (Gomez) to steal Spanish gold shipments and seize the seat of government from Mario Scaccia, the French monarch. Leading lady Pier Angeli plays twins Consuelo and Grazia; Consuelo's a corsair, kidnapped at birth and raised as a buccaneer, while Grazia is a reluctant wallflower, jealous of her sister's upfront bearing; their assumed father was hanged by Alda's confederates and Consuelo seeks retribution. Consuelo enlists with Pollock's gang in Maracaibo and, after a string of adventures, it transpires that Scaccia, in fact, is the twins' true father. After snaring Alda on the tip of his rapier in a frenzied shipboard tussle, Pollock and company are pardoned by the king and he marries Consuelo—or is it her twin, Grazia? Pollock isn't curious enough to find out, happy enough that he's snapped up one of the dark-haired beauties all for himself!

A French poster for *Musketeers of the Sea*

Torture sequences, much swordplay, fights on ships, daring escapes from the noose—all add up to an effervescent sea adventure marred by the horseplay of Ray (in a ridiculous long wig) and lugubrious Clay, the duo clowning it up far too much. Carlo Rustichelli's score propels things along in a picture that flounders a bit from over-length in the middle section. Pan and scan plus uneven color balance is also what you'll have to put up with if you can obtain a copy of the film, whose unavailability presents a real problem to avid collectors of the obscure.

Tiger of the Seven Seas [*La tigre dei sette mari*]

Liber Film/Euro Intl. (Italy/France); Totalscope/Eastmancolor; 90 mins; Producer: Ottavio Poggi; Director: Luigi Capuano ✝✝✝

London-born actor Anthony Steel, popular square-jawed heartthrob of countless British dramas of the 1950s (particularly war films), was 42 when he starred in this derivative pirate opus, his second peplum movie, giving the distinct impression of being completely out of his comfort zone among the predominantly Italian cast; he didn't swash a buckle all that well either. Steel played buccaneer William Scott, wrongly accused of sticking a dagger into the heart of "Tiger," a pirate skipper (Carlo Ninchi), who has decided to call it a day by handing over command of the *Santa Maria* to his daughter, Consuelo (Gianna Maria Canale, looking ravishing in pirate costume). Andrea Aureli, true to type, is the transgressor Robert, not only jealous of Canale's new role as the self-proclaimed Tiger of the Seven Seas (that should read Tigress!) but thirsting after her father's treasure. Beauty Maria Grazia Spina (Anna de Cordoba) features as a shady Spanish lady hand in glove with Aureli, longing for more and more golden riches to run her well-manicured fingers through, while her powder-puff husband, Ernesto Calindri (Governor Inigo), floats around court like a dandy, under the misguided impression that every woman is in lust with him—nothing could be further from the truth!

There's a full quota of fencing/parrying face-offs, an explosive clash of ships at sea, deck fighting and an amusing masked ball sequence in the Spanish fortress, where Canale turns up dressed as a pirate (which, of course, she is!) and coerces gullible Calindri (also in pirate attire) to show her the prisoners in the dungeon, Steel one of their number. Steel and his men bust out, and with the ball still in full sway, the *Santa Maria* fires a broadside at the fortress, prelude to a vigorous 10-minute fracas which lifts the movie out of the depths of mediocrity; it's pirates versus Spaniards, noisy and exciting, the Spanish victorious after the lawless seafarers have swarmed all over the shore batteries and battlements like ants, casting every cannon off the topmost walls. Captured, Steel and Canale are spared the noose (Aureli has been killed) on condition they tell Spina where the treasure lies hidden; the closing few minutes shows the Spanish diva salivating over the spoils, while Steel and Canale sail off to new adventures aboard the *Santa Maria*, bickering over who will be the ship's new captain.

This was Canale's second crack at playing a pirate queen (see *The Queen of the Pirates*) and Italy's answer to Ava Gardner (as one critic described her) took center stage, eclipsing all those around her including Steel, looking older than his 42 years. Carlo Rustichelli's score from Canale's first pirate flick was used for a second time, one of pepla's most instantly recognizable

An Italian poster for *The Devil Pirate*

soundtracks (and a good one), and Capuano directed with pace, trying to inject freshness into what was by now very familiar piratical themes. It's bright and breezy enough but could have been a whole lot better with perhaps a touch more in the way of character depth; Canale carries the day here (the actress unexpectedly quit acting two years after completing this picture).

1963

The Devil Pirate [*Il pirata del diavolo*] aka *Flag of Death*; *The Saracens*

Walmar Cinematografica/Triglav Film (Italy/Yugoslavia); Totalscope/Eastmancolor; 89 (84) mins; Producers: Aldo Piga, Gisleno Procaccini; Director: Roberto Mauri ††††

In the 16th century, Turkish hordes are overflowing into Europe, conquering people along the Dalmatian coast. Swarthy pirate chief Rabanek, played with sly contemptuousness by Demeter Bitenc, invades Count Gino Turini's castle during a gathering held in honor of his son's homecoming (catch that spectacular firework display), his white-caped corsairs streaming into the palace and slaughtering practically everyone, ferrying the women plus a few survivors aboard their ship. Richard Harrison, the count's son (Marco Trevisan), and soldier friend Walter Brandi (Ranieri) then have two pieces of business on their hands: to rescue Harrison's betrothed, Liana Dori (Velia), from prison and overthrow the devilish corsair to prevent any further bloody massacres.

Obscure, faded, wobbly prints available on the gray market, English-dubbed with Greek subtitles, do little justice to Roberto Mauri's violent pirate-cum-swashbuckler, in which two things stand out: Aldo Piga's vibrant score and the almost perverse acts of bestiality toward women. Piga's music pounds incessantly in the background, but never becomes intrusive, melding with the action rather than detracting from it, a brilliant piece of film scoring from pepla's golden age. As for the female cast, from the opening raid on the village to the castle assault, they're stabbed, feel the keen edge of a sword, molested, fondled and raped, breasts almost spilling out of bodices, dresses torn, even a bare shoulder bitten in one moment of madness. Later on, Turkish beauty Annamaria Ubaldi (Alina), who has unwisely fallen for Harrison and been accused of treachery, is buried up to her neck in mud (along with her maid); horsemen trample their exposed heads to pulp, killing both. Mauri also includes, for titillation purposes only, a near-naked bath scene. Today, this content could be viewed as rather disturbing; back then, the Italians reveled in it.

Sandwiched between this "cruelty to females" subtext is a pretty exciting narrative that moves like wildfire. Harrison, captured, fever-ridden and incarcerated in a dungeon, is cared for by Ubaldi, who helps him escape with the women (but not Dori), the girl resigned to the fact that the Christian hunk loves another. When she's callously tried, convicted and put to death by Bitenc, second-in-command Luigi Batzella, her father, changes sides, determined to slay the pirate boss in revenge. Bitenc's vessel is blown out of the water, refugees are herded to an old mill for safety and a standoff takes place in a desert ravine, Bitenc demanding an exchange, Dori for Batzella. During the ensuing battle, Piga's music is replaced by the sound of the keening wind, a nice touch that adds to the flavor. Dynamite decimates most of the pirates—Harrison and Bitenc engage in a scuffling four-minute duel inside the castle, the pirate succumbing to Harrison's steel blade. On the castle balcony, Harrison kisses Dori, the Turks defeated—for the time being.

Harrison, unusually for him, turns in a lackluster performance, not really coming alive until the movie is two-thirds over. It's Bitenc who comes out tops, a memorable, lip-smacking villain given all the picture's best lines, as when he turns his nose up at a troupe of cavorting male dancers: "I much prefer buxom girls," he grins, salaciously. *The Devil Pirate* may be formulaic in content, but it's noisy, energetic fodder put together with pace and style, filmed in and around Kamerlengo Castle at Trogir, although perhaps not ideal for the more feminine of clientele.

1964

The Masked Man Against the Pirates [*L'uomo mascherato contro i pirati*] aka *The Black Pirate*

Titanus/Rio Film (Italy); CinemaScope/Eastmancolor; 90 mins; Producer: Pino Addario; Director: Vertunnio De Angelis †††

Wearing the latest in fashionable (for 1659) pirate headgear (black wide-brimmed hat, black plumes, the skull and crossbones emblem placed neatly dead center), burly, bearded brigand of the seas, Giovanni Vari (Captain Pedro Ramon Garcia), drinks, eats, fights and roars his way through a piratical "shiver me timbers" farce of such pantomime proportions that you half-expect the entire cast to take a curtain call at the end. Peplum high seas adventures don't come much pottier than this one.

An Italian poster for *The Masked Man Against the Pirates*

sword in mistress Gina Rovere, tired of her clinging ways, and is eliminated by Hilton who, having previously revealed his true identity to Dantes, places the mask over his head, electing to stay on the island to tend to unfinished business. ("We'll meet again in Spain.") His bogus wife sails off in the Albatross, the ship now under Spanish command, with Vari and his crew captives, awaiting the hangman's rope in Spain.

"Goofy fun" best describes *The Masked Man Against the Pirates*; the acting is adequate (how Hilton and Kendall managed to keep straight faces dressed like third-rate superheroes lord alone knows) while Alessandro Nadin's score drifts like the ocean currents, going nowhere; and on current prints, the color photography lacks sparkle. One or two online sites give the film's length at 105 minutes, but the present (2015) English-dubbed DVD issue containing Greek subtitles (hard to find) comes in at 90 minutes, with no evidence of cuts or breaks in continuity.

Toto Against the Black Pirate [*Toto contro il pirata nero*]

Liber Film (Italy); Totalscope/Eastmancolor; 102 (94) mins; Producer: Ottavio Poggi; Director: Fernando Cerchio †††

Italian sad-faced funnyman Toto stars as José, a petty dockside thief hiding from the law in an empty rum barrel, who finds himself on a pirate ship commanded by Mario Petri, the dreaded Black Pirate. In a rash of daft adventures performed strictly on slapstick lines (although to his credit, Petri just about plays

Vari, captain of the super-swift *Albatross* (why are all these pirate vessels named *Albatross*?), closes in on a Spanish man-o'-war, fires a warning shot across her bow, lets fly a broadside and overcomes the Spaniards, burning their galleon for good measure; among his hostages is pretty-but-dumb Princess Anne (Claude Dantes), the lady coming to the attention of second-in-command George Hilton (Suarez). All female prisoners are to be sold into slavery, the male captives hanged, but to prevent Dantes falling into bondage, Hilton marries her, the wedding null and void due to stuttering friar Pietro Vico not officiating properly (in fact, this bumbling ex-pirate can't do *anything* properly). Down in the hole, Dantes is visited by a strange cloak-and-dagger figure sporting a green balaclava, blue/green outside pants and mustard yellow tights, who promises to help her and the captives (photobustas depict the balaclava as red, to catch the eye of the paying customer!). From the moment this refugee from a *Batman* movie appears, you know it's Hilton in disguise; when the *Albatross* calls at Vari's island stronghold, Hilton carries on with this laughable subterfuge, even enlisting the aid of Spanish captain Tony Kendall (Ruiz), who *also* leaps around on set in identical getup; yes, we now have *two* masked men against Vari's cutthroats, looking like a couple of 17th-century terrorists! Enter Lucio De Santis, a slave merchant demanding that Dantes, related to the King of Spain, be included in his job lot negotiations. Naturally, Hilton objects and masterminds a successful mass escape from the grotto prison. De Santis sticks a

An Italian poster for *Toto Against the Black Pirate*

A Spanish lobby card for *The Adventurer of Tortuga*

it dead straight), the diminutive clown enters into the thick of battle with the Spanish, is promoted to hero status and infiltrates the governor's court to pave the way for a pirate attack, winding up rescuing his daughter, Maria Grazia Spina (Isabella), from Petri's clutches. The pirates defeated, Toto is last seen back to his old ways, stealing a chicken from a stallholder.

Even if you're not Italian, some of the antics on display in this handsomely mounted spoof will bring a smile to the face. Naturally, Toto converses with a talking parrot; he disguises himself (one of many disguises) as a white-sheeted ghost to jump ship; as he's hanged, his neck stretches to the top mast and he's reprieved on orders from Petri's crew; he fights the Spaniards with a magnetized sword, a colander perched on his head and a saucepan lid acting as a shield for protection, acclaimed for his daring deeds. In the guise of a marquis, he worms his tiny figure into court, plays a tune on flexible prison bars, defeats Petri (first camouflaged as a chair, then in an acrobatic seesaw duel) and reunites Spina with her beloved. Carlo Rustichelli's score, matching the scenario, veers from stirring to screwy, Alvaro Mancori's pristine photography coats the production in a high-gloss sheen and Cerchio directs his third and final *Toto* outing with purpose, where so easily he could have let things slip into total absurdity. Prints are only available in Italian, so Toto's humorous patter will mean absolutely nothing to non-Italian viewers, not a loss as this is a sight gag movie, not a dialogue-driven one, amusing after downing a few beers. It's certainly a lot better than its predecessors, *Toto Against Maciste* and *Toto and Cleopatra*.

1965

The Adventurer of Tortuga [*L'avventuriero della Tortuga*]

Liber Film/Eichberg Film (Italy/West Germany); Eastmancolor; 97 mins; Producer: Gino Fanano; Director: Luigi Capuano ☦

American Guy Madison, sporting one of peplum's worst-ever hair pieces, stars as Alfonso di Montélimar, governor of New England colony Santa Cruz, vying for the attention of half-breed Ingeborg Schöner (Princess Soledad Quintero), along with brawny pirate chief Rik Battaglia (Pedro Valverde); Madison desires to lay his hands on the girl's rumored treasure while the pirate, a self-confessed "dowry hunter" (he woos rich women and ditches them at the altar, absconding with their fortunes to finance a fleet of ships), falls in love for the first time, wishing to marry Schöner for her dusky beauty as well as her wealth.

Ninety-seven minutes of piratical tosh sums up Luigi Capuano's turgid offering, a rare misfire from this usually dependable action director, in which very little in the way of shipboard action takes place, considering it's meant to be a pirate adventure. Apart from one cutting line, "I've forgotten that the brain of a woman is incapable of logical thought," the confusing script will have you scratching your head for the first half hour, wondering what on earth is going on, and who is who. Why does that monosyllabic Indian follow Schöner around? One minute the cast is off to the Court of Spain in Madrid, the next there are "redskins" appearing all over the place, and then we're in a temple standing in the middle of thick jungle—where are we supposed to be? Why does dastardly Madison desire those riches anyway? What happened to the proposed raid on the Island of Tortuga by Battaglia's buccaneers? That rarest of rarities in a peplum seagoing flick (or *any* peplum flick), the back-projected image (back-projection, on the whole, was commendably avoided like the plague by Italian filmmakers, deemed a cheating distraction from action scenes presented in gritty, realistic fashion) crops up in only one of three brief moments on board Battaglia's vessel, and a madcap tavern brawl performed on slapstick lines is thrown in to quicken the deadly slow pace. Fair enough, the closing five minutes livens up, featuring a pretty ferocious whipping set-to between Madison and Battaglia and an out-of-context Indian raid on a fort, which looks as though it's materialized from an entirely different production altogether, but it comes much too late in the day to save this rambling muddle of a movie (as does Carlo Rustichelli's fine marching-type score, reprised from *The Queen of the Pirates*). At the end of it all, you care nothing for Madison, his long-suffering mistress (Nadia Gray), that granite-faced Indian servant (Mino Doro) or Battaglia and his Indian bride, as they set sail for far more exciting adventures than are on offer here.

The Mystery of the Evil Island [*Il mistero dell'isola maledetta*] aka *Giant of the Evil Island*

Romana Film (Italy); Totalscope/Eastmancolor; 85 mins; Producer: Fortunato Misiano; Director: Piero Pierotti ☦☦☦

Peter "Rock Stevens" Lupus played Captain Pedro Valverde, taking over the command of Spanish galleon *Rio Tinto* from Arturo Dominici (Don Alvarado), tasked with routing a gang of cutthroats led by Nello Pazzafini (Malik), their fortified refuge the aptly named Evil Island. Pazzafini, sailing under the skull and crossbones, is looting Spanish vessels for their goods and terrorizing the seas around Puerto Suarez, but where, and from who, is he obtaining information regarding ships' manifestos and their movements? Creole Halina Zalewska (Dona Alma Morales) is the stooge, posing as a rich plantation owner and a respected member of the governor's entourage; in fact, she's a former slave girl and branded as such, nursing an almighty

and blessed with the same amount (or lack) of acting talent, smooches with De Santis. And there is no "Giant" on the island; Lupus is about the only male on set to fit that description!
1966

Surcouf, Hero of the Seven Seas** [Surcouf, l'eroe dei sette mari]* aka ***The Sea Pirate; ***The Fighting Corsair***; ***Thunder Over the Indian Ocean***

Arco Film/Balcazar Producciones/EDIC (Italy/Spain/France); Techniscope/Technicolor; 98 (85) mins; Producers: Roy Rowland, Nat Wachsberger, Francisco Balcazar, Georges de la Grandiere; Directors: Roy Rowland, Sergio Bergonzelli ††

In 1795, young Frenchman Robert Surcouf (Gérard Barray) is banned from marrying sweetheart Marie-Catherine (Genevieve Casile) because of his impoverished state. Enlisting with a gang of French freebooters, he becomes the scourge of the Indian Ocean, raiding British ships for their bounty. When the governor informs Barray that any loot taken will not be shared out with his corsairs, he travels to Paris to fight his cause, encountering American Margaret Carruthers (Antonella Lualdi) en route when their carriage is attacked by bandits. The pair fall in love, but she's betrothed to Lord Blackwood (Terence Morgan). At a luxurious ball, Barray converses with Napoleon's mistress, Josephine (Monica Randall), and a truce is made between France and Great Britain. Refusing to go to the States with Lualdi, Barray returns to pirating, 27 British ships under his belt, a reward of 20,000 guineas on the feared corsair's head. Taking possession of a 60-cannon English warship, he discovers Lualdi and Morgan on board, now wed. The pirate emerges victorious in a duel with his rival but doesn't deliver the *coup de grace*. "Thank you for sparing my husband," are Lualdi's final words as Barray heads back to a shipyard, second rival Antonio Molino Rojo expiring in agony when a vat tips boiling lead over him, a fitting and unusual demise; the villain was all set to marry Casile counter to her wishes and take control of her valuable assets. Barray and Casile are reunited in love and sail off to new adventures.

An Italian poster for *The Mystery of the Evil Island*

grudge against the town's rich ladies. Her dream is to see Puerto Suarez stripped of its treasures and every white woman given the brand of slavery on her left breast. When Lupus appears on the scene, she falls for the strapping officer and her loyalties are divided; should she spill the beans to Lupus or go along with Pazzafini's plans to carry out a mass raid on the town, kidnapping all the women, to be sold into bondage.

A spirited "ho ho, me hearties" nautical jaunt of the early afternoon matinee type enjoyed in cinemas 50 years ago bellows, and Pierotti's colorful costume swashbuckler is acceptable entertainment for the kids: plenty of swordfights, authentic galleons, black-hearted malefactors, public house uproars, a cave hideout, a minimum of violence and pirate chief Pazzafini wearing black gloves tipped with blades. Governor's daughter Dina Da Santis (Blanca) also has eyes for Lupus. When she's taken to Evil Island and left to rot in a dungeon after spotting the telltale mark on Zalewska, he comes to the girl's rescue by deceiving the Creole spy into thinking he's in love with her. Eventually the Spanish fleet blockades Evil Island, the pirates' lair blown sky-high when Lupus ignites the store of powder kegs. Zalewska dies under falling masonry and Lupus stabs Pazzafini to death. Following a confrontation at sea (footage from *The Adventures of Mary Read* is utilized), the pirate flotilla is destroyed, cannons obliterating what's left of the island. Dominici is promoted to admiral, while Lupus, resembling a young Sylvester Stallone

Bookended by a woeful sea shanty tune warbled by French folk group Les Compagnons de la Chanson, *Surcouf, Hero of the Seven Seas* is uninvolving, messy and strangely dislikeable (rare DVDs come in blurred widescreen). Barray tries much too hard to be the all-grinning, all-action romantic hero, up against wooden performances from the support cast, and doesn't pull it off. A great deal of stock footage from *The Son of Captain Blood* (1962) is included (some scenes repeated twice), and in one instance, a badly constructed model ship is seen sinking, a rarity in peplum where, by and large, real full-sized ships were used. There is some dispute over Roy Rowland's involvement. In 2003, Barray stated that Sergio Bergonzelli's input was negligible; other sources claim that Rowland tidied the product up for American distribution, his name added because Western audiences couldn't relate to an Italian nomenclature. A sequel, *Big Chief Surcouf* (*Il grande colpo di Surcouf*), was released in 1967 featuring the same cast and technicians, but it seems to have sunk without trace. Not one of the normally dependable Barray's finest moments, this soggy nautical actioner is as limp as that floating prop mentioned earlier, and fans will only want to experience that ghastly pseudo-jaunty title song once—and once is well and truly enough!

16
Swashbucklers, Historical and Costume Dramas

Outside of the traditional *fusto*/mythological hero sphere of pepla, nowhere else did the genre flourish as much as it did in the *cappa e spada* adventures. Here you had everything on offer, from Robin Hood to medieval knights, from caped crusaders in red masks to wild women on board ships, from noble swordsman to not-so-noble traitors, from Sir Francis Drake to Marco Polo, from the Normans to the Saxons, from the son of El Cid to Scaramouche, from the Cossacks to the Cavaliers, from Sandokan to Ivanhoe, from the Russian steppes to the Venice canals and the jungles of Malaysia via Corsica and Sardinia and from Stewart Granger to Rod Taylor. Gothicism spilled over into *cappa e spada* more than anywhere else in pepla, surfacing in productions such as *The Terror of the Red Capes*, *The Revenge of the Iron Mask* and *The Invincible Masked Cavalier*, a near-merging of Italian horror and swashbuckler, resulting in moments of sublimely atmospheric cinematography. Italian directors, photographers and composers rose to prominence during this halcyon period, shooting around authentic location sites and real castles to enrich their works, adding that highly important medieval/Renaissance atmosphere; this, allied with imaginative musical tones, resulted in a cinematic eruption of bold, colorful, flamboyant escapades that even Hollywood's pots of gold and depth of personnel couldn't match in such a short space of time—61 films are included in this chapter, made between 1960 and 1967, an incredibly creative output displaying a remarkably high standard given the occasionally derivative material to work on. Here can be found lost classics such as *The Lion of St. Mark*, *Sign of the Avenger*, *The Black Duke*, *Revolt of the Mercenaries*, *Genoveffa of Brabant*, *The Bridge of Sighs*, *Terror of the Red Mask*, *The Corsican Brothers*, *The Executioner of Venice*, *The Magnificent Adventurer* and *The Prisoners of Devil's Island*, costumers and swashbucklers which remain unknown and have been overlooked by mainstream film writers but deserve much more recognition. And if Tanio Boccia's scatty take on English history, *The Revenge of Ivanhoe*, doesn't bring a smile to the face, then nothing will!

1960

The Cossacks [*I cosacchi*]
Explorer Film '58/Comptoir Francais CFPC (Italy/France); Totalscope/Eastmancolor; 114 (100) mins; Producer: Giampaolo Bigazzi; Directors: Viktor Tourjansky, Giorgio Venturini (credited as Giorgio Rivalta) ††††

Bookended by two sweeping battles straight from the pages of Leo Tolstoy's *War and Peace*, *The Cossacks* presents a lavish depiction of Russian court life against a background of the mid-1800s Chechen conflict. Edmund Purdom plays Chechen leader Shamil, who sends his young son Jemel to St. Petersburg as a hostage guarantee to prevent further hostilities. Twelve years later, Jemel (John Drew Barrymore) is undergoing officer training at a military academy, attending lavish balls with pal Pierre Brice (Boris) and courting Lady Georgia Moll (Tatiana), appreciating the finer delights of Russian life and forgetting all about childhood sweetheart Maria Grazia Spina (Alina), stuck pining for her absent lover in his father's peasant hilltop fortress. Barrymore's esteem rises considerably in the eyes of his superiors when he prevents an assassin from putting a bullet in Tsar Alexander II (Massimo Girotti), receiving a citation and medal. But when news filters through to Girotti and his advisors that Purdom is becoming restless, sitting around doing nothing and champing at the bit for war, Barrymore's divided loyalties are tested to extreme limits. He returns to Chechnya to dissuade his father from taking up arms in a war he cannot possibly win, getting embroiled in a personal power struggle as Russian forces close in on Purdom's stronghold, their objective to wipe him and his rebels off the map.

If you think the initial battle is a corker, Russian cannons bombarding Chechen villages on the slopes (a woman and child killed; a telling shot of a dead shepherd lying next to his surviving goat), stay around for the final 10-minute skirmish. Russian infantry in white tunics take holy mass before battle commences, then attack in force, Tourjansky and Venturini's camera tracking over hundreds of charging horses amid shellfire (one soldier has both legs blown off), the Chechens cut to pieces,

Hard to tell whether or not Liana Orfei is enjoying Livio Lorenzon running his hands all over her delectable body! From *The Knight of 100 Faces*

completely outnumbered. Barrymore ties a white flag to his sword; Purdom, wounded, shoots him in the back for this perceived act of cowardice but, realizing his campaign is doomed to failure, surrenders himself as a Russian troop approaches; the film quickly fades to the end credits, an abrupt but tragic conclusion. Between the mayhem, *The Cossacks* is soap opera-ish and talky, although the palace scenes look magnificent, photographed in Massimo Dallamano's subdued period colors. It's an exemplary production all round, bolstered by Giovanni Fusco's Russian-themed music and a trio of incisive performances from Purdom (he doesn't smile once), Barrymore and Brice. The one scene that jars is when Barrymore has to prevent Brice and his girlfriend from being torn to ribbons by voracious eagles, shot rather clumsily on an obvious stage set. Not seen for many years, this movie deserves a decent DVD release with subtitles; current prints are in Italian-only.

The Knight of 100 Faces [*Il cavaliere dai cento volti*] aka *The Return of Robin Hood*; *The Revenge of the Red Knight*

Romana Film (Italy); Totalscope/Technicolor; 91 (75) mins; Producer: Fortunato Misiano; Director: Pino Mercanti ✞✞✞

Gaudy fluff of the medieval variety sums up this Robin Hood-type escapade (the film's French title was *The Return of Robin Hood*), in which the body count is surprisingly low—only one fatality, not even wicked knight of the piece Livio Lorenzon getting his just deserts. And Lex Barker, the good knight, doesn't really possess 100 faces, only about four disguises, including one in hilarious drag. Nevertheless, the movie's a pleasant-enough time waster, sporting bright, sharp color (Carlo Bellero) and a fine score (Michele Cozzoli); it canters rather than gallops, more for the kids than the grown-ups.

Barker (Riccardo d'Arce), with goatee beard, is a do-gooder who robs the rich to pay the poor. In his imposing chateau (Italy's Castello Sarriod de la Tour was used for location work), Herbert A. E. Bohme (Duke Ambrogio Di Pallanza) sides with growling bandit leader Lorenzon (Count Fosco Di Vallebruna),

hoping to put an end to Barker's annoying pranks, failing to realize that his scheming partner covets the Duchy himself. Meanwhile, the duke's young son, Alvaro Piccardi (Ciro), has secretively formed a close bond with the outlaw, bordering on hero-worship. Tossed into the convoluted broth comes flame-haired Gypsy temptress Liana Orfei as Zuela (peplum actress Moira Orfei's cousin), an outrageous flirt wearing a scarlet dress to match her hair and showing acres of leg. Piccardi gets the hots for her, as does Lorenzon and Barker's lieutenant Roberto Altamura (Rino), his senses also aroused at the sight of those shapely pins and heaving bosom. Barker isn't interested—he only has eyes for Bohme's winsome daughter, Annie Alberti (Bianca), who just happens to be betrothed, contrary to her express wishes, to womanizing Lorenzon. A tangled muddle to be sure, the announcement of a jousting tournament the only way to sort out the mess by Barker attending and winning back an opulent gold ruff belonging to the shrine of St. George, thereby restoring Bohme's family honor *and* stealing Alberti from Lorenzon's clutches. Almost added as an afterthought, Gérard Landry is way down on the cast list, playing the captain of the guards.

Even when Piccardi dies from an arrow wound (Lorenzon's hit-men are responsible) and Barker blamed, the mood turns down the chance to become just that little bit deeper. Barker's Merry Men waylay various knights on their way to the games to reduce the competition (one prank involves the ex-Tarzan star dressing up in woman's garb), Barker recovers from an injury in his stalactite-infested blue-lit cave dwelling and the pageant gets underway. After a couple of clattering bouts of crossing lances, the righteous outlaw arrives and challenges his sworn enemy to a hand-to-hand contest, sword versus a two-ball flail. Barker triumphs but spares Lorenzon's life, returns the ruff to Bohme and chases after Alberti, who is just about to fling herself off a cliff, thinking her beloved dead. Saved in the nick of time, the couple embraces and kiss, the curtains descending on a colorful but fairly forgettable swashbuckler of the old school. Regular Franco Fantasia, starring as Captain d'Argentero, was also the movie's fencing coach.

The Last Czar [*L'ultimo zar*] aka *Nights of Rasputin*; *The Night They Killed Rasputin*

Faro Film/Explorer Film '58/Comptoir Francais CFPC (Italy/France); Eastmancolor; 95 (87) mins; Producer: Giampaolo Bigazzi; Director: Pierre Chenal ✞✞✞

A highly dramatized telling of events leading up to the assassination of Father Grigori Rasputin, the vagrant monk imbued with almost supernatural healing powers, who inveigled himself into the Russian court in 1907, becoming a huge embarrassment to the aristocracy because of his scandalous lifestyle. Edmund Purdom was an odd choice to play the female-obsessed holy man, but he pulled it off, giving Christopher Lee, who starred in Hammer's 1966 *Rasputin the Mad Monk*, a real run for his money; maniacal eyes stare out of a heavily bearded face perpetually breaking into gales of raucous laughter. Rasputin first came to the attention of the Czar (Ugo Sasso) when his son was bedridden with a leg tumor; in strides the peasant from the steppes and cures the swelling by simply placing his hands on the boy's limb and chanting a few words. Thereafter, Rasputin was given the freedom of the palace court and his own apartments, which he used to entertain ladies only too eager to jump into his bed in return for favors. He also advised the Czar on affairs of state, including the war with Germany, and caused a young officer to

Edmond Purdom's Rasputin casts his hypnotic eyes over Gianna Maria Canale in *The Last Czar*.

commit suicide, warning officials that if they ever for one moment thought of getting rid of him, "the Romanovs will forfeit their thrones and their lives." Several attempts were made on Rasputin's life, all uncannily abortive, until the night of December 16, 1916 when "The Dark Force that is ruining Mother Russia" was poisoned, shot several times, half-strangled and dumped in the frozen Malaya Nevka river.

Peplum masquerading as wildly dramatic semi-horror, distributed by MGM, the picture, retitled *Nights of Rasputin*, surfaced on the English Sunday one-day cinema circuit in 1962, double billed with Boris Karloff's *Corridors of Blood*; it's one of only three films in this book to be awarded the British "X" certificate, the others being *Sodom and Gomorrah* and *Maciste Against the Vampire* (*Goliath and the Vampires*). Hammer's *The Pirates of Blood River*, although U-rated, was originally to have been an "X"; current DVD issues contain the uncut version (see chapter 19). Very difficult to track down today, existing DVD copies are in monochrome only and present the edited version, making it impossible to evaluate Adalberto "Bitto" Albertini's rich period photography. Angelo Francesco Lavagnino's Russian-based, doom-laden music is in sharp contrast to his much grander, more buoyant, torch and toga scores, while Livio Lorenzon looks slightly uncomfortable in his role of a Russian police inspector. Elsewhere, Gianna Maria Canale is the empress keeping her hunger in check, yearning for Rasputin's iron embrace, and almond-eyed Jany Clair plays the femme fatale luring the lustful monk to her husband's (John Drew Barrymore) rooms to meet his doom. But this is Purdom's show; never the most lauded of actors despite his extensive repertoire, he shows his mettle here, carousing through the scenario like a shaggy bear, roaring his head off, seducing one female after another and downing enough wine to sink a ship. A remastered issue in color would be most welcome for fans of the obscure.

Terror of the Red Mask [*Il terrore della maschera rossa*]

Jonia Film (Italy); Totalscope/Eastmancolor; 92 (88) mins; Producer: Jacopo Comin; Director: Luigi Capuano
††††

Three quarters of the way into Luigi Capuano's extravagant costumer, Gypsy temptress Karima (Chelo Alonso) decides to get rid of clinging boyfriend Ivan (Marco Guglielmi). Dipping his hand into a foodbag, he's bitten by a poisonous viper, placed there by Alonso who's also stolen his dagger, just in case he wants to cut the wound open and save himself. "You'll never embrace me again," she spits as he falls to the ground in agony. "You're finished. Seeing you die makes me pleased." He looks up at her, gasping. "Why has it taken you so long to die?" she says, glaring at his pain-wracked features before riding off. Yes, not only is the hot tamale as venomous as that snake, but she performs two sex-charged dance routines, among her best, writhing all over Livio Lorenzon's palace floor in a display of such overt lasciviousness that it even renders him speechless, making the tyrant forget, for a brief moment, the devil in the red mask, who is tormenting him to the verge of mental frenzy.

Who is The Red Mask, a caped crusader on horseback appearing out of nowhere, fighting with Lorenzon's gorillas and vanishing into thin air? Lorenzon (Astolfo) turns crimson and foams at the mouth at the mere mention of his name; the lord

Chelo Alonso strikes a sensuous pose in *Terror of the Red Mask*.

of the manor has murdered niece Liana Orfei's (Jolanda) father in his corrupt rise to power, scared stiff that the phantom figure will unmask *him* as the pitiless go-getter he is (a torture scene, in which a man is burned with a white-hot iron for refusing to reveal The Red Mask's identity, is not for the squeamish). Second-in-command Franco Fantasia (Egidio) is aware of the truth but remains loyal to the ranting bully, even when threatened with banishment. Into this devil's brew strides soldier Lex Barker (Marco) and two semi-comical compatriots (their interlude in the castle, dressed as monks and trying to retrieve a pet monkey, is a hoot but doesn't ruin the mood), plus Alonso and her clan, and soon the fiery Gypsy is making eyes at Barker, who in turn makes eyes at Orfei, while Lorenzon's evil heart pounds at the charms Alonso has to offer ("I'm bored to death. I don't want to be alone tonight," he tells Fantasia, after watching the Gypsy queen dance erotically). Capuano, a true craftsman of Italian cinema when it came to this kind of swashbuckling material, manufactures a romantic drama played out against a tangled web of treachery and court intrigue, evocative set and costume design adding immensely to the rich medieval aura on show. "I'm in love," states Alonso to Barker. "My sword is my love," is his cold response. Picking up a snake, she continues. "Venom is like loving. It brings pain or pleasure," but still Barker isn't interested. The ex-Tarzan star is thrown into a dungeon, viciously flogged (number 22 in Alvin Easter's *Lash! The Hundred Great Scenes of Men Being Whipped in the Movies*) and sentenced to be put to death inside an infernal spike-lined cage, but the all-knowing Red Mask incites a rebellion, Barker liberated when insurgents flood into the castle. Lorenzon replaces Barker in the cage, and The Red Mask turns out to be Orfei, although how she can manage to change out of her voluminous gowns into a red suit and back again in the space of a few minutes is anyone's guess. Alonso, alone and panicking, convinced she's cursed through killing her lover, makes the mistake of donning The Red Mask's outfit, galloping toward freedom but receiving a dagger in the back from Lorenzon before he meets his end. The crowds cheer loudly as Barker and Orfei embrace on the balcony, bringing to a close a very satisfactory, and very snappy, romp saturated in Carlo Montuori's vibrant color tones and enlivened by Carlo Innocenzi's bubbly score.

1961

Bandits of Orgosolo **[*Bandita a Orgosolo*]**

Titanus (Italy); B&W; 92 mins; Produced and Directed by Vittorio De Seta ✞✞✞

Can Vittorio De Seta's tale of two sheep farmers on the run from the police be classed as peplum? Some sites and literature on the subject have included the movie in their listings because of its underlying genre ideals, so it's included here. Italian Neorealism meets modern-day peplum would best describe this harsh-looking fable, documentary filmmaker De Seta (this was his first full-length feature) casting local people in the three principal roles: Michele Cossu and Peppeddu Cuccu, the two honest shepherd brothers, and Vittorina Pisano, the girl from crime-ridden Orgosolo, who helps them. The story is minimal as the brothers (the bandits of the title) are wrongly accused of stealing pigs and murdering a paramilitary policeman; taking flight over the Sardinian mountain ranges with their flock, they eke out a meager existence amid bleak, punishing surroundings, hunted by law officers. Toward the end of the movie, half their

A bleak scene set in the mountain regions of Sardinia from *Bandits of Orgosolo*

flock is stolen, and the other half is dying from exhaustion and hunger. In revenge, Cossu steals back his sheep from the thief responsible, knocking him senseless and is last seen herding his flock toward an uncertain future.

Winner of four international awards, including Best New Film at the 1961 Venice Film Festival, *Bandits of Orgosolo* is stunningly shot by De Seta amid the barren mountain scenery of Sardinia's Barbagia region, the director/cinematographer placing his two fugitives in an uncompromising rocky terrain that mirrors their grim odyssey, man versus elemental forces. But ultimately, while worthy, it verges on the side of boring. A great deal of the picture is taken up by sheep scrambling up and down rocky slopes, and of Cossu staring thoughtfully into the distance. Yes, their trek is arduous and full of hardship, but dramatic impetus is almost totally absent, the result of depression served up on a cold platter. Valentino Bucchi supplies a sparse, evocative musical score to a little-seen pseudo-peplum that is poetic in mood, yet difficult to digest and enjoy.

Captains of Ventura **[*Capitani di Ventura*] aka *Rampage of Evil***

Artix Cinema (Italy); Totalscope/Ferraniacolor; 90 mins; Producers: Aldo Piga, Angelo Dorigo; Director: Angelo Dorigo ✞✞

Peplum regular bad guys Mario Petri (Captain Hans) and Paul Muller (Count Falcino) take center stage in Angelo Dorigo's talkative medieval potboiler regarding a papal treasure due to be delivered to the pontiff under the care of Prince Luigi Batzella; he carries letters of credentials from the Holy See in order to collect the riches from the Primate of the Church of the East. In a mountain pass, wily Petri's Slavic allies ambush the party and Batzella is captured. Muller assumes the role of Batzella, as

An Italian poster for *Captains of Ventura*

A French poster for *The Corsican Brothers*

Petri has admitted that he can't read a single word of what's on those documents. Consequently, the devious count picks up the treasure under an assumed name. On discovering the deception, the church council instructs Captain Gérard Landry (Brunello) to go in pursuit of the stolen treasure; during a fight, he's wounded and left for dead. Ambitious Muller is out to rule the Duchy, also demanding the "right of the first night" from bride Franca Parisi (Rosalba), while beautiful but drippy Wandisa Guida (Belinda) plays the Duchess Belinda, Landry's love interest.

There's a great deal of standing around and plotting in this film, meaning that producer/composer Aldo Piga's decent score goes nowhere fast and ends up wasted. Petri and Muller, both attired in almost laughable fetish leatherware (get those thigh-hugging boots!), do their utmost to score points off one another in the acting stakes, trying their hardest to inject some life into the proceedings. Things perk up slightly in the finale. Landry sneaks into Muller's castle via a secret passage to rescue Batzella, is captured and sentenced to death; his old artist friend (he revealed Muller's true identity to Landry in a portrait he completed), disguised as a monk, saves the chivalrous captain from the axeman's block, culminating in a swordfight between Landry and Petri. Guess who triumphs? Parisi, in turn, stabs Muller in the stomach, her revenge for being defiled (almost) on her wedding night. As might be expected, Landry and Guida become an item. And that troublesome treasure is turned over safely to the Pope.

The Corsican Brothers [*I fratelli Corsi*] aka *Lions of Corsica*
Flora Film/Variety (Italy/France); Dyaliscope/Eastmancolor; 102 mins; Producers: Leo Cevenini, Georges Cheyko, Vittorio Martino; Director: Anton Giulio Majano ††††

Adapted from Alexandre Dumas' 1844 novel, *The Corsican Brothers* is a world away from director Majano's dark, malignant *Seddok, Son of Satan*; filming took place in sunny Corsica, Adalberto "Bitto" Albertini's cinematography bathing the production in pastel hues and bright, sunlit seascapes. Dumas' tale (commencing in 1822) concerned the Franchi twins, separated following their baptism. The neighboring Sagona clan annihilates the Franchis in their home after the ceremony, killing all family members and the entire household, and razing the mansion to the ground. The twins, however, are spared death. Bandit chief Orlandi takes in Leon, while Doctor Dupont raises Paul in Parisian high society, with Paul living among the very people who massacred his mother and father. 23 years later, each is unaware of the other's existence, although sharing a psychic link (when Leon is wounded in the shoulder, Paul feels an identical pain in the same spot); eventually, they meet on a clifftop when mutual love interest Edith is chased by Sagona soldiers, leading to a tragic conclusion in which Leon's intervention prevents Edith from being shot dead, taking a bullet in her place, thus leaving his brother in a position to marry the heiress.

To start the ball rolling, Angelo Francesco Lavagnino treats us to one of the loveliest title themes ever to grace a peplum production, a powerfully emotive melody that lingers long in the mind, a truly wonderful piece of scoring from this criminally underrated composer. Buenos Aires-born actor Geoffrey

An Italian poster for *Crown of Fire*

Horne played the parts of the twins with a mixture of bravado and angst. As Leon, masked and carrying out sorties to antagonize the Sagonas with Gypsy bandit boss Amedeo Nazzari (as Orlandi) from the rebels' cavern bolthole, he's an energetic, macho swashbuckler. Paul, on the other hand, appears nervous and twitchy, a court-loving dilettante puzzled as to why he should be experiencing, and dreaming about, the thoughts and ills of "another person." In this respect, the movie went against the grain by having Edith (Valérie Lagrange) getting hitched to the less heroic and less-manly of the two brothers, something she herself didn't appear to be all that pleased about.

Majano's pace is leisurely on occasions, content to wallow in Corsica's rugged mountain scenery and positioning his cast, bedecked in their finery, on balconies overlooking the scintillating blue Mediterranean, then livening things up with sporadic bursts of action. The gradual dawning on the twins that each had a sibling is expertly done and not hurried; needless to say, a jealous Gypsy wench is involved (Paola Patrizi), furious at Horne's romantic liaisons with Lagrange. Old-stalwarts Alberto Farnese, Germano Longo, Nando Tamberlani, Jean Servais, Mario Feliciani and Nerio Bernardi were on hand to ensure that Horne, looking ever so slightly out of his depth, stayed with it. Best of all, Gérard Barray starred against type as the principal villain (Jean Sagona), wanting rid of the interfering twins, aware of their true origins (Horne, as Leon, shoots him dead after a dagger duel). Nazzari's rebels (wearing red bandanas) besiege the Sagona residence in the climax, the family members exterminated, Horne (as Paul) taking up residence in the stately manor house with Lagrange. The final, almost supernatural image is of the twins, with Lagrange sandwiched between them, superimposed over the rugged Corsican sea and landscape, Lavagnino's plaintive notes guaranteeing that female members of the audience felt the need to reach for their tissues and wipe away the tears. Talkative, yes, but more intelligently handled than similar efforts and stunning to look at, even though decent widescreen copies are very difficult to obtain today.

Crown of Fire [*La corona di fuoco*]

S.I.A.T. Italia (Italy); Cinepanoramic/Eastmancolor; 90 mins; Producer: Urbano Natali; Director: Luigi Latini de Marchi (as Louis Mané)

In the year 1020, King Rudoph III of Burgundy rules the fiefdoms with his spouse, Ermengarda, by his side. Ermengarda is secretly in love with Count Umberto Biancamano, the king's vassal, the bravest knight in the kingdom. However, he loves the Lady Ancilla and marries her. The treacherous tyrant Oddone Di Blois, plotting against the king, ambushes Umberto on his way to meet the monarch, stealing vital papers bestowing upon him the title of governor of the province. Umberto escapes death but Ancilla is killed in the skirmish. The imposter takes over the governorship promised to Umberto, who vows vengeance, Oddone threatening the queen with torture and death if she refuses to share the throne with him, following the murder of her husband. In a climactic battle outside the castle walls, Umberto slays Oddone in a duel to the finish and hands the Burgundy crown to Ermengarda, who eyes the gallant warrior up as her next partner.

Starring Victor Chassiu as Umberto, Germana Paolieri as Ermangarda, Gino Turini as Oddone, Wally Salio as Ancilla and Oreste Grandi as the king, *Crown of Fire* (the plot is similar to the storyline in *Captains of Ventura*, 1961), partly based on factual events and filmed around Fenis Castle, is unobtainable on tape or disc; an online download was withdrawn in 2014.

Drakut the Avenger [*Drakut il vendicatore*] aka ***Revenge of the Conquered***

Jonia Film (Italy); Colorscope/Eastmancolor; 93 (84) mins; Producer: Felice Felicioni; Director: Luigi Capuano †††

Burt Nelson stars as Drakut, champion of the Gypsy clans, who leads the fight against wrong-doings and repression in Luigi Capuano's long-forgotten Renaissance potboiler, a movie that remains virtually unobtainable today; hard-to-come-by DVD copies are in a lamentable state, the color fading in and out, with repeated jumps in continuity. All right, the story is nothing new, but viewing the picture under more favorable conditions would greatly add to the pleasure of catching it—regrettably, *Drakut the Avenger*, like many, many other titles included in this book, is condemned through neglect to a level of anonymity quite unknown to those who follow only mainstream cinema and expect pristine digital prints on their menu, and nothing else.

Nelson gallops to the rescue of carriage-driven Princess Irina (Wandisa Guida), who is under attack from bandits, and he quickly gets around to kissing the lady after a protracted bout of flirting, taking her to his mother's camp. Mum Carla Calò just happens to be the Queen of the Gypsies. Guida's father, benevolent Walter Barnes, is regent of the realm, manipulative Grand Duke Mario Petri (Atanas) scheming to get rid of him and the Gypsy travelers inhabiting his land. There's also the little matter of the Gypsy treasure which Calò and her followers are desper-

An Italian photobusta for *Drakut the Avenger* showing (top) Wandisa Guida, Franco Fantasia and Mario Petri; (bottom) Moira Orfei

ately trying to hide from the unwelcome attentions of Petri and Franco Fantasia's troops, the Red Mountains being their chosen location, in a cave policed by a hairy dwarf (not, as they claim, a dragon). Moira Orfei plays betrayer Edmea, siding with Petri for her own ends; the Gypsy village is twice razed to the ground (and the same sequence is repeated twice!), Calò tortured, whipped and burned at the stake, branded a witch (a harrowing scene). On the day of their enforced wedding, Petri and Guida are interrupted by fatally wounded Orfei, who spills the beans on who actually murdered the princess's father (it was Petri's paid assassin, organized by Guida's treacherous maid, Maria Grazia Spina) before flopping down dead; in charge the Gypsy rabble dressed as monks, skirmishing with the guard, while Nelson and Petri go eyeball-to-eyeball in a splendidly staged duel, Nelson delivering the death thrust just as his protagonist is about to club him over the head with a large axe. Nelson rides off with his own people but Guida chases after him, performs a brief ceremony and entrusts upon his shoulders the rank of prince, one sure way of making the soldier of fortune eligible for marriage and luring him back to her castle *and* her bed!

Among the cast, Alberto Lupo, Nando Tamberlani and Ugo Sasso lend strong support. As stated, Sergio Pesce's cinematography has deteriorated over the passage of time, rendered to a mix of greens, mauves, reds and even monochrome, although in compensation, Carlo Innocenzi's ebullient score remains more or less intact. This one is for purists only, and those who must have everything, however obscure, in their peplum collection.

The Mutiny [*L'ammutinamento*] aka *White Slave Ship*; *Wild Cargo*

Illiria Film/Gladiator/Champs-Elysées Prods. (Italy/France); Totalscope/Eastmancolor; 98 (92) mins; Producer: Giorgio Agliani; Director: Silvio Amadio †††

Newgate Prison, London, 1675: Women of loose morals are given a cursory medical inspection in front of magistrates and placed on board *HMS Albatross*, bound for New England, to be sold into slavery. Below their deck is a hold containing male convicts, mistreated by a bestial warden. Above deck, aristocrats Lord and Lady Graveston walk around with their snooty noses stuck in the air, while a brother and sister also join the voyage. Yes, the scene is set for an overheated shipboard yarn that makes the most of its confined setting, testing the strengths and weaknesses of the various characters, as they come into discord with one another. It's low on action but strong on the theatricals and pithy dialogue (the script written by Sandro Continenza, Marcello Coscia and Ruggero Jacobbi), Aldo Giordani's color photography imbuing the vessel in rich shades of brown, a pleasure to behold. Angelo Francesco Lavagnino's nautical score is also a bonus.

One-time Hollywood starlet Pier Angeli (billed as Anna Maria Pierangeli) is Polly, the women's unofficial spokesper-

The U.S. one-sheet poster for *White Slave Ship* (aka *The Mutiny*)

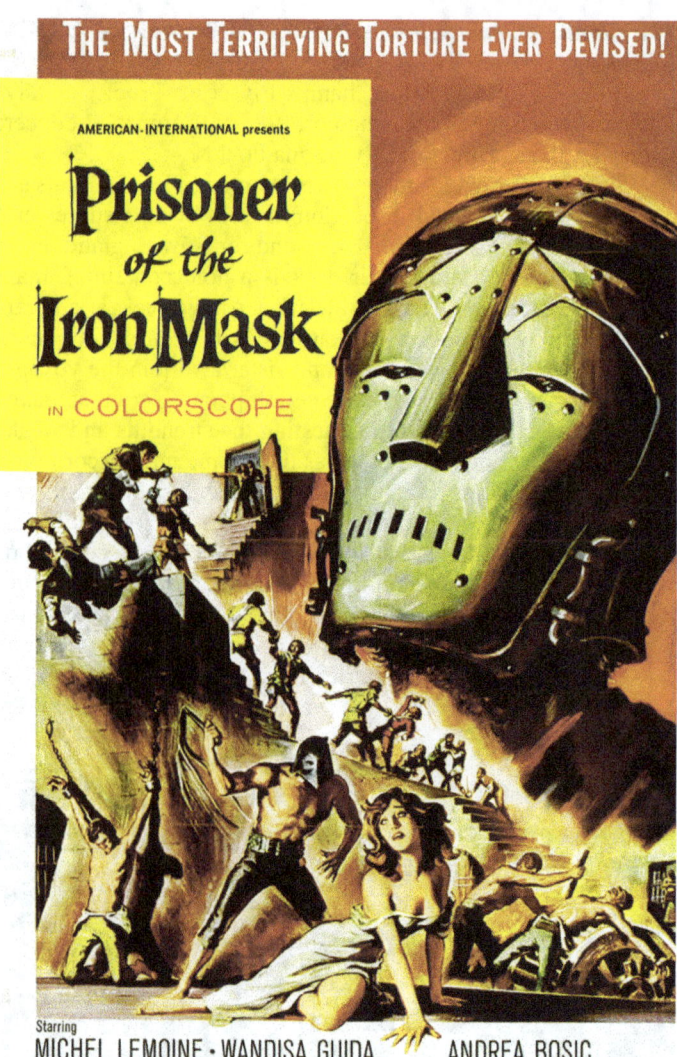

A U.S. one-sheet poster for *Prisoner of the Iron Mask* (aka *The Revenge of the Iron Mask*)

son, a coltish wench who has great difficulty in preventing her bosom from spilling out of her low-cut dress (as do all the other leggy girls). Directly beneath the women's quarters, Edmund Purdom (Doctor Bradley), a political prisoner, stands chain-to-chain with Calico Jack, a salty seadog played with lip-smacking relish by Armand Mestral, and Angeli's spineless pimp, Renato Speziali. Flogged for protesting about the unpalatable victuals, Purdom recovers and attends to Ivan Desny's (Captain Cooper) septic arm, falling for Michele Girardon (Anna), her young brother (Franco Capucci) furious at the blossoming liaison; he later rakes Purdom's back with a poker. One of the women gives birth and Angeli, after an abortive attempt, sets the men free; murdering some of the crew and tossing the rest overboard, but holding Desny hostage, Mestral takes command, forcing his swarthy attentions on Franca Parisi (Lady Graveston), who commits suicide in disgust, and entering into a difference of opinion with Purdom. The doctor objects to the convicts' roughhouse behavior. Following a storm in which Desny is reinstated because of his seafaring skills, the ship steers a course for Tortuga, 5,000 miles away. Mestral then decides to dump the ladies in shark-infested waters to save on food and water; on hearing this, Angeli and her lasses revolt, leading to a pitched pistol fight in which the bandit gets a pike in his stomach; Angeli stabs Speziali and the convicts are routed. Officers from a passing British frigate board the *Albatross*, and Desny pardons Purdom and Angeli (left holding the baby) because of their help in overthrowing Mestral and his mutineers; Purdom is reunited with love Girardon.

The Revenge of the Iron Mask [*La vendetta della maschera di ferro*] aka *Prisoner of the Iron Mask*

Mida/CI.AS./Comptoir France CFPC (Italy/France); Techniscope/Eastmancolor; 89 mins; Producers: Robert de Nesle, Francesco Thellung; Director: Francesco De Feo ††††

In 1703, a mysterious figure known popularly as the Man in the Iron Mask died in Paris' Bastille prison. The man, whose identity has never fully been established by historians, was arrested in 1670 and incarcerated in various jails, including the Italian fortress of Pignerol, where this film takes place in 1679. De Feo gives his own slant on the version of events, coming up with the idea that an evil count was the prisoner, his punishment for placing the iron mask on the son of a duke he had slowly poisoned, to keep him out of the way in his corrupt climb to power. Fanciful, maybe, but the movie is entertaining enough, worth hunting down (copies are as rare as hen's teeth) for Raffaele Masciocchi's color photography alone, clear evidence of how superbly the Italians dressed their period dramas and horror features during the 1960s in rich inky shades of reds, blues, greens and purples. In the frequent dungeon sequences, beautifully lit and imagined, we stray into Gothic semi-horror territory anyway, tormented Pietro Albani howling in agony behind bars, unable to eat or drink properly because of that monstrous contraption covering his head. How did it get there?

Albani (Marco) and friend Michel Lemoine (Andrea) are on the run from Count Andrea Bosic's men, having obtained documentary proof that he's poisoning the local bigwig (Albani's father) in order to rule the Duchy of Pignerol. Galloping past a roadside shrine, the scroll is flung behind an icon before rapiers are drawn; Lemoine is wounded, and Albani captured. Taken to the citadel at Pignerol, he's locked up inside a dank dungeon, a bucket-mask locked on his head, and left to molder. The old duke is poisoned, Bosic (Count Astolfo) makes a play for his daughter, Wandisa Guida (Christina, Albani's sister), and the turnkey's niece Jany Clair brings gruel and water to the wretched internee, who is unable to communicate but can only groan in abject misery. Meanwhile, a good-natured bandit gang attends to Lemoine; recovering, he leads a small resistance group against Bosic's gorillas, taking on the guise of a Robin Hood-type do-gooder by carrying out raids at random intervals. When Clair brings Lemoine a note from Albani written in blood on cloth, he organizes a raiding party, attired in soldiers' uniforms, to infiltrate the castle and release his friend from a living hell. Their first attempt flounders, Clair shot dead in the struggle. "Marry me and I'll spare him," states Bosic to Guida, which she reluctantly concedes to when she learns of her brother's impending fate. On their wedding day, Lemoine and his merry men burst in on the ceremony, grab the bride and hightail it out of the castle, chased by a posse of soldiers led by Bosic (the Monte Gelato waterfalls and mill buildings appear in many of these scenes). Albani is in a coach, on its way to the Bastille; after collecting the scroll from the shrine and reading the damming evidence to the congregating villagers, Lemoine's outfit overpowers Bosic's regiment and the count takes the place of Albani, yelling in fright as the iron mask is removed from the young duke and fixed on *his* head. Lemoine gets to keep Guida all to himself.

An Italian photobusta for *Revolt of the Mercenaries*

An enjoyable romp with a nod in the direction of Alexandre Dumas (Carlo Innocenzi's score is a delight), *The Revenge of the Iron Mask* is spoiled in some instances by too much contrast in tone between the harrowing dungeon scenes and the joviality of Lemoine's troops, sporting yellow pantaloons, skirmishing within the citadel walls. Peplum's resident funny man, clown-faced Silvio Bagolini, also gets a few minutes' worth of screen time to lighten the mood. The deep Eastmancolor photography's the thing here, a golden reminder of what color used to be like on celluloid before the advent of 21st-century practices of digital shooting direct to hard drive. Digital disc rendered the whole color process as dull as ditchwater.

Revolt of the Mercenaries [*La rivolta dei mercenari*] aka *The Mercenaries*

Prodas Film/Chapalo Films (Italy/Spain); Totalscope/Eastmancolor; 98 (90) mins; Producer: Antonio Canelli; Director: Piero Costa ††††

In Fruili, Italy during the Renaissance period, Captain Lucio Di Rialto and his band of merry mercenaries find themselves caught up in a land struggle between two prosperous nobles: Lady Patricia, Duchess of Rivalta, and Count Keller Paroli. To ward off Paroli's aggressive land-grabbing intentions, she plans to wed foppish Stefano, Prince of Siena, thus forming a dynasty that will repel Paroli. But the count resorts to violence and intimidation in his ambition to rule the roost, Di Rialto and his men siding with the duchess to bring about the downfall of the felonious count.

After years of neglect, *Revolt of the Mercenaries* is now available in German-dubbed, bright-as-a-button letterbox format, Julio Ortas and Godfredo Pacheco's cinematography restored to its former glory. Piero Costa brought a panoramic sweep to the scenario, capturing splendidly the wide-open Spanish/Italian landscapes and two imposing edifices, the Castle of Mendoza (or Manzanares el Real Castle, Madrid) and a medieval fortress manor house near Fruili. Livio Lorenzon (Paroli) inhabits the first, Virginia Mayo (Patricia) the other. At age 41 former Hollywood vamp Mayo, although exuding poise and glamour, came off slightly second-best to younger Carla Calò, playing Miriam, the girlfriend of Conrado San Martin (Captain Lucio) and Anita Todesco (Prisca), Alfredo Mayo's (Marco) raven-haired lady. San Martin assists Mayo in turning back Lorenzon's first offensive on her castle by setting a pack of hundreds of dogs onto his horsemen, an unusual turn of events which would have animal rights campaigners howling, like the dogs, in protest today. The mercenary leader then pretends to take up arms with Lorenzon (as usual, an overripe turn from the actor), putting Mayo's nose so much out of joint (she loves him) that she decides to proceed with her nuptials to Luciano Benetti, a prissy dandy, thinking that San Martin has betrayed their trust. There are some graphic torture/flogging scenes in Lorenzon's Gothic dungeon, not for the fainthearted; Todesco, grieving for her slain boyfriend, is caught, lashed and branded, her back running with blood. San Martin's trick is uncovered, his men placed behind bars, but Lorenzon's hard-faced mistress, Susana Canales (Katia), is sympathetic to their cause, releasing them; for her good deed, she's stabbed in the back by deputy Franco Fantasia (as Ilario, listed on the credits as Master of Arms; he taught most of the cast to wield a sword). In the 80th minute, Lorenzon stages a final launch on Mayo's fortress, his soldiers scaling the walls but repulsed; San Martin duels with Lorenzon on the battlements, the pair hard at it in the novel confines of a pigeon loft. The count receives a spike in the chest; staggering toward a door, he pushes it open and collapses, surrounded by dozens of fluttering, wheeling birds that fly off over his body. Mayo gets a kiss from San Martin, but that's all—he rides off with his mercenaries, picking up Calò on the way, to the sound of Carlo Innocenzi's choral-marching score, which has been the backbone of the narrative throughout. This is a colorful, scintillating Renaissance swashbuckler that hits all the right notes where it matters most, in acting, direction, photography and scope of vision.

The Robbers [*I masnadieri*] aka *Rome, 1585*; *The Mercenaries*

Leda Film (Italy); Dyaliscope/Eastmancolor; 110 (85) mins; Producer: Mario Pellegrino; Director: Mario Bonnard ††

Mario Bonnard's final film is a muddled costume melodrama relating the adventures of mercenary leader Antonio Cifariello (Leonetto), from Siena, as he attempts to remove from power Livio Lorenzon (Fabrizio), up to no good in Rome at the time of Pope Gregory XIII's death in 1585. The picture (DVDs are taken from scratchy 16mm prints) is hardly the hotbed of political intrigue it was meant to represent, what with Cifariello vying for the attentions of three ladies and jovial friar Folco Lulli (Silenzio) using his ham-sized fists to appreciable effect on all those that upset him. Simply a catalogue of protracted swordfights interspersed with a lot of mumbo jumbo concerning matters of state, Bonnard directs with hectic pace but opts for a tongue-in-cheek approach verging on daftness at times, the hero's band of merry, drink-guzzling mercenaries hardly the type

A publicity shot of Debra Paget from *The Robbers*

to strike fear into a seasoned tough guy like Lorenzon. Daniela Rocca plays bland princess-cum-political hostage Alba, who's rescued along with her father from Lorenzon's evil clutches; dark-haired Debra Paget is Gypsy Esmeralda, performing sexy, thigh-revealing dance numbers but unable to stoke the fires of passion in Cifariello, looking too boyish for the part and not knowing a good thing when he sees one and Yvonne Sanson stars as Lorenzon's slightly more mature woman, also flirting with the rebel leader.

Roman citizens get hot under the collar when flour supplies are withheld by Lorenzon's bully boys, and Cifariello and his gang are smuggled into Lorenzon's castle in sacks; there's a fight in which the bald-headed tyrant is killed and Cifariello, in the public square with a noose around his neck, is pardoned by the new Pope, waltzing off with Rocca in the dying seconds. Considering that *The Robbers* (also called *The Mercenaries* in Italy) was produced during peplum's golden period, there's a distinct lack of "oomph" which, together with the disjointed narrative flow, makes for uninteresting viewing. (Note: In 1968, only 38, Cifariello tragically died in a plane crash in Zambia on his way to a shoot.)

Sword in the Shadows [*Una spada nell'ombra*]

Romana Film (Italy); Totalscope/Eastmancolor; 89 (80) mins; Producer: Fortunato Misiano; Director: Luigi Capuano ✝✝✝

Livio Lorenzon was up to his frilly laced neck in all manner of swashbucklers during this golden period in Italian swashbuckling, a bad guy that producers could rely on to put in the required mean performance, whatever the material; here, he's meaner than mean, hacking his way through the Altavila family in the opening, noisy few minutes (Michele Cozzoli's score batters the eardrums into submission) with undisguised relish. Contessa Ottavia della Rocca (Tamara Lees) has given orders that the neighboring rivals to her domain be wiped off the face of the map; Lorenzon (Captain Mellina) and his gorillas do just that, with zest—however, the young heir to the Altavila estate, Fabrizio, is spirited away through a secret passage, while the orphaned, bastard son (Braccio), caught hiding upstairs, is taken into care by Lees in a fit of remorse. Fifteen years later, rightful heir Mario Valdemarin is living with Gypsies while sham heir Germano Longo is being groomed as the future duke. As for scorned Lorenzon, he skulks and schemes, harboring an unrequited craving for Lees, now cutting a matronly figure but still behaving like a fire-breathing dragon.

Full credit must go to Luigi Capuano for bringing his expertise and experience to the *cappa e spada* subgenre and knocking out something that, though derivative, gives the impression of being freshly painted. From the moment Longo starts acting like a prima donna and Gypsy wench Pina Cornel (Iolanda) flashes her lashes at Valdemarin, you know exactly what to expect and how it will all turn out: Valdemarin steals horses from Lees' corral; Longo visits the Gypsy camp, accuses them of theft and has a hand-to-hand tussle with his half-brother, losing the contest; Lorenzon fronts a night raid on the Gypsies, destroying their camp; Valdemarin, masked, fights back, attacking Lorenzon's troops;

A Belgian poster for *Sword in the Shadows*

Leonora Ruffo as Lady Gigliola, a real peolum beauty, in *Swords Without a Flag*

Swords Without a Flag [*Spade senza bandiera*] aka *Sword Without a Country*

A.D. Cinematografica (Italy); Totalscope/Eastmancolor; 88 (82) mins; Producer: Lello Luzi; Director: Carlo Veo ✝

"They say that a great motion picture score can hold up a not-so-great movie." These are my exact opening words to *Ursus and the Tartar Girl*. But that's not the case here. Carlo Innocenzi's thumping music loses the battle in trying its hardest to inject some life and soul into Carlo Veo's lifeless, soulless peasants versus bandits Renaissance potboiler which, after a promising 25 minutes, disassembles itself in spectacular fashion. In that opening 25 minutes, Lady Leonora Ruffo (Gigliola) disobeys her father's wishes that she marries a bearded ruffian twice her age to cement an alliance, instead romancing troubadour Renato Speziali (Cino); Speziali and Piero Lulli (Benedetto) are joint leaders of a pack of robbers lying low in a cave. Speziali's bandits meet the prospective bridegroom in the open; Speziali accidentally stabs him to death, is arrested, found guilty of murder (Folco Lulli as Diego, Ruffo's father, implicates him), sentenced to be beheaded but freed from jail by Ruffo, who runs off to his hideout where she plays house with stolen loot. All fine and dandy, the film containing rich Gothic color tones by Aldo Greci, Innocenzi's score moving things along nicely, although the scenario is far from original, even for 1961.

Then it all goes horribly wrong. Folco Lulli disappears from the picture (he returns later), replaced by Claudio Gora (Baron Belvarco) and his peasant mistress, Mara Berni (Isabella). Why the change isn't made clear. Peplum bad boy Ivano Staccioli crops up, uncomfortably against type, as a court jester, joining the brigands; Speziali and his Robin Hood-type Merry Men raid the rich in a succession of limp, static holdups and use a white horse as a go-between, relaying messages to the nearby peasants, one of whom has betrayed the gang, leading to the torture and death of one of their number. Speziali's demand of "100 pieces of silver or we raze your village to the ground" is reluctantly met as the peasants, headed by blank-looking Gérard Landry (Constanzo), asks Gora for military support or at least a quantity of arms. While viewers may be scratching their heads, wondering what is occurring in the Ruffo/Speziali storyline, or the plot

a carriage arrives at the castle from a convent, Lees' daughter Gabriella Farinon (as Lavinia) alighting with Gianni Rizzo and Loris Gizzi, her rotund uncle and cousin; Farinon is betrothed to Longo, but as soon as she encounters Valdemarin, her affections change, arousing jealousy in Cornel's broken heart; Valdemarin is captured and incarcerated in a dungeon, later freed by Cornel, who visits the castle, pulls the wool over Longo's eyes and arranges for her clan to enter the dungeons via a hidden tunnel; Longo, now as mad as a march hare, stabs Lees in the back *and* Lorenzon, the two doomed lovers clasping hands in death; and after saving Farinon from a neck-stretching by his own people (Cornel gets wounded and dies), Valdemarin, aware of his true identity, storms the fortress and duels with Longo, the usurper receiving a well-aimed dagger in *his* back. Now the new lord of the manor, Valdemarin, rides off with Farinon, surrounded by his cheering partisans.

Like Lewis Carroll's Tweedledum and Tweedledee, Rizzo and Gizzi pamper and preen, in the picture for decorative purposes only; they contribute absolutely nothing to the plot, but are a delight to watch. Attractively shot amid wooded scenery (photography: Carlo Bellero), *Sword in the Shadows*, one of pepla's rarer offerings, is available (as at 2015) in unspoiled, letterbox prints from Germany, hence the German dubbing and lack of subtitles. Lorenzon, as so often was the case, pinches the acting carpet from under everyone else's feet—where, one wonders, would these Italian swashbucklers be without his bulldozing presence to liven things up (look out for the end banquet scene; Lorenzon's brother, Gianni Solaro, is seated at the table, made up to resemble his sibling who has just been murdered).

A Spanish lobby card for *The Black Invaders*

per se, we get a two-minute longshot of that white stallion trotting along a mountain path, followed by two minutes showing a peasant family bemoaning their lot, followed by two minutes of Ruffo and Speziali romping in the waves, Innocenzi's music virtually absent (had the noted composer thrown in the towel at this juncture?). Speziali (one of pepla's weakest heroes) is finished off by an assassin's arrow, leaving the way clear for Piero Lulli to make his move on Ruffo, the lass changing into a raving harridan, assuming joint leadership: "Go and destroy. Burn their village to the ground. I want revenge!" she rants. Swindling Gora agrees to help Landry's serfs on condition he reclaims their land and the whole disorganized concoction ends with Landry's settlement put to the torch, Folco Lulli plunging a dagger into Ruffo, Piero Lulli dispatching his off-screen brother and he himself falling over a cliff during a fight. The curtain closer is of Landry (unaccountably elevated to leading man) standing in a field, looking bemused (as well he might), while peasants till the land, a woman telling tales to her children about the events that have unfolded throughout the film; it is to be hoped that she made far more sense of them than scriptwriter/director Veo managed to do. This one is for diehard completists only.

1962

The Black Invaders [*Odio mortale*] aka **Knights of the Gray Galley**

Morino Film/France Cinéma Productions (Italy/France); Totalscope/Eastmancolor; 89 (82) mins; Producers: Alfredo Mirabile, Massimo Patrizi; Director: Franco Montemurro ††

On December 31, 1660 the Spanish, under the orders of Dominique De Gourges, attack the small French colony of Fort Carolina in the Caribbean while they are celebrating the New Year. Most are massacred, but André Leboeuf, a French knight, escapes with his three-year-old daughter. 15 years later, Leboeuf is a red-masked pirate chieftain known as Ruiz, causing traitor De Gourges, now self-imposed governor, no end of problems in repeated sorties on his ships and, in one instance, saving three serfs from the gallows. De Gourges, carrying out a reign of persecution on the local peasantry with the aid of conniving mistress Conchita, is in league with Englishman Lord Simmons, promising the British fleet a hoard of Aztec treasure, to be taken from the vessel of Captain Carlos, busy starting up a relationship with Leboeuf's tomboy daughter, Solange. When Carlos and Leboeuf get wind of this, they do their utmost to scupper the duo's plans, becoming involved in a plethora of fights, near-escapes, breakouts from prison, black-clothed disguises (hence the title) and galleon clashes. Eventually, after faithful Conchita has been shot in the back, Leboeuf reveals his true identity to De Gourges and runs him through in a duel on board ship; the English throw in the towel, and Carlos, once thought of as a turncoat, resumes his romance with Solange.

Filmed in and around Castel dell'Ovo in the Bay of Naples, peplum rarity *The Black Invaders* (distributed worldwide by Paramount) is *almos*t a pirate adventure … but not quite. An abundance of swordfights, tavern brawls, ship skirmishes, castle set-tos and fistfights, adorned in Aldo Scavarda's sunny colors, paper over the cracks in a mediocre, seen-it-all-before plot, as does Nino Oliviero's ear-splitting score. Amedeo Nazzari (Ruiz/Leboeuf) appears at odds with his surroundings, stepping out of his rowing boat onto the burnished shore in his bright red full-faced mask, while Renato Baldini puffs his cheeks in anger

An Italian poster for *Blood and Defiance*

as bad guy De Gourges. Elsewhere, pretty Danielle De Metz turns in a limp performance as Solange, Peter Meersman is the token English noble-cum-dandy and busty Angela Luce tries her hardest to smolder as dark-haired Conchita, singing and dancing to entice the men; it's left to Aldo Bufi Landi to steal the acting honors as a lively and relatively interesting Captain Carlos. There's nothing intrinsically wrong with the way it's been put together by Franco Montemurro, the movie just happens to be missing a few key elements to raise it to a more invigorating exercise in swashbuckling. Current German DVDs come without subtitles and are scratchy, although clear enough if you're not a perfectionist, something that most peplum addicts cannot afford to be!

Blood and Defiance [*Il sangue e la sfida*]

Pampa Cinematografica (Italy/Spain); Dyaliscope/Eastmancolor; 96 mins; Producer: Armando Morandi; Director: Nick Nostro

In a small Latin American country, Madariaga, the tyrannical governor, is maltreating the local citizens, imprisoning those who step out of line and oppose his doctrines, and lusting after Lady Carmencita. Juanito Santander assumes command of a revolt against the dictator, resulting in an uprising and a massacre of the insurrection's leaders instigated by Madariaga's officers. In a duel to the finish, Juanito runs through the governor, and afterwards he retires to his country estate with Carmencita as his bride, after peace has been restored to the area.

An Italian photobusta for *Captain of Iron* (notice Barbara Steele in between the two males on the left)

Starring Gérard Landry (Juanito), Rossella Como (Carmencita), Andrea Checchi (Madariaga), José Greci, Rosalba Neri, Andrea Bosic and Aldo Bufi Landi, *Blood and Defiance* remains commercially unavailable on disc or tape as of 2015.

Captain of Iron [*Il capitano di ferro*] aka *Revenge of the Mercenaries*; *Rampage of Evil*

Taurisano Film/Dubrava Film (Italy/Yugoslavia); Iscoscope/Eastmancolor; 94 mins; Producer: Lello Luzi; Director: Sergio Grieco ♱♱♱

Captain of Iron treads a wobbly tightrope between being deadly serious drama one minute, none-too-serious skylarking the next, ending up a major disappointment. It starts off brilliantly with the violent destruction of a village and its inhabitants: men and children hanged, houses burned, women rounded up, raped, herded into a church and put to the sword and dagger. Into this ghastly tragedy rides soldier of fortune Gustavo Rojo (Furio), friend Fred Williams (aka Friedrich Locherer) and their mercenaries; Rojo's entire family has been slaughtered, his mother and father tied to a railing and adorned with arrows. A harrowing first 10 minutes then, Rojo determined to exact vengeance on the monster responsible for this terrible act, the arch peplum baddie Mario Petri. But the movie (shot in Yugoslavia's cold-looking wooded terrain) goes all silly on us, not helped in this respect by Carlo Savina's chirpy score. With a grin on his face (after witnessing that massacre?), Rojo sets off with his men on their quest, the soldier spending an inordinate amount of time romancing (and bedding) two feisty females, Gypsy Silvana Jachino (aka Susan Terry) and noblewoman Barbara Steele, who he steals from her fiancé Petri. Grieco also treats the audience to one too many tavern knockabouts, assisted by the tomfoolery of Relja Basic, dressed up like a court jester and behaving like one.

Petri's vocation, it transpires, is to conquer large parts of 16th-century Italy and assassinate the Pope, wanting to become head of state. The second part of the movie is shot in and around Ljubljana Castle, each party converging on Andrea Aureli's splendid fortress without realizing the other is there. Steele (she received second billing instead of Petri because of her reputation in Italy) flits between Rojo and Petri, scheming and romping half-naked on her bed with both, while Jachino boils with jealousy. After much coming and going in rococo, low-vaulted castle sets (beautifully photographed by Guglielmo Mancori, one of the genre's ace cinematographers and brother of Alvaro Mancori, another fine photographer), Petri's detachments are slaughtered in a muddy, confusing skirmish, Jachino felled by an arrow; the tyrant goes head-to-head with Rojo in the castle, succumbing to two sword thrusts. Collapsing in agony, he grabs a curtain, bringing down five lances that pin his body to the floor, a suitably grisly demise. Steele, after being chased around the lofty halls by a one-eyed, cackling, hopping and skipping hunchback, who ravishes and nearly rapes her, waves goodbye to Rojo as he disappears on the horizon with his band, while Williams trots off with damsel Lilly Darelli.

Picturesque location filming (it must have been freezing; check the actors' breath in many scenes) and buoyant art direction maintain interest and enjoyment levels, but if *Captain of Iron* (nigh on impossible to obtain) had kept with that somber tone created in its opening spell, the picture would have been a classic. Instead, the numerous free and easy interludes and genial ambience let it down.

The Defeat of the Barbarians [*Lo sterminatore dei barbari* aka *Re Manfredi*] aka *The Scourge of the Barbarians*

Retix Cinematografica (Italy); Supercinescope/Ferraniacolor; 90 (69) mins; Producer: Vitaliano Natalucci; Directors: Paolo Lombardo, Piero Regnoli ♱

In 14th-century Italy, upon the death of the country's German autocrat (another German), Berthold of Staufenholer (Aldo Peri) is sent to get rid of Prince Albert, the young heir-in-waiting (played by Daniela Regnoli; the director cast his daughter in the part!), and reign as monarch. Prince Manfredi (Piero Lulli), enraged at these arrangements that interfere with his own agenda, kidnaps Peri's daughter, Grenda (Moira Orfei), holding her hostage in reprisal. Infuriated at her treatment, snooty, preening Orfei uses her feminine wiles on Lulli's devious second-in-command, Riccardo (Gérard Landry). He's to convince Lulli that Regnoli has died; thus Lulli, who lusts after Orfei, can ascend to the throne, releasing her from captivity (even though she appears not to be all that bothered with her plight). Rudolph of Bavaria (Vittorio André), another contender for the seat of power, gets wind of the plot via treacherous Landry and takes advantage, staging an uprising to eliminate Lulli and his army. Lulli discovers Landry's betrayal and that the child prince is actually alive, but too late—André's coup is successful, the German's forces wiped out by the Bavarian's cavalry on the Plateau of Roka. Lulli's not-so-faithful servant, Astolfo (Ken Clark, first seen rolling in the hay with girlfriend Renata Monteduro, play-

An Italian poster and French book cover for *The Defeat of the Barbarians*

Duel in Sila [*Duello nella Sila*] aka *Duel of Fire*

Romana Film (Italy); Totalscope/Technicolor; 85 mins; Producer: Fortunato Misiano; Director: Umberto Lenzi ††

One of Umberto Lenzi's dullest and lesser films, taking place in Sicily, 1855. Fernando Lamas (Antonio Franco) plays a killer on the run, who vows to eliminate ruthless bandit chief Armand Mestral (as Rocco) and his accomplices for raping and murdering his sister (Daniela Igliozzi) during a coach robbery. Getting rid of lecherous nobleman Gino Buzzanca after a protracted opening 15 minutes in which Lamas avoids capture during a religious ceremony, the fugitive infiltrates Mestral's brigands, along with British journalist Lisa Gastoni (Miss Parker); the lady wants to run a piece in her newspaper on the lives and exploits of those caught up in banditry and what makes Mestral tick. Lamas falls for redheaded Liana Orfei (Maruzza), sister of a gang member, but eventually he's unmasked as well as Gastoni, who's obtained a list of the names Lamas requires to carry

ing Arabelle), escapes from Orfei's clutches, rescues Monteduro from a dungeon after she's been brutally whipped, forms a rebel group and in his own insurrection defeats schemer Landry and his partisans in an ambush. When Orfei is tossed off her horse into a ravine, Landry, who also loved her, throws in the towel after dueling with Clark (a clumsily shot slice of non-action, the sound of clashing swords replaced by the sound of someone hitting a wooden block) and the young prince is crowned king, while Clark is elevated to the position of Royal Protector.

Perhaps the missing 21 minutes has something to do with it, but *The Defeat of the Barbarians* (in pan and scan, the color transfer atrocious) is a shambolic muddle of a swashbuckler, dubbed in comical English with Greek subtitles. Scenes jump alarmingly from one confusing piece of court intrigue to another (you are never quite sure who is on the side of good, and who isn't), a few of the short battle sequences are filched from *The Night of the Great Attack* and Carla Calò's role as Bibiana makes no sense whatsoever in the scheme of things. Is she in love with Clark, or Lulli, or both? Who, in fact, is she? This was the first of five peplum outings for American Clark, famous for his role in American International's cult B classic *Attack of the Giant Leeches* (1959), and he performs adequately in a movie that is far from adequate, only Aldo Piga's marching-type score rising above it all. Director Regnoli, responsible for the hokey 1960 Italian horror flick *The Playgirls and the Vampire*, was on poor form here, as were peplum regulars Orfei, Landry and Lulli. This is *not* one of the finer examples of *cappa e spada*.

out his act of vengeance; she's shot dead, Lamas fleeing across country with Orfei, the pair in love. She sides with Lamas, even though he's been forced to kill her brother. Both perish after a bloody showdown involving a duel between Lamas and Mestral in a darkened cabin on the Sila Mountains. Lamas, wounded in the face-off, guns down five of Mestral's men and is then shot by henchman Vincenzo Musolino, who uses Orfei's body as a shield; approaching gendarmes finish him and Mestral off. The lovers are last seen lying dead in the dust, clasped in each other's arms.

An Italian photobusta for *Duel in Sila*

Stephen Boyd makes love to Gina Lollobrigida in *Imperial Venus*.

Muddy color (Augusto Tiezzi) further deflates a downbeat period costumer, a middling score (Gino Filippini) and Lamas' performance, as dour as the action. Full marks to Lenzi for concocting a tragic finale where everyone meets his/her Maker; however, one cares little for the characters themselves and the overall result is a plodding melodrama that struggles to maintain the interest.

Imperial Venus [*Venere imperiale*]

Royal Film/France Cinéma Prods. (Italy/France); Super Technirama 70/Technicolor; 140 (121) mins; Producer: Guido Giambartolomei; Director: Jean Delannoy ††

An Italian/French take on Fox's 1954 *Désirée*, *Imperial Venus* (current DVDs are 19 minutes shorter than the original) is a long-winded historical melodrama constructed on soap opera lines, charting the sexual exploits of Napoleon Bonaparte's frisky sister Paulette (or Pauline), played by Italian screen goddess Gina Lollobrigida. Lollobrigida flits from one besotted beau to the next, much to her brother and mother's annoyance, marrying Massimo Girotti (General Leclerc), who succumbs to the plague in the fever-ridden Antilles, then toying with the rampant emotions of Hussar Stephen Boyd (Jules de Canouville) before rashly getting hitched to unsuitable Guilio Bosetti (Prince Camillo Borghese); he refuses to divorce her when she tires of him. Bonaparte's conquests are only glimpsed as the aftermath of battle—there isn't a single scene of conflict in the whole picture which, over 140 minutes, would have led at the time to restless bums on seats, one reason for the film's lack of success. Bonaparte (a decent performance from Raymond Pellegrin) has his own problems trying to cope with Empress Josephine (Michele Presle), eventually divorcing the headstrong nymphomaniac who's unable to produce a son and heir; the emperor then weds Marie Louise of Austria in an ornate ceremony, Lollobrigida roped in as a reluctant bridesmaid. Eventually in a position to romance Boyd, Lollobrigida goes into mourning when he enlists to join in the upcoming war with Russia and dies on the battlefield, her portrait in a locket clasped in his hand. The film closes with Bonaparte's abdication and exile to Elba.

A U.S. one-sheet poster for *Seven Seas to Calais* (aka *King of the 7 Seas*)

Unusually for a composer of his repute, Angelo Francesco Lavagnino's score is as spiritless as the narrative (disjointed in edited prints), while Gabor Pogany's color is dark and muddy. Lollobrigida emotes in true Italian fashion and, posing for a sculptor, strips naked (back-shot only!), Boyd running his fingers over her statue, anticipating the real thing—if she allows it! No doubt the good intentions were there to drum up a grand historical epic, but overall the result was a failure; *Imperial Venus* rarely gets mentioned in film compendiums and has never been granted a restored, full-length DVD release, which says a lot for its low standing among fans.

King of the 7 Seas [*Il dominatore dei 7 mari*] aka *Seven Seas to Calais*

Adelphia/MGM (Italy/US); CinemaScope/Eastmancolor; 102 mins; Producer: Paolo Moffa; Directors: Rudolph Maté, Primo Zeglio ††††

Australian actor Rod Taylor was very popular both with directors and the moviegoing public during the 1960s, personable and underrated, a beguiling mix of charm, rugged good looks and beefcake, with an ever-present twinkle in his eyes. Historically inaccurate *Seven Seas to Calais* (its more common MGM-released title) had Taylor taking on the role of one of England's greatest naval heroes, Sir Francis Drake. It worked because of his charismatic screen presence. The narrative covered Drake's 1577 voyage to plunder Spanish ships and ports for their gold, a conspiracy by the Spanish to dethrone Elizabeth I and replace her with Mary Queen of Scots and Drake's notorious victory in 1588, defeating the Spanish Armada off the French coast. Another Australian, Keith Michell, was drafted to star as Taylor's lieutenant, location filming taking place in the scenic Bay of Naples. Directors Rudolph Maté (it was his second-to-last picture) and Primo Zeglio switched effortlessly between Taylor's foreign exploits and court intrigue, Irene Worth spot-on in her portrayal of Queen Elizabeth, berating the "King's Pirate" in front of her subjects but, behind closed doors, admiring him from afar (Elizabeth's unrequited passion for Drake, and their almost forbidden relationship, is subtly hinted at in a series of intimate, hand-kissing encounters, beautifully played by the two leads). It's an entertaining, colorful package; decent widescreen copies can be found with perseverance.

To the sound of Franco (Francesco) Mannino's noisy "Rule, Brittania!" score, Taylor sets sail for Spanish gold to fill Worth's near-empty coffers, puts down a ship's mutiny, raids a gold mine, strips clean a Spanish vessel, encounters non-hostile Indians (Michell accidentally promises marriage to six girls, predating his lead role in BBC's 1970 *The Six Wives of Henry VIII*, made into a feature film in 1972) and discovers potatoes and tobacco. Back in England, the hero of the day receives a knighthood at the same time Spanish ambassador Arturo Dominici is being given the runaround regarding a peace treaty. After thwarting an assassination attempt on the monarch in order to supplant Esmerelda Ruspoli on the English throne (Michell's sweetheart, Edy [aka Hedy] Vessel, is one of 15 people arrested, but she's innocent and later released), King Philip of Spain (Umberto Raho), who masterminded the plot, declares war, sick and tired not only of the English Queen's continual procrastinations but her favorite privateer running riot, wrecking his warships. In one of England's most famous of all naval victories, Taylor hoists his battle ensigns, crushes the Spanish fleet (well-staged, an expert combination of model shots and real ships, filmed at night) and has a final audience with Worth. "No man has ever served his Queen more truly than you. What shall I give you as a reward?" she asks him, smiling. "Nothing, ma'am," he replies. "Only your leave to return to sea." And are those two kisses he plants on Her Majesty's hand just a little too lingering, as is her regal gaze on his broad back when he walks off? A fine effort from start to finish and a worthy reminder of Rod Taylor's undisputed, often overlooked, talents in front of the camera (the actor unexpectedly died in January 2015, aged 84).

The Last Charge [*La leggenda di Fra Diavolo*]

Era Cinematografica (Italy); Totalscope/Eastmancolor; 143 (90) mins; Producers: Giovanni Addessi, Felice D'Alisera; Director: Leopoldo Savona

Leopoldo Savona's costume epic (drastically cut for U.S. release and retitled *The Last Charge*) chartered the exploits of legendary robber/military man Fra Diavolo (1771-1806), who antagonized the authorities in Naples. Tony Russel has the title role and Haya Harareet serves as his love interest, Fiamma. A very rare peplum, *La leggenda di Fra Diavolo* is often confused

An Italian poster for *The Last Charge*

with Savona's *The Last Charge* (*L'ultima carica*), issued in 1964 by Telefilm International and also starring Russel and Harareet. In this, Russel took on the part of Rocco Vardarelli, a bandit chief leading his men in the fight against Napoleon Bonaparte's invading French forces, Harareet playing Claudia, the girl he loves. Sources suggest that *The Last Charge* was never released outside of its native Italy. As at 2015, both films are unavailable on the market.

Marco Polo [*Marco Polo*]

Panda Film/Alta Vista/Filmorsa (Italy/France); CinemaScope/Technicolor; 103 (95) mins; Producers: Luigi Carpentieri, Ermanno Donati; Directors: Piero Pierotti, Hugo Fregonese ✝✝✝

A revamp of the old Gary Cooper/Samuel Goldwyn 1938 vehicle *The Adventures of Marco Polo*, this Italian/French effort stars Rory Calhoun as the 13th-century Venetian trader/explorer, which had a moderately successful run in England during the early months of 1963, double billed with Keelou's *The Young and the Cool* (1961). Leisurely paced, more like a travelogue in

places than a motion picture (the voice-over narration at the beginning is thankfully dropped after 10 minutes), Calhoun drifts through the scenario with a smile on his handsome face, first seen boarding a ship after jilting his bride at the altar, rescuing Michael Chow (Ciu-Lin) from brigands (the lad becomes his devoted servant), viewing the Great Wall of China, saving the life of Yoko Tani (Princess Amurroy) from more bandits, encountering Great Khan Camillo Pilotto in Peking and liaising with rebel chief Pierre Cressoy (Cuday) to put an end to villainous aide Claudio Undari (billed as Robert Hundar), who plans to depose the khan and become Peking's head of state. Calhoun also discovers the benefits of gunpowder from a hermit, constructing three hefty cannons which are used to telling effect when Cressoy's men charge into Peking during the movie's closing stages; an explosion sends Undari to meet Buddha, and Calhoun rides off to experience further adventures with Chow, deciding not to wed Tani, who he's romanced throughout the entire film.

The lavish sets left standing from *Marco Polo* were made use of by Panda in the production of *Maciste at the Court of the Great Khan*, both movies shot during 1961; these are indeed impressive, as is Riccardo Pallottini's rich color photography and Angelo Francesco Lavagnino's Chinese-themed score (as usual, augmented by Les Baxter for U.S. release). One or two skirmishes, an eye-catching Chinese dance routine, scary torture devices, picturesque Far East locations, opulent, spacious palaces, baroque temples and Japanese actress Tani delightfully prim and proper—despite these laudable credentials, *Marco Polo* would probably empty a cinema today. The film's too laid-back for its own good, a lackluster, rambling costumer that, unlike the gunpowder Calhoun messes around with in the final reel, fails to ignite as it should have done; 1965's *The Marvellous Adventures of Marco Polo* (*Marco the Magnificent*) probably fared better in the entertainment stakes, although it remains a peplum rarity difficult to obtain these days.

Night of the Unnamed [*La notte dell'innominato*] aka *Night of the Nameless*

Tabor Film/S.I.A.T. (Italy); Totalscope/Eastmancolor; 90 mins; Producers: Urbano Natali, Otello Colangeli; Director: Luigi Latini de Marchi (as Luigi Demar) †††

Based on a character in Alessandro Manzoni's 1827 novel *The Betrothed*, *Night of the Unnamed*, taking place in the 1620s, tells the tale of Esteban the Unnamed (Bruno Piergentili, billed as Dan Harrison, in his first and best peplum role), a Robin Hood-type champion of the people. On the night of the abduction of his love Lucia Mondella (Lorella De Luca) by Governor Don Rodrigo's men (Mirko Ellis played the tyrannical dictator), he recalls his life in flashback as a freedom fighter, where he waged war on the Spanish authorities who were abusing the rights of the Andalusian Gypsy clans by robbing the rich for their grain and gold, and giving it to the poor. Maria Dolores' devious, jealous sister Carmencita (Anita Todesco), also in love with Esteban, thwarted his marriage to Maria. In a struggle, Don Rodrigo's hyenas killed Maria, the Gypsy camp attacked and destroyed by his soldiers wearing Ku Klux Klan-hooded robes after Carmencita had disclosed its whereabouts. The survivors fled, power-mad Carmencita marrying Don Rodrigo to become joint ruler of the Spanish-occupied province. When his mother was tried for witchcraft and executed, tormented Esteban, in exile, turned to banditry and violence, rallying a force of peasants behind him (Howard Ross among them), determined to rescue Lucia from Don Rodrigo's clutches and end his reign of terror. Following a series of skirmishes, castle swordfights, attacks on carriages and dungeon escapes, Esteban, the mysterious benefactor of the people, finishes off the evil governor (Carmencita is also run through) and finally pardoned by Cardinal Federico, marrying Lady Lucia.

Bruno Piergentili attempted to get under the skin of Manzoni's complex character, at odds with his unscrupulous life, a

The Italian VHS cover for *Night of the Unnamed*

An Italian poster for *The Normans*

An Italian poster for *The Prisoners of Devil's Island*

swashbuckling schizophrenic if ever there was one, and was only partially successful in a *cappa e spada* that remains very difficult to lay hands on, as do the director's two other obscure swashbucklers, *Crown of Fire* and *Captain Tempest* (aka *Sword of Vengeance*), the latter released by Stellor Films/Classic Film in 1961 and starring Frank Latimore in the title role. The film was issued on Italian VHS in 1983; as at the time of writing, copies of this tape remain unavailable—Russian DVD issues taken direct from the tape can be sought out at considerable expense, in faded, lamentable quality; Carmelo Petraglia's photography is lusterless and faded while Aldo Piga's score sounds wonky on occasions. The picture is also believed to exist on 35mm film. A series of film cells could be obtained from Germany in August 2015 on various auction sites, plus a number of German lobby cards.

The Normans [*I normanni*] aka *Attack of the Normans*; *Conquest of the Normans*

Galatea Film/Lyre (Italy/France); CinemaScope/Eastmancolor; 79 mins; Producer: Paolo Mercuri; Director: Giuseppe Vari ✝

Utilizing a great deal of stock footage from both *The Last of the Vikings* and *The Invaders* (*Erik the Conqueror*) to knock up its running time and save on costs, *The Normans* is cheapskate fare for the undiscriminating fan, the gaudy color photography a complete mismatch with the inserted scenes. In some instances,

George Ardisson (who starred in the first two) can be glimpsed, and it's a miracle that in the final sortie on the castle, the producers didn't have blond Cameron Mitchell, the Viking, fighting black-haired Cameron Mitchell, Wilfred, the Duke of Saxony!

Villainous Mitchell, forever hatching plans and conspiring at court, arranges for the Saxon king to be captured and hopefully done away with by the restless Normans (who, thanks to the ham-fisted merging of two other movies, resemble Vikings most of the time) so that he can wed Franca Bettoia (Queen Patricia) and rule the kingdom. Watch out for Gianni Solaro, Livio Lorenzon's brother, in the minor role of King Dagobert and Paul Muller's Thomas, skulking around court with a grimace on his face. Ettore Manni stars as Olivier D'Anglon, the token Norman hero coming to the aid of the English sovereignty and winning the hand of damsel Genevieve Grad (Svetania), who's lusted after by bullying Piero Lulli (Barton), made up to look like Kirk Douglas in *The Vikings* (1958). The movie is performed mainly on pantomime castle stage sets and consists of Mitchell toadying up to Bettoia, Manni being imprisoned, then escaping, Lulli double-crossing his brethren and the inevitable comeuppance for all concerned. Mitchell dispatches Lulli after he has served his purpose, and Grad emerges as the king's daughter, thought killed years ago, and following a siege, the obligatory duel between hero and baddie sees Mitchell clutching the hilt of a sword, wedged firmly in his stomach. Manni now has free rein to marry Grad and become the latest addition to the monarchy, the king having escaped torture and death, and a cessation of hostilities is declared with the Normans (should that read Vikings?), bequeathing upon them the same rights as normal English citizens. Not one of peplum's (or Mitchell's) finest hours—he was more believable playing Vikings than Saxon schemers.

The Prisoners of Devil's Island [*Le prigioniere dell'isola del diavolo*] aka *Women of Devil's Island*

Documento Film/Le Louvre (Italy/France); CinemaScope/Technicolor; 88 mins; Producer: Gianni Hecht Lucari; Director: Domenico Paolella ♱♱♱♱

An Italian photobusta for *The Seven Swords of the Avenger*

Or, some might say after watching it, *Papillon on Heat*. Practically the entire production team from *Executioner of the Seas* was assembled to make this female prisoners/sexploitation opus that took place during the French Revolution—director, producer, composer, cinematographer and several members of the cast. Opening with an oddly disturbing collage of bloodied arms and hands frantically reaching out through a grate covering the ship's hold, Michele Mercier (Martine) and her fellow captives are offloaded onto the infamous penal colony known as Devil's Island, there to pan for gold in a crocodile-infested swamp, get bad-mouthed and whipped by taskmaster Tullio Altamura (Dubois) and trade sexual favors with Lieutenant Paul Muller (Lefevre) in exchange for a day off work: "I must have rest for tomorrow" is the salient phrase for hopping into leering Muller's bed. And what a bunch these girls are. Showing acres of bosom and stocking top, flawless complexions unblemished by the tropical sun, hair coiffured, make-up neatly applied, they'd look more at home on the streets of Paris than toiling in a Cayenne backwater. The "cruelty toward women" content is on a much higher level than most: One blonde babe, stripped to the waist, is flogged and tethered to a wooden frame; Altamura a little too handy with his whip and fists; a group of women receiving 20 strokes of the lash and left to "dry out" in the blazing sun; the prisoners chained to each other for a night; the girls allowed to run for it so that they can be hunted down like wild animals and many shot or blasted by cannon fire. Even a crocodile gets to feast on female flesh. Is all lost for these degraded female internees?

No! In marches Guy Madison (Captain Henri Valliere) from a docking French warship, takes command over Muller and changes things around for the better: No mistreatment of the prisoners; get rid of those whips; anyone found abusing a female will be hanged and Muller must stand trial for the murder of Mercier's sister, headstrong Federica Ranchi, who was shot in the back. But Madison isn't all that he's cracked up to be. The man's a resistance fighter, in cahoots with rascally sea captain Roldano Lupi, wanting to lay his hands on the vast quantities of gold stored in strongboxes only reached by negotiating a secret passage. The gold is essential for furnishing the Revolution back home with new arms. Naturally, Madison falls in love with Mercier about two seconds into meeting her, the pair winding up in each other's arms after Muller and his soldiers are wiped out. Marisa Belli, a spy in the camp, torches the gunpowder store ("I was the one who betrayed them!"), blowing almost everybody to kingdom come, while Fernando Piazza hideously strangles Altamura with a chain, a fisherman sympathetic to Madison's cause. Even stout Lupi (wearing oversized false teeth) gets a piece of French skirt to himself as his ship heads away from the accursed island with the surviving prisoners (and the gold) on board, bound for France.

Strikingly photographed in vivid, sun-bleached colors by Carlo Bellero (dark glasses are needed throughout), Egisto Macchi's grandiose score reaching operatic heights, *The Prisoners of Devil's Island* is male titillation fare masquerading as peplum costume drama. A lot of what's in it wouldn't get past the censor in these more conservative times, but back in the early 1960s, audiences didn't bat an eyelid at all that exposed female flesh on display, brutalized, whipped and ogled at by Muller and his lascivious acolytes. How times have changed!

The Seven Swords of the Avenger [*Le sette spade del vendicatore*] aka *The Seventh Sword*

Adelphia/Francisco Film/Comptoir Francais CFPC (Italy/France); Dyaliscope/Technicolor; 94 (84) mins; Producer: Cino Del Duca; Director: Riccardo Freda ♱♱♱

As of 2015, Riccardo Freda's swashbuckler set in the reign of Philip III (1598-1621) is only available on French video in the edited cut; due to France's SECAM system, it is difficult to evaluate the movie shorn of its color and cursed with annoying breaks in continuity. The French authorities excised several minutes from the scene where a group of performing players enacts Cardinal Mario Scaccia's leaden, pompous drama *A Christian*

An Italian poster for *Sign of the Avenger*

Heart's Temptation, based on the morals of Catholics, reasoning that the full version would upset the Catholic Church. Viewed beyond the jumps and grainy images, Freda's movie, blessed with a tuneful flamenco score from Franco Mannino, comes into its own in the dungeon sequences, vast underground chambers crammed to the rafters with any manner of giant fiendish devices designed to inflict the maximum amount of pain on the sufferer, the set worthy of inclusion in any Italian horror film. Otherwise, it's very much routine fare, Brett Halsey (as Don Carlos of Bazan) and his band of rebels foiling a plot by his cousin, Giulio Bosetti (the Duke of Saavedra), to overthrow the Spanish monarch and take over as regent.

Playing the philandering king, Gabriele Antonini mainly appears at the beginning and end, the rest given over to Halsey encountering masked, hooded conspirators, rescuing Béatrice Altariba (Lady Isabella) from a carriage holdup and romancing her, getting involved in umpteen duels and scrapes, raiding gunpowder supplies hidden in champagne barrels needed by Bosetti in his covert plans, tussling with scar-faced Gabriele Tinti, surviving a firing squad (rifles contain harmless powder), engaging in a frivolous affray dressed in knight's armor and avoiding being caged and lowered into a well of flesh-hungry piranhas (that's reserved for crooked attendant Jacopo Tecchio, later on). Halsey is forced to marry Altariba so that he's implicated in the plot, but dispatches his cousin in a thrilling set-to within the confines of that grand torture chamber, huge guillotine-type blades smashing down while the two fight to the death; Bosetti receives a dagger in his chest, falling backwards into the piranha pit. To the cheers of the crowd, Halsey and his new bride ride off for pastures new after being honored by Antonini.

The Seven Swords of the Avenger was a remake of Freda's directorial debut in 1942, *Don Cesare of Bazan* (Elica Film); Freda, in interviews, admitted that he favored sword and sandal over horror, although he was to make his considerable mark in both genres. Many of his early forays into the realm of pepla are almost impossible to obtain (*The Black Eagle*, 1946; *The Mysterious Rider*, 1948; *The Iron Swordsman*, 1949; *Son of D'Artagnan*, 1950), and as for this example of his work, it will probably never be issued on disc, a fate which has befallen many rare peplum features that survive on old French VHS tapes, and nowhere else.

Sign of the Avenger [*Il segno del vendicatore*] aka *The Masked Cavalier*

Mecurfilm (Italy); Schermopanoramic/Eastmancolor; 74 (66) mins; Producer: Aurelio Serafinelli; Director: Roberto Mauri ✞✞✞✞✞

Of the plethora of "Masked Avenger" *cappa e spada* movies to have come out of the Italian film studios during the early 1960s, Roberto Mauri's offering remains one of the least recognized and little seen. A scratchy print containing shortened scenes is available in Italian (no subtitles), a shame as *Sign of the Avenger* is a classic of its type, bubbling with energy and excitement, filmed with real gusto by Mauri and blessed, behind that curtain of scratches, by Ugo Brunelli's atmospheric color photography, not to mention Aldo Piga's humdinger of a score. Permission was granted to shoot in and around the imposing Palazzo dei Consoli in Gubbio, Central Italy, a medieval palace/fortress town built between 1332-1349, imbuing the production with that all-important period feel and authentic backdrop. With bad guy Claudio Undari hamming it up for all it's worth (the tall, lean saturnine actor was underused as a villain in pepla) and rotund Alfredo Rizzo turning in a wonderfully timed performance as a rascally padre, this is one to seek out and revel in, and perhaps mourn the fact that the picture will never be issued commercially in its original pristine form.

The evil Duke de Hauteville (Undari) tortures and kills Count Arvedi to gain the rights to his land and possessions. In steps the count's son Antonio (Gabriele Antonini; his character is Zorro in some listings), bent on retribution. After being given coaching lessons from fencing master Luigi Batzella, he takes on the guise of The Masked Cavalier, a Zorro-type avenger who cuts down Undari's thuggish lackies when they're caught treating the local populace like vermin, terrorizing, pillaging and assaulting at leisure. In addition, the enigmatic caped horseman sends razor-edged messages to Undari via arrow, warning the duke of the dire consequences if he continues his vile reign of oppression. Furtive rebel gatherings are held behind blacksmith Vincenzo Musolino's workshop, wily priest Rizzo ferrying weapons backwards and forwards to the insurgents concealed under his habit and indulging in swordplay himself under the watchful eyes of a figure of Christ on the cross (which the monk hastily covers with a cloth to avoid chastisement in the hereafter). Frustrated by the activities of the masked interloper, Undari imprisons Antonini's girlfriend Velia (Graziella Granata) and

has her viciously flogged; the girl won't give in to his advances, but Undari's mistress, Dorothée Blanck, puts up with his infidelities for a life of riches and comfort. A turbulent, noisy climax has townsfolk storming the palace, armed with standard two-pronged pitchforks, their numbers boosted by Batzella, Musolino and the rebels. In a prolonged duel, Antonini runs Undari through, the usurper's body slumping into an ornamental pool; Granata, marked by her savage lashing, staggers into her savior's arms as the curtain falls (in the uncut print, the couple marry and Antonini is declared rightful ruler). Unfortunately, the immensely likeable Rizzo perishes in the affray, meeting his Maker with sword in hand, just as he would have liked. Another in a long line of lost peplum must-haves, *Sign of the Avenger* trounces many higher-budgeted films of this nature by sheer force of execution for the by-now routine material in hand; it's short, snappy and very sweet.

The Sword of El Cid [*La spada del Cid*] aka *The Daughters of El Cid*

Alexandra Produzioni/Cintera (Italy/Spain); Supercinescope/Eastmancolor; 86 mins; Producer: Nino Milano; Director: Miguel Iglesias ††

Legendary Spanish nobleman El Cid's two daughters (Chantal Deberg as Maria, and Daniela Bianchi as Elvira) travel to meet their nephew, José Luis Pellicena (Felix), accompanied by their two despicable husbands of three years (Fernando and Diego) in tow. En route, the women are each tied to a tree and whipped by their spouses for "unreasonable behavior." Pellicena discovers them, escorts the semi-conscious pair to a convent for safekeeping and becomes embroiled in a convoluted plot to restore Sandro Moretti (Ramon) as the rightful King of Catalonia, Andrés Mejuto (Berenguer) having usurped the throne with the assistance of henchman Roland Carey (Bernardo). The two squabbling husbands also have to return their swords and take on three champion combatants in order to restore their not-so-good names after this wicked act of cowardice.

The Sword of El Cid was the only peplum movie made by Spanish director Miguel Iglesias and it shows in his lack of grasp of the material in hand. The disjointed narrative wanders all over the place, leaving you to try and figure out just who is who, and what on earth is happening. At one stage the script leads the audience to believe, or infers, that Moretti is the son of El Cid, when he plainly isn't, a plethora of names, titles, towns and ranks bandied about at random to confuse the issue, not only from Moretti, Pellicena and compatriot Andrea Fantasia (brother of peplum regular Franco Fantasia), but from the women seeking sanctuary in the convent. A 10-minute sword/axe fight in the middle section drags, there are too many meaningless shots of horsemen riding through countryside, Fantasia receives an arrow in the back from Carey (some movie sites claim that Carey plays the hero in this film; in fact, he's the villain), Mejuto desires El Cid's fabled broadsword as a symbol of power and Deberg, her husband slain, gives up any pretence of becoming a grieving widow by falling in love with boyish Moretti. All credit to Iglesias for conjuring up a bustling five-minute battle, staged at Spain's magnificent Belmonte Castle in the province of Cuenca. Moretti's men (the Knights of Cid) besiege the fortress, Carey is stabbed by Moretti and flung from a turret and the rebels rejoice in victory. A flat anticlimax wraps up the muddled action, Mejuto branded a murderer for doing away with Moretti's father and banished to the Holy Lands by church officials; the youngster is crowned King of Catalonia and

Hollywood swashbuckling legend Stewart Granger takes to the dance floor with a smitten Christine Kaufmann in *Swordsman of Siena*.

The Italian Peplum Phenomenon 1950-1967

Count of Barcelona, winning the hand of Deberg, much to the delight of the torch-waving crowds. In all honesty, *The Sword of El Cid* is a bit of a shambles; not even Carlo Savina's resounding score and Francisco Marin's super widescreen photography can cement the pieces of this particular uncoordinated jigsaw.

Swordsman of Siena [*La congiura dei dieci*] aka *The Mercenary*

Monica Film/CIPRA (Italy/France); CinemaScope/Metrocolor; 97 mins; Producer: Jacques Bar; Directors: Baccio Bandini, Etienne Périer ††††

Distributed worldwide by MGM as *Swordsman of Siena*, Stewart Granger's final swashbuckler is 97 minutes of pure pleasure thanks to the star himself. Granger was one of Hollywood's more self-effacing actors, who never quite took the movie capital's scene too seriously, his light, elegant touch blessing many a

A Belgian poster for *The Triumph of Robin Hood*

costume production during the 1950s. Taking up fencing lessons during the making of *Scaramouche* (1952) left him in good stead to play the role of English mercenary Thomas Stanwood, whose deadly sword is on offer to the highest bidder, in this case Spanish overlord Riccardo Garrone (Don Carlos). Garrone needs a bodyguard for his fiancée, Tuscan noblewoman Sylva Koscina (Orietta), and Granger fits the bill nicely. But the Spaniard should have noticed that twinkle in the Englishman's eye. From the opening scene, when Granger is pursued by soldiers because he's run out on his latest fling, we know that the man's a one for the ladies and very soon, he's casting those eyes on unhappy Koscina, who remains standoffish in his company, but yearns for his embrace. Casting *her* eyes on Granger is Koscina's young sister, Christine Kaufmann (Serenella); the lass develops an almighty crush on the handsome mercenary, dreaming of an idyllic life with her gallant back in England. Garrone has other ideas, to marry the girl to his sadistic cousin, Fausto Tozzi (Hugo), and thus secure Spanish dominance over the subjugated inhabitants of Siena. The despot is being terrorized by "The Ten," a cloak-and-dagger group led by Alberto Lupo (Andrea), who are hell-bent on usurping him from power and he's a worried man; unbeknown to Garrone, Koscina is a member. When Kaufmann is callously brought down by a crossbow bolt during a curfew imposed by the Spaniard, Granger, enraged at the act, ceases to think about filling his purse and joins the rebels in their lair, approached by a hidden passage; he also takes part in a murderous annual horse race, riders having to avoid a gauntlet of spears, spikes, pointed staves and blades. Tozzi is usually the winner but this time around, Granger plans to be number one *and* put an end to Garrone's martial rule.

Easygoing Granger makes it look all so simple, showing genuine dexterity using the blade, his witty repartee matched by that renowned ready smile, an effortless performance that beguiles. The torture and murder by strangulation of Lupo is savage and unnecessary in a frothy gambol of this nature; although Tozzi is set upon by a mob, we never witness his beating, while Garrone's parting shot as he's steamrollered out of Siena is, "I was never partial to Italian food." "Goodbye, my lady," says Granger to Koscina, before galloping off, but the climax is a carbon copy of the beginning. Soldiers intercept Granger, and he is forced to dismount when he meets Koscina in a wooded glade. "Attack me," she invites. "With pleasure," is his response, and we know that this is one gal who Granger won't want to run from, not for now! Yes, what we have here, courtesy of the Italian film studios, is the Stewart Granger show—where are the actors of his disarming caliber today, one wonders.

The Triumph of Robin Hood [*Il trionfo di Robin Hood*]

Buona Vista/Triglav Film (Italy/Yugoslavia); Totalscope/Eastmancolor; 86 (77) mins; Producer: Tiziano Longo; Director: Umberto Lenzi ††

Umberto Lenzi's entrant into the Robin Hood tale of old contained the same ingredients as most other movie versions: Robin and his Merry Men, the Sheriff of Nottingham, Maid Marian, King Richard the Lionheart and Sherwood Forest. Only here, Maid Marian becomes plain Anna and English viewers, if they could lay their hands on this rare movie, would surely cringe at the sight of a Sherwood Forest containing caves and waterfalls (location shooting took place at Umbria's Marmore cascades and around Grad Otočec, Slovenia), plus a backdrop composed of the snow-capped Italian Alps. Too much glaring sunshine reflecting off white-stoned medieval Italian village walls dispels any sense of Englishness, as Scottish-born Don Burnett (it was his final feature before quitting the film industry to become a stockbroker) takes on Sheriff Arturo Dominici, deputy Germano Longo, bungling henchman Nello Pazzafini and their mob in 1194; the dastardly villains are busy trying to wrest the throne from King Richard and hand it to Prince John. Burnett's wife at the time, Gia Scala, fresh from playing Anna in Columbia's enormously popular *The Guns of Navarone*, stars as (you might have guessed) Anna, who does little but to run across meadows shouting, "Robeeeen. Robeeeen Hooood!" while kittenish Gaia Germani's Lady Isabella is a preening, pouting Italian Barbie doll, decorative but vacuous. Bodybuilder Samson Burke is celluloid's unlikeliest Little John, his infamous riverside duel rendered laughable by the fact that Burnett, his caveman op-

The battlefield in *With Iron and Fire*, showing a fallen horse. Horses generally came in for a lot of rough treatment throughout peplum history.

ponent, makes the Canadian giant look small; in the meantime, jolly glutton Friar Tuck rolls around, food in one hand, club in the other, dishing out slapstick whacks over the heads and feet of his enemies. Mythical knight Ivanhoe is mentioned in passing but fails to turn up for the party.

It sounds like a complete disaster perhaps, yet Lenzi has the expertise to manufacture a number of half-decent action sequences to stop everyone from debating whether or not this is the worst treatment of the legendary archer's exploits ever committed to celluloid. There's a great deal of leaping from trees, Germani is saved from marrying an inappropriate suitor, a pretty exciting clash between Dominici's soldiers and Burnett's men, trapped in a mill, raises the excitement levels and a colorful skirmish between red-cloaked and white-cloaked knights of opposing factions tops it all off. Oh yes, the rebel leader in the blue/green tights is trapped in that classic peplum pose, cornered on all sides by a ring of lances. Burnett gets Scala all to himself, probably going down in celluloid history as (to put it kindly) the least memorable of all Robin Hoods, proving that when it came to English history and its heroes, the Italians could get it all so horribly wrong; watch this in tandem with 1965's *The Revenge of Ivanhoe* and you'll see precisely what I mean.

With Iron and Fire [*Col ferro e col fuoco*] aka *Invasion 1700*; *With Fire and Sword*

Film Europa/Comptoir Francais CFFP/Avala (Italy/France/Yugoslavia); Euroscope/Eastmancolor; 112 mins; Producer: Giampaolo Bigazzi; Director: Fernando Cerchio ✝✝✝

An overlong drama set during the time of the Ukraine Khmelnytsky uprising of 1666-1671 in which the Polish military had to face up to not only the Ukrainians but Tartar armies

from Central Asia. The movie is basically a romance played out against a warlike background. Polish officer Pierre Brice (Jan Ketusky), on his way to take command of the Jurak garrison, stops over at Rosloghi Castle where he meets Elena Zareschi (Princess Kurzevich), her ward Jeanne Crain (Helen), eye-patched warrior Akim Tamiroff (Mielski Zasloba), blind Raoul Grassilli (Basilio) and John Drew Barrymore (Bohun). Barrymore is a Ukrainian Cossack, an ally to the Poles, promised in marriage to Crain as part of a peace alliance. The snag is, Crain detests him. Caressing his pet monkey, bushy hair flopping over glinting eyes, his homicidal temper barely held in check, Barrymore is only one step away from lunacy and the madhouse, hardly a young girl's fancy. It goes without saying that Brice and Crain become lovers, Cerchio focusing on their covert liaison and Barrymore's increasingly diseased state of mind, when he discovers what his fiancée is up to behind his back.

It's a talkative affair, just about keeping clear of dry-as-dust, a few raids by the Tartars, ambushes and scenes of torture chucked in to keep the momentum flowing (Gordon Mitchell, although billed as one of the main stars, makes only a brief guest appearance as a Polish officer, torn to pieces by an angry mob), and Bruno Nessi wields peplum's biggest broadsword; disappointedly, the battle set pieces (short by these standards) don't commence until the 80th minute. Crazed Barrymore, after committing a string of atrocities and abducting Crain, switches allegiance, throwing in his lot with the Tartars when the Poles refuse to capitulate; there's a sweeping confrontation between the opposing contingents, the Tartars' giant war machines firing off rockets, and Brice, out in the field, is wounded. Barrymore meets his Maker, trussed up and dragged to his death by a horse, and Crain is reunited with Brice on the corpse-strewn battlefield following the defeat of the joint Tartar and Ukrainian forces. Pier Ludovico Pavoni's flawless photography and Francesco De Masi's resonating soundtrack add immeasurably to a picture that, despite a mesmerizing central performance from Barrymore, appears strangely lethargic given the inspirational subject matter.

1963

The Adventures of Scaramouche [*Le avventure di Scaramouche*] aka **The Mask of Scaramouche**

CCM/Fides/Producciones Benito Perojo (Italy/France/Spain); Dyaliscope/Eastmancolor; 98 mins; Producer: Juan Campos; Director: Antonio Isasi-Isasmendi ✝✝✝

MGM's $3,500,000 production of Rafael Sabatini's 1921 novel *Scaramouche* was a massive commercial success in 1952; the Italian remake had Gérard Barray and Alberto de Mendoza taking over the roles of Stewart Granger and Mel Ferrer as hero and villain, the action set during the French Revolution. Isasi-Isasmendi's version was far more happy-go-lucky in approach, with Barray (as Robert Lafleur/Scaramouche), an actor with the Commedia dell'Arte troupe, spending most of his free time bedding other men's wives/mistresses. One day, he receives an unannounced visit from the Marquis de Souchil (Rafael Brugera), who questions him about an unusual birthmark on his left shoulder; when the old man is murdered, Barray is arrested as the chief suspect but later escapes with the help of Brugera's niece, Michele Girardon (Diana). Barray then discovers that he is the legitimate son of the Duke de Froissart, who died under questionable circumstances, and that de Mendoza (Roger), the illegitimate son of Froissart's scheming brother, was substituted at birth, a duplication of Barray's birthmark etched on his shoulder. This deception would enable the counterfeit son to inherit the real son's title and wealth. At a masked ball, Barray, pal Gonzalo Canas and their performing troupe act out de Mendoza's charade, exposing him as an imposter, leading to his death. Now the lawful recipient to the family fortune, Barray is free to marry Girardon.

Two thrilling seven-minute bouts of balletic swordplay between Barray and de Mendoza highlight *The Adventures of Scaramouche*. The first takes place on the ornate bastions of Burgos Cathedral in Leon, Spain, a vertigo-inducing duel executed with a genuine feel for the swashbuckling genre; the second is the final confrontation in the great hall, almost equalling the infamous Granger/Ferrer showpiece in MGM's movie, spectators tripping over themselves to avoid the line of fire as the two protagonists leap from stairway to balcony to alcove, cold steel clashing. Alejandro Ulloa's color photography, taking in the vibrant hustle and bustle of Parisian street life, is exemplary and Barray makes an ever-smiling, engaging hero, donning a variety of masks to outwit his enemies. And as a bonus, deeply sensuous Gianna Maria Canale (Suzanne) is on hand to play one of Barray's many love toys. But the accent is on practical jokes, fun, frivolity and buffoonery (except for an eerie graveyard sequence), and by emphasizing this comical playacting, the film, which after all is supposed to be a tale of vengeance, becomes draggy and a little

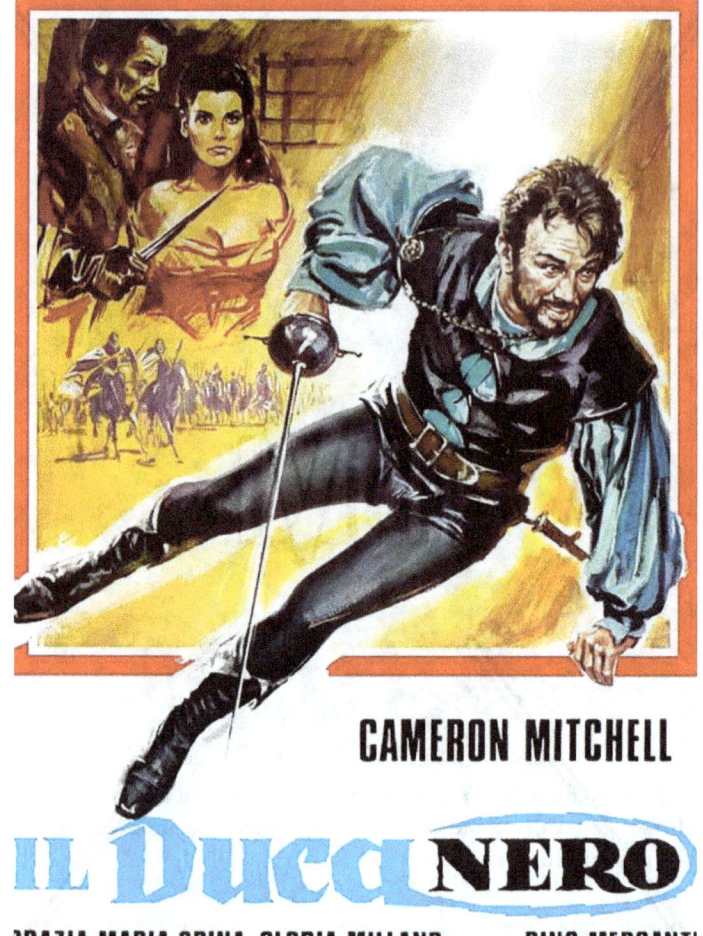

An Italian poster for *The Black Duke*

bit tiresome in places. Those two tremendous duels, among the greatest in pepla, are really the main reason to watch.

The Black Duke [*Il duca nero*] aka *Cesare Borgia*

Rodes Cinematografica/Hispamer (Italy/Spain); Dyaliscope/Eastmancolor; 105 (89) mins; Producer: Tullio Bruschi; Director: Pino Mercanti ✝✝✝✝

Hamming it up to the hilt of his sword, Cameron Mitchell plays Cesare Borgia, the infamous nobleman, politician and soldier, who attempted to rule the whole of Northern Italy in the early years of the 16th century. Constantly manipulating dignitaries to his own advantage, Mitchell (first seen in bed caressing a semi-nude sex kitten) plots, schemes and puts in place stratagems aimed at outwitting his opponents, both in love and war. For example, at one point, he flirts with an ambassador's wife, forcing the man to creep into his room to catch them *in flagrante delicto*. The enraged husband draws a knife and stabs dead, not Mitchell, but his own brother; the brother was an adversary of Mitchell who wanted him out of the way. Unscrupulous Mitchell also wishes for his cold, aloof sister Gloria Osuna (as Lucrezia, their complex relationship is only hinted at) to marry into the French royalty to cement an alliance and, as a consequence, strengthen his considerable forces. Also a hindrance in his relentless march to power is one of peplum's most scrumptious of leading ladies, Gloria Milland (Caterina Sforza), a haughty, determined countess whose majestic fortification (a medieval castle at Brescia was made use of for location shooting) and prosperous principality Mitchell desires. Another thorn in his side comes in the form of The Red Carnations, a group of red-hooded mercenaries led by the mysterious Red Carnation; they persistently upset Mitchell's machinations and he wants to get to the bottom of who runs the outfit once and for all. Working for The Red Carnations, Maria Grazia Spina (Ginerva) infiltrates Mitchell's court, bent on revenge for the murder of her father, but falls in love with the man she thinks did it, while second-in-command Conrado San Martin (Riccardo), a pawn in Mitchell's game plan, is instructed to uncover the identity of The Red Carnation and bring him to heel.

The Black Duke may be short on action (there's the occasional fencing scene, choreographed by Franco Fantasia, who appears as Venerio), appearing like a 1940s Gothic melodrama, but the beautiful color (Antonio Macasoli), twisty-turny narrative and Mitchell's scenery-chewing star turn atones for it; he makes a rascally scoundrel that's difficult not to like. Following a racy moment in which Mitchell grabs Spina, freshly bathed, and disrobes her, the girl confesses to him who she really is but cannot carry out The Red Carnation's orders to kill him. "Go back to those who plot against me in the dark. Go, you strumpet of death," Mitchell barks before she drinks poisoned wine meant for him, the ultimate love sacrifice, dying in his arms. San Martin is revealed as The Red Carnation, more power hungry than his boss, hankering after Mitchell's position and dominions. Caught out at a gathering in which wily Mitchell has somehow managed to attend (complete with red hood), the quisling is imprisoned but released, defecting to Milland's camp; he draws his last breath at the hands of Mitchell in the exciting closing mass swordfight (yes, a secret tunnel *is* involved, as is scaling the castle walls), his corpse tossed from the battlements like a rag doll. And after Milland's forces capitulate, does the lady seem bothered? Not one bit of it. Grinning from ear to ear, she escorts Mitchell on the victory parade toward his tent, no doubt wondering whether or not, under all that black armor, he's the legendary Lothario everyone claims he is.

Non-peplum movie fans would probably be completely unaware that Mitchell, an accomplished player with 240 listings to his name (including TV series), ever appeared in these Italian historical features. Best known as rancher Buck Cannon in 97 episodes of *The High Chaparral* (1967-1971), he demonstrated that out of cowboy gear, he was perfectly able as a character actor; here, he brings to life one of history's most brutal figureheads, a solid performance that is shamefully overlooked in a lot of film compendiums to this day.

Catherine of Russia [*Caterina di Russia*]

Romana Film/SNC/Zagreb Film (Italy/France/Yugoslavia); Totalscope/Eastmancolor; 105 (92) mins; Producer: Fortunato Misiano; Director: Umberto Lenzi ✝✝✝

An Italian photobusta for *Catherine of Russia*

Beautiful to look at (cleaned-up unedited prints in Italian/widescreen are available) but devoid of dramatic thrust, *Catherine of Russia*, set in Petersburg, 1761, starred Hildegard Knef in the title role of the woman who, from 1762 to her death in 1796, became Russia's greatest female leader. German husky-voiced actress Knef, 38 at the time of filming, was no raving beauty, but perhaps the part didn't call for one. Forcible rather than overtly sexy, she carried her own weight by assuming an air of lofty superiority, upstaged at every turn of events by Raoul Grassilli's Grand Duke Peter III, her husband. Taking on the characteristics of a demented Nero (like the mad emperor, he even fiddles while Petersburg falls to the Cossacks), petty-minded Grassilli scuttles, plots, grabs his violin in times of stress and rolls his eyes, a lip-smacking performance of certifiable villainy to top 'em all. The narrative doesn't amount to much. Cossack captain Sergio Fantoni (Orloff) is sent to a Siberian labor camp for defying Grassilli's orders to open fire on a threatening crowd, escapes when on a burial detail, returns to take up his old position, is jailed again and set free from the gallows by Knef. The two join forces to overthrow Grassilli's troops, which they achieve in an action-packed epilogue; the Cossack regiments are repulsed three times but gain victory on the fourth attempt. Grassilli is deposed and arrested, Knef taking up her position as Tsarina of Russia, or Catherine the Great, with Fantoni by her side, the crowds jubilant in their celebrations.

Due to her unhappy marriage, Knef launches herself at any good-looking male in uniform that takes her fancy (Giacomo Rossi-Stuart is one of her victims), while Fantoni is nice but a tad stilted as Orloff the Cossack (regal-looking Knef could eat him for breakfast). It's the sensational costume design (Walter Patriara) and baroque set details (Franco D'Andria) that bring the movie to life, given a sumptuous gloss by experienced peplum cinematographer Augusto Tiezzi. Yes, as stated, *Catherine of Russia* is a joy to behold but in many ways remains an empty vessel.

A Spanish lobby card for *The Devils of Spartivento*

The Devils of Spartivento [*I diavoli di Spartivento*] aka ***Arms of the Avenger***; ***Curse of the Haunted Forest***; ***Weapons of Vengeance***; ***The Fighting Legions***

Cinecompagnia Romana/Comptoir Francais CFFP (Italy/France); Euroscope/Eastmancolor; 95 (89) mins; Producer: Alberto Chimenz; Director: Leopoldo Savona ✝✝✝

A long-forgotten peplum, available in rough, jumpy prints if you can track them down from obscure outlets—Pier Ludovico Pavoni's color photography is all but ruined in the transfer. In 15th-century Italy, the three swashbuckling cavalier-type Duchesca brothers, Lothar (John Drew Barrymore), Demetrio (Romano Ghini) and Vannozzo (Giacomo Rossi-Stuart), return from the wars to discover their family estate ransacked by villains Michel Lemoine and Franco Balducci, both employed by the Duke of Collinalto (Ugo Silvestri) but working against his specific orders to practice leniency on the oppressed country folk. Vowing vengeance and donning masks, the brothers embark on a rampage of sedition to upset Lemoine's hyenas, encountering duchess-in-distress Scilla Gabel in their mission, as well as treacherous Jany Clair.

A standard "let's get the usurper who has stolen our property" scenario is made different by the inclusion of eccentric hermit Mario Pisu and young assistant Giampiero Calasso, both disciples of that great inventor Leonardo Da Vinci. Pisu inhabits an alchemist's cave in the so-called Devil's Forest where the brothers end up after being chased by Lemoine's men, constructing various unique weapons in his workshop, very useful for repelling the baddies: a multiple arrow-shooter and a rocket launcher (note how distressed the horses are when the brothers use Pisu's weapons to shatter the enemy ranks). When the trio are captured and incarcerated in Silvestri's castle keep, Pisu concocts three sets of mechanical wings (canvas membranes spread over frames), takes them to the castle on the pretext that Lemoine can use them himself ("They're good for the army!"), gasses the guards and delivers the contraptions to the keep; the brothers strap themselves in, jump from the parapets and fly away, much to the amazement, and anger, of Lemoine. A huge, lumbering war machine belching flames enables the vigilantes to storm the castle. Balducci is run through by Rossi-Stuart, but Silvestri spares Lemoine's life, banishing him from his domain. Gabel hitches her skirts to Barrymore, who bids farewell to his two siblings and gallops off to sample the female delights on offer. A tremendous score from Francesco De Masi boosts a rather flat narrative, and Barrymore, Rossi-Stuart and Ghini play off each other delightfully. However, the movie needed more zip and pace to make it a better all-round effort.

The Executioner of Venice [*Il boia di Venezia*] aka ***Blood of the Executioner***

Liber Film (Italy); Totalscope/Eastmancolor; 90 mins; Producer: Ottavio Poggi; Director: Luigi Capuano ✝✝✝✝✝

Out of the many peplum swashbucklers set in the Renaissance city of Venice, Luigi Capuano's gloriously evocative costumer must rank as the finest. It's a historical caper that contains everything you could wish for in a picture of this type: a dazzling array of colors (Alvaro Mancori), a magisterial score (Carlo Rustichelli), eye-popping Venetian locations, solid performances, lush production design and ornate sets, all assembled and directed with rattling pace by Capuano; not a dull second in sight. Lex Barker (a captivat-

A German poster for *The Executioner of Venice*

ing star turn as Sandrigo Bembo), adopted son of Doge (Duke) Feodor Chaliapin, Jr., crosses swords with Grand Inquisitor Guy Madison (Rodrigo) over who should be sanctioned the next Doge of Venice, when the senior official passes on. Madison tries his damnedest to blacken Barker's good name and eliminate him, desiring marriage with his fiancée, Alessandra Panaro (Leonora); in his campaign of hate and point-the-finger, Madison utilizes the services of traitor Alberto Farnese (Michele) and elusive pirate-cum-executioner Mario Petri (Guarnieri) who may not be all that he appears to be. Watching out for Barker's back is pal Franco Fantasia and Giulio Marchetti, a blind fatherly figure who has been at Barker's side since he was a young lad.

A wacky opening contest of "who can bury this axe the deepest in that log," Barker cleaving the log in two, much to the dismay of Petri (sporting a deep, livid scar across his surly face); golden shots of gondolas being rowed down canals and under classical-designed bridges in warm sunlight; Barker branded an enemy of the Republic and served with a warrant on his wedding day; Petri, his abode a cave stacked with booty, showing Madison a distinctive tattoo of the Madonna on his left shoulder; a tremendous rapier-rattling set-to in the grounds of a convent; beheadings; court intrigue; treasonable twists and turns involving the Venetian council; fashionable corteges; dungeon close calls and a terrific climax, Barker and Panaro facing a double execution but saved from the axeman's block by Petri, who happens to be Barker's real father (Petri, 41 at the time, was in fact three years younger than Barker!)—Barker wears an identical tattoo on *his* shoulder, the revelation poleaxing Petri on execution day. Madison gets what's coming to him, decapitated by Petri, the pirate chief sailing off with his corsairs, content to leave Barker in the loving arms of Panaro and Marchetti. This is one peplum package to savor over and over again, a feast of goodies to titillate the senses; it also serves as a reminder to fans that good-looking Barker in his prime was a personable, much underrated, actor deserving more credit than he was given.

An Italian poster for *The Invincible Masked Cavalier*

The Invincible Masked Cavalier [*L'invincible cavaliere mascherato*] aka ***The Invincible Masked Rider***; ***Terror of the Black Mask***

Romana Film/SNC (Italy/France); Totalscope/Eastmancolor; 96 (91) mins; Producer: Fortunato Misiano; Director: Umberto Lenzi ✞✞✞✞✞

Umberto Lenzi's long-forgotten take on the Zorro legend contains some of pepla's richest color photography; with Augusto Tiezzi and Adalberto "Bitto" Albertini behind the lens, how could it not. Watch the scene in which Hélène Chanel leaves her bedroom and creeps down a castle corridor. Brief, maybe, but the veteran cinematographers imbue this short poetic episode with such vivid color tones and artful lighting that it stays in the memory, making fans appreciate the consummate artistry behind many of these Italian swashbucklers. The color throughout, in fact, is as lush as Chanel herself; never has the French actress looked more downright sexy than she does here, her red locks, luminous eyes and heaving cleavage (Lenzi dwells on that cleavage a little *too* much sometimes) guaranteed to raise any man's blood pressure.

Chanel (Carmencita) finds herself an unwanted guest in Daniele Vargas' (Don Luis) castle. The tyrant has just arranged the murder of her father, planning to have the lass wed to his stepson, effete Pierre Brice (Don Diego). With Chanel in the family, the sadistic nobleman can take possession of her father's capital and continue trampling all over the plague-ridden population without interference, aided by a trio of vicious henchmen, Massimo Serato, Carlo Latimer and Nello Pazzafini. But Brice isn't as incapable as people think; in black hat, full-faced black mask and black attire, he swings into action, carving a cross on his protagonists' foreheads and dispatching the people's aggressors, all the while ensuring that no harm comes to Chanel, who goes completely orgasmic at the slightest touch of his black-gloved fingers, longing to kiss him, mask or no mask. Brice kills the three terrorizing thugs one at a time over the course of 90 minutes, Vargas falling to the tip of his rapier during a masked party, crashing to the floor clutching a suit of armor after his stepson has revealed his true identity. Chanel, naturally, is as pleased as punch: The foppish young nobleman she was being forced to marry turns out to be that strange, but highly desirable, man in black; no wonder her grin lights up the screen when she gets to engage in lip action with her benefactor *minus* his mask!

You'd be wrong in thinking that *The Invincible Masked Cavalier* was yet another formulaic *Zorro* rip-off. Lenzi strayed into Gothicism at times (Britain's Hammer Films could have come up with something similar to this in the 1950s), presenting Brice as a figure of mystery, his pitch-black form a stark, almost spooky, contrast against the deep rich interior color hues, a twilight phantom rescuing the damsel in distress in her hour of need (Angelo Francesco Lavagnino's mood music expertly strikes the right somber note in Brice's alter-ego scenes, par-

An Italian photobusta for *The Lion of St. Mark*

ticularly when the Masked Man appears at night during a thunderstorm). Elsewhere, the director threw in small doses of horror (he directed several slasher/horror flicks following his bout in pepla): plague victims carried through the streets by cowled monks, their corpses cremated on pyres; a bloody, contaminated slice of skin delivered to Vargas, the carrier put to death; a lurid dungeon torture interrogation; and terrified women herded up by Vargas' thugs, stripped, fumigated and shared out among his leering, groping acolytes at a drunken banquet. Lenzi also found time to orchestrate a fantastic castle siege, rebellious townsfolk swarming over rocky slopes toward Vargas' fortress, scaling the walls and mown down by pistol fire, plus a sex-charged dance number. The closing shot is of Brice and Chanel, on one steed, riding off to play house, the curtain coming down on a relatively obscure but extremely rewarding costume feature that is a lot meatier, and darker in tone, than most of its ilk.

The Lion of St. Mark [*Il leone di San Marco*] aka *The Marauder*

Liber Film (Italy); Totalscope/Eastmancolor; 106 (90) mins; Producer: Ottavio Poggi; Director: Luigi Capuano ✟✟✟✟

If only we had scores in motion pictures these days to equal Carlo Rustichelli's fabulous music in Luigi Capuano's definitive "pirates invade Venice" actioner. Reminiscent of a classical overture by an Old Master, the noted Italian composer's soundtrack enhances, lulls, delights and pulverizes at each turn of the sprocket hole; his leitmotif in the romantic interludes between Gordon Scott and Gianna Maria Canale is a sublime piece of mood music in any cinemagoer's book, a form of cinematic art that, by and large, has faded from 21st-century filmmaking. But Rustichelli isn't the only reason to catch this superior medieval swashbuckler. Capuano's forceful, full-on direction ensures that there's more than enough furious swordplay on hand to satisfy all fight addicts, taking you right into the midst of the slashing, ringing action. Scott is bang on form, the ensemble cast give great value for money and the whole richly embroidered tapestry comes dressed up in ace cinematographer Alvaro Mancori's rich, sumptuous color wash. Yes, *The Lion of St. Mark*, much like the same team's *The Executioner of Venice*, is a feast for the eyes *and* the ears.

In Venice, 1620 Doge Feodor Chaliapin, Jr. is holding an engagement party—son Gordon Scott (as Manrico) is due to be betrothed to vacuous French noblewoman Franca Bettoia (Isabella); it is hoped that the union will cement relations between Venice and France and act as a calming influence on Scott, more used to soldiering than joining the diplomatic corps and taking on the role of a future ambassador. Into the reception bursts pirate Alberto Farnese (Tiffa) and his gang of cutthroats, including Gianna Maria Canale (Rosanna); the rich are robbed of their jewelry, the pirates make a dash, the Doge's son shows his true metal by carving bloody tramlines on a captive and Captain Giulio Maculani's mercenary force goes in hot pursuit. But Scott is not to be outdone. He wants the Venetians to put an end to the ongoing pirate scourge and claim the glory, not allowing foreign mercenaries who are in it for the money to do so. Reinventing himself as The Lion of St. Mark, a masked, Zorro-type figure that is fully able to swash a very fine buckle, Scott soon proves himself to be a thorough nuisance to Farnese and his corsairs. In only a matter of days, this fearless, charismatic champion takes on the mantle of the people's idol, a fast-growing legend that has already managed to put Venice's enemies to flight where others have failed. A lively opening 25 minutes occurs then. Capuano has treated us to a lavish ballroom feast, a pirate attack and Scott now transformed into a daring Venetian masked crusader. Where do we go from here? In a night sortie on a pirate boat, Scott comes face to face with Canale ("A daughter of pirates."), who flees and is then captured by Maculani; Scott buys her off and, out of the blue, it's fireworks; the two fall in lust, Bettoia forgotten as Scott tries to convince Canale to mend her ways and marry him, freeing her in the process. However, Bettoia isn't to be left out in the cold. Rik Battaglia (Giandolo), Scott's bosom buddy, fancies his chances with her ("You don't love him and he doesn't love you."), while Scott's canny uncle, Giulio Marchetti, thought the Scott/Bettoia liaison doomed anyway. Cross and double-cross follows. Canale lures Farnese to a masked gala ball (The Feast of the Savior; Rustichelli's music is absolutely exquisite in these sequences), Bettoia spots her and Scott kissing, and the piratical tigress pretends to be abducted so that she can be seen in a more favorable light by those present. In a rendezvous with Scott the day after, the fledgling lovers are taken by surprise when Farnese, second-in-command Franco Fantasia (as Vipera, unrecognizable under heavy pirate make-up) and their men turn up. Battaglia, dressed as The Lion of St. Mark (he's one of the few to be in on Scott's secret), and his compatriots leap off a wall and a terrific rapier versus cutlass fight ensues; Farnese escapes while Canale feels betrayed: "I won't remain at your side," she storms at Scott, flouncing off to Farnese's castle and promising to marry the wine-guzzling ruffian instead.

An Italian photobusta for *The Magnificent Adventurer*

The final 20 minutes centers on the raid on Farnese's hilltop bastion, Capuano utilizing stock footage from his 1962 pirate outing, *Tiger of the Seven Seas*. Maculani's two galleons open fire as Scott, while Battaglia and local insurgents rush the fortress walls, Canale realizing her grave error in promising the pirate chief wedlock by blowing up the castle gates. Mercenaries and rebels stream in, Farnese surrenders, but what about Canale, who is sentenced to be exiled. Crafty Marchetti, who joined in the battle for the sheer fun of it, adopts her as his daughter—legally, she's now entitled to get hitched to Scott, leaving the way open for Battaglia to make his move on Bettoia. The film ends with the newlyweds on board a gondola, sailing off in bright sunshine to the sound of Rustichelli's magnificent score and leaving you with the one thought: Boy, this must have looked really something screened in a large, dark auditorium all those years ago.

The Magnificent Adventurer [*Il magnifico avventuriero*] aka ***The Burning of Rome***
Panda Societa/Les Films du Centaure/Hispamer (Italy/France/Spain); Technicolor; 93 mins; Producers: Luigi Carpentieri, Ermanno Donati; Director: Riccardo Freda ††††

Fortunately, a restored color copy of Riccardo Freda's 16th-century joyride that encompasses political intrigue, romance, skulduggery, comedy, spectacle, history and action has recently surfaced on a German triple-DVD set entitled *Die Grosse Mantel und Degen* (*The Big Cloak and Dagger*), although the film's credits remain in monochrome; previously, faded black-and-white issues taken from 16mm prints were all that you could get (with difficulty). Featuring an acrobatic Brett Halsey on full throttle, Freda's foot also stays firmly on the gas pedal in an energetic cloak-and-dagger offering, directing without pausing for a second, the narrative driven admirably by Francesco De Masi's powerful score and awash in Julio Ortas and Raffaele Masciocchi's rich Technicolor schemes.

Halsey's character (Benvenuto Cellini) is just that little bit different from your run-of-the-mill hero. He's a dishonest Florentine ne'er-do-well, a gifted artist/goldsmith not averse to stealing his rivals' gold (which he does in the opening minutes), forging counterfeit coins and seducing any woman who crosses his path. Branded a thief during an amusing ceremony in which the king takes his first-ever bath, his studio subsequently burned to the ground by jealous competitors, Halsey is taken on as Felix Dafauce's (Count Fragipani) bodyguard due to his skill with the sword; he quickly makes a play for Dafauce's aloof, unhappy wife Francoise Fabian (Lucrezia), romances volatile tavern wench Claudia Mori (Piera) and is caught forging gold coinage. Escaping the gallows on the pontiff's pardon, the reprobate ends up Captain of the Vatican guard and a key player in a battle over Rome's riches. The mercenaries of King Charles V are congregating outside the city, waiting to pounce on Pope Clemente VII's (Bernard Blier) minions, and the primate needs all the help he can get. Halsey's brother, Giampiero Littera (Francesco), tags along for the ride while his sibling organizes the city's defense lines and militia. There's a spectacular siege on the hour, cannonades filling the air with smoke (Naples' Nuovo Castle was used in some shots); the jubilant enemy breaks through into Rome and sacks the city, plundering, crucifying and raping, Halsey leaving the turmoil behind through a hidden gallery with orders to deliver a peace message from the Pope to the king in his residence at Subiaco. The monarch (Diego Michelotti) gave strict instructions to his troops that no atrocities were to take place on occupying Rome and has had a change of heart, wanting to withdraw his forces. Dafauce proves to be a colluder and is dispatched, along with devious constable José Nito, but cold-as-ice Fabian, now a widow, still won't give in to Halsey's roguish charms. The knave decides instead on earthy, buxom Mori as his next partner and is last seen working on his new masterpiece, a life-sized bronze model of Perseus holding the head of Medusa.

Halsey, as was shown in *The Bridge of Sighs* (*The Avenger of Venice*), seemed quite at home in the peplum *cappa e spada* medium, more so than in many of his American B-features. Here, he jumps over tables, eyes up the women, swishes his blade and finds himself entangled in one dangerous scrape after another, all performed with a swagger and a disarming smile. He carries a gratifying actioner on his shoulders in one of famed Italian director Riccardo Freda's rarest, lesser-seen pieces of work.

Revenge of the Black Knight [*La cieca di Sorrento*] aka ***Mission of Revenge***; ***The Black Cavalier***; ***Vendetta at Sorrento***
CI.AS (Italy); Techniscope/Technicolor/B&W; 102 (93) mins; Producer: Mario Damiani; Director: Nick Nostro ††††

In 1848, a noblewoman is murdered and, because of the incident, her daughter Isabella di Rionero, through shock and trauma, goes blind. Fifteen years later, George, the son of the doctor wrongly executed for the murder, meets Isabella, now in the charge and tutorship of Amedeo Aniante, the tyrannical ruler of Sorrento, handing out bribes to keep local servile dignitaries in his pocket. The orphan's guardian is haughty Gloriana,

An Italian poster for *Revenge of the Black Knight*

in this instance, that remains an impossibility. Among the vast number of gray-market DVDs I have reviewed in compiling this book, *Revenge of the Black Knight* stands out as the ropiest digital transfer of the lot. No color—black-and-white or brown-and-white (granted, in some areas of Europe, it was released in a monochrome print) replaces Colli's sumptuous tones (seen to their full advantage in online posters and stills), Savina's exceptional music sounding like a wonky record (his score is so highly thought of on the Continent that it's available as a limited soundtrack recording). At least the widescreen ratio remains more or less intact. I won't repeat what I've written in the Foreword about the sad condition of this film, just glad I've had the golden opportunity to catch one of pepla's rarest offerings, whatever lamentable state it is in. Look through the sea of fog and the irritating blemishes that have reduced Nostro's actioner to an almost unviewable fog and you will appreciate, with difficulty, what this movie once looked like

hopelessly in love with Amedeo, but the cruel despot is infatuated with the blind heiress and plans to marry her. However, George, a distinguished doctor, decides to treat Isabella and restore her sight; by doing so, she'll be able to reveal Amedeo as her mother's real killer. Isabella undergoes surgery, wearing a silk bandage to protect her sensitive eyes; on realizing his predicament, the dictator savagely beats Gloriana, who assisted in the operation and resolves to eliminate the doctor, including an attempt to burn him alive, unaware that his adversary heads a gang of masked vigilantes opposed to his iron-fisted regime, the rebels carrying out a number of surprise raids. George falls for Isabella, but during a masked ball, Amedeo announces his forthcoming nuptials to the girl. Gloriana, seething with jealousy, confronts her lover and is done away with, George and a compatriot captured and incarcerated in a dungeon. Breaking out, they overcome the guards, release prisoners, get caught up in a blazing shoot-out and interrupt Amedeo's forced marriage. Amedeo grabs Isabella and rides off to his castle, followed by George. In a furious duel, the steel tip of the doctor's rapier finds Amedeo's evil heart; dead, he topples from the parapets. Isabella suddenly regains her sight and embraces George, her savior.

Previously filmed in 1916, 1934 and 1953, Francesco Mastriani's popular novel, *The Blind Woman of Sorrento*, published in 1852, was given the big screen treatment by Nick Nostro, a Gothic romantic mystery on Hitchcockian lines featuring betrayals, swordfights, secret rooms, the Monte Gelato falls, Lazio's grand Orsini-Odescalchi fortress and a full throttle final 25 minutes when Anthony Steffen (George) and his buddy Pierre Vivaldi (father of nine children; his pregnant wife smuggles in a pistol) bust out of prison and engage in a shooting match with guards, Nostro climaxing the whole affair with an epic five-minute duel between Steffen and the villain of the piece, Alberto Farnese. Carlo Savina also pulled out all the stops to present a wondrous score packed with melodious leitmotifs, while Diana Martin shone as the blind blonde, in stark contrast to brunette Leontine May's ranting guardian.

It would be nice to mention Franco Delli Colli's cinematography (he was photographer Tonino Delli Colli's cousin) but,

A U.S. poster for *Sandokan the Great* (aka *Sandokan, the Tiger of Mompracem*)

54 years ago. In all probability, it will never again be seen in its original pristine format.

Sandokan, the Tiger of Mompracem [*Sandokan, la tigre di Mompracem*] aka *Sandokan the Great*

Filmes S.A./Comptoir Francais CFFP/Ocean Films (Italy/France/Spain); Techniscope/Technicolor; 105 (95) mins; Producer: Thomas Sagone; Director: Umberto Lenzi ††

Filmed in Singapore, the first of two *Sandokan* outings for Steve Reeves (two others appeared in 1964 starring Ray Danton and Guy Madison) is a lazily paced trot through picturesque jungle/coastal locations, containing very little of any substance. Taking place in the period when British colonialism governed in Malaysia, the flimsy yarn has Reeves, playing the turban-headed rebel leader, pinching British general Leo Anchóriz's (Lord Hillock) niece, Genevieve Grad (Mary Ann), from a fortress and holding her hostage as a trade-off for his imprisoned father. En route to Mompracem, Grad falls in love with her captor, Reeves' father dies, nullifying the whole exercise, there's an informer in the camp, a tame elephant stampede forces the group to climb dwarfish trees and bad guy Anchóriz is eventually overthrown in a roller-coaster six-minute finale that atones for the sluggishness that has preceded it. The smoke-filled gunfights seem out of context in a peplum movie (there *are* swords and spears, wielded by headhunters, but never used) and Reeves only bares his magnificent torso once.

Acting honors go to Andrea Bosic, playing Reeves' brother-in-law Yanez, speaking his clipped lines in a phony dubbed English accent; the main man himself is stiff, putting negligible effort into his part, while Grad never was one of the genre's more arresting female leads, pretty enough but not gorgeous. Halfway through the leaden trek to their destination at Mompracem, our hero wrestles with a stuffed tiger, putting one in mind of an old Johnny Weissmuller *Jungle Jim* potboiler from the '50s, as does the repeated use of wildlife stock footage and a performing chimp. The trite dialogue is also a distraction.

Grad, gushingly: "I love you, Sandokan."

Reeves, woodenly: "I love you too."

Appearing near the end of Reeves' 14-movie stint in pepla, *Sandokan, the Tiger of Mompracem* is slightly depressing fare, especially when compared to the two classics that came before, *The Son of Spartacus* and *The Legend of Aeneas*. Those were essential Reeves; this one isn't. Take him out of the picture (literally) and you are left with a colonial actioner that steadfastly demurs at lighting the fuse of excitement.

The Sign of the Coyote [*Il segno del coyote*] aka *The Avenger of California*

Produzioni Europee Associati/Hispamer/Copercines (Italy/Spain); Totalscope/Eastmancolor; 85 mins; Producers: Aldo U. Passalacqua, Norberto Solino; Director: Mario Caiano †††

El Coyote was a Zorro-type Spanish fictional character created by José Mallorquí; between 1944 and 1953, 192 pulp novelettes were written featuring the masked crusader fighting for the rights of the downtrodden Hispanic population in Old California, circa 1846-1875. Mario Caiano (he wrote the screenplay with Mallorquí) was too experienced a director with this kind of by-now familiar material to allow it to lapse into tedium, even though leading man Fernando Casanova, playing the black-clad avenger El Coyote and his simpleton alter-ego César de Echague was, in some scenes, as stiff as a plank. The storyline had new

An Italian poster for *The Sign of the Coyote*

regional administrator Mario Feliciani (Parker), in cahoots with corrupt partners Arturo Dominici and Giuseppe Fortis, trampling their well-heeled boots over the local citizens in a land-grab operation of epic proportions, following the annexe of the State of California into Union hands. Maria Luz Galicia (Leonora) was the lady of the manor, snubbing her pretty nose at her fiancé's meek and mild ways, attracted instead to the chivalrous hero in black on his magnificent ebony steed who so happened to be that selfsame fiancé, while Giulia Rubini (Beatrice) and Nadia Marlowa (Lupita) completed a trio of highly vivacious female leads. Shoot-outs, bad guys led by wolf-faced Piero Lulli (Lenny), much skulking around in corridors by El Coyote, a bust-out from jail, a hidden cave, Marlowa impersonating the avenger to lead his pursuers off the scent and all three miscreants getting their just desserts (Casanova and Feliciani duel furiously in the climax, rapiers replacing pistols) result in an entertaining 85 minutes shot in bright color by Aldo Greci, Francesco De Masi's Spaghetti Western score trumpeting merrily along in the background. Yes, as the curtain comes down, Casanova removes his mask before a startled Galicia who smothers him in kisses, the pair framed in a window as the camera draws back, a nice storybook touch in homage to Mallorquí's novels.

And Spaghetti Western is the operative term here: *The Sign of the Coyote* is a classic example of the hybrid peplum Western, the two genres crossing swords (and pistols) as early as 1963

A German poster for *The Terror of the Red Capes*

before eventually morphing into the Spaghetti horse opera per se, from 1964 onwards. It sometimes makes for an uneasy mix, swashbuckling swords replaced by gun and holster, and maybe it's not for purists. However, Caiano's opus still comes under the peplum banner, an essential ingredient if a somewhat misaligned one. Note—it must have been bitterly cold on Spanish location, judging by the amount of vapor issuing from the cast, even in the interior shots.

The Terror of the Red Capes [*Il terrore dei mantelli rossi*] aka Knights of Terror

Pamec Cinematografica/Radius/Hispamer (Italy/France/Spain); Iscoscope/Eastmancolor; 86 mins; Producer: Francesco Paolo; Director: Mario Costa ††††

One thing distinguishes Mario Costa's peplum swashbuckler from so many others of its ilk—cinematographer Julio Ortas' deep inky color hues, prevalent in exterior shots of old buildings, castles and woodland, the interior furnishings, the night scenes and the rakish costumes. Luckily, VHS prints in widescreen haven't dimmed his work (the film isn't available on DVD as at 2015), which adds immeasurably to a frisky tale, set in the Duchy of Pretsch, Germany in 1600, concerning a band of red-caped hoodlums wearing pug-ugly latex masks spreading alarm and death throughout the countryside by tossing experimental explosives here, there and everywhere. Local duke Alf Marholm, under pressure from the irate citizens, has little choice but to hire arrogant captain Yves Vincent (Mirko) to uncover the identities of this murderous gang (named the Red Knights); Vincent agrees on condition that the duke's daughter Cristina (Scilla Gabel at her loveliest) marries him. Naturally, Vincent's mistress, wench Carla Calò, fumes at this forced liaison, and so does Gabel; she's taken with Tony Russel (Paolo), handsome leader of *another* bunch of red-robed masked riders (only black eye masks this time), who are attempting to put an end to the Red Knights' reign of terror.

There's an awful lot of tearing around on horseback in this movie, swords waving in the air, not a bad thing as the striking locales (filmed in Spain) are pleasing on the eye, as are the baroque castles and rustic buildings (Lazio's Collalto Sabino Castle was used for principal location shooting). Carlo Rustichelli's score also hammers wonderfully in the background, driving the action to perfection. Caught after gaining entrance into the castle via a concealed corridor, Russel is clapped in irons, lashed and beaten but rescued by his compatriots after a fierce struggle. The commoners then swarm en masse over the duke's fortress, wielding wooden implements (mainly pitchforks), in protest at their ruler's dithering stance; Jacques Dacqmine (Vladimir), Vincent's ambitious lieutenant, takes the opportunity during the mayhem to shoot an arrow into Marholm's back. However, assassins knife Dacqmine; Vincent is too aware that he knows more than he should about his own shady agenda and won't take any chances. The conclusion takes place in the Red Knights' underground vaulted domain, an artfully lit set straight out of the pages of Edgar Allan Poe—in fact, these Gothic surroundings combined with the Red Knights' hideous rubber masks makes you think that the picture has changed course and taken on the mantle of a glossy Hollywood '50s horror feature. Vincent emerges as the ringleader of the Red Knights, engineering the whole escapade to become duke of the kingdom and marry Gabel into the bargain. In a furious exchange between Vincent's mob and Russel's men, the caped menaces are vanquished, their leader dying from a rapier thrust after he's sunk his blade into poor spurned Calò. Russel is last seen on the castle's battlements with new bride Gabel, waving to the villagers who he now commands.

Unfortunately, the German video copy doesn't come with subtitles, but that doesn't really detract from a rollicking slice of swaggering derring-do enriched, as stated, by Ortas' sterling photography. This is a rarity that's well worth tracking down.

The Tyrant of Castile [*Sfida al re di Castiglia*] aka Kingdom of Violence; The Battle of Toledo

Alexandra Produzioni/Procinsa (Italy/Spain); Techniscope/Technicolor; 100 mins; Producer: Virgilio De Blasi; Director: Ferdinando Baldi ††††

Partly hinged on fact, Baldi's *El Cid*-type extravaganza is handsomely photographed by Francisco Marin; the director elected to shoot location work at a selection of real Spanish castles, not stage sets, endowing the production with an air of medieval authenticity. The multi-turreted Alcazar of Segovia and Belmonte Castle were the two main sites chosen. Set in Toledo in 1360, Mark Damon stars as Pietro the Cruel, the King of Castile, good-looking but as mad as a hatter, at loggerheads with half-brother Paolo Gozlino, playing Enrique di Trastamara, the King of Aragon. Who should be overall dynastic autocrat? Each desires the other's throne, and each provokes the other. When right-hand man Carlos Estrada staggers into Damon's court,

A Spanish lobby card for *The Tyrant of Castile*

1964

The Bridge of Sighs [*Il ponte dei sospiri*] aka *The Avenger of Venice*

Panda Societa/Estela Films (Italy/Spain); Totalscope/Technicolor; 91 mins; Producer: Piero Donati; Directors: Carlo Campogalliani, Piero Pierotti ✝✝✝✝

There's enough skulduggery going on in Carlo Campogalliani and Piero Pierotti's plush 16th-century Venetian falsely charged-jailed-escape-revenge romp to make the head spin. As Doge (Duke) of Venice, Jean Murat's (Candiano) proposed new rules for the city are bitterly resented by bad guys José Marco Davo (Bembo Altieri, the Grand Inquisitor), henchmen Paolo Gozlino and Andrea Bosic and Captain Conrado San Martin. Murat's son, Brett Halsey (Rolando), is accused of plotting against the Republic (forged documents are produced in evidence) and framed for the subsequent murder of Bosic, Gianna Maria Canale (Imperia), his courtesan ex-lover, testifying in court to discredit him, lying her head off if she wants her daughter Lilly Darelli (Bianca)

bloody and seared with a "T" (the branding of Estrada and two soldiers is one of several graphic torture sequences in the movie), the enraged king orders a night sortie on his brother's castle, slashing *his* right-hand man across the face with a spiked metal glove. Then Anna Maria Surdo (Bianca di Borbone) arrives at Damon's fortress, an arranged marriage; discovering that en route his betrothed fell in love with another of his bastard brothers, she's slapped across the face and banished. Damon already has a young wife whom he wed in secret, Maria Teresa Orsini (Maria), also in exile (he carries out regular clandestine trysts with the lass), and dallies with the more mature Rada Rassimov (Anna), a deposed queen. Quite the ladies' man, in spite of his cruel streak!

The scenario develops into a war of attrition between the two mentally unbalanced brothers, Baldi's camera sweeping over the arid Spanish terrain and taking in those sun-blasted fortresses as showy knights on horseback scurry from one confrontation to the next, marvelous blood and thunder stuff, assisted by a pounding drumbeat Carlo Savina score. Orsini is murdered by an assassin, a crossbow bolt embedded in her back, and in the 77th minute, the director orchestrates a pulse-racing battle, Damon and Gozlino's knights clashing head-on, a rain of arrows from both camps causing widespread death and destruction. Under a flag of truce, the two brothers meet and cross swords, Damon stabbed to death. If that wasn't enough, Gozlino's horsemen use his body for target practice, over 20 lances pitched into his corpse. Not to be outdone, an archer puts paid to Gozlino, therefore ending, for the time being, hostilities, with the two provinces entering into an uneasy moratorium. It's Damon who carries the day, demonstrating vulnerability under his cloak of near-insanity, a tidy performance in a flashy spectacle urgently in need of a digital release containing subtitles; current issues are in Italian only.

The Italian DVD cover for *The Bride of Sighs*

to live a longer life. Murat, indicted for having collaborated on the trumped-up conspiracy, is flung into a torture chamber and blinded by a spiked iron mask wedged over his face (Mario Bava's *Black Sunday*, anyone?). With the elderly Doge and his son out of the picture, Davo can turn his slimy attentions in the direction of Canale's daughter, even if he's old enough to be her grandfather, while ordering magistrate José Nieto to sanction the marriage of his daughter, Vira Silenti (Leonora), to San Martin. She's engaged to Halsey, but if Nieto gives in to the torturer's demands, he could become the next Doge of Venice, serving as a puppet to Davo's crooked ambitions.

Beautifully shot mostly at night among Venice's waterways and alleys by Rafael Pacheco and Luciano Trasatti, noted Italian directors Campogalliani and Pierotti expertly manipulate light and shadows cast by the Venetian Gothic architecture to create a sense of mood and danger at every dark corner; *The Bridge of Sighs* looks wonderful, blessed with a semi-classical score by Angelo Francesco Lavagnino, borrowed from the old masters. Thirty-one-year-old Halsey, veteran of countless Hollywood B-programmers, plays the hero with dash, getting into all manner of scrapes; tunneling out of his prison cell, he emerges into thief Burt Nelson's cell and the two form a close bond, escaping the gallows and enlisting the aid of Nelson's flighty wife to lure Davo out of his city territory on a gondola where Halsey, in a moment of fury (his father expires in agony in Nelson's homestead), bashes him into oblivion. The pair return to Venice and, in a convoluted showdown, Nelson throttles Gozlino, Canale is stabbed in the back by San Martin after telling Nieto the truth about the whole scandalous affair, after which San Martin engages in a thrilling five-minute duel with Halsey amid the striking stonework of the deserted Piazza San Marco, succumbing to the business end of his rapier thrust on the senate steps. "Long live the newlyweds," roar the approving crowd as Halsey poses on the balcony with Silenti and beaming Nieto, the newly appointed Doge of Venice.

The Bridge of Sighs turned out to be Carlo Campogalliani and Gianna Maria Canale's personal swansong; both director and actress left the film industry after completion of the picture (Canale starred in 27 peplum movies, going back to 1946's *The Black Eagle*, where she first met her future husband, Riccardo Freda). This is a well-crafted, enjoyable costume swashbuckler, available in 2015 in widescreen with subtitles from one or two independent outlets, and in great condition.

Genoveffa of Brabant [*Genoveffa di Brabante*] aka *The Revenge of the Crusader*

Imprecine/Hispamer (Italy/Spain); Techniscope/Eastmancolor; 89 mins; Producers: José Luis Monter, Riccardo Freda (both uncredited); Director: José Luis Monter ✟✟✟✟✟

Knight Alberto Lupo (Count Sigfrido di Treviri) wades into a bandit raid on a shipment of gold coin, is wounded and carried to Andrea Bosic's castle, where Maria José Alfonso (Genoveffa, or Genevieve) tends to his injuries. The two fall in love and

An Italian photobusta for *Genoveffa of Brabant*: Alberto Lupo protects Maria José Alfonso from madman Stephen Forsyth.

marry, returning to Treviri in wedded bliss. When Lupo is unexpectedly instructed by his king to join the Crusades in the Holy Lands, he places his new bride in the hands of second-in-command Stephen Forsyth (Golo) for safekeeping, a big mistake. Forsyth is a psychopathic sadist suppressing deep homosexual leanings, the very last person you would want protecting a fragile young bride constantly pacing the battlements, wondering whether she'll ever see her husband alive again. What's more, he's been infatuated with her for years, so as soon as Lupo disappears on the horizon, Alfonso falls prey to Forsyth's twisted morals, threatened with death of the horrible kind if she doesn't give in to his depraved yearnings.

Sharp-featured Forsyth lays on the wickedness with stark raving relish, one of the genre's vilest of all villains: piercing blue eyes glinting insanely, his slight frame shakes in rage as he punishes anyone who doesn't share his distorted views. The castle's coffers are empty of coinage, therefore tribute must be exacted from the peasants, whatever the cost. The first noble to storm out of one of his heated conferences winds up stabbed, his body thrown over the battlements; another is chained to a plank and beaten. Creeping into Alfonso's boudoir, Forsyth tries to assault her; when a servant intervenes, the unhinged noble smashes an axe into the man's face, dumps his blood-soaked corpse on the bed, summons the other servants and accuses the hysterically sobbing woman (now pregnant) of adultery, flinging her into a cell where she witnesses a screaming female flogged without pity (no wonder Mario Bava cast the actor as a deranged killer in his 1970 slasher flick *Hatchet for the Honeymoon*). Alfonso's also given a dagger to kill herself. Can this perverted monster do any more harm? Yes. Two men are told to take Alfonso and her baby into the woods and murder the pair. As one man brings his blade down toward the wriggling infant, the other, stricken with horror, stays his hand and kills him. Alfonso, child clasped to her breast, wanders off, discovers a cave, home to a friendly deer, and lives there for four long years. Meanwhile, Lupo and his crusaders, captured by Muslims, break out of a stockade, the knight eventually working his way back to the castle where

Guy Madison confronts his childhood sweetheart Lisa Gastoni in this Italian photobusta from *The Masked Avenger*.

The Masked Avenger [*Il vendicatore mascherato*]

Lux-Ultra Film/Sicilia (Italy/France); Eastmancolor; 93 mins; Producer: Danilo Marciani; Director: Pino Mercanti ††††

At the age of 42, Guy Madison (as Massimo) was perhaps a wee bit long in the tooth to play the dashing young hero that he portrayed here, overthrowing Doge Gastone Moschin's despotic rule in Renaissance Venice, 1542. In Pino Mercanti's run-of-the-mill costumer, everyone at some stage in the proceedings seems to be either wearing a black cloak, a red hood or a black mask, or all three, so it comes as something of a surprise to note that Madison's light blue cloak and mask isn't all that prepossessing; he only dresses up in the garb once anyway.

Madison's childhood sweetheart Lisa Gastoni (Elena), whom he hoped to marry, has wedded loathsome Moschin, while he's been absent fighting the Turks. In harness with reptilian deputy Jean Claudio, Moschin is governing with an iron fist, the locals simmering with hatred, all set to revolt. Gastoni sets eyes on Madison at a lavish reception and wants him back; Madison sets eyes on blonde Ingrid Schoeller (Katarina) and decides he'd rather have her. Claudio, who fancies Schoeller himself as a wife in waiting, sees the two together and boils over in rage, infiltrating the outlaws' clandestine meetings and flushing out Madison's buddy Vanni Materassi; he's captured, imprisoned, tortured and garroted. Madison, initially against the idea of a rebellion, now shakes off his indifference and becomes the conspirators' leader but is caught and flung into a cell. Schoeller visits him with a dagger concealed in a book; Madison makes good his escape over the rooftops, chased by soldiers, just as his scaffold is being erected and he joins in a mass skirmish, leading to the collapse of a bridge into a canal and the death of Claudio, who also tumbles into the canal, and the arrest of disgraced Moschin. As for those two lovely women in Madison's life; with Gastoni bestowing her reluctant blessing, he walks off with Schoeller, leaving his ex-girlfriend to reflect on what might have been. A pleasant-enough undemanding swashbuckler, Madison strolls through the proceedings without ruffling a hair on his well-groomed head, available (in 2015) in an unblemished Italian print lacking English subtitles.

Forsyth, convinced that Lupo is dead, has taken on the role of commander-in-chief. When Lupo learns of the true facts behind his wife's disappearance, we know that Forsyth's game is up; he's run through by Lupo following a bout of exciting swordplay (what a pity, though, that the lunatic didn't meet a more fitting, violent death), the count eventually reunited with wife and son. As Carlo Rustichelli's lovely score murmurs in the background, Lupo, Alfonso and their lad, all perched on one horse, ride toward that magnificent castle and home, a quite moving climax.

José Luis Monter worked with Riccardo Freda on *Romeo and Juliet* (1964) as assistant director, helping out on a number of other films yet never really making his mark; Freda, notorious for walking off set during mid-production, had a major hand in writing both story and script (based on a popular European legend), also producing alongside Monter (neither receive a credit, although the movie has "made by Riccardo Freda" on the titles). The result is a "Knights of Old" saga containing touches of pure Italian X-rated horror within its stylish visual framework, yet at the same time possessing a strange ethereal quality, a medieval tragedy rooted in barbaric realism (it was originally filmed in 1947, Primo Zeglio directing). Stelvio Massi and Julio Ortas' cinematography is out of this world, every color tone painted in pastel shades; not to be outdone, composer Rustichelli contributes a beautifully sweet score that underlines the movie's tragic elements. Location shooting was carried out at Manzanares el Real Castle near Madrid, a formidable citadel now a major tourist attraction in the area, imbuing the picture with a real sense of "time and place" period atmosphere. Without doubt, this was Spanish director Monter's finest hour (his one and only peplum) and an important piece of the jigsaw puzzle that represented Freda's varied career in cinema. Pristine prints in Italian with Greek subtitles are rare but can be found at some specialist outlets. Many obscure peplum features come under the heading of "little-known classic." *Genoveffa of Brabant* is one such film.

100 Horsemen [*I cento cavalieri*] aka *Son of El Cid*

Domiziana Int./Procusa/Intl. Germania Film (Italy/Spain/West Germany); Techniscope/Technicolor; 115 (85) mins; Producer: Eduardo de la Fuente; Director: Vittorio Cottafavi ††

It's very hard to be over-critical of Cottafavi's Spanish peasants in defiance of the Moors saga set around 1000 AD. The location shooting is superb, filmed at Pedraza's medieval village, Segovia, the huge Spanish fortress at La Mota and the mountainous, chasm-riven hinterland near Madrid, all highlighted in sharp relief by cinematographer Francisco Marin. Cottafavi directs fluidly and with purpose, the production design faultless, using real-life castles instead of stage sets. But whatever convinced all concerned to go for the half-humorous,

An Italian poster for *100 Horsemen*

A French poster for *The Pirates of Malaysis*

tongue-in-cheek approach? Six scriptwriters were involved in turning what on paper was a medium-budget variation of *El Cid* into a Spaghetti Western-type frolic. Even Antonio Pérez Olea's score is of the kind heard in the countless Italian Westerns that followed the death of pepla in 1966/1967, totally out of context in this particular scenario; the film needed a thunderous Carlo Rustichelli or Francesco De Masi soundtrack to add bite and impetus. *100 Horsemen*'s often inane approach, the cast overacting in madcap fashion both vocally and in excitable hand gestures, torpedoes what could have been a really great action motion picture, reducing it to the level of an 11th-century farce.

Bookended by a garrulous artist painting a fresco of the events about to unfold (and addressing the audience), the film opens with Arab chief Wolfgang Preiss (Abengalbon), son Manuel Gallardo (Halaf) and their blue-robed regiments marching into Hans Nielsen's village, breaking a peace treaty and thereby forcing the peasants to retreat into the mountains to form a popular army with the purpose of bringing about the downfall of the troublesome occupiers. Mark Damon (Don Fernando Herrera y Mecendez) and Antonella Lualdi (Sancha) play the squabbling Romeo/Juliet lovers, schooling their citizens in the arts of tactical warfare (giant pitchforks appear to be their only weapons), along with a group of streetwise kids, white-robed monks bossed by ex-warrior Gastone Moschin, Damon's wily father Arnoldo Foà and comical dwarf lookout Salvatore Furnari. Against the grain, Cottafavi chucks in two painful-to-watch torture sequences featuring a well, multiple hangings and a couple of stirring battle sequences, the last presented in a monochrome wash to give the action a timely, much-needed dose of grit. But the ridiculous scene in which a nobleman pontificates on waging future wars with one giant soldier, only for the cumbersome armored figure to fall flat on its back, sums up the overall jovial mood, as does rightful head of the community Damon signaling "Fine" on his fingers as the film closes. Thoroughly disheartening and, in some ways, depressing—an invigorating Middle Ages swashbuckler was in here somewhere, buried under that oddball silly-one-minute/profound-the-next mix. A classic case of what might have been …

The Pirates of Malaysia [*I pirati della Malesia*] aka ***Sandokan, the Pirate of Malaysia***; ***The Pirates of the Seven Seas***

Euro Intl. Films/Sirius/Lacy Intl. (Italy/Spain/France/West Germany); Techniscope/Technicolor; 110 (90) mins; Producer: Solly V. Bianco; Director: Umberto Lenzi ††††

Steve Reeves bowed out of pepla cinema on a high note in a superior follow-up to *Sandokan, the Tiger of Mompracem*, Umberto Lenzi's camerawork much more fluid, the tropical Singapore scenery bathed in Angelo Lotti's lush colors. Reeves was to make only one other picture after this, the Spaghetti Western *A Long Ride From Hell* (1968), before leaving the film industry, beset with injuries sustained in his earlier torch and toga outings (he had turned down the roles of James Bond in 1962's *Dr. No* and the Man With No Name character in 1964's *A Fistful of Dollars*). A Boy's-Own caper revolving around Reeves' quest to set

The hillside fortress of Castello Piccolomini, Balsorano featured frequently in many peplum productions, such as here in *The Rebel of Castelmonte*.

free the ruler of Sarawak, Giuseppe Addobbati (Muda Hassin), held captive in a remote monastery perched on a precipitous cliff, the action is performed in helter-skelter style, beginning with an explosive attack on the British quarters, then moving on to a raucous fight aboard the schooner *Young India*, followed by Reeves posing as a Rajah, gate-crashing his way into blackguard Leo Anchóriz's (Lord Brook) consul buildings (Anchóriz played a different wrong 'un to his character in the first *Sandokan* movie) before being unmasked, arrested, saved from the firing squad by Jacqueline Sassard (Princess Hada); she agrees to give in to Anchóriz's physical needs on condition that the prisoners are not terminated; he's then sent to work in a salt mine. It's here, in the 74th minute, that Mr. Muscles shows us, for about the last time, the rippling torso that promoted him to this kind of thick-ear fodder during a blazing breakout from the labor camp, Reeves manning a Gatling gun mounted on an ore wagon. He has the Malayan revolutionary reuniting with chain-smoking confederate Andrea Bosic (Yanez) and his men and circumnavigating the monastery to find a route to the top to emancipate Addobbati, thus restoring the nobility to Sarawak.

Reeves' concluding peplum feature may be comic book stuff, but it's entertaining and pleasing on the senses, a real popcorn and Coke movie if ever there was one (Giovanni Fusco's score stomps along merrily). Chain-smoker Bosic, sporting pith helmet, supplies the gravitas and a nice line emphasizing dry humor ("I hope the water doesn't put my cigarette out," he grimaces as he wades in to board the *Young India*), and a crocodile almost makes a meal out of Mimmo Palmara (Tremal-Naik), staked in a river. There's a fabulous Malayan rock temple adorned with exotic stone idols, savage tribesmen butcher a bunch of slaves on the run and a heart-thumping episode on a rope spanning a deep ravine ups the excitement level. Anchóriz snarls, rolls his eyes and sneers, and there are uproarious shoot-outs a-plenty. It goes without saying that Addobbati is rescued, Anchóriz falls over a sheer cliff to his doom and Reeves winds up with forever grateful Sassard's lithe brown arms entwined around his neck, climaxing a satisfying colonial frolic and the curtain closer to the ex-Mr. America and Mr. Universe's rewarding time in the sword and sandal arena.

The Rebel of Castelmonte [*Il ribelle di Castelmonte*] aka *Sword of Rebellion*

Industrie Cinetelevisive (Italy); Totalscope/Technicolor; 83 mins; Producer: Luigi Massarini; Director: Vertunnio De Angelis ††

Shot in and around Italy's imposing hilltop citadel of Castello Piccolomini, Balsorano, *The Rebel of Castelmonte* is strictly routine fare, only available in monochrome pan and scan as I write. Gérard Landry stars as daredevil highwayman Marco Degli Ammannati in 17th-century Spain, embarking on a personal vendetta with Duke Ivano Staccioli (Alberto); the reptilian varlet murdered his family, stole his castle, treats the peasants with contempt and arranges a marriage between a protesting Annie Alberti (Bianca) and duplicitous Gino Turini (Count Kurt Von Utrecht) to further his own ends. It goes without saying that Landry has already met Alberti and her equally charming maid, Liana Trouche, in a carriage holdup and has fallen for her, and she for him. In a game of tit for tat, Staccioli offers a reward of 100 gold escudos for Landry's capture; the rebel reciprocates, offering 500 gold escudos for the duke's head. Lying low in the Cave of the Owl, Landry and his followers carry out numerous raids to the sound of Aldo Piga's deafening score, a score that beats you over the head with a sledgehammer, while Staccioli prowls the castle rooms, figuring out ways to get Landry out of his neatly coiffured hair.

Much galloping about through meadows and woods, the planning of tactics in taverns, Staccioli and Turini constantly two-timing each other, swordfights and Alberti bemoaning her fate from the battlements, her big brown eyes brimming with

A Belgian poster for *Sandok, the Maciste of the Jungle*

tears, is formulaic stuff to the extent that, by 1964, fans of swashbucklers could easily tell what was coming next without too much trouble. In one of two climactic clashes, Landry runs Staccioli through, John Kitzmiller, Turini's black servant, is shot and Landry finally fences with the count who has double-crossed both camps, Piga's music rising to new heights of intensity, the loudest score ever to accompany a duel in pepla. Turini expires, Alberti cosies up to Landry, the pair kiss and the curtain comes down on a costumer that is pleasant enough but instantly forgettable. The castle is the star of this particular movie.

Sandok, the Maciste of the Jungle [*Sandok, il Maciste della giungla*] aka *Temple of the White Elephant*

Filmes Rome/Capitole Films (Italy/France); Techniscope/Technicolor; 85 mins; Producer: Solly V. Bianco; Director: Umberto Lenzi †††

Produced around the same time as *Sandokan, the Tiger of Mompracem* and *The Pirates of Malaysia* (both directed by Lenzi), *Sandok, the Maciste of the Jungle* was a so-so colonial jungle outing set in India in which wan-looking hero Sean Flynn (son of Errol) played second fiddle to Mimmo Palmara's exuberant musclebound Sandok. The Sikkim rebels, a religious sect whose devotees are marked by a white elephant tattoo on their bodies, have captured Lieutenant Giacomo Rossi-Stuart (Milliner) and viceroy's daughter Alessandra Panaro (Cynthia) in a ravine ambush. In order to infiltrate their temple, Colonel Andrea Bosic cashiers Flynn (Dick Ramsey) out of the army on a spurious charge of insubordination in full view of his regiment on the parade ground. The idea behind this carefully orchestrated ruse is that any spies present will report back to the sect's masked leader that a disgraced Englishman *could* be in a position to work on their side. Flynn, in native costume, wrestles with a large python and encounters Marie Versini (Princess Dhara) and her fist-happy servant Palmara on his way to the sect's hideout; all three soon find themselves prisoners in a vast red-lit temple, where a blue-robed white elephant is glorified as a deity and prisoners have molten gold tipped over their faces. Rossi-Stuart is found tied up behind a curtain, encircled by blades, while Panaro staggers around in a trance, the new queen of this domain. Can Flynn, Palmara and Versini escape, unmask the sect's leader and save the two captives from a life of misery?

Lenzi keeps the action bubbling by having Flynn balance on a plank over a leopard pit while being lashed, Palmara bending prison bars like rubber and the white elephant smashing down prison walls when Bosic's division attacks the temple. Maharajah Arturo Dominici turns out to be the cult's boss, strangled by Flynn as the insurgents are routed by troops perched on a herd of decoratively attired elephants. Panaro, restored to normal, makes a beeline for Rossi-Stuart and Flynn (once again an officer) decides to woo dusky Versini. A colorful native dance and spasmodic inclusions of wildlife footage contribute to a moderately entertaining time waster, one that Lenzi and company must have drummed up in their sleep; current pan and scan prints in a ragged, faded condition do the film very little justice.

Sandokan Against the Leopard of Sarawak [*Sandokan contro il leopardo di Sarawak*] aka *Throne of Vengeance*; *The Return of Sandokan*

Liber Film/Eichberg Film (Italy/West Germany); Totalscope/Eastmancolor; 88 mins; Producer: Ottavio Poggi; Director: Luigi Capuano ††††

An Italian poster for *Sandokan Against the Leopard of Sarawak*

Although Sandokan as a character carried on in later years, notably in television serials, the peplum *Sandokan* movies stopped right here with, in all honesty, nowhere else to go. Luigi Capuano shot the last of the four adventures back-to-back with *Sandokan to the Rescue* (same cast and technicians), the events having moved on two years. The action commences with an unpalatable tiger hunt that wouldn't get past the cruelty to animals brigade in this day and age; the censor would never allow it. Ray Danton now occupies the throne of Sarawak and is about to announce his wedding to Princess Franca Bettoia (as Samoa; why it's taken him two years to get around to marriage is anyone's guess). In steps fly-in-the-ointment Mario Petri, playing Sir Charles Brooks, the son of the tyrant of the previous film; he's the self-styled Leopard of Sarawak and wants his father's throne back. Bettoia is abducted, her minders brutally shot dead, and taken to Petri's subterranean dominion in the distant Mountains of Kimbaloo; there she's put into a trance by hypnotist Aldo Bufi Landi (Rajani), Petri hoping that in this state, she'll forget all about the Tiger of Malaya and fancy him instead. Danton gets together compulsive smoker Guy Madison (as Yanez, promoted to Rajah of Assam for his unswerving devotion to duty), close friends Alberto Farnese and traitor-turned-ally Franco Fantasia, plus a squadron of men, and heads off toward the mountains to bring his beloved back to Sarawak and eliminate Petri.

Cliffhangers by the dozen enliven Capuano's colorful oriental joyride, with Danton penetrating Petri's domain, emerging

An Italian poster for *Sandokan To The Rescue*

played previously by Andrea Bosic. A simplified storyline has Danton, the son of a dethroned Rajah, involved in an insurgence to regain the sovereign power of Sarawak; 25 years previously, his family, Sarawak nobility, had been murdered but he alone survived, thanks to the quick-thinking of his nurse. Horrible white usurper Mario Petri (Sir Charles Brooks), at present the incumbent, wishes to marry his niece, Franca Bettoia (Princess Samoa), to his son and thus become, by proxy, king of the realm. Rallying together his red-turbaned warriors from Mompracem, the Tiger of Malaya finds himself immersed in one scrape after another before putting a stop to Petri's reign and bagging Bettoia for himself.

In all four *Sandokan* outings, it's not the plot that matters most, but it's how to top one action sequence after the previous one has ended. Luigi Capuano keeps things on a roll by having an elephant crush a prisoner's head; two schooners clashing in combat; Danton saying wryly to Madison after a skirmish, "Why don't you have a cigarette? You deserve it!"; a wildlife hunt; cutlass duels in the palace; an avalanche ambush in a ravine; a marvelous temple housing the giant gold statue of the Goddess Kali; a noisy cannonade on Petri's fortress; Danton and Bettoia saved from incineration by her pet elephant, Jumbo and a fight to the death between Danton and Petri in an underground cavern. Shot against a backdrop of enchanting Malayan jungle backdrops and containing a very apt Oriental-type score from Carlo Rustichelli, *Sandokan To the Rescue* is 91 minutes of harmless (the violence is minimal) family fun that doesn't tax the brain; the vivid color is worth the price of a DVD copy alone.

unscathed from a cave of pythons, leaping into a raging river from a vertical cliff and rescuing Bettoia from Landi's tent (he's killed; she regains her senses). The whole shebang climaxes in a 10-minute gun/saber affray (there's a nasty shot-in-the-face scene), Petri sinking in quicksand after running from his nemesis through a bamboo thicket. Back in Sarawak, ensconced once again on the throne, Danton shows an act of mercy by releasing those who conspired against him and tells his loyal multitudes that the wedding is back on! Full marks to photographer Adalberto "Bitto" Albertini and composer Carlo Rustichelli for expertly bringing this slice of Southern Seas blarney to vivid life.

Sandokan to the Rescue [*Sandokan alla riscossa*] aka *The Revenge of Sandokan*; *Sandokan Fights Back*; *Vengeance of Sandokan*; *Terror of Sandokan*

Liber Film/Eichberg Film (Italy/West Germany); Techniscope/Eastmancolor; 91 mins; Producer: Ottavio Poggi; Director: Luigi Capuano ☨☨☨

You'll need sunglasses to sit through the credits of the third *Sandokan* movie, and for most of the running time—Adalberto "Bitto" Albertini's gorgeous photography is a patchwork of color tones, matching Singapore's verdant landscapes and sun-drenched seascapes. Steve Reeves having hung up his curled-toed Baboosh slippers, Ray Danton took over the role of Sandokan, the self-styled Tiger of Malaya, reuniting with his European partner, cigarette-addicted Guy Madison's Captain Yanez,

A German VHS cover for *The Three Sergeants of Bengal*

A Spanish poster for *Captain from Toledo*

ground prison chamber when the three undisciplined sergeants are caught in a fight, and much wildlife footage is slotted into the narrative to remind us all that we are supposed to be in India during the British colonial years, not Italy.

Three bouts of aggressive action liven matters up considerably—the breakout from the rebels' bolt-hole (Sasso obligingly assembles a machine gun for the benefit of Sambrell's inquisitive natives, then turns the weapon on them with murderous results), the blazing saber/gun attack on Fort Victoria and the final explosive incursion on Fort Madras where Sambrell's followers are lured into a cunning trap and decimated, their chief falling onto an upturned bayonet. Harrison and company receive their deserved pardons from Bosic, and Guida nabs Harrison in an amusing closing wedding ceremony. A fun-packed wet Saturday afternoon romp expertly put together by Umberto Lenzi, available (as at 2015) in clear-as-crystal widescreen *and* dubbed in English.

1965

Captain from Toledo [*L'uomo di Toledo*] aka *The Knights of Seville*; *The Avenger of Seville*

Italcine/Procusa/Petraka Film (Italy/Spain/West Germany); Techniscope/Technicolor; 96 mins; Producers: Franco Palombi, Gabriele Silvestri; Director: Eugenio Martin ✝✝✝

In between spending his leisure hours chewing on chicken drumsticks and wenching, Captain Stephen Forsyth (as Knight Miguel) finds time to hunt down the black-cloaked, iron-gloved assassin who is murdering the Spanish army's leading commanders in 1491, also nipping in the bud an assault by Moors on a Spanish fortification (Belmonte Castle was the setting used for location filming). Never mind the well-worn plot, just relax and take in the sight of a tasty selection of ladies in various states of undress all throwing themselves at Forsyth, Ann Smyrner (Rosita) and Norma Bengell (Myriam) among their number. To the trumpet-based sounds of Angelo Francesco Lavagnino's Spanish score, Forsyth cavorts through the easygoing action with amiable sidekick Enrique Avila (Pancho) in tow, thwarting Moorish warriors wearing grotesque rubber masks and armed with miniature crossbows, getting himself involved in Ivan Desny's (Don Felipe) Christian organization meetings, kissing a succession of busty females, uncovering a plot by Carl Mohner (Don Ramiro) to bring Spain to its knees with the aid of the Arabs, dabbling with experimental pistols and cannon shot and engaging in a pillow fight with another two girls, who have been paid to kill him but end up fancying the good-looker, romping on the bed with wide grins on their faces.

It's an entertaining cloak-and-dagger swashbuckler that doesn't tax the brain or go out of its way to press the excitement button, obviously shot on a low budget judging by the two battle scenes which feature a cast of a few dozen, not hundreds or thousands. Bad guy Mohner is blown sky-high when he stands too close to an exploding wagon, Forsyth and Smyrner ending up in a smooching session, although with his track record, she won't be the last of his conquests. Available pristine DVD copies are in German only and lack subtitles.

The Three Sergeants of Bengal [*I tre sergenti del Bengala*] aka *Adventures of the Bengal Lancers*

Olimpic Pic S.A. (Italy/Spain); Techniscope/Technicolor; 92 mins; Producer: Solly V. Bianco; Director: Umberto Lenzi ✝✝✝✝

Faced with up to a year in prison on charges of drunken disorderly behavior, Sergeants Richard Harrison (Frankie Ross), Ugo Sasso (Burt Wallace) and Nazzareno Zamperia (John Foster) are handed an olive branch by Andrea Bosic (Colonel McDonald). Go across land to Fort Madras via Fort Victoria, treat and rescue the personnel, currently in the grip of a typhoid epidemic and capture rebel leader Sikki Dhama (played by Aldo Sambrell); if successful in their undertaking, all charges will be dropped. What follows is a none-too-serious jungle adventure full of pitfalls and close calls in which the whole cast seems to be enjoying itself immensely. Secretive guide Gamal turns out to be Sikki Dhama in disguise, bent on sabotaging the expedition, while whiskey-loving physician Sasso keeps hitting the bottle (and somehow finding plenty of liquor along the way) but stays sober long enough to cure a headhunter's sick son, while a rampaging elephant almost flattens Zamperia's head with its foot (he's saved by a typhoon springing up). Blonde Wandisa Guida (Mary), sole survivor of a massacre, is discovered in an under-

A glamour portrait of Italian actress Elsa Martinelli who appeared in *The Marvellous Adventures of Marco Polo*

An Italian poster for *The Mountain of Light*

The Marvellous Adventures of Marco Polo [*Le meravigliose avventure di Marco Polo*] aka ***Marco the Magnificent***; ***Kublai Khan***

Prodi Cinematografica/Avala/Italaf Kaboul/ITTAC (Italy/France/Afghanistan/Egypt/Yugoslavia); Franscope/Eastmancolor; 112 (100) mins; Producer: Raoul Lévy; Directors: Denys de la Patelliere, Raoul Lévy ††††

Filmmakers weren't always entirely successful when it came to putting the Oriental travels of the renowned 13th-century Venetian merchant up on the big screen; *The Marvellous Adventures of Marco Polo*, an international production with international stars, remains one of the best of the bunch, fluidly directed by Frenchman Denys de la Patelliere against captivating Asian backdrops including, naturally, the Great Wall of China. German actor Horst Buchholz starred as 17-year-old Marco Polo, setting off for the Far East in 1271, his father, uncle and two Knights Templar among their caravan, after being briefed by tutor Orson Welles and Pope Gregory X; both wish for Western philosophy founded on peace to be imparted to Kublai Khan and his warmongering Mongol tribes so, in addition to all his other duties, Buchholz finds himself the Pope's official envoy.

A bedroom scene showing womanizer Buchholz stroking the back of his naked dark-haired sweetheart guaranteed a British "A" classification when the film was released in the United Kingdom, entitled *Marco the Magnificent*, in 1966 (as did the later sequence of a deserted town clogged with corpses); from then on, unlike previous *Marco Polo* outings, the pace never really flagged. In the arid wilds of the Holy Land, Buchholz encounters the golden masked "Old Man of the Mountains" (Akim Tamiroff), a cruel lord residing in spacious caverns housing gigantic statues hewn from the sandstone rock with a race of leather-clad muscular androids (the one female specimen is very scantily attired, her outfit defying the laws of gravity), bringing a touch of fantasy/sci-fi to the proceedings. One Knight Templar dies in agony after having a huge glass bell placed over his body, the ringing tones sending him to madness and oblivion. Omar Sharif (Sheik Alla Hou), taking time off from wenching at his oasis, rescues Buchholz, who continues on his hustle-bustle exploits, crossing the Gobi Desert and snow-laden mountains and indulging in a brief (but torrid) fling with the mysterious "Woman with the Whip" (Elsa Martinelli); the dominatrix saves him from a gang of Mongolian bandits but gets an arrow between the shoulder blades. Eventually, the fresh-faced explorer meets Kublai Khan (a shaven-headed Anthony Quinn), busy selecting a bride from a bevy of young, exotic Chinese beauties. Quinn's angry young son (Robert Hossein) advocates war over peace, thirsting for power, leading to his rebels clashing with Quinn's forces. Buchholz scatters the enemy by firing a barrage of rockets into their ranks using newly discovered gunpowder, Hossein dying in his father's arms. Mission accomplished, Bu-

A French poster for Tanio Boccia's tacky take on English medieval history, *The Revenge of Ivanhoe*

chholz elects to stay in China as his caravan heads westward to Venice; Marco Polo remained in the country until 1295 when he returned home to Venice and wrote his famous memoirs.

The movie was panned by critics when first issued, mid-'60s film writers rejecting badly dubbed foreign features of this type in favor of the in-vogue X-rated Westerns and crime dramas. Viewed five decades on, *The Marvellous Adventures of Marco Polo* has overlooked merit. It's a colorful, fast moving, decently acted and densely plotted adventure of the kind that long since has vanished from cinema auditoriums. Only copies containing Arabian dialogue overlaying the indistinct English dubbing are available as I write.

The Mountain of Light [*La montagna di luce*] aka *Sandok*; *Jungle Adventurer*

Filmes Rome (Italy); Techniscope/Technicolor; 87 mins; Producer: Solly V. Bianco; Director: Umberto Lenzi ††

After completion of *Sandok, the Maciste of the Jungle* and *The Three Sergeants of Bengal*, director Lenzi and producer Bianco continued their cinematic sojourn in Malaysia, quickly knocking out *The Mountain of Light*, a Saturday morning-type serial romp featuring Richard Harrison in his final peplum before he entered the world of Spaghetti Westerns. About the only two things sparkling in this limp jungle effort were Angelo Lotti's dazzling cinematography and the huge diamond Harrison pinches from the forehead of the God of Dharmaraja, a 20-foot-high statue of an Indian goddess. Harrison plays Alan Foster, an American master thief down on his luck, fond of gambling and whiskey, who is cajoled into stealing the million-dollar jewel to clear his debts, totaling $250,000, from the very man he owes the money to, Rajah Daniele Vargas (Sindar). Along for the ride is smelly, wily fakir Wilbert Bradley (Sitama), the pair pursued by growling Andrea Scotti and his heavies. En route to the rat-infested Pagoda of Kipni, where the statue stands, dusky maiden Luciana Gilli (Lilamani) crops up to supply the love interest.

The *Topkapi*-styled robbery, performed by rope through the temple roof, is reasonably intense; afterwards, Harrison leaves his not-to-be-trusted buddy to fester in an animal pit, disguises himself as an Indian and hides the precious stone in Gilli's diamond-encrusted waistband. Bradley scrambles out of the pit and is captured by Scotti, along with Harrison and Gilli; eventually, following a couple of street/bar brawls, the jewel is returned to its proper place in the statue's forehead, Harrison awarded the Order of Dharmaraja after escaping with Gilli from a flooded cave. But is the replaced diamond the *real* McCoy? Apparently it's not. Telling moody, argumentative Gilli that he loves her in a windswept field, Harrison then addresses the audience in a cockeyed epilogue, informing them that the jewel will be sold to Queen Victoria to pay off what he owes; a few minutes of grainy black-and-white footage hinting that the stone found a new home in the British Crown Jewels during the Coronation of Elizabeth II rounds off the proceedings.

Harrison breezes through this waffle like the Far East trade winds, likeable and energetic without exerting too much effort, yet the whole enterprise has a jaded air, despite Lenzi's proficient camerawork, Lotti's rich color tones, a fantastically ornate temple and some beautiful scenic shots. Even Francesco De Masi's pleasant-enough score is strangely (for this composer) muted, and Gilli leaves no impression whatsoever as the one and only female on display. Peplum jungle movies' days were almost over by mid-1965, and it showed in this tame addition to a fading genre.

The Revenge of Ivanhoe [*La rivincita di Ivanhoe*]

Tevere Film (Italy); Totalscope/Eastmancolor; 100 (90) mins; Producers: Roberto Capitani, Néstor Gaffet; Director: Tanio Boccia (Amerigo Anton) †† or ††††† for lovers of camp schlock

Minus MGM's $3,800,000 budget, stars Robert Taylor, Elizabeth Taylor and Joan Fontaine and Richard Thorpe's directorial expertise, all contributing factors in making 1952's *Ivanhoe* a glossy Middle Ages adventure of some merit, what we are left with in Tanio Boccia's cut-down take on the famous tale, set in 1199, is a cardboard jaunt through Sir Walter Scott's Saxons against Normans novel. Sunny glades stand in for dense English woodland, the action is hampered by comical dubbing and one of the poorest castle sets in peplum raises its minimalistic turrets into a distinctly Mediterranean blue sky. It receives two stars instead of one because Boccia's heraldic horror show is so hilariously awful it *is* good, a guilty pleasure of the first order!

We know we're in for a good/bad time when one of a troop of soldiers cantering through that sunlit Italian forest opens his mouth and says, in a New York accent, "We gotta getta move on." "Who orders thus?" the soldier inquires as a masked Rik Van Nutter (Ivanhoe) rides up and demands the release of prisoner Marco Pasquini. The two make a dash for it during a storm, Pasquini secreted away in a native outlaw village hidden behind a curtain of foliage, while Van Nutter acquaints himself with rotund hermit Renato Terra, playing Friar Tuck (straight out of Robin Hood). Meanwhile, over in that makeshift chateau, smarmy Duilio Marzio (Sir Cedric of Hastings), his psycho son Andrea Aureli (Bertrand of Hastings) and hobgoblin-like counselor Wladimiro Tuicovich (Redbourne) have kidnapped Gilda Lousek (The Lady Rowena) and issued her with *two* peplum ultimatums: Marry Sir Brian of Godwald (Franco Pasquetto) to establish an alliance, forget about your betrothal to Ivanhoe, and your brother (Pasquini, captured and behind bars) will be saved; later, when the very attractive damsel in deep distress is tried and found guilty of high treason, she is told, marry Sir Brian and *you* will avoid execution. Van Nutter (on white steed) defeats Aureli (on black steed) in a jousting tournament, deciding not to deliver the *coup de grace*, abiding by the rules of chivalry, and turns up at the wedding to Lousek posing as Pasquetto, who happens to be on his side in the strife. Tullio Altamura plays a sneaky turncoat, Marzio is after a third of Lousek's dowry, the other two-thirds going to Prince John to keep the autocrat in favor, and in the outlaws' leafy camp, an Alan-a-Dale cloned minstrel warbles a medieval ditty, strumming a lute. "You dog! Die!" shouts wooden Van Nutter in a Californian accent during the obligatory siege, putting Aureli to the sword, the bandits having gained entry via a secret tunnel through the solitary castle wall on display. "Ivanhoe! My love!" cries Lousek, kissing her knight in shining armor before the assembly, gathered to hear a proclamation read out that age-old feudal animosities should forthwith cease, along with serfdom. Utterly risible hokum that almost defies serious critique, just about rising above the level of ineptitude; Romolo Garroni's pastel-hued color photography, together with Giuseppe Piccillo's Olde English score, just about make Boccia's cockeyed Italian simplification of British legend-cum-history bearable. But it *will* bring a smile to the face, particularly if you're an Englishman!

1967

The Adventurer [*L'avventuriero*] aka *The Rover*

Arco Film/ABC/Selmur Prods. (Italy); Eastmancolor; 103 mins; Producer: Alfredo Bini; Director: Terence Young ✝

Adapted from Joseph Conrad's 1921/1922 novel *The Rover*, Terence Young's soggy seafaring drama is the cinematic equivalent of watching paint dry. Pirate captain Anthony Quinn

An Italian photobusta for *The Adventurer*

(Peyrol), master of the stolen British frigate the *Marigalante*, is tasked with delivering sealed orders to the French on promise of a free pardon. Creating a smokescreen to avoid a run-in with a British warship and cannonade from French shore batteries, Quinn disembarks at Toulon with the papers but is not granted that free pardon by the French authorities. Disgusted, Quinn takes off to a remote part of the coast where he rescues Rosanna Schiaffino (Arlette) from a mob of itinerant, sex-crazed youths. Up to this point in the proceedings, the movie is moderately interesting thanks to grizzled 52-year-old Quinn giving the rambling plot all he's got and picturesque location work. But when he becomes embroiled in a tedious relationship with mentally disturbed Schiaffino (she suffered a traumatic event as a child), her gray-haired Aunt Caterina (one-time Hollywood sex bomb Rita Hayworth) and crazy guardian Ivo Garrani, things become very turgid, and very boring, indeed. French naval officer Richard Johnson (as Real) appears on the scene, Schiaffino transferring her suppressed on/off desires from Quinn (who's alarmed at her predations) to him, much to his delight (the girl's a stunner, especially in that rear-framed nude shot). Meanwhile, Quinn is busy restoring an old wreck moored in a cove—eventually, he casts off alone with falsified documents that will put Admiral Nelson off the scent of Napoleon Bonaparte's proposed invasion of Egypt. Sailing straight into the arms of a British ship as planned, he's killed by a cannon blast. The last we see of him is his corpse draped over the tiller, drifting on the ocean currents.

Not released in America until 1971, *The Rover* (its U.S. title) was screened in Cinerama in a last-ditch effort to recoup production losses, which were considerable, over $1,500,000. It's hard to like a film that goes nowhere fast; Quinn looks tired throughout, the lengthy middle section hits rock bottom and Ennio Morricone's repetitive music seems to belong elsewhere. By 1967, the peplum nautical adventure had had its day; attempting to watch the once mighty Quinn struggling against the tide in one of his most forgettable pictures conclusively proves it.

17
The Conquerors and the Vikings

To be honest, the handful of Italian Viking features made in the wake of Kirk Douglas' rousing, brutal *The Vikings* (which narrowly avoided a British "X" certificate when first released in the United Kingdom) were a bit hit-and-miss, and the same could be said about Conquerors (as opposed to all those pagan/Roman/Greek warlords mentioned elsewhere). Giacomo Gentilomo's *The Last of the Vikings* emerges as the best of the Viking bunch, *Treasure of the Petrified Forest* is without doubt the weirdest, while *Suleiman the Conqueror* is, in this writer's view, one of the top 10 peplum productions ever made. How this bone-crunching, rousing epic has languished in the vaults for over 50 years is beyond all cinematic comprehension. Can someone, somewhere, *please* rescue Mario Tota's stirring saga from obscurity and release it in a pristine, letterbox digital copy so that it can be viewed in all its former glory?

1960

The Conqueror of the Orient [*Il conquistatore dell'Oriente*]
PEA/Tabos Film (Italy/West Germany); Dyaliscope/Ferraniacolor; 102 (74) mins; Producer: Giuliano Simonetti; Director: Tanio Boccia (Amerigo Anton) ††

In which poor fisherman Rik Battaglia, residing in Oriental Stone Age dwellings, becomes Nadir, Conqueror of the Orient, resplendent in turban and radiant tunic and armed to the teeth, holding a council of war in a swanky battle tent and leading out his regiments to establish peace and justice in the Holy Lands. Where this sudden influx of luxury and substance appeared from, only Allah knows—perhaps the explanation lies in the full-length version, not the 74-minute cut that appears to be the only copy available in 2015 (an 85-minute edit on VHS also exists but is extremely scarce). Shorn of 28 minutes, the second half of the film suffers from major scissor work and has a rushed air. In the finale, Franco Balducci leaps up the palace steps, kisses Gianna Maria Canale (lucky man), professes his undying love and is waved goodbye at the end by the beauty, when Battaglia rides off with fresh conquests in mind; as the actor has only been glimpsed briefly in previous scenes (Battaglia's comrade-in-arms), what role did he play in the Arab hero's venture to overthrow fraudulent sultan Paul Muller (Dakar) and regain his right to the throne?

Battaglia was brought up by kindly Fosco Giachetti, following the death of his royal father by Muller the usurper. A male chauvinist of the highest order, Muller tramples all over everybody's feelings, including Canale's, in his determination to wed statuesque Irene Tunc (Fatima) and bring her to heel; the girl, carried into the palace in a sedan, was offered as a peace gift but repels at the thought of betrothal to the black-hearted pig. Fawning court advisor Giulio Donnini (as Rato; he specialized in playing loathsome peplum characters) is on hand to make sure nobody stands in his master's way. When Battaglia learns of his true birthright from Giachetti, he organizes an army made up from sympathetic tribes with two main objectives in mind: to eliminate Muller and rid the Middle East of the yoke of persecution. First, he has to undergo a trial of strength, pulling two

An Italian poster for *The Conqueror of the Orient*

poles of men together and hitting a log thrown at him with his sword … end of test! Tunc escapes, is recaptured, Battaglia is imprisoned, *he* escapes and the mandatory showdown has the rebels crushing Muller's men-at-arms in the City of the Golden Domes; Battaglia finishes off Muller in a pretty exciting scimitar fight, while Balducci, for reasons probably made clear in the uncut print, slowly pushes his sword into hated enemy Donnini's back.

The sets, by peplum standards, are a bit stagy in this production, not the usual lavishly decorated palace rooms normally seen; Battaglia just about scrapes through as Nadir; Canale hardly ever smiles, looking cold and disinterested; and Tunc, possessing a fulsome figure, is lifeless, her part hampered by corny dubbing ("Nadir, my only beloved. I love you."). Muller virtually carries a picture short on action, adding to a long list of repulsive peplum villains of the type *you* wouldn't mind plunging a blade into. Not quite an Oriental disaster, but almost.

1961

The Invaders [*Gli invasori*] aka Erik the Conqueror; Fury of the Vikings

Galatea Film/Lyre/Criterion (Italy/France); Dyaliscope/Technicolor; 90 (89) mins; Producer: Ferruccio De Martino; Director: Mario Bava ✝✝✝

Mario Bava (he was one of three scriptwriters) showed his true mettle, not only in organizing the stirring battle scenes in this Viking swashbuckler, but in his renowned use of atmospheric lighting. The cave sets are painted in phosphorescent greens, blues, reds and purples, while a beach shot showing Queen Alice (Francoise Christophe) collecting a blond-haired baby from the surf has a stunning backdrop of red-tinged billowing clouds at sunset. Bava's artistic creativity as a cinematographer also manifested itself in *Hercules at the Center of the Earth*, but that was far more fantasy-orientated than *The Invaders*; some might say that his poetic cave interludes made for uncomfortable bedfellows within the grittier Viking framework. The movie flags in the middle section—admittedly, it looks superb, but nevertheless loses vital pace and, with it, a certain degree of interest.

Set in 786 AD, a siege on England's Dorset coast kicks off the action, a bloody massacre filmed in gratuitous close-up (spear through a woman clasping a child to her chest; head cleaved by an axe; rape); in the fracas, two baby brothers, Eron and Erik, are separated. Eron is hauled off in a longship to Norseland while the English queen finds Erik. Twenty years later Eron (Cameron Mitchell) is a Viking tribal chief, vowing vengeance on his father's death by organizing an all-out raid on the English castle near to where he was slain; Erik (George "Giorgio" Ardisson) has been raised by Christophe as a royal son and is made king, setting sail to intercept the Viking armada. Meanwhile, lurking in the background, Andrea Checchi (Sir Rutford) and his flunkies are conspiring to remove Christophe from office so that he can rule as regent of the kingdom; the reptile also proposes marriage to her but is turned down flat. Following the ensuing clash of ships, Christophe is held prisoner by Mitchell and taken back to his homestead; Ardisson, battered and bruised, is washed ashore near Mitchell's abode and instantly falls in love with Rama (Alice Kessler), a winsome vestal virgin whose twin sister Daya (Ellen Kessler ... Bava presents them as guardian angels) happens to be the sweetheart of Mitchell. So now, two blond brothers are dating two blonde sisters. Nice!

It's at this point that *The Invaders* loses momentum. We have Mitchell's wedding feast, revelries and Ardisson, bound to a cross overshadowed by the branches of a vast tree, used as target practice, all taking place in Bava's wondrously lit cavern. Rama unbinds Ardisson, the pair joining Christophe on

Andrea Checchi feels the edge of Cameron Mitchell's blade in *The Invaders*.

a longship, fleeing back to England to regain the royal castle from Checchi and his cohorts, with Mitchell and his Vikings in pursuit. Note the castle in longshot—it's the same edifice that features in *The Normans* and *The Last of the Vikings*. Bava then increases the tempo and wraps up the scenario in rousing style, the inevitable tussle between Mitchell and Ardisson revealing to both, via identical dragon tattoos, that they are indeed brothers. Checchi lets loose an arrow into Mitchell, who goes to meet his God in a far-too-lengthy death scene, clutching his sword; Ardisson scales the fortress walls, unshackling Daya in her cell, and the Vikings storm the fortress. In the battle's dying stages, Checchi topples from the ramparts, his body riddled with 10 arrows. The closing seconds are of Mitchell's body on a longship surrounded by flames, given a time-honored Viking burial, Daya staying by his side to the bitter end. Ardisson stands watching in a second longship, sailing off to Viking land with Rama.

Two sadistic moments highlight the way for what Bava later became famous for—European horror. In one, a half-naked couple who have sinned (she was a vestal virgin, promised to Odin) are tied back to back by thorny vines on a stake, to be sacrificed at leisure; in the other, Checchi has a poisonous spider housed in a glass cage positioned over Daya's face, a threat to what will happen to her if the queen and Ardisson don't play ball. Derived very much from Richard Fleischer's landmark Viking movie, *The Vikings* (as most of these films were), *The Invaders* is excellent in parts, rather ponderous in others, lacking overall the robust, gutsy approach that showcased Mitchell's other big Viking picture, *The Last of the Vikings*. And Bava was to have one more stab at a Viking flick in 1966's *Knives of the Avenger*, also starring Mitchell.

The Last of the Vikings [*L'ultimo dei vichinghi*]

Tiberius Films/Galatea/Criterion (Italy/France); Totalscope/Eastmancolor; 103 (98) mins; Producers: Roberto Capitani, Luigi Mondello; Director: Giacomo Gentilomo ✝✝✝✝✝

Cameron Mitchell and a scarred Andrea Aureli in *The Last of the Vikings*

Before he started on his role as Norwegian King Sveno, Edmund Purdom must have sat down, watched a screening of the Laurence Olivier classic *Richard III* and thought, "Hmmm. Maybe I could do something like that." What Purdom came up with was a black-robed, hand-wringing, twitching idiot, limping across set on a left leg that was twisted one minute, normal the next (his "hunchback," a flagrant imitation of Olivier's stooped Richard Crookback, also came and went with the tide). Allied to Purdom's carpet-chewing performance was Cameron Mitchell's hard-as-nails turn, playing Harald the Viking chief, complete with beefed-up torso, skimpy tunic and short blond rinse. A recipe for disaster? Surprisingly, no; the two leads plus Gentilomo's forceful directorial technique (Mario Bava also had a hand in directing but didn't receive a credit) ensured that this roughhouse Viking saga maintained the interest, incorporating enough head-splitting set pieces to satisfy all peplum gore freaks. (The film ran into censorship problems in Italy; the British film censor ordered cuts and passed it with an "A" certificate but allowed the sequence showing the massacre of a group of Viking women by a lake to stand. As we have seen, many peplum features contained what some would regard as unnecessary scenes of violence toward women, and this was one such example.)

Returning home after a 10-year crusade, the Danish court ambassador held captive on board his longship, Mitchell finds his homestead wrecked, his father murdered. Swearing vengeance, he gathers together the various tribes to plan a blitz on Purdom's medieval castle and overthrow the crazy Norwegian usurper. But there's a troublemaker in the ranks—Andrea Aureli (Haakon) is scheming to replace Mitchell as head of the Viking clans, convinced that he'll perish when he launches his offensive on Purdom's impregnable stronghold. The first strike is successful; Mitchell decides to impersonate a Danish prince and gain access to Purdom's court and the Viking chief's excitable brother George Ardisson (as Guntar, suffering from a severe case of overacting) adds fuel to the fire of insurrection by wanting to lead his own charge on the fortification. For his pains, he's captured and nailed to a cross. In the meantime, Mitchell has fallen for Norwegian princess Isabelle Corey (Hilde), betrothed (against her inclinations) to the King of Denmark, promising her female liberation if she joins with him. When the Danish envoy, freed by Aureli after being scarred with a burning torch, staggers into court, the game is up for Mitchell; dragging Ardisson off the cross (a painful moment), he leaps through a window into the sea and makes it to shore, his brother dead. Back in camp, two-timing Aureli has declared himself *de facto* leader but his reign doesn't last long; in walks Mitchell with his brother's body and promptly disembowels the Judas using his father's sword. With a battle cry of "Odin! Odin!" ringing out, the Vikings march on Purdom's castle, a giant catapult in tow. "Yes, he's mad! Mad with love!" shrieks the loony monarch as blazing logs are propelled into the compound, the walls are breached, hatchets bury themselves in heads, arrows fly into eyes, heads are sliced open, spears find their mark and Purdom himself succumbs to a Shakespearean tragedy-type death, slumping on his throne, an axe embedded in his chest, flaming timbers crashing over his prone body. The closing moments see Mitchell, Corey and the Vikings sailing off into the sunset, mission accomplished, to the sound of Roberto Nicolosi's noisy but effective score. And full marks to photographer Enzo Serafin for imbuing the whole boisterous yarn in a relevant gritty color wash. *The Last of the Vikings* remains the topmost of all the Viking pepla, almost on a par with Kirk Douglas' classic tale of Norse derring-do.

Suleiman the Conqueror [*Solimano il conquistatore*]

Cine Produzione Astoria/CFS Kosutnjak (Italy/Yugoslavia); Totalscope/Eastmancolor; 99 (83) mins; Producers: Adriano Merkel, Vatroslav Mimica; Directors: Vatroslav Mimica, Mario Tota ††††††

Based on the real-life exploits of Suleiman the Magnificent, the Sultan who ruled over the Ottoman Empire in the early to middle years of the 16th century, carrying out 13 campaigns from the age of 25, Vatroslav Mimica and Mario Tota's joint Italian/Yugoslavian barnstormer is an action-filled cracker, rarely seen these days except by peplum devotees, a staggering achievement in any filmmaker's book. As a curtain raiser, master composer Francesco De Masi's magisterial title music establishes precisely the right tone, an exceptional score to die for (he conducted the Milan Philharmonic Orchestra). In 1566, the marauding Turkish army, the mightiest ever assembled during this period, is moving steadily but surely toward Vienna and only the fortress of Szigetvar near Siklos, surrounded by pestilent marshes, its people going about their daily rituals, stands in the way of its line of advancement. Suleiman the Second (Loris Gizzi), overweight and suffering from gout, wants to annihilate the settlement; second-in-command, Edmund Purdom (as Ibrahim Pasha), looking grim in a black tunic, is averse to the idea—why risk good men in a fever-ridden wasteland when a much bigger prize is on the horizon. But Gizzi argues the case with Purdom to press on, determined to swat this "mere grain of sand" off the map, thereby setting up the scenario for a titanic Alamo-type confrontation between opposing forces that lasts almost the entire length of the movie. Inside the fortress, leader Stane Potokar (Captain Nicholas Orlovich) adopts a "fight to

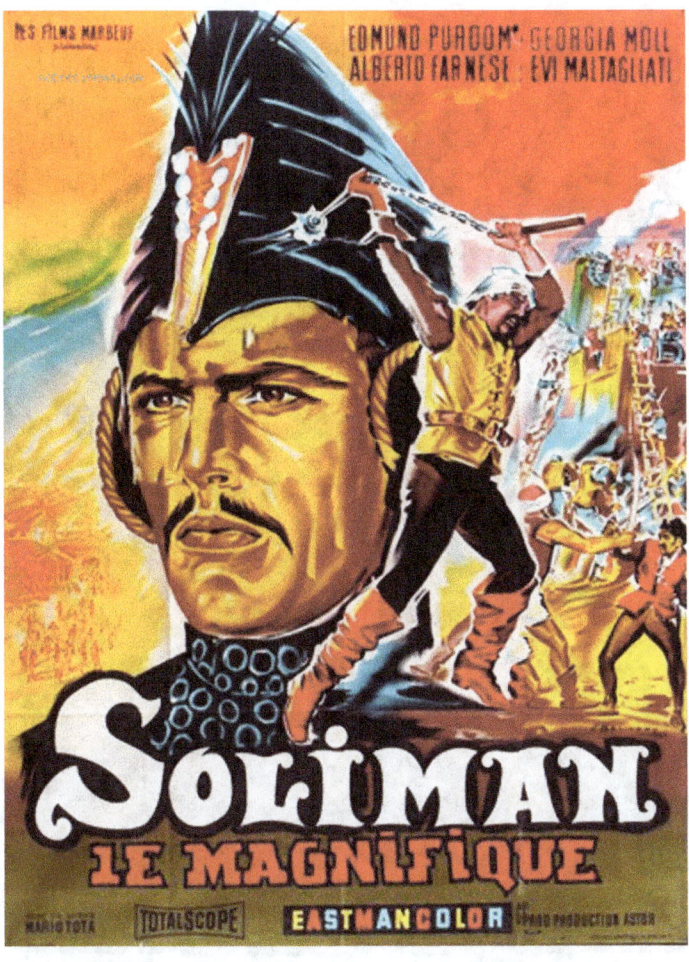

A French poster for *Suleiman the Conqueror*

A French poster for *The Legendary Conqueror*

the bitter end" stance, refugees from neighboring villages pour in, young Luciano Marin (Ivan) manages to reach Vienna, only to face rejection from the Viennese court in his request for reinforcements, and Potokar's daughter, Giorgia Moll (Vesna), spurns the overtures of tough soldier Alberto Farnese (Gaspard), longing for Marin to return from his perilous assignment.

With a budget of almost $400,000 dollars to play with, Croatian directors Mimica and Tota (it was Tota's one and only action feature as director; he acted as assistant director on four other movies, including *The Giant of Metropolis* and *The Son of the Sheik*) piled on the large-scale spectacle with gusto and flair, the fortress under continual bombardment from siege engines, the invaders repeatedly repulsed with crossbows, spears, cannons and vats of boiling oil. When Gizzi dies from a sudden heart seizure (the Turkish conqueror was 72), Purdom takes command, deciding upon an all-out blitz on Potokar's battered, vastly outnumbered, battalions. Farnese drowns in quicksand after trying to kill his love rival Marin, who is then given the task of ferrying the women and children to Vienna before the final assault. And that final assault is monumental in size and scope, Potokar and his beleaguered warriors standing their ground, dying to the last man as hundreds of Turks breach the fortress walls and swarm all over the defenders. After this ferocious set piece, Purdom surveys the hundreds of corpses lying in the dust with resignation, rain begins to fall and he makes the decision not to march on Vienna as intended but to turn back. Enough is enough. "A contradiction of war," he says to his puzzled commanders, "Victors are often losers." The evocative closing panoramic shot shows the Turkish army departing in their thousands from the smoking remains of Szigetvar under a blanket of mist and rain, the croaking of marsh frogs heard above the marching of the troops. There are several moving moments in this rousing, almost operatic, tragedy—Potokar's wife (Evi Maltagliati) collapses with a fatal arrow wound, bemoaning on her deathbed that she didn't tell her husband she loved him enough, while the women gather up dirt from the compound ground prior to leaving, a reminder of their native soil. De Masi's soundtrack reverberates during the fabulous battle sequences, while Giuseppe La Torre's cinematography bathes the bleak landscape in a gray wash, imbuing the film with the necessary grittiness it deserves. Yes, there's the obligatory two-minute dancing scene (in Gizzi's tent) but it doesn't hold up the pulverizing narrative flow. A long-lost classic that should be hunted down by all sword and sandal lovers. If ever a peplum motion picture deserved an urgent digital makeover, it's this one.

1963

The Legendary Conqueror [*Il leggendario conquistatore*] aka *Balboa*; *Balboa, Conquistador of the Pacific*

Capitol Film/CCU (Italy/Spain); Eastmancolor; 96 mins; Producer: H.S. Valdés; Director: José Maria Elorrieta ✝✝✝

A semi-historical romp relating the exploits of Vasco Nunez de Balboa who, in 1513, crossed the Isthmus of Panama and discovered the "Great Southern Sea," later named the Pacific Ocean. The opening few minutes presents us with Frank Latimore (as Balboa) engaged in a swordfight on cantina tables with three of his creditors, the mood far-from-serious, almost farcical; the tone becomes more somber when the destitute conquistador is smuggled on board Commissioner Carlos Casaravilla's ship, bound for the New World. Casaravilla demands that Latimore be thrown into chains, claiming he's a deserter following an Indian raid on the fortress of San Sebastion; Latimore promises that once they land, he'll take him and his crew to the ruined stockade and show them the gold the Spaniards managed to hoard, thereby proving his innocence. Famed explorer Francisco Pizarro (Jésus Puente) is picked up in a boat containing the survivors of a previous expedition, the ship hits a reef and goes under and the Spaniards, safely ashore, troop into the jungle to find fame and fortune. From here on in, the picture becomes episodic and slightly disjointed, the men encountering one warlike Indian tribe after another in their twin quest: gold and the rumored sea that lies to the west. Latimore hitches up with sultry Indian beauty Pilar Cansino (Anayensi), and there are several bloody skirmishes and a couple of suggestive native Indian dances; Latimore shows his compassionate side by preventing the brutish Casaravilla from butchering the natives, and the explorers suffer from exhaustion, thirst and hunger in the latter stages of their trek through jungles, swamps and over mountains harboring hostile tribes. Finally, after struggling up a steep hillside, the Pacific is reached, Latimore taking possession of the sea by marching into the waves and planting the flag of Spain in the surf.

The Legendary Conqueror is most definitely *not* in the same league as Werner Herzog's spellbinding *Aguirre, the Wrath of God* (1972), *the* classic "Spanish conquistadors searching for gold in the South American jungles" opus, but it's colorful and enjoyable enough, even though Puente would have made a far more forceful Balboa than the stiff-as-a-board Latimore, and the facts, as presented, are open to question. Sidney W. Pink, the man responsible for one of monster cinema's most dire creature-features, *Reptilicus* (1962), took up the production rights for U.S. distribution and the picture played spasmodically in England during the early part of 1964.

1965

Erik, the Viking [***Erik, il vichingo***] aka ***Vengeance of the Vikings***

AS Films/Triglav Film (Italy/Spain); Cinepanoramic/Eastmancolor; 95 mins; Producers: Luigi Mondello, José Maria Ramos; Director: Mario Caiano ☦☦☦

Vinland was the name given to a subtropical region of North America discovered by the Norse Vikings circa 1000 AD. It's here that Erik (Giuliano Gemma) wants to uproot his tribe and go to live, sick of Danish interference in his affairs. Sailing west with a handpicked crew, he leaves behind his betrothed beauty Gudrid (Eleonora Bianchi) and cousin Erloff (Lucio De Santis) in their Scandinavian fjord enclave, unaware that bitter and twisted De Santis has designs on Bianchi and has planted two assassins (Gordon Mitchell as Sven and Eduardo Fajardo as Olaf) among the crew to dispose of his hated cousin.

Boosted by a great Carlo Franci score and Mario Caiano's workmanlike direction, *Erik, the Viking* opens in true Viking fashion, two warring factions engaged in a vicious set piece, strongman Mitchell hacking left, right and center with double axes, emitting a maniacal cackle. Lured by the promise of gold

An Italian poster for *Erik, the Viking*

by De Santis, a group of thugs attacks Gemma but he kills all except one, who's caught; afraid that the ruffian will talk, Mitchell directs a well-aimed axe at his head. On the long sea voyage to find new lands, Gemma survives a murder attempt by Mitchell and snarling cohort Fajardo, and eventually the adventurers come ashore in the tropics, their unexpected arrival bringing out of the jungle a tribe of friendly Indians. Saving one of the Indian maidens—the chief's daughter Wa-ta-wa (Elisa Montés)—from being mauled to death by a bear, the young leader is latched onto by the doe-eyed squaw, who takes an instant shine to her hero; "Me kiss," she coos delightfully at him. But Redskins and Vikings do not a good mix make, the two milieus poles apart. The contrast between bleak, gray Scandinavian locale to blue, sunny coastline jars, the movie lapsing into silliness at times (Greek Aldo Bufi Landi teaching the natives how to make wine and getting them blind drunk in the process) and suffering from over-length. Mitchell and Fajardo hatch plans to kill Gemma and stir up trouble with Montés' bullying intended, a brute of a Redskin who stumbles around with a perpetual glare on his face and Gemma forgets all about Bianchi in favor of the chief's delightful daughter. However, on their wedding day, Mitchell shoots Montés with an arrow; in reprisal, two axes are sunk in his back, and pal Fajardo is stabbed to death with a sword. Disillusioned with the whole disastrous enterprise, Gemma heads back home to engage in single combat with De Santis; the be-

Composite photograph from *Treasure of the Petrified Forest* showing Gordon Mitchell (center), Eleanora Bianchi and Ivica Pajer

trayer informed Gemma's mother and Bianchi that he was dead, having brought down Gemma's carrier pigeon and destroyed the message that he was, in fact, very much alive. De Santis slides over a cliff edge after his cousin slashes him with a blade; the returning head of the clan then promises to his people (after getting back with Bianchi) that they will stay where they are for all time—the grass isn't always greener over the horizon.

Treasure of the Petrified Forest [*Il tesoro della foresta pietrificata*] aka *The Stone Forest*

Asteria/Avis Film (Italy); Asterscope/Eastmancolor; 111 (89) mins; Producer: Olga Chart; Director: Emimmo Salvi ††††

Any peplum movie starring the great Gordon Mitchell is worth a look. His acting technique may have amounted to little more than scowling, shouting and throwing that huge frame of his around set, but the man's terrifying persona could light up the screen a hundredfold, as it did in Emimmo Salvi's devil's brew of a picture combining Viking chicanery and Old Norse fantasy; cinematographer Mario Parapetti highlighted the actor's formidable shark's grin and flinty eyes to great effect, in garish blues and reds, promoting Mitchell's Hunding, King of the Vikings, to a commanding figure of monstrous power that no man dares cross.

Yet Ivica Pajer (Sigmund, billed as Ivo Payer), guardian of the Black Forest, the Petrified Forest and the Valley of the Sun, does just that, refusing Mitchell and his warriors access to the land on which the fabulous treasure of Valhalla and god Woden's golden sword is buried near an inscribed stone obelisk (the scriptwriters took their inspiration from the Germanic/Norse mythological tales of Nibelungen). Also keeping watch over the mystical site are the Valkyries, an all-female tribe led by Pamela Tudor—whenever they appear, Richard Wagner's "Ride of the Valkyries" is played (as it is in the opening credits). Mitchell's having none of it; with Pajer's spurned lover (Luisa Rivelli) in his bed (Pajer is romancing her sister, Eleonora Bianchi, playing Siglinde), supplying him with inside information, plus a spy (Luigi Tosi) from the other side's camp, the Vikings' resident soothsayer shows Mitchell the exact spot where the treasure lies, thus setting up a conflict between Pajer's people and the bloodthirsty Vikings. Pillaging, raping, killing and burning their way toward the fabled forest (bathed in an eerie blue light), the Vikings have Pajer's men on the run; Pajer is imprisoned ("I will kill your woman and take out your eyes," threatens Mitchell) but hauled out of his cell on the end of a rope by midget Franco Doria, setting the scene for a remarkable last act in a forest glade. A gigantic revolving pivot of blades, worked by a wheel, confronts the Vikings, scything them down in droves. Mitchell's fighters disable the machine, Tudor and her Valkyries join in the affray, traitors Rivelli and Tosi are brought down by arrow and sword, and Mitchell gets the sword of Woden, but not how he envisaged; Pajer plunges the carved blade into his belly. Their leader dead, the Vikings are captured but liberated, told to go back to their own lands and practice love and peace. Forlorn Tudor watches in anguish as Pajer departs with Bianchi—she fancied him all along, but his heart belongs to another. All she has to look forward to is a life with her Valkyries.

Salvi's surrealistic 11th-century Viking opus with a difference is difficult to come by these days, a shame as Mitchell is on highly watchable form. His barnstorming performance, combined with eye-catching photography, offbeat set design (Peppino Ranceri and Antonio Fratalocchi) and bloody clashes, promotes the movie to essential status for buffs looking for something slightly more unusual in their peplum diet.

1966

Knives of the Avenger [*I coltelli del vendicatore*]

Sider Film (Italy); Techniscope/Technicolor; 85 mins; Producer: Alfredo Leone; Director: Mario Bava †††

Queen Karin and her son Moki are on the run from the barbarian Hagen. Her husband, King Arald, has been missing for three years on a visit to Britain, and Hagen wants to marry her to attain leadership of her kingdom. A mysterious Viking, Helmut, who turns out to be the very man that raped her many years ago, now protects Karin and her son; Moki *could* be his son. Helmut eventually defeats his sworn enemy, Hagen, and rides off, leaving Karin in the arms of her returned husband.

In other hands, *Knives of the Avenger* would have turned out a mundane, even boring, affair, but Mario Bava's expert camera strokes imbue the production with nuances it might otherwise not have received. Although commencing atmospherically on a beach, where Karin (Elissa Pichelli, the hot new Italian hopeful of the time) and her lad Moki (Luciano Pollentin) are informed of impending danger by a wizened old soothsayer, the movie sags on occasions, the couple befriended by Helmut (Cameron Mitchell, his final liaison with Bava), who bonds with the boy and wants to play house, but receives only cold indifference from the woman. Mitchell is handy with a knife, dispatching his victims by throwing a variety of blades hidden under his tunic to bring down Hagen's (Fausto Tozzi, billed as Frank Ross) henchmen; he also uses the axe and acrobatic drop kicks to great effect. As well as a nod in the direction of Sergio Leone's *Dollar* movies, (Marcello Giombini's Spaghetti Western-based score seems out of context, trotting along harmlessly in the background), George Stevens' *Shane* (Paramount, 1953) is

An Italian poster for *Knives of the Avenger*

the other major influence. Mitchell's relationship with Pollentin is mirrored in the Alan Ladd/Brandon de Wilde relationship in Stevens' masterpiece, while the six-minute cat-and-mouse standoff between Mitchell and Tozzi in a tavern is a blatant copy of the classic Ladd/Jack Palance standoff, even right down to the mangy dog slinking beneath a table. In flashback, Mitchell, wearing a helmet, assaulted Pichelli on her wedding night in wrongful retribution against Giacomo Rossi-Stuart's (King Arald) tribe, instead of Tozzi's; he's aware of this, but she isn't. Following Tozzi's death, Mitchell decides not to pursue his right to claim Pollentin as his own and rides off into the setting sun, leaving the family to get on with their lives.

Bava inserts a few snatches of gore (decapitated heads; a knife through the neck) and his stylish use of color tones (with Antonio Rinaldi) is evident in the final cavern scenes; he also artfully frames his protagonists in such a way as to bring punch to the proceedings. Mitchell, not really known for his work within the peplum genre, is highly watchable as the brooding, blond Viking and Tozzi is your archetypal peplum bad guy. Elsewhere, Rossi-Stuart is stoically heroic, while Pichelli (her career nose-dived after this picture) is nice to look at but wooden. Overall, it's a thoughtful mood piece, short on action, the pace sluggish, and it just about manages to keep its head above water, thanks to the leading man's performance and Bava's revered name behind the lens.

1967

Massacre in the Black Forest [*Il massacro della foresta nera*] aka ***Arminius the Terrible***

Debora Film/Avala/Peter Carsten Prod. (Italy/West Germany/Yugoslavia); Totalscope/Technicolor; 89 (82) mins; Producer: Moris Ergas; Directors: Ferdinando Baldi, Rudolf Nussgruber (uncredited) †††

Produced in the dying stages of the Italian peplum era and made back-to-back with the inferior *Shadow of Eagles* (1966), *Massacre in the Black Forest*'s storyline is rooted in factual events. Arminius (or Hermann) did exist, a chieftain of the Cherusci clan who united Germany's Teutonic tribes in an endeavor to throw off the shackles of Roman rule during the 1st-century AD and reclaim "our sacred homeland." The brutal massacre occurred in the Teutoburg Forest in the year 9 AD, Arminius' forces annihilating three entire divisions under the command of Varus, resulting in heavy casualties, 20,000 Roman troops losing their lives. Varus in shame fell on his own sword; as a consequence of this crushing rout, Rome inflicted savage retribution and eventually, after numerous battles, succeeded in breaking Arminius' stranglehold on the tribes, leading to an uneasy truce, but not overall Roman dominance.

Baldi's interpretation of events takes place in cold, wintry locations (much like the first half of *The Fall of the Roman Empire*) and features a morose turn from Cameron Mitchell as consul Aulus Sessina, ordered by Rome to put a stop to the activities of this German troublemaker (played by Hans von Borsody). Trouble is, von Borsody and Mitchell were centurion friends in the legion before he defected to his own side, and this friendship culminates in the two calling it quits after a prolonged siege on the Roman garrison's winter quarters, attacked first by von Borsody's warriors who capture it, then retaken by Mitchell's legionnaires, a thrilling set piece staged with bravura. Mitchell's gloomy countenance may have been due to his enforced presence in Italy following IRS investigations into his affairs; whatever the reason, he looks pale and dispirited, and not appearing, bar a brief opening spot, until 40 minutes have gone by. The forest wipeout is violent and well staged, as is the aftermath, hundreds of skeletons, skulls and bones littering the marshland near a broken-up wooden causeway. But can anyone explain how Mitchell can receive four savage lash marks across the face and, a few days later, emerge from his tent without a single mark? That final encounter is a humdinger, fought to the drum-thumping score of Carlo Savina, Lucky Satson's cinematography accentuating the snow-laden wooded landscapes beautifully. Two tasty ladies (Antonella Lualdi and Beba Loncar), hired for love interest, look pretty but contribute very little, German actor Peter Carsten, whose production company provided funds for the project, makes a brief appearance while von Borsody makes a headstrong conqueror, a sort of blond beach hunk in battle armor with attitude. If Mitchell had put a bit more "oomph" into his part, the movie would have developed into something far worthier than mere comic book theatrics, which on the odd occasion and to its detriment, it resembles.

18
Zorro and The Musketeers

The Italian *Zorro* adventures are, in most cases, a barrel of laughs, not peplum presented at its finest (*Zorro the Rebel* and *The Three Swords of Zorro* come out tops) or gravest, simply lighthearted fare for a good night in. After all, there are only so many alternative forms of fluctuations in plot that you can carry out on what amounts to basically one storyline—the masked crusader versus the oppressors of the people. Likewise, the Latin take on French heroes D'Artagnan and his Musketeers can come across as fun-packed nonsense, especially when the masked avenger in black meets up with all four swashbucklers in *Zorro and the Three Musketeers*. But give these films their due, they got on with the business instead of hanging around for hours on end, as in 1998's multi-million dollar, 136-minute *The Mask of Zorro*. Italian filmmakers didn't have that kind of money to throw around, having to budget with care. The results were sometimes amateurish (as in *The Oath of Zorro*), but the flicks were short and snappy, moved briskly enough and were, in the long run, enjoyable, perhaps more suitable for a younger, less critical, audience.

1962

The Secret Mark of D'Artagnan [*Il colpo segreto di d'Artagnan*]
Liber/Les Films Agiman (Italy/France); Totalscope/Technicolor; 95 (91) mins; Producer: Ottavio Poggi; Director: Siro Marcellini ††††

There is only one of the Three Musketeers in Siro Marcellini's lively romp, and that's Porthos, played by peplum regular Mario Petri. Other genre stalwarts on hand include Georges Marchal, Massimo Serato, Franco Fantasia and his brother, Andrea. American George Nader was drafted in to take on the D'Artagnan role and he makes a good fist of it, energetic, romantic and amusing in equal measures. Nader and Petri are commissioned by Serato (as Cardinal Richelieu, on his old foe's side this time) to eliminate an assassination attempt on King Louis XIII of France, the conspirators led by Marchal (the Duke of Montserrat) and Franco Fantasia. This involves the pair in bucketloads of derring-do as they fence their way from one sticky situation to another, Nader carving a cross with the tip of his rapier on the foreheads of the king's enemies. At the beginning, Nader is wounded in a fight and cared for by Marchal's niece, Alessandra Panaro (Diana); they fall in love, as does the noblewoman's busty maid, Magali Noel (Carlotta), with Petri, forming an appealing, forever-kissing foursome throughout the scenario. Clambering into the girls' bedrooms, crossing a moat on a rickety ladder, scaling castle walls, scurrying through secret passages, engaging in tavern duels and bursting in on Marchal's gatherings, Nader and Petri make thorough nuisances of themselves, giving rise to two tremendous pieces of stuntwork. During a duel at the start, a victim of Nader's deadly sword thrust falls through banisters, flips over in midair and crashlands onto a table, followed by Nader (or his stunt double) swinging through a window into the street below in a cascade of broken glass; a similar sequence occurs halfway through the picture. Marchal arrests his niece on suspicion of aiding and abetting Nader, her

An Italian poster for *The Secret Mark of D'Artagnan*

left hand crushed in a torture device; most of his cohorts wind up with a bloody cross etched on their features, the action climaxing in a Parisian mansion with a balletic swordfight carried out on a curved staircase between Nader and Marchal. King Louis' blue-caped troops enter the hall, the conspirators throw down their weapons and Marchal inches down the stairway, his blade across Panaro's delicate neck, looking for a means of escape. Coming up from behind, Serato presses a dagger into his back and he's arrested, condemned to death. A happy ending to a good-natured romp sees Nader and Petri entwined in the loving arms of their two gorgeous women.

Easy to digest and agreeable, *The Secret Mark of D'Artagnan* benefits from Alvaro Mancori's colorful photography and a "Best of Carlo Rustichelli" score. The composer seamlessly assembled snippets from his Roman, Egyptian and Pirate ventures to come up with a composite soundtrack; keen-eared aficionados of movie music will be able to detect from which film a particular piece harks. It works in this context, adding considerably to 95 minutes of classic peplum swashbuckling mayhem of the extremely obscure variety.

An Italian poster for *The Shadow of Zorro*

bad guys and restoring fair play to the locals. Howard Vernon played the villainous Union boss El General, determined to unmask Latimore, not too difficult as this particular Zorro only wears a black bandanna covering the lower portion of his face, and no eye mask. In *Zorro the Avenger*, the crusader is trying to live the quiet life after dispatching a criminal sergeant during a clash between Mexican revolutionaries and the U.S. cavalry. One of the sergeant's bandit cohorts disguises himself as Zorro (Claudio Undari), terrorizing the countryside with sidekicks Paul Piaget and Raf Baldassarre in an attempt to flush out the real article; it works, Latimore donning his bandanna and black hat to eliminate the imposter and his gang and clear his tarnished reputation in the eyes of his adoring public.

The Shadow of Zorro contained scenes from *Zorro the Avenger* (noticeably the battle segment) and saw Latimore once more crossing swords (or rapiers) with Vernon: A new, amenable governor (José Marco Davo) arrives from Washington with pacifist daughter Maria Silva (Irene). To incite trouble and unrest among the citizens, Vernon orders the murder of a priest by three henchmen (Zorro is blamed) and, in the end, he kills Latimore's close friend Carlos Romero Marchent (as Fred; he was the director's younger brother); the closing minutes sees the black-clad savior swing across a room by chandelier and run his rapier blade into the colonel's stomach.

To be honest, Latimore doesn't cut it as Zorro, at 37 looking a little too mature for the role, and lacking the requisite dash. The set pieces are lackluster, the photography muddy (even of Spain's splendid Manzanares el Real Castle), and even composing maestro Francesco De Masi, in tandem with Manuel Parada, is unable to lift the mood, his score at best disappointingly tame. A tepid cross between pepla and the Italian Spaghetti Western, these two Iberian-based cowboy hybrid *Zorro* outings, patched up together to make one movie and very hard to come by in their originally conceived forms (some compendiums list the films separately or as one and the same but under differing titles), should be avoided by all but diehard fanatics.

The Shadow of Zorro [*L'ombra di Zorro*] aka *Zorro the Avenger*; *The Mark of Zorro*

Explorer Film '58/PEA/Copercines (Italy/Spain/France); Dyaliscope/Eastmancolor; 87 mins; Producers: Eduardo Manzanos Brochero, Alberto Grimaldi; Director: Joaquin Luis Romero Marchent ††

In 1962, American actor Frank Latimore starred as Don José de la Torre (El Zorro) in the Spanish production of *Zorro the Avenger* (*La venganza del Zorro*; Italy: *Zorro il vendicatore*); the same year, *The Shadow of Zorro* was drummed up (with Italian involvement), both movies having been shot back-to-back. *Zorro the Avenger* was reissued in 1975 as *The Mark of Zorro*, containing clips from each film, while in England, to further confuse the issue, *The Shadow of Zorro* was released as *Zorro the Avenger*, which also combined footage from both features. Baffled? The production teams responsible for this pair of humdrum, mix 'n' match *Zorro* offerings were virtually the same, and that goes for the basic plots. Zorro fights for justice in an Old California overrun by troublesome Yankees and corrupt dictators, triumphing in the end by vanquishing the

A Spanish poster for *Zorro at the Spanish Court*

A Spanish poster for *Sign of Zorro*

Zorro at the Spanish Court [*Zorro alla corte di Spagna*] aka ***The Masked Conqueror***

Jonia Film (Italy); Dyaliscope/Eastmancolor; 94 mins; Producer: Ferdinand Felicioni; Director: Luigi Capuano ♰♰♰

With Luigi Capuano's expertise at the helm and a cutback on the sillier interludes that mar many of these Italian *Zorro* swashbucklers, *Zorro at the Spanish Court* is better than most, setting the action back in Spain rather than the Old West. Blond George Ardisson starred as Riccardo Di Villa Verde, alias Zorro, returning to the Duchy of Lusitania in 1843 to find it in the illegal hands of Don Carlos (Gianni Rizzo), the Grand Duke's slippery brother who plans to overthrow the monarchy, led by Andreina Paul (Maria Cristina), and abduct the young infanta Isabella (Maria Letizia Gazzoni), using her as a trade-off for the right to absolute power.

Excellent use of locations and visual color, plus a spot-on Carlo Savina score and a plethora of handsomely attired females make for an entertaining ride, if a little on the "I've seen it all before" side, but then, how many variations on the Zorro theme can you tinker around with before a sense of déjà vu and mild boredom sets in? Ardisson, effete as Riccardo, looks a bit too hefty for Zorro-type acrobatics, but he performs well enough, his duels with villain Alberto Lupo (Miguel) staged with vigor. Fencing master Franco Fantasia escapes the hangman's rope thanks to the crusader in black, Capuano tosses in umpteen fights/chases with soldiers and a rollicking knockabout finale, while poor old Capitano Morales (Livio Lorenzon with hair!) has the mark of Zorro slashed across his face, not once but twice—forehead and right cheek. Ardisson even gets to marry noblewoman Nadia Marlowa (Bianca) without the lady realizing that he's her hero of the hour in the black mask—no wonder the Russian-born beauty looks mighty relieved at the end when Zorro reveals his real identity. Zorro receives a peck on the cheek from youngster Gazzoni in gratitude for restoring her to the hot seat and Maria Grazia Spina (Consuelo) is the other Spanish honey on show, hitching up with boyish Antonio Gradoli (L'Oste) in the final reel. This is a fun-packed adventure in which the entire cast seemed to be enjoying themselves immensely, a feeling that filters over to the viewer.

1963

Sign of Zorro [*Il segno di Zorro*] aka ***Duel at the Rio Grande***

Mondiale C.C./Fides/Producciones Benito Perojo (Italy/Spain/France); Dyaliscope/Eastmancolor; 90 (84) mins; Producers: Benito Perojo, Harry Joe Brown; Director: Mario Caiano ♰♰♰

Yelling a bizarre Basque high-pitched cry of "Yi-Yi-Yi-Yi-Yi-Ya-Ya-Hey-Hey-Ha-Haha!" Errol Flynn's son Sean stars in this *Zorro* rip-off, in which there is scant evidence of the legendary black-clad crusader. In the 38th minute, Flynn dons a dark green mask and cape, fencing with guards in a mine, and on the hour, "Z" is scrawled on a prison wall. That's it, then, a *Zorro* picture without Zorro. However, Mario Caiano knew how to put an action movie together, coaxing to the surface what latent talent Flynn, Jr. possessed as an actor and coming up with a solid adventure that lapsed into farce at times before rapidly switching to bulldozing excitement. Don sunglasses before you view: Adalberto "Bitto" Albertini and Antonio Macasoli's super-bright photography fully captures the renowned glare of that harsh Mediterranean light. You can almost feel the sweltering heat and taste the dust.

Flynn (Don Ramon Martinez) travels to Mexico to meet the father who deserted him 21 years ago, taking grizzled, jovial mountain peasant Folco Lulli (José) as company (a juicy performance: Brother Piero is also on the cast list). Once there, he discovers his father's unmarked grave; he hanged himself in prison after being accused of crimes against the state. But was he really a traitor? Armando Calvo (General Gutiérrez) instructed Lieutenant Mario Petri (Martino) to murder him in order to lay his hands on the man's silver mine and has taken over his palace of residence with wife Gaby André, unjustly governing with a rod of iron. Flynn, dressed as a dandy, gains entrance to what is rightfully his, gets chatted up by seductress André, flaunting acres of cleavage, and wins the admiring glances of Danielle De Metz (Manuella). Helga Liné (Mercedes) is another beauty flitting in and out of the decorative scenery. In retribution, he then blows the mine to smithereens, forcing Calvo to raise taxes through loss of revenue and bring forward the due date by six months. The locals are now under pressure; blood will be spilt if they don't pay on time. A prolonged street fight that unfortunately lapses into slapstick is followed by Flynn forming an alliance with priest-cum-insurgent Giulio Bosetti (Gomez) and bear-like ruffian Walter Barnes (Mario), a Basque who, with his two pals, likes nothing better than a good scrap when he can find

A Belgian poster for *The Three Swords of Zorro*

one; he also (irritatingly) howls that discordant war cry heard in the opening seconds, a Basque call-to-arms of sorts.

A tax convoy reaches the Rio Grande, due to be robbed by Petri's gang to finance Calvo's personal coffers; Flynn's men gallop in to prevent the theft and in an ensuing duel with Petri, on horseback and on foot, Flynn displays agile, fleet-footed swashbuckling traits inherited from Flynn, Sr., whose bravura at handling the blade became part of Hollywood folklore (note the two horses colliding in this sequence; both steeds appear to be overly stressed). Petri is cut down, toppling into one of Monte Gelato's striking cascades, while back in town, Caiano masterminds a bloody seven-minute siege, the townsfolk, armed with pitchforks, flaming torches and rocks, congregating on Calvo's massed ranks of militia, who open fire with devastating results. Through pure weight of numbers, the mansion walls are breached, the rooms invaded. Calvo is arrested and from the balcony, Flynn, flanked by Barnes, Lulli and Bosetti, tells the crowd that the yoke of subjugation has been lifted; he will now take charge and adopt those same liberal policies advocated by his father. André, free of her domineering husband, heads off to the court at Madrid, leaving De Metz to wed Flynn and start a family. One of Flynn's better acting roles, he puts in an engaging, carefree show and holds the narrative throughout with a measure of poise and self-assurance, something lacking among the nine other pictures he made between and 1957 and 1967.

The Three Swords of Zorro [*Le tre spade di Zorro*] aka *Sword of Zorro*

Rodes Cinematografica/Hispamer (Italy/Spain); CinemaScope/Technicolor; 89 mins; Producers: Tullio Bruschi, Sergio Newman; Director: Ricardo Blasco ††††

In Baja, California in 1830, Governor Antonio Prieto (Don Manuel Parades) pays no heed to central authority, imposing his will on the downtrodden farmers by instructing his soldiers to kill, rape and exact unreasonable tribute. Following a village raid, Diego's wife is murdered, their baby son (also Diego) taken to the sanctuary of the church and placed in a confessional. Years later, Diego (Julio Cesar Sempere) is hunted down and left to rot in a dungeon, but not before carving a "Z" on Prieto's forehead as his calling card. 10 years on, there's no more talk of a "Zorro" in the province, not until a group of inebriated military men accost a farmer in Mikaela Wood's tavern, knocking him from pillar to post. "If you want to enjoy yourselves, here I am." Lash in one hand, rapier in the other, Zorro Mark II (Guy Stockwell) announces his presence, leaping into the fray, reducing the soldiers to quivering cowards, lining them up and instructing the farmer to hit every single one of them hard around the face. Thus a new legend is born; Prieto has another Zorro on his hands, one that falls in love with his unwilling bride-to-be Virginia (the lovely Gloria Milland) and one that carves another "Z" on his acned features to add to the scar of the first one.

Yes, over 30 years before Martin Campbell's $65,000,000 *The Mask of Zorro* hit the screens, Italian movie producers were knocking out their own string of adventures starring the black-masked crusader, some just as good, if not better. Leading lady Milland even resembles Catherine Zeta-Jones! Stockwell, mild-mannered brother of Wood one minute, fearsome freedom fighter the next, wields a blade with zip, the fencing scenes filmed in energetic quick-edits by Blasco. It's tongue-in-cheek stuff, despite Prieto's glum persona and devil-type features, Stockwell playing it just short of laughs, both as Zorro and his alter-ego, although you have to smile at the finish when *three* Zorros appear on the scene: Stockwell, Sempere (reunited with his son) and Wood. If you count one of Prieto's henchmen monkeying around in a Zorro outfit during the climactic masked ball, it makes four! Naturally, Prieto, second-in-command Franco Fantasia (Martinez) and their hyenas get their comeuppances, a newly arrived legislator arresting them for gross misconduct, leaving Marquis Giuseppe Addobbati to grant his blessing for Milland to marry Stockwell; she was only due to wed Prieto as a trade-off for her father's mortgage debts anyway, so she's well rid of the louse.

Horseback skirmishes, coach raids, chases, swordfights, romance—*The Three Swords of Zorro* may appear unpolished by today's standards (the DVD issue is annoyingly blighted by a uneven audio track, reducing Antonio Ramirez Angel's strident

A German poster for *Zorro and the Three Musketeers*

delight and cinematographer Carlo Bellero lit each scene to perfection, especially during the ballroom dance.

Fine credentials, yes, but overall, Capuano's *Zorro* offering is flat-footed and uninteresting. As mentioned, Scott in Zorro guise is only glimpsed twice in shadows and he isn't all that animated in his non-Zorro persona. Accused of treachery against the state by Bernardi, Scott is imprisoned halfway through the movie after a protracted sequence set in a castle courtyard, where nothing of any note occurs. Also prolonged is Scott's head-on-the-block scene, the executioners plied with drink and the citizens clashing with Rizzo's guards, thus allowing the innocent victim to be freed. Capuano also shoots predominantly in longshot, therefore scuppering any hope of intimate drama (but then, does a *Zorro* flick have call for it?); not once is Scott or any of the cast seen in close-up. To be fair, there are a few humorous tavern brawls and briskly fought duels (Scott doesn't at first get on with the Musketeers, then enrolls as one of their number), but it's all done on a comic book level without an iota of depth. The finale, whereby the real turncoat of the piece, Franco Fantasia (the Count of Sevilla), has to do battle with Zorro, the Musketeers *and* D'Artagnan amid the multitude of fountains in the Italian Renaissance gardens of Villa d'Este, Cernobbio, shows Capuano at his best, but by then it's too late in the day, Scott waltzing off with Greci as the Musketeers and D'Artagnan wave goodbye for more adventures. Not one of Gordon Scott's better peplum efforts, or Capuano's either.

1964

D'Artagnan Against the Three Musketeers [*D'Artagnan contro i 3 moschettieri*] aka *Revenge of the Musketeers*

Jonia Film (Italy); Dyaliscope/Eastmancolor; 97 (90) mins; Producers: Felice Felicioni, Jacobo Savina; Director: Fulvio Tului ✝✝

D'Artagnan (Fernando Lamas) has split with the Three Musketeers, Aramis, Porthos and Athos (Roberto Risso, Walter Barnes and Franco Fantasia), both parties finding themselves charged with identical missions, but with a major difference: Lamas is instructed by Folco Lulli (Cardinal Mazarini) and Re-

score to a screech), but it's highly amusing and Stockwell, grinning from ear to ear, appears to be enjoying himself as much as those watching Blasco's swashbuckler will be.

Zorro and the Three Musketeers [*Zorro e i tre moschettieri*] aka *Mask of the Musketeers*

Jonia Film (Italy); Totalscope/Pathécolor; 100 (83) mins; Producer: Marino Vacca; Director: Luigi Capuano ✝✝

Long before a time in current cinematic fads where filmmakers pit one superhero against another, or had them combine forces to overthrow evil, Luigi Capuano and his team had Zorro meeting up with the Three Musketeers and D'Artagnan during the Spanish/French conflict of the early 1800s. Beefcake actor Gordon Scott donned the black cape, riding boots, wide brimmed plumed hat and mask of the avenger, but only twice (and very briefly), at the beginning and end of the action (those muscles are kept firmly under wraps!). Livio Lorenzon, Giacomo Rossi-Stuart, Roberto Risso and Nazzareno Zamperia played Porthos, Athos, Aramis and D'Artagnan respectively, Gianni Rizzo (a good guy for a change) was King Philip of Spain and Nerio Bernardi appeared as Cardinal Richelieu. José Greci (Isabella) and Maria Grazia Spina (Manuella) provided female glamour, Carlo Savina's exuberant score was a noisy

A Spanish lobby card for *D'Artagnan Against the Three Musketeers*

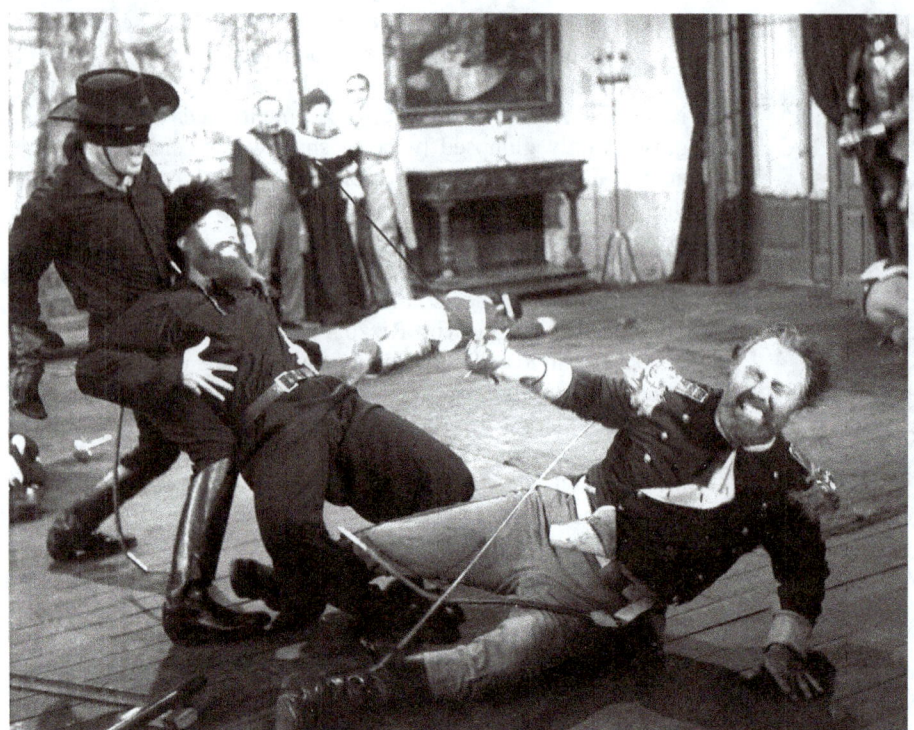

Tony Russel as the masked avenger in a rough and tumble sequence from *The Oath of Zorro*

gent Gloria Milland (Olimpia) to deliver exiled King Charles II of England (Gabriele Antonini) into their safekeeping, as are the Musketeers. At present, he's roaming around at a loose end, chatting up the girls. Moreover, the infamous trio are fully aware that Lulli and Milland plan to hand the king over to Oliver Cromwell for disposal, form an alliance with the country's puritanical Lord Protector and grab the English throne. However, Lamas isn't, hence a clash of interests. When one band of villains after another tries to thwart repeated attempts to steer the king away from a string of beautiful women and face up to his responsibilities, the cry of "All for One! One for All!" goes up; Lamas and his buddies reunite to prevent Charles II from returning to England unguarded, straight into the arms of his anti-Royalist enemies. They also have to rescue him from a hastily arranged wedding, one proposal that has gone a step too far!

Despite a strong cast which includes Lulli's brother, Piero, Carla Calò, Andreina Paul and Ugo Sasso, Fulvio Tului's entry into the list of Italian *Musketeer* outings is a little on the ordinary side, an over-emphasis on talk at the expense of exciting swordplay (it was Tului's one and only stab at direction; he wrote the screenplay to 1964's *Sword of the Empire*). It's handled a little too lightly, Antonini's Charles a dithering libertine forever suggesting wedded bliss to his lady friends without the slightest intention of marrying them. Lamas is as stiff as a pikestaff, nowhere near as animated as Barnes, Fantasia and Risso; Milland is her usual entrancing self (her resemblance at times to Catherine Zeta-Jones is uncanny) and what knockabout fare there is comes in semi-comic style. Charles II is offered safe conduct to England in the end but seems more intent on seeking marriage with the Infanta of Spain than riding away with the Musketeers, retaining to the final curtain the film's humorous tone. On the plus side, Carlo Savina's score, especially the title theme, is a winner.

1965

The Oath of Zorro [*Il giuramento di Zorro*] aka *Behind the Mask of Zorro*

Duca Film/Hispamer (Italy/Spain); Technicolor; 96 mins; Producers: Tullio Bruschi, Sergio Newman; Director: Ricardo Blasco †

Blasco's latter-day slice of peplum *Zorro* hokum featuring Tony Russel, in the dual role of foppish manservant and the audacious masked avenger in black, nosedives into tedium because of its unrelenting humorous approach. Even the principal bad guy doesn't get finished off in the end. Shot in the manner of a Spaghetti Western (arid landscapes and adobe dwellings in glaring sunshine), Russel, to his credit, runs through the stan-

An Italian DVD cover for *Zorro the Rebel*

dard genre tropes with a certain amount of cocky verve, routing bandits who have waylaid a carriage, saving Governor Jesus Puente's (Esteban Garcia) neck more than once from dastardly Capitano Agustin Gonzalez and his mob of comical men-at-arms and finding time to dally with Maria José Alfonso (Manuela), Puente's daughter. Aiding him in his fight for justice is equally foppish Pepe Rubio (Marcel), a young entomologist-cum-inventor who could be mistaken for Russel's double in bad light.

Yes, there's a glut of fencing and parrying, with much bounding over tables and jumping off stairways; Zorro's supporters dress up in nun's outfits to haul Alfonso out of jail, and don Russian outfits in the closing minutes to outwit Gonzalez's rogues at a reception, but it's all rather predictable, a waning cycle with nothing new to say and nowhere to go. To the sound of Angel Arteaga's irritating happy-go-lucky music, Gonzalez is last seen scampering over the horizon with his tail between his legs, accompanied by two henchmen, while Russel, as if we hadn't guessed already, gets the girl. Instantly forgettable *Zorro* fodder, surprisingly so when you consider that Blasco and his producers had fared a whole lot better in 1963's *The Three Swords of Zorro*.

1966

Zorro the Rebel [*Zorro il ribelle*]

Romana Film (Italy); Technicolor; 93 (89) mins; Producer: Fortunato Misiano; Director: Piero Pierotti ✝✝✝✝

Considering that Pierotti's *Zorro* offering was made at the very tail end of the peplum boom, *Zorro the Rebel* was spiffy, energetic and surprisingly fresh, a difficult task as practically every movie featuring the black-clad masked crusader centered on the same storyline. But somehow, the director pulled it off. Howard "Red" Ross, in his final peplum (he starred in 14 if you include the ultra-rare *La notte dell'innominato* [*Night of the Unnamed*, 1962]), turned in a robust, pleasing performance, taking on the twin roles of spineless Don Ramiro (he hates fighting, horses and is always sniffing into a handkerchief) and his dashing alter-ego, Zorro, who metes out rough justice to those deserving of it. Set in the Mexican Spanish colony of La Paloma, the story had accommodating Don Miguel (Edoardo Toniolo) handing local peons the deeds to the land on which they had worked so hard for centuries, much to the disgust of Governor Don Alvarez (Arturo Dominici) and his foul son, whose mind is "clouded by madness" (a lesson in vile villainy from Charles Borromel). The pattern of events from then on differs no more from many, many other *Zorro* flicks. Borromel, spouting lines of Shakespeare in times of stress and drunkenness, desires Toniolo's daughter, busty blonde Lady Isabella (Dina De Santis), who loathes him on sight ("I'll have her! I'll tame her! I'll master her!"). Dominici reckons the marriage might bring his unstable son to his senses; the peons are persecuted by Nello Pazzafini's gorillas, acting for Borromel; Toniolo is arrested and imprisoned, to be released on condition his daughter weds Borromel; a pair of lovers (Valentino Macchi and Gabriella Andreini) assist the vigilantes in their secret cave hideout and, every so often, Ross swings into action, displaying nimbleness of foot when on his rapier parries, proving an annoyance to Dominici, Borromel and company.

"A mole on her left shoulder. A pleasant inspection of each one of you," leers Borromel to a group of terrified nuns, in a convent scullery searching for De Santis, who sports that distinctive mark, the poor girl stating to her maid, "Not every man can be as handsome and courageous as Zorro," unaware that prissy would-be beau Don Ramiro is, in fact, her handsome, courageous hero. To prevent the betrothal of Borromel and De Santis from taking place, she gets hitched to Ross (as Ramiro), but this bogus state of wedlock doesn't even get as far as the bedroom ("Are you a man or a jellyfish? Thank heavens this marriage hasn't been consummated!" she fires at him), leaving the door wide open for Borromel to annul the union and arrange his own nuptials ("Kill him. Then you can marry a widow," suggests Dominici). The action climaxes in a terrific fight at the wedding ceremony. Ross' men, disguised as monks (The Venerable Order of the Black Virgin!), infiltrate the palace carrying candlesticks, which turn out to be spears; unusually, during the fracas, not one of the main bad guys gets finished off, Pazzafini split across the cheek by Zorro's blade, while Borromel and Dominici are tied up and detained in cages. Ross and De Santis, to the cheers of the crowd, gallop off to exercise their conjugal rights—that "jellyfish" has turned into the man of her dreams!

Colorful photography by veteran Augusto Tiezzi, a noisy, castanets-laden Spanish score from Angelo Francesco Lavagnino and forceful lens work from Pierotti breathed new life, if but for an instant, into a fast-fading area of cloak-and-dagger Italian cinema. These three proven experts of pepla alone ensured that *Zorro the Rebel* would end the series with a bang, not a whimper. Although *Zorro* carried on up to 1970 in *Zorro the Fox* (1968), *The Nephew of Zorro* (1968), *Zorro, the Navarra Marquis* (1969), *The Avenger, Zorro* (1969) and *Zorro in the Court of England* (1970), *Zorro the Rebel* marked the final stages of the classic peplum movies featuring the masked champion of the downtrodden poor, an entertaining closing shot featuring one of Howard Ross' best performances.

19
It Wasn't Only the Italians

As the peplum explosion gained pace, film companies outside of Italy, even those in the United Kingdom, jumped on the bandwagon and came up with their own versions of sword and sandal, *fusto* and *cappa e spada*. The French and the Spanish had cooperated with the Italians on a vast number of projects covering a vast number of subjects but, on occasion, were the main driving force in their own productions. For instance, *King of the Vikings* and *Marie of the Isles* are both peplum (and long-forgotten ones) but made in Spain and France respectively, working jointly with the Italians; thus the reason why these particular films are featured in this chapter. All except *The 300 Spartans* and *The War Lord* can be classed as low-to-medium budget, although Rudolph Maté's $8,000,000 Ancient Greek saga and Franklin J. Schaffner's $3,500,000 overlooked Middle Ages masterpiece aren't that high on cost, even for 1962 and 1965. All credit to Hammer Film Productions for flying the peplum flag in Britain, mostly in a string of dynamic pirate, Robin Hood and swashbuckling costume actioners, while the United States came up with their own variation on the Robin Hood legend, a neglected Biblical classic and Ali Baba; B-movie maestro Roger Corman even "tried it on" with *Atlas*, probably the cheapest, tattiest muscleman movie ever foisted onto an unsuspecting paying public, and that includes the very worst of Latin examples. In sharp comparison, Fox's *The 300 Spartans* is as close to authentic sword and sandal spectacle as you can possibly get without Italian involvement. So the following pages present a varied selection of 30 motion pictures produced between 1958 and 1967, each in its own fashion embodying the Italian spirit of pepla, while not being Italian in origin; like the Italian craze, they more or less petered out toward the end of 1967 as X-rated crime, gangster, Western and social sex dramas took prominence in theaters. Applaud them for the colorful, innocent, entertaining nonsense they purported to be, before cinema audiences rejected them in favor of more unsavory fare. In this particular chapter, I have put the English release title first on foreign productions to avoid confusion.

1958

Son of Robin Hood

20th Century Fox/Argo (US/UK); CinemaScope/Technicolor; 81 mins; Produced and Directed by George Sherman ✝✝✝

Often cited as the worst *Robin Hood* film ever made, *Son of Robin Hood* is, in fact, one of the most pleasurable to sit through, thanks to a short running time, decent photography (Arthur Grant), a rousing Olde English score (Leighton Lucas) and incisive camerawork from veteran George Sherman, director of over 100 movies dating back to 1937, many of them B-Westerns. David Hedison, fresh from his triumph in Fox's hugely successful X-rated *The Fly* in the same year, was the token pretty-boy American among a cast of English stalwarts: June Laverick, David Farrar, Philip Friend, Delphi Lawrence, George Coulouris, Marius Goring, George Woodbridge, Humphrey Lestocq and Noel Hood. Overall performances were adequate rather than spectacular (the Italians put far more conviction into

their villainy than Farrar, Friend and Lestocq managed here), while Laverick was as pretty as a peach in an innocent English way, not a smoldering, sluttish, uninhibited Italian way. Acting honors went to burly George Woodbridge; doyen of scores of British features going right back to 1937 and a Hammer regular, his gruff Little John stole the show from the bigger names, proof that the industry relied on support actors of his caliber to fill in the cracks and ensure matters were running on an even keel.

Robin Hood's son is actually a daughter! Pert Laverick plays Deering Hood; Hedison is Jamie, the brother of the deposed Earl of Chester (Goring), who festers in Farrar's (Simon Des Roches) castle. Hedison returns from Spain, learns of his brother's plight and trades places with Laverick ("I pledge my bow to your cause"), joining Robin Hood's old band to bring justice to the persecuted foresters, but not before the pair have slipped into Farrar's court masquerading as a marquis and his wife to find out the lay of the land and who is disclosing the rebels' plans to the enemy. Unfortunately (or fortunately?) for Hedison, the real marquis has the prestige of being a serial female seducer of some note and is pounced upon by man-eater Lawrence, betrothed to Friend, leading to a midnight tryst in her secret love den reached by a hidden passage under the moat. George W. George and George F. Slavin's witty script then comes into its own when Hedison returns to Laverick's bedchamber. "Well," she fumes, "we're here to find a traitor, not for you to spend half the night with Lady Sylvia!"

"I told you De Valle had a reputation and I've got to live up to it. It was for the cause. You sound like a jealous wife," is his grinning riposte, calling her "Sir Fair Legs," which annoys the lass even further (the actress flashes those legs up to and beyond the thighs in one revealing scene). The effervescent Hedison/Laverick relationship keeps things on the boil—she loves him,

310 *Heroes Never Die!*

A French poster for *The Captain*

Adapted from Michel Zevaco's 1906 novel *Le Capitan*, André Hunebelle's enjoyable actioner cast renowned French heartthrob (and director Jean Cocteau's muse) Jean Marais in the role of famed swordsman Francois de Capestan, championing King Louis XIII's cause in 1616. The 15-year-old boy monarch is being threatened on all sides: by his scheming mother Marie de Medicis (Lise Delamare), by his treacherous consultant Concini (Arnoldo Foà) and by untrustworthy Gisele of Angouleme (Elsa Martinelli), who covets the throne for her father Raphael Patorni. An unlikely assistant to Marais in his mission to put paid to the king's enemies is French comedian Bourvil, otherwise André Robert Raimbourg, a street player performing card tricks with the aid of his horse and useless with a sword; Marais has to instruct him in the finer details of the art later on.

Marais was one of Hunebelle's favorite actors, the director using him as a lead in eight of his productions, three of which included Bourvil: this picture and two further swashbucklers, *The Hunchback* (1959) and *Miracle of the Wolves* (1961). French swashbucklers, although slightly more refined, lacked the visceral blood and guts attitude that hallmarked the volatile Italian *cappa e spada*; they looked great, but, in terms of British film classification, were nearer the friendlier "U" for everyone than the adult "A" and "X" ratings. *The Captain*, filmed on location in six real medieval castles, is no exception. Hunebelle ups the pace most, if not all, of the time; Marcel Grignon's diamond-hard cinematography throws into relief every stone block in those ancient gray edifices, while adding sparkle to the court and its costumes and Marais, as might be expected, made an energetic, dashing heroic caped figure, taking on most of his own stunts, including scaling the walls of the magnificently imposing Chateau de Val at Lanobre, Cantal, to free Martinelli from her cell. This tense, sweat-inducing 15-minute segment, coming slap bang in the middle of the film, had Marais climbing the walls using daggers as pitons to gain a foothold, then swinging over a vertiginous gulf from a buttress by way of a grappling hook to gain entry into the fortress. Undertaken without the aid of back projection or digital chicanery, Marais (aged 47) seemed distinctly nervous during this lengthy, taut sequence, and who could blame him! The climactic mass bout of swordplay amid the fortifications and rooftops of the Chateau de Pierrefonds, Oise, was an exciting slice of action-packed cinema. It compensates for Bourvil's cheesy singing interludes with girlfriend Jacqueline Porel, a weird few minutes where a dwarf alchemist concocts a poisoned liquid, mildly amusing comical/magic sketches in the palace and blonde Annie Anderson (Beatrice) wandering around set like a French Barbie doll. Foà and confederate Guy Delorme are put to the sword in the end, Martinelli redeeming herself by preventing the young king, Christian Fourcade, from being shot in the back; she canters off with gay cavalier Marais to get wed after the swordsman has been lauded for his bravery.

he loves her, but neither will admit it, an engaging double act from the attractive pair. The action rattles through its paces. Goring is branded with a red-hot iron, prioress Hood is the informer, relaying messages to Lestocq via carrier hawk, Coulouris (Alan-a-Dale) is almost stretched on the rack, Hedison is imprisoned in a cell adjacent to his brother and the castle is stormed at the end by Sherwood Forest's Merry Men, led by Laverick in smart, Robin Hood Lincoln green tights. The trio of knaves all perish, Goring is free to become a future English king and Hedison vows to marry Laverick before the sun sets.

What a pity the production team chose to depict the castle as a painted backcloth. With England chock-a-block full of castles of every age, shape, size and description, they could easily have taken a leaf out of Italian filmmakers' book and had the cast perform in a real edifice, a black mark for the production team. But there were a lot worse films of this type around in the late '50s, early '60s, and although *Son of Robin Hood* may be classed as lightweight and cheap-looking, it's fun and never boring, a picture for the whole family to enjoy.

1960

The Captain [*Le capitan*] aka Captain Blood; The King's Captain

Pathé Consortium/Da.Ma. Cinematografica (France/Italy); Dyaliscope/Eastmancolor; 105 mins; Producers: René Bezard, Pierre Cabaud; Director: André Hunebelle ✝✝✝

King of the Vikings [*El principe encadenado*]

Europa de Cine S.A. (Spain/Italy); CinemaScope/Technicolor; 100 (81) mins; Producer: Miguel A. Martin; Director: Luis Lucia ✝✝✝✝

What a dilemma facing King Gudrun of Denmark. When his son is born, his wife (half Dane, half Viking) dying in childbirth, it is prophesied that the prince will, in years to come, cause war between the Danes and their Viking neighbors, bring death and misfortune to the land and kill the King of Denmark, a curse brought upon the monarch's head by barbaric acts of slaughter

A Spanish poster for *King of the Vikings*

cus) challenges Prendes to a fight to the death in front of both factions. Prendes, disarmed in the duel, grabs Mahor round the throat, dagger poised. A well-aimed lance thrown by a Danish commander sends him to his doom. In effect, Escriva has, as the prophecy foretold, killed the King of Denmark; it just so happens to be Prendes, not Vilar! "Long live the King of the Danes *and* the Vikings" roar the soldiers and peasants as Escriva, reconciled with his father, cuddles Mahor, no doubt waiting to indulge in the delights that lie waiting underneath that fetching blue outfit she fills so enticingly.

At a Spanish Film Awards ceremony in 1960 (The National Union of the Spectacle), *King of the Vikings* won an award for best cinematography (Alejandro Ulloa). The color *is* first-rate, as is Luis Lucia's artistic control of the camera and Cristobal Halffter's rumbustious music. Yes, it's wordy in parts, but the four main leads bounce off each other with aplomb, Mahor adding to the sense of drama with an androgynous mix of cute sexiness and steely resolve. Escriva was a noted Spanish actor of his day, tragically dying in an automobile accident in 1996, aged 65. Here, he burns up the screen, his intense performance positive-

against the Vikings. To prevent this catastrophic chain of events from taking place, little Harald is banished to a cave in a remote valley guarded by 100 archers. And this is where the movie begins—Danish consul Luis Prendes and his troops try to enter the forbidden valley, are driven back and return to court with a ring embossed with the royal seal. In a fit of conscience, Gudrun (Antonio Vilar) orders that Harald, now 30, be released from exile and given a chance to rule the throne as the rightful heir ("Bring him here and observe his actions."), prophesy or no prophesy. Prendes, his own designs on the throne thrown into confusion, boils with indignation while Javier Loyola, Harald's lifelong guardian, calls into doubt the king's decision and, as it turns out, rightly so. When Harald (Javier Escriva, one of three scriptwriters) turns up in the palace minus his shackles, he rants, raves, questions everything around him ("What am I doing here? I've lived 30 years in a filthy cave, a living death!"), declares his hatred for Vilar ("You fear my Viking blood! My sad destiny was to have you as a father.") and storms around court like a crazed maniac, throwing the dungeon keeper out of a window to his death and releasing Viking prisoners. In the space of one hour, the madman has wreaked havoc ("I'll be King of the Vikings! I won't be a Danish king!") and Vilar, thoroughly alarmed, has unwisely given his unhinged sibling three days to prove his worth. When will this unexpected nightmare end?

It's a novel twist on the old "son has returned to reclaim the throne" scenario by having that returned son behave like a certifiable lunatic, not a sensible, upstanding king-in-waiting. Tormented Escriva is anything but sensible and upstanding, finding solace in the arms of warrior girl Maria Mahor, who soothes his troubled brow and tries to convince him that buried under all that angst is a true monarch with the strength of character to rule. Needless to say, Prendes seizes the opportunity to force Vilar into abdication and crown himself king, marching off to the valley where Escriva, drugged and carried back to his grotto, is inciting a rebellion against the usurper. Following a mass scrimmage among the valley's odd, mushroom-shaped rocks (filmed at Spain's La Ciudad Encantada area with its bizarre rock formations), Escriva (resembling a beefed-up Kirk Douglas in *Sparta-*

A Spanish poster for *Marie of the Isles*

ly mesmerizing in a buoyant Spanish/Italian peplum offering that is extremely difficult to come by these days; DVD issues contain jumps in continuity at the start, the credits are truncated and the widescreen format lost to pan and scan.

Marie of the Isles [*Marie des Isles*] aka *The Filibusters of Martinique*

Radius Prod./Tibre Film (France/Italy); Dyaliscope/Technicolor; 111 (103) mins; Producers: Georges and Yvette Combret; Director: Georges Combret ♱♱ (♱ if Lee wasn't in it)

Continuing her movie career sojourn in Italy, Belinda Lee took star billing in Georges Combret's French/Italian seafaring saga set in 1635 (copies are extremely difficult to lay hands on) in which the plot appeared to be cut into pieces, tossed in the air and the pieces stuck back together at random; much of it is totally incomprehensible, particularly in the middle section where Lee disappears for around 10 minutes, there's frequent mention of a pirate named Barracuda who's only spotted briefly toward the closing stages and one is never quite sure who is good, and who is bad, or what they're up to. It's a real mess, saved by Lee's in-your-face sexed-up presence; without her, the film wouldn't be worth a light.

Lee is Marie Bonnard, your archetypal buxom tavern wench (and so is her pal, Magali Noel) dreaming of a better life in sunnier climes, sick of customers ogling and brawling over her cleavage. She gets the hots for Alain Saury (Jacques), a young officer due to take up a post in the Caribbean, but fights shy of his advances (Lee—shy? That's a bit hard to swallow!). Her father is ordered to build a ship, *La Belle France* (why isn't made clear), and Lee marries starchy Jacques Castelot (Count Cheneau de Saint-André), the sole reason to escape her Dieppe surroundings, refusing to consummate the union. In the Caribbean, the new but unhappy (despite all her jewelry and sudden wealth) Madame de Saint-André finds that Saury is Governor of Martinique, while her frustrated husband is pirating goods to the natives, in league with pirate boss Barracuda (Noel Roquevert). The whole plot unravels alarmingly after 40-odd minutes, exacerbated by continuity jumps. Lee teases and flirts with ruffian Folco Lulli and his randy mate, their attempts to untie her blouse thwarted by a giggle and a slap; there's a grotesque tribal dance, the white-painted natives intoxicated on contraband rum; and Saury flits in and out of the scenario after his ship is scuppered, trying to pin down the restless natives and Lee (whom we are led to believe is still a virgin). Sweaty overweight traitor Dario Moreno offers to save Lulli from being hanged if Lee will surrender her charms to him; Lulli and arch rival Philippe Hersent constantly bicker, forever grabbing the hilts of their swords; and Castelot is up to all kinds of tricks known only to himself, not the audience (peplum nasty Ivano Staccioli lurks in the background but doesn't do a lot). It all climaxes in a mass scrimmage inside the governor's fortress between Roquevert's pirates, Castelot's men, Saury's followers, Lulli's brigands and a few natives who have stated to Saury, "We will go with big white chief." The fortress is blown sky-high, Castelot perishing under rubble, and Lee finally weds her man.

Director Combret takes full advantage of Lee's heavily promoted sexual lust allure, probably to pull in the punters. She's shown peeling off black stockings, his camera zooms in on those wanton features, and there are two nude silhouette shots, one nipple is briefly exposed and she's forever flashing her legs and thighs, on top of emoting like crazy. The girl had it and knew how to flaunt it! Take her out of the equation, and you are left with one of the most head-scratching, awkwardly constructed semi-piratical romps of all time; even Georges Van Parys' fine score and Pierre Petit's lush photography can't haul the picture out of its watery grave.

The Story of Ruth

20th Century Fox (US); CinemaScope/DeLuxecolor; 132 mins; Producer: Samuel G. Engel; Director: Henry Koster ♱♱♱♱♱

In the land of Moab of long ago, the people worship the stone god Chemosh, offering up children as human sacrifice. Ruth, being groomed as a priestess in Hedak's temple, meets Judaean goldsmith Mahlon, who plants the seeds of religious doubt in her mind, the stimulus for her to question the Moabites' barbaric faith in a stone idol; Mahlon advises that she should take up the Hebrews' beliefs in a more compassionate being. During a ceremony in which an eight-year-old is brutally sacrificed, Ruth recoils in horror, imprisoned six months for disruption, to be cleansed of her subversive feelings; Mahlon is apprehended and forced to work in a quarry, his brother and father killed in custody. Released from her cell, Ruth arranges Mahlon's escape, but he's fatally wounded in the attempt; Ruth, Mahlon and Naomi, his mother take refuge in a cave, where the couple exchange marriage vows before he expires. Ruth, as a sign of her new faith, sets free her slave, Kera; with Naomi, she crosses the River Jordan, taking up residence in Naomi's run-down homestead near Bethlehem. The Moabitess then becomes the subject of malicious gossip mongering, treated like a pariah by the women in the city marketplace. Naomi's two kinsmen, Boaz and Tob, figure prominently in Ruth's life; she loves Boaz but, under Hebrew law, Tob has first rights on her as a wife. Counter to his will, Boaz has to testify against Ruth's former idolatry ways to the Council of Elders; however, she's vindicated when two eye witnesses lie on oath. At the harvest festival, Ruth is about to marry Tob but declares to the crowd that she doesn't love him; dejected, Tob relinquishes his claim on her and Ruth marries Boaz, as foretold to Naomi by the prophet Jehoam. Their children's children will result in the birth of David, future King of Bethlehem and Israel.

The pages of the Old Testament sprang vividly to life in Henry Koster's lengthy, involving, intelligent Biblical yarn which boasted a worthy cinematic pedigree among its team. Koster, who directed *The Robe* (1953), was nominated for an Oscar several times in his career, while composer Franz Waxman won two and cinematographer Arthur E. Arling one. There was also a strong Jewish connection: Koster's family came from a Jewish background, scriptwriter Norman Corwin was Jewish and female lead Elana Eden was an Israeli. Pictorially, the film dazzles the eye, particularly during the first 48 minutes with the depiction of the Asian-looking Moabite city, its gigantic stone idol and the colossal quarry that the slaves toil in. Corwin's script is pithy and straight to the point, cutting out all the sermonizing and sanctimonious air that blights many such Biblical essays by getting down to the nitty-gritty. "To die with Chemosh is to live forever," states Eden (Ruth) to Tom Tryon (Mahlon) at their first secret meeting, the idea of an "invisible god" amusing her. "I was at peace before I met you," she moans after they kiss, confused, especially as the temple has previously announced that she's a possible king's favorite. Burly Thayer David plays High Priest Hedak as a smarmy, shaven-headed bully, High Priestess Viveca Lindfors (Eleilat) a poisonous viper ready to stamp on anyone who dares disagree with her unholy opinions. A riveting scene shows slaves crushed under the pedestal of Chemosh's statue before Tryon scrambles to freedom, Eden forming an intimate bond with his mother, Naomi, following his death; the heartbroken mother is beautifully realized by veteran actress Peggy Wood, her tentative relationship with her daughter-in-law, already a widow, touching and soul-stirring.

The Story of Ruth's second half moves away from Moab into Israel. Of the two men in Eden's troubled life, Stuart Whitman (Boaz) is the more upright and honest, Jeff Morrow (Tob) a ruthless landowner overfond of wine (it makes a change to see Morrow in Biblical garb and not combating various monsters as he did in his run of classic '50s horror/sci-fi flicks). Corwin's screenplay focuses on this triangular relationship and the cruel attitudes of the Judaean women who, in promoting their god as an all-seeing, all-believing deity, appear as bad as the Moabites in their worship of a stone idol, confirmation that over the centuries, gods, in one shape or another, have caused nothing but trouble. Another touching interlude is when Wood breaks down, praying for Eden to be spared any further suffering and an end to the drought. Eduard Franz appears (as Jehoam, a holy man sent from God), assures her that everything will work out for the best, sends forth rain and ordains that Eden will marry God's chosen partner. After being cleared of heresy, marriage plans are made. At her wedding ceremony, Eden announces to Morrow, "It's true that I do not love you, but I will try," going on, "Last

Television's most famous Robin Hood, Richard Greene, makes it to the big screen in *Sword of Sherwood Forest.*

night I sought out Boaz on the threshing floor," although nothing untoward happened. Morrow admits defeat and Eden and Whitman are then wed, Franz mingling with the onlookers, smiling to Wood—his prophecy has come true, as predicted.

Resembling Haya Harareet's Esther in *Ben-Hur*, Eden, her oval features lit by huge brown almond eyes, positively radiates enchanting grace and tough inner resolve as Ruth, a young woman in torment from choosing one god over another (the part was originally offered to Susan Strasberg before Koster decided on an unknown); amazingly, the actress only ever made one other motion picture before quitting the business in 1966. Wood as Naomi, her life of hardship finally rewarded by the marriage of the two people closest to her, is truly wonderful, a tissue-inducing turn if ever there was one. On the production front, Franz Waxman's horn-laden score resonates and tingles the spine, while Arling's photography glows as much as Eden's refined features. Over 132 minutes, Koster pitches the pace perfectly, never allowing the dialogue-driven plot to lapse into tedium. Even for those not addicted to two-hour-plus Biblical movies, *The Story of Ruth* is an overlooked treasure that deserves far wider recognition than it has ever been afforded, shunted aside in the wake of far costlier '60s epics based on similar themes.

Sword of Sherwood Forest

Hammer/Columbia (UK); Megascope/Eastmancolor; 80 mins; Producers: Sidney Cole, Richard Greene; Director: Terence Fisher ✞✞✞

Star of 143 television episodes of *The Adventures of Robin Hood* (1955-1960), Richard Greene made his Robin Hood swansong in the second of Hammer's four *Robin Hood* excursions (the first, 1954's *The Men of Sherwood Forest*, was the company's debut color production, Don Taylor in the title role—see chapter two). The man in green tights crossed longbows and broadswords with Peter Cushing's dastardly Sheriff of Nottingham in a tale of treachery. Richard Pasco (Edward, Earl of Newark), impressed by Greene's archery skills, tries to employ the Sherwood Forest outlaw chief as an assassin without him realizing it, the aim to murder the Archbishop of Canterbury (Jack Gwillim) and take possession of Bortrey Castle and its estates, being on the market due to the death of the owner in the Crusades campaigns. Members of Pasco's sect sport a gold emblem depicting a falcon clutching a daisy; Greene has spotted one before, on a dying stranger whose last breath was to warn him of great danger. Greene meets up with Sarah Branch (as Maid Marian), marrying the frisky blonde in the end and receiving a free pardon after Cushing is stabbed three times in the back by sulky, glowering Oliver Reed (Lord Melton: His peculiar Irish accent was the result of bad dubbing), Pasco run through by Greene in a frantic skirmish inside a priory.

Attractively shot in County Wicklow, Ireland, Terence Fisher was no stranger to the *Robin Hood* legend, having directed 11 entrants in the television series in 1956/1957. There isn't a great deal of dramatic thrust on offer here, the action suffering from a lack of dynamics, Fisher content to dwell on Ireland's green and pleasant wooded scenery rather than swashbuckling savagery (a graphic flogging on a whipping post *is* shown). However, the experienced cast makes it all so watchable. Greene (42 at the time) sailed through the role, as well he might with all those TV shows under his belt, while Cushing *never* turned in a bad performance throughout his extensive, varied career, always worth the price of admission. Nigel Green (Little John), Niall MacGinnis (Friar Tuck), Vanda Godsell (the evil prioress), Edwin Richfield (the sheriff's lieutenant), Pasco, Branch and Reed acted with conviction, and British crooner Denis Lotis warbled a medieval ditty, playing troubadour Alan-A-Dale. Originally released in England on a double bill with Columbia's *The 3 Worlds of Gulliver*, *Sword of Sherwood Forest* is a typical medium-budget Hammer non-horror offering of the day, entertaining but, in the long run, leaving very little impression on the senses.

1961

Atlas

Beacon Films/Filmgroup (US); Vistascope/Eastmancolor; 79 mins; Produced and Directed by Roger Corman ††

To the sound of wooden swords hitting plastic shields and two armies, each composed of around 20 warriors, throwing sticks at one another, Roger Corman's $70,000 ode to peplum opened to much cynical abuse from critics in 1961. Noting the success of the Italian *Hercules* features, the resourceful director of '50s B-horror movies and his entourage of regulars flew to Greece for six weeks shooting, concocting a low-budget peplum pastiche in between sunbathing and taking in the sights. We're not talking Mario Caiano, Domenico Paolella, Alberto De Martino or Carlo Campogalliani here—we're talking Roger Corman, where the City of Thenis is a collection of stone ruins, where forces totalling 40 men clash, the dead quickly rising to keep the numbers going, where weapons are of the type made by kids in their back gardens and where Charles B. Griffith's modernistic screenplay, spoken in broad American accents, destroys any sword and sandal ambience *Atlas* may have nurtured. Six-foot-three-inch Corman bit player Michael Forest

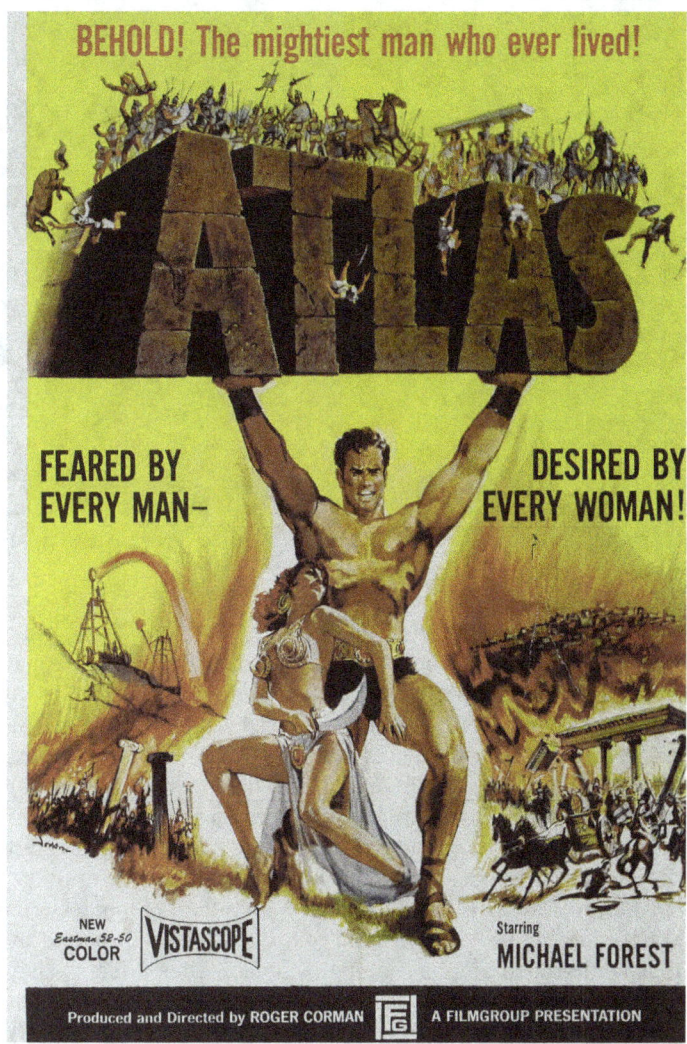

starred as the titular hero, the actor *not* possessing the physique of a Steve Reeves or Gordon Scott, wiry rather than muscular, while Frank Wolff did a corny impersonation of mad emperor Commodus, even though Commodus wasn't in it. All credit to composer Ronald Stein for conjuring up an ear-battering score, following in the musical footsteps of Carlo Rustichelli, Angelo Francesco Lavagnino and others, although for some strange reason, his soundtrack disappears for 10 minutes after half an hour. Ultimately, *Atlas* is cheap and downright dreary, warranting two stars because of Stein's score, Griffith's hilarious dialogue, picturesque Greek temples overlooking the blue Aegean and a sassy performance from Barboura Morris as female love interest Candia, the girl, knickers permanently on show, behaving as though she's just stepped off the streets of New York after lunch with her mates.

Praximedes the Tyrant (Wolff) plans to invade Thenis. King Telektos (Andreas Filippides) declares a duel of champions from opposing sides; if Wolff's man triumphs, his troops can take over the state. In a less-than-packed arena (about a dozen citizens), Wolff chooses Forest as his representative when he emerges an Olympic winner, although the athlete abhors violence. During a banquet (yes, Corman includes a Chelo Alonso look-alike dancer), a drunken reveler converses with Forest: "Atlas—when you fight a really strong man, with sinews like iron, with flesh like marble and you defeat him, how does it make you feel?"

Hammer stalwart Peter Cushing is Squire Trevenyan, up to his neck in smuggling in *Fury at Smugglers' Bay*.

"Tired," Forest retorts.

The nuisance then ogles Morris, flaunting her full figure and flashing smile. "Who's that brazen harlot?"

"She's my sister," Forest shoots back, irritated. "Were you ordered to work on me?" Forest enquires of Morris as she devours him with her eyes. On the march to Thenis, an ambush takes place, dreadfully choreographed by Corman (even the worst of pepla never came up with anything as lame as this) before Forest defeats Christos Exanchos (Prince Indros) in the battle of titans, but he refuses to kill him. "The city is yours," Filippides tells Wolff, the ranting victor treated to a clumsy dance routine by four white-robed virgins tripping over each other's feet ("They dance like my grandmother."). We then get a sustained 10-minute bout of confusing double-cross and intrigue, the film rapidly going downhill (Stein's music vanishes again for a second time). Wolff is unveiled as an unhinged creep, blonde maiden Miranda Kounelaki (Ariana: She's no Wandisa Guida, that's for sure!) is marked for sacrifice and Corman wraps matters up with another bloodless, punchless skirmish in another empty amphitheater (although we do get the standard peplum "slashed face" wheeling toward camera). The director enters the fray, dressed as a soldier; well, why not, everyone else was joining in the fun and games. During a struggle, Forest breaks Wolff's neck, and peace is restored to Thenis (and sanity to the viewer), the hero riding off to Egypt with Morris in the setting sun to set up house. It is sad to note when watching the picture that both Wolff and Morris died at the early age of 43: Wolff from suicide, Morris from heart seizure.

Fury at Smugglers' Bay

Regal Films Intl. (UK); Panascope/Eastmancolor; 92 (82) mins; Producer and Director: John Gilling ✝✝✝

British film producers began a run of late 18th-century swashbucklers around this period, ranging from the good to the commonplace. John Gilling, who wrote the script and story in addition to producing and directing, came up with one of the better examples, a variation on Daphne du Maurier's *Jamaica Inn*, featuring a strong cast: Peter Cushing, Bernard Lee, John Fraser, William Franklyn, June Thorburn, Liz Fraser, George Coulouris and star of four Italian pepla, French actress Michele Mercier. Although set in Cornwall, shooting took place in the picturesque locale of Abereiddy, Pembrokeshire, Wales (the rugged Welsh and Cornish coastlines bear a marked similarity); Harry Waxman's sharp photography brings out the best of the rocky, indented seascapes. It's a fast-moving adventure containing bags of incident and fireworks, although one is left with the impression that given a bigger budget, the picture could have been a minor classic of its type.

Cushing plays Squire Trevenyan, a strict magistrate residing in the Cornish seacoast village of Tarn, home to a gang of smugglers led by Lee (Black John). Fraser is Cushing's illegitimate son, in love with Mercier (Louise), his father frowning upon the relationship ("She's the daughter of a tradesman."), while highwayman Franklyn, when not rolling in the straw with busty barmaid Fraser (Betty) and nibbling her delectable neck, is busy defending the locals from Cushing's tyranny in the guise of The Captain. Tavern brawls, wrecked ships, storms, skirmishes on the beach between smugglers, villagers and the military, Coulouris (Mercier's father) threatened with deportation for receiving stolen contraband, Franklyn and Fraser dueling on a windswept tor and lovely June Thorburn's talents *not* put to better use (she should have had Mercier's part, not wasted as Cushing's daughter)—Gilling's action-packed yarn merrily bulldozes its way through the motions, the only plot surprise being that Cushing is in cahoots with Lee, blackmailed because of Fraser's illegitimacy and the fact that Lee, once the squire's groom, was thrashed regularly by him when in service; the leering seadog has never forgotten his harsh treatment. The finale occurs in a large sea cave, soldiers versus smugglers, the air blue with pistol smoke. Lee is stabbed to death after shooting Cushing, Fraser is reunited with Mercier and likeable Franklyn, pardoned of his crimes, rides off to rob another area of its riches, for some reason leaving the luscious Liz Fraser behind. A few niggling jumps in continuity point to the British censor's scissors having trimmed the movie of some of its more violent elements (the same thing happened with *The Pirates of Blood River* in 1962); Cushing is quoted as saying that he enjoyed working on the film, and it shows in his usual keenly observed character study, the full quota of Cushing mannerisms on display, a real delight for the actor's legions of admirers. *Fury at Smugglers' Bay* is an agreeable British costume swashbuckler that proved popular on U.K. circuits in the early 1960s, Peter Cushing and the solid support cast on top form.

Pirates of Tortuga

20th Century Fox (US); CinemaScope/DeLuxecolor; 97 mins; Producer: Sam Katzman; Director: Robert D. Webb ✝✝✝

King of the B-quickies producer Sam Katzman and director Robert D. Webb's pirate caper is a bright and breezy family affair: colorful photography (Ellis W. Carter), a salty, tuneful score (Paul Sawtell, Bert Shefter) and believable performances from the players. After three years at sea, Captain Bart Paxton (Ken Scott) docks in London and is immediately commissioned by King Charles II to about face and sail to the West Indies, there to dispose of Henry Morgan and his buccaneers (we get a "peplum pose" moment here, three swords at Scott's throat to prevent him leaving the city in a hurry). The privateer is creating havoc in the colonies and the king wants an end to it all. Stowing on board the Mermaid is dancing street thief Meg (Leticia Roman), for-

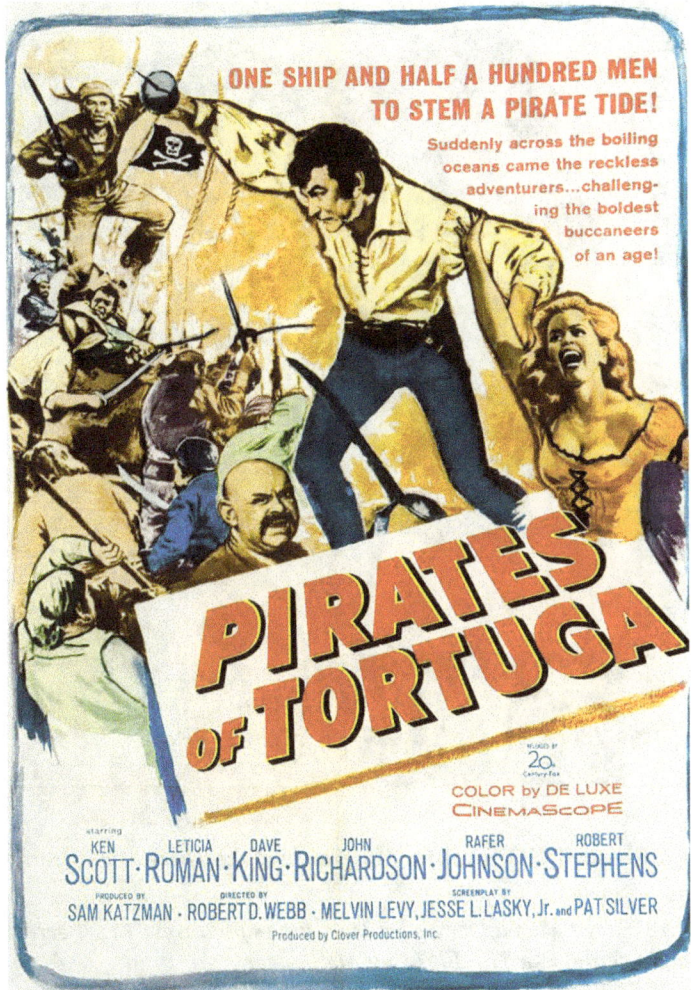

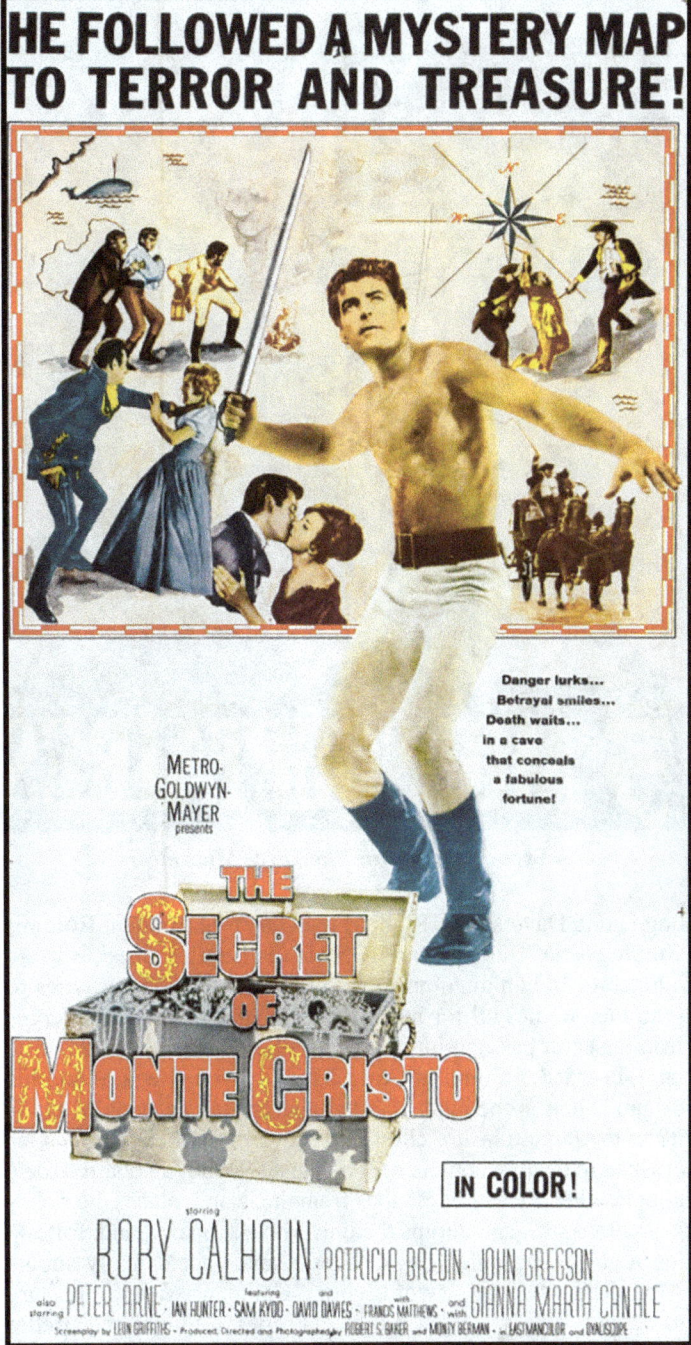

ever dreaming of one day becoming a lady of leisure. She falls for the captain but he doesn't want to know, their on/off spats continuing all the way to Jamaica where plans are drawn up to apprehend the pirate in his stronghold on Tortuga.

There's nothing particularly original here, but the 97 minutes goes by fast enough and sustains the interest. Among the cast, British singer/comedian Dave King (the author bumped into him in Cheam, Surrey in 1962 and obtained his autograph) in his first major film role, is excellent as Jack the Lad Pee Wee, while another Brit, Robert Stephens, makes a dashing, not-all-that-evil Henry Morgan. The real star of the show, however, is Roman. The hyperactive Italian actress mugs her way furiously throughout the entire proceedings, speaking in a weird Italian/American/Cockney accent, fobbing herself off as "Lady Margaret" and flashing her cleavage and shapely legs at every given opportunity in a desperate attempt to stir Scott (slightly wooden) to life (she had minor parts in *Pontius Pilate* and *The Black Lancers*). The feisty lass nearly weds elderly Sir Thomas Mollyford (Edgar Barrier) to achieve her aims before Scott, after defeating Stephens in a storming battle at his island fortress, which is blown up, is exonerated on a conspiracy charge and grabs her for his own pleasure. Notwithstanding a fake-looking mock-up of London and galleons that in some shots don't appear to move on the ocean waves, *Pirates of Tortuga* is easy on the eyes, the kind of good-natured movie kids used to yell, stomp their feet and cheer at during Saturday matinee performances in the 1960s.

The Secret of Monte Cristo aka ***The Treasure of Monte Cristo***

Mid Century/Regal Films/MGM (UK); Dyaliscope/East-mancolor; 95 mins; Produced and Directed by Robert S. Baker and Monty Berman †††

Baker and Berman, responsible for a clutch of lurid '50s horror movies (*Blood of the Vampire*; *Jack the Ripper*; *The Trollenberg Terror*), turned to *Boy's Own Adventure* in this agreeable though superficial costumer. In 1815, a bunch of disparate characters, each possessing one quarter of a treasure map, converge on the Island of Monte Cristo in search of a fabulous hoard of riches. Rory Calhoun (Captain Adam Corbett) has been paid £2,000 to escort Ian Hunter and daughter Patricia Bredin (Pauline) to Italy to locate the 300-year-old loot, servant Sam Kydd along for the ride (and comic relief). Hunter is murdered by mountain bandits when the trio meets devious Francis Matthews (Louis Auclair) in a ruined temple, then proceed with sea

A French poster for *The Three Musketeers*

A French DVD cover for *Vengeance of the Three Musketeers*

dog David Davies (Van Ryman) to Peter Arne's (Count Boldini) Gothic castle, Gianna Maria Canale (as Lucetta, hired to bring a touch of Italian glamour to the production) using her wiles to grab the goodies all for herself. At one point she even emerges from a secret passage into Calhoun's bedroom. Once on the island, bearded, onion-munching John Gregson (Renato) and his brigands join in the hunt ("You come for the treasure? Where is it?"); the huge treasure chest is discovered in a cavern, Davies crushed to death when the roof collapses. Kydd, on board Arne's clipper when the varlet escapes from the island, places the riches in a potato sack and dumps them overboard; on dry land, following a chase and numerous clashes, Canale accidentally shoots Arne dead when he's swordfighting Calhoun. With no treasure to be had, simply a chest full of old ropes, Calhoun and Bredin head back to England to play house, even though she's blown hot and cold over our hero during the movie's entire running length, while Kydd and Gregson ride off in a hay wagon.

Filmed in the Bay of Naples (Columbia's *Jason and the Argonauts* used some of the same locales around Palinuro), Baker and Berman's potboiler canters instead of gallops, superficial stuff indeed, albeit nice to take in. There's a complete lack of spark between Calhoun (at 39, looking worn around the edges) and snooty, upper-crust English lass Bredin; Gregson's scallywag of a bandit makes up for it, as does the attractive scenery and Canale, using her haughty peplum Queen Bitch act to good effect. Clifton Parker's score is a welcome plus, and likeable, diminutive Sam Kydd, one of British cinema's most familiar faces with over 300 pictures and TV shows to his credit, is a joy whenever he appears. Containing moderate amounts of violence, *The Secret of Monte Cristo* is one for the kids; even seasoned buffs will find some measure of enjoyment in it.

The Three Musketeers [*Les trois mousquetaires: Les Ferrets de la reine*] aka ***The Fighting Musketeers***

Les Films Modernes/Le Film d'Art (France/Italy); Franscope/Eastmancolor; 95 mins; Producer: Raymond Borderie; Director: Bernard Borderie ††††

Vengeance of the Three Musketeers [*Les trois mousquetaires: La vengeance de Milady*]

Les Films Modernes/Le Film d'Art (France/Italy); Dyaliscope/Eastmancolor; 91 mins; Producers: Raymond Borderie, Henri Jaquillard; Director: Bernard Borderie ††††

Bernard Borderie shot his epic 186-minute version of the classic Alexandre Dumas novel at the Chateau de Guermantes in Seine-et-Marne, and around Semur-en-Auxois in the French Burgundy region; the movie was then split into two and released theatrically as separate titles in October 1961. Jean Marais was approached to play D'Artagnan but contractual obligations forced him to pull out, Gérard Barray taking on the role of the dashing cavalier. A stellar cast included Mylene Demongeot (Milady de Winter), Georges Descrieres (Athos), Bernard Woringer (Porthos), Jacques Toja (Aramis), Jean Carmet (Planchet), Guy Delorme (Rochefort), Daniel Sorano (Cardinal Richelieu) and Perrette Pradier (Constance). Paul Misraki provided a rumbustious score to match the rumbustious action, while Armand Thirard's photography brought those picturesque French locations to vivid life.

The first part was marginally better than part two, introducing us to young soldier of fortune D'Artagnan and his initial involvement with the Three Musketeers, when on the road to Paris; at first, he antagonizes them but they quickly bond as comrades-in-arms after Richlieu's guards interrupt their dueling: "All for One! One for All!" D'Artagnan then proceeds to have an affair with Constance, a royal dressmaker, and travels to England to retrieve a diamond pendant and jewels given to Anne of Austria, Consort of France, by King Louis XIII, but they are passed on to her secret lover, Prime Minister the Duke of Buckingham. The jewels are brought back safely, thus saving the monarch from scandal and exile and preventing a possible war between France and England, which is what Richelieu, deputy Rochfort and secret agent Milady de Winter had hoped for. Part Two saw D'Artagnan teamed up with his three jovial compatriots and amiable wine-guzzling friend Planchet, becoming more romantically entangled with the deadly, dagger-happy Milady (as well as rekindling his heated relationship with Constance); the temptress was out for personal revenge, as was Richelieu and Rochefort, the narrative encompassing escapes from prison, coach chases, swordfights and an inordinate amount of bedroom hopping by the leading man. The picture closed with the demise of the murderous Milady by Athos, the musketeer plunging a rapier blade into her beautiful body, *his* revenge for the death of Constance, poisoned in a convent, at the hands of the blonde agent.

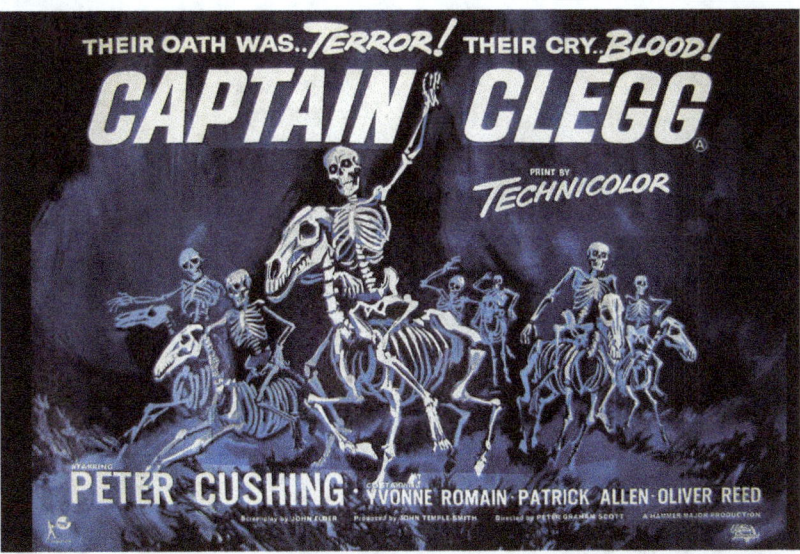

Putting the two films together, you have one of the finest adaptations of Dumas' famous yarn ever committed to celluloid, a swashbuckler filmed with passion and zest, and an eye for flamboyant period detail. Barray makes an irrepressible hero, while Demongeot lives up to her reputation (at the time) as one of France's sexiest leading ladies. At over three hours, the narrative sags in places and in some instances the comedic element jars, but in such an ambitious undertaking, these quibbles can be forgiven. The entire package can be purchased today in two DVD issues, both dubbed pan and scan versions and not, regrettably, in widescreen.

1962

Captain Clegg aka ***Night Creatures***
Hammer/Major Pictures/Universal (UK); Eastmancolor; 82 mins; Producer: John Temple-Smith; Director: Peter Graham Scott ✞✞✞✞✞

Released in the United Kingdom in June 1962, *Captain Clegg* must be the only occasion where a Hammer co-feature received higher critical and public acclaim than the main Hammer feature it went the rounds with, *The Phantom of the Opera*. Both films were rated "A" but Hammer diehards were bitterly dismayed and felt let down when *The Phantom of the Opera*, bloodless despite Hammer's usual faultless production values, wasn't X-certified. A loose remake of Gaumont British's *Dr. Syn* (1937), *Captain Clegg* was promoted as a semi-horror outing, based mainly on the opening sequence where Milton Reid is left to rot on a desert island after having his tongue cut out and ears sliced open. It's a startling curtain raiser to one of the company's unsung treasures from this heady period in their history, a tale of smuggling, dark deeds and night phantoms centered on the creepy, misty Romney Marshes in Kent, 1792, with Peter Cushing in fine fettle (filming actually took place around Bray, Berkshire, in hilly countryside—Kent's Romney Marsh area is as flat as a pancake).

Cushing (superb in the role) starred as the feared pirate chief of the title, Parson (Doctor) Blyss, preaching to the congregation from his pulpit by day, scourge of Her Majesty's revenue officers by night, selling contraband brandy to locals in Dymchurch. Patrick Allen (Captain Collier) and his scruffy brigade (plus Reid in chains) march into this smuggler's paradise, suspecting everyone of being involved in the racket. They all are, of course, but how does stern-faced Allen prove it, and his sneaking suspicion that Clegg is still alive, what with scarecrows signaling to the smugglers when he's sniffing about and luminescent skeletal figures on horseback prowling the marshes. Enlivened by Don Banks' slam-bang score and Arthur Grant's needle-sharp photography, *Captain Clegg* crams one incident after another into its briskly directed 82 minutes, bolstered by a great cast: Cushing, Allen, Oliver Reed, Martin Benson, Derek Francis, David Lodge and the ever-dependable Michael Ripper, playing a crafty coffin-maker.

Reid, the hulking, scarred mulatto, supplied the horror element, grunting and sweating every time he sees his hated enemy Cushing (who ordered his tongue to be ripped out in 1776), and the final plot twist was a neat one, the parson (his neck bears the mark of the hangman's noose) receiving a pike in the back from the mulatto, ironically ending up buried in the empty grave that was supposed to be the final resting place of the dreaded captain; all those present, including Allen and his men, raise their hats to a man whose only aim in life was to better the lot of his impoverished parishioners, even if it was by illegal means. Yvonne Romain, as ale house wench Imogene, Cushing's secret daughter, looked like a rabbit caught in the headlights on occasions, up against a raft of heavyweight acting talent, especially when she's romping in the hay with hellraiser Reed, but she was attractive enough, the token Hammer piece of eye-candy. And there were *two* secret passages in the movie, plus Benson trying to rape Romain on the threat of disclosing her true identity, more nods in the direction of Italian pepla. A full-blooded costumer made at a time when Hammer Films triumphed over all other competitors in the British film industry, *Captain Clegg* could well qualify as the company's best-ever co-feature, it's that good; in fact, this spiffy little picture is a classic of its type.

The Knight of Pardaillan [*Le chevalier de Pardaillan*] aka ***Clash of Steel***
Florida Films/Lux (France/Italy); Franscope/Eastmancolor; 89 (79) mins; Producers: André Haguet, André Legrand; Director: Bernard Borderie ✞✞✞✞

A Spanish poster for *The Knight of Pardaillan*

A French poster for *Mandrin*

Sprightly Gérard Barray fences, duels, fights, romances, leaps and laughs his way through Bernard Borderie's energetic period swashbuckler, set in Paris 1588, playing almost the same character he did in the director's *Three Musketeers* movies. As Jean de Pardaillan, a D'Artagnan-type figure, he pits his wits against Duke Henri de Guise, a surly, sour-faced performance from Jean Topart. The corrupt nobleman has abducted bohemian dancing girl Michele Grellier (Isabelle) from a group of traveling performers, knowing full well she's no Gypsy—the girl happens to be heiress to the French throne. He plans to marry her to gain access to the monarchy without letting on to haughty mistress Gianna Maria Canale (Princess Fausta Borgia), busy supplying him with financial support to further his rise to power. When it becomes plain that Barray is to be a continual thorn in his side, henchman Guy Delorme (Maurevert) is given orders to eliminate the knight and his small band of troublemakers, which includes Kirk Morris (as Hercules!), pint-sized Claude Vega (as Picouic, very handy with a slingshot) and dashing cavalier Philippe Lemaire (Charles d'Angouleme). But getting rid of this foursome, who love nothing better than engaging in a good scrap, is easier said than done.

Morris (in need of a haircut and shave) sets the picture's knockabout tone in the opening scene, knocking over Delorme's gorillas like bowling pins with a bench when they attempt to kidnap Grellier; Barray hops out of a good-time girl's bed, joins in the fracas and demolishes the traveler's rickety caravan in the process. From thereon in, Barray and his friends involve themselves in one stunt after another in trying to extricate Grellier from Topart's fortress, while Topart has to fend off the enquiries of jealous, ambitious Canale; the action set pieces rattle by, Canale's coach heaved into a river after Barray saves her from an attack orchestrated by Topart, a rumbustious set-to in a flour mill, slam-bang palace duels and a pulsating, noisy climax in which Grellier is snatched from the hangman's noose, resulting in a colossal swordfight. Barray dispatches Delorme, and Topart and Canale are left to stew in their own corrupt juices as Barray, Morris, Lemaire, Vega and Grellier row down a river to freedom, after a wooden hut on a bridge has collapsed like matchwood into the water.

Borderie, as shown in his *Three Musketeers* outings, chose to shoot in real-life French medieval locations (Dordogne's Chateau de Hautefort stood in for Topart's castle), imparting a true sense of historical time and place to a none-too-serious narrative boosted by Paul Misraki's thumping military score. Everyone (especially Barray) appears to be having a ball and, at one point, Borderie inserts the classic peplum pose, Barray pinioned to a door by eight pikestaffs. We also (thankfully) get to behold a great deal of Canale's mouth-watering figure when she takes a bath. Barray went on to star as the fun-loving knight one more time, in Borderie's *Hardi Pardaillan!* (1964), with the movie retaining virtually the same cast, technicians and plot. While this is available on DVD from France, *The Knight of Pardaillan* can only be found on old French VHS tapes, meaning that outside of France, that country's SECAM system renders Henri Persin's color photography redundant; all you'll get is a black-and-white image, unless it's converted.

Mandrin aka *The Indomitable*

Films Gibé/Franco London/Titanus (France/Italy); Dyaliscope/Eastmancolor; 100 mins; Producers: Pierre Gout, Jean-Paul Le Chanois; Director: Jean-Paul Le Chanois ††††

In 1748, Louis Mandrin, a cooper in the village of Saint Etienne de Saint Geoirs on the French-Swiss border, took up arms against King Louis XV's inspector of taxes, spearheading a struggle for justice and becoming a legendary figure, the Robin Hood of France as he was known. His execution in 1755 attracted 6,000 onlookers, but is not shown in Jean-Paul Le Chanois' vibrant, colorful picture; the director instead skilfully concentrates on Mandrin's numerous confrontations with the military, who are dead set on putting an end to his mischief-making ways.

Georges Riviere starred as Mandrin, a masculine, handsome ponytailed man of action sharing two beautiful females in his turbulent life: virtuous noblewoman Jeanne Valérie (Antoinette) and amorous Gypsy Silvia Monfort (Myrtille). Blonde, doe-eyed stage actress Monfort oozed animal magnetism and earthy sex appeal, assisting Riviere in his many scrapes and falling for him in the process. Shot around a panoramic backdrop of the French-Swiss Alps in pristine sunny color by Marc Fossard, *Mandrin* is one of those running, jumping and standing still kind of movies, where skirmishes with the enemy on mountain trails and meadows are interrupted by Gypsy dances, escapes from taverns, romantic interludes, secretive liaisons in castles and in-fighting among the insurgents, a beguiling, highly enjoyable concoction underscored by Georges Van Parys' memorable music that lingers long in the mind. Not only is Riviere averse to unreasonable rises in tax, tobacco and livestock duties to finance the French army, who are constantly at war, but also rival chief Armand Mestral (Sigismond de Moret); in a three-minute slugging match, Riviere emerges the victor, the two then forging a close friendship. Mestral is later shot dead while participating in a horse race; Riviere is captured but rescued from the hangman's noose, leading up to, in the 85th minute, *Mandrin*'s 10-minute showcase, and an exciting one: A regiment swarms into a village to quell the uprising once and for all and is met with a hail of assorted missiles—apples, barrels, rocks, burning hay, boiling water, scalding treacle and feathers. Soldiers caught in the sticky mess throw down their arms in surrender, Riviere putting to the point of his rapier an assassin who has nearly killed Monfort in a bell tower. The rather sudden ending sees Riviere galloping off on a peace mission (and to his death), leaving behind his two gorgeous admirers, Monfort clutching a pendant he has left behind. A real treasure of a French/Italian swashbuckler, infused with a unique rustic character; Riviere has never been better, and as for Monfort, she's worth the price of a ticket all on her own, French glamour of the 1960s variety that really does set the screen smoldering in its intensity.

The Pirates of Blood River

Hammer/Columbia (UK); Megascope/Eastmancolor; 87 (82) mins; Producer: Anthony Nelson Keys; Director: John Gilling ††††

Few if any among the packed audiences who had queued in their droves to watch one of the United Kingdom's top-grossing double bills of 1962, *Mysterious Island* c/w *The Pirates of Blood River*, would have guessed that, originally, Hammer's lively pirate adventure was earmarked for an "X" certificate, chief censor John Trevelyan putting his foot down after viewing the completed product. Hammer then decided to agree on a less prohibitive rating to draw in a wider clientele; cuts were made, and the film passed with an "A" rating. Following further discussions, more trimming resulted in a general "U" classification, words such as "adulterer" and "harlot" overdubbed to avoid being heard by children and those of a sensitive nature. In all, around five minutes was excised from the original edit: the piranha attacks on Marie Deveraux and Andrew Keir; the blindfolded cutlass duel to the finish between Oliver Reed and Peter Arne, Reed expiring in agony; a graphic flogging scene; two pirates impaled on spits; Kerwin Mathews strung up in the sun; the attack on the farm, two women molested, a husband stabbed to death; a shot of a hanged man's legs; bloodied corpses and other glimpses of violence. In his book *What the Censor Saw* (Michael Joseph, 1973), Trevelyan relates how the two piranha attacks, the victims thrashing about in pools of blood, were shown in their entirety in the "X" version; in the "A" edit, the fish rushed toward Deveraux and Keir, but no blood was seen; and in the "U" version, the piranhas never appeared at all. I caught this double bill twice in 1962, and once in 1963, and although 50 years have elapsed, the current DVD issue of *The Pirates of Blood River* is definitely the X-rated cut; I cannot recall any of the above sequences all those years ago in the "U" version.

All this gave John Gilling's pirates-on-land feature (a galleon is seen in longshot only) a typical Hammer vicious streak, unsuitable for youngsters. Christopher Lee starred as Captain LaRoche, an eye-patched, black-clad corsair, left hand twisted into a gloved claw, who comes to the aid of Mathews (Jonathon Standing), lying wounded beside a swamp; he's just escaped from a brutal labor camp, serving 15 years for having a scandalous affair with a married woman (Deveraux). Mathews agrees to escort Lee and his ragbag outfit to the Huguenot settlement on Devon Island, the pirate boss stating that he needs a

safe retreat for his men, although the untrustworthy brigand of the seas is after plunder and the treasure he believes lies hidden there. Mathews' puritanical father, Keir, knows exactly where that treasure is; it's the statue of a Huguenot leader in his hall of justice, paint covering the pure gold construction. Following a bloody, all-musket blazing skirmish and brutal countermeasures, Lee and his mob drag the statue toward the swamp where, during a fracas, Arne is dispatched by Mathews, Keir gets eaten alive by piranhas, Lee receives a sword in the guts and the gold statue sinks into the mire, Mathews, sister Marla Landi and her lover Glenn Corbett reunited.

A word about that swamp, or the polluted pond bordering Black Park near Bray; its stinking, mud-filled waters proved the downfall of several of the cast. Reed suffered a severe eye and ear infection, Michael Ripper almost drowned, Mathews hated the place, stuntmen refused to immerse themselves in it and Lee was floored with a stomach complaint, saying later that he couldn't walk upstairs for months afterwards because of wading through four feet of silt. (It's plain he doesn't appear particularly happy soaked up to his chest in these waterlogged scenes.) Film detectives with a partiality for cine-facts and trivia take note: Mathews, playing Keir's son, was in fact three months older than Keir, although looking at them, you would never have believed it. *The Pirates of Blood River*, directed with pace by Gill-ing, containing a tuneful Gary Hughes title theme and glistening photography from Arthur Grant, is one of the best and more hard-edged of the Hammer swashbucklers, mostly because of its highly unusual triple-certificate pedigree, besides which any movie starring Lee, Mathews, Reed and even habitual Hammer support actor Ripper (Lee's wily trusted servant) is worth a look in any cinemagoer's book.

The Son of Captain Blood [*El hijo del capitan Blood*]

Producciones Benito Perojo/CCM (Spain/Italy/US); Dyaliscope/Eastmancolor; 88 mins; Producers: Benito Perojo, Harry Joe Brown; Director: Tulio Demicheli ††

Not a chip off the old block—that would be the verdict handed out on Errol Flynn's son Sean after observing him attempt to take on the mantle of his legendary father, who shot to fame following his role as Peter Blood in Warner Bros.' classic *Captain Blood* (1935). Flynn, Jr. played Peter Blood in this predictable swashbuckler, reluctantly becoming a pirate, romancing blonde Alessandra Panaro (Abigail), rescuing slaves on board a British slave ship and saving his mother during an earthquake that destroyed Port Royal, Jamaica in 1692. A flashing smile and androgynous looks do not a good pirate chief make, even though every woman (or in this film, schoolgirl) swoons at the sight of him, just as they did with Flynn, Sr. It's a decent stab at following in his father's footsteps, but it doesn't quite come off.

Flynn boards ship at the same moment his mother (Ann Todd) is being told by Governor José Maria Caffarel to ditch her friendly attitude toward slavery and return her workforce to bondage. Flynn wows a party of giggling schoolgirls, Panaro falls for him and the ship is hijacked by pirates, José Nieto (Captain De Malagon) calling the shots; he orders the lash for Flynn's insolence (no marks are on his back when he walks away from the flogging; if this was an Italian-only production, they would be shown in gory detail). After a couple of swordfights (Flynn doesn't really swash a buckle all that convincingly), Flynn, contra to his own wishes, eventually takes command of the pirate vessel, with Roberto Camardiel (Olivier) his jovial second-in-command, the buccaneers clashing with a slave galleon carrying a cargo of black prisoners, including Todd's faithful servant, John Kitzmiller, among them. Laying down cannon fire on Port Royal as a protest against slavery and Todd's ill-treatment (her plantations have been burnt, her servants rounded up), Flynn and his men go ashore, invade Caffarel's fortress and rescue Todd in a crumbling church as an earthquake and tsunami hit the island, a nine-minute sequence proficiently handled in the special effects department. The final few minutes has Flynn, Panaro, Todd and the corsairs at a banquet given by the new legate, who presents pardons to the would-be pirates.

Gregorio Garcia Segura delights with a breezy seafaring score and director Demicheli orchestrates a few stimulating ocean sequences, but overall the family-friendly *The Son of Captain Blood* (distributed by Paramount and U-rated in England, when it appeared in cinemas on a double bill with *The Scarlet Blade* in August 1963) lacks the hard-edged bite of the Italian pirate films, which in most cases were A-rated and unsuitable for the very young. And Flynn was short by a mile on the sheer force of character and animal magnetism that placed his father among Hollywood's immortals. (On April 6, 1970, Flynn, aged 28, and war correspondent Dana Stone disappeared while on a photo shoot for *Time* magazine and CBS News in Cambodia. It is thought that they were captured by Vietnamese communist guerrillas manning a checkpoint and subsequently murdered. Their remains have never been found.)

The 300 Spartans aka *Lion of Sparta*

20th Century Fox (US); CinemaScope/DeLuxecolor; 114 mins; Producers: Rudolph Maté, George St. George; Director: Rudolph Maté ††††

In 480 BC, the Persians, led by King Xerxes, invade Greece. Themistocles of Athens strongly advocates linking up with Sparta, whose forces are stronger than those of his country's, the men possessing a fiercer warlike nature than the Greeks. The pact is reluctantly passed, King Leonidas of Sparta deciding to hold the vital narrow pass at Thermopylae against Xerxes' invaders, numbering 200,000, until the Greek armies are mobilized by land and by sea. However, Sparta's Council of Elders pronounces that no fighting must take place during their religious festival. Ignoring their edict, Leonidas deploys 300 of his personal bodyguard, augmented by a handful of Greek warriors, to defend the pass, no quarter given. After several days of ferocious combat in which the Persians are repeatedly repelled, a treacherous shepherd, in exchange for gold, shows the Persians a hidden goat trail, enabling a regiment of Xerxes' elite troops, the Immortals, to sneak up behind the Spartans. Trapped on both sides of the pass, Leonidas and his gallant men are wiped out by volleys of arrows, but their valiant sacrifice hasn't been in vain. The Greek armies have amassed in their thousands, annihilating the mighty Persian army at the Battle of Platea, which took place in 479 BC.

Produced on a budget of $8,000,000, *The 300 Spartans*, in about-face fashion, is probably the closest a Hollywood studio ever came to duplicating an Italian sword and sandal mini-epic, an Italian film in all but name only. In some areas, the Italians could have come up with improvements: David Farrar (Xerxes) was no match for the likes of Andrea Aureli, Alberto Lupo, Claudio Undari and other peplum heavies; he simply wasn't evil enough, far too stoically English to play a despotic Persian king. Likewise, Diane Baker (Ellas) was winsome but lacked the exotic beauty of Rosalba Neri, Gloria Milland, Daniela Rocca and all those delectable Italian babes. Manos Hatzidakis' score more or less aped the colossal musical talents of Carlo Innocenzi, Francesco De Masi and their ilk, while Rudolph Maté's direction occasionally flagged in the first hour, devoid of the grit and bite that hallmarked the classic pepla made around this time.

Nevertheless, Fox's Ancient Greek saga, viewed years later, is truer to its peplum roots than Warner's flashy version of events, *300*, made 44 years later. No computers to boost troop numbers here—10,000 extras were employed, impressive to watch ("An army far bigger than you can imagine."), especially in the long opening sequence where rows of Persian infantry file past Farrar, filmed on location in the Gulf of Corinth by veteran cinematographer/double Oscar-winner Geoffrey Unsworth. The numerous exciting battle clashes, commencing in the 73rd minute, are tough, bloody and authentic, Maté's camera glued to the charging chariots in a spate of tight shots as they home in on the closed Spartan ranks, ensuring audiences are right there in the thick of the action. Richard Egan put in a solid, charismatic turn as Leonidas, knowing that his stand at Thermopylae would result in his death, his farewell scenes with radiant wife Anna Synodinou intimately touching; Ralph Richardson's eloquent Themistocles was a lot less preachy than other senators who were on Egan's side in the war; Barry Coe played Baker's betrothed, Phylon, like a teenage, lovesick colt, kicked out of the Spartan army because of his father's connivance with the enemy but reinstated when he shows his mettle during a night raid on Farrar's camp and able support came in the form of British actors Donald Houston, Kieron Moore, Laurence Naismith and Robert Brown. Throw in a fight to the finish between two champions, a couple of sexy court dances, a wicked queen (Anne Wakefield), an amusing script ("A woman's tongue is far deadlier than the sword.") and striking, sunlit Greek scenery (The Gulf of Corinth; Perachora) and you have a rousing picture overlooked in the wake of mega-bucks spectacles like *Ben-Hur*, *El Cid* and *The Fall of the Roman Empire*. Unpretentious and largely forgotten, *The 300*

Spartans is great sword and sandal entertainment; not Italian in origin, but near enough to it in spirit.

1963

The Scarlet Blade aka The Crimson Blade

Hammer/ABPC (UK); Hammerscope/Technicolor; 83 mins; Producer: Anthony Nelson Keys; Director: John Gilling ✟✟✟

In 1648 a gang of Royalists, led by The Scarlet Blade, is getting to be a thorn in the side for Colonel Judd and his regiment of Roundheads, busy trying to enforce Oliver Cromwell's puritanical laws throughout the land. To complicate matters, The Scarlet Blade has fallen for Judd's Royalist-sympathetic daughter, the headstrong lass also being pursued by Judd's bullish second-in-command, Captain Tom Sylvester. To win her hand, Sylvester is willing to "change coats" and assist the outlaws in saving King Charles I from execution; however, on discovering that his beloved has hitched her skirts to another, he issues her with an ultimatum—him or me. How can the girl juggle two men in the palm of her hand and save both the king and the Scarlet Blade's band of brothers from being wiped out by her father's troops?

Oliver Reed, in his seventh Hammer appearance, glowered as only he could glower, playing the two-timing Sylvester, who turns ever more evil when delectable English rose June Thorburn, the woman he assumes will be his for the asking (or taking, which was more Reed's style!), decides she loves Jack Hedley (The Scarlet Blade) after being in the Robin Hood-clone's company for about one hour ("I've fallen in love with this vagabond," she tells Reed whose dark good looks grow darker by the second). That's not the only peplum-based trope here; there are final demands by the bucketload, everyone out to hold someone to ransom on some pretext or another ("Tell me where I can find the king and you'll both be granted a free pardon.") *and* a secret passage. Hammer produced a number of swashbucklers during the early '60s, all stocked with the company's standard retinue of character actors, all colorfully photographed (Jack Asher was the cinematographer on this occasion), all having a catchy score (composer Gary Hughes on duty) and all entertaining, ideal fare for a family outing to the pictures (most were "U" rated). *The Scarlet Blade*, briskly directed by John Gilling, went the rounds in England in August 1963, double billed with *The Son of Captain Blood*, and was quite successful, due partly to Reed's box-office clout and a standout performance from Lionel Jeffries as the cold-hearted Colonel Judd, unable to reconcile the bald truth that Thorburn is a Royalist, as he once was. In fact, the Jeffries/Reed double act is the best reason for tuning into this movie, the duplicitous duo relegating the good guys to the shadows, although Hammer stalwart Michael Ripper's knife-happy Gypsy, Pablo, is an absolute hoot. The ending is unusually downbeat. Having been torn to pieces in a Cavaliers versus Roundheads battle, Hedley and his survivors go undercover in Ripper's Gypsy camp; Jeffries (who has shot Reed for treason) gallops by with his regiment, dismounts, recognizes Thorburn and Hedley in disguise but has second thoughts, letting the pair get on with their lives: "I advise you Gypsies to keep to the forest," he says in resignation, riding off, knowing that he has lost his precious daughter to the Royalist cause.

Scheherazade [Schéhérazade] aka The Slave of Bagdad

Ciné-Alliance/Filmsonor/Dear Film/Speva (France/Italy/Spain); Superpanorama 70/Eastmancolor; 124 (117) mins; Producers: Michael Safra, Serge Silberman; Director: Pierre Gaspard-Huit ✟✟✟✟

A film of two halves, set in 809 AD. In the first part, three emissaries (Gérard Barray, Giuliano Gemma, Gil Vidal) employed by the French emperor Charlemagne, on a peace treaty to Bagdad in order to cement Christian/Islamic dogma, rescue Princess Scheherazade (Anna Karina) from Bedouin bandits. Barray (Renaud de Villecroix) and the girl fall in love, although she's betrothed to Caliph Haroun-al-Raschid, played by Antonio Vilar. Barray's mission, to pave the way for religious tolerance, thereby allowing pilgrims to visit the Holy Land, is jeopardized when Vilar bursts in on Barray and Karina smooching after she's undergone a form of Arabian Nights lie test with two other women (all attired in fetching oriental bikinis) to prove her love for the caliph. As punishment for her deception, Karina is thrown to the street beggars, Barray publicly flogged (painful to watch). Barray and his knights then snatch the girl and make off into the desert, where they separate, Barray and Karina left to proceed on their own.

Up to this stage, *Scheherazade* possesses a languid, ethereal quality, scenes bathed in André Domage and Christian Matras' rich color wash. Vilar's opulent palace is a riot of gold, contrasting brightly with the exotic costumes worn by the dancing maidens and court officials; André Hossein's evocative music also matches the carefully visualized Middle Eastern mood perfectly; the movie must have looked and sounded swell on the giant screen all those years ago. Barray is personable as the knight

tormented by love, while Karina, although no lustful beauty, has an Audrey Hepburn quality about her, innocence combined with fragility, enough to melt any French knight's heart. The second half of the film lapses into standard goodies against baddies action. Barray and Karina, suffering from exposure following their enforced sojourn in the desert wastes, are allowed to recuperate inside the Sultan's palace on condition that Karina joins the caliph's 200-strong harem. Jealous mistress Marilù Tolo (Shirin), in cahoots with Grand Vizir Jorge Mistral (Zaccar), is up to her pretty neck in plans to overthrow Vilar, leading to an assault on the palace where insurgents burst in on the harem; for a few seconds, bare breasts are on view, cut from the British print. On the plains outside of Baghdad, Mistral's forces are eventually routed by a combined army of Vilar's troops and Barray's knights, the treacherous vizir falling off a cliff, a spear embedded in his stomach after a broadsword versus scimitar clash with Barray. Severely wounded, Vilar grants his blessing on the two lovers, stating that there will be no repercussions between his country and France; Barray and Karina ride off with the knights to report back to Charlemagne. This is an enjoyable quasi-Arabian Nights romantic adventure, wonderfully shot in arid desert locations and featuring top performances from the entire cast.

Siege of the Saxons aka ***King Arthur's Adventurer***

Columbia (UK); Technicolor; 85 mins; Producers: Charles H. Schneer, Jud Kinberg; Director: Nathan Juran ††

On Saturday, August 17, 1963, at the ABC theater, Falmouth, this writer distinctly remembers fidgeting throughout the entire length of *Siege of the Saxons*, waiting patiently for the main feature, *Jason and the Argonauts*, to come on. It seemed a middle-of-the-road effort then, and still does 50 years later. *Robin Hood Meets King Arthur* would have been a more apt title for Nathan Juran's cobbled-together slice of medieval blather, in which a miscast Ronald Lewis (Robert) in brown leathers (the jobbing actor committed suicide in 1982, at age 53) starred as a lone rebel living in the woods, coming to the rescue of Princess Janette Scott (Katherine), when her father King Arthur (Mark Dignam) is murdered by bogus Saxons, the coup instigated by power-mad Ronald Howard, playing Edmund of Cornwall. He wants the throne for himself and has thrown in his lot with England's hated enemies to achieve his goal.

You would have thought that with Merlin and Excalibur thrown into the scenario, things would have heated up, but they don't, most of the picture consisting of Lewis and Scott (dressed to resemble a scruffy lad) on the run from Howard's soldiers and villain Jerome Willis, a black-hearted assassin limping heavily on one leg. The lengthy battle sequence from Alan Ladd's justly maligned camp classic *The Black Knight* (1954) was inserted to save on budgetary costs, while location filming centered around Castell Coch in South Glamorgan, Wales (standing in for Camelot), a striking, multi-turreted edifice that added immeasurably to production values; the same can be said of the authen-

A stark and at times graphically violent version of the Lancelot/Guinevere relationship, Cornel Wilde partly financed his pet project, as well as starring as the legendary French knight. At 51, Wilde may have been a tad too mature to portray Lancelot as the dashing hero-cum-lover, bringing a great deal of gravitas to the role as well as a suspect French accent. But his film has to be commended for its refreshingly realistic approach to the familiar subject matter. A-rated in Britain, it contains a couple of steamy love trysts, and the two major battles depict things as they were: the clash of steel on armor, arrows piercing flesh, faces slashed and helmets battered to bloody pulp. Guinevere, played by Jean Wallace, is no virtuous maiden either, rather a wilful, self-centered go-getter, her sham marriage to King Arthur (Brian Aherne) not preventing the blonde lass from dragging her unprotesting lover into her bedchamber when the mood (and hunger) takes her … which here is often (as Wallace, 40, had been married to Wilde since 1951, those sweaty bedroom scenes were probably not faked!). Wilde strengthened the bleak scenario with the selfsame earthiness that Franklin J. Schaffner achieved so admirably in *The War Lord*, the nuts and bolts of English medieval life laid bare, eschewing the rosy romantic glow so prevalent in other productions (shooting was carried out in Yugoslavia).

The story tells of Lancelot's illicit affair with Queen Guinevere, daughter of King Leodogran, carried out within the walls of Camelot, with his conquest of the barbarian hordes, his betrayal by Modred, Arthur's bastard son, his banishment to Brittany, his return from exile and a final confrontation with Modred's troops following Arthur and Merlin's deaths. Lancelot's men emerge triumphant, but Guinevere takes her vows, electing to live life under God's holy orders. Lancelot and Guinevere's last moments together are touchingly realized in Wilde and Richard Schayer's intelligent screenplay. "What's happened to you? What do I see in your eyes?" Wilde asks of his beloved, attired in a nun's habit. From her guarded response, he knows that he has lost the battle to God. "I'll leave to my atonement. Perhaps that's what this all means. Farewell, my golden-headed one."

Three moments of shocking bloodshed were guaranteed to jolt audiences of the day out of their seats. The first appears in an unflinching, no-holds-barred duel of king's champions near the start, fought with lance, axe, mace and broadsword; Wilde brings his hefty blade crashing down on his opponent's helmet, cleaving his skull in two. The second is after the fabulously staged assault on the barbarians; Wilde is talking to Iain Gregory (Sir Tors) when an arrow suddenly transfixes itself straight through the young soldier's head. The third is the climactic scrimmage between Wilde and Michael Meacham (Modred); Wilde furiously launches his sword at the traitor in a flurry of hacking lunges, slicing off his opponent's left arm at the shoulder joint. The eight-minute grand finale, Wilde and Meacham's regiments clashing on the open field, is a blinder, one of the '60s finest, undertaken without Ron Goodwin's musical accompaniment, massed ranks of bowmen causing havoc on both sides before Meacham's men are overwhelmed. Among the sterling cast, jovial Archie Duncan is Sir Lamorak, Wilde's old fighting/drinking comrade; George Baker plays Sir Gawaine, out to exact revenge when the noble French knight accidentally kills his brother and Mark Dignam's interpretation of wizard Merlin brings dignity to a role that is so often hammed up to the full. It's also unusual to show a series of tinted stills from the movie behind the opening credits. Cornel Wilde deserves a huge round

tic costume wardrobe, colorful in the extreme. Unfortunately, the movie skimped on its own action set pieces, the ultimate skirmish made up of obvious stock footage with just a couple of castle altercations to its name. As a nod in the direction of Italian peplum, a secret passage in Camelot is mentioned but never seen, there's the obligatory ultimatum (Howard to Scott: "Marry me and you can return to Camelot in safety.") and halfway through, Lewis is cornered by several archers, longbows drawn at the ready, *the* classic peplum "we've got you" shot. "Why an outlaw?" Dignam asks Lewis. "Because I enjoy it" is the riposte, one example of a pretty amusing script by John Kohn and Jud Kinberg, ably delivered by the cast who, all credit to them, give it everything they've got. But the material is routine and slackly handled by director Juran, Laurie Johnson's score forgettable, Wilkie Cooper and Jack Mills' photography less-than-sparkling. Yes, even as far back as 1963, you had a two-star film teamed with a five-star—no wonder there was a feeling of restlessness in the auditorium when *Siege of the Saxons* was being screened; everyone was on tenterhooks, waiting for Ray Harryhausen's mythical monsters to appear!

Sword of Lancelot aka **Lancelot and Guinevere**

Emblem/Universal (US/UK); Panavision/Technicolor; 116 mins; Producers: Bernard Luber, Cornel Wilde; Director: Cornel Wilde †††† of applause for adding grit to the Arthurian legend instead of coating it in sugar: *Sword of Lancelot* is an underrated gem.

Valley of the Swords [*El valle de las espadas*] aka *The Castilian*; *The Lion of Castile*

M.D. Producciones/Cinemagic Inc. (Spain/US); Panacolor; 128 mins; Producers: Espartaco Santoni, Sidney W. Pink; Director: Javier Seto †††

Based on the legendary exploits of Castilian Fernan Gonzales, who united the provinces of Leon and Navarre in the 10th century and quashed the Moorish invasion of Spain, *Valley of the Swords* (distributed worldwide by Warner Bros. as *The Castilian*) is what was once termed years ago a sprawling epic, similar to a moderately budgeted version of *El Cid* in many ways. But sprawling is the operative word—interspersed with superfluous shots of minstrel Frankie Avalon (Jerifan) warbling the sequence of events as they unfold (American producer Pink's idea), director Javier Seto treats the audience to a Spanish soap opera of mammoth proportions, topped off by a spectacular 12-minute battle sequence shot around Spain's Arlanza river basin region. Other points in the movie's favor: authentic location filming on the actual medieval sites that Gonzales trod, including the mighty fortress at Berlanga de Duero in Soria, exquisite costume and set design detail, plus Mario Pacheco's lush cinematography. But Espartaco Santoni (he was executive producer) makes a lackluster hero in Fernan Gonzalez, as does Teresa Velazquez's heroine, Sandra (or Sancha). Together, this pair of moonstruck lovers don't exactly set the screen on fire with youthful passion; it's left for old-stagers Cesar Romero and Broderick Crawford to ham it up, steal the acting honors and inject some life into the occasionally flaccid proceedings.

Appointed Count of Castile on the death of his brother, Santoni has three items on his agenda that require urgent attention: Call a halt to the yearly tribute by Castile of 100 maidens gifted to the marauding Moors to keep them at arm's length ("The coward's peace."); inform neighboring province Leon that Castile will cease to obey her orders and visit the province of Navarre to make overtures of appeasement. Only by uniting all three nations in a triple alliance will Spain be in a position to drive out the infidels. In between teen idol Avalon singing his ditties, Santoni, Romero (as Jeronimo!) and their small army disguise themselves as maidens, slaughtering an entire camp (a violent episode); there's a risqué semi-nude bathing scene (a trap to lure the Moors), the Moorish castle is besieged and over 1,000 enemy troops are put to death in a series of skirmishes. Moors' chieftain German Cobos (Abderraman) declares war on Spain, Leon's king (Fernando Rey) falls in with Santoni, while wine-guzzling Crawford (Velazquez's father, Don Sancho), along with venomous wife Alida Valli (Teresa), opposes the marriage of his daughter to the Castilian upstart. In a challenge to sort out who's top dog, Santoni kills ball and chain-wielding bully Crawford with an axe, incurring the wrath of his beloved's brother, Angel del Pozo and, for a brief moment in time, Velazquez (del Pozo incarcerates Santoni in a dungeon as he prepares for his marriage). After one hour and 50 minutes of intrigue, plotting and incident, Seto manufactures his showpiece finale within a dramatic canyon setting, Santoni's troops joined by Rey's men, del Pozo's cavalry and the phantoms of two patron saints, facing the might of Cobos' massed battalions. The Spaniards file slowly forward in the formation of a giant cross, the enemy led into a pincer movement and annihilated to a man, by spears, arrows and the flaming swords of the two saints, who dish out divine retribution, incinerating hundreds of foot soldiers. "It is written in the stars. This land will never be ours," intones Cobos as he leads his survivors away from the carnage. Romero expires with that trademark flashing-grin on his bloodied face, while Santoni says to Velazquez, "With a kiss, I will build an empire." The two ghostly saints ride off into the sunset, accompanied by Romero's spirit, and Avalon wraps the whole shebang up by singing a song that seems several centuries out of context with the events of 939 AD, a song more appropriate for John Wayne's *The Alamo*, in which the young crooner starred. If shorn by 20 minutes, this could have been a classic of its type and era; as it stands, the picture is an overlong, verbose historical essay let down by mediocre central performances from the leads and a wandering narrative flow.

1964

The Devil-Ship Pirates

Hammer/Columbia (UK); Megascope/Eastmancolor; 86 mins; Producer: Anthony Nelson Keys; Director: Don Sharp †††

Hot on the heels of *The Pirates of Blood River*, Christopher Lee took on another pirate role, that of Captain Robeles, a Spanish privateer who steers his crippled galleon Diablo away from the Battle of Armada in 1588, holing up in an English backwater for repairs. Hoodwinking a local village into believing that the English were defeated, he lords it over the local squire's domain, uses villagers to put right his ship and lusts after Suzan Farmer (Angela), the squire's daughter. When news comes out that the Spaniards actually lost the massive naval conflict, the locals plot to get rid of Lee and his cutthroat gang and destroy their stricken ship.

Any film with Christopher Lee was guaranteed a decent box-office return in the '60s, whether it was lurid "X" certificate

A U.S. poster for *The Castilian* (aka *Valley of the Swords*)

An Italian poster for *The Devil-Ship Pirates*

horror or straightforward "U" certificate period adventure. Attired in crimson and black, he chews the scenery with aplomb, even though the piratical clichés come thick and fast. Able support comes in the form of Barry Warren as Don Manuel, a Spaniard who nurses a conscience about Lee's rough treatment of the serfs and does his utmost to save them from unfair punishment; Hammer regular Michael Ripper plays skirt-chasing Pepe; Andrew Keir leads the revolt against Lee; John Cairney (he was the young Greek flattened by Talos in *Jason and the Argonauts*) plays Farmer's embittered boyfriend, the Spaniard responsible for his disabled left arm; Ernest Clark appears as snooty Sir Basil and heavyweight Duncan Lamont plays the bosun. Duels, furtive shootings in the dark, tavern brawls, Farmer avoiding Lee's mesmeric, lustful gaze and a hectic finale in which the Spanish vessel (a specially constructed full-sized model) explodes and sinks in the mire—Hammer's pirate caper kept the interest going over 86 minutes, although in retrospect it's nothing really special. The mighty Lee, Don Sharp's tight direction and watchable role-playing from the entire support cast ensure that audiences won't get restless; however, Jimmy Sangster's screenplay in fact is ever-so-slightly ordinary.

East of Sudan

Columbia/Ameran Films (UK/US); Techniscope/Technicolor; 85 mins; Produced and Directed by Nathan Juran ††

In 1885, Anthony Quayle (Private Richard Baker), Sylvia Syms (Miss Margaret Woodville), Derek Fowlds (Murchison) and Jenny Agutter (Asua) flee from Fort Barash in the Sudan, under attack by Mahdist troops, and head for Khartoum. Avoiding crocodiles, rhinos, lions, Moslem dervishes and Arab slave traders, they encounter Johnny Sekka's tribe, ruled by Joseph Layode (King Gondoko), eventually reaching their destination after General Gordon's famous defeat. Despite their differences, prim and not-so-proper Syms hitches her skirt to rough-but-nice Quayle.

A typical British support feature of the 1960s, *East of Sudan* is performed entirely on studio sets, extensive footage from London Film Productions' *The Four Feathers* (1939) tagged on at the start and finish, plus copious wildlife shots of various African animals, many of whom would never have been seen within 100 miles of the River Nile—at times, it's like being at the zoo. Scriptwriter Jud Kinberg's attempts at introducing a Humphrey Bogart/Katharine Hepburn spat-filled relationship between Quayle and Syms is only partially successful; Fowlds does little but moon over Syms, telling her he loves her, while 12-year-old Agutter, in her film debut, is quite enchanting as a dark-haired native girl. There's a solitary peplum moment, Quayle trapped by a semicircle of spears, and Syms yells the genre's much-used phrase, "Follow me!" Its limitations exposed by those stage-

bound vignettes, *East of Sudan* is a tedious non-starter, particularly when considering the amount of talent involved (and wasted) here. Quayle and Syms were big British box-office stars at the time, while Nathan Juran, cinematographer Wilkie Cooper and executive producer Charles H. Schneer came up with much better pictures than this. *East of Sudan* will make even kids yawn, it's that uninteresting.

1965

The Brigand of Kandahar
Hammer/Columbia (UK); Hammerscope/Eastmancolor; 81 mins; Producer: Anthony Nelson Keys; Director: John Gilling ††

Hammer's long association with Columbia ended with a sour-faced colonial adventure set in 1850, as did Oliver Reed's involvement with Hammer, his last appearance for the company that made his name. Using extensive battle footage from Terence Young's *Zarak* (Warwick, 1956), John Gilling's program filler had an unusually high body count for what, after all, was viewed as family entertainment; cardboard studio sets; too-obvious back-projection work; Reed overacting like a madman and a downbeat *Duel in the Sun* ending, lovers Ronald Lewis and Yvonne Romain clutching hands before expiring from gunshot wounds. Director Gilling's story and literate screenplay centered on half-caste Ronald Lewis (Lieutenant Richard Case), discharged from the British army operating out of Fort Kandahar on the Indian frontier, given 10 years for supposedly deserting his commanding officer *and* having an affair with the man's wife (Katherine Woodville). Embittered Lewis, innocent of the charge of cowardice, escapes from prison through the help of native Sean Lynch (Rattu), enlisting with fanatic Oliver Reed (Eli Khan) and his Gilzhai brigands in their mountain den ("Join me to fight those that betrayed you."), one thought uppermost in his mind—to kill Duncan Lamont (Colonel Drewe), the martinet responsible for his unreasonable, prejudiced treatment.

A meaty scenario, then, is sabotaged by its stage-bound confines, Lewis' dour performance (not once does he smile), Gilling's plodding camerawork (a real surprise, considering his other Hammer features) and the non-appearance of Reed. The greased-up star of the show doesn't walk on set until 15 minutes have dragged by, vanishes for around 10 minutes in the middle section and is then strangled to death by Lewis on the hour during a "let's see who's leader around here" tussle to the finish. Glyn Houston's cynical newspaper reporter, Marriott, is a nice turn, the war correspondent sympathizing with Lewis' plight but appalled at his callous disregard for human life, especially when he guns down Woodville's tortured husband to put him out of his misery. Romain, playing Reed's exotic sister Ratina, actually stirs Lewis into some semblance of life by wrapping her lithe brown arms around him, questioning Reed's acceptance of the half-caste into his white-robed ranks: "You trust this man?" "Like my own brother." "You killed our brother." "That is why I trust him." A couple of blazing ambushes and saber clashes leave the studio floor littered with corpses. Inigo Jackson is venomous racist Captain Boyd, and Lewis and Romain perish holding hands. It's left to Houston to report back to the *London Times* on Lamont's unethical activities and to restore Lewis' tarnished reputation, a man "destroyed, piece by piece." Muddy photography and Don Banks' jaunty military score dispel any mood of seriousness; perhaps it would have worked better, and been more of a success, as a comedy. After all, Rank's *Carry On Up*

Ali Baba (Peter Mann, resembling Douglas Fairbanks in his prime) is leading the 40 thieves on a string of raids against the Mongols, wearing the seal of Bagdad. Attractively shot around California's Red Rock Canyon area, incorporating vivid painted backdrops, this early part of the narrative moves briskly and looks fine. Mann bumps into Amara (Jocelyn Lane) at an oasis where she's bathing nude; he then finds himself locking horns with Gavin MacLeod (Hulagu Khan), the vicious despot desiring marriage to redhead Lane; Lane's treacherous father, Frank Puglia (as Prince Cassim), does his best to outwit Mann, who is aided by amiable slave Greg Morris (Yusuf). The whole topsy-turvy escapade ends at the Feast of Ramadan. Forty big jars of oil are brought into MacLeod's wedding ceremony but they don't contain, as suspected, the 40 thieves, but only sand. The brigands spring out of the rebellious crowd, there's a five-minute scimitar clash, MacLeod stabs Puglia to death and then falls to the ground, a dagger wedged between his shoulder blades. The Mongol guards are overpowered, and peace is restored to the city. "We are pledged," whispers Lane to Mann. "Forever," he confirms, the two now joint rulers of Bagdad.

A genuine Hollywood B-movie in an age where B-movies ceased to exist, *The Sword of Ali Baba* is enjoyable nonsense that seems to belong, as do much of the crew involved, in the 1950s, not 1965. Disengaging the brain while watching it will help enormously!

The War Lord

Universal (US); Panavision/Technicolor; 123 mins; Producer: Walter Seltzer; Director: Franklin J. Schaffner ☥☥☥☥☥

Of the five big-budget spectacles starring Hollywood legend Charlton Heston to have appeared on the screen from 1956 up to 1965—*The Ten Commandments*, *Ben-Hur*, *El Cid*, *55 Days at Peking* and *The War Lord*—Franklin J. Schaffner's $3,500,000 Middle Ages yarn tends to get overlooked, a strange anomaly; the mighty Heston gave one of the best performances of his long and illustrious career in a movie that commendably got down and got dirty, doing away with rose-tinted medieval romanticism, presenting everyday life in 11th-century Britain as unglamorous, grimy, smelly and harsh, the superstitious populace indulging in Druidic rituals while trying to come to terms with nascent Christianity. Adapted from Leslie Stevens' play *The Lovers*, Heston played battle-weary knight Chrysagon de la Cruex who, as reward for 20 long years' service to the country fighting in the Crusades, is given his own piece of land to rule on England's desolate northeast coast, a curiously suffocating community surrounded by misty fens and marshes, overlooked by a lofty stone tower and open to attack from the warmongering Frisian raiders across the sea. "A queer moody place," observes Richard Boone (superb as Heston's gruff protector, Bors), while younger brother Guy Stockwell (Draco) is more succinct in his appraisal: "A dung heap. You deserve better. Much better."

Expertly photographed in a hazy, watery light by Russell Metty (winner of an Oscar for best cinematography, *Spartacus*) to reflect the bleak locations (actually filmed in California, although many English critics found this difficult to believe), John Collier and Millard Kaufman's intelligent screenplay, tackling complex themes, focused on the fractious relationship between Heston's solid machismo Lord and Stockwell's excitable sib-

the Khyber (1968), which in some ways it vaguely resembles, is a classic of British mirth. A little light humor wouldn't have gone amiss.

The Sword of Ali Baba

Universal (US); Eastmancolor; 81 mins; Producer: Howard Christie; Director: Virgil W. Vogel ☥☥☥

A virtual remake of Arthur Lubin's *Ali Baba and the Forty Thieves* (Universal, 1944) and utilizing stock footage from it, *The Sword of Ali Baba*, bolstered by a complement of '50s B-movie actors, just about muddles through as a Saturday morning offering for the kids, containing mild doses of Eastern mayhem and a few violent moments. The other two '50s connections are Frank Skinner's stock score, lifted from numerous soundtracks he composed throughout that decade, and director Virgil W. Vogel, the man responsible for two Universal classic monster yarns: *The Mole People* (1956) and *The Land Unknown* (1957).

In Old Bagdad, young Ali and Princess Amara, after pledging themselves with a blood pact and promised in marriage, are separated when Mongols conquer the city and the caliph is killed. Ali escapes into the desert, taken care of by Old Baba and his 40 thieves in their treasure-laden cavern. 15 years later,

ling. The idolatrous peasants practice their ancient doctrine and fertility rites, and Heston develops an infatuation with virgin bride Rosemary Forsyth (Bronwyn). She's betrothed to James Farantino (Marc), but on their tribal wedding day, Heston, tired and in urgent need of female company, invokes the pagan law of *droit de seigneur*, the right of a feudal nobleman to take the bride to his bed on her wedding night on condition she's returned at dawn. Village elder Niall MacGinnis grudgingly bows to this unforeseen order, but come morning, Heston refuses to let his lovely-as-a-rose prize go, besides Forsyth is smitten with him ("She is mine!" Heston roars to the waiting serfs). Heston's selfish actions are the catalyst for all kinds of disasters. Jilted Farantino, seething with hatred, rows to the Frisians to enlist their aid in ousting Heston and his Norman knights (the Frisian prince's son has been captured in an earlier skirmish), Stockwell fumes in frustration and jealousy over his brother's little "witch," priest Maurice Evans spells doom and gloom and taciturn Boone tries to keep the peace. When the Frisians arrive, Schaffner orchestrates several exciting attacks on the tower featuring siege machines, Stockwell eventually turning up with reinforcements, just as the stronghold is about to be taken. For his sex-motivated folly, Heston's role as Lord of the Manor has been passed to his brother, who brings news of the change in command, sanctioned by the ruling duke; ever vindictive, Stockwell claims to have lived too long under Heston's formidable shadow and relishes being top dog. The two come to blows and, in a violent scuffle, Stockwell receives Heston's dagger in his ribs, tumbling into the cellar to his death. Hostilities over, Heston releases the child to the grateful Frisian prince (Henry Wilcoxon) and is asked to join them, with a promise of land and wealth—his leadership qualities are far more appreciated by the Frisians than the peasant rabble under his authority. Declining the offer for now, he asks Wilcoxon to take Forsyth with him and is then wounded by vengeful Farantino; in turn, the spurned bridegroom is brutally dispatched by Boone. Together, the warlord and his battle-scarred companion ride off to face the duke's wrath and hopefully sort out the mess he's made before joining the Frisians and Forsyth.

Blessed by a lovely score from Jerome Moross (British instrumental group The Shadows reached number 18 in the charts in December 1965 with their jaunty version of the title theme), *The War Lord* is one of those films that rewards on repeated viewings, inch perfect in performances, direction, vision, set design (that striking stone tower takes on a life of its own) and atmosphere. Heston was a giant among actors, both in physical stature and screen presence; here, at age 42 and looking in great shape, he fits that chain mail suit like a glove in a role that was tailor-made for his artistic talents, one of celluloid's finest-ever medieval knights portrayed by an artist at the very top of his form.

1967

A Challenge for Robin Hood
Hammer/Seven Arts (UK); DeLuxecolor; 96 (85) mins; Producer: Clifford Parkes; Director: C.M. Pennington-Richards ††

The Italian peplum genre was virtually dead in the water, and with it the *Robin Hood* cycle of films, when Hammer gave the story a last-gasp shot, tinkering with the legend in an effort to produce something different. Robin Hood was now a Norman, and Maid Marian was traveling incognito as her own maid. Otherwise, it was down the familiar route of Robin de Courtenay (Barrie Ingham) pitting his wits against Sir Roger (Peter Blythe) and the Sheriff of Nottingham (John Arnatt) by joining a band of Norman (?) Sherwood Forest outlaws armed with longbows and quarterstaffs, forced to live the rough life due to their property having been commandeered to line the bailiff's pockets.

Strikingly filmed in and around East Sussex's massively constructed Bodiam Castle, built in 1385 (photography by Arthur Grant), the plot had Ingham enlisting into the rather depleted ranks of the Merry Men after John Gugolka's father is callously slain by Blythe for poaching deer. When Blythe's own father collapses and dies, the neurotic weed tears up the will, murders his brother (Eric Woofe) with Ingham's dirk, thus blaming him for the killing, and cosies up to Arnatt, the sheriff casting his sly eyes on Gay Hamilton's slim figure (as Maid Marian). Douglas Mitchell (Will Scarlett) is arrested and sentenced to have his neck stretched at a fair; Ingham, posing as The Masked Monk, wrestles Leon Greene (Little John); tearing off his mask, he's ordered to take his place beside Mitchell on the scaffold; roly-poly James Hayter (Friar Tuck) is their unlikely savior, coming to the pair's aid by engaging in a pie-throwing battle with the guards, Ingham and Mitchell escaping the rope. Eric Flynn (Alan-a-

Dale) gets to warble a melancholy ditty in a forest glade, Hamilton drifts waif-like through the narrative, her bright blue eyes completely void of any emotion, Jenny Till, her blonde stand-in, is even less active (where's that Italian fire when you need it? Buck up, girls!), goofy British comedian Alfie Bass plays a crooked pie seller and Arnatt is coldly arrogant. A secret passage crops up under the castle moat, there are several leaden bouts of swords versus quarterstaffs and a debauched banquet complete with two musclemen wrestlers, the whole shebang closing with Ingham's bandits entering the great hall via the scullery serving hatch. Blythe meets his Maker (a knife embedded in the back), Arnatt gallops off to safety and Ingham marries Hamilton, at last bringing a smile to those wan features.

It's harmless and charmless: Jovial Hayter (he played Friar Tuck in Disney/RKO's *The Story of Robin Hood and His Merrie Men* in 1952) acts everyone else off screen, his rotund monk forever gorging on all manner of juicy medieval goodies; Ingham is so-so, not quite hitting it off as the feather-capped, Lincoln green-clad hero; Hamilton is poor as the female love interest, registering little interest and highly strung Blythe rants, raves, rolls his eyes in pantomime fashion but still manages to appear like a cowardly weasel, not the blaggard you wouldn't want to cross broadswords with. A low-budget *Robin Hood* caper that is unable to doff its cap in the direction of the far more robust Italian versions; they may, in most instances, have been dafter in approach, but the passion and energy was there. In *A Challenge for Robin Hood*, it's sadly missing.

The Viking Queen

Hammer/Seven Arts (UK); DeLuxecolor; 91 (80) mins; Producer: John Temple-Smith; Director: Don Chaffey ††††

For those who have never experienced a peplum barbarian flick, *The Viking Queen* comes across as hokey, coarse and historically suspect. But if you have sat through stuff like 1960's *The Queen of the Tartars*, you can spot the influences; Hammer's half-a-million pound movie is the closest a British film studio ever came to during the 1960s in replicating an Italian barbarian picture. Shot, not around Bray as usual, but in County Wicklow, Ireland, Chaffey chucks forward every Italian Roman versus pagan plot/visual device you can throw a sword at. A barbarian queen, Salina (Carita, one of her only two movie appearances), falls for centurion Justinian (Don Murray) in Roman-occupied Britain and then leads her warriors on a rampage against Roman rule, psychotic Druids stirring up trouble, sacrificing troublemakers in a fiery pit. An ambitious officer (Andrew Keir), out to cause mischief in his insane quest to become governor general, murders those who stand in his path; semi-nudity and violence toward women on display; religious fanaticism; Carita stripped to the waist and graphically flogged; a peasant revolt; savage in-your-face spear-throwing skirmishes; a wild boar hunt; chariots armed with deadly scythes and a Roman corps marching over bleak moorland. Even a waterfall is included, not Monte Gelato but the Powerscourt waterfall at Enniskerry, picturesque enough in this setting.

On his deathbed, King Priam (Wilfred Lawson) passes the throne to daughter Carita; the Druids, led by Donald Houston, are determined to undermine her authority. She falls in love with Murray after sex on a riverbank and Keir argues incessantly with Murray, undermining *his* authority; Murray goes to Anglesey to quell a Druid rebellion, leaving Keir and his followers to create havoc with the Iceni. On his return, Murray has to face Carita and her Iceni fighters who, sick of Keir's brutal command, attack the Romans in their war chariots; Keir is stabbed to death; and Carita, her forces defeated, falls on a soldier's blade, dying in Murray's arms.

A strong support cast comprising Niall MacGinnis, Patrick Troughton, Adrienne Corri, Nicola Pagett, Percy Herbert and Denis Shaw contribute to a fantastic Hammer peplum that in many ways doesn't resemble a typical Hammer production of that period. Shorn by 11 minutes in some parts of Europe because of its near-rape scenes and bloody mayhem (it just about escaped an "X" certificate in England, where it was rated "A"), *The Viking Queen* is a well-crafted pagan actioner that doesn't set a sandal in the wrong direction, a wickedly underrated picture that looks great in every scene (as does the bewitching Carita)—it could so easily have had "Made in Italy" stamped all over it, it's that true to its roots.

20
The Spirit Lives On

The spirit of peplum lives on, not so much in the multi-million dollar computerized epics such as *Gladiator*, *Troy*, *300*, *Alexander* and *Kingdom of Heaven*, but in those movies produced on much tighter finances (and less reliance on CGI for their effects) that go largely unnoticed on the national circuits. It is here that you can find and really participate in the true ethos of pepla: tightly knitted dramas embodying within their narrative heroic leaders, motifs and intrigues, bloody fights, gut-wrenching violence, beautiful women, devious villains, a touch of fantasy, warlike scenarios and that all-important Italian bravura that has trickled down through the decades, still influencing filmmakers to this day. What is sadly missing is a glorious score to back up the action, but regrettably the days of Carlo Savina, Carlo Rustichelli, Angelo Francesco Lavagnino, Carlo Innocenzi and their ilk are long gone, never to be replaced. There has been a glut of these peplum-type pictures since 2001 (in Britain, the majority are age 15-rated), made on budgets of around $100,000 to $70,000,000, small change when compared to the amount of coin lavished by the big studios on crowd-pleasing blockbusters (*Troy* cost a staggering $175,000,000). So check out the following and you'll discover that the Italian way of doing things perpetuates in multinational releases that echo to the clash of steel and the roar of the arena crowd; that wallow in the spilling of blood and Christian uprising in Ancient Egypt; that tell tales of Mongol warlords, Knights of the Crusade and lost legions; that have medieval castles under siege; that include Vikings and Spanish Musketeers; that have Romans battling heathen hordes; that have warriors embarking on a nightmarish journey to the Holy Lands and that contain moments of superstition and horror. Yes, perhaps peplum hasn't completely vanished from modern-day cinema screens after all; it still lingers on, but in a different guise.

Agora [Mod Producciones/Himenoptero, 2009] Director: Alejandro Amenabar
The Arena [Juga Films, 2001] Director: Timur Bekmambetov
Arn: The Knight Templar [AMC Pictures, 2007] Director: Peter Flinth
Barbarossa: Siege Lord [Martinelli Film, 2009] Director: Renzo Martinelli
Black Death [Egoli Tossell/Hanway, 2010] Director: Christopher Smith
Captain Alatriste: The Spanish Musketeer [Estudios, 2006] Director: Augustin Diaz Yanes
Centurion [Pathé, 2010] Director: Neil Marshall
Clash of Empires [KRU Studios, 2011] Director: Yusry Abd Halim
Crusade of Vengeance [Drotcroft, 2002] Director: Byron W. Thompson
Cyclops [New Horizons, 2008] Director: Declan O'Brien
The Eagle [Focus Features/Film4, 2011] Director: Kevin Macdonald
Henry of Navarre [Ziegler Film, 2010] Director: Joe Baier
Iron and Blood: The Legend of Taras Bulba [Telecanal Rossiya, 2009] Director: Vladimir Bortko
Ironclad [Mythic Intl./ContentFilm, 2011] Director: Jonathan English
Ironclad: Battle for Blood [Mythic Intl./ContentFilm, 2014] Director: Jonathan English
Iron Lord [Anno Domini, 2010] Director: Dmitriy Korobkin
The Last Legion [Dino De Laurentiis Co., 2007] Director: Doug Lefler
Mongol: The Rise to Power of Genghis Khan [CTB/Kinofabrika, 2007] Director: Sergey Bodrov
Season of the Witch [Atlas Ent., 2011] Director: Dominic Sena
1612 [CPFACC/Golden Eagle, 2007] Director: Vladimir Khotinenko
Shadow of the Sword [Allegro Film/Eurofilm, 2005] Director: Simon Aeby
Soldier of God [Anabasis, 2005] Director: W.D. Hogan
Solomon Kane [Davis-Films/Czech Anglo Prods., 2009] Director: Michael J. Bassett
Valhalla Rising [BBC Films/Belle Alle Prods., 2009] Director: Nicolas Winding Refn
Vercingetorix/Druids aka *The Gaul* [CNC/Eiffel Prods., 2001] Director: Jacques Dorfmann,
Vikingdom [KRU Studios, 2013] Director: Yusry Abd Halim

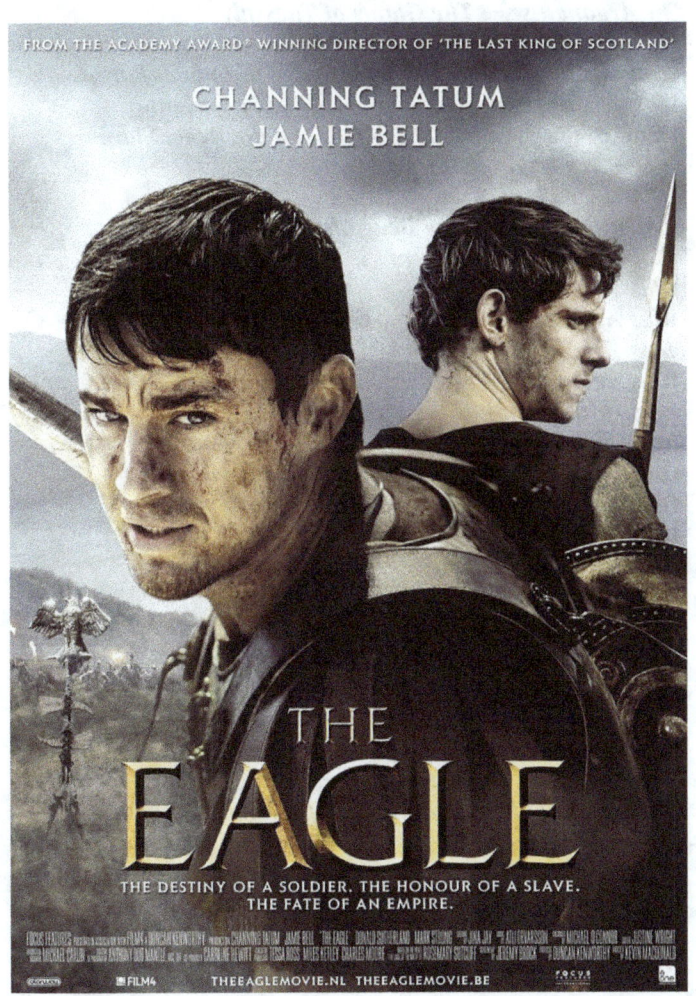

21
Index of Film Titles

Each film title is followed by the book chapter and year of release. Alternative titles are cross-referenced against the release title.

Achilles see *The Fury of Achilles*
The Adventurer 16.67
The Adventurer of Tortuga 15.65
The Adventures of Hajji Baba 2.54
The Adventures of Mary Read 15.61
Adventures of Scaramouche 16.63
Adventures of the Bengal Lancers see *The Three Sergeants of Bengal*
The Affairs of Messalina see *Messalina*
Ali Baba and the Sacred Crown see *The 7 Tasks of Ali Baba*
Ali Baba and the Seven Saracens see *Sinbad Against the Seven Saracens*
Alone Against Rome 12.62
Amazons of Rome 12.61
Anne of the Indies 2.51
Anthar the Invincible 13.64
Aphrodite, Goddess of Love see *The Venus of Cheronea*
Aphrodite, Goddess of Love 4.58
Archimedes see *Siege of Syracuse*
The Argonauts see *The Giants of Thessaly*
Arm of Fire see *The Colossus of Rome*
Arminius the Terrible see *Massacre in the Black Forest*
Arms of the Avenger see *The Devils of Spartivento*
Arrow of the Avenger see *Goliath and the Rebel Slave*
At Sword's Edge 3.52
At Sword's Point 2.52
L'Atlantide see *Journey Beneath the Desert*
Atlantis the Lost Continent see *Siren of Atlantis*
Atlas 19.61
Atlas Against the Cyclops see *Maciste in the Land of the Cyclops*
Atlas Against the Czar see *Maciste at the Court of the Czar*
Atlas in the Land of the Cyclops see *Maciste in the Land of the Cyclops*
Attack of the Moors see *The Kings of France*
Attack of the Normans see *The Normans*
Attila 3.54
Attila the Hun see *Attila*
The Avenger see *The Legend of Aeneas*
The Avenger of California see *The Sign of the Coyote*
The Avenger of Seville see *Captain from Toledo*
Avenger of the Seven Seas see *Executioner of the Seas*
The Avenger of Venice see *The Bridge of Sighs*
The Bacchantes 9.61
Balboa see *The Legendary Conqueror*
Balboa, Conquistador of the Pacific see *The Legendary Conqueror*
The Bandit of Sherwood Forest 2.46
The Bandit of Zhobe 2.59
Bandits of Orgosolo 16.61
The Barbarians see *Revak, the Slave of Carthage*

The Barbarians see *The Sack of Rome*
The Battle of Marathon 4.59
Battle of the Spartans see *Brennus Enemy of Rome*
Battle of the Titans see *Vulcan, Son of Jupiter*
Battle of the Valiant see *Brennus Enemy of Rome*
The Battle of Toledo see *The Tyrant of Castile*
Battles of the Gladiators see *Gladiator of Rome*
The Beast of Babylon Against the Son of Hercules see *The Hero of Babylon*
Behind the Mask of Zorro see *The Oath of Zorro*
The Black Archer 4.59
The Black Arrow 2.48
The Black Arrow Strikes see *The Black Arrow*
The Black Brigand see *The Secret of the Black Falcon*
The Black Captain 3.51
The Black Cavalier see *Revenge of the Black Knight*
The Black Devil 4.57
The Black Duke 16.63
The Black Invaders 16.62
The Black Knight 2.54
The Black Lancers 14.62
The Black Pirate see *Gordon, the Black Pirate*
The Black Pirate see *The Masked Man Against the Pirates*
The Black Shield of Falworth 2.54
Blood and Defiance 16.62
Blood of the Executioner see *The Executioner of Venice*
Blood Over Rome see *The Sack of Rome*
The Boatmen see *The Volga Boatmen*
Bondage Gladiator Sexy see *The Bacchantes*
Brennus Enemy of Rome 12.63
The Bridge of Sighs 16.64
The Brigand of Kandahar 19.65
Buccaneer's Girl 2.50
The Burning of Rome see *The Magnificent Adventurer*
Caesar and the Pirates see *Julius Caesar Against the Pirates*
Caesar the Conqueror see *Julius Caesar the Conqueror of Gaul*
The Captain 19.60
Captain Blood see *The Captain*
Captain Clegg 19.62
Captain Falcon see *Captain of Fire*
Captain from Castile 1.47
Captain from Toledo 16.65
Captain Kidd and the Slave Girl 2.54
Captain of Fire 4.58
Captain of Iron 16.62
Captain Phantom 3.53
Captains of Ventura 16.61
Caribbean Hawk see *Hawk of the Caribbean*
Carthage in Flames 12.60
The Castilian see *Valley of the Swords*
Catherine of Russia 16.63
Cavalier in Devil's Castle see *Cavalier in the Devil's Castle*
Cavalier in the Devil's Castle 4.59
Cavalier of the Devil's Castle see *Cavalier in the Devil's Castle*

The Centurion see *The Conqueror of Corinth*
Cesare Borgia see *The Black Duke*
A Challenge for Robin Hood 19.67
Challenge of the Giants 5.65
Challenge of the Gladiator 10.65
The Charge of the Black Lancers see *The Black Lancers*
Clash of Steel see *The Knight of Pardaillan*
Cleopatra's Daughter see *The Tomb of the Kings*
Colossus and the Amazon Queen see *Queen of the Amazons*
Colossus and the Headhunters see *Maciste Against the Headhunters*
Colossus and the Huns see *Tharus Son of Attila*
The Colossus of Rhodes 9.61
The Colossus of Rome 12.64
Colossus of the Arena see *Maciste, the World's Strongest Gladiator*
Colossus of the Stone Age see *Maciste Against the Monsters*
The Conqueror of Atlantis 13.65
The Conqueror of Corinth 12.61
Conqueror of Maracaibo 15.61
The Conqueror of the Orient 17.60
The Conquest of Mycenae see *Hercules Against Moloch*
Conquest of the Normans see *The Normans*
Constantine and the Cross see *Constantine the Great*
Constantine the Great 12.61
Coriolanus: Hero Without a Country 12.64
The Corsican Brothers 16.61
The Cossacks 16.60
The Count of Matera-The Tyrant 4.58
The Count of Saint Elmo 3.51
The Crimson Blade see *The Scarlet Blade*
Crossed Swords 3.54
Crown of Fire 16.61
Curse of the Haunted Forest see *The Devils of Spartivento*
Damon and Pythias see *The Tyrant of Syracuse*
Dangerous Exile 2.57
D'Artagnan Against the Three Musketeers 18.64
Daughter of Cleopatra see *The Tomb of the Kings*
The Daughters of El Cid see *The Sword of El Cid*
David and Goliath 11.60
Day of Vengeance see *The Ten Invincible Gladiators*
The Defeat of the Barbarians 16.62
Demetrius and the Gladiators 2.54
The Desert Lovers 4.57
Desert Raiders see *The Ruler of the Desert*
Desert Raiders see *Valley of the Thundering Echo*
Desert Warrior see *The Desert Lovers*
Devil of the Desert Against the Son of Hercules see *Anthar the Invincible*
The Devil Pirate 15.63
The Devil-Ship Pirates 19.64
The Devil's Cavaliers 4.59
The Devil's Daughter 3.52
The Devils of Spartivento 16.63
Drakut the Avenger 16.61
Duel at the Rio Grande see *Sign of Zorro*
Duel Before the Mast see *The Pirate's Revenge*
Duel in Sila 16.62
Duel of Champions see *Duel of the Champions*
Duel of Fire see *Duel in Sila*
Duel of the Champions 12.61

Duel of the Titans see *Romulus and Remus*
East of Sudan 19.64
Erik the Conqueror see *The Invaders*
Erik, the Viking 17.65
Esther and the King 11.60
The Executioner of Lille 3.52
Executioner of the Seas 15.62
The Executioner of Venice 16.63
Fabiola 1.49
The Face That Launched a Thousand Ships see *The Loves of Three Queens*
Falcon of the Desert see *The Magnificent Challenge*
The Fall of Rome 12.63
The Fighting Corsair see *Surcouf, Hero of the Seven Seas*
The Fighting Gladiator see *Fabiola*
The Fighting Legions see *The Devils of Spartivento*
The Fighting Musketeers see *The Three Musketeers*
The Filibusters of Martinique see *Marie of the Isles*
Fire Monsters Against the Son of Hercules see *Maciste Against the Monsters*
The Fire of Rome 12.65
Fire Over Rome see *The Fire of Rome*
Flag of Death see *The Devil Pirate*
Flame of Araby 2.51
Fortunes of Captain Blood 2.50
Fury at Smugglers' Bay 19.61
The Fury of Achilles 9.62
The Fury of Hercules 5.62
The Fury of Samson see *The Fury of Hercules*
Fury of the Barbarians 14.60
Fury of the Pagans see *Fury of the Barbarians*
Fury of the Vikings see *The Invaders*
Genoveffa of Brabant 16.64
The Giant of Marathon see *The Battle of Marathon*
The Giant of Metropolis 13.61
Giant of the Evil Island see *The Mystery of the Evil Island*
Giant of the Lost Tomb see *Maciste at the Court of the Czar*
The Giants of Rome 12.64
The Giants of Thessaly 9.60
Gideon and Samson see *The Great Leaders*
Gladiator of Rome 10.62
Gladiators 7 10.62
Goddess of Love see *The Venus of Cheronea*
Gold for the Caesars 12.63
The Golden Arrow 13.62
The Golden Blade 2.53
The Golden Falcon 3.55
The Golden Hawk 2.52
Goliath Against the Giants 8.61
Goliath and the Barbarians see *Terror of the Barbarians*
Goliath and the Dragon see *The Revenge of Hercules*
Goliath and the Masked Rider 8.63
Goliath and the Rebel Slave 8.63
Goliath and the Sins of Babylon see *Maciste, the World's Greatest Hero*
Goliath and the Vampires see *Maciste Against the Vampire*
Goliath at the Conquest of Bagdad 8.64
Goliath at the Conquest of Damascus see *Goliath at the Conquest of Bagdad*
Goliath, King of the Slaves see *The Hero of Babylon*
Gordon, the Black Pirate 15.61

The Great Leaders 11.65
The Green Flags of Allah 13.63
Guns of the Black Witch see *The Terror of the Seas*
Hadji Murad The White Devil 4.59
Hannibal 4.59
Hawk of Bagdad see *Sinbad Against the Seven Saracens*
Hawk of the Caribbean 15.62
Head of a Tyrant see *Judith and Holofernes*
Helen of Troy 2.56
Hell Below Deck see *The Adventures of Mary Read*
Hercules see *The Labors of Hercules*
Hercules Against Moloch 5.63
Hercules Against Rome 5.64
Hercules Against the Barbarians see *Maciste in Genghis Khan's Hell*
Hercules Against the Mongols see *Maciste Against the Mongols*
Hercules Against the Moon Men see *Maciste and the Queen of Samar*
Hercules Against the Sons of the Sun 5.64
Hercules Against the Tyrants of Babylon 5.64
Hercules Against the Vampires see *Hercules at the Center of the Earth*
Hercules and the Black Pirate see *Samson Against the Black Pirate*
Hercules and the Captive Women see *Hercules and the Conquest of Atlantis*
Hercules and the Conquest of Atlantis 5.61
Hercules and the Masked Rider see *Goliath and the Masked Rider*
Hercules and the Pirates see *Samson Against the Black Pirate*
Hercules and the Princess of Troy 5.65
Hercules and the Queen of Lydia 4.59
Hercules and the Ten Avengers see *The Triumph of Hercules*
Hercules and the Treasure of the Incas see *Samson and the Treasure of the Incas*
Hercules at the Center of the Earth 5.61
Hercules Attacks see *Hercules Against Moloch*
Hercules Challenges Samson 5.63
Hercules Conquers Atlantis see *Hercules and the Conquest of Atlantis*
Hercules in the Haunted World see *Hercules at the Center of the Earth*
Hercules in the Vale of Woe see *Maciste Against Hercules in the Vale of Woe*
Hercules of the Desert see *Valley of the Thundering Echo*
Hercules, Prisoner of Evil see *Ursus, the Terror of the Kirghiz*
Hercules Returns see *Hercules, Samson, Maciste and Ursus: The Invincibles*
Hercules, Samson and Ulysses see *Hercules Challenges Samson*
Hercules, Samson, Maciste and Ursus: The Invincibles 5.64
Hercules the Avenger see *Challenge of the Giants*
Hercules the Invincible 5.64
Hercules Unchained see *Hercules and the Queen of Lydia*
Hercules vs. The Giant Warriors see *The Triumph of Hercules*
Hercules vs. The Hydra see *The Loves of Hercules*
Hercules vs. the Sea Monster see *Hercules and the Princess of Troy*
The Hero of Babylon 13.63
Hero of Rome see *The Colossus of Rome*

Herod the Great 4.59
The Highwayman 2.51
The Huns see *The Queen of the Tartars*
I, Semiramis 13.63
Imperial Venus 16.62
In the Shadow of the Eagles see *Shadow of Eagles*
The Indomitable see *Mandrin*
The Invaders 17.61
Invasion 1700 see *With Iron and Fire*
The Invincible Brothers Maciste 6.64
The Invincible Gladiator 10.61
The Invincible Gladiators see *The Invincible Brothers Maciste*
The Invincible Masked Cavalier 16.63
The Invincible Masked Rider see *The Invincible Masked Cavalier*
The Invincible Seven 9.63
The Invincible Three 8.64
Island of Monte Cristo see *Sword of Venus*
Ivan the Conqueror see *The Seven Challenges*
Jacob and Esau 11.63
Jacob, The Man Who Fought With God 11.63
Jason and the Golden Fleece see *The Giants of Thessaly*
Jerusalem Set Free 4.58
Jesus, the Son of Man see *The Son of Man*
Joseph and His Brethren see *Joseph Sold By His Brothers*
Joseph Sold By His Brothers 11.60
Journey Beneath the Desert 13.61
Judith and Holofernes 4.59
Julius Caesar Against the Pirates 12.62
Julius Caesar and the Pirates see *Julius Caesar Against the Pirates*
Julius Caesar the Conqueror of Gaul 12.62
Jungle Adventurer see *The Mountain of Light*
Kerim, the Son of the Sheik see *The Son of the Sheik*
Kindar, the Invulnerable 13.65
King Arthur's Adventurer see *Siege of the Saxons*
King of the 7 Seas 16.62
King of the Vikings 19.60
The Kingdom in the Sand see *The Conqueror of Atlantis*
Kingdom of Violence see *The Tyrant of Castile*
The King's Captain see *The Captain*
The Kings of France 4.59
The Knight of 100 Faces 16.60
The Knight of Pardaillan 19.62
Knight of the Black Sword 3.56
Knight Without a Country 4.59
The Knights of Seville see *Captain from Toledo*
Knights of Terror see *The Terror of the Red Capes*
Knights of the Gray Galley see *The Black Invaders*
Knives of the Avenger 17.66
Kublai Khan see *The Marvellous Adventures of Marco Polo*
The Labors of Hercules 4.57
Lady in the Iron Mask 2.52
Lancelot and Guinevere see *Sword of Lancelot*
The Last Charge 16.62
The Last Czar 16.60
The Last Days of Pompeii 3.50
The Last Days of Pompeii 4.59
The Last Days of Sodom and Gomorrah see *Sodom and Gomorrah*
The Last Gladiator 10.64

The Last Glory of Troy see *The Legend of Aeneas*
The Last of the Vikings 17.61
The Legend of Aeneas 9.62
The Legendary Conqueror 17.63
The Legions of Cleopatra 4.59
Legions of the Nile see *The Legions of Cleopatra*
The Lion of Amalfi 3.50
The Lion of Castile see *Valley of the Swords*
The Lion of St. Mark 16.63
Lion of Sparta see *The 300 Spartans*
The Lion of Thebes 9.64
Lions of Corsica see *The Corsican Brothers*
The Lost Kingdom see *Journey Beneath the Desert*
The Lost Treasure of the Aztecs see *Samson and the Treasure of the Incas*
The Lost Treasure of the Incas see *Samson and the Treasure of the Incas*
The Loves of Cleopatra see *Serpent of the Nile*
The Loves of Hercules 5.60
The Loves of Salammbo see *Salammbo*
The Loves of Three Queens 3.54
Maciste Against Hercules in the Vale of Woe 6.61
Maciste Against the Headhunters 6.62
Maciste Against the Mongols 6.63
Maciste Against the Monsters 6.62
Maciste Against the Sheik 6.62
Maciste Against the Vampire 6.61
Maciste and the Queen of Samar 6.64
Maciste and the Women of the Valley see *Valley of the Thundering Echo*
Maciste at the Court of the Czar 6.64
Maciste at the Court of the Great Khan 6.61
Maciste, Avenger of the Maya 6.65
Maciste, Gladiator of Sparta 6.64
Maciste in Genghis Khan's Hell 6.64
Maciste in Hell 6.62
Maciste in King Solomon's Mines 6.64
Maciste in the Land of the Cyclops 6.61
Maciste in the Valley of the Kings 6.60
Maciste, The Avenger of the Mayans see *Maciste, Avenger of the Maya*
Maciste the Mighty see *Maciste in the Valley of the Kings*
Maciste, the Strongest Man in the World 6.61
Maciste, the World's Greatest Hero 6.63
Maciste, the World's Strongest Gladiator 6.62
The Magnificent Adventurer 16.63
The Magnificent Challenge 13.65
The Magnificent Gladiator 10.64
Mandrin 19.62
The Marauder see *The Lion of St. Mark*
Marco Polo 16.62
Marco the Magnificent see *The Marvellous Adventures of Marco Polo*
Marie of the Isles 19.60
The Mark of Zorro see *The Shadow of Zorro*
Mars, God of War 9.62
The Marvellous Adventures of Marco Polo 16.65
Mary Magdalene see *The Sword and the Cross*
The Mask of Scaramouche see *The Adventures of Scaramouche*
Mask of the Avenger 2.51
Mask of the Musketeers see *Zorro and the Three Musketeers*
The Masked Avenger 16.64
The Masked Cavalier see *The Highwayman*
The Masked Cavalier see *Sign of the Avenger*
The Masked Conqueror see *Zorro at the Spanish Court*
The Masked Man Against the Pirates 15.64
Massacre in the Black Forest 17.67
Medusa Against the Son of Hercules see *Perseus the Invincible*
The Men of Sherwood Forest 2.54
The Mercenaries see *Revolt of the Mercenaries*
The Mercenaries see *The Robbers*
The Mercenary see *Swordsman of Siena*
Messalina 3.51
Messalina see *Messalina Venus Empress*
Messalina Against the Son of Hercules see *The Last Gladiator*
Messalina Venus Empress 12.60
Michael Strogoff 3.56
The Mighty Crusaders see *Jerusalem Set Free*
The Mighty Khan see *The Plunderers of the Steppe*
The Mighty Ursus see *Ursus*
The Mighty Warrior see *The Revenge of Ursus*
Milady and the Musketeers see *The Executioner of Lille*
The Minotaur see *Theseus Against the Minotaur*
Mission of Revenge see *Revenge of the Black Knight*
Mole Men Against the Son of Hercules see *Maciste, the Strongest Man in the World*
The Mongols 14.61
Monster from the Unknown World see *Maciste in the Land of the Cyclops*
Morgan, the Pirate 15.60
The Mountain of Light 16.65
Musketeers of the Sea 15.62
The Mutiny 16.61
My Son, The Hero 9.62
The Mysterious Swordsman 3.56
The Mystery of the Evil Island 15.65
Nefertiti, Queen of the Nile 11.61
Nero and Messalina 3.53
Nero and the Burning of Rome see *Nero and Messalina*
Nero, Tyrant of Rome see *Nero and Messalina*
Night Creatures see *Captain Clegg*
The Night of the Great Attack 4.59
Night of the Nameless see *Night of the Unnamed*
Night of the Unnamed 16.62
The Night They Killed Rasputin see *The Last Czar*
The Nights of Lucretia Borgia 4.59
Nights of Rasputin see *The Last Czar*
Nights of Temptation see *The Nights of Lucretia Borgia*
The Normans 16.62
The Oath of Zorro 18.65
The Old Testament 11.63
100 Horsemen 16.64
Orlando and the Knights of France 3.56
The Pagans see *The Sack of Rome*
The Patriarchs see *Jacob, The Man Who Fought With God*
Perseus Against the Monsters see *Perseus the Invincible*
Perseus the Invincible 9.63
The Pharaohs' Woman 11.60
Phryne, Courtesan of the East 3.53
Pia of Ptolomey 4.58

The Italian Peplum Phenomenon 1950-1967

The Pirate and the Slave Girl see *The Scimitar of the Saracen*
The Pirate Captain see *Buccaneer's Girl*
The Pirate of the Black Hawk 4.58
Pirate of the Half Moon 4.57
The Pirate's Captive see *The Scimitar of the Saracen*
The Pirate's Revenge 3.51
The Pirates of Blood River 19.62
The Pirates of Malaysia 16.64
Pirates of the Barbary Coast see *Pirates of the Coast*
Pirates of the Coast 15.60
The Pirates of the Seven Seas see *The Pirates of Malaysia*
Pirates of Tortuga 19.61
Plains of Battle see *Taras Bulba the Cossack*
The Plunderers of the Steppe 14.64
Pontius Pilate 12.62
The Prince in the Red Mask 3.55
Prince Valiant 2.54
Princess of the Nile 2.54
The Princess of the Nile see *The Pharaohs' Woman*
Prisoner in the Tower of Fire 3.53
Prisoner of the Iron Mask see *The Revenge of the Iron Mask*
Prisoner of the Volga see *The Volga Boatmen*
The Prisoners of Devil's Island 16.62
The Purple Mask 2.55
A Queen for Caesar 11.62
The Queen of Babylon 3.54
The Queen of Sheba 3.52
Queen of the Amazons 2.47
Queen of the Amazons 9.60
Queen of the Nile see *Nefertiti, Queen of the Nile*
The Queen of the Pirates 15.60
Queen of the Seas see *The Adventures of Mary Read*
The Queen of the Tartars 14.60
Rage of the Buccaneers see *Gordon, the Black Pirate*
Raiders of the Seven Seas 2.53
Rampage of Evil see *Captain of Iron*
Rampage of Evil see *Captains of Ventura*
The Rape of the Sabine Women 12.61
The Rebel Gladiators see *Ursus, the Rebel Gladiator*
The Rebel of Castelmonte 16.64
The Rebel of Naples see *The Count of Saint Elmo*
The Red Cloak 3.55
The Red Eagle see *The Prince in the Red Mask*
The Red Sheik 13.63
The Return of Robin Hood see *The Knight of 100 Faces*
The Return of Sandokan see *Sandokan Against the Leopard of Sarawak*
Revak the Rebel see *Revak, the Slave of Carthage*
Revak, the Slave of Carthage 14.60
The Revenge of Hercules 5.60
The Revenge of Ivanhoe 16.65
The Revenge of Sandokan see *Sandokan To The Rescue*
The Revenge of Spartacus 12.64
Revenge of the Barbarians 14.60
Revenge of the Black Eagle 3.51
Revenge of the Black Knight 16.63
Revenge of the Borgias see *The Night of the Great Attack*
Revenge of the Conquered see *Drakut the Avenger*
The Revenge of the Crusader see *Genoveffa of Brabant*
Revenge of the Gladiators 10.64
Revenge of the Gladiators see *The Fire of Rome*

Revenge of the Gladiators see *The Revenge of Spartacus*
The Revenge of the Iron Mask 16.61
Revenge of the Mercenaries see *Captain of Iron*
Revenge of the Musketeers see *D'Artagnan Against the Three Musketeers*
Revenge of the Pirates see *The Pirate's Revenge*
The Revenge of the Red Knight see *The Knight of 100 Faces*
The Revenge of Ursus 8.61
Revolt of the Barbarians 14.64
Revolt of the Barbarians see *Revak, the Slave of Carthage*
The Revolt of the Gladiators 4.58
Revolt of the Mercenaries 16.61
Revolt of the Praetorians 12.64
Revolt of the Seven 10.64
Revolt of the Slaves 12.60
Rivak the Barbarian see *Revak, the Slave of Carthage*
The Robbers 16.61
Robin Hood and the Pirates 15.60
Robin Hood, the Rebel see *Captain of Fire*
Rogues of Sherwood Forest 2.50
Roland the Mighty see *Orlando and the Knights of France*
Rome Against Rome 12.64
Rome, 1585 see *The Robbers*
Romulus and Remus 12.61
Romulus and the Sabines see *The Rape of the Sabine Women*
Rosamund and Alboino 14.61
The Rover see *The Adventurer*
The Ruler of the Desert 13.64
The Sack of Rome 3.53
Salammbo 12.60
Samson 7.61
Samson Against the Black Pirate 7.64
Samson Against the Pirates 7.63
Samson Against the Sheik see *Maciste Against the Sheik*
Samson and Delilah 1.49
Samson and His Mighty Challenge see *Hercules, Samson, Maciste and Ursus: The Invincibles*
Samson and the Sea Beast see *Samson Against the Pirates*
Samson and the Seven Miracles see *Maciste at the Court of the Great Khan*
Samson and the Seven Miracles of the World see *Maciste at the Court of the Great Khan*
Samson and the Slave Queen see *Zorro Against Maciste*
Samson and the Treasure of the Incas 7.64
Samson in King Solomon's Mines see *Maciste in King Solomon's Mines*
Samson vs. the Giant King see *Maciste at the Court of the Czar*
Sandok see *The Mountain of Light*
Sandok, the Maciste of the Jungle 16.64
Sandokan Against the Leopard of Sarawak 16.64
Sandokan Fights Back see *Sandokan To The Rescue*
Sandokan the Great see *Sandokan, the Tiger of Mompracem*
Sandokan, the Pirate of Malaysia see *The Pirates of Malaysia*
Sandokan, the Tiger of Mompracem 16.63
Sandokan To The Rescue 16.64
Sappho—Venus of Lesbos 9.60
The Saracen Blade 2.54
The Saracens see *The Devil Pirate*
Saul and David 11.64
The Savage Hordes see *Ursus and the Tartar Girl*
The Scarlet Blade 19.63

The Scarlet Coat 2.55
Scheherazade 19.63
The Scimitar of the Saracen 4.59
The Scourge of the Barbarians see *The Defeat of the Barbarians*
The Sea Pirate see *Surfouf, Hero of the Seven Seas*
The Secret Mark of D'Artagnan 18.62
The Secret of Monte Cristo 19.61
The Secret of the Black Falcon 15.61
The Secret Seven see *The Invincible Seven*
Semiramis, Slave Queen see *The Queen of Babylon*
Serpent of the Nile 2.53
Seven Against All 10.65
The Seven Challenges 14.61
Seven from Thebes 9.64
Seven Rebel Gladiators see *Seven Against All*
The Seven Revenges see *The Seven Challenges*
Seven Seas to Calais see *King of the 7 Seas*
Seven Slaves Against Rome see *The Strongest Slaves in the World*
Seven Slaves Against the World see *The Strongest Slaves in the World*
The Seven Swords of the Avenger 16.62
The 7 Tasks of Ali Baba 13.62
The Seven Thunderbolts of Assur 13.62
The Seventh Sword see *The Seven Swords of the Avenger*
7th Thunderbolt see *The Seven Thunderbolt of Assur*
79 AD see *79 AD: The Destruction of Herculaneum*
79 AD: The Destruction of Herculaneum 12.62
Shadow of Eagles 12.66
The Shadow of Zorro 18.62
Sheba and the Gladiator see *Sign of Rome*
The Ship of Condemned Women 3.53
Ship of Lost Women see *The Ship of Condemned Women*
Siege of Syracuse 12.60
Siege of the Saxons 19.63
Sign of Rome 4.59
Sign of the Avenger 16.62
The Sign of the Coyote 16.63
Sign of the Gladiator see *Sign of Rome*
Sign of the Pagan 2.54
Sign of Zorro 18.63
The Sign of Zorro 2.58
Sinbad Against the Seven Saracens 13.64
Sins of Pompeii see *The Last Days of Pompeii*
Sins of Rome, Story of Spartacus see *Spartacus*
Siren of Atlantis 2.49
Siren of Atlantis see *Journey Beneath the Desert*
Siren of Bagdad 2.53
The Slave see *The Son of Spartacus*
The Slave Girls of Carthage see *The Slaves of Carthage*
The Slave Girls of Sheba see *The Green Flags of Allah*
The Slave Merchants see *Anthar the Invincible*
The Slave of Bagdad see *Scheherazade*
Slave of Rome 12.61
Slave of the Orient see *Aphrodite, Goddess of Love*
Slave Queen of Babylon see *I, Semiramis*
The Slave Woman see *The Queen of Babylon*
Slave Women of Corinth see *Aphrodite, Goddess of Love*
The Slaves of Carthage 3.56
Sodom and Gomorrah 11.62

Sold into Egypt see *Joseph Sold By His Brothers*
Son of Ali Baba 2.52
The Son of Captain Blood 19.62
Son of Cleopatra 11.64
Son of D'Artagnan 3.50
Son of El Cid see *100 Horsemen*
Son of Hercules in the Land of Darkness see *Hercules the Invincible*
Son of Hercules in the Land of Fire see *Ursus in the Land of Fire*
The Son of Hercules vs. Venus see *Mars, God of War*
The Son of Man 3.54
Son of Robin Hood 19.58
Son of Samson see *Maciste in the Valley of the Kings*
The Son of Spartacus 12.62
Son of the Red Corsair 4.59
Son of the Red Pirate see *Son of the Red Corsair*
The Son of the Sheik 13.62
Sons of the Musketeers see *At Sword's Point*
Sons of Thunder see *My Son, The Hero*
Soraya, Queen of the Desert see *Anthar the Invincible*
Spartacus 3.53
Spartacus and the Ten Gladiators see *The Ten Invincible Gladiators*
The Spartan Gladiators see *Revolt of the Seven*
The Stone Forest see *Treasure of the Petrified Forest*
The Story of Robin Hood and His Merrie Men 2.52
The Story of Ruth 19.60
The Strongest Slaves in the World 10.64
Suleiman the Conqueror 17.61
Surcouf, Hero of the Seven Seas 15.66
The Sword and the Cross 4.58
The Sword and the Cross see *The Slaves of Carthage*
Sword in the Shadows 16.61
The Sword of Ali Baba 19.65
The Sword of Damascus see *The Golden Blade*
Sword of Damascus see *The Thief of Damascus*
The Sword of El Cid 16.62
Sword of Lancelot 19.63
The Sword of Monte Cristo 2.51
Sword of Rebellion see *The Rebel of Castelmonte*
Sword of Sherwood Forest 19.60
Sword of the Conqueror see *Rosamund and Alboino*
Sword of the Empire 12.64
Sword of Venus 2.53
Sword of Zorro see *The Three Swords of Zorro*
Sword Without a Country see *Swords Without a Flag*
Swords Without a Flag 16.61
Swordsman of Siena 16.62
Taras Bulba the Cossack 14.62
The Tartar Invasion see *Ursus and the Tartar Girl*
The Tartars 14.61
The Tartars see *Taras Bulba the Cossack*
Taur, The King of Brute Force 13.63
Taur the Mighty see *Taur, The King of Brute Force*
Tempest 4.58
Temple of the White Elephant see *Sandok, the Maciste of the Jungle*
The Ten Desperate Men see *The Ten Gladiators*
The Ten Gladiators 10.63
The Ten Invincible Gladiators 10.64

Terror of Rome Against the Son of Hercules see *Maciste, Gladiator of Sparta*
Terror of Sandokan see *Sandokan to the Rescue*
Terror of the Barbarians 4.59
Terror of the Black Mask see *The Invincible Masked Cavalier*
The Terror of the Red Capes 16.63
Terror of the Red Mask 16.60
The Terror of the Seas 15.61
Terror of the Steppes see *The Plunderers of the Steppe*
Tharus Son of Attila 14.62
Theodora, Empress of Byzantium 3.54
Theodora, Slave Empress see *Theodora, Empress of Byzantium*
Theseus Against the Minotaur 9.60
The Thief of Baghdad 13.61
Thief of Damascus 2.52
The Thief of Damascus 13.64
The Thief of Venice 3.50
Thor and the Amazon Women see *Women Gladiators*
The Three Avengers see *The Invincible Three*
The Three Centurions 12.64
The 300 Spartans 19.62
The Three Musketeers 19.61
The Three Pirates 3.52
The Three Sergeants of Bengal 16.64
Three Swords for Rome see *The Three Centurions*
The Three Swords of Zorro 18.63
Throne of Vengeance see *Sandokan Against the Leopard of Sarawak*
Thunder of Battle see *Coriolanus: Hero Without a Country*
Thunder Over the Indian Ocean see *Surcouf, Hero of the Seven Seas*
Tiger of the Seven Seas 15.62
The Titans see *My Son, The Hero*
The Tomb of the Kings 11.60
The Tomb of the Pharaoh see *The Tomb of the Kings*
Tor: Mighty Warrior see *Taur, The King of Brute Force*
Toto Against Maciste 6.62
Toto Against the Black Pirate 15.64
Toto and Cleopatra 11.63
The Treasure of Monte Cristo see *The Secret of Monte Cristo*
Treasure of the Petrified Forest 17.65
The Triumph of Hercules 5.64
The Triumph of Maciste 6.61
The Triumph of Robin Hood 16.62
Triumph of the Son of Hercules see *The Triumph of Maciste*
The Triumph of the Ten Gladiators 10.64
The Trojan Horse see *The Trojan War*
The Trojan War 9.61
The Two Gladiators 10.64
Two Nights With Cleopatra 3.54
The Tyrant of Castile 16.63
The Tyrant of Lydia Against the Son of Hercules see *Goliath and the Rebel Slave*
The Tyrant of Syracuse 9.62
Ulysses 3.54
Ulysses Against Hercules 5.62
Ulysses vs. the Son of Hercules see *Ulysses Against Hercules*
Ursus 8.61
Ursus and the Tartar Girl 8.61
Ursus and the Tartar Princess see *Ursus and the Tartar Girl*
Ursus in the Land of Fire 8.63
Ursus in the Valley of the Lions 8.61
Ursus, Son of Hercules see *Ursus*
Ursus the Invincible see *The Invincible Three*
Ursus, the Rebel Gladiator 8.62
Ursus, the Terror of the Kirghiz 8.64
Valley of the Lions see *Ursus in the Valley of the Lions*
Valley of the Swords 19.63
Valley of the Thundering Echo 6.64
The Veils of Bagdad 2.53
Vendetta at Sorrento see *Revenge of the Black Knight*
Vengeance of Sandokan see *Sandokan To The Rescue*
Vengeance of the Gladiator see *Alone Against Rome*
Vengeance of the Musketeers see *The Executioner of Lille*
Vengeance of the Three Musketeers 19.61
Vengeance of the Vikings see *Erik, the Viking*
The Vengeance of Ursus see *The Revenge of Ursus*
Venus Against the Son of Hercules see *Mars, God of War*
The Venus of Cheronea 4.57
The Viking Queen 19.67
The Violent Patriot 3.56
The Volga Boatmen 4.59
Vulcan, God of Fire see *Vulcan, Son of Jupiter*
Vulcan, Son of Jupiter 9.62
War Gods of Babylon see *The Seven Thunderbolts of Assur*
The War Lord 19.65
War of the Trojans see *The Legend of Aeneas*
War of the Zombies see *Rome Against Rome*
Warlord of Crete see *Theseus Against the Minotaur*
The Warrior and the Slave Girl see *The Revolt of the Gladiators*
The Warrior Empress see *Sappho—Venus of Lesbos*
Warrior Women see *Amazons of Rome*
Weapons of Vengeance see *The Devils of Spartivento*
White Slave Ship see *The Mutiny*
The White Warrior see *Hadji Murad The White Devil*
Wild Cargo see *The Mutiny*
The Witch's Curse see *Maciste in Hell*
With Fire and Sword see *With Iron and Fire*
With Iron and Fire 16.62
Women Gladiators 13.63
Women of Devil's Island see *The Prisoners of Devil's Island*
The Wonders of Aladdin 13.61
The Wooden Horse of Troy see *The Trojan War*
Zarak 2.56
Zorikan see *Zorikan the Barbarian*
Zorikan the Barbarian 14.64
Zorro Against Maciste 6.63
Zorro and the Three Musketeers 18.63
Zorro at the Spanish Court 18.62
Zorro the Avenger see *The Shadow of Zorro*
Zorro the Rebel 18.66

22
Source References/Author Biography

Source references for peplum movies are very few and far between, and very much hit and miss, even in the information-mad climate of the 21st-century we live in. As emphasized in the Foreword, online knowledge, statistics, facts and figures relating to Italian pepla can be incorrect, misleading, scant and contradictory. Even DVD covers (those discs that come supplied with one, that is!), when translated from Italian, Spanish, French, Greek, Russian and German into English, can give inaccurate data (it is highly doubtful whether the published review of *any* Italian peplum corresponds *exactly* with other published reviews of the same title). The one major work to be issued on the subject (before 2017) is Patrick Lucanio's *With Fire and Sword: Italian Spectacles on American Screens 1958-1968* (Scarecrow Press, 1994). However, the author was battling against the odds from the start. Written 23 years ago, particulars and hard-copy material on pepla in those days was 100 times more difficult to obtain and fathom out than it is now, and many films not seen by Lucanio, or given a very brief résumé, can now be procured with difficulty, and at a sometimes exorbitant cost, from gray-market dealers. Wikipedia has a pretty comprehensive 20-page article on the broader aspects of Sword-and-Sandal (*sic*), listing many titles under their various categories, while Cool Ass Cinema details, over 54 illustrated pages, the 26 Best Sword and Sandal strongman adventures featuring pepla's leading beefcake players, prefaced with a concise introductory chapter on the genre and its recurrent themes. IMDb generally lists titles under their alternative American/English name or in Italian only. To obtain the accuracy one is striving toward, a myriad of obscure non-English sites have to be sought out and navigated with the patience of a detective, then translated and compared, not only with each other but with what appears on the film's credits, *if* said credits are there in the first place *and* correct. In the absence of any substantial reading matter on the subject, combined with a plethora of inconsistent media facts spread right across the board, this, and only this, is the sole method of sourcing and making heads or tails of the complex cinematic world of Italian pepla.

Author Biography

Barry Stephen Atkinson was born in Brighton, Sussex England in 1947 and spent his formative years growing up in Leatherhead, Surrey, with his sister and two brothers. Barry self-published his wayward adventures during the austere climate of 1950s postwar Britain in *Out: Growing Up in the 1950s* (Trafford Press, 2006), a defining period in his life which he looks back on with affection. Moving to the West Country in the harsh winter of 1963, he was educated at Cornwall Technical College, his interest in writing rewarded when he came runner-up in a Brooke Bond-sponsored essay competition carried out among West Cornwall's secondary schools in March 1963. On leaving college in June 1965, he joined the merchant navy with the P & O Orient shipping line to see the world before taking up a career in credit management and legal administration, his numerous jobs encompassing lengthy spells with both England's largest scaffolding company and biggest removals outfit. The last 10 years of his working life saw him driving all over England, including a great deal of time spent in London and Brighton, for a variety of delivery companies, before he retired in 2006.

His first published book, *Mining Sites in Cornwall and South West Devon* (Dyllansow Truran, 1988), eventually became a bestseller in its chosen field, as did the follow-up, *Mining Sites in Cornwall Volume 2* (Dyllansow Truran, 1994). Since the successful publication of *You're Not Old Enough Son* (Midnight Marquee Press, 2006), Barry has had several books issued by his present publishers: *You Are Old Enough Son*, *Indie Horrors!*, *Atomic Age Cinema* (nominated for a Rondo award in 2015) and *Six-Gun Law*. His film-based work can also be found in *Reel Mad Doctors*, *Cinematic Hauntings*, *Popcorn Prozac* and *Midnight Marquee*'s 50th Anniversary issue. In addition, he has, since 1981, been writing the occasional article for a Plymouth-located mining club. After a four-year sojourn on the Greek island of Crete, Barry and Janet, his wife of 21 years, returned to England in 2010 where they now live in North Cornwall, with their six Greek cats. When not busy writing, Barry enjoys reading, collecting 1950s memorabilia (his revised book *Off Out to the Woods*, published by Novum/United P.C. in 2016, chronicles his childhood years during the 1950s), walking, nature, music ranging from the 1930s to hard rock, exploring Cornwall's rugged coastline and industrial archaeological remains and, naturally, watching movies of every description and category, not just peplum!

If you enjoyed this book,
write for a $2.00 catalog
of Midnight Marquee Press titles
or visit our website at
http://www.midmar.com

Midnight Marquee Press, Inc.
9721 Britinay Lane
Baltimore, MD 21234
410-665-1198
mmarquee@aol.com

www.ingramcontent.com/pod-product-compliance
Lightning Source LLC
Chambersburg PA
CBHW081718100526
44591CB00016B/2414